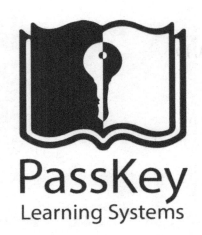

PassKey
Learning Systems

EA Review
Part 1: Individuals

Enrolled Agent Study Guide

May 1, 2024 - February 28, 2025

Testing Cycle

Joel Busch, CPA, JD

Christy Pinheiro, EA, ABA®

Thomas A. Gorczynski, EA, USTCP

Executive Editor: Joel Busch, CPA, JD

Contributors:

Joel Busch, CPA, JD

Christy Pinheiro, EA, ABA®

Thomas A. Gorczynski, EA, USTCP

PassKey Learning Systems EA Review Part 1 Individuals; Enrolled Agent Study Guide, May 1, 2024 - February 28, 2025 Testing Cycle

ISBN 13: 978-1-935664-99-4

First Printing. April 1, 2024.

This study guide is designed for exam candidates who will take their exams in the May 1, 2024, to February 28, 2025, testing cycle.

Note: Prometric will NOT TEST on any legislation or court decisions passed after December 31, 2023. For exams taken between May 1, 2024, to February 28, 2025, all references on the examination are to the Internal Revenue Code, forms and publications, as amended through December 31, 2023. Also, unless otherwise stated, all questions relate to the calendar year 2023. Questions that contain the term 'current tax year' refer to the calendar year 2023.

Table of Contents

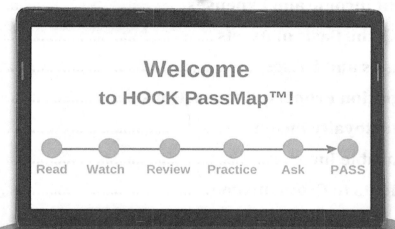

Recent Praise for the PassKey EA Review Series

(Real customers, real names, public testimonials)

Perfect review book!
A. Bergman
The [PassKey] EA Review is great! Goes into detail and explains why. When you do the practice test, it actually tells you details of the answer for learning and retaining! Definitely recommend!

Fantastic textbooks and video resources.
Vino Joseph Philip
Comprehensive and accurate video lessons are available online, and testing is also available for each course. I passed all three exams on the first attempt after using Passkey's resources.

Helped me to pass faster
Mohamed Helemish
I highly recommend Passkey if you are looking for something simple, and easy to understand, and if you want a good reference for your future career in taxes. I passed the exam with confidence and I used it with the three parts.

I Highly recommend these materials
Tosha H. Knelangeon
Using only the [PassKey] study guide and the workbook, I passed all three EA exams on my first try. I highly recommend these materials. As long as you put in the time to read and study all the information provided, you should be well-prepared.

I passed on the first try.
Jake Bavaro
I recently passed the first part of the EA exam using just the textbook and a separate practice test workbook. The textbook is very easy to read and understand. Although I have a background in accounting and tax, someone with little or no knowledge of either should be able to grasp all of the various topics covered in the book. I really do believe that it is a superior preparation resource.

I passed all three parts the first time taking them.
Sheryl Reinecke
I passed all three parts the first time. I read each chapter and the review quiz at the end of each chapter. Before taking the real exam, I did the practice exams in the additional workbook. I feel the material adequately prepared me for success in passing the exam.

You can pass.
Vishnu Kali Osirion
I really rushed studying for this section. These authors make tax law relevant to your day-to-day experiences and understandable. You can pass the exam with just this as a resource. I do recommend purchasing the workbook as well, just for question exposure. The questions in the book and in the workbook are pretty indicative of what's on the exam. This is a must-buy. Cheers.

Absolute Best Purchase
Sharlene D.
This book was definitely worth the purchase. The layout was great, especially the examples! Reading the book from front to back allowed me to pass [Part 2]. I also recommend purchasing the workbook or subscribing to the material on their website for this section.

Excellent explanations!
Janet Briggs
The best thing about these books is that each answer has a comprehensive explanation about why the answer is correct. I passed all three EA exams on the first attempt.

PassKey was the only study aid that I used
Stephen J Woodard, CFP, CLU, ChFC
The [PassKey] guides were an invaluable resource. They were concise and covered the subject matter succinctly with spot-on end-of-chapter questions that were very similar to what I encountered on the exams.

Amazing!
Sopio Svanishvilion
PassKey helped me pass all three parts of the Enrolled Agent exam. They are a "must-have" if you want to pass your EA exams.

I passed all three with Passkey.
Swathi B.R.
I went through the online membership, read the whole book, solved all the questions, and passed the EA exam on my first attempt. For all three [parts], I referred to Passkey EA Review. Wonderful books.

Passed all 3 Parts!
Kowani Collins
Thank you so much for providing this resource! I have passed all 3 parts of the SEE exam. PassKey allowed me to study on my own time and take the exam with confidence. Thank you for providing such thorough and easy-to-follow resources!

Introduction

Congratulations on taking the first step toward becoming an enrolled agent, a widely respected professional tax designation. The Internal Revenue Service licenses enrolled agents, known as EAs, after candidates pass a competency exam testing their knowledge of federal tax law. As an enrolled agent, you will have the same representation rights as a CPA, with the ability to represent taxpayers in IRS audits and appeals—an EA's rights are unlimited before all levels and offices of the IRS.

The PassKey study guide series is designed to help you study for the EA exam, which is formally called the *IRS Special Enrollment Examination* or *"SEE."*

EA Exam Basics

The EA exam consists of three parts, which candidates may schedule separately and take in any order they wish. The computerized exam covers all aspects of federal tax law, with Part 1 testing the taxation of individuals; Part 2 testing the taxation of businesses, and Part 3 testing representation, practice, and procedures.

Each part of the EA exam features 100 multiple-choice questions, with no written answers required. The exam will include some experimental questions that are not scored. You will not know which of the questions count toward your score and which do not.

> **Computerized EA Exam Format**
> **Part 1: Individual Taxation–100 questions**
> **Part 2: Business Taxation–100 questions**
> **Part 3: Representation, Practice, and Procedures–100 questions**

You will have 3.5 hours to complete each part of the exam. The actual seat time is four hours, which allows time for a pre-exam tutorial and a post-exam survey. An on-screen timer counts down the amount of time you have to finish. The testing company Prometric exclusively administers the EA exam at thousands of testing centers across the United States and in certain other countries. You can find valuable information and register online at *https://www.prometric.com/IRS*.

Prometric Testing Center Procedures

The testing center is designed to be a secure environment. The following are procedures you will need to follow on test day:

1. Check in about thirty minutes before your appointment time and bring a current, government-issued ID with a photo and signature. If you do not have a valid ID, you will be turned away and will have to pay for a new exam appointment. Refunds will not be issued by Prometric if you forget to bring a proper ID with you.
2. The EA exam is a closed-book test, so you cannot bring any notes or reference materials into the testing room. The center supplies sound-blocking headphones if you want to use them.
3. No food, water, or other beverages are allowed in the testing room.
4. You will be given scratch paper and a pencil to use, which will be collected after the exam.

5. You can use an on-screen calculator during the exam, or Prometric will provide you with a handheld calculator. You cannot bring your own calculator into the examination room.
6. Before entering the testing room, you may be scanned with a metal detector wand.
7. You must sign in and out every time you leave the testing room.
8. You cannot talk or communicate with other test-takers in the exam room. Prometric continuously monitors the testing room via video, physical walk-throughs, and an observation window.

Important Note: Violating any of these procedures may result in the disqualification of your exam. In cases of cheating, the IRS says candidates are subject to consequences that include civil and criminal penalties.

Break Policy: The Special Enrollment Exam (SEE) now includes one scheduled 15-minute break. You may decline the scheduled break and continue testing. If you choose to take the scheduled break, you will leave the testing room, adhering to all security protocols. You can take additional unscheduled breaks; however, the exam clock will continue to count down during any unscheduled break.

Exam-takers who require special accommodations under the Americans with Disabilities Act (ADA) must contact Prometric directly to obtain an accommodation request. The test is administered in English; a language barrier is not considered a disability.

Exam Content

Each year, using questions based on the prior calendar year's tax law, the IRS introduces multiple new versions of each part of the EA exam. If you fail a particular part of the exam and need to retake it, do not expect to see identical questions the next time.

Prometric's website includes broad content outlines for each exam part. When you study, make sure you are familiar with the items listed, which are covered in detail in your PassKey guides. Questions from older exams are available on the IRS website for review. Be aware that tax laws change yearly, so be familiar with recent updates.

Your PassKey study guides present an overview of all the major areas of federal taxation that enrolled agents typically encounter in their practices and are likely to appear on the exam. Although our guides are designed to be comprehensive, we suggest you also review IRS publications and try to learn as much as possible about tax law in general, so you are well-equipped to take the exam. In addition to this study guide, we highly recommend that all exam candidates read:

- **Publication 17,** *Your Federal Income Tax* (for Part 1 of the exam), and
- **Circular 230,** *Regulations Governing Practice before the Internal Revenue Service* (for Part 3 of the exam)

You may download these publications for free from the IRS website.

Note: Some exam candidates take *Part 3: Representation, Practice, and Procedures* first rather than taking the tests in order, since the material in Part 3 is considered less complicated. However, test-takers should know that several questions pertaining to taxation of *Individuals* (Part 1) and *Businesses* (Part 2) are often included on the Part 3 exam.

Exam Strategy

Each multiple-choice question has four answer choices. There are several different question formats. During the exam, you should read each question thoroughly to understand precisely what is being asked. Be particularly careful when the problem uses language such as "not" or "except."

Format One–Direct Question
Which of the following entities are required to file Form 709, United States Gift Tax Return?
A. An individual B. An estate or trust C. A corporation D. All of the above
Format Two–Incomplete Sentence
Supplemental wages do not include payments for:
A. Accumulated sick leave B. Nondeductible moving expenses C. Vacation pay D. Travel reimbursements paid at the federal government's per diem rate
Format Three–All of the Following Except
Five tests must be met for you to claim an exemption for a dependent. Which of the following is *not* a requirement?
A. Citizen or Resident Test B. Member of Household or Relationship Test C. Disability Test D. Joint Return Test

If you are unsure of an answer, you may mark it for review and return to it later. Try to eliminate clearly wrong answers from the four possible choices to narrow your odds of selecting the right answer. But be sure to answer every question, even if you have to guess, because all answers left incomplete will be marked as incorrect. Each question is weighted equally.

There may also be a limited number of questions that have four choices, with three incorrect statements or facts and only one with a correct statement or fact, which you would select as the right answer. With 3.5 hours allotted for each part of the exam, you have about two minutes per question. Try to answer the questions you are sure about quickly, so you can devote more time to those that include calculations or that you are unsure about. Allocate your time wisely. To familiarize yourself with the computerized testing format, you may take a tutorial on the Prometric website. The tutorial illustrates what the test screens look like.

Scoring Methods

The EA exam is not graded on a curve. The IRS determines scaled scores by calculating the number of questions answered correctly from the total number of questions in the exam and converting to a scale that ranges from 40 to 130. The IRS has set the scaled passing score at 105, which corresponds to the minimum level of knowledge deemed acceptable for EAs.

After you finish your exam and submit your answers, you will exit the testing room, and Prometric will send your results to your email, showing whether you passed or failed. Test results are automatically shared with the IRS, so you do not need to submit them yourself. Test scores are confidential and will be revealed only to you and the IRS. If you pass, your printed results will show a passing designation but not your actual score. The printout also will not indicate which specific questions you answered correctly or incorrectly.

If you fail, you will receive diagnostic information to help you know which subject areas to concentrate on when studying to retake the exam:

- Level 1: Area of weakness where additional study is necessary.
- Level 2: Might need additional study.
- Level 3: Clearly demonstrated an understanding of the subject area.

These diagnostic indicators correspond to various sections of each part of the exam. If necessary, you may take each part of the exam up to four times during the current testing window. You will need to re-register with Prometric and pay fees each new time you take an exam part. Due to the global pandemic, the IRS extended the two-year carryover period to **three years** for passing all three parts of the exam.

> **Example:** Randall, an EA exam candidate, successfully passed Part 1 on November 15, 2021. Subsequently, he passed Part 2 on February 15, 2022. Randall has until November 15, 2024, to pass the remaining part. Otherwise, he loses credit for Part 1. Randall has until February 15, 2025, to pass all other parts of the examination or he will lose credit for Part 2.

Applying for Enrollment

Once you have passed all three parts of the EA exam, you can apply to become an enrolled agent. The process includes an IRS review of your tax compliance history. Failure to timely file or pay personal income taxes can be grounds for denial of enrollment.

The IRS Return Preparer Office will review the circumstances of each case and make determinations on an individual basis. You may not practice as an EA until the IRS approves your application and issues you an enrollment card, a process that takes up to 60 days or more.

Successfully passing the EA exam can launch you into a fulfilling and lucrative new career. The exam requires intense preparation and diligence, but with the help of PassKey's comprehensive *EA Review*, you will have the tools you need to learn how to become an enrolled agent.

We wish you much success!

Ten Steps for the EA Exam

STEP 1: Learn

Learn more about the enrolled agent designation, and explore the career opportunities that await you after passing your EA exam. In addition to preparing income tax returns for clients, EAs can represent individuals and businesses before the IRS, just as attorneys and CPAs do. A college degree or professional tax background is not required to take the EA exam. Many people who use the PassKey study guides have had no prior experience preparing tax returns, but go on to rewarding new professional careers.

STEP 2: Gather Information

Gather more information before you launch into your studies. You will find valuable information about the exam itself on the Prometric testing website at www.prometric.com/IRS. Be sure to download the official Candidate Information Bulletin, which takes you step-by-step through the registration and testing process.

STEP 3: Obtain a PTIN

PTIN stands for "Preparer Tax Identification Number." Before you can register for your EA exam, you must obtain a PTIN from the IRS. The PTIN sign-up system can be found at www.irs.gov/ptin. You will need to create an account and provide personal information. Foreign-based candidates without a Social Security number are also required to have a PTIN to register to take the exam; they will need to submit additional paperwork with their Form W-12 (PTIN Application and Renewal).

STEP 4: Register with Prometric

Once you have your PTIN, you may register and schedule your exam on the Prometric website by creating an account to set up your user ID and password. Alternatively, you can schedule an appointment to take the exam by calling 800-306-3926 (toll-free) or 443-751-4193 (toll), Monday through Friday, between 8 a.m. and 9 p.m. (ET); or by submitting IRS Form 2587.

STEP 5: Schedule Your Test

After creating an account, you can complete the registration process by clicking on "Scheduling." Your exam appointment must be scheduled within one year from the registration date. You can choose a test site, time, and date that is convenient for you. Prometric has test centers in most major metropolitan areas of the United States, as well as in many other countries.

You may schedule your exam through the website or call Prometric directly Monday through Friday (some centers have Saturday testing). The testing fee is nonrefundable. Once you have scheduled, you will receive a confirmation number. Keep it for your records because you will need it to reschedule (which may incur a charge), cancel, or change your appointment.

STEP 6: Adopt a Study Plan

Focus on one exam part at a time and adopt a study plan that covers each unit of your PassKey guides. The period of time you'll need to prepare for each exam is truly unique to you, based on how much prior tax preparation experience you have and your current level of tax knowledge, how well you understand and retain the information you read, and how much time you have to study for each test.

For those without prior tax experience, a good rule of thumb is to study *at least* 60 hours for each of the three exam sections. Part 2: Businesses may require additional study preparation, as evidenced by the lower pass rates. One thing is true for all candidates: for each of the tests, start studying well in advance of your scheduled exam date.

STEP 7: Get Plenty of Rest and Good Nutrition

Get plenty of rest, exercise, and good nutrition before the EA exam. You will want to be at your best on exam day.

STEP 8: Test Day

Be sure to arrive early at the test site. Prometric advises arriving at least 30 minutes before your scheduled exam time. If you miss your appointment and cannot take the test, you will forfeit your fee and must pay for a new appointment. Remember to bring a government-issued ID with your name, photo, and signature. Your first and last name must exactly match the first and last name you used to register for the exam.

STEP 9: During the Exam

This is when your hard work finally pays off. Focus and don't worry if you don't know the answer to every question, but make sure you use your time well. Give your best answer to every question. All questions left blank will be marked as wrong.

STEP 10: Congratulations. You Passed!

After celebrating your success, you need to apply for your EA designation by filling out Form 23, *Application for Enrollment to Practice Before the Internal Revenue Service*. Once your application is approved, you will be issued an enrollment card and you will officially be a brand-new enrolled agent!

Essential Tax Law Figures for Individuals

Here is a quick summary of some important tax figures for the enrolled agent exam cycle that runs from May 1, 2024, to February 28, 2025.

Study Note: The IRS has stated in the most recent version of the official Prometric SEE Candidate Bulletin that candidates should not take into account any legislation or court decisions made after December 31, 2023.

Legislation Affecting the 2023 Tax Year:

- The **SECURE Act 2.0** was signed into law on December 29, 2022, as part of the *Consolidated Appropriations Act of 2023.* The Act included dozens of provisions affecting retirement plans. Most of the provisions in the SECURE Act 2.0 went into effect in 2023.

- The **Corporate Transparency Act (the "CTA")** was enacted by Congress as part of the National Defense Authorization Act. The CTA establishes a beneficial ownership reporting requirement for corporations, limited liability companies, and other similar entities formed or registered to do business in the United States. Starting on January 1, 2024, the CTA will mandate certain types of entities to submit a beneficial ownership information (BOI) report to the Financial Crimes Enforcement Network (FinCEN). Note that according to the testing specifications for the EA exam for this testing window, BOI reports are not included as a testable item on the exam.

Individual Income Tax Return Filing Deadline: April 15, 2024.[1] Taxpayers residing in Maine or Massachusetts have until **April 17, 2024,** because of the Patriots' Day and Emancipation Day holidays in those states. The extended filing deadline is **October 15, 2024.**

FBAR Due Date: The due date for the FBAR (FinCen 114, Report of Foreign Bank and Financial Accounts) coincides with the filing of the federal tax return. An automatic 6-month extension is allowed, typically until October 15.[2] FBARs must be timely e-filed separately from federal tax returns, on the FinCEN website.

2023 Tax Rates and Brackets: The individual tax rates for 2023 for U.S. citizens and U.S. residents are: 10%, 12%, 22%, 24%, 32%, 35%, and 37%. Nonresident aliens filing Form 1040-NR are taxed at a flat 30% rate on US-sourced income unless a tax treaty specifies a lower rate.

---

[1] Taxpayers are automatically granted a 2-month extension of time to file (to June 15) if the taxpayer lives outside the U.S. and their tax home is outside the U.S.

[2] FBAR refers to FinCEN Form 114, Report of Foreign Bank and Financial Accounts, that must be filed with the Financial Crimes Enforcement Network (FinCEN), which is a bureau of the Treasury Department. The FBAR is not filed with the IRS, but the IRS is responsible for FBAR enforcement.

2023 Standard Deduction Amounts (by Filing Status):

- Single/MFS: $13,850
- MFJ or QSS: $27,700
- Head of Household: $20,800
- Additional Standard Deduction for Age 65 and over and/or blindness
    - MFJ, QSS or MFS: $1,500
    - Single or HOH: $1,850

2023 Filing Thresholds Based on Filing Status and Gross Income

Filing Status	Age	Filing threshold
Single	Under 65	$13,850
	65 or older	$15,700
Married Filing Joint and Qualifying Surviving Spouse (QSS)	Under 65 (both spouses)	$27,700
	65 or older (one spouse)	$29,200
	65 or older (both spouses)	$30,700
Married Filing Separate	Any age	$5 (not a typo)
Head of Household	Under 65	$20,800
	65 or older	$22,650
Any filing status	The taxpayer had net earnings from self-employment of at least $400.[3]	
Any filing status	Church employee income of $108.28 or more.	

2023 Retirement Plan Contribution Limits: Roth and traditional IRAs: $6,500 (additional catch-up contribution of $1,000 for taxpayers age 50 or older)[4]

Qualified Small Employer HRA Limits (QSEHRA): $5,850 Single/ $11,800 family coverage

2023 "Kiddie Tax" Threshold: The "Kiddie Tax" age limit is for those under 18 and certain dependents under 24. The unearned income threshold is $2,500. The kiddie tax only applies to unearned income.[5]

---

[3] Table source: Publication 501, Filing Requirements for Most Taxpayers. Taxpayers who have gross income under these thresholds may still be required to file a return. This chart is not comprehensive. There are situations where a taxpayer may be required to file a return, even with income below these thresholds, for example, if the taxpayer owes special taxes, or those who received advanced payments of the premium tax credit (APTC).

[4] ROTH IRAs: Starting in 2023, SIMPLE and SEP IRAs may now accept Roth contributions. Previously, SIMPLE IRAs and SEP IRAs could only accept pre-tax funds.

[5] The kiddie tax is reported on Form 8615, which is attached to the child's Form 1040. Alternatively, parents can elect to include the child's unearned income directly on their own return, using Form 8814, if certain requirements are met.

2023 Maximum Compensation Subject to FICA

- OASDI maximum wage base: $160,200[6]

- Employee and employer portion: 7.65% (6.2% Social Security + 1.45% Medicare)

- Self-employed 15.30% (12.4% Social Security + 2.9% Medicare)

- Additional Medicare Tax: 0.9% on earned income exceeding the following thresholds:

    - Married filing jointly: $250,000[7]

    - Married filing separately: $125,000

    - Single, HOH, and QSS: $200,000

2023 Capital Gains and Long-Term Dividends: Short-term capital gains and ordinary dividends are taxed at ordinary income rates. The top rates for qualified dividends and long-term capital gains are as follows:

Long-Term Capital Gains & Qualified Dividends Tax Rates for 2023			
Filing status	**0% rate**	**15% rate**	**20% rate**
Single	Up to $44,625	$44,626 – $492,300	$492,301 and over
Married filing joint & QSS	Up to $89,250	$89,251 – $553,850	$553,851 and over
Married filing separately	Up to $44,625	$44,626 – $276,900	$276,901 and over
Head of household	Up to $59,750	$59,751 – $523,050	$523,051 and over
Trust & Estates	Up to $3,000	$3,001 - $14,650	$14,651 and over
Other long-term gains rates			
Gain on sale of collectibles		Maximum 28%	
Unrecaptured Sec. 1250 gain		Maximum 25%	

2023 Net Investment Income Tax: A 3.8% tax applies to individuals, estates, and trusts with net investment income above certain threshold amounts. The MAGI thresholds are:

- Married filing jointly and Qualifying Surviving Spouse: $250,000
- Single and HOH: $200,000
- Married filing separately: $125,000
- Estates and trusts: $14,450

---

[6] "OASDI" is the official name for Social Security in the United States, and the terms are often used interchangeably. The acronym stands for "Old-Age, Survivors, and Disability Insurance." Church employee income is wages received as an employee of a church or qualified church-controlled organization that has a certificate in effect electing an exemption from employer social security and Medicare taxes.

[7] Earned income of spouses is combined towards this Additional Medicare Tax threshold for MFJ returns. Employers must withhold this tax from wages or compensation when they pay employees more than $200,000 in a calendar year, regardless of the employee's filing status.

2023 Foreign Earned Income Exclusion: $120,000 per person.

2023 Bonus Depreciation and Section 179: Bonus Depreciation ramps down to 80% starting January 1, 2023. In 2023, the maximum Section 179 expense deduction is **$1,160,000.** This limit is reduced by the amount by which the cost of Section 179 property placed in service during the tax year exceeds **$2,890,000.** Once qualifying Section 179 assets placed in service during the year exceed **$4,050,000,** the Section 179 election is no longer available.[8]

2023 QBI deduction Limits: The Section 199A limitation phase-in ranges increased and are as follows:

- Married Filing Joint: $364,200-$464,200
- All other filing statuses: $182,100-$232,100

2023 Standard Mileage Rates:

- Business use: 65.5 cents a mile
- Medical and moving: 22 cents a mile
- Charitable: 14 cents a mile

2023 HSA Limits: To qualify to contribute to a health savings account, the taxpayer must have a high-deductible health insurance policy. The plan must also have an annual limit on out-of-pocket expenses (not including premiums).[9]

HSA contribution limit (employer + employee)	Self-only: $3,850 Family: $7,750
HDHP minimum deductibles	Self-only: $1,500 Family: $3,000
HDHP maximum out-of-pocket amounts (not including insurance premiums)	Self-only: $7,500 Family: $15,000

2023 FSA Limits:
- Health Care FSA (HCFSA): $3,050
- Dependent Care FSA (DCFSA): $5,000 for unmarried filers and couples filing jointly, and $2,500 for MFS filers.

2023 QSEHRA Limits: Maximum payments and reimbursements through the QSEHRA are: $5,850 for an employee only and $11,800 for an employee plus family.

---

[8] Section 179 and bonus depreciation are covered more extensively in the PassKey EA Review Part 2, Businesses.
[9] The IRS also announced an increase to the Excepted Benefit HRA (EBHRA), which is now $1,950. An EBHRA stands for Excepted Benefit HRA. It is a health reimbursement arrangement that pays qualified medical expenses for excepted benefits like dental and vision coverage. This can be offered in addition to group health coverage. An employee can participate in an EBHRA, even if they decline participation in the employer's group health plan.

2023 Long-Term Care Premiums Maximum Deduction (Per Person): The maximum amount of qualified long-term care premiums includible as medical expenses has increased. The limit on the deduction for premiums is for *each* person (not per tax return). Long-term care premiums up to the amounts below can be included as medical expenses on Schedule A.

Taxpayer's Age At the End of Tax Year	Deductible Limit
40 or less	$480
More than 40 but not more than 50	$890
More than 50 but not more than 60	$1,790
More than 60 but not more than 70	$4,770
More than 70	$5,960

2023 Alternative Minimum Tax (AMT) Exemption Amounts:
- Single or Head of Household: $81,300
- Married filing jointly or QSS: $126,500
- Married filing separately: $63,250
- Estates and Trusts: $28,400

2023 AMT Exemption Beginning Phaseout Range:
- Single or Head of Household: $578,150 to $ 903,350
- Married filing jointly or QSS: $1,156,300 to $ 1,662,300
- Married filing separately: $578,150 to $831,150
- Estates and Trusts: $94,600 to $208,200

2023 Estate and Trust *Exemption* Amounts
- Estates: $600[10]
- Simple trusts: $300
- Complex trusts: $100
- Qualified disability trusts: $4,700

2023 Estate and Gift Tax Exclusion Amounts
- Estate and gift tax (highest rate): 40%
- Combined Estate tax and lifetime gift/GST exemption: $12.92 million ($25.84 million per married couple).
- Gift tax annual exclusion: $17,000
- Annual exclusion for gifts to noncitizen spouse: $175,000

---

[10] For estates and trusts, the exemption amount is not allowed in the entity's final tax year (the year of dissolution).

2023 Retirement Savings Contributions Credit (Saver's Credit): This credit[11] is between 10% to 50% of eligible contributions to IRAs and qualifying retirement plans up to a maximum credit of $1,000 ($2,000 MFJ). The income limitations are as follows:

Credit %	MFJ	HOH	All other filers
50%	AGI not more than $43,500	AGI not more than $32,625	AGI not more than $21,750
20%	$43,501- $47,500	$32,626 - $35,625	$21,751 - $23,750
10%	$47,501 - $73,000	$35,626 - $54,750	$23,751 - $36,500
No Credit	more than $73,000	more than $54,750	more than $36,500

---

[11] The IRS uses two different names for this particular credit: the "Saver's Credit" and the "Retirement Savings Contribution Credit." However, they are the same credit.

2023 Tax Credit Changes

2023 Earned Income Tax Credit (EITC)

- **Investment income:** The investment income limit in 2023 is $11,000. The investment income limitation is now increased and indexed for inflation.

- **Social Security Numbers:** Taxpayers with valid Social Security numbers can claim the credit, even if their children do not have SSNs. In this instance, they would get the smaller credit available to taxpayers without qualifying children (the "childless EITC"). In the past, these filers did not qualify for the credit.

- **Special rule for separated spouses.** Taxpayers who file married filing separately may qualify for the EITC in limited circumstances (explained later).

Children Claimed	Maximum AGI (all filing statuses except MFJ)	Maximum AGI (MFJ filers only)
Zero ("childless EITC")	$17,640	$24,210
One	$46,560	$53,120
Two	$52,918	$59,478
Three or more	$56,838	$63,398

Maximum amount of the EITC in 2023:
- No qualifying children: $600 (the "childless EITC")
- 1 qualifying child: $3,995
- 2 qualifying children: $6,604
- 3 or more qualifying children: $7,430[12]

2023 Child and Dependent Care Credit (CDCTC): The Child and Dependent Care Credit or "Daycare credit" is a percentage ranging between 20% to 35% of up to $3,000 in qualifying expenses (for one dependent) or $6,000 (for two or more dependents). This credit is not refundable in 2023.

2023 Child Tax Credit (CTC): The maximum Child Tax Credit in 2023 is $2,000 per qualifying child. The Additional Child Tax Credit is the refundable component, of which a maximum of $1,600 is refundable in 2023. The CTC phaseout begins at $400,000 (MFJ) and $200,000 for all other filing statuses.

---

[12] The IRS cannot issue refunds claiming the Earned Income Tax Credit (EITC) and the Additional Child Tax Credit (ACTC) before mid-February. This is a congressional provision in the Protecting Americans from Tax Hikes (PATH) Act. This time frame applies to the entire refund, not just the portion associated with these credits.

2023 Adoption Credit: $15,950. The AGI phaseout range starts at $239,230 and ends at $279,230 for all filing statuses.[13] The exclusion for employer-paid adoption reimbursement is the same. The adoption credit applies per each adopted child. It is non-refundable, but any unused credit can be carried forward for five years.

2023 Credit for Other Dependents/Other Dependent Credit (ODC): The ODC is a tax credit available to taxpayers for dependents who do not qualify for the Child Tax Credit. The maximum credit amount is $500 for each dependent. There is no refundable portion.

2023 Premium Tax Credit: The American Rescue Plan Act temporarily removed the 400% FPL ceiling (commonly called the "subsidy cliff") and increased the amount of the credit to qualifying households. For 2023, the repayment caps range from $350 to $3,000, depending on the taxpayer's income and filing status. The ACA subsidy cliff is scheduled to come back in 2026.

Energy Efficient Tax Credits: Starting in 2023, the *Inflation Reduction Act* expands two tax credits focused on energy efficiency. Previously called the Nonbusiness Energy Property Credit, the updated credit is now called the *Energy Efficient Home Improvement Credit*. This updated credit can provide a maximum annual credit of $1,200 for qualifying property placed in service during the year. Unlike the previous credit with a lifetime limit of $500, this new one has an increased *annual* limit. Additionally, investments in heat pumps, biomass stoves, and boilers can earn a $2,000 credit.

New 2023 Clean Vehicle Credit: The credit for new qualified plug-in electric drive motor vehicles has changed. In 2023, this credit is now known as the *Clean Vehicle Credit*. The maximum amount of the credit and some of the requirements to claim the credit have changed. The credit is reported on Form 8936 and Schedule 3, line 6f.

---

[13] Unlike most other credits, the adoption credit has the same phaseout range for all filing statuses.

2023 Education-Related Credits and Deductions

American Opportunity Credit: The credit is up to $2,500 per student for the first four years of higher education expenses paid. The credit phases out for unmarried taxpayers with MAGIs between $80,000 and $90,000 ($160,000 and $180,000 for MFJ).

Lifetime Learning Credit: 20% of tuition paid up to a credit of $2,000 per return. In 2023, the credit phases out for unmarried taxpayers with MAGIs between $80,000 and $90,000 ($160,000 and $180,000 for MFJ).

Coverdell Education Savings Accounts (also called an "Education IRA"): The maximum contribution limit is $2,000 per beneficiary in 2023. Contributions must be made in cash, and are not deductible. Earnings grow tax-free and the amounts can be used for qualifying educational costs.

Section 529 Plans (Qualified Tuition Programs or QTP): The IRS does not specify a specific dollar amount for annual contribution limits to 529 college savings plans, but contributions are considered gifts for tax purposes and are subject to gift tax limits. This means that in 2023, up to $17,000 per beneficiary qualifies for the annual gift tax exclusion.

Student loan interest deduction: Student loan interest includes both required and voluntary interest payments. The maximum deduction per return is $2,500, regardless of filing status. The 2023 phaseout limits are:
- Married filing jointly: $155,000 - $185,000
- Single, HOH, QSS $75,000 - $90,000
- MFS filers cannot take this deduction.

Educational Savings Bond Expense Exclusion: The savings bond education tax exclusion allows taxpayers to exclude interest income upon redeeming eligible savings bonds when the bond owner pays qualified higher education expenses at an eligible institution. This exclusion is subject to the following income limitations in 2023:
- Married filing jointly: $137,800 – $167,800
- Unmarried filers: $91,850 – $106,850
- MFS filers cannot take the deduction.

Educator Expense deduction: The deduction for educator expenses, also known as the "teacher credit," is set at $300 for the year 2023. If two teachers are married and file taxes jointly, they can claim a total deduction of $600 ($300 each).

Other Essential Tax Law Updates for Individuals in 2023

Insurance premiums for retired public safety officers: Retired public safety officers can receive a tax break on their retirement distributions. They can exclude up to $3,000 of distributions from income from an eligible retirement plan if the funds are used directly for health insurance premiums.

Direct File Pilot Program: Direct File is a new IRS tool that provides taxpayers with relatively simple returns to e-file their federal tax return for free. Taxpayer eligibility to participate in the pilot will be limited to 13 states in the initial pilot, but the IRS plans to expand the service in future years.

Increase in penalty for failure to file: The penalty for failure of an individual to file a tax return that is more than 60 days late shall not be less than the lesser of (1) $485 or (2) 100% of the tax due on the return.

Student Loan Forgiveness: Exclusion from gross income is available for student loan forgiveness after 2020 and before 2026 for most forgiven student loans. In addition, an employer may contribute up to $5,250 annually toward an employee's student loans, and such payment is excluded from the employee's income through 2025. The $5,250 cap applies to both the student loan repayment benefit and other educational assistance (e.g., tuition, fees, books) provided by the employer.

Required Minimum Distribution Changes: The SECURE Act 2.0 has changed the rules for RMDs. For 2023, the age at which account owners must start taking required minimum distributions goes up from age 72 to age 73.

Excess Business Losses: The *Inflation Reduction Act* extended the provision for excess business losses through 2028. Non-corporate taxpayers, including sole proprietors, are limited in their offset use of overall business losses to offset nonbusiness income. The excess business loss limitation is $578,000 for MFJ, and $289,000 for all other filing statuses in 2023.

Personal and Dependency Exemptions: The deduction for all personal exemptions is suspended (reduced to zero) through 2025. For 2023, the gross income limitation[14] for a qualifying relative is $4,700 (also called the "deemed exemption" amount).

2023 "Nanny Tax" on Household Employees: The nanny tax threshold is $2,600 in 2023. A household employer is normally obligated to withhold and pay federal FICA (Social Security and Medicare) taxes for any household employee above this threshold. A household employer is required to pay FUTA taxes if they paid a household employee $1,000 or more in a calendar quarter in the current or prior year. These thresholds are on a per-employee basis.

---

[14] A "deemed personal exemption" is used for purposes of determining who is a "qualifying relative" under IRC Sec. 152(d)(1)(B). An exemption amount still applies to Qualified Disability Trusts, which were not subject to an exemption repeal under the Tax Cuts and Jobs Act.

2023 Tax Form Changes

Publication 535, Business Expenses, is now historical. The 2022 edition will be the final revision available.

The new Form 7206, *Self-Employed Health Insurance Deduction*, will be used by self-employed individuals to calculate and claim the deduction for health insurance as an above-the-line deduction.

Form 1040-X, Amended U.S. Individual Tax Return, now includes the option to select direct deposit of their refund.

IRIS Platform for Information Return filings: The Taxpayer First Act required the IRS to develop an Internet portal that allows taxpayers to file Forms 1099 electronically. On January 25, 2023, this new platform, called the *Information Returns Intake System (IRIS)* went live. Filers must register with the IRS before using IRIS.

E-file Mandate for Information Returns: On February 21, 2023, the IRS issued final regulations requiring most businesses to e-file beginning in 2024. This mandate applies to individuals and businesses who submit 10 or more information returns, such as Form 1099, W-2, and 1099-MISC. Failure to e-file, when required, may result in penalties imposed on taxpayers and businesses who file their information returns on paper instead.

2023 Rules for Form 1099-K: The reporting requirement for Form 1099-K, Payment Card and Third-Party Network Transactions, was reduced by the *American Rescue Plan of 2021*. However, on November 21, 2023, the IRS announced an additional delay in the new 1099-K reporting threshold for third-party settlement organizations (TPSOs). As a result, reporting will not be required unless the taxpayer receives over $20,000 and has more than 200 transactions in 2023. These reporting requirements do not apply to personal transactions such as birthday or holiday gifts, sharing the cost of a car ride or meal, or paying a family member or another for a household bill.

Unit 1: Preliminary Work with Taxpayer Data

More Reading:
Publication 17, *Your Federal Income Tax*

The enrolled agent exam, Part 1, covers a wide range of topics related to preparing tax returns for individual taxpayers. This includes essential knowledge of filing status, requirements, and deadlines; taxable and nontaxable income; deductions, credits, adjustments to income; determining the basis of property; calculating capital gains and losses; reporting rental income; understanding retirement income; and navigating estate and gift taxes. In this section, we will cover the initial steps that tax return preparers must take in order to ensure accuracy when filing taxes for their individual clients.

For the current exam cycle, Part 1 of the exam is broken down into the following sections and corresponding number of questions:

1. Preliminary Work with Taxpayer Data – 14 questions
2. Income and Assets – 17 questions
3. Deductions and Credits – 17 questions
4. Taxation – 15 questions
5. Advising the Individual Taxpayer – 11 questions
6. Specialized Returns for Individuals – 12 questions[15]

We will cover preliminary work with taxpayer data, as well as the importance of a taxpayer's biographical information in this unit.

Use of Prior Year Returns

When preparing tax returns for clients, tax professionals are expected to diligently gather and verify all necessary taxpayer information. This includes reviewing prior-year tax returns for accuracy, completeness, and compliance with tax laws.

If any errors or omissions are discovered on a prior-year return, the preparer is required by law to inform the taxpayer of the mistake and explain the potential consequences if it is not corrected. However, the preparer is not obligated to fix the error. Utilizing prior-year returns can help identify and prevent major mathematical mistakes and alert the preparer to any issues that may impact the current year's return.

During this review process, the preparer must also consider any items from previous years that may affect the current year's return, such as:

- Carryovers,
- Net operating losses,
- Tax credit carryovers, of which examples include the prior year AMT tax credit and the adoption credit.
- Prior-year depreciation and asset basis.

---

[15] The current exam specifications are listed in the official *Enrolled Agent Special Enrollment Examination Candidate Information Bulletin,* which is available for download on the official Prometric website.

Taxpayer Biographical Information

When filing tax returns, certain biographical information of the client is required. A tax professional must collect this information from each taxpayer to prepare an accurate tax return:

- Legal name, date of birth, and marital status
- Residency status and/or citizenship
- Dependent information
- The taxpayer's identification number (SSN, ITIN, or ATIN)

In order to prevent fraudulent tax filings, it is important for tax preparers to request identification from taxpayers. Photo IDs are preferred and should include the taxpayer's name and current address. It is also crucial for tax preparers to verify social security cards, ITIN letters, and other documents to ensure that the correct TINs are used for the taxpayer, their spouse, and any dependents listed on the return.

Additionally, taxpayers have the option to request an Identity Protection Personal Identification Number (IP PIN) which must be entered into software for the IRS to accept an electronically filed tax return. This service is now available to anyone, regardless of whether they have been a victim of identity theft or not. The IRS requires all individuals listed on a federal income tax return to have a valid Taxpayer Identification Number (TIN), including the taxpayer, their spouse (if married), and any dependents listed on the return. The types of TINs are:

- **Social Security number (SSN)**
- **Individual taxpayer identification number (ITIN)**
- **Adoption taxpayer identification number (ATIN)**[16]

Note: The personal and financial information of taxpayers is considered highly sensitive and confidential. It is crucial for tax preparers to understand the importance of protecting this information and to take all necessary precautions to ensure it remains secure. A preparer who wrongfully discloses a taxpayer's information could face civil and criminal charges.

A taxpayer who cannot obtain an SSN must apply for an ITIN in order to file a U.S. tax return. Generally, only U.S. citizens and lawfully admitted noncitizens authorized to work in the United States are eligible for a Social Security number.

Nonresident aliens with a U.S. tax liability generally have ITINs, although not always. For example, an ITIN would be required when a U.S. soldier marries a foreign spouse and wishes to file jointly. In order to file a joint return, the couple would need to request an ITIN for the alien spouse. People who do not have lawful status in the United States may obtain an ITIN for tax reporting purposes only.

The issuance of an ITIN does not affect an individual's immigration status or give the taxpayer the right to work in the United States. A taxpayer with an ITIN is not eligible to receive Social Security benefits or the Earned Income Tax Credit. ITINs are for federal tax reporting only and are not intended to serve any other purpose.

---

[16] A special form is used for ATIN requests; Form W-7A, *Application for Taxpayer Identification Number for Pending U.S. Adoptions.* This form is used to apply for an ATIN for a child who is placed in the taxpayer's home for legal adoption.

Example: Umberto is an Italian citizen who has never been to the United States. On January 20, 2023, he inherited a rental property from his deceased aunt, Giuseppina, a green-card holder who was living in the U.S. On his accountant's advice, Umberto decides to keep the rental property as a passive income source. He hires a management company to receive the rents and manage the property in his absence. Umberto requests an ITIN for tax reporting purposes. He will report his U.S. rental income on Form 1040-NR. He will not be taxed on his worldwide income, only his income from U.S. sources.

Example: Kristal is a U.S. citizen living in Norway. In 2023, she met and married Trond, a Norwegian citizen. The couple plans to live in Norway. Trond does not plan to apply for U.S. residency, but Kristal and Trond can make the election to file jointly and treat Trond as a U.S. resident alien by attaching a statement to their joint return. To make this election, Trond must request an ITIN.

ITIN Application Process

Taxpayers who need an individual taxpayer identification number (ITIN) must fill out Form W-7, also known as the Application for IRS Individual Taxpayer Identification Number. Along with submitting this form, taxpayers must provide documentation that proves their foreign status and verifies their identity.[17] There are three ways to apply for an ITIN.

- Using Form W-7
- Using an IRS-authorized Certified Acceptance Agent (CAA) or
- In-person at a designated IRS Taxpayer Assistance Center

A taxpayer can also engage the services of a CAA, or Certified Acceptance Agent,[18] to request an ITIN. CAAs can authenticate a passport and/or birth certificate for taxpayers who want to request an ITIN, but do not wish to mail their original documents to the IRS. All ITINs expire unless they are renewed.

Example: Adriana, a U.S. citizen with a Social Security number, currently resides in Mexico and is employed by an international manufacturing firm. She recently married Santino, a Mexican citizen, who has a daughter named Lucia from a previous marriage (both Santino and Lucia are Mexican citizens). Adriana and Santino decide to file their taxes jointly as a married couple and claim Lucia as a dependent. To do so, they need to apply for Individual Taxpayer Identification Numbers (ITINs) for Santino and Lucia. Adriana may enlist the help of a Certified Acceptance Agent (CAA) in obtaining these ITINs for her husband and stepdaughter.

Note: Typically, the process for obtaining an ITIN involves submitting an application (Form W-7) by mail along with a taxpayer's initial tax return. This must be done on paper. The Form W-7 *cannot* be filed electronically. There are limited situations where a foreign person may apply for an ITIN without filing a tax return, such as when claiming tax treaty benefits or providing an ITIN for reporting purposes to a third party, such as a bank or financial institution. A full list of exceptions can be found in the Form W-7 instructions.

---

[17] When a taxpayer applies for an ITIN, the Form W-7 must include original documentation such as: an original passport, birth certificate, or certified copies of these documents from the issuing agency. Notarized copies are no longer accepted.
[18] A Certified Acceptance Agent (CAA) is an individual or organization that is authorized by the Internal Revenue Service to assist alien individuals and with obtaining ITINs. The IRS maintains a list of CAAs on its website.

Adoption Taxpayer Identification Number (ATIN)

ATINs are designed explicitly for adopted children who are not yet eligible for a Social Security number. An ATIN is requested using Form W-7A, *Application for Taxpayer Identification Number for Pending U.S. Adoptions.* For an adopted child who does not have an SSN, a taxpayer may request an ATIN if:

- The child is placed in the taxpayer's home for legal adoption.
- The adoption is a domestic adoption, or the adoption is a foreign legal adoption, and the child has a permanent resident alien card or certificate of citizenship.
- The taxpayer cannot obtain the child's existing SSN, even though they made a reasonable attempt to obtain it from the birth parents, the placement agency, and other persons.
- The taxpayer cannot obtain an SSN for other reasons, such as the adoption not yet being final.

An ATIN issued for an adoptive child will expire after two years from the date it is issued, although an extension can be requested, using IRS Form 15100, *Adoption Taxpayer Identification Number Extension Request.* An ATIN cannot be used to obtain the Earned Income Tax Credit, the Child Tax Credit, or the American Opportunity Tax Credit.

Special Rules for a Deceased Child

If a child is born and dies within the same tax year and is not granted an SSN, the taxpayer may still claim that child as a dependent.

> **Example:** On October 9, 2023, Diane had a newborn son. Sadly, he faced health complications and passed away just one week later. The child was issued both a birth certificate and a death certificate, but no Social Security number. When filing her taxes for 2023, Diane can still claim her son as a qualifying child. She will need to submit a paper return in order to do so. Her son will still be considered a "qualifying child" for tax purposes, even though he only lived for a short time.

The tax return must be filed on paper with a copy of the birth certificate or a hospital medical record attached. The birth certificate must show that the child was born alive; a stillborn infant does not qualify. The taxpayer should enter the word "DIED" in the space for the dependent's Social Security number on the tax return.

Recordkeeping Requirements for Individuals

It is the responsibility of taxpayers, with or without the assistance of a tax preparer, to maintain copies of their tax returns and related records for as long as necessary for the administration of federal tax laws. Typically, it is required that taxpayers retain copies of their tax returns and supporting documentation for at least three years from either the date they were filed or the due date, whichever is later.

There are no specific guidelines set by the IRS on how these records should be kept, but individuals are advised to maintain good records for several purposes. These include identifying sources of income, keeping track of expenses for potential deductions, documenting the cost and improvements made to owned property, substantiating items reported on tax returns in case of an audit, and aiding in the accurate preparation of future tax returns. In cases of an IRS audit, it is the responsibility of the taxpayer to provide proof and documentation for their claimed expenses. Even if a tax professional prepares and signs a tax return, the *taxpayer* is the one ultimately responsible for the accuracy of their own return. The IRS allows taxpayers to maintain records in any way that will help determine the correct tax. Electronic records are acceptable as long as a taxpayer can reproduce the records in a legible format. Necessary records that all taxpayers should keep include items related to:

- **Income:** Forms W-2, Forms 1099, bank statements, pay stubs, brokerage statements, Schedules K-1.
- **Expenses:** Sales slips, invoices, receipts, credit card statements, canceled checks or other proof of payments, written communications from qualified charities, Forms 1098 to support mortgage interest and real estate taxes paid (if the taxes are paid through an impound account).
- **Home purchase and sale:** Closing statements, HUD statements, purchase and sales invoices, proof of payment, insurance records, receipts for improvement costs.
- **Investments:** Brokerage statements, mutual fund statements, Forms 1099-DIV.

Basic Tax Forms for Individuals

Form 1040: The Form 1040 is the primary tax form used by U.S. taxpayers to file their annual income tax returns. The Form 1040 includes three numbered schedules:

- **Schedule 1, Additional Income and Adjustments to Income**: Schedule 1 is used to report types of income that are not listed directly on the Form 1040, such as taxable alimony, unemployment compensation, and gambling winnings. Schedule 1 also includes adjustments to income, like the student loan interest deduction, the self-employed health insurance deduction, and the deduction for educator expenses.
- **Schedule 2, Additional Taxes:** Schedule 2 is used to report additional taxes owed, such as the alternative minimum tax, self-employment tax, or household employment taxes.
- **Schedule 3, Additional Credits and Payments:** Schedule 3 has two main sections: nonrefundable credits, and other payments and refundable credits.

Form 1040-SR: This form is specifically for use by seniors who are age 65 or older. This form is essentially the same as the standard Form 1040 but is designed to be easier to read with a bigger font.

Form 1040-NR: Form 1040-NR is used by nonresident aliens to report their U.S. source income. Form 1040-NR uses Schedules 1, 2, and 3, just like Form 1040. The 1040-NR is *never* used by U.S. citizens or U.S. residents. The IRS defines an "alien" as any individual who is not a U.S. citizen or U.S. national. A *nonresident* alien is an alien who has not passed the green card test or the substantial presence test. Form 1040-NR is used by foreign investors, as well as nonresident taxpayers who earn money while in the U.S.

Example: Angelo, a Filipino citizen and world-famous boxer, receives permission to enter the U.S. on a special visa in order to participate in a champion boxing match. He earns a substantial income of $900,000 for his appearance, but only stays in the U.S. for six days before returning to his home country. As he is not eligible for a Social Security Number (SSN), Angelo must request an Individual Taxpayer Identification Number (ITIN) to report his U.S. earnings. Without the ITIN, he would face automatic backup withholding on his income. Thankfully, Angelo's tax accountant requests the ITIN and correctly files his income taxes using Form 1040-NR, which only requires him to report the income he earned while in the United States and not his worldwide income.

Example: Ferdinand, a Canadian citizen, travels to the United States on a visitor's visa. During his visit, he goes to Atlantic City and happens to win $45,000 while playing Baccarat. Since Ferdinand is not a resident alien of the U.S. for tax purposes and does not have an SSN, he falls under the category of nonresident alien. Generally, gambling winnings for nonresident aliens are subject to a flat rate of 30% in taxes, and they are usually unable to claim deductions for gambling losses. However, a beneficial tax treaty exists between the U.S. and Canada. Ferdinand chooses to request an ITIN, so he can file a Form 1040-NR to receive a partial refund of the U.S. taxes withheld from his gambling winnings.

Form 1040-X, *Amended U.S. Individual Income Tax Return*: This form is used to correct errors in a previously filed Form 1040, Form 1040-SR, or 1040-NR. Form 1040-X can now be filed electronically. In 2023, taxpayers electronically filing amended returns may now choose direct deposit to obtain a faster refund.

Federal Income Tax Rates

An individual's federal taxable income is taxed at progressive rates in the United States. The IRS groups individuals by ranges of their taxable income level, or *brackets*, and applies increasing tax rates at each successive level. For tax year 2023, there are seven tax brackets for individuals: 10%, 12%, 22%, 24%, 32%, 35%, and 37%. The bottom rate is 10% in 2023.

	2023 Federal Income Tax Brackets and Rates			
Tax rate	Single Filers	Married Filing Joint & QSS	Head of Household	Married Filing Separately
10%	$0 to $11,000	$0 to $22,000	$0 to $15,700	$0 to $11,000
12%	$11,001 to $44,725	$22,001 to $89,450	$15,701 to $59,850	$11,001 to $44,725
22%	$44,726 to $95,375	$89,451 to $190,750	$59,851 to $95,350	$44,726 to $95,375
24%	$95,376 to $182,100	$190,751 to $364,200	$95,351 to $182,100	$95,376 to $182,100
32%	$182,101 to $231,250	$364,201 to $462,500	$182,101 to $231,250	$182,101 to $231,250
35%	$231,251 to $578,125	$462,501 to $693,750	$231,251 to $578,100	$231,251 to $346,875
37%	$578,126 or more	$693,751 or more	$578,101 or more	$346,876 or more

The applicable tax rate for each successive bracket that is applicable to the taxpayer applies only to the additional amounts of taxable income that fall within that particular bracket.

Example: Melissa is unmarried, and she earned $32,000 of taxable income in 2023. This means she is in the 12% tax bracket. But that does not mean she will pay 12% on all her income. Instead, she would pay 10% on the first $11,000 plus 12% on the remaining amount.

In addition to the regular tax in the United States, there is a "parallel tax" called the alternative minimum tax (AMT). Taxpayers must pay *either* the regular tax or the AMT, depending on whichever amounts to the greater amount of tax. The AMT is covered in detail later.

Tax Return Due Dates and Extensions

The *normal* due date for individual tax returns is April 15. If April 15 falls on a Saturday, Sunday, or legal holiday, the due date is extended until the next business day. The IRS will accept a postmark as proof of a timely filed return.

A tax return is considered filed "on time" if the envelope is properly addressed, postmarked, and deposited in the mail by the due date. For example, if a tax return is postmarked on April 15 but does not arrive at an IRS service center until April 30, the IRS must accept the tax return as having been filed on time. This is also called the "mailbox rule." E-filed tax returns are given an "electronic postmark" to indicate the day they are accepted and transmitted to the IRS. In cases where a tax return is filed close to the deadline, it is highly advisable for a taxpayer to pay for proof of mailing or certified mail.

Example: Seraphina is an enrolled agent who specializes in handling tax returns. One of her clients, Watson, is a single father to his 14-year-old daughter, Emily, and provides all financial support for her. On April 15, 2024, Seraphina attempts to electronically file Watson's 2023 tax return but it is rejected due to someone else already claiming Emily as a dependent. Watson suspects that his estranged ex-wife may have tried to claim their daughter, but he has no way of confirming or contacting her. Upon realizing the issue cannot be resolved electronically, Seraphina advises filing a paper return instead. She prints out the necessary forms for Watson and he signs them with an original ink signature before they are sent via certified mail before the post office closes. The return is considered timely and undergoes regular processing. Approximately eight weeks later, Watson receives his full refund.

If a taxpayer cannot file by the due date, the taxpayer may request an extension by filing Form 4868, *Application for Automatic Extension of Time to File*, which may be filed electronically. The extension must be filed by the original due date. An extension grants an additional six months to file a tax return.

Note: Although an extension gives a taxpayer extra time to *file* a return, it does not extend the time to *pay* any tax due. Taxpayers must estimate and pay taxes by the original filing deadline.

Filing Deadline Exceptions

Federal Disaster Areas: Taxpayers in federally declared disaster areas (FEMA disasters) are granted postponements to file and pay their income taxes and to make estimated tax payments. The IRS may also abate interest and any late filing or late payment penalties that apply to taxpayers in these disaster areas. This type of tax relief generally includes:

- Individuals and businesses located in a disaster area,
- Those whose tax records are located in a disaster area, and
- Relief workers who are working in the disaster area.

A taxpayer does not have to be *physically* located in a federally declared disaster area to qualify as an "affected taxpayer." Taxpayers are also considered "affected" if the records necessary to meet a filing or payment deadline postponed during the relief period are located in a covered disaster area. Therefore, disaster relief also applies to tax preparers (and their clients) who are unable to file returns or make payments on behalf of their clients because of a disaster.

> **Example:** Declan owns a 30% interest in a partnership that is located in a federally-declared disaster area. However, Declan himself does not live in the disaster zone. Since he must rely on the information (Schedule K-1) from the partnership to file his individual tax return, he qualifies as an "affected taxpayer" for purposes of receiving filing and payment relief. Declan's filing and payment deadlines are suspended until the end of the postponement period, just like the affected partnership.

June 15 Deadlines (Automatic Two-Month Extension)

Three groups of taxpayers are granted an automatic two-month extension to file:

- Nonresident aliens who do not have wage income subject to U.S. withholding,
- U.S. citizens or legal U.S. residents who are living outside the United States or Puerto Rico, and their main place of business is outside the U.S. or Puerto Rico,
- Taxpayers on active military service duty outside the U.S.

A citizen or resident alien living abroad must attach a statement to their tax return, explaining which situation qualifies for this special two-month extension. Even if allowed an extension, the taxpayer will have to pay interest on any tax not paid by the regular tax deadline of April 15.

December 15 filing extension: For most Americans and U.S. residents living abroad, the six-month extension to October 15 is sufficient. However, a taxpayer who resides outside the United States can request an additional "discretionary" two-month extension of time to file their tax return beyond the regular six-month extension of October 15.

For calendar-year taxpayers, the "additional" extension date would be December 15.[19] Unless the extension request is denied, the taxpayer will not receive a response from the IRS.

> **Example:** Isabella is a U.S. citizen residing and working in Portugal. She has already requested a 6-month extension for filing her tax return using Form 4868. However, she realizes that she may require more time to ensure the accuracy and completeness of her return, as she is still waiting on essential financial documents from a Portuguese bank that has paid her interest during the year. Without these documents, Isabella fears that her income tax return will not be accurate. Luckily, as an expatriate living abroad, she has the option to obtain an additional 2-month extension, giving her until December 15th to file her U.S. tax return.

Special Exception for Combat Zones: The deadline for filing a tax return, claim for a refund, and the deadline for payment of tax owed, is automatically extended for any service member, Red Cross personnel, accredited correspondent, or contracted civilian serving in a combat zone.

These taxpayers have their tax deadlines suspended from the day they started serving in the combat zone until 180 days after they leave the combat zone. The deadline postponement provision also applies to estate, gift, employment, and excise tax returns. These deadline extensions also apply to the spouses of armed service members serving in combat zones. The extension applies to both spouses whether joint or separate returns are filed.

---

[19] In addition to the normal 6-month extension, taxpayers who are out of the country can request a discretionary 2-month additional extension of time to file their returns (to December 15). See Publication 54 for complete instructions on how to request this extension.

Example: Ramon is a U.S. Marine who has served in a combat zone since March 1, so he is entitled to extra time to file and pay his taxes. The 46 days between the date he entered the combat zone and the normal April 15 filing deadline are added to the normal extension period of 180 days, so he has a 226-day extension period *after* he leaves the combat zone. IRS deadlines for assessment and collection are also suspended during any period that a U.S. service member is in a combat zone.

Penalties and Interest

The IRS can assess a penalty on individual taxpayers who fail to file, fail to pay, or both. The failure-to-file penalty is greater than the failure-to-pay penalty. If someone is unable to pay all the taxes they owe, they are better off filing on time and paying as much as they can. The IRS will consider payment options for taxpayers. These penalties can be abated if the taxpayer qualifies for an administrative waiver, or can establish that there was a reasonable cause for not paying or filing on time. Common penalties include:

- **Failure-to-file**: When a taxpayer does not file their tax return by the return due date (or extended due date, if an extension to file is requested and approved).
- **Failure-to-pay**: When a taxpayer does not pay the taxes reported on their return in full by the due date, April 15. An extension to *file* does <u>not</u> extend the time to *pay*.
- **Failure to pay properly estimated tax**: When a taxpayer does not pay enough taxes due for the year with their quarterly estimated tax payments (or through withholding) when required.
- **Interest on the amount due:** In addition to filing penalties, the taxpayer will also be charged interest on the amount due.

Failure-to-File Penalty: The penalty for filing Form 1040 late is usually 5% of the unpaid taxes for each month or part of a month that a return is late. The penalty is based on the tax that is not paid by the due date. This penalty will not exceed 25% of a taxpayer's unpaid taxes.

If both the failure-to-file penalty and the failure-to-pay penalty apply in any month, the 5% failure-to-file penalty is reduced by the failure-to-pay penalty. For the tax year 2023 (for returns filed in 2024), the failure-to-file penalty is as follows:

- 5% of the unpaid balance per month (or part of a month) for a maximum penalty of 25% of the unpaid tax. However, if the failure to file on time is determined to be fraudulent, the penalty is 15% of the unpaid balance per month (or part of a month) for a maximum penalty of 75% of the unpaid tax.
- For returns filed more than 60 days late, the penalty shall not be less than the *lesser* of (1) $485 or (2) 100% of the tax due on the return.

Example: Lenny does not file his tax return on time, or request an extension, because he believes that he does not owe any income tax this year. When he finally gets around to filing his return, Lenny discovers that he owed $25 in taxes. He files his return on July 30, and pays the amount due, but his return is over 60 days late. He later receives a bill with a late filing penalty of $25, which is 100% of the tax that was due on his return. He will also owe a small late payment penalty of $2, as well as interest on the amount due.

Failure-to-Pay Penalty: If a taxpayer does not pay their taxes by the original due date (determined without regards to any extension), the taxpayer could be subject to a failure-to-pay penalty of ½ of 1% (0.5%) of unpaid taxes for each month, or part of a month, after the due date that the taxes are not paid. This penalty can be as much as 25% of the unpaid taxes on the return. The failure-to-pay penalty rate increases to a full 1% per month for any tax that remains unpaid the day after a demand for immediate payment is issued, or ten days after notice of intent to levy certain assets is issued.

Note: A taxpayer may request penalty abatement due to "reasonable cause." Acceptable reasons for abatement include: fire, casualty, natural disaster or other disturbances, inability to obtain records due to a casualty or a disaster, death, serious illness, incapacitation, or unavoidable absence of the taxpayer or a member of the taxpayer's immediate family.

The failure-to-file penalty is reduced by the failure-to-pay penalty if both penalties apply. No penalty will be assessed if the taxpayer is due a refund. If a taxpayer files their return on time, but does not pay on time, then only the 0.5% failure-to-pay penalty will be assessed, which will increase per month until 25% is reached.

Example: Ximena does not have all her paperwork ready to file her return on April 15, so she requests an extension. She is not sure if she owes taxes or not, because she is waiting for a copy of a brokerage statement that was lost in the mail. Ximena finally receives her missing documents and files her return on October 1, before the extended deadline. She owes $1,000 in tax, which she pays electronically when she files her return. She does not owe a late *filing* penalty, because her return was filed on time (on extension). However, she will owe a late payment penalty of approximately $30. She will also owe a small amount of interest on the amount due.

Interest on the Amount Due: In addition to penalties, the taxpayer will also be charged interest on the amount due. Generally, interest accrues on any unpaid tax from the due date of the return until the date of payment in full. The interest rate is determined quarterly and is the federal short-term rate plus 3%. Interest compounds daily.

Unlike late filing penalties, interest cannot be reduced or abated for reasonable cause. Taxpayers may request abatement of interest by filing Form 843, *Claim for Refund and Request for Abatement*, or by submitting a request by letter. Interest will only be abated in extremely unusual circumstances, such as in the case of a mathematical error made by the IRS.

Example: Nicole died two years ago. She had a filing requirement when she passed away. However, Nicole died without a will, and an executor was not named by the probate court until November 10, 2023. Nicole's brother, Ezequiel, was named the executor. Ezequiel filed two years of delinquent tax returns on behalf of his deceased sister, and also requested a penalty abatement for filing Nicole's final tax returns late. The IRS granted the penalty abatement, although the interest on the amount due was not abated and still had to be paid by Nicole's estate. As the executor, Ezequiel would be responsible for filing and signing all his late sister's tax returns and making sure her estate pays any assessed tax.

Note: These are the penalties that apply to individual taxpayers only. Different penalty amounts apply to business entities, which are covered in detail in *Book 2, Businesses.*

Estimated Taxes for Individuals

The federal income tax is a "pay-as-you-go" tax. This means that people need to pay most of their tax during the year, as they earn income. This can be done either through withholding or estimated tax payments. Estimated tax payments can be used to pay income tax, self-employment tax, and alternative minimum tax. For taxpayers who are working as employees and wish to increase (or decrease) their withholding amounts, they must use Form W-4, *Employee's Withholding Certificate*. The Form W-4 is not submitted to the IRS. Instead, it is submitted to the taxpayer's employer.

Safe Harbor Rule: Taxpayers can avoid making estimated tax payments by ensuring they have enough tax withheld from their income. A taxpayer must generally make estimated tax payments if:

- They expect to owe at least $1,000 in tax (after subtracting withholding and tax credits)
- They expect the total amount of withholding and tax credits to be less than the *smaller* of:
  - 100% of the tax liability on their prior-year return
  - 90% of the tax liability on their current year return

Example: Harvey earned $95,000 during 2023 and paid $8,200 in tax, which was enough to cover his tax liability for the year. Although Harvey expects his income to increase in 2024, he will not be assessed a penalty for underpayment of estimated taxes, provided he pays at least $8,200 in estimated tax during the year (100% of the tax liability on his prior year return).

Safe Harbor Rule for Higher-Income Taxpayers: If the taxpayer's adjusted gross income was more than $150,000 ($75,000 if MFS), the taxpayer must pay the *smaller of* 90% of their expected tax liability for the current year or *110%* (instead of the normal 100%) of the tax shown on their prior-year return to avoid an estimated tax penalty.

Example: Massimo earned $205,000 in 2023. After applying all his deductions and credits, he had a $30,000 tax liability for the year. In 2024, he expects his income to increase substantially. He estimates that he will earn over $450,000. As long as Massimo pays at least 110% of his tax liability for the prior year (110% × $30,000 = $33,000), he will not owe an estimated tax penalty, regardless of how much he owes when he files his 2024 return.

A taxpayer will not face an underpayment penalty if the total tax liability on their return (minus the amounts of tax credits or paid through withholding) is under $1,000.

Example: Yvonne is a full-time secretary. She also earns money part-time as a self-employed manicurist. She did not make any estimated payments during the year. However, Yvonne made sure to increase her withholding at her regular job to cover any amounts that she would have to pay on her self-employment earnings. When she files her tax return, she discovers that she still owes $750. She files her return and pays the full amount of tax ($750) on April 15, which is the filing deadline. Although she is responsible for paying the additional tax that she owes, she will not owe an underpayment penalty because her total tax liability, after withholding, is still less than $1,000 for the year.

A U.S. citizen or U.S. resident is not required to make *any* estimated tax payments if they had zero tax liability in the prior year. However, late payment penalties will generally apply if a taxpayer does not pay the taxes they owe by April 15, 2024 (the filing deadline), regardless of whether an extension is filed or not.

Example: Edgar, 27 and single, earned $4,700 in wages before he was laid off in the prior year. He did not file a tax return or pay any income tax that year because his income was below the filing requirement. In 2023, he started working as a self-employed rideshare driver. He paid no estimated tax during the year. He files his 2023 return on March 30, 2024, and discovers that he owes $5,000 in tax. Although Edgar owes the full amount of tax, he will not owe an underpayment penalty as long as he pays the full amount due by April 15, 2024, because he had zero tax liability in the prior year.

Estimated Tax Due Dates for Most Individuals

The year is divided into four payment periods for estimated taxes, each with a specific payment due date. If the due date falls on a Saturday, Sunday, or legal holiday, the due date is the next business day. A taxpayer must complete Form 1040-ES, *Estimated Tax for Individuals*, to pay estimated tax. If a payment is mailed, the date of the U.S. postmark is considered the date of payment.

- First Payment Due: April 15
- Second Payment Due: June 15
- Third Payment Due: September 15
- Fourth Payment Due: January 15 (of the following year)

To calculate an estimated tax penalty, or to request a waiver of the penalty, taxpayers use Form 2210, *Underpayment of Estimated Tax by Individuals, Estates and Trusts*. The IRS may waive the underpayment penalty in certain situations, such as when a taxpayer's income varies throughout the year. For instance, if a taxpayer's business operates on a seasonal basis or if a person receives a large capital gain towards the end of the year. This is called the "annualized income installment method."

Example: Camila is self-employed as a hairdresser. She usually makes estimated payments throughout the year. Her income doesn't usually fluctuate much during the year, and she usually makes estimated payments of $500 each quarter. However, at the very end of the year, on December 25, 2023, she receives a large sum from a bridal contract where she was hired to do makeup and hairstyling for a big wedding party. Because of this, she will owe a lot more tax for the year. She plans to increase her final estimated tax payment for the year, but she also wants to avoid an estimated tax penalty. Since a large sum was received by her in December, she can use Form 2210 to report the large variance in her taxable income. By using the annualized income installment method, she can avoid a penalty.

Estimated Taxes for Farmers and Fishermen

Special rules apply to the payment of estimated tax by qualified farmers and fishermen (those who file on Schedule F). If at least two-thirds of the taxpayer's gross income in the current year comes from (or in the prior year came from) farming or fishing activities, the following rules apply:

- **March 1 deadline:** The taxpayer does not have to pay estimated tax if he files his return and pays all tax owed by the first day of the third month after the end of his tax year (generally, this is March 1).
- **January 15 deadline:** If the taxpayer must pay estimated tax, he is required to make only one estimated tax payment (called the "required annual payment") by the fifteenth day after the end of his tax year (for individuals, this is usually January 15).

For this special tax treatment, "qualified farming income" includes gross farming income on Schedule F, gross farming rental income, gains from the sale of livestock, and crop shares for the use of a farmer's land. This rule also applies to qualified fishermen.

Note: If a qualified farmer (or fisherman) files their 2023 Form 1040 by March 1, 2024, and pays all the tax they owe at that time, they do not need to make <u>any</u> estimated tax payments during the year. This rule does not apply to *any other type* of business activity—it only applies to farmers and fishermen.

Example: Naomi's sole source of income is her organic strawberry farm, and she reports all of her business profits on Schedule F. Since she is a qualified farmer, she is not required to make quarterly estimated tax payments. On February 28, 2024, Naomi filed her 2023 tax return, including a check for the full balance of $9,900. Because she submitted her return and paid the full amount due before March 1, 2024, she will not face any penalties for underpaying estimated taxes, regardless of the amount she owes.

Example: Granville is a self-employed owner of a commercial oyster farm. He reports his income and loss on Schedule F. All his income is from farming, so he is not required to pay quarterly estimated taxes. However, his bookkeeper quits at the end of the year, and Granville's bookkeeping records are incomplete, so he asks his tax accountant to file an extension on his behalf. Granville tells his accountant that he will be unable to file his 2023 tax return by March 1, 2024. Since he cannot comply with the March 1 deadline, and he did not make any estimated payments during the previous year, Granville is required to make a single payment of estimated taxes by January 15, 2024 to avoid an underpayment penalty.

Example: Aaron is a farmer who grows hothouse orchids and sells them to florists in his community and online. He makes a tidy profit selling the flowers every year. Aaron also earns a considerable sum as an occasional handyman. In 2023, his net income from farming is $47,000. His net income from his handyman business is $33,000. Since two-thirds of his income is not from farming activities, Aaron is not eligible for the special rule for estimated payments. He is required to pay quarterly estimates throughout the year, just like every other business.

Note: This special estimated tax rule also applies to a person's share of gross income from partnerships, where the majority of the income is derived from farming or fishing. This safe harbor for estimated payments *does not* apply to C corporations, regardless of the business activity.

Backup Withholding

There are times an entity is required to withhold certain amounts from a payment and remit the amounts to the IRS. For example, the IRS requires backup withholding if a taxpayer's name and Social Security number on Form W-9, *Request for Taxpayer Identification Number and Certification*, does not match its records.

The IRS will sometimes require backup withholding if a taxpayer has a delinquent tax debt, or fails to report all their interest, dividends, and other income. Payments that are subject to backup withholding may include: wages, interest, dividends, rents, royalties, and payments to independent contractors.

Backup withholding also applies following notification by the IRS, where a taxpayer underreported interest or dividend income on their federal income tax return. To *stop* backup withholding, the payee must correct any issues that caused it. They may need to give the correct TIN to the payor, resolve the underreported income and pay the amount owed, or file a missing return.

The current **backup withholding rate** in 2023 is **24%** for all U.S. citizens and legal U.S. residents. Generally, backup withholding applies only to U.S. citizens, and resident aliens; not to *nonresident* aliens. However, a nonresident alien may be subject to withholding, as well. Most types of U.S. source income received by a foreign person are subject to withholding of 30% (unless an exemption or tax treaty applies).

Under the current backup withholding rules, a business, financial institution, or bank *must* withhold taxes from a payment if:

- The individual did not provide the payor with a valid taxpayer identification number;
- The IRS notified the payor that the taxpayer's SSN or ITIN is incorrect;
- The IRS notified the payor to start withholding on interest and dividends because the payee failed to report income in prior years; or
- The payee failed to certify that he was not subject to backup withholding for underreporting of interest and dividends

Backup withholding is not a penalty, and taxpayers may report the backup withholding amount as taxes withheld when filing their tax return. As with any overpayment, backup withholding tax can be refunded.

Example: Marco is a frequent visitor to the local casino, where his favorite activity is playing slot machines. One day, he hits it big and wins over $20,000 from one of the machines. However, when he goes to collect his winnings, he is asked for his SSN by the casino. Marco declines, expressing concerns about privacy. As a result, the casino is legally required to withhold 24% of his winnings and remit them to the IRS. Marco will later receive a Form W-2G, *Certain Gambling Winnings,* and it reflects his winnings as well as the withheld amounts. Marco reports the backup withholding amount as taxes when filing his tax return. Marco does not earn very much income for the year, other than the gambling winnings, so he receives a tax refund of most of the withheld amounts.

Example: Dario is a U.S. citizen with investments through Interactive Brokers. The IRS notifies the brokerage firm that Dario's Social Security number is incorrect., Dario fails to update it despite being informed by mail and email. A month later, Interactive Brokers starts backup withholding on his investment income until the issue is resolved, resulting in a 24% withholding that will be taken from any future payments to ensure the IRS receives the tax due on this income.

Example: Federico is a citizen of Spain who also lives in Spain. He does not have a green card or live in the U.S., but he visits the United States occasionally. He owns several U.S. investments, including a limited partnership interest and U.S. Treasury bonds. He is a nonresident for U.S. tax purposes, but he is required to provide an ITIN to his investment firm, where his U.S. investments are held. If he does not provide a tax identification number, the investment firm will be required to automatically withhold 30% from all his U.S.-source income.

Gross Income and Filing Thresholds

Not everyone is obligated to file a tax return. The determination of whether a taxpayer must file a federal income tax return is based on several factors. According to the IRS, "gross income" includes all forms of taxable income received by a taxpayer, including money, goods, property, and services that are not exempt from taxes.

"**Earned income**" encompasses all taxable income earned through work, such as wages, salaries, tips, and other forms of employee compensation. This category also includes self-employment earnings from business or farm ownership. Other types of income, such as interest income, dividends, capital gains, retirement income, gambling winnings, and prizes, are considered "**unearned income.**"

The **2023 filing requirement** thresholds for most taxpayers, expressed as levels of gross income, are as follows:

2023 Filing Thresholds Based on Filing Status and Gross Income		
Filing Status	**Age**	**Filing Threshold**
Single	Under 65	$13,850
	65 or older	$15,700
Married filing joint and Qualifying Surviving Spouse (QSS)	Under 65 (both spouses)	$27,700
	65 or older (one spouse)	$29,200
	65 or older (both spouses)	$30,700
Married Filing Separate	Any age	$5 (not a typo)
Head of Household	Under 65	$20,800
	65 or older	$22,650
Any filing status	The taxpayer had net earnings from self-employment of at least $400.	
Any filing status	Church employee income of $108.28 or more.	

The gross income filing thresholds are adjusted for inflation each year, and they vary by age and filing status.

Example: Elena is 65, married, and had $3,500 of wage income in 2023. Her husband, Ricardo, age 65, had $19,600 in wage income. They have no dependents. Normally, Ricardo and Elena would not have a filing requirement because their gross income is under the filing threshold for joint filers age 65 and over. However, Elena wants to file separately from her husband this year. They are both required to file a tax return because the filing threshold for MFS taxpayers of any age is $5 in 2023. Ricardo must file a separate tax return because his filing status is MFS by default. Ricardo cannot choose to file jointly with his wife unless she agrees, since both spouses are required to sign a joint return.

Example: Francine and Kevin are married and file jointly. Francine is 66 and had gross income of $18,000 for the year. Kevin is 68 and had gross income of $10,900 for the year. All their income is from Social Security and wages. Since their combined gross income is $28,900, they are not required to file a tax return for 2023. The filing requirement threshold for joint filers when both spouses are 65 or older is $30,700 in 2023.

Filing Requirements for Dependents

Sometimes, dependents are required to file their own tax returns. A dependent child must file a tax return if their earned income is more than the standard deduction for their age and filing status. The filing thresholds are different for taxpayers that can be claimed as dependents, than for those that cannot, and they are also different depending on whether a dependent has "earned income" or "unearned income."

The filing threshold is much lower for those with "unearned" income. *Earned* income includes wages, tips, and self-employment income. *Unearned* income includes interest, dividends, and capital gain distributions.

For a child with only **unearned** income, the first $1,250 of unearned income is not taxed in 2023. The next $1,250 is taxed at the child's rate. Anything above $2,500 is then taxed at the parents' rate. This means that normally a dependent child 18 or under (23 or under if a full-time student) with only unearned income for the year will have to file a return if their unearned income is greater than $1,250 for the year.

Example: Chloe is 10 years old and lives with her mother, Louise. Chloe inherited some stock when her father died a few years ago. Chloe receives $1,100 in dividends in 2023. She has no other sources of income. She is not subject to the kiddie tax, and she is not required to file a return, because her investment income is less than the filing threshold that would trigger a filing requirement.

Example: Javier is a 17-year-old high school student who is claimed as a dependent on his parents' tax return. He worked as a pizza delivery driver 10 hours a week and earned $6,200 of wages in 2023. He also had $2,850 of interest income from a certificate of deposit that his grandmother gave him last Christmas. Javier is required to file a tax return because his unearned income exceeded the filing threshold, and he is subject to the kiddie tax. If Javier did not have any interest income, he would not be required to file a return; his investment income is what triggers his filing requirement.

For 2023, a dependent child who has received more than $13,850 of **earned** income (like wages or tips) needs to file a return (i.e., the total cannot be more than the standard deduction for their filing status, which is $13,850 for most dependents in 2023).

Example: Barrett is a 17-year-old high school student living with his parents. He earned $5,650 from a part-time job and received $200 of dividends from stocks gifted by his grandmother. Barrett's parents claim him as a qualifying child. Barrett's total income is below the gross income filing threshold for dependents. His investment income is also below the filing requirement for the kiddie tax. Barrett is not required to file a tax return in 2023, and his parents can claim him as a qualifying child on their tax return. Even if Barrett is not required to file a tax return, he may still choose to file to receive a refund of any taxes he had withheld from his wages.

Example: Elizabeth is 19 and is claimed as a dependent on her parents' tax return. She is a full-time college student. She works part-time at an ice cream parlor during the year, and earned a total of $14,000 in wages in 2023. She had no other income, and her parents provide the majority of her financial support, as well as pay for her college tuition and her food and housing. Elizabeth is not subject to the kiddie tax, because all her income is from wages, but she must file a tax return because her total *earned* income is more than $13,850 (the normal standard deduction amount in 2023 for single filers), but her parents can still claim her as a dependent.

Filing Requirements for Self-Employed Taxpayers

There are different filing requirements for self-employed taxpayers. Generally, a taxpayer is required to file a tax return if they have net self-employment earnings of $400 or more. Net self-employment earnings are calculated by subtracting any business expenses from your total self-employment income. Most self-employed taxpayer report their business income on Schedule C, *Profit or Loss from Business,* which is for reporting income and expenses related to their business. For self-employed farmers, there is a different form called Schedule F, specifically for reporting profit or loss from farming.

Do not confuse the filing threshold amount for self-employed taxpayers with the filing requirement for information returns (most notably, Form 1099-NEC and 1099-MISC). The Form 1099-NEC is used to report payments to an independent contractor who is paid at least $600 during the year. This $600 "reporting threshold" has nothing to do with the income tax filing requirement for a self-employed person. Form 1099-MISC is still used to report other types of payments, such as rents, royalties, prizes, and awards.

Example: Santiago is 67 years old and single. He has no dependents. Santiago is retired and receives $12,600 in Social Security. Normally, he would not have to file a tax return, but he also earned $2,100 in self-employment income working as a rideshare driver on the weekends. He has a profit motive in the rideshare activity and received a Form 1099-K from the rideshare service. His gross income is $14,700, which is less than the filing threshold for filing status (single, *plus* he is over the age of 65). However, his self-employment income exceeds $400, which will trigger a filing requirement. Santiago is required to file an income tax return. He will report his Social Security as well as his self-employment income on Schedule C.

Example: Janessa is 32 and earns $11,800 in wages during the year. Normally, she would not have a filing requirement, but she also has $590 in self-employment income for two modeling gigs that she did during the year. She had a profit motive in the modeling activity and hopes to pick up more modeling gigs in the future. Although she did not receive a 1099-NEC for the contract work, any taxpayer that has $400 or more in self-employment income during the year is required to file a return. Therefore, Janessa must file Form 1040. She will report her wages, and she must also attach a Schedule C to report her self-employment income.

Note: The Social Security Administration uses the information from tax returns (specifically Schedule SE) to figure a person's benefits under the social security program. Not reporting a taxpayer's self-employment income could cause their social security benefits to be lower when they retire.

Additional Filing Requirements

Sometimes, a taxpayer is required to file a tax return even if the gross income threshold is not met, such as in the previous example, when a taxpayer has self-employment earnings of $400 or more. Other filing requirements include the following:

- A taxpayer who earned $108.28 or more as a church employee. For the purposes of this rule, a "church employee" is an employee of a church or religious organization that has a certificate electing an exemption from employer social security and Medicare taxes.[20]
- If the taxpayer owes Social Security tax or Medicare tax on unreported tips.
- If the taxpayer must pay the alternative minimum tax.
- If the taxpayer owes additional tax in connection with a retirement plan, such as an IRA, 401(k), or 403(b).
- If the taxpayer received a distribution from a Medicare Advantage MSA, Archer MSA, or health savings account (HSA).
- If the taxpayer owes household employment taxes for a household worker, such as a nanny. If a taxpayer is filing a return only because they owe this tax, the taxpayer can also choose to file Schedule H by itself.
- If the taxpayer must recapture an education credit, investment credit, or other credit.
- If the taxpayer received advance payments of the Premium Tax Credit. The taxpayer should receive Forms 1095-A showing the amount of the advance payments, if any.[21]

Example: Calhoun is 32 and single. In 2023, he was unemployed for most of the year. He only earned $9,100 in wages for the year. Normally, he would not have a filing requirement. However, he withdrew $1,200 from his traditional IRA account at the beginning of the year to pay his bills. The IRA withdrawal triggers a filing requirement for Calhoun. He must file a tax return and report the distribution as taxable, even though his income is less than the filing threshold for single filers.

Even if an individual is not legally obligated to file a tax return, it is still advisable to do so if they are eligible for a tax refund.

Filing a tax return is recommended if taxes were withheld from their income, or had overpayments from the previous year that would result in a refund, or if they qualify for any refundable tax credits, such as the Earned Income Tax Credit (EITC).

Example: Susie is 32 and unmarried. She has a 9-year-old son and qualifies for head of household filing status. She can claim her son as a dependent. In 2023, she earns $10,050 of wages and $1,900 of self-employment income from cleaning houses on the weekends. Although Susie makes less than the filing threshold for her filing status, she must file a tax return because her earnings from self-employment exceed $400. Even if Susie did not have self-employment earnings, she should still file a tax return, because she likely qualifies for the Earned Income Tax Credit as well as the Child Tax Credit. The EITC and CTC are valuable credits that could give Susie a sizable tax refund.

---

[20] For the purposes of this rule, a "church employee" does not include an ordained minister, a member of a religious order (such as a nun or a monk), or a Christian Science practitioner.

[21] This list is not exhaustive. A detailed list of filing requirements can be found in Publication 501.

Relief from Joint Tax Liability

In some instances, a spouse can be relieved of the tax, interest, and penalties on a joint return. When spouses file a joint return, they are both legally responsible for the entire tax liability. However, a taxpayer can file a claim for spousal relief under three different grounds:

- Innocent Spouse Relief
- Separation of Liability Relief
- Equitable Relief

The same form, Form 8857, *Request for Innocent Spouse Relief*, is used to request all three types of relief. Note that all of these types of relief apply to joint filings. If a married taxpayer files a separate return (MFS) then there is no joint liability.

Innocent Spouse Relief: This is when a joint return has understated tax liability due to "erroneous items" attributable to a taxpayer's spouse or former spouse. Erroneous items include income received by a spouse that is omitted from the return. Deductions, credits, and property basis are also "erroneous items" if they are incorrectly reported on the joint return. To be considered an "innocent" spouse, the taxpayer must establish that they did not know (or have reason to know) there was an understated tax liability at the time of signing the joint return. In other words, a taxpayer could seek innocent spouse relief from the IRS if they later become aware of a tax liability and they believe that it is not theirs.

Example: Salma and Barton have always filed joint returns throughout their marriage. On February 2, 2023, Salma leaves Barton and files for divorce. Their divorce became final on December 20, 2023. On January 10, 2024, *after* her divorce was finalized, Salma receives an IRS notice for a prior-year joint return, indicating that $25,000 in gambling income was not reported. Salma discovers that Barton was hiding a gambling problem, and he had won that money during their marriage and failed to report it. Salma had no knowledge of the gambling winnings because Barton hid the money in a separate bank account and never told her about it. Salma immediately files for innocent spouse relief by filing Form 8857, *Request for Innocent Spouse Relief.*

The taxpayer must generally request relief within two years after the date on which the IRS begins collection activity. In most cases, innocent spouse relief is limited to taxpayers who are no longer married, including when one spouse is deceased.

Separation of Liability Relief: The restrictions mentioned above also apply to "separation of liability" relief. The taxpayer must either no longer be married or legally separated from their spouse, be widowed, or have lived apart for at least a year from the spouse with whom they filed a joint return. Any unpaid taxes, along with any additional interest and penalties, will be separated and allocated to each spouse based on their individual responsibility. Separation of liability relief only applies to amounts owed that have not yet been paid. Separation of liability relief will not generate a refund.

In order to qualify for separation of liability relief, the requesting spouse cannot have had knowledge of the tax item leading to the deficiency unless the return was signed under duress or if the spouse can establish (1) that they were a victim of spousal or domestic violence before signing the joint return, and (2) because of that abuse they feared retaliation from their spouse if they challenged any items on the return.

Example: Athena and Roman have always filed joint returns. In 2021, they filed a joint return together, reporting Roman's $42,000 salary and self-employment income of $10,000 for Athena. On January 3, 2023, Athena and Roman file for divorce, and begin living in separate homes. Their divorce becomes final on May 1, 2023. The IRS later audits their 2021 joint return, and finds that Athena claimed over $20,000 of improper business deductions. This results in understated tax, plus interest and penalties for the 2021 tax year. Roman was not involved in Athena's business and was unaware of the improper deductions when he signed their joint return. Athena had been hiding all of her business records and did not permit Roman to view her business bank statements. Since Roman is now legally divorced from Athena, he can file Form 8857 to request separation of liability relief. Roman must generally be able to prove that he didn't know about his ex-wife's improper business deductions at the time he signed the joint return with his wife. In the event that separation of liability is approved, the IRS will divide the underpayment of taxes on their joint return between Roman and his ex-wife, and any understatement of tax shall be allocated as if they had filed separate returns for the year.

Equitable Relief: If a taxpayer does not qualify for the first two types of relief, they may be eligible for "equitable relief." The IRS will review the facts and circumstances of the taxpayer's case and determine whether it would be unfair to hold the taxpayer liable for the understated tax.

Unlike the other two forms of relief, equitable relief may be granted for an underpaid tax, meaning it was *properly* reported on a tax return but not paid. Further, in some cases, the spouse requesting relief may have known about the understated or underpaid tax but did not challenge the treatment for fear of their spouse's retaliation.

Example: Margot is a victim of domestic violence, and she now lives apart from her husband. When she signed her joint return, she knew her husband was underreporting income from his business but was afraid of what would happen if she refused to sign. After the IRS discovered the understated tax, Margot filed for equitable relief and was able to document her history of spousal abuse using affidavits from family members and other legal proof. The IRS granted her request for relief of her portion of the understated tax, penalties, and interest.

If the tax was paid, the taxpayer has until the expiration of the refund statute of limitations to request equitable relief. If the tax is unpaid, the taxpayer has until the expiration of the collection statute of limitations (ten years) to seek equitable relief.

Injured Spouse Claims

An "injured spouse" claim and "innocent spouse" relief have similar-sounding names, but they are very different. To be considered an *injured* spouse, the taxpayer must meet all the following criteria:

- Have filed a joint return
- Have paid federal income tax or claimed a refundable tax credit
- All or part of the taxpayer's refund was, or is expected to be, applied to the other spouse's past financial obligations, and
- Not be responsible for the debt

Injured spouses can file Form 8379, *Injured Spouse Allocation*, to request their portion of the refund on a joint return.

Example: Gerard and Kimberly got married in 2023 and decided to file jointly. Kimberly has delinquent student loan debt. Kimberly incurred the student loan debt before she married her husband. Gerard files Form 8379 to request his portion of their tax refund as an injured spouse. The IRS will retain Kimberly's share of the couple's tax refund to offset her debt but will allow Gerard to obtain his portion of the refund.

Refund Claims and Amended Returns

To claim a refund, a taxpayer must generally file an amended tax return (Form 1040-X) within three years from the date the return was filed, or two years from the date the tax was paid, whichever is later. This is also called the **refund statute expiration date**, or RSED. The RSED is the last day a taxpayer can request a refund. If a taxpayer finds an error on a previously-filed return, and wants a refund, then the amended return must generally be filed within three years of the due date in order to preserve the right to those amounts.

Example: Myles e-filed his 2019 Form 1040 early, on February 1, 2020. He later discovered that he failed to claim the American Opportunity Credit on his return, which would result in a substantial refund. Myles mailed an amended return on April 15, 2023. Since returns filed on or before the due date are considered filed timely, as of the original due date, for purposes of the amended return refund claim period, his amended return was filed within the three-year statute period. He will receive a tax refund for the 2019 tax year.

If a refund claim is not filed within the applicable period, a taxpayer generally will not be entitled to a refund, unless an exception applies.

Example: Jenny self-prepared her 2019 tax return and filed it late, after the deadline, on November 5, 2020. She did not request an extension, and the return was considered delinquent when she filed it. She later discovered that she had forgotten to claim the Earned Income Tax Credit. Almost three years later, she files an amended return on October 5, 2023. Jenny's refund claim is denied because she filed her original return *past* the filing date *without* a valid extension. Therefore, since her amended return was not considered timely, her refund from the 2019 tax year is forfeited.

However, if the taxpayer files an extension and files his original return prior to the October 15 extension deadline, the three-year period begins on the date that the taxpayer originally filed his return.[22]

Example: Arnold has not filed a tax return for a long time. Arnold hires Patricia, an enrolled agent on January 23, 2024, and tells her he wants to file all his delinquent tax returns, including his current year return: 2018 through 2023. Patricia prepares and files all the returns. The most recent three years can be e-filed, but all the other delinquent returns must be mailed. Arnold files all the back tax returns and his current-year return before the 2023 filing deadline (April 15, 2024). All the returns show a refund. While he will receive refunds for his 2020-2023 tax returns, he will not be receiving refunds for any older years, because the refund periods for those years have expired. He will not receive a refund for those years unless an exception applies.

---

[22] If the taxpayer had an extension to file (for example, until October 15), but the taxpayer filed earlier and the IRS received it July 1, the return is considered *filed on* July 1 (Form 1040-X instructions).

Extended Statute for Filing Late and Claiming Refunds

In some cases, a late-filed tax return and claiming a tax refund beyond the deadline will be honored. Sound reasons, if established, include:

- Fire, casualty, natural disaster, or other disturbances
- Financial disability, death, serious illness, incapacitation, or unavoidable absence of the taxpayer or a member of the taxpayer's immediate family

In the case of a taxpayer who is "financially disabled," the time period for claiming a refund will be extended. This typically refers to individuals who are mentally or physically unable to handle their financial responsibilities. For a joint income tax return, only one spouse has to be financially disabled for the time period to be suspended. Note that a lack of funds, in and of itself, is not considered "reasonable cause" for failure to file or pay one's taxes on time.

Example: Samantha timely-filed her tax return for 2019 on April 15, 2020. Her CPA later finds an error on the return that would result in a refund, and he notifies her that she should amend the return. The last date for Samantha to file a refund claim under the statute of limitations for the 2019 taxable year would normally be April 15, 2023. Before she can file an amended return, on March 10, 2023, Samantha is involved in a terrible car accident. The doctor did not expect her to survive, and she was in a coma for nine months (until December 10, 2023). If Samantha can prove that she meets the qualifications to be considered financially disabled, the statute of limitations for filing a refund claim would be extended by the nine-month duration of her disability.[23]

Several unique scenarios allow a taxpayer to request a refund beyond the "normal" deadline. These unique scenarios involve:

- A bad debt from worthless securities (up to seven years prior)
- A payment or accrual of foreign tax (up to ten years prior)
- A net operating loss (NOL) carryback
- A carryback of certain tax credits
- Exceptions for military personnel
- Taxpayers in federally declared disaster areas or taxpayers who have been affected by a terroristic or military action

---

Example: Garth has been helping his elderly mother, Alma, file her tax returns. Over time, she has become forgetful of things. In 2023, Garth discovers a file in his mother's home filled with old brokerage statements. Several of the brokerage statements show losses from worthless securities, dating back many years. Alma had been putting the statements away unopened because she believed that they were unimportant. Alma's Form 1099-B from 2017 shows a significant loss from worthless stock (over $18,000 in losses that were never reported). Even though the brokerage statement is six years old, Alma is still allowed to amend her 2017 tax return to claim the stock losses. That is because the IRS allows up to seven years to amend a tax return for losses from worthless securities. Alma can file a Form 1040-X to claim the losses and receive a refund under this extended statute of limitations.

---

[23] To claim financial disability, the taxpayer (or their representative) must complete the appropriate income tax return or amended income tax return and also submit a statement of proof of the financial disability. For full instructions, read the section on financial disability in Publication 17.

Statute of Limitations for IRS Assessment and Collection

The IRS is generally required to assess tax within three years after the return is filed or, if filed early, the due date of the return. If a taxpayer files their return on extension, or files their tax return late, then the IRS has three years from the actual filing date.

Example: Alexandrina e-filed her 2019 tax return on February 27, 2020. Since she filed her return before the actual due date, the three-year statute period for audit began April 15, 2020, (the actual due date of her tax return) and ends on April 15, 2023. After that date, the IRS must be able to prove fraud or a substantial understatement of gross income (over 25%) in order to assess additional tax on Alexandrina's 2019 tax return.

The IRS has six years to assess tax on a return if a "substantial understatement" is identified, meaning that gross income was understated by more than 25%. If a taxpayer never files a return, or if a return is fraudulent, then there is no statute of limitations for an additional assessment of tax.

Example: Margot had a particularly good year and earned $100,000 in income. However, when she filed her tax return, she only reported $70,000 of income. She did not include $30,000 that she received as a sweepstakes prize, mistakenly believing it was non-taxable. This is a "substantial understatement" because Margot understated her income by 30% ($30,000 is 30% of her actual income of $100,000). The IRS could audit Margot's return up to six years from the filing date because of the substantial understatement, and force Margot to pay the additional tax owed on the understated amount, plus interest and penalties.

The statute of limitations for IRS *collection* of tax is ten years from the date tax is assessed. The ten-year collection statute period begins to run on the date of the tax assessment, not on the date of filing. So, for example, if the taxpayer owes when they file their tax return, the IRS will send a bill. The bill date is the assessment date. The IRS can attempt to collect unpaid taxes for up to ten years from the date the taxes are *assessed*.

This is also called the **Collection Statute Expiration Date**, or **CSED**. The ten-year CSED period begins to run on the date of the tax assessment, not on the date of filing. The IRS assigns a collection statute expiration date or "CSED" to every delinquent taxpayer account. Once the CSED expires, the IRS loses its right to seize assets or make payment demands. Certain events can extend the amount of time the IRS has to collect.

Example: Franco has always filed his tax returns on time. Five years ago, Franco was self-employed and did not understand how to manage his money or pay estimated taxes. He had a large tax bill from that year. Franco still filed his tax return on time and correctly reported the amount due, intending to make monthly payments. The IRS issued its assessment and sent Franco a bill for $24,000 (the amount that Franco owed, including penalties and interest). Franco requested an installment agreement and began making monthly payments toward his tax debt. Shortly thereafter, Franco had a car accident and became disabled. He no longer has the means to work or pay the bill. The IRS has five years left to collect on the debt, and after that, the statute for collection expires. Although the interest and penalties will continue to accrue, if Franco does not have any assets or any means to pay the bill, the debt will likely be deemed uncollectible.

Once again, if a taxpayer fails to file a return, the statute of limitation on assessment remains open indefinitely.

Example: Joan is 45 years old and unmarried. She makes very little money working part-time at a grocery store. She is usually under the filing requirement and therefore does not file a return. In 2023, she receives an audit notice for 2018, 2019, and 2020, stating that she may have underreported income for those years. Since Joan did not file tax returns for those years, the statute is still open, and she is forced to respond to the IRS audit notices. Unfortunately, she already shredded all her records for those years, so it may be more difficult to properly file those returns, if in fact she is required to do so. If Joan had filed her returns when they were due (even if not required to do so because of her low income), the assessment statute would have already been closed (unless there was a substantial understatement or the returns were fraudulent).

Unit 1: Study Questions

(Test yourself first, then check the correct answers at the end of this quiz.)

1. What is the normal statute of limitations for an IRS assessment on a tax return from which more than 25% of the taxpayer's gross income was omitted?

A. There is no statute of limitations on the return.
B. Three years from the date the return was filed.
C. Six years from the date the return was filed.
D. Ten years from the date the return was filed.

2. Roksana and Baptiste file a joint return. Their tax refund will be applied toward Baptiste's unpaid child support obligations from an earlier relationship. To request her portion of a joint refund, Roksana should file:

A. As an innocent spouse.
B. As a damaged spouse.
C. As an injured spouse.
D. For equitable relief.

3. Milla, age 26, and Leonardo, age 31, are married and live together. Leonardo's income was $45,000 in wages. Milla did not work and had no taxable income for the year. Milla refuses to file a joint tax return with Leonardo. Based on this information, which of the following statements is correct?

A. Leonardo is required to file a tax return. He must file MFS. Milla is not required to file a return.
B. They are both required to file tax returns, whether they file jointly or separately.
C. Leonardo is required to file a tax return, and he can claim his wife as a dependent.
D. Neither is required to file a tax return.

4. Which of the following taxpayers must have an individual taxpayer identification number (ITIN)?

A. A nonresident alien with a J-1 visa and a Social Security number who moves to the U.S.
B. Anyone who does not have a Social Security number but has U.S.-source income.
C. A nonresident alien who must file a U.S. tax return and is not eligible for a Social Security number.
D. All nonresident aliens that are physically present in the U.S. for 183 days.

5. Generally, how long should taxpayers keep the supporting documentation for their tax returns?

A. Four years from the date the return was filed, or the return was due, whichever is later.
B. Three years from the date the return was filed, or the return was due, whichever is later.
C. Two years from the date the return was filed, or the return was due, whichever is later.
D. Ten years from the date the return was filed, or the return was due, whichever is later.

6. Cristiano is single and earned $350,000 as a self-employed software developer during the year. Under the estimated tax safe harbor rules for high-income taxpayers, he can avoid an underpayment penalty if he pays *what percentage* of his prior-year tax liability?

A. 50%
B. 90%
C. 100%
D. 110%

7. Isabella files as single and has no dependents or refundable credits. All her income is from wages. Based on the figures below, is she required to pay estimated taxes in the current year?

AGI for prior tax year (2022)	$73,700
Total tax on her prior-year return (2022)	$9,224
Anticipated AGI for the current year (2023)	$82,800
Total current-year estimated tax liability (2023)	$11,270
Tax expected to be withheld in the current year	$10,250

A. Yes, she is required to make estimated tax payments.
B. No, she is not required to make estimated tax payments.
C. She is not required to make estimated tax payments because she is not self-employed.
D. None of the above is correct.

8. Catalina, age 20, is single and a full-time college student who is claimed as a dependent on her parents' tax return. Her parents provide the majority of her support and pay for all her college tuition and books. In 2023, Catalina earned $13,990 in wages from her part-time job. She had no other income. Is she required to file a tax return?

A. Yes.
B. No.
C. Catalina is only required to file a tax return if she is self-employed.
D. Catalina should file a return because she will receive a refund, but she is not required to file.

9. Which of the following is not an acceptable reason for extending the statute of limitations for claiming a refund past the normal filing deadline?

A. A bad debt from worthless securities.
B. Living in a federally declared disaster area.
C. Exceptions for military personnel.
D. Living outside the country for three years.

10. Bibiana, age 28, paid estimated tax in the prior year totaling $2,560. On December 10, 2023, she closed her business as a self-employed wedding planner. She is now unemployed and living with her parents. Bibiana expects to have zero tax liability in 2024. Which of the following statements is correct?

A. She is still required to make estimated tax payments.
B. She is not required to make any estimated tax payments in 2024.
C. She must pay a minimum of $2,560 in estimated tax payments in 2024, or she will be subject to a failure-to-pay penalty.
D. She must make a minimum of $1,000 in estimated tax payments in 2024, or she will be subject to an underpayment penalty.

11. Alice requests an extension (Form 4868) to give herself an extra six months to file her tax return. She chooses not to pay any taxes with the extension because her records are disorganized and she is uncertain of the amount she owes. On October 10, when she finally prepares her return, she discovers that she owes $3,000 in income tax. She pays the full amount when she files her return, before the extended due date. What penalties, if any, will Alice have to pay?

A. She will owe interest on the amount owed and a late payment penalty.
B. She will owe interest on the amount owed and a late filing penalty.
C. She will owe interest on the amount owed, a late payment penalty, and a late filing penalty.
D. She will not owe any penalties because she filed before the extended due date and paid the taxes owed along with the return.

12. When does the 10-year collection statute period for the IRS begin to run?

A. On the date the tax is assessed.
B. On the date of the IRS acceptance of filing a tax return.
C. On the date the taxpayer receives the bill.
D. On the date the taxpayer pays the tax.

13. Durant files his 2023 tax return on February 25, 2024. He has a balance due of $800 on the return. How long can he wait to pay the amount owed and not incur a late payment penalty?

A. He will owe a late payment penalty unless he pays his tax liability when he files his return.
B. He has until the due date of the return (not including extensions) to pay the amount owed and not owe a penalty.
C. He has until the due date of the return (including extensions) to pay the amount owed and not owe a penalty.
D. He does not have to pay the amount due by a certain date because it is less than the safe harbor amount of $1,000.

14. The 2023 backup withholding rate for U.S. taxpayers is:

A. 10%
B. 24%
C. 25%
D. 30%

15. Which of the following documents will be accepted as a valid means of identification for a taxpayer applying for an ITIN?

A. Notarized copies of birth certificates and passports.
B. Color copies of birth certificates and passports.
C. Original birth certificates and passports.
D. Photocopies of birth certificates and passports.

Unit 1: Quiz Answers

1. The answer is C. If a taxpayer omitted more than 25% of their gross income on his return, the IRS has up to six years to assess a deficiency.

2. The answer is C. Roksana should file a claim as an injured spouse to request her portion of their tax refund. She would do so by filing Form 8379, *Injured Spouse Allocation.* If the request is granted, the IRS will retain her husband's portion of their tax refund to offset his unpaid child support but will allow Roksana to obtain her portion of the refund. In contrast, innocent spouse relief is when tax has been incorrectly reported on a joint return, and one spouse is relieved of the obligation to pay the other spouse's portion of the tax liability.

3. The answer is A. Leonardo is required to file a tax return. Milla is not required to file a return. Leonardo will be required to file MFS (married filing separately) because Milla will not file jointly with him. Milla does not have any taxable income and therefore does not have to file a return.

4. The answer is C. A nonresident alien must request an individual taxpayer identification number if the person is not eligible for an SSN and they are required to file a tax return.

5. The answer is B. Taxpayers should keep the supporting documentation for their tax returns for at least three years from the date the return was filed, or three years from the date the return was due, whichever is later. This includes applicable worksheets, receipts, and other forms.

6. The answer is D. To avoid an underpayment penalty, Cristiano must pay the smaller of:

- 110% of his prior-year tax liability or
- 90% of his expected tax for the current year.

This estimated tax safe harbor rule applies to higher-income taxpayers with an adjusted gross income of more than $150,000 ($75,000 if filing an MFS return).

7. The answer is B. Isabella does not need to pay estimated tax because she expects her income tax withholding in the current year ($10,250) to be *greater* than both—90% of the tax to be shown on her current year return ($11,270 × 90% = $10,143) and 100% of her prior-year tax liability ($9,224). Therefore, Isabella qualifies for the safe harbor rule and is not required to make estimated tax payments. A taxpayer is not required to pay estimated tax if:

- The taxpayer was a U.S. citizen or resident alien and had no tax liability in the prior year, and
- The prior tax year covered a twelve-month period.

A taxpayer also does not have to pay estimated tax if she pays enough through withholding so that the tax due on the return is less than $1,000. In most cases, a taxpayer must pay estimated tax if she expects withholding (plus any refundable credits) to be less than the smaller of:

- 90% of the tax to be shown on the current year tax return, or
- 100% of the tax shown on the prior-year tax return.

8. The answer is A. Catalina must file a tax return. A single dependent whose earned income was more than $13,850 in 2023 must generally file a return. Her parents may still claim Catalina as a dependent and a qualifying child because she is a full-time student and under age 24 at the end of the year, and did not provide more than one-half of her own support.

9. The answer is D. Living outside the country is not a valid reason to extend the statute of limitations for claiming a refund. In some cases, a request for a tax refund will be honored past the normal three-year deadline. Exceptions exist for military personnel, individuals who are financially disabled, taxpayers who live in federally-declared disaster areas, and taxpayers who have bad debts from worthless securities.

10. The answer is B. Regardless of the amount she owed in a prior year, Bibiana is not required to pay estimated tax if she expects, and in fact has, a zero tax liability for the current tax year.

11. The answer is A. Even though she filed an extension request using Form 4868, Alice may owe interest and a late payment (i.e., failure-to-pay) penalty on the amount owed if she does not pay the tax due by the regular due date. However, she will not be assessed a late filing penalty (failure-to-file) because she filed her tax return before the extended due date.

12. The answer is A. The statute of limitations for IRS collection of tax is ten years from the date tax is assessed. If the taxpayer owes when they file their tax return, the IRS will send a bill. The bill date is the assessment date. The IRS can then attempt to collect unpaid taxes for up to ten years from the date the taxes are assessed.

13. The answer is B. Durant has until the original due date of the return (not including extensions) to pay the amount owed and not incur a late payment penalty. Taxpayers should submit their payment of taxes due on or before the unextended due date. For the 2023 tax year, Durant has until April 15, 2024, to pay the amount he owes.

14. The answer is B. The 2023 backup withholding rate is 24%. The IRS may require backup withholding if a taxpayer has a delinquent tax debt; if he fails to report all his interest, dividends, and other income, or if his Social Security number does not match records provided to the IRS.

15. The answer is C. Only original documents of birth certificates and passports are accepted (or documents that have been "certified" by the *original* issuing agency). Notarized copies are not accepted.

Unit 2: Determining Filing Status and Residency

For additional information, read:
Publication 17, *Your Federal Income Tax*
Publication 54, *Tax Guide for U.S. Citizens and Resident Aliens Abroad*
Publication 519, *U.S. Tax Guide for Aliens*

The IRS uses a taxpayer's filing status to determine filing requirements, standard deductions, eligibility for certain credits, and the amounts of tax owed.

There are **five filing statuses**, with specific rules governing each. Some taxpayers are eligible to use more than one filing status; usually, these taxpayers may choose the filing status that will result in the lowest overall tax.

In general, a taxpayer's marital status on the last day of the year (December 31) determines their marital status for the entire year. However, there are special rules that apply to annulled marriages, widowed taxpayers, and surviving spouses who have dependent children.

Note: Federal law does not allow Registered Domestic Partners (RDPs) to file a joint return. This rule also applies to civil unions.[24] However, the IRS *does* recognize common-law marriages. Currently, the only states that recognize common-law marriage are: the District of Columbia, Colorado, Iowa, Kansas, Montana, Oklahoma, Rhode Island, and Texas. Common-law marriage laws vary from state to state, and cohabitation alone does not constitute a common-law marriage. Several states now recognize same-sex common-law marriages. You must be familiar with the marital laws of your state in order to correctly determine filing status.

Example: Chauncey and Archibald are a same-sex couple living together in South Dakota. Both are U.S. citizens. On May 20, 2023, they took a one-month trip to Canada and got married in a civil ceremony. The United States recognizes foreign marriages performed in Canada, so Chauncey and Archibald are now legally married for federal tax law purposes. They may file either Married Filing Jointly, or Married Filing Separately for the tax year. Neither one can file "single."

Example: Dwight and Charlotte live together in Texas, which is a common-law state. Although Dwight and Charlotte never applied for a marriage license[25] or went through a formal marriage ceremony, they tell their family and friends that they are married, use the same last name, own a house together, and have three children together. In the state of Texas, their conduct rises to the level of "holding oneself out to the public" as a married couple. Therefore, they are considered "married" under the common-law statutes and can file a joint federal return together.

---

[24] Per Revenue Ruling 2013-17, although RDPs are legally treated in the same manner as marriages in the state of California for *state* income tax purposes, for federal tax law purposes, they are not. On the EA exam, you will not be tested on the matrimonial laws of any particular state, but you must know that only a legal marriage is recognized for IRS purposes, and not any other type of civil union or registered domestic partnership.

[25] Marriages are usually created by a legal ceremony. Some states, however, recognize common law marriage. A common law marriage may be defined as an informal marriage by agreement entered into by two individuals having capacity to marry, ordinarily without compliance with statutory formalities such as marriage licenses (IRM 25-018-001). For example, a common law marriage in Texas entitles couples to the ability to file taxes jointly. Couples who live in a common law marriage state can also choose to register their common law marriage by filing a declaration with the county clerk, if they wish.

Single

Marital status is generally determined on the last day of the year. A taxpayer is considered single for the entire tax year if, on the <u>last day</u> of the tax year, he or she was:

- Unmarried,
- Legally separated under a decree of divorce or separate maintenance,
- Legally divorced by the end of the year.

Example: Reuben and Natasha lived together until July 30, when they separated. Reuben filed for divorce on August 1, and their divorce became final on December 30, 2023. They do not have any dependents. They each must file as "single" for 2023. It does not matter that they were legally married and lived together during much of the year. The fact that the divorce became final before the end of the year means that they are *unmarried* for tax purposes in 2023.

Example: Margot and Juliet are a same-sex couple living in California. They have been registered domestic partners (RDPs) since 2004. Under California law, they can file a joint *California* return. However, for federal tax purposes, they are considered "unmarried." They must file "single" federal returns. Margot and Juliet are both high-income earners. They decide not to get married, and instead to remain registered domestic partners, because in their particular situation, their overall tax rate would increase if they were to marry and file jointly.

Married Filing Jointly (MFJ)

The "married filing jointly" status typically offers more tax advantages than filing separately. This option allows both spouses to report their combined income, expenses, exemptions, and deductions on one return. Spouses can file a joint return even if only one spouse has income.

This filing status is an election, <u>not</u> the default. This is because *both* spouses must agree to sign a joint return, and *both* are responsible for any tax owed, even if all the income was earned by only one spouse. If one spouse does not wish to file jointly, then both spouses must default to MFS (unless one qualifies for a different filing status). In the event of a subsequent divorce, both spouses are still held liable for any taxes owed from the original joint return, with exceptions for innocent spouse relief. As long as marriage was valid on December 31st, taxpayers can file jointly if they:

- Live together as married spouses, or
- Live together in a common-law marriage recognized in the state where they now reside or in the state where the common-law marriage began, or
- Live apart but are not legally separated or divorced,[26] or
- Are separated under an interlocutory (not final) divorce decree.

In addition, a widowed taxpayer may use the married filing jointly status and file jointly with their deceased spouse, if the taxpayer's spouse died during the year and the taxpayer has not remarried as of the end of the year.

---

[26] State law governs whether a taxpayer is married or legally separated under a divorce or separate maintenance decree. Single filing status generally applies if the taxpayer is not married, divorced, or legally separated according to state law.

Example: Osvaldo and Jessamine separated on October 9, 2023. Neither Osvaldo nor Jessamine filed for divorce yet, but they plan to file for divorce in the future. They do not have any children or dependents. Since their divorce was not final before the end of the year, and they are not legally separated, they are considered "married" for tax purposes. They must either file jointly or separately. Neither one qualifies to file as "single" or "head of household."

Nonresident Alien Spouses: Special rules apply to nonresident alien spouses. A U.S. resident or U.S. citizen who is married to a *non*resident alien can elect to file a joint return as long as *both* spouses agree to be taxed on their worldwide income. An election statement must be attached to the joint return.[27]

Example: Patricia is a U.S. citizen living in Indonesia. She is married to Vikal, a nonresident alien and citizen of Indonesia. The spouses elect to treat Vikal as a U.S. resident (for tax purposes). Patricia and Vikal must request an ITIN for Vikal and report their worldwide income for the year they make the choice, and for all later years unless the election is ended or suspended. Although Patricia and Vikal must file a joint return for the year they make the election, as long as one spouse is a U.S. citizen or U.S. resident, they can file either joint or separate returns for later years.

Married Filing Separately (MFS)

The MFS status is for taxpayers who are married and either:
- Choose to file separate returns or
- Do not agree to file a joint return.

If one spouse chooses to file an MFS return, the other is forced to do the same, since a joint return must be signed by both spouses. The MFS filing status means the two spouses report their own income, exemptions, credits, and deductions on separate returns, even if one spouse had no income. This filing status may benefit a taxpayer who wants to be responsible only for their own tax, or if it results in less tax than filing a joint return.[28] Typically, a married couple will pay more tax on a combined basis when filing separately, than they would by filing jointly.

Example: Arush and Namita have always filed jointly in the past. However, Namita has chosen to separate her finances from her husband this year, even though they are still living together. Arush wants to file jointly with Namita, but she has refused. Namita files her tax return using married filing separately as her filing status; therefore, Arush is forced to file MFS, as well.

Specific features of the MFS filing status include the following:
- The tax rates are generally higher at the same levels of taxable income than those applicable to MFJ, but there are some scenarios where filing separate returns can produce a better tax result.
- The exemption amount for the AMT is half that which is allowed on a joint return.
- Various credits are either not allowed or they are more limited than on a joint return.
- The capital loss deduction is limited to $1,500; half of what is allowable on a joint return.
- The standard deduction is half the amount allowed on a joint return and cannot be claimed if the taxpayer's spouse itemizes deductions.
- Neither spouse can deduct student loan interest on an MFS return.

---

[27] This is called a "§6013(g) election," and a required election statement must be attached to the return.
[28] Special rules apply for community property states.

Example: Harrison and Regina are married and live together. They have always kept their assets and finances separate and always file separate tax returns. Harrison plans to itemize his deductions this year, so Regina is forced to either itemize her deductions or claim a standard deduction of zero.

Married taxpayers sometimes choose to file separate returns when one spouse does not want to be responsible for the other spouse's tax obligations, or because filing separately may result in a lower total tax. For example, the couple's overall tax liability may be lower on a separate return when one spouse has significant medical expenses or large miscellaneous itemized deductions (such as a casualty loss). Couples have the ability to change their filing status between MFJ (married filing jointly) and MFS (married filing separately) every year without limitations. This allows for flexibility and potential tax benefits depending on the couple's tax scenario.

Example: Daniel and Inara are married and live together in Florida. They usually file jointly. Daniel earns $120,000 in wages, while Inara earns much less; $40,000. This year, Inara had very high medical expenses due to a hip replacement procedure. If they file jointly, the medical expenses cannot be deducted, because the out-of-pocket medical expenses do not exceed 7.5% of their joint AGI, so they do not qualify as a deduction. However, if Daniel and Inara file separate returns, Inara's medical expenses are deductible on her separate tax return, eliminating her tax liability entirely and resulting in a large tax refund. They calculate their taxes both ways, and find that their overall tax liability will be several hundred dollars less by filing separate returns, so they choose to file separately.

Another common reason a taxpayer may choose the MFS filing status is to avoid a refund offset against the other spouse's outstanding prior debt. This might include delinquent child support or student loans, or a tax liability one spouse incurred before the marriage. This is especially true if the taxpayers reside in a state that does not recognize injured spouse provisions.

Example: Phillip and Dinah were married in 2023. Dinah owes $80,000 in delinquent student loans. Phillip chooses to file separately from Dinah, so his refund will not be offset by her overdue tax debts. If they were to file jointly, their entire refund might be retained in order to pay Dinah's delinquent debt. Phillip files a separate return from Dinah. He retains his entire refund, which is deposited into his separate bank account.

Example: Hillard and Ingrid were married in 2023. They reside in Georgia. Ingrid owes $15,000 in back child support and delinquent state income taxes. Georgia law does not contain a provision for injured spouse relief. Hillard decides to file a separate return from Ingrid, so he can retain both of his federal and state tax refunds. Hillard does not have to file any injured spouse forms, because he did not file a joint return with Ingrid. He receives both of his separate refunds. Ingrid files her own separate return, and her federal and state tax refunds are offset to pay her delinquent debts.

Amending Filing Status

There are rules for when married taxpayers are allowed to change their filing status. Although it is possible to amend a person's filing status, there are strict rules for doing so. Taxpayers generally cannot change from a joint return to a separate return *after the unextended due date* of the return.

For example, if a married couple files a joint (2023) return on February 1, 2024, and subsequently decide they wanted to file separately instead, they would have only until April 15, 2024 (the unextended due date of their original return) to file amended returns using the MFS filing status.

Example: Alvin and Ivana are married and live in Montana. They e-file their 2023 tax return jointly, on February 5, 2024. A few weeks later, Ivana discovers that Alvin has a hidden bank account and a second set of books for his business. Ivana is concerned that Alvin may not be reporting all the income from his business, and she is afraid of being audited in the future. Ivana confronts her husband, and he refuses to discuss the issue. Ivana decides to quickly amend her joint return to a separate return. She files Form 1040-X on March 3, 2024, to file a separate return for herself. Since she filed her amended return *before* the April 15 filing deadline, the IRS will process the return, and her filing status will be adjusted to MFS, making her responsible only for her own tax liability.

A notable exception to this strict deadline allows a personal representative for a deceased taxpayer to change from a joint return, elected by the surviving spouse, to a separate return for the decedent for up to a year after the filing deadline.[29]

Example: Landon and Bianca have always filed jointly. Bianca dies suddenly on November 16, 2023, and her last will and testament names Laura, her daughter from a previous marriage, as the executor of her estate. Landon files a joint return with Bianca for the tax year 2023, but Laura, as the executor, decides that it would be better for her deceased mother's estate if Bianca's final tax return were filed as MFS. Laura files an amended return claiming MFS status for Bianca and signs the return as the executor. Laura has a full year after the filing deadline to submit the amended return.

To change from separate returns *to* a joint return (MFS to MFJ), taxpayers must file an amended return using Form 1040-X, and may do so at any time within three years from the due date of the separate returns (not including extensions).

Example: Jackie and Kaleb are married, but have been physically separated for two years. They did not file for divorce and have been working on their marriage with a counselor. They choose to file separate returns for 2021 and 2022. On January 2, 2023, Jackie and Kaleb reconcile and move back in with each other. Jackie and Kaleb decide to file jointly for 2023. They can also choose to amend their prior-year separate tax returns to "married filing joint" by filing a Form 1040-X. They have up to three years to amend their previously-filed separate returns to joint returns.

Head of Household (HOH)

A taxpayer who qualifies to file as head of household will usually have a lower tax rate than a single or MFS taxpayer and will receive a higher standard deduction. The head of household status is available to taxpayers who meet all of the following requirements:

- The taxpayer must be single, divorced, legally separated, or "considered unmarried" on the last day of the year.
- The taxpayer must have paid more than half the cost of keeping up a home for the year.
- The taxpayer must have had a qualifying person living in his home for more than half the year. There are exceptions for temporary absences, as well as for a qualifying parent, who does not have to live with the taxpayer. This would include hospitalization and stays in a nursing home.

---

[29] The IRM outlines the procedure for returns that are amended from MFJ to MFS (IRM 21.6.1.5.6) by only one of the spouses. The IRS creates a "dummy" MFS return for the other spouse for return processing, and then that dummy return can be amended by the second spouse, if desired.

For IRS purposes, "temporary absences" include time away from home going to college, vacation, business, medical care, hospitalization, military service, summer camp, and detention in a juvenile facility. It must be reasonable to assume that the absent person will return to the home after the temporary absence.

> **Example:** Rhonda is unmarried. Her son, Nathaniel, was eighteen years old at the end of the year. Nathaniel lived away from his mother all year because he was going to college. He lived on campus, in the dorms, returning home only on holidays. Nathaniel does not work and does not provide any of his own support. Since his time away from home to attend school is considered a "temporary absence," Rhonda may claim head of household filing status, and claim Nathaniel as her dependent.

When determining head of household filing status, valid household expenses used to calculate whether a taxpayer is paying more than half the cost of maintaining a home include:

- Rent, mortgage interest, property taxes
- Home insurance, repairs, and utilities
- Food eaten in the home

Valid expenses do *not* include clothing, education, medical treatment, vacations, life insurance, or transportation. Welfare payments are not considered amounts that the taxpayer provides to maintain a home.

The "qualifying person" for the HOH filing status must generally be related to the taxpayer either by blood, adoption, or marriage. However, a foster child also qualifies if the child was legally placed in the home by a government agency. For purposes of the head of household filing status, a "qualifying person" is defined as:

- A qualifying child,
- A married child who can be claimed as a dependent, or
- A dependent parent,
- A qualifying relative that meets certain relationship tests

A taxpayer's qualifying person may include: a child or stepchild, sibling or step-sibling, or a descendant of any of these. For example, a niece or nephew, stepbrother or stepsister, or grandchild may all be eligible as qualifying persons for the HOH filing status.[30]

> **Example:** Kevin is unmarried and age 64. He earns $49,000 in wages during the year. His disabled sister, Francesca, has lived with him since their parents passed away six years ago. Francesca is 42 and has severe autism. She cannot engage in any substantial gainful activity, but she does receive a small amount of State Disability Assistance every month. These amounts are not taxable and Francesca does not have a filing requirement. Kevin can file as head of household and claim Francesca as his qualifying child, because she meets the relationship test (she is his sibling), and she meets the age test for a qualifying child, because she is permanently disabled.

---

[30] A taxpayer cannot file HOH if their only dependent is a Registered Domestic Partner. To see a full list of these rules, see: https://apps.irs.gov/app/vita/content/globalmedia/head_of_household_qualifying_person_4012.pdf

Example: Lamonte is 71 years old and unmarried. His daughter, Brooke, lived with him the entire year. Brooke turned 29 at the end of the year. She does not have a job, did not provide any of her own support, and cannot be claimed as a dependent by anyone else. She is not disabled. Although she cannot be Lamonte's qualifying child, because of her age, she is a qualifying relative. As a result, Lamonte may use the HOH filing status.

Example: Asmara is unmarried and age 52. Asmara's 23-year-old son, Ziyad, lives with her all year long. He has a part-time job and earns $9,800 in wages during the year. He is not disabled or a college student, so he does not meet the age test for a qualifying child. Since he made over the "deemed exemption" amount,[31] he is also not a qualifying relative. As a result, Asmara cannot file as head of household because her son is not a dependent (he does not qualify under the rules for a "qualifying child" or for a "qualifying relative"). Asmara is forced to file as Single.

An unrelated individual, and even certain family members, may still be considered a "qualifying relative" for dependency purposes but will not be a qualifying person for the HOH filing status.[32]

An example of someone who could be a qualifying relative, but not a qualifying person for the head of household filing status, are cousins. A cousin is not a close enough relative to be a qualifying child (unless the cousin is placed in the taxpayer's home as a qualifying foster child). A cousin can be a qualifying relative, but only if the cousin lives with the taxpayer the entire year. A spouse or registered domestic partner also cannot be a qualifying person for head of household purposes.

Example: Constantina is age 36, unmarried, and does not have any children. On January 2, Constantina's 15-year-old cousin, Bailey, is put into foster care because her mother is arrested for drug trafficking and later convicted. Constantina does not want her cousin Bailey to be in foster care, so she applies to be Bailey's foster parent, and she is approved. On March 1, Bailey is placed in Constantina's home as her foster child. Constantina may file as head of household and claim Bailey as a qualifying *child*, because Bailey is her foster child.

Example: Adina and Paola are registered domestic partners (RDPs) who live together in California. They do not have any children or other dependents. Adina works full-time and earns $90,000 in wages for the year. Paola does not have a job and has no taxable income. Adina fully supports Paola, but she cannot file as head of household because a registered domestic partner is not a "qualifying person" for head of household status. Adina may be able to claim Paola as a qualifying relative on her federal income tax return, but she will be forced to file "single."

Example: Richard is unmarried and age 54. He earns $62,000 in wages for the year working for a grocery store. His old Army friend, Emmet, lives with Richard all year long. Emmet does not work, because he is disabled. Emmet and Richard are not related, but they are best friends. Richard pays for all the household costs as well as food and utilities for both of them. As a result, Richard can claim Emmet as a "qualifying relative" dependent, but Richard cannot file as "head of household" because Emmet is not a qualifying person for HOH filing status (i.e., Emmet is not related to Richard by blood, marriage, or adoption).

---

[31] In determining who is a qualifying relative, the "deemed exemption" amount is $4,700 for 2023. We will cover this topic later.
[32] The rules for qualifying children and qualifying relatives will be covered in detail in the next unit, Personal and Dependency Exemptions.

Example: William is unmarried and age 42. He earns $60,000 as a self-employed contractor. William's cousin, Jimmy, age 22, has lived with William all year. Jimmy is attending junior college and also has $3,100 in wages from a part-time job on campus. William cannot file as head of household, because Jimmy cannot be a qualifying child. However, William can claim Jimmy as his qualifying relative, because Jimmy earned less than the deemed exemption amount and lived with William all year.

Divorced and Noncustodial Parents: A taxpayer can qualify as HOH, even though they may not claim a qualifying child as their dependent. This happens most often with divorced parents. This is because the head of household filing status applies to the taxpayer who maintains the main home of a qualifying child.

However, a custodial parent may choose to *release* the dependency exemption to a noncustodial parent. In this scenario, the custodial parent would claim head of household filing status, while the noncustodial parent would claim the dependency exemption.

Example: Nicolas and Vivian have been divorced for two years and they live apart. They have a twelve-year-old daughter named Cristina, who lives with her mother during the week and only sees her father on weekends. Therefore, Vivian is considered Cristina's custodial parent. The parents agree, however, to allow Nicolas to claim the dependency exemption for Cristina on his tax return. Nicolas correctly files as "Single" and claims Cristina as his dependent. This entitles him to the Child Tax Credit. Vivian may still file as HOH if she otherwise qualifies, but she will not claim the dependency exemption for Cristina.

"Considered Unmarried" for HOH Status

There are some instances where a taxpayer can be "considered unmarried" for tax purposes only. To be "considered unmarried" on the last day of the tax year, a taxpayer must meet all of the following conditions:

- File a separate return from their spouse.
- Pay more than half the cost of keeping up a home for the tax year, and maintain the home as the main residence of a qualifying child, stepchild, or foster child for more than half the year.
- Not live with a spouse in the home during the last six months of the tax year.
- Be able to claim an exemption for the child (although there is an exception for divorced parents, explained later).

The "considered unmarried" rules apply in determining who can claim a child for dependency and head of household purposes. A couple, if not formally separated or divorced, must live apart for *more than half the year* for either spouse to claim HOH status.

Example: Austin and Cayla physically separated on February 10, 2023, and lived apart for the remainder of the year. They do not have a written separation agreement and have not filed for divorce. Their six-year-old daughter, Brigid, lived with her father all year, and Austin paid more than half the cost of keeping up the home. Austin claims Brigid as his dependent because he is the custodial parent. Austin can claim head of household status. Although Austin is still legally married, he can file as head of household because he meets all the requirements to be "considered unmarried."

> **Example:** Darya and Craig physically separated on November 4, 2023. Neither spouse had filed for divorce or legal separation by the end of the year. They have one minor child, Krissy, age eight. Even though Krissy lived with her mother Darya, Darya does not qualify for head of household filing status because she and Craig did not live apart for the last six months of the year, and are not legally separated or divorced.

Death or Birth during the Year: A taxpayer may still file as head of household and claim a child as a dependent if the child is born or dies during the year. The taxpayer must have provided more than half of the cost of keeping up a home that was the child's main home while he or she was alive.

> **Example:** Brigitta is unmarried and lives alone. Brigitta gives birth to a son on September 1, 2023. She takes her child home, but the child is sickly. The infant dies one month later. Brigitta can claim her deceased son on her tax return, and file as Head of Household, even though the child only lived a short time. Assuming Brigitta qualifies, the child would also be a qualifying child for the Child Tax Credit and the Earned Income Tax Credit. This is true even if Brigitta is unable to obtain a Social Security number for the child.[33]

Dependent Parents: If a taxpayer's qualifying person is a dependent parent, the taxpayer can file as HOH even if the parent does not live with the taxpayer. The taxpayer must pay more than half the cost of keeping up a home that was the parent's main home for the entire year. This rule also applies to a parent in a retirement home. A qualifying "parent" may be a stepparent, in-law, or grandparent who is related to the taxpayer by blood, marriage, or adoption.

> **Example:** Theodore, age 55, is unmarried and lives alone. Theodore has financially supported his elderly mother, Susan, for many years. Susan is 82 and lives in a senior living facility. Susan does not have any taxable income, and Theodore provided more than one-half of her support. Theodore may file as head of household, and claim his elderly mother as his dependent.

> **Example:** Janie is single and fully financially supports her elderly mother, Leona, who is age 78 and lives in her own apartment. Leona dies on February 12, 2023. Janie can claim her mother as a dependent and file as head of household for 2023, even though Leona was not alive for the entire year.

> **Example:** Caroline is 54 years old and single. She pays the monthly bill for Shasta Pines Nursing Home, where her 79-year-old mother lives. Caroline's mother, Greta, has lived at Shasta Pines for two years and has no income. Since Caroline pays more than one-half of the cost of her mother's living expenses, Caroline qualifies for head of household filing status, even though her mother lives in a retirement home.

Special Rules for Nonresident Alien Spouses

A taxpayer who is married to a nonresident alien may elect to file as head of household by "disregarding" the nonresident alien spouse. This is true even if both spouses <u>lived together</u> throughout the year. This is a *unique* rule that only applies to taxpayers who are married to nonresident aliens. In order to take advantage of this special rule, the U.S. taxpayer cannot file jointly with the nonresident alien spouse (by electing to treat the nonresident alien spouse as a U.S. resident).

---

[33] If a child was born and died in the same year and was not issued an SSN, the taxpayer may enter "DIED" on the Form 1040, and attach a copy of the child's birth certificate. The tax return must be filed on paper.

The taxpayer must *also* have a qualifying child (or another qualifying dependent, such as a parent) to qualify for head of household status.

Remember, a U.S. citizen or resident who is married to a nonresident alien <u>must have</u> another qualifying person in order to "disregard" their nonresident alien spouse in order to be eligible to file as a head of household.

Example: Two years ago, Wharton, a U.S. citizen, met and married Esmeralda, a nonresident alien who is a citizen of Ecuador. The couple lived together in Ecuador while Wharton was on sabbatical from his university teaching position. They had a son, who was born on June 18, 2023. Esmeralda does not wish to file jointly with Wharton and does not wish to make the election to be treated as a U.S. resident, because she does not want to pay tax on her worldwide income, as she would be required to do if she filed jointly with Wharton. Wharton can file as head of household and claim his infant son as a dependent, even though he and Esmeralda lived together all year, because Esmeralda is a nonresident alien.

Example: Leanne is a U.S. citizen. She is married to Nunzio, a citizen of Italy. Leanne and Nunzio reside in Italy together, along with Leanne's 62-year-old mother, Margaret. Margaret is also a U.S. citizen. Leanne supports her mother financially, because Margaret has no taxable income. Nunzio does not want to file jointly with Leanne, because he owns a successful business in Italy and he does not want to pay U.S. income tax on his worldwide income, or have to file an FBAR for his Italian bank accounts. Nonetheless, Leanne may choose to "disregard" her nonresident alien spouse, and file as head of household, claiming her mother as a dependent.

Qualifying Surviving Spouse

Qualifying Surviving Spouse (QSS)[34] is the least common filing status. A qualifying surviving spouse receives the same standard deduction and uses the same tax brackets as married taxpayers who file jointly. This filing status <u>only applies</u> if the surviving spouse remains unmarried *and* has a qualifying dependent. In the year of the spouse's death, a taxpayer can generally file a joint return. However, if the surviving spouse *remarries* before the end of the year, the deceased spouse's return must be filed MFS (married filing separately).

Example: Daphne and her husband, Vince, have a 12-year-old son named Oscar. Vince dies on February 1, 2023. A few months later, Daphne meets Adam, and she remarries on December 20, 2023. Since Daphne remarried in the same year her late husband died, she no longer qualifies for the MFJ status with her deceased husband. However, Daphne does qualify to file jointly with her new husband, Adam. Therefore, Vince's (the deceased) filing status for his final tax return must be MFS. The executor of Vince's estate would be responsible for filing his final tax return.

For each of the two years following the year of the spouse's death, the surviving spouse can use the qualifying surviving spouse filing status if the survivor has a qualifying dependent and does not remarry. After two years, the taxpayer's filing status converts to single or HOH, depending upon which status applies.

---

[34] The former filing status qualifying widow(er) (QW) name was recently changed to qualifying surviving spouse (QSS), but you may see either term on the IRS website and IRS publications.

For example, if a taxpayer's spouse died in 2023 and the survivor did not remarry, the taxpayer could file a joint return with their deceased spouse in 2023, then use the qualifying surviving spouse (QSS) filing status for tax year 2024 *and* 2025 (two years *following* the year of death). After this two-year period has ended, the surviving spouse may no longer file as QSS.

Filing Status After the Death of a Spouse (with Dependent Child)	
Tax Year	**Filing Status**
Year of death	MFJ or MFS
1st year after death	Qualifying surviving spouse*
2nd year after death	Qualifying surviving spouse*
3rd and subsequent years after death	Head of household or single

To be eligible for the "qualifying surviving spouse" filing status, the taxpayer normally must:

- Not have remarried before the end of the year.
- Have been *eligible* to file a joint return in the year the spouse died; (it does not matter if a joint return was actually filed).
- Have a qualifying child[35] for the year. A qualifying child can be a child, adopted child, or a stepchild, but does *not* include a foster child for the purposes of this filing status.
- Have furnished over half the cost of keeping up the child's home for the entire year.

Example: Sampson and Rosie are married and have always filed jointly. Rosie dies on July 3, 2023. Sampson has one daughter, Angie, who is ten years old. Sampson did not remarry before the end of the year. Therefore, Sampson's filing status for 2023 is MFJ or MFS, since 2023 is the last year his wife was alive. For 2024 and 2025, Sampson can claim Angie as his dependent and file as a "qualifying surviving spouse," which is a more favorable filing status than single or head of household. For 2026, Sampson could file as HOH, assuming Angie is still his dependent child and he remains unmarried.

Example: Patrick and Janet are married and have always filed jointly. They have one 15-year-old foster child named Ramona, who they claim as a dependent. They do not have any other children or dependents. Patrick dies on June 10, 2023. Janet plans to file jointly with Patrick in 2023. Assuming she does not remarry, Janet would qualify for Head of Household filing status in 2023. She would not qualify for the "qualifying surviving spouse" filing status, because Ramona is a foster child, and that is not a qualifying relationship for the QSS filing status.

Example: Scott and Noelle are married. Scott has a 17-year-old son named Toby, from a prior relationship. Scott dies suddenly on October 4, 2023. Toby continues to live with his stepmother and Noelle supports her stepson financially. Noelle files jointly with her late husband Scott and claims Toby as a dependent for 2023. If Noelle does not remarry, she can file as a "qualifying surviving spouse" in 2024 and 2025, as long as Toby continues to qualify as her dependent, because a stepchild is a qualifying child for the QSS filing status.

---

[35] While the taxpayer still needs a qualifying child that meets the qualifications listed above, the child does not have to be claimed as a dependent on the tax return. The taxpayer must only provide the child's name on the return.

Annulments

Annulment is a legal procedure for declaring a marriage null and void.[36] If a taxpayer obtains a court decree of annulment that holds no valid marriage ever existed, the couple is considered *unmarried* even if they filed joint returns for earlier years. Unlike divorce, an annulment is retroactive. Taxpayers who have annulled their marriage must file amended returns (Form 1040-X), claiming single (or head of household status, if applicable) for all the tax years affected by the annulment that are not closed by the statute of limitations.

Example: Norah and Remington were granted an annulment on October 31, 2023. They were married for two years. Remington has sole custody of one son from a prior relationship. For 2023, Norah must file as single and must amend the prior two years' tax returns to "single" as well. Remington must also amend his returns. If he otherwise qualifies, Remington can amend his returns to head of household filing status, claiming his own son as a dependent.

Example: Howie and Cassie were married in Alaska three years ago. They do not have any children or other dependents. Cassie discovers that Howie was already legally married in Canada to a different woman and has been living a double life. Cassie files for an annulment on December 1, 2023 on the grounds of bigamy. Their marriage is annulled on March 8, 2024. Howie and Cassie filed joint returns for every year that they were married. Cassie must amend her prior-year tax returns to "single" because her marriage has been legally annulled.

Determining Residency for Tax Purposes

To accurately file their taxes, a taxpayer must determine their residency status. For the IRS, an "alien" refers to an individual who is not a U.S. citizen. Aliens are divided into two categories: **"nonresident alien"** and **"resident alien."** This classification is crucial because it determines how these taxpayers are taxed.[37]

Residency status is important because these taxpayers are taxed in different ways:

- **Resident aliens** are typically taxed on all of their income worldwide, similar to U.S. citizens.
- **Nonresident aliens** are only taxed on income earned within the United States and certain income related to conducting business in the country.
- **Dual-status aliens** have both nonresident and resident alien statuses during the same tax year. Different rules apply for the parts of the year when they were a U.S. resident and nonresident. The most common dual-status years are the year of arrival and departure from the U.S.

Residency for IRS purposes is <u>not the same</u> as legal immigration status. Do not confuse residency for federal tax purposes with:

- Immigration residency
- Residency requirements for college tuition or earning a degree, etc.
- Residency requirements for state income taxes

---

[36] Fraud is the most common basis for annulment petitions, but depending on the jurisdiction, other legal reasons for an annulment include bigamy, forced marriage, impotence, undisclosed infertility or sterility, and mental incompetence.
[37] Nonresidents who are married to U.S. Citizens or U.S. resident aliens can make an election to file a joint return for tax purposes and file as Married Filing Jointly.) If both married taxpayers are nonresident aliens, they CANNOT file as Married Filing Jointly, they must file as Married Filing Separately.

An individual may be considered a U.S. resident for tax purposes, based upon the time spent in the United States, regardless of their immigration status. A nonresident alien could be someone who lives outside the U.S., and simply invests in U.S. property or stocks, and is therefore required to file a tax return to correctly report their U.S. income.

Tax Residency Tests

Certain rules exist for determining the residency for aliens. If a taxpayer is an alien (not a U.S. citizen), the taxpayer is considered a nonresident alien for tax purposes unless he or she meets one of two tests: the **green card** test or the **substantial presence** test.

Green Card Test: An alien taxpayer is automatically considered a U.S. resident if they are "lawful permanent residents" of the United States at any time during the tax year. A lawful immigrant that has been issued an alien registration card, also known as a "green card" is a U.S. resident by default.

With a green card holder, their residency "start date" is the first day during the calendar year on which the alien is physically present in the United States as a lawful permanent resident. However, an alien who has been present in the U.S. any time during a calendar year as a lawful permanent resident may opt to be treated as a resident alien for the entire calendar year.

Example: Hector is a citizen of Portugal. Hector meets and marries Theresa, an American citizen, while she was visiting family on an extended visit in Portugal. They decide to live in the United States, rather than Portugal. Two weeks after their marriage, Hector applies for a green card at a U.S. consulate in his home country. On December 20, 2023, Hector is issued his permanent resident card (green card). Hector and Theresa fly back to the United States together and land in New York City on January 10, 2024. Hector's official residency start date is January 10, 2024, his first date of physical presence in the United States.

Figure 1-Permanent Resident Card Sample, (courtesy of USCIS)

Substantial Presence Test: An alien without a green card is considered a U.S. resident for tax purposes only if they meet the substantial presence test for the calendar year. To meet this test, they must be physically present in the United States for at least:

- 31 days during the current tax year (2023), and
- 183 days during the three-year period, which includes the current year (2023) and the two years immediately *preceding* the current year (2021 and 2022).

For purposes of the 183-day requirement, all the days present in the current year are counted, along with:

- 1/3 of the days present in the previous year (i.e., 2022), and
- 1/6 of the days present in the second year *before* the current year (i.e., 2021).

Example: Juliana is a citizen of Brazil. Her brother, Victor, is a naturalized U.S. citizen living in the United States and Juliana visits him frequently. She obtains a visitor's visa and was physically present in the U.S. for 120 days in each of the years 2021, 2022, and 2023. To determine if she meets the substantial presence test for 2023, she must count the full 120 days of presence in 2023, 40 days in 2022 (1/3 of 120 days), and 20 days in 2021 (1/6 of 120 days). Since the total for the 3-year period is 180 days (and therefore under the 183-day requirement for the substantial presence test), Juliana is not considered a U.S. resident under the substantial presence test for 2023.

If an individual meets the requirements of the "substantial presence" test, the taxpayer is considered for federal tax purposes a resident alien of the United States, even though they may not have legal residency in the United States.

A taxpayer who does not meet either the **green card test** or the **substantial presence test** is considered a nonresident alien for tax purposes and is subject to U.S. income tax only on their U.S.-source income.

Exempt Individuals

Numerous exceptions are considered when counting days for the substantial presence test. The following days within the United States are <u>not counted</u> if the alien:

- Regularly commutes to work in the U.S. from a residence in Canada or Mexico, generally more than 75% of the workdays during the applicable working period (this is deemed a "closer connection to home country").
- Is present in the U.S. as a crew member of a foreign vessel.
- Is unable to leave because of a medical condition that arose while in the United States.
- Is a professional athlete in the U.S. to compete in a charitable sports event. These athletes exclude only the days in which they competed in the sporting event, but do not exclude days used for practice, travel, or to participate in promotional events.
- Is an exempt individual. Exempt individuals include aliens who are:

  o Foreign government officials in the U.S. temporarily[38] under an "A" or "G" visa (such as foreign ambassadors and other important diplomats);
  o Teachers on temporary visas; visiting scholars or researchers (scholars are exempt from the substantial presence test for two years); and *au pairs* on a J-1 visa;
  o Foreign students on temporary visas who do not intend to reside permanently in the U.S. (foreign students are exempt from the substantial presence test for five years).

---

[38] A foreign government-related individual is considered "temporarily" present in the United States *regardless* of the actual amount of time present in the United States. An example would be an individual who had full-time diplomatic or consular status, such as a foreign ambassador to the United States.

Example: Amelia is a folk singer and a popular recording artist in her home country of Poland. Amelia comes to the U.S. on tour, playing a variety of different venues during the month of May. Afterward, she returns to her home country. Amelia is not a U.S. resident for tax purposes, although she entered the U.S. legally on a P-2 Visa, and has the right to earn money from her musical performances in the U.S.[39] She is required to report her U.S. source income. Amelia hires a professional accountant to file a Form 1040-NR to report the income that she earned while she was touring in the U.S. She will only report and be taxed on her U.S. source income.

Example: Diego is a wealthy citizen of Panama. He entered the U.S. for the first time on August 29, 2021 on a E-2 investor visa, because he wanted to purchase a few rental properties. Since his initial entry, Diego has returned to the U.S. several times to purchase more investment properties. He uses a management company to manage the properties, which are profitable and trigger a filing requirement. He remained physically present in the United States for 12 days in 2021, 90 days in 2022, and 175 days in 2023. Diego meets the physical presence test in 2023, and must file a Form 1040 (not Form 1040-NR) in that year. The substantial presence test for Diego is calculated as follows:

Current year (2023) days in the United States (175) × 1 = 175 days
Prior year (2022) days in the United States (90) × 1/3 = 30 days
Year before that (2021) days in the United States (12) × 1/6 = 2 days
Total for 2023 = **207 days (physical presence test is met)**

This means that in 2021 and 2022, Diego will file Form 1040-NR as a nonresident. But in 2023, Diego will file Form 1040 as a U.S. resident.

Example: Ayla is a French citizen and a professional translator who was physically present in the United States for 19 days in each of the years 2021, 2022, and 2023. Ayla is not a green card holder or a U.S. resident, but she has a special O-2 visa because she works for a famous tennis champion. In 2023, Ayla earned $32,000 in the United States as a translator for this famous sports star, who traveled to the U.S. to play in an international tennis match. Since the total days she was present in the U.S. for the three-year period do not meet the substantial presence test, Ayla is not considered a U.S. resident for tax purposes, and her earnings are taxed as a nonresident alien. Ayla is required to obtain an ITIN and file Form 1040-NR, *U.S. Nonresident Alien Income Tax Return*.

International Students and Scholars

Most foreign students and scholars fall under the status of nonresident aliens. An international student is anyone who is temporarily in the U.S. on an F, J, M, or Q visa. Immediate family members of a student, including spouses and unmarried children under age twenty-one who reside with the student, are also considered nonresidents for tax purposes. International students holding specific visas are exempt from the substantial presence test for the first five calendar years they are in the U.S.[40] The five calendar years need not be consecutive. Any part of a calendar year in which the student is present in the U.S. counts as a full year. Nonresident Aliens in F-1 or J-1 visas do not have to pay Social

---

[39] This is a type of temporary visa issued to individual performers, artists or entertainers.
[40] In some circumstances a student may still be considered a nonresident alien and eligible for benefits under an income tax treaty between the U.S. and their home country. Foreign tax treaties are outside the scope of the EA exam, but these exceptions do exist.

Security tax or Medicare Tax. For example, if an international student's very first F-1 or J-1 entry date to the U.S. was in 2018, their five exempt years will be 2018-2022. The student will become a resident alien for tax purposes in tax year 2023. Once a person becomes a U.S. resident alien for tax purposes, they will be required to pay Social Security tax and Medicare tax on their earnings.

Example: Woong, a citizen of South Korea, is in the U.S. as a graduate student on F-1 visa status, enrolled in a doctoral degree program at Stanford University. She has resided in the U.S. since arriving on February 15, 2018, going back to her home country only for short visits between semesters. She was in the U.S. continuously all of 2023. Because international students are exempt from the substantial presence test for five years, Woong became a U.S. resident alien for federal income tax purposes in 2023. Woong is married to Quim, who lives in South Korea and is a nonresident alien. Beginning in the 2023 tax year, Woong and Quim can both elect to be treated as U.S. residents for tax purposes on a jointly-filed return. If they choose to make that election and file jointly, Woong and Quim will be forced to report all their worldwide income and pay U.S. income tax on it, as well as report their foreign bank accounts and other reportable foreign assets.

Example: Kalinda's first visit to the United States was as a foreign student on an F-1 visa from India. She attended Purdue University from 2016 until the end of 2018 and then returned to her home country on December 31, 2018. She remained in India during that time. On January 5th, 2023 she re-entered the U.S. on a J-1 visa to pursue graduate studies. As a student under this visa, she is permitted to work for the university as a teaching assistant. Since she has been in the U.S. for less than five years as a student, Kalinda is still considered a nonresident alien for federal income tax purposes in 2023. She will need to file Form 1040-NR, not Form 1040, to report her earnings from her on-campus job. This is true even if she stays in the U.S. for the entire year.

Remember, there are numerous exceptions that result in individuals who pass the substantial presence test still being classified as nonresident aliens for tax purposes. For example, foreign students, visiting scholars and diplomats, au pairs, and other types of exempt individuals are generally considered nonresident aliens, even if they spend the entire taxable year in the United States. In addition, noncitizens who pass the substantial presence test can still be deemed a nonresident alien if they claim a "closer connection" to their home country.[41]

Tax Residency through Marriage

A nonresident alien who does not meet the substantial presence test and does not have a green card, may still elect to be treated as a resident for tax purposes if they are married to a U.S. citizen or resident. This election can be made only if:

- At the end of the year, one spouse is a nonresident alien, and the other is a U.S. citizen or resident, and
- Both spouses agree to file a joint return and treat the nonresident alien as a resident alien for the entire tax year.

---

[41] Nonresident aliens may use Form 8840, *Closer Connection Exception Statement for Aliens* (Form 1040-NR) to claim the "closer connection to a foreign country" exception to the substantial presence test. To establish a closer connection, a taxpayer must have maintained more significant contacts with a foreign country other than the US.

Example: Azalea and Sergio are married, and both are citizens of Ecuador. They do not have any dependents. Sergio is a cardiac physician who is legally present in the U.S. on an H-1B work authorization visa. On February 1, 2023, Sergio obtains a green card and becomes a legal U.S. resident. Azalea is not eligible for a Social Security number yet, because her immigration paperwork is still being processed. Sergio may choose to file a separate return and report only his income. Since Azalea is a nonresident alien and has no U.S. source income, she does not have a filing requirement. Azalea does not work and has no taxable income, but she may file jointly with her husband if she requests an ITIN. If Azalea and Sergio may also choose to file jointly, they must attach an election statement to their joint return.[42]

Example: Vanessa is a U.S. citizen living in Spain. She works online as a professional editor. In 2023, she meets and marries Hugo, a citizen of Spain. Vanessa has a filing requirement, and she wants to file jointly with Hugo, but Hugo refuses. Hugo owns a successful business in Spain, and has no desire to report his worldwide income, or pay U.S. tax on his income. Vanessa does not have any dependents, so she will be forced to file MFS. Since Hugo is a nonresident alien and does not have an SSN or ITIN, and she needs to file her tax return using Married Filing Separately status, Vanessa would enter "NRA" in the space for her husband's identifying number.

Example: Vladimir is a citizen of Serbia. He arrived in the United States on January 4, 2023, as a college student on an F-1 visa. Vladimir meets Belinda, a U.S. citizen, in one of his college courses. After a whirlwind romance, on March 20, 2023, Vladimir marries Belinda. Vladimir immediately petitions USCIS for a change in immigration status to that of a lawful permanent resident based upon his marriage to Belinda. USCIS approves Vladimir's petition to become a lawful permanent resident of the United States and issues him a green card on December 20, 2023. Vladimir passes the Green Card Test on December 20, 2023. Although he is not required to do so, Vladimir could *elect* to be taxed as a U.S. resident for the entire tax year by filing jointly with his U.S. citizen spouse, Belinda.

Dual Status Aliens: An alien is considered a "dual-status" alien when the person has been both a resident alien and a nonresident alien in the same tax year. "Dual status" is only used for tax purposes, and has no bearing on a person's legal immigration status. The most common dual-status tax years are the years of arrival and departure.

A taxpayer's status on the last day of the year determines whether a person is a resident alien or a nonresident alien for the tax year. For the part of each year the taxpayer is a *nonresident* alien, the person is taxed only on their U.S.-source income.

Example: Humphrey is a citizen of England and unmarried. Despite having a green card and a steady job as a graphic designer, he always planned to permanently return to his home country after living in the U.S. for several years. Humphrey seeks assistance from an immigration lawyer to officially renounce his green card status. He officially relinquishes his green card and departs from the United States on May 1, 2023, permanently returning to England. As a result, Humphrey will be classified as a dual-status resident for the 2023 tax year.

---

[42] The spouse who is a nonresident alien for U.S. income tax purposes can elect to be treated as a U.S. taxpayer and the married couple can file a joint tax return. This is a Section 6013(g) election, and it is used when one spouse is a U.S. taxpayer and the other is not. In the example, Sergio is a green card holder, so he is a U.S. resident by default.

For the part of each year the taxpayer is a *U.S. resident alien*, they are taxed on their worldwide income. This applies even if the income was earned earlier in the year while the taxpayer was a nonresident alien but was received after they became a resident for tax purposes.

> **Example:** Ismael applied for an adjustment of status and became a legal U.S. resident (a green card holder) on January 25, 2023. A few weeks later, on February 16, 2023, he received $2,000 of income for some online contract work he did during the previous tax year. Even though the income was *earned* while he was a nonresident alien, it was received *after* he became a U.S. resident. This income must be reported and taxed on Form 1040, not on Form 1040-NR.

Tax Treaties

The United States has income tax treaties with many foreign countries. Under these treaties, residents of foreign countries may be taxed at reduced rates or be exempt from U.S. income taxes on certain items of income they receive from U.S. source income. These reduced rates and exemptions vary among countries and specific items of income. Treaty provisions are generally reciprocal.

Therefore, a U.S. citizen or resident who receives income from a treaty country and who is subject to taxes imposed by foreign countries may be entitled to certain credits, deductions, exemptions, and reductions in the rate of taxes of those foreign countries. However, it is important to note that many tax treaties contain a "saving clause" that limits the ability of U.S. citizens and residents to use treaty provisions to mitigate their U.S. tax liability.

Income received by a nonresident alien that is effectively connected with a trade or business in the United States is, after allowable deductions, taxed at the rates that apply to U.S. citizens and residents. Withholding would be made at the highest applicable rate.

> **Note:** For nonresident aliens, income or gains from U.S. sources is generally subject to backup **withholding at 30%**, unless a lower treaty rate applies. The normal backup withholding rate for U.S. citizens and U.S. residents in 2023 is a flat 24% rate.

Unit 2: Study Questions

(Test yourself first, then check the correct answers at the end of this quiz.)

1. Tatiana is 41 years old and divorced. She files as head of household and has two dependent children. Tatiana is a citizen of Canada and a legal U.S. resident (a green card holder). She lived in Canada for the entire tax year and earned all her income working in Canada. She earned $63,000 in 2023 and plans to itemize her deductions. Which tax form should Tatiana use to report her income?

A. Form 1040
B. Form 1040-NR
C. Form 1040-X
D. Form 1040-SR

2. Ezequiel and Candra are married, but they choose to file separate returns for 2023 because the IRS is auditing Ezequiel for a previous tax issue. Ezequiel and Candra file their MFS returns on time. A few months after filing their separate returns, the audit is over, and Ezequiel's previous tax issue has been resolved. He then wishes to file amended returns and file jointly with his wife to claim the Earned Income Tax Credit (EITC). Which of the following statements is correct?

A. Taxpayers are prohibited from changing their filing status to claim the EITC.
B. Ezequiel and Candra can amend their MFS tax returns to MFJ in order to claim EITC.
C. Ezequiel and Candra can amend their MFS tax returns to MFJ, but they cannot claim the EITC on an amended return.
D. Candra cannot file jointly with Ezequiel after she has already filed a separate tax return.

3. Taxpayers are considered to be "married" for the entire year if:

A. The spouses had their marriage annulled during the tax year.
B. The spouses are legally separated under a separate maintenance decree.
C. The spouses are divorced on December 31 of the tax year.
D. One spouse dies during the year, and the surviving spouse does not remarry.

4. Nikkie's marriage was annulled on February 5, 2023. She filed jointly with her husband in the previous two years. She has not yet filed her 2023 tax return. Nikkie has no dependents. Which of the following statements is correct?

A. She must file amended returns, claiming single filing status for all open years affected by the annulment. She will file as single for 2023.
B. She is not required to file amended returns. She can file jointly with her husband in 2023, because she was still married to him during the year.
C. She is not required to amend any tax returns. She must file as married filing separately in 2023.
D. She is not required to amend returns for any prior years, but she must file as single in 2023.

5. Tania's divorce became final on October 30, 2023. She has sole custody of her two children, who lived with her the entire year. Her children are both under the age of 18, and Tania provided more than half of the cost of keeping up the home. What filing status should she use?

A. Single
B. Married Filing Separately
C. Head of Household
D. Qualifying Surviving Spouse

6. Elvira's husband died on November 3, 2023. She has one dependent son, who is eight years old. She did not remarry during the year. What filing status should Elvira use in 2023?

A. Married filing jointly or Married filing separately.
B. Single.
C. Qualifying surviving spouse.
D. Head of household.

7. Madison and Franco are not married and do not live together, but they have a two-year-old daughter named Ivette. Madison and her daughter lived together all year, while Franco lived alone in his own apartment. Franco cares for his daughter two days a week. Madison earned $17,900 working as a grocery store bagger. Franco earned $48,000 managing a hardware store. Franco paid over half the cost of Madison's apartment for rent and utilities, where his daughter Ivette lives. He also gave Madison child support and extra money for groceries. Franco does not support any other family member. Which of the following statements is correct?

A. Franco can file as head of household.
B. Madison can file as head of household.
C. Franco and Madison can file jointly.
D. Neither Franco nor Madison can claim head of household filing status.

8. Rosemarie, age 65, and Lionel, age 72, were married on December 26, 2023. They have no dependents. Rosemarie had wages of $2,000, and Lionel had Social Security income of $19,000 for the year. Lionel wants to file jointly, but Rosemarie wants to file separately. Which of the following statements is correct?

A. Lionel must file a tax return using the MFS status. Rosemarie is not required to file a return.
B. Lionel may claim Rosemarie as a dependent, as long as she does not file her own separate return.
C. Lionel and Rosemarie are both required to file tax returns, and they must both file MFS.
D. Lionel and Rosemarie may both file as single since they were married for less than one month during the taxable year.

9. In 2023, Clarence took legal and physical custody of his ten-year-old grandson, Breton. Breton's parents were both incarcerated all year, and do not have the right to claim Breton as a dependent. How long must Breton live in Clarence's home for Clarence to qualify for head of household status?

A. At least three months.
B. More than half the year.
C. The entire year.
D. More than twelve months.

10. When may a taxpayer amend a joint tax return from "married filing jointly" to "married filing separately" after the original filing deadline?

A. Never.
B. Only within the statute of limitations for filing amended returns.
C. Only when a marriage has been annulled.
D. An estate's personal representative may amend a joint return to MFS for the decedent, if elected by the surviving spouse.

11. A U.S. citizen who is married to a nonresident alien can file a joint return as long as both spouses:

A. Sign the return and agree to be taxed on their worldwide income.
B. Are living overseas and do not plan to reside in the United States.
C. Have valid Social Security numbers.
D. Are physically present in the United States.

12. Liza and Stuart were married for many years. Stuart died on May 3, 2021. Liza and Stuart qualified to file MFJ in the year he died, with Liza signing the tax return as a surviving spouse. Liza did not remarry after her husband's death. Liza has one dependent son, age 14. Which filing status should Liza use for her 2023 tax return?

A. Single.
B. Married filing jointly.
C. Head of household.
D. Qualifying surviving spouse.

13. Which of the following statements is correct regarding head of household filing status?

A. The taxpayer must be unmarried to qualify for the head of household filing status.
B. The taxpayer's spouse must be deceased, or a nonresident alien.
C. A dependent parent does not have to live with the taxpayer to qualify for head of household status.
D. The taxpayer must have paid roughly half of the cost of keeping up the house for the entire year.

14. The married filing separately (MFS) status is for taxpayers who:

A. Are married and choose to file separate returns.
B. Are legally divorced on the last day of the year.
C. Are unmarried but engaged to be married.
D. Are unmarried but have a dependent child.

15. Camille is 26 years old and an international student at Tulane University. She first came to the U.S. in 2013 from France in F-2 student immigration status with her father while he was completing his doctorate. They remained in the U.S. in the same status until he completed his doctorate in 2015, and then returned home to France. Camille reentered the U.S. as a J-1 student immigration status in 2021, and has not left the U.S. nor changed her immigration status. Camille works on-campus as a part-time tutor and earns $15,700 in wages during the year. For federal income tax purposes, what is Camille's residency status in 2023?

A. Camille is a nonresident alien.
B. Camille is a resident alien.
C. Camille is an undocumented alien.
D. Camille is a dual-status alien.

16. All of the following individuals are required to file an income tax return except:

A. A taxpayer who owes household employment tax for a nanny.
B. A church employee who is exempt from FICA taxes, who earned $101 of wages in 2023.
C. A 66-year-old unmarried taxpayer who is blind and earned $19,200 in 2023.
D. A 26-year-old taxpayer with $8,500 in wages in 2023 who owes a 10% penalty on withdrawals from a traditional IRA account.

17. Adrienne and Troy are married and lived together all year. Adrienne earned $1,900 in wages during the year, and Troy earned $72,000. Adrienne wants to file a joint return, but Troy refuses to file with Adrienne and instead files a separate return on his own. Which of the following statements is correct?

A. Adrienne can file a joint tax return and e-file it if Troy refuses to provide his signature.
B. Adrienne can file as single because Troy refuses to sign a joint return.
C. Adrienne does not have a filing requirement because her income is below the filing threshold.
D. Adrienne and Troy must both file separate returns.

18. Which dependent relative may qualify a taxpayer for head of household filing status?

A. An adult stepdaughter who lives in her own apartment who is supported by the taxpayer.
B. A cousin who lives with the taxpayer all year.
C. A parent who lives in his own home and not with the taxpayer.
D. A foster child who lived with the taxpayer for five months of the tax year.

19. Harish is 39 years old and has lived apart from his wife, Eleanor, since February 1, 2023. Their divorce was not yet final at the end of 2023, and they were not legally separated under a separate maintenance decree. They have two children, a son, age fifteen, and a daughter, age sixteen. After Harish and Eleanor split up, their son lived with Harish. Their daughter chose to live with Eleanor. Harish provides all the support for the minor child living with him. Eleanor refuses to file jointly with Harish in 2023. The most beneficial filing status that Harish qualifies for is:

A. Married filing separately
B. Single
C. Head of household
D. Married filing jointly

20. Baylee is an 18-year-old high school senior in her last year of high school. She worked at a toy store during the Christmas holiday and earned $1,400 in wages in December 2023. She also received $4,600 for a winning scratch-off lottery ticket. Her parents claim Baylee as a dependent on their joint tax return. Does Baylee have to file her own return?

A. Yes, because of the amount of her unearned income.
B. Yes, because of the combined amount of her unearned and earned income.
C. No, because her earned income is below the threshold for a dependent.
D. No, because it is illegal for a high school student to play the lottery.

21. Which of the following dependency relationships would _not qualify_ a taxpayer to claim "qualifying surviving spouse" as their filing status after the death of a spouse?

A. A biological child.
B. A foster child.
C. An adopted child.
D. A stepchild.

22. Alexandra's younger brother, Sebastian, is 18 and a full-time student. Sebastian lived with a friend from January through February of 2023. From March through July, Sebastian lived with his sister, Alexandra. On August 1, 2023, Sebastian moved back in with his friends and stayed with them for the rest of the year. However, since Sebastian did not have a job, Alexandra gave him money every month and provided the majority of his financial support for the entire year. Alexandra has no other dependents. Which of the following statements is correct?

A. Alexandra can file as head of household.
B. Alexandra can file jointly with Sebastian.
C. Alexandra cannot file as head of household.
D. Sebastian can file as head of household.

23. Louisa legally separated from her husband in 2023. They share custody of a 13-year-old son. Which of the following facts would *prevent* Louisa from filing as head of household?

A. Louisa has maintained a separate residence from her husband since February 1, 2023.
B. Her son's principal home is with Louisa.
C. Louisa's parents assisted her with 40% of her household costs.
D. Louisa's son lived with her for four months. He lived with his father for the rest of the year.

24. Elisabete and Sirius were married in 2018. They have no children or other dependents. They split up two years ago but never officially filed for divorce. Although they lived apart all of 2023, they are neither divorced nor legally separated. Which of the following filing statuses can they use?

A. Single or married filing separately.
B. Married filing jointly or married filing separately.
C. Married filing separately or head of household.
D. Single or qualifying surviving spouse.

25. Huang is an international student temporarily in the U.S. on an F-1 Visa. Huang arrived in the U.S. on January 3, 2023, and was present in the U.S. all year, studying at Yale University. How long is he exempt from the substantial presence test?

A. One year.
B. Three years.
C. Five years.
D. There is no exemption to the substantial presence test.

Unit 2: Quiz Answers

1. The answer is A. Tatiana must file Form 1040. Form 1040-NR is only for nonresident taxpayers, and Form 1040-SR is for seniors who are 65 years of age or older. With few exceptions, green card holders are taxed as U.S. citizens and do not file Form 1040-NR, regardless of where they live.

2. The answer is B. Ezequiel and Candra are allowed to amend their separate returns to a joint return. If a married couple files separate returns, the spouses may elect to amend the filing status to "married filing jointly" at any time within three years from the due date of the original return. However, the same does not hold true in reverse. Once a married couple files a joint return, the spouses cannot amend to separate returns for that year after the due date of the return (an exception exists for deceased taxpayers).

3. The answer is D. Taxpayers are considered "married" for the entire year if:
- They were married on the last day of the tax year, or
- One spouse died during the year, and the surviving spouse has not remarried as of the end of the year.

4. The answer is A. Nikkie must file amended tax returns for the previous two years. She must file single in 2023. If a taxpayer obtains a court decree of annulment, the taxpayer must file amended returns (Form 1040-X), claiming single or head of household status for all tax years affected by the annulment that are not closed by the statute of limitations.

5. The answer is C. Because she was legally divorced by the end of the year, Tania is treated as unmarried for the entire tax year. However, because she has children and meets the requirements for head of household, she should use this as her filing status because it will result in a lower tax.

6. The answer is A. If a taxpayer's spouse died during the year, the taxpayer is considered married for the whole year and can file as married filing jointly or married filing separately in 2023.

7. The answer is D. Although Franco provided over half the cost of maintaining a home for Madison and Ivette, he cannot file as head of household since Ivette (his daughter) did not live with him for more than half the year. Madison cannot file as HOH either because she did not provide more than one-half the cost of keeping up the home for her daughter. However, either Franco or Madison may still claim Ivette as a dependent and file as "Single." Generally, a child is the qualifying child of the custodial parent, so Madison would have the primary right to claim Ivette. But Madison may also choose to release the dependency exemption to Franco (who is the noncustodial parent) by using Form 8332.

8. The answer is C. Since Lionel and Rosemarie are married, they can file either jointly or separately. If Rosemarie does not agree to file jointly with Lionel, both taxpayers must file MFS. The filing requirement threshold for married filing separately in 2023 is $5, so both spouses have a filing requirement.

9. The answer is B. Breton must live with his grandfather, Clarence, for more than half the year (over six months) in order to qualify as his qualifying child. There are exceptions for temporary absences.

10. The answer is D. An executor for a deceased taxpayer can amend a joint return to an MFS return up to one year after the filing deadline. This is the only exception to a rule that generally prevents a taxpayer from amending a joint return to a separate return past the filing deadline. Answer "C" is incorrect because if a marriage has been annulled, the filing status would be amended to "single" rather than "MFS" because an annulment invalidates the original marriage contract.

11. The answer is A. A U.S. citizen (or U.S. resident), who is married to a nonresident alien, can elect to file a joint return as long as both spouses sign the return and agree to be taxed on their worldwide income. A Social Security number is not required for the nonresident spouse because a nonresident spouse that is ineligible for an SSN may request an ITIN to file jointly with a U.S. resident spouse. An election statement must be attached to the return.

12. The answer is D. In 2023, Liza is eligible for "qualifying surviving spouse" filing status. The year of death is the last year for which a taxpayer can file MFJ. For each of the *two tax years* following the year of the spouse's death, the surviving spouse can use the "qualifying surviving spouse" status, if she has a qualifying dependent and does not remarry.

13. The answer is C. A dependent parent does not have to live with a taxpayer for the taxpayer to elect the head of household filing status. This special rule applies to parents who are related to the taxpayer by blood, marriage, or adoption if the taxpayer pays more than half of the qualifying parent's household costs. Answer "A" is incorrect because a married person can still qualify for head of household if they are "considered unmarried" for tax purposes. A married person can be "considered unmarried" in certain circumstances if they live apart from their spouse and can file as head of household.

14. The answer is A. The married filing separately (MFS) status is for taxpayers who are married and either:
  • Choose to file separate returns, or
  • Do not agree to file a joint return.

15. The answer is B. Camille is classified as a U.S. resident alien for tax purposes in 2023 because she has already been in the U.S. during five previous calendar years in exempt student immigration status (three years with her father in F-2 status from 2013-2015, and two years as a student herself in 2021 and 2022). Camille should file Form 1040 in 2023, not Form 1040-NR (this question is based on a case study in the IRS' VITA tax training program).

16. The answer is B. Church employees who are exempt from Social Security and Medicare taxes and have wages of $108.28 or more for the year are required to file a tax return. In answer "B," the church employee's wages are below that threshold. In all of the other answers, the taxpayer would be required to file a return.

17. The answer is D. Married couples must agree to file jointly. If one spouse does not agree to file jointly, they are individually subject to the MFS filing threshold. In this case, Adrienne and Troy are both required to file separate tax returns because both are above the applicable earnings threshold for MFS.

18. The answer is C. A parent is the only dependent relative who does not have to live with the taxpayer for the taxpayer to claim "head of household" status. In order to file for head of household, the "qualifying person" must be one of the following: a birth child, adopted child, grandchild, stepchild, foster child, brother, sister, half-brother, half-sister, stepbrother, stepsister, or a descendant of any of those, or a parent. The qualifying person must also <u>live with</u> the taxpayer (unless the absence is temporary). The only exception to the "residency test" is a parent who <u>does not</u> have to live with the taxpayer. A cousin does not qualify because they do not meet the relationship test. The foster child in answer "D" does not qualify because the child lived with the taxpayer for less than half of the year.

19. The answer is C. Harish qualifies for head of household filing status because he can be "considered unmarried" for tax purposes. His son lived with him for more than six months, he did not live with his spouse the last half of the year, and he paid more than half the cost of keeping up a home for the year for a qualifying child. Couples who are living apart but not yet divorced or legally separated are allowed to file jointly, but both spouses must agree to do so. Therefore, if Eleanor refuses to file jointly with Harish, the most beneficial filing status for Harish is head of household.

20. The answer is A. Baylee has to file a tax return because of the amount of her unearned income: i.e., the $4,600 lottery prize. Her earned income—$1,400 in wages—was not high enough to trigger a filing requirement, but the lottery winnings (unearned income) do trigger a filing requirement. Answer "D" is incorrect because most U.S. states allow 18-year-olds to play the state lottery because they are legal adults. However, even if playing the lottery was illegal in her state, it would still be considered taxable income, and it would not change her filing requirement for the year. Despite the fact that Baylee has to file her own return, her parents can still claim her as a qualifying child.

21. The answer is B. To be eligible for the qualifying surviving spouse filing status, the taxpayer normally must have a dependent child. For the purposes of the "qualifying surviving spouse" filing status, a qualifying child can be an adopted child, biological child, or stepchild, but does *not* include a foster child. This special rule for dependents that excludes foster children only pertains to the qualifying surviving spouse filing status.[43] Answer "C" is incorrect because legally adopted children are always treated the same as biological children for federal tax law purposes.

22. The answer is C. Alexandra cannot claim head of household status because Sebastian lived with her for only five months, which is less than half the year.

---

[43] Note that this is a unique rule that applies to the qualifying surviving spouse filing status ONLY. For a surviving spouse (a taxpayer whose spouse has died) a "qualifying child" does not include a foster child. Please be aware that this filing status is very rare and a scenario where you would have a surviving spouse with a foster child would be even more so. It is unlikely that you would ever see this scenario in actual practice, but we briefly cover it here, because on the EA exam the IRS does test on exceptions, in addition to the general rules.

23. The answer is D. For Louisa to file as head of household, her home must have been the main home of her qualifying child for more than half the tax year (i.e., over six months). Since her son lived with her for only four months, he would not have been in the household sufficient time to qualify her for this filing status.

24. The answer is B. As long as they are married and are neither divorced nor legally separated, Elisabete and Sirius can file a joint return or file separately. Neither spouse can file as head of household (even though they lived apart) because they do not have any dependents. They are also not eligible to file as single, because they were legally married on the last day of the tax year.

25. The answer is C. Huang is exempt from the substantial presence test for five years. In determining residency status for tax purposes, students temporarily in the U.S. on an F, J, M, or Q visa are exempt from the substantial presence test for five years.

Unit 3: Dependency Relationships

For additional information, read:
Publication 501, *Dependents, Standard Deduction, and Filing Information*
Publication 504, *Divorced or Separated Individuals*

Personal and dependency exemptions are suspended (reduced to $0) through tax year 2025. However, the ability to *claim* a dependent can make taxpayers eligible for other tax benefits. For example, the following tax benefits are all associated with a dependent:

- Child Tax Credit (CTC),
- Earned Income Tax Credit (EITC),
- Child and Dependent Care Credit,
- Head of household filing status (HOH),
- Credit for Other Dependents (ODC) and other tax benefits.

Although the Tax Cuts and Jobs Act eliminated the benefit of the dependency exemption itself, the law remains unchanged on who qualifies as a dependent for tax purposes. For 2023 tax year filings, taxpayers can determine a dependent's eligibility by using the "deemed exemption" amount of $4,700.[44] Dependents are either a "qualifying child" or a "qualifying relative" of the taxpayer. Examples of dependents include a child, stepchild, brother, sister, or parent.

Primary Tests for Dependency

Identifying and determining the correct number of dependents is a critical component of completing a taxpayer's return. To determine if a taxpayer can claim a dependent, there are three primary tests:

- **Dependent taxpayer test**
- **Joint return test**
- **Citizenship or residency test**

Test #1: Dependent Taxpayer Test

A person who may be claimed as a dependent by another taxpayer, may not claim anyone as a dependent on their own tax return. In other words, the dependent taxpayer test specifies that any taxpayer who can be claimed as a dependent cannot claim a dependent themselves.

Example: Evie is an 18-year-old single mother who has an infant son who is three months old. Evie and her son live with her parents. Evie has a small part-time job, but she only earned $2,300. She does not make enough money to support herself or her infant son. Evie is claimed as a dependent by her parents, so she is prohibited from claiming her infant son as a dependent on her own tax return.

Sometimes, an individual meets the rules to be a qualifying dependent of more than one person. Regardless, only one person can claim the same individual as a dependent.

---

[44] In 2023, the gross income limitation for a qualifying relative is $4,700. This amount is used for purposes of determining a qualifying relative under IRC Sec. 152(d)(1)(B).

Example: Pearce and Annika are an unmarried couple with one daughter, named Juliana, age 10. They all live together in the same home. Juliana is a qualifying child for both Pearce and Annika, but only one of them can claim her as a dependent. Although only one parent can claim Juliana as a dependent, the two parents can agree on which parent should claim the child to achieve the best tax outcome, because Juliana lived with both her parents the entire year.

Test #2: Joint Return Test

If a married person files a joint return, that individual normally cannot be claimed as a dependent by another taxpayer. Even if the other dependency tests are met, a taxpayer is generally not allowed to claim a dependent if that person files a joint return with their spouse.

Example: Irina is 19 years old and had no income in 2023. Irina lived with her father for the whole year. Irina got married on December 30, 2023, to Rafferty, who is 24 years old. Irina's new husband earned $28,700 during the year. Irina and Rafferty choose to file jointly. Irina's father supported his daughter the entire year and even paid for her wedding. However, her father cannot claim Irina as his dependent because she is filing jointly with her new husband, Rafferty.

There is only one narrow exception to this test. The joint return test *does not apply* if the joint return is filed by the dependent only to claim a refund, and neither spouse would have a tax liability, even if they filed separate returns.

Example: Robbie and Rosalie are both 18 years old and recently married. They both live with Rosalie's mother, Sylvia. In 2023, Robbie earned $2,950 from a part-time job. That was the only income that Robbie and his wife earned all year. Neither Robbie nor Rosalie is required to file a tax return, but they decide to file a joint return to obtain a refund of the income taxes that were withheld from Robbie's wages. Robbie and Rosalie correctly check the box next to "Can anyone claim you as a dependent?" on their joint tax return. As the exception to the joint return test applies, Sylvia can claim both Robbie and Rosalie on her tax return, if all the other tests for dependency are met.

Test #3: Citizenship or Residency Test

A dependent must be a citizen or resident of the United States, Canada or Mexico. Exceptions exist for foreign-born adopted children.[45] If a U.S. citizen or U.S. national legally adopts a child who is not a U.S. citizen, U.S. resident alien, or U.S. national,[46] this test is met if the child lives with the taxpayer as a member of the household all year.

If all other dependency tests are met, the child can be claimed as a dependent. This also applies if the child was lawfully placed with the taxpayer for legal adoption.

Example: Tressa, who is a U.S. citizen, is in the process of adopting an infant boy from Mexico, Alejandro, who lived with her for the entire tax year. Even though Tressa's child is not yet a U.S. citizen, he meets the "citizen or resident test" because he was a member of Tressa's household for the entire year.

---

[45] Foreign exchange students generally are not U.S. residents and generally do not meet the citizen or resident test, so they cannot be claimed as dependents, even if they live in the taxpayer's home all year.

[46] A "U.S. national" is an individual who, although not a U.S. citizen, owes their allegiance to the United States. U.S. nationals include American Samoans and Northern Mariana Islanders who chose to become U.S. nationals instead of U.S. citizens.

Dependency Relationships

A dependent may be either a **"qualifying child"** or a **"qualifying relative."** Both types of dependents have unique rules, but some requirements are the same for both. Remember, a person must meet the requirements of either a qualifying child or a qualifying relative to be claimed as a dependent. There are very specific tests to identify the difference between the two.

> **Note:** Both, **"qualifying children"** and **"qualifying relatives"** must *first* meet all the primary dependency requirements already specified: the dependent taxpayer, joint return, and citizenship or residency tests. If these three tests are met, the person is a dependent.[47]

Rules for a Qualifying Child

The tests for a "qualifying child" are more stringent than the tests for a "qualifying relative." Having a qualifying child entitles a taxpayer to claim refundable tax credits, including the Earned Income Tax Credit and the Additional Child Tax Credit. Having a qualifying relative, on the other hand, does not qualify a taxpayer for these special credits. There are five tests for a qualifying *child*:

- **Relationship Test**
- **Age Test**
- **Residency Test**
- **Support Test**
- **Tiebreaker Test (for a qualifying child of more than one person)**

Test #1: The Relationship Test

The qualifying child must be related to the taxpayer by blood, marriage, or legal adoption. Qualifying children include:

- A child, stepchild, or adopted child.[48]
- A sibling, half-sibling, or stepsibling (includes; half-brother, half-sister, stepbrother, etc.)
- A descendant of one of the above (such as a grandchild, niece, or nephew)
- A foster child

For the purposes of this test, an adopted child is always treated the same as a natural child.

Test #2: The Age Test

In order to be a qualifying child, the dependent must be:

- Under the age of 19 at the end of the tax year, or
- Under the age of 24 at the end of the tax year and a full-time student,[49] or
- Permanently and totally disabled at any time during the year, **regardless of age.**

---

[47] A taxpayer's spouse cannot be claimed as a dependent; however, a taxpayer's registered domestic partner may qualify as a dependent, assuming all the tests for dependency are met. A taxpayer cannot file as head of household if the taxpayer's only dependent is their registered domestic partner.
[48] An adopted child also includes a child who was lawfully placed with a person for adoption, even if the adoption is not yet final.
[49] To qualify as a "full-time" student, the child must be enrolled in the number of hours or courses the school considers full-time during some part of at least five months of the year. See Publication 17 for additional details.

A child who is claimed as a dependent must be *younger* than the taxpayer who is claiming him, except in the case of dependents who are disabled. For taxpayers filing jointly, the child must be younger than one spouse listed on the return but does not have to be younger than both spouses.

Example: Gordon and Denise are both 21 years old, married, and file jointly. Denise's 23-year-old stepbrother, Benjamin, is a full-time student and lives with Gordon and Denise, who provide all of his financial support while he is going to college. Benjamin is not disabled. Gordon and Denise are both younger than Benjamin. Therefore, Benjamin is not their qualifying child, even though he is a full-time student.

Example: Stavros, age 30, and Audrey, age 21, are married and file jointly. Audrey's 22-year-old brother, Brayden, is a full-time college student, is single, and lives with Stavros and Audrey. They provide all of Brayden's support. In this case, Stavros and Audrey can claim Brayden as a qualifying child on their joint tax return because he is a full-time student and is *younger* than Stavros.

Example: Jerrik is 55 years old and mentally disabled with Down syndrome. Agnes, his 38-year-old sister, provides all of Jerrik's support and cares for him in her home, where he lives with her full-time. Despite Jerrik's age, he is considered a qualifying child and a dependent for tax purposes because he is disabled. Agnes can claim Jerrik as her qualifying child, and she can also file as head of household.

Example: Elwin and Hortense file jointly. They have one daughter named Stacy, age 28. Stacy earned $4,900 in wages before she was laid off in February and moved back in with her parents. Elwin and Hortense provided most of Stacy's financial support for the year. Stacy got a new job at the end of December and moved out. She is not a qualifying child for federal tax purposes. Although Stacy meets the support test and the residency test, she does not meet the age test to be claimed as a qualifying child.

Test #3: The Residency Test

A qualifying child must live with the taxpayer for more than half the tax year (over six months). The taxpayer's home is any location where they regularly live; it does not need to be a traditional home. For example, a child who lived with the taxpayer for over half the year in a homeless shelter would meet the residency test.[50]

Example: Leonardo and James are brothers. They have joint legal custody of their 17-year-old nephew, Jonah, whose parents tragically passed away in a car accident three years ago. Leonardo and James both support Jonah financially, but Jonah lives full-time with his uncle Leonardo, because Leonardo's home is closer to Jonah's high school. Since Jonah lives primarily with Leonardo, then Jonah passes the residency test to be Leonardo's qualifying child. Leonardo may claim his nephew as his dependent, and file as head of household.

In most cases, because of the residency test, a child is automatically the qualifying child of the custodial parent. However, exceptions to the residency test apply to children of divorced parents, kidnapped children, children who were born or died during the year,[51] and temporary absences.

---

[50] See IRS Publication 596, *Earned Income Credit*, for similar examples and scenarios.
[51] A stillborn child cannot be claimed as a dependent. The child must be born alive, even if they lived only for a short period of time.

A "temporary absence" includes illness, college, vacation, military service, institutionalized care for a child who is permanently and totally disabled, and incarceration in a juvenile facility. It must be reasonable to assume that the child will return to the home after the temporary absence.

> **Example**: Martino is widowed and has one 10-year-old son named Davian. The child lives with his father, and Martino provides all his son's financial support. On January 10, Davian was diagnosed with a rare form of pediatric cancer and was hospitalized continuously for ten months. Davian is still considered Martino's qualifying child because the hospitalization counts as a temporary absence from home. Martino can claim Davian as his qualifying child, and he can also file as head of household.

> **Example:** Jonathan, age 21, is a full-time college student and lived in the on-campus dorms at his university for the entire year. Jonathan worked part-time and earned $4,000 in wages during the year. He did not pay over one-half of his own support. Instead, his mother, Camille, supported him and his tuition and living expenses. Jonathan's time spent in the dorms counts as a "temporary absence." Camille is unmarried, and therefore, she can file as "head of household" and claim Jonathan on her tax return as her qualifying child because he meets the relationship, age, residency, and support tests.

> **Example:** Denise is 18 years old and disabled. She is institutionalized at a long-term care facility for severely disabled children. Denise cannot work and does not provide any of her own support. Denise's parents, Charlie and Cindy, both work full-time, and only see their daughter on weekends. However, they can claim their daughter Denise as a qualifying child, even though she does not live with her parents most of the time, because institutionalized care for a child who is permanently and totally disabled is considered a temporary absence under the law.

Test #4: The Support Test

A qualifying child cannot provide more than one-half of their own support. This test is different from the support test for a qualifying relative and should not be confused as such. State benefits provided to a person in need, such as welfare, food stamps, or subsidized housing, are generally considered support provided by the state. However, if a child receives Social Security benefits and uses the benefits for their own support, the benefits are considered to be provided by the child, not by the parents.

> **Example**: Ernesto is 46 and unmarried. He has an 18-year-old daughter named Gladys, who is single. Ernesto contributes $5,100 toward his daughter's support for the year. Gladys is no longer in school, and she has a full-time job as a waitress, earning $19,500 for the year. Gladys spends all her wages and tips on her own support. Since Gladys supplied over half of her own support for the year, Gladys does not pass the support test, and consequently, she is not Ernesto's qualifying child. Ernesto cannot claim his daughter as a dependent. Gladys should file her own tax return as "single."

A full-time student does not take scholarships (whether taxable or nontaxable) into account when calculating the support test.

> **Example**: Anton is 54, and a single parent with a 21-year-old daughter named Catia. Catia is a full-time college student at the University of Nevada. Anton contributes $11,000 to his daughter's support. Catia receives a $10,900 scholarship during the year, and has no other income. The scholarship is not counted for the support test for a qualifying child, so Catia can be claimed as Anton's qualifying child.

Note: The definition of "**support**" includes only income that is used for living expenses. A person's own funds are not "support" unless they are *actually spent* for support. For example, if a child earns income that is saved in a bank account rather than spent on the child's living expenses, the amounts saved are not included for the purposes of the support test.

Example: Mikhail, age 12, had a small role in a television series. He earned $69,000 as a child actor, but his parents put all the money in a trust fund for him. Mikhail lived at home with his parents all year. Mikhail meets the support test since none of his earnings were used for his own support. He meets the tests for a qualifying child, so he can be claimed as a dependent by his parents. Mikhail must file a tax return to report his wages, but he is still treated as a "qualifying child" for tax purposes.

Foster parents may claim a foster child if the child is legally placed in their home by the courts or a government agency. Payments received from a child placement agency for the support of a foster child are considered support provided by the agency, rather than support provided by the child.

Example: Hilda is an unmarried foster parent who provided $3,500 toward the support of Devon, her 8-year-old foster son. The state of Nevada also provided $6,000 in foster care payments, which was considered support provided by the state, not by the child. Devon did not provide more than half of his own support for the year. Therefore, Hilda can claim her foster son as a qualifying child.

Test #5: Tie-breaker Test

Sometimes a child meets the rules to be a qualifying child of more than one person. Only one taxpayer can claim a qualifying child. If more than one taxpayer *attempts* to claim the same child under the dependency rules, the tie-breaker rules apply in the following sequence:

- By the child's parents if they file a joint return.
- By the parent, if only one of the taxpayers is the child's parent.
- By the parent with whom the child lived the longest during the year.
- By the parent with the highest AGI, if the child lived with each parent for the same length of time during the tax year.
- By the taxpayer with the highest AGI, if neither of the child's parents can claim the child as a qualifying child.
- By a taxpayer with a higher AGI than either of the child's parents who can also claim the child as a qualifying child, but does not.

Example: Isabel is a single mother who has a three-year-old son named Jeffrey. They live with Isabel's father, Robert (the child's grandfather). Robert made $65,000 in wages during the year. Isabel made $19,000 in wages during the year, and she has a filing requirement. Robert wants to claim his grandson as a dependent, but Isabel plans to claim her son as a dependent on her own return. If Robert and Isabel both *attempt* to claim Jeffrey, the IRS will apply the tie-breaker tests and disallow Robert's claim, because as the child's mother, Isabel has the primary right to claim Jeffrey as her qualifying child.

Note: The tiebreaker test only applies when two people <u>attempt</u> to claim the same child. If two or more taxpayers have the same qualifying child, <u>they can choose</u> which of them will claim the credit using that child. If more than one taxpayer actually *attempts* to claim the same child, *only then* will the IRS apply the tie-breaker rules. In cases where the parents are in agreement, there is no tiebreaker test.

Example: Rosita and her sister, Evita, live together. Their seven-year-old nephew, Alex, lived with his aunts all year while Alex's mother was incarcerated in a maximum-security prison. Rosita's AGI is $18,600. Evita's AGI is $29,000. Alex is a qualifying child of both Rosita and Evita because he meets the relationship, age, residency, and support tests for *both* of his aunts. However, Evita has the primary right to claim Alex as her qualifying child because her AGI is higher than Rosita's.

The tie-breaker test applies when two taxpayers *attempt* to claim the same child, but all of the primary tests for dependency still apply. For tax purposes, the person with whom the child lives (i.e., the taxpayer with primary physical custody) generally has the decisive right to claim the child as a dependent. Many times, these cases will go into audit, or even to litigation in the U.S. Tax Court.

Example: Carol Griffin claimed her nieces and nephews as her dependents. The children's father, Robbie, was a single father and disabled, and kept the children only two days a week. The IRS selected Ms. Griffin's tax return for audit, and disallowed the dependency exemptions for the children. Ms. Griffin disagreed with the IRS examiner's audit findings, and she subsequently petitioned the U.S. Tax Court. At trial, Ms. Griffin provided evidence and credible testimony that the children lived with her the majority of days during the year. The Tax Court awarded the three dependency exemptions to Ms. Griffin because she had the children for the majority of the year. In this case, Ms. Griffin proved that her nieces and nephews were her qualifying children by virtue of the residency test.[52]

Rules for a Qualifying Relative

A person who is not a qualifying child may still qualify as a dependent under the rules for qualifying relatives. Unlike a qualifying child, even an individual of any age who is not a family member can be a qualifying relative. The tests for a qualifying relative are applied only when the tests for a qualifying child are not met. To be claimed as a qualifying relative, the following four tests must be met:

- **Not a qualifying child test**
- **Member of household or relationship test**
- **Gross income test**
- **Support test**

Test #1: "Not a Qualifying Child" Test

If a child is already a qualifying *child* for any taxpayer, the child cannot be a qualifying *relative* of another taxpayer. In other words, a taxpayer cannot claim an individual who can be claimed as a dependent on another tax return.

Example: Nigel lives with his girlfriend Madeline and her 3-year-old daughter, Ainsley. They all live together in Nigel's home. Nigel is not the father of the child. Nigel owns the home and pays all the costs for keeping up the home, including the mortgage and property taxes. Nigel earned $56,000 in wages, while Madeline earned only $16,500 in wages during the year. Madeline has a filing requirement, so she files Single (not HOH) and claims her own daughter, Ainsley. Madeline also claims the Earned Income Tax Credit and the Child Tax Credit on her return. Madeline's daughter is *her* qualifying *child*, so Nigel cannot claim Ainsley as his qualifying *relative*.

---

[52] Based on U.S. Tax Court case Griffin v. Comm'r. The Tax Court held that a child's aunt was entitled to dependency exemption based on the time spent living with her, which was determined by the court to be more than half the year.

Under the tests for a qualifying relative, a child may qualify as the taxpayer's dependent, even if that child is the qualifying child of another taxpayer. This is allowed *only* when the child's parent is not required to file an income tax return and either does not file a return or only files to get a refund of income tax withheld or estimated tax paid.

> **Example:** For more than a year, Thorne has shared a home with his girlfriend, Daisy, and her two sons. Daisy is unemployed and does not have any taxable income, so she is not obligated to file a tax return. Thorne has a full-time job, and he provides all the support for the household. In this situation, Daisy and her children meet the criteria to be considered Thorne's "qualifying relatives." Thorne can claim Daisy and her two sons as "qualifying relative" dependents.

Test #2: "Member of Household" or "Relationship" Test

A dependent that is not related to the taxpayer must have lived with the taxpayer the *entire tax year* in order to meet the "member of household" or "relationship" test. However, a family member who is related to the taxpayer in any of the following ways <u>does not</u> have to live with the taxpayer to meet this test:

- A child, stepchild, foster child, or descendant of any of them (for example, a grandchild)
- A sibling, stepsibling, or half-sibling
- A parent, grandparent, stepparent, or another direct ancestor (but not a foster parent)
- A niece or nephew, son-in-law, daughter-in-law, father-in-law, mother-in-law, brother-in-law, or sister-in-law

> **Example:** Felton is 45 and single. Felton's 12-year-old nephew, Chilton, lived with him for two months. For the remainder of the year, Chilton lived with his mother, Inga, in a nearby town. Inga is Felton's 32-year-old sister. Inga did not have a job during the year and does not have any taxable income, or a filing requirement. Felton and Inga do not live together, but Felton still provides all of Inga and Chilton's financial support. Chilton is not Felton's qualifying child because he did not live with his uncle for more than half the year and therefore, does not meet the residency test. However, both Chilton and Inga would meet the requirements to be Felton's qualifying *relatives*.

For the relationship test, "family members" do not include cousins, who are treated as unrelated persons for tax purposes. A cousin must live with the taxpayer for the entire year and also meet the gross income test to qualify as a dependent, and even then, a cousin cannot be a qualifying child—only a qualifying relative. Also, a taxpayer may not claim a housekeeper or other household employee as a dependent, even if the employee lives with the taxpayer all year.

> **Example:** Faith lived all year with her boyfriend, Oscar, and his two children in her home. Faith is not the mother of Oscar's children. Oscar was unemployed for the entire tax year and has no taxable income and no filing requirement. Oscar and his two children are not related to Faith as family members, but they may be qualifying relatives if they meet all the other tests. If Faith and Oscar were later to marry, then Faith would be able to claim Oscar's children as her stepchildren, and they would be qualifying *children*, instead of qualifying *relatives*.

Example: Albert is 62 and single. Albert has lived with his first cousin, Elizabeth, the entire year. Elizabeth is 54 and has no taxable income. She is not required to file a tax return. Albert provided all the household support for Elizabeth. Therefore, Elizabeth passes the "not a qualifying child test" to be Albert's dependent. If Albert meets all other tests, Elizabeth may be claimed on Albert's tax return as a qualifying *relative*.

Example: Melanie is 21 years old and works as a live-in nanny for Vicente, a widowed taxpayer with two small children. Melanie lives with Vicente all year and takes care of his two toddlers. Vicente pays Melanie wages and properly reports her as his household employee on Schedule H, which he attaches to his Form 1040. Regardless of how little or how much he pays his nanny, Vicente cannot claim Melanie on his tax return as a dependent, because a household employee can never be claimed as a dependent.

Any relationship that is established by marriage does not end as a result of death or divorce.[53] For example, if a taxpayer supports his mother-in-law, he can continue to claim her as a dependent even if he and his spouse divorce, or even if he later becomes widowed.

Example: Celeste and Carlos have always financially supported Celeste's elderly mother, Rose, and claimed her as their dependent on their jointly filed returns. In 2021, Celeste died, and Carlos became a widower. Carlos remarries in 2023, but he has continued to support his late wife's mother. Carlos can continue to claim his late wife's mother, Rose, as a qualifying relative, even though he has remarried.

Test #3: Gross Income Test

To meet the gross income test, the dependent's gross income for the tax year must be less than the threshold amount. A qualifying relative cannot earn more than the "deemed exemption" amount, which is $4,700 in 2023. For the purposes of this test, "gross income" includes all income in the form of money, property, and services that are not exempt from tax.[54]

Example: Beatrice is 56 and earned $67,000 in wages. She financially supported her nephew, Jacob, who is 28 and a full-time college student, earning his Master's degree. Jacob is not disabled. Jacob has a small part-time job, and he earned $5,900 in 2023. Although Beatrice financially supported Jacob, she cannot claim him as a dependent because Jacob does not meet the age test for a qualifying child. Jacob also does not meet the test for a qualifying relative because his income exceeds the gross income test.

Note: Remember that there is no "gross income test" for a qualifying **child**—only for a qualifying **relative**! A person may be a qualifying child if they are permanently and totally disabled at any time during the year, regardless of age.

---

[53] Treasury Regulation section 1.152-2(d) currently provides that "the relationship of affinity once existing will not terminate by divorce or death of spouse."

[54] For purposes of this test, the gross income of an individual who is permanently disabled does not include income from a sheltered workshop. Sheltered Workshops provide a supervised work environment for disabled individuals to learn job skills.

Example: Keegan is 31 and has lived on his own for many years. He earns $14,000 in wages until February 16, 2023, when he is involved in a horrible car accident, rendering him permanently disabled. Keegan moves in with his mother, Annika, on April 3, 2023, after he gets out of the hospital. Keegan is in a wheelchair now and needs nursing care. Keegan's mother cares for him in her home and hires a home healthcare aide to care for Keegan when she is working. Keegan continues to live with his mother until the end of the year, with his mother providing the majority of his financial support. Annika earns $79,000 in wages during the year. Although Keegan was not a dependent in prior years, he is now Annika's qualifying child, because he lived with his mother for more than six months in 2023, he does not provide his own support, and he is permanently disabled. He is Annika's qualifying child in 2023.

Test #4: Support Test

To claim an individual as a qualifying relative, the taxpayer must provide *more than one-half* of the dependent's total support during the year. Support includes:

- The costs for necessities, such as food, housing, clothing, healthcare, education, and other similar expenses. Support can include the fair market value of housing.
- It also includes amounts from Social Security and welfare payments, even if that support is nontaxable.

Note that this "support test" is very different from the one for a qualifying child. The support test for a qualifying relative considers all income, taxable and nontaxable.

Example: Alexi, 27, is a full-time graduate student who lives with his parents. He is not disabled. He worked part-time, earning $4,100 in wages. He did not pay over half of his total support. Alexi meets the relationship, residency, and support tests for a qualifying *child*, but he does not meet the *age* test, because even though he is a full-time student, he is not under 24 years of age. Therefore, Alexi can be claimed as a qualifying *relative* by his parents.

Example: Cherise, age 35, financially supports her father, Asmund, who lives with her. Cherise earns $59,000 in wages during the year. Asmund is 62 and received $2,800 from Social Security during the year. He spent only $700 for his own support and put the rest in a savings account. Cherise spent $6,600 of her own income for Asmund's support, so she has provided over half of her father's support for the year. Cherise can claim Asmund as her qualifying relative and file as head of household.

Example: Angela's son, Darwin, is 22 years old. Darwin does not go to college, so he is no longer a student, and he is not disabled. Angela provides the majority of her son's support. Darwin's gross income is $3,960 for the year from a small part-time job. Darwin is not Angela's "qualifying child" because he fails the age test (because he is not a full-time student). However, he is still Angela's dependent because he is a qualifying relative. Darwin meets the relationship test because he is Angela's child, and he meets the gross income test because his income is under the "deemed exemption" amount for the year ($4,700 for 2023), and he meets the support test because Angela provides the majority of his support.

Special Rules for Divorced and Separated Parents

Generally, to claim a child as a dependent, the child must live with the taxpayer for more than one-half the year. However, special rules apply if the dependent is supported by parents who are divorced, separated, or live apart. In most cases, the child is the qualifying child of the custodial parent.

However, a custodial parent may permit the noncustodial parent to claim the child. The noncustodial parent must attach Form 8332, *Release/Revocation of Release of Claim to Exemption for Child by Custodial Parent*, to their tax return. A child may be treated as the qualifying child of the noncustodial parent if *all* the following conditions apply:

- The parents are divorced or legally separated, or if they lived apart during the last six months of the year.
- The child received over half of their support for the year from the parents.
- The child is in the custody of one (or both) parents.
- The custodial parent signs Form 8332 (or a similar statement), and the noncustodial parent attaches this declaration to their return.

This rule is an exception to the normal residency test for a qualifying child. It does not apply to the determination of head of household filing status or to eligibility for the Earned Income Tax Credit. The EITC and HOH filing status can be claimed only by the custodial parent, even if the noncustodial parent claims the child. If a divorce decree does not specify which parent is the custodial parent or which parent is allowed to claim the child, the dependent should be claimed by the parent who has *physical custody* for the majority of the year.

> **Example**: Johan and Penelope are legally divorced and live in separate homes. They share equal custody of their 8-year-old son, Lucas. During the year, Lucas stayed with Johan for 195 nights and with Penelope for 170 nights. Therefore, for federal tax purposes, Johan is considered the custodial parent and has the primary right to claim Lucas as his qualifying child.

> **Example:** Anders and Wilma are divorced and have one son, who is 10 years old. Wilma is the custodial parent, but she allows Anders to claim the child by signing Form 8332. Anders correctly files as "single" and claims his son as his dependent. Wilma may still file as head of household, even though she does not claim her son as a dependent, because she maintained the home where the child lived for most of the year.

If the child lived with each parent for an equal number of nights during the year, the custodial parent will be deemed to be the parent with the higher adjusted gross income.

The custodial parent can also revoke the release by using Form 8332. A copy of the revocation must be attached to the tax return for each year the child is claimed after the revocation. The custodial parent must also provide the noncustodial parent with a copy of the revocation, or make a reasonable effort to provide the noncustodial parent with a copy of the revocation.

The earliest the revocation will apply is the year *following* the year the revocation was provided (or a reasonable effort was made to provide) to the noncustodial parent. The custodial parent must keep a copy of the revocation and evidence of delivery of the notice to the noncustodial parent, or of reasonable efforts to provide actual notice.

Multiple Support Agreements

A *multiple support agreement* is when two or more people jointly provide for a person's support. This happens commonly when adult children are taking care of their parents.

Under a multiple support agreement, family members together must pay *more* than half of the person's total support, but no one member individually may pay more than half.

Taxpayers use Form 2120, *Multiple Support Declaration,* to report a multiple support arrangement. When a taxpayer uses this form, they acknowledge that they do not pay more than half the cost of supporting a dependent, but that the other individuals who share the costs allow the taxpayer to claim that person as a dependent.

In addition, the taxpayer who claims the dependent must provide more than 10% of the person's support. Only one family member can claim a dependent in a single year, but different qualifying family members can agree to claim the dependent in other years.

Example: Betty and Elinor are sisters who help financially support their 66-year-old father, Grayson. Each pays approximately 20% of his care in a residential facility for elderly people. The remaining 60% is paid for by a wealthy friend of the family, who is not related to Grayson. Because more than half of Grayson's support is provided by someone unrelated to him, no one can claim Grayson as a dependent.

Example: Altair, Gerry, and Hettie support their disabled mother, Leanne. Leanne is 83 years old and lives in a nursing home. In 2023, Leanne receives 20% of her financial support from Social Security, 40% from Gerry, 30% from Altair, and only 10% from Hettie. Under the IRS rules for multiple support agreements, either Gerry or Altair can claim their mother as a dependent if the other signs a statement agreeing not to do so. Hettie cannot claim her mother as a dependent, because she does not provide *more than* 10% of the support for Leanne during the year.

Unit 3: Study Questions

(Test yourself first, then check the correct answers at the end of this quiz.)

1. Ursula and her son, Kayden, live together. Kayden is 27 years old, not disabled, and has a part-time job. Ursula provides more than half of Kayden's support. Ursula can claim Kayden as a qualifying relative, as long as he does not earn _____ or more in 2023.

A. $1,100
B. $3,500
C. $4,700
D. $12,400

2. Apollonia and Wesley file for divorce. Apollonia has one teenage son from a prior relationship named Jeremy, age 17. After the divorce is final, Apollonia develops a drug problem and disappears. In 2023, Jeremy lives for nine months with his (former) stepfather, Wesley, who provides all of Jeremy's support. Which of the following statements is correct?

A. Wesley can claim Jeremy as his qualifying child.
B. Wesley can claim Jeremy as his dependent but not as a qualifying child because the divorce dissolved any legal relationship between them.
C. Wesley cannot claim Jeremy as his dependent because they are not related persons.
D. Only Apollonia can claim Jeremy as her dependent.

3. Waylen, 52, is unmarried and lives with his son Wyatt, who has Down syndrome. Wyatt is 32 years old and permanently disabled. Wyatt had $800 of interest income and $6,200 of wages from a part-time job at a sheltered workshop. Waylen provided more than one-half of his son Wyatt's support. Which of the following statements is correct?

A. Waylen can file as head of household, with Wyatt as his qualifying child.
B. Waylen does not qualify for head of household, but he could still claim Wyatt as his qualifying relative because Wyatt does not meet the age test for a qualifying child.
C. Waylen can file as head of household, with Wyatt as his qualifying relative.
D. Waylen must file as single, and he cannot claim his son because of the amount of Wyatt's income.

4. Khristina's son, Eugene, lives with her. Eugene is 18 years old and does not go to school. She provided $5,100 toward her son's support for the year. Eugene also has a part-time job and provided $14,950 toward his own support. He also paid part of the utilities and rent on the home. Can Khristina claim her son as a dependent?

A. Yes, she can claim Eugene as a qualifying child.
B. Yes, she can claim Eugene as a qualifying relative.
C. No; Eugene provided more than half of his own support for the year.
D. No; Eugene is 18-years-old.

5. Becky is 22 and a full-time college student. During the year, she lived at home with her parents for four months and lived in the college dorms for the remainder of the year. She worked part-time and earned $6,500, but that income did not amount to half of her total support. Can Becky's parents claim her as a dependent?

A. No, because Becky earned more than the gross income threshold.
B. No, Becky did not live with her parents for half the year, and she did not meet the age test.
C. Yes, her parents can claim her as a dependent, but only as a qualifying relative.
D. Yes, her parents can claim her as a qualifying child.

6. Which of the following is _not_ one of the tests that must be met for a child to be considered a qualifying child?

A. Relationship test
B. Passport test
C. Age test
D. Joint return test

7. All of the following statements are correct about the rules of dependents except:

A. One spouse is never considered the dependent of the other spouse.
B. A taxpayer may not claim a stillborn child as a dependent.
C. A housekeeper can be a dependent, as long as the housekeeper lives with the taxpayer all year.
D. A child is considered to have lived with the taxpayer during periods when the child is temporarily absent.

8. Astrid and Sergey divorced ten years ago. They have twelve-year-old twins who live with Astrid. Her AGI is $41,000, and Sergey's AGI is $48,000. Although Astrid is the custodial parent, their divorce decree states that Sergey can claim the children on his tax return. However, Astrid refuses to sign Form 8332. Which of the following statements is correct?

A. Sergey can claim one child as a dependent, and Astrid can claim the other.
B. Sergey cannot claim either child.
C. Sergey and Astrid can each claim the children as dependents on their respective tax returns.
D. Neither Astrid nor Sergey can claim the children as dependents.

9. Kingston provides the sole support for his mother. To claim her as a dependent on his Form 1040, Kingston's mother must be a resident or citizen of which of the following countries?

A. United States
B. Mexico
C. Canada
D. Any of the above

10. Cheryl is 46 and unmarried. Her nephew, Bradley, lived with her all year and turned 18 years old on December 28, 2023. Bradley is not a student anymore because he finished high school last year and did not go to college. Bradley did not provide more than one-half of his own support. He had $4,200 of income from wages and $1,020 of investment income. Which of the following statements is correct?

A. Bradley is Cheryl's qualifying child.
B. Bradley is not a qualifying child; however, Cheryl can claim him as a qualifying relative.
C. Bradley is neither a qualifying child nor a qualifying relative.
D. Cheryl can claim Bradley only if he goes back to college.

11. Orion is 22 years old, single, and a full-time graduate student. During the year, he studied on a student exchange program in Costa Rica and did not have any taxable income, although he was awarded a scholarship of $6,000, which he used for his tuition. He did not live at home with his parents a single day during the tax year. Orion's parents provided the majority of his financial support and want to claim him as a dependent. Which of the following is true?

A. His parents may claim Orion as a qualifying child.
B. His parents may claim Orion as a qualifying relative.
C. His parents may not claim Orion as a dependent.
D. Orion should file his own tax return.

12. A taxpayer cannot claim a qualifying child as a dependent if that child provides more than _____ of their own support.

A. 25%
B. 33%
C. 50%
D. 75%

13. Greta is 80 years old. She has three children: Luther, Silas, and Caprice. Each child contributes financially towards her support. Luther and Silas each provide 45%, and Caprice provides 10%. Which taxpayer would be eligible to claim Greta as a dependent parent under a multiple support agreement?

A. Luther or Silas.
B. Caprice or Silas.
C. Luther, Silas, or Caprice.
D. No one is eligible to claim Greta.

Unit 3: Quiz Answers

1. The answer is C. Kayden cannot be a qualifying child for Ursula because he does not meet the age test, but he can be claimed as a qualifying relative. The 2023 limit for gross income for qualifying relatives is $4,700. Therefore, if Kayden earns less than this amount during the year, his mother can claim him as a "qualifying relative" dependent on her tax return.

2. The answer is A. A qualifying child must be related to the taxpayer by blood, marriage, or legal adoption. A "step" relationship formed by marriage is not dissolved by divorce or death for federal tax purposes. Since Jeremy did not live with his mother but *did* live with his stepfather, Wesley, for more than half the year, Wesley is considered the custodial parent for tax purposes, and he can claim his stepson as a qualifying child.

3. The answer is A. Even though Wyatt is over the normal age threshold for a qualifying child, he is considered Waylen's qualifying child. This is because Wyatt is permanently disabled, and Waylen provides the majority of his financial support and care. The normal age thresholds for "qualifying children" do not apply in the case of permanently disabled individuals. The wages earned by Wyatt were earned in a sheltered workshop. Income earned in a sheltered workshop does not count as gross income for an adult child for the purposes of determining dependency.

4. The answer is C. Eugene provided more than one-half of his own support for the year, so he is not Khristina's qualifying child or her qualifying relative. To meet the support test, the child cannot have provided more than half of his own support for the year.

5. The answer is D. Becky meets all the qualifying child tests: the relationship test, the age test (because she is under 24 and a full-time student), the residency test (because the time spent at college is a legitimate temporary absence), and the support test (because she did not provide over half of her own support). Therefore, her parents can claim Becky as a qualifying child.

6. The answer is B. The passport test is not one of the tests for a qualifying child. In general, to be a taxpayer's qualifying child, a dependent must satisfy four tests:

- **Relationship:** The taxpayer's child or stepchild (whether by blood or adoption), foster child, sibling or step-sibling, or a descendant of one of these.
- **Residence:** Has the same principal residence as the taxpayer for more than half the tax year.
- **Age:** Must be under the age of 19 at the end of the tax year, or under the age of 24 if a full-time student, or be permanently and totally disabled at any time during the year.
- **Support:** Did not provide more than one-half of their own support for the year.
- **Tie-breaker test:** A child may meet all the other tests to be a qualifying child of two or more individuals, however only one of them can treat the child as a qualifying child.

7. The answer is C. A taxpayer may not claim a housekeeper or other household employee as a dependent, regardless of whether or not the employee lived with the taxpayer.

8. The answer is B. Since Astrid is the custodial parent and refuses to sign Form 8332, Sergey cannot claim either child. Without Form 8332, *Release/Revocation of Release of Claim to Exemption for Child by Custodial Parent,* signed and attached to the return, Sergey does not have the primary right to claim the children, since he is not the custodial parent.

9. The answer is D. A dependent must be a citizen or resident alien of the United States, Canada, or Mexico. Generally, you can't claim a child as a dependent who lives in a country other than the United States, Canada, or Mexico unless the child is a U.S. citizen, U.S. resident alien, or U.S. national. There is an exception for certain adopted children who live in a taxpayer's home as a member of their family for the entire taxable year.

10. The answer is A. Bradley is Cheryl's qualifying child because he meets the age test, support test, and relationship test. Also, because Bradley is single, he is a qualifying person for Cheryl to claim head of household filing status. Bradley is not required to be a full-time student because any child <u>under the age of 19</u> at the end of the tax year will be treated as a qualifying child if all the other tests are met. Bradley is only 18 years old and therefore passes the age test.

11. The answer is A. His parents may claim Orion as a qualifying child. He was a full-time student, and temporary absences for education are allowed and do not count as time living away from home. The scholarship does not have to be counted as part of the support test.

12. The answer is C. A taxpayer cannot claim another person as a dependent if that person provided more than one-half of their own support (more than 50%).

13. The answer is A. Only Luther or Silas are eligible to claim Greta under a multiple support agreement. Caprice is not eligible because she does not provide more than 10% of her mother's support. Either Luther or Silas may use Form 2120, *Multiple Support Declaration,* to report their multiple support arrangement.

Unit 4: Taxable and Nontaxable Income

For additional information, read:
Publication 525, *Taxable and Nontaxable Income*
Publication 15-B, *Employer's Tax Guide to Fringe Benefits*
Publication 3, *Armed Forces Tax Guide*

According to federal tax law, all income is taxable except for specific exclusions. It is important to understand the difference between an *exclusion* and a *deduction*, as some deductions and credits are phased out at higher gross income levels. Excluded income, however, remains nontaxable regardless of the taxpayer's income level.

Most excluded income does not need to be reported on a tax return, although there are exceptions, such as interest from municipal bonds.[55]

Example: Javier is a software engineer who works for a tech company and earns a salary of $80,000 a year. His salary is fully taxable. He also receives $15,500 in municipal bond interest, which is tax-exempt at the federal level. Although he must report the municipal bond interest on his tax return, it is not taxed.

Example: Marcus is a popular recording artist who earned more than $2 million of taxable income during the year. Because of his high income, many deductions and credits are phased out for him. However, on July 1, 2024, Marcus is involved in an auto accident and sustains major injuries. Marcus sues the other driver and receives an insurance settlement of $900,000 related to his injuries resulting from the accident. The settlement is excluded from his gross income because compensation for physical injuries is not taxable to the recipient, regardless of his taxable income level. Marcus does not even have to report the injury settlement on his tax return.

Calculating Taxable Income

In order for a taxpayer to calculate their tax owed, they must first determine their **gross income.** Gross income includes all forms of taxable compensation such as wages, salaries, commissions, tips, and self-employment income. It also encompasses non-monetary forms of compensation like goods, property, services, and taxable fringe benefits such as interest, dividends, capital gains, and stock options.

Next, the taxpayer calculates their **adjusted gross income (AGI)** by subtracting from gross income certain specific deductions or adjustments. Examples of some of these "for AGI" (commonly referred to as "above the line") deductions include certain IRA contributions, certain expenses for self-employed individuals, deductible student loan interest and penalties paid to banks on early withdrawals of savings. The amount of a taxpayer's AGI is important because it helps determine eligibility for certain deductions and credits.

Finally, the taxpayer calculates their **taxable income** by subtracting additional deductions (standard or itemized) from AGI. The next table is a simplified example of how to calculate income tax.

---

[55] Municipal bonds are debt securities issued by state, city, and local governments. Municipal bond interest is tax-free at the federal level but can be taxable at state or local income tax levels.

> **How to Calculate Taxable Income and Tax Liability for Most Individuals**
> Start with gross income
> Subtract adjustments to income ("above the line" deductions)
> = <u>Adjusted gross income (AGI)</u>
> Subtract greater of itemized deductions or the standard deduction
> = Taxable income
> × Tax rate
> = Gross tax liability
> <u>Subtract credits</u>
> **= Net tax liability or refund receivable (based on the amount of prepaid tax, if any)**

Earned Income vs. Unearned Income

Earned income such as wages, salaries, tips, professional fees, or self-employment income is received for services performed. *Unearned income* includes interest, dividends, retirement income, taxable alimony, and disability benefits. Earned income is generally subject to Social Security and Medicare taxes (also called FICA taxes). Investment income and other unearned income are generally not subject to FICA taxes. The amount of taxable income is used to determine the taxpayer's gross income tax liability before applicable credits.

Constructive Receipt of Income

The doctrine of constructive receipt requires that cash-basis taxpayers be taxed on income when it becomes available and is not subject to substantial limitations or restrictions, regardless of whether it is in their physical possession.[56] Income received by an agent for a taxpayer is constructively received in the year the agent receives it.

Example: Logan is a landlord who owns several rental properties. On December 30, 2023, a tenant delivers a $750 rent check to Logan's payment lockbox. Logan does not collect the rental deposits in the lockbox on December 30 and instead leaves town later that day to celebrate New Year's Eve. Logan does not actually take physical possession of the check until January 5, 2024, the same day he deposits the check in his bank account. He is considered to have constructive receipt in 2023, and must include the $750 of gross income on his 2023 tax return because the check was available to Logan at that time without any substantial limitations or restrictions.

If there are significant restrictions on the income, or if the income is not accessible to the taxpayer, it is not considered to have been constructively received. According to the IRS, constructive receipt requires that an amount credited to an individual's account be subject to "unqualified demand."

The doctrine of constructive receipt requires the <u>actual receipt</u> of property or the right to receive property. Economic benefit applies when assets are unconditionally and irrevocably paid into a fund or trust to be used for a taxpayer's sole benefit.

---

[56] Most individuals are cash-basis taxpayers who report income when it is actually or constructively received during the tax year. This concept of constructive receipt would not apply to accrual basis taxpayers who recognize income when it is earned rather than when it is received. We will cover accrual basis taxpayers in Book 2, Businesses.

Example: Raakel owns a large plot of land in Chicago, IL. On January 2, 2023, the county filed a condemnation action to acquire Raakel's land in order to build a public highway. Raakel does not want to sell her land and decides to fight the condemnation. On May 5, 2023, the county deposited $800,000 as "probable compensation" for the property with the IL state treasurer. Raakel could have withdrawn the funds, but to do so would have jeopardized her ability to sue. She does not accept the funds, and a month later, on June 3, 2023, Raakel files a lawsuit against the county, challenging the government's right to take her property. Raakel eventually settles the lawsuit, but not until the following year, when she and the county eventually agree to a financial settlement. Raakel finally accepts the condemnation award for her property on March 3, 2024 (the following year). In this case, the IRS determined that constructive receipt occurred in 2024.[57]

Income is also not considered to have been "constructively received" if a taxpayer declines to accept an item, such as a prize or an award, or if the prize is not received by the taxpayer.

Example: Lucia won front-row concert tickets valued at $1,200 from a local radio station. The value of the tickets is clearly printed on the tickets. Lucia would be required to pay taxes based on the fair market value of the tickets. However, on the day of the concert, the radio station does not receive the tickets in time from the promoter, and Lucia is not able to attend the concert. Since she never received the tickets, the prize is not taxable to her because she never had constructive receipt of it.

Example: Wendy purchased a $1 ticket for a raffle conducted by her Methodist church, an exempt organization. The drawing was held, and Wendy won $900. The church offers her a check for her winnings, but Wendy declines the prize and does not accept the check, preferring that her church use the funds to help needy families. Since she never had constructive receipt of the funds, the prize is not taxable to Wendy.

When determining the value of a prize or an award, the IRS defines fair market value (FMV) in this way: the price at which a property would change hands between a buyer and a seller when both have reasonable knowledge of all the necessary facts and neither is being forced to buy or sell. If parties with adverse interests place a value on property in an arms-length transaction, that is strong evidence of FMV. If there is a stated price for services, this price is treated as the FMV unless there is evidence to the contrary.

The "Claim of Right" Doctrine

In the event that a taxpayer is required to pay back an amount over $3,000 which they had included in income in a previous year, they may be eligible for a deduction or a tax credit.[58] Under IRC section 1341, if a taxpayer reports income in one year, but then has to repay that income in a future tax year, and the repayment exceeds $3,000, the taxpayer may claim a tax credit on Schedule 3 (Form 1040) in

---

[57] This example is based on Private Letter Ruling 200944012, where the IRS concluded that a taxpayer was not in constructive receipt of condemnation proceeds that had been deposited with the state treasurer during the time the taxpayer was contesting the condemnation in a legal action.

[58] Per Publication 525, the repayment is deducted on the same form or schedule on which it was previously included. If it had been included as self-employment income on Schedule C, Profit or Loss from Business, it is deducted on Schedule C. If it had been included as capital gain on Schedule D, Capital Gains and Losses, it is deducted on Schedule D. If it was reported as wages, taxable unemployment compensation, or other non-business ordinary income, it is deducted on Schedule A, Itemized Deductions (but only if the repayment is over $3,000). If the amount repaid was $3,000 or less, the Claim of Right under IRC Section 1341 does not apply. See IRS Publication 525, under *Repayments Under Claim of Right.*

the repayment year equal to the tax change caused by the income inclusion in the prior year if it results in less tax.

If the repayment is $3,000 or less, section 1341 does not apply and the repayment is generally deducted on the same form or schedule on which it was previously included. If the income had been included as self-employment income on Schedule C, *Profit or Loss from Business*, it may be deducted directly on Schedule C in the year the repayment occurs. A taxpayer should not amend their reported gross income for the earlier year.

> **Example:** Marilyn is a fine art dealer who is self-employed and owns her own art gallery. In 2023, Marilyn sells a painting in her art gallery for $28,000. She properly includes $28,000 in her gross income and pays taxes on the income. On February 2, 2024, the customer discovers the painting is a forgery and returns the painting, demanding a full refund of $28,000. Marilyn promptly refunds the customer. Since Marilyn pays back the $28,000 in 2024, she is entitled to deduct the amount from her gross income in 2024 on her Schedule C. She does not have to amend her prior-year tax return.

However, if the income was previously reported as wages, taxable unemployment compensation, or other nonbusiness ordinary income, and the repayment is less than $3,000, the repayment cannot be deducted.

> **Example:** Josie was fired from her job on October 3, 2022 (the prior year). She filed for unemployment a week later, and began receiving unemployment benefits. Josie received a Form 1099-G for $7,000 in unemployment compensation that she received during the year and reports the amounts on her tax return. On January 2, 2023, Josie's former employer appeals the decision, claiming that Josie made false statements on her unemployment application, and submits evidence that Josie had been fired for employee theft. On March 30, 2023, the state's Department of Unemployment Assistance sides with Josie's employer, and determines that Josie was not eligible for unemployment. The state forces her to repay the entire $7,000 in unemployment benefits in 2023 (the following year). Since the amount of the repayment exceeds $3,000, she can take a deduction or an IRC 1341 credit in 2023 for the repaid amounts.

> **Example:** Webster, age 64. He retired from his teaching job several years ago and started receiving pension payments. On February 3, 2023, Webster receives a letter from his pension administrator informing him that the administrator made a mistake and overpaid his pension benefits by $2,300 in 2022 (the prior year). The administrator requests that Webster repays the overpayment by writing a check back to the pension plan. Webster writes a check for the full amount and remits it to his pension administrator on February 20, 2023. Since the amount Webster repaid was less than $3,000, he cannot deduct the repayment.

Self-Employed Taxpayers

Self-employment income is earned by taxpayers who work for themselves. A taxpayer who has self-employment income of $400 or more in a year must file a tax return and report the earnings to the IRS. Taxpayers who are independent contractors usually receive Form 1099-NEC from their business customers showing the income they were paid for the year (if $600 or more).

The amounts reported on Forms 1099-NEC, along with any other business income, are reported by most self-employed individuals on Schedule C, *Profit or Loss from Business*, of Form 1040. Self-employed farmers report their earnings on Schedule F, *Profit or Loss from Farming,* of Form 1040. Self-employment income also includes:

- Income of ministers, priests, and rabbis for the performance of services such as baptisms and marriages.
- The distributive share of trade or business income allocated by a partnership to its general partners or, in certain circumstances, by a limited liability company (LLC) to its members. The income is reported to the individual partners on Schedule K-1 (Form 1065).

Example: Carmen operates a popular taco truck with her brother, Orlando. They both split profits and losses equally, and they operate their business as a general partnership. They request a partnership EIN from the IRS and correctly file Form 1065, *U.S. Return of Partnership Income*, to report the gross income from the taco stand. Carmen and Orlando both receive a Schedule K-1 from the partnership every year. Carmen and Orlando must each report their distributive share of income from the taco stand on their respective Forms 1040, Schedule E (Part 2). The income is considered self-employment income and is subject to self-employment tax.

A taxpayer does not have to conduct regular full-time business activities to be considered self-employed. A taxpayer may have a side business in addition to a regular job, and this is also considered self-employment.

Example: Gavin earned $49,000 in wages as a full-time employee for Royal Roofing, Inc. He also advertises general handyman services online and performs household repair services for various local businesses. During the year, Gavin did several handyman side-jobs on the weekends for private clients. Gavin received payments of $9,000 from several different individuals for his handyman work. He did not receive Forms 1099-NEC for the $9,000 (because they were individuals who are not required to issue Forms 1099-NEC), but he must report the payments as self-employment income on Schedule C.

FICA Tax (Payroll Taxes)

The Federal Insurance Contributions Act (FICA) tax includes two separate taxes: one is Social Security tax, and the other is Medicare tax. The current rate for Social Security is 6.2% for the employer and 6.2% for the employee, or 12.4% total. The current rate for Medicare is 1.45% for the employer and 1.45% for the employee, or 2.9% total.

The combined FICA tax rate for 2023 is 15.3% and applies up to $160,200 of a taxpayer's combined earned income, including wages, tips, and 92.35% of net earnings from self-employment.[59] If the taxpayer's combined earned income exceeds $160,200 in 2023, a rate of 2.9%, representing only the Medicare portion, applies to any excess earnings over the earned income threshold.

Note: The 7.65% FICA tax rate is the *combined* rate for Social Security and Medicare. The Social Security portion (also called "OASDI") is 6.2% on earnings up to the applicable taxable maximum amount ($160,200 in 2023). *Remember:* the Medicare portion is 1.45% on *all* earned income: there is no yearly maximum for Medicare tax.

---

[59] A 7.65% deduction is taken from the total amount of net self-employment income before applying the applicable Social Security and Medicare tax rates for self-employment tax purposes.

For certain high-income individuals, an *additional* Medicare surtax of 0.9% is applied to wages and self-employment income above certain thresholds.[60]

Example: Bernadette is a registered nurse who works for a medical office. To calculate her FICA tax contribution as an employee, her payroll department multiplies Bernadette's gross pay by the current Social Security and Medicare tax rates. Bernadette's taxable wages are $80,000 in 2023, so all her wages would be subject to FICA tax. Bernadette's social security contribution would be: $80,000 × 6.2%, or $4,960, which is credited to her Social Security account. Her Medicare contribution would be: $80,000 × 1.45%, or $1,160. These are also the amounts her employer would pay.

Note: If a taxpayer works for more than one employer and their total compensation is over the $160,200 Social Security base limit for 2023, too much Social Security tax may have been withheld. For tax year 2023, a taxpayer will have excess Social Security withholdings if the sum of multiple employers' withholdings exceeds the annual maximum. This usually occurs when a person changes jobs mid-year, or works multiple jobs. In this case, the taxpayer can claim the excess as a credit against his income tax. This is officially called the **"Credit for Excess Social Security and RRTA Tax Withheld"** and is fully refundable on a taxpayer's individual return.

Example: Kiyoshi is a civil engineer working for Surety Engineering. Kiyoshi earns $98,000 in wages working for his employer until August 5, 2023, when he gets a better job offer from another company. Kiyoshi gives notice and begins working at the new engineering firm on August 25, earning $75,000 in wages from September to the end of December. He has earned a total of $173,000 in wages for the year ($98,000 + $75,000). Social Security and Medicare tax was withheld by both employers, because employers are required by law to withhold payroll tax from each employee's wages. As a result of having two jobs, Kiyoshi has "excess" Social Security withholdings. When Kiyoshi files his individual tax return, he will receive a credit for the over-withheld amounts on Schedule 3 (Form 1040).

Schedule 3 (Form 1040) 2023   Page **2**

Part II   **Other Payments and Refundable Credits**

9	Net premium tax credit. Attach Form 8962	9
10	Amount paid with request for extension to file (see instructions)	10
11	Excess social security and tier 1 RRTA tax withheld	11
12	Credit for federal tax on fuels. Attach Form 4136	12
13	Other payments or refundable credits:	
a	Form 2439	13a
b	Credit for repayment of amounts included in income from earlier years	13b
c	Elective payment election amount from Form 3800, Part III, line	

Self-Employment Tax

Self-employment tax (SE tax) is imposed on self-employed individuals in a manner similar to the Social Security and Medicare taxes that apply to wage earners. Self-employed individuals are responsible for paying the entire amount of Social Security and Medicare taxes applicable to their net earnings from self-employment. Self-employment tax is calculated on Schedule SE, *Self-Employment*

---

[60] The Additional Medicare Tax applies to wages, railroad retirement (RRTA) compensation, and self-employment income over certain thresholds. This tax will be covered in more detail later.

Tax. If a taxpayer has wages in addition to self-employment earnings, the Social Security tax on the wages is paid first. There are two adjustments related to the self-employment tax that reduce overall taxes for a taxpayer with self-employment income.

- First, the taxpayer's net earnings from self-employment are reduced by 7.65%. Just as the employer's share of Social Security tax is not considered wages to the employee, this reduction removes a corresponding amount from the net earnings before the SE tax is calculated.
- Second, the taxpayer can deduct the employer-equivalent portion of his self-employment tax in determining his adjusted gross income.

More Than One Business: If a taxpayer owns more than one business, he or she must net the profit or loss from each business to determine the total earnings subject to SE tax. However, married taxpayers cannot combine their income or loss from self-employment to determine their individual earnings subject to SE tax.

Example: Brian is a sole proprietor who owns a popular barbershop. He has $49,000 of net income from the business in 2023. His wife, Ellen, has a candle-making business, which has overall losses of ($12,000) for the year. Brian must pay self-employment tax on $49,000, regardless of how he and Ellen choose to file. That is because married couples cannot offset each other's income from self-employment, even if they file jointly, for self-employment tax purposes. The income of each business is allocated to each individual.

Example: Kangiten is a married taxpayer who is a sole proprietor of two small businesses, a computer repair shop and a car wash business. Kangiten's wife, Akemi, is a homemaker and does not work in either business. Kangiten's computer business has net income of $50,000, while the car wash has a net loss of ($23,000) for the year. Kangiten only must pay self-employment tax on $27,000 ($50,000 - $23,000) of income because he may "net" the income and losses from both his businesses.

Employee Compensation and Worker Classification

Wages, salaries, bonuses, tips, and commissions are compensation received by employees for services performed. Employee compensation is taxable income to the employee and a deductible expense for the employer. For federal tax purposes, the IRS classifies "workers" in two broad categories: **employees** and **independent contractors**. These workers are taxed in different ways, and businesses must identify the correct classification for each individual to whom it makes payments for services.

In general, a business must withhold and remit income taxes, Social Security and Medicare taxes (payroll taxes), and pay unemployment tax on salaries and wages paid to an employee. Employers are required by January 31 to issue Forms W-2, which shows the amounts of wages paid to employees for the previous year. A business generally does not have to withhold or pay taxes on payments to independent contractors, because the earnings of a person working as an independent contractor are subject to self-employment tax. The general rule is that an individual is an independent contractor if the payor has the right to control or direct only the result of the work, not what will be done and how it will be done.

If a worker receives a Form 1099-NEC, but believes that they are an employee and should have received a Form W-2 instead, they can file Form SS-8, *Determination of Worker Status for Purposes of*

Federal Employment Taxes and Income Tax Withholding with the IRS, and if a determination is made that they are an employee, they will file Form 8919, *Uncollected Social Security and Medicare Tax on Wages*, with their tax return. Wages from Form 8919 also are reported on the Form 1040 on line 1g.

Example: Stella was hired to work as a file clerk for a small car wash company in 2023. The business classified Stella as an independent contractor in order to avoid having to pay payroll taxes. Stella worked in the office every day from 9-5, under the full control of the company, and was clearly an employee. The business issued Stella a 1099-NEC at the end of the year. Stella disagrees with her classification, so she fills out Form SS-8 and files it with the IRS. The IRS will investigate the classification issue, and if they determine that she was an employee, they will make sure that her employer pays the payroll taxes that were their responsibility, and Stella will be liable for the income tax on the amount that she earned, just as she would have been, had she been classified correctly. She would file Form 8919 with her tax return to account and pay for her share of Social Security and Medicare taxes on her wages.

Example: Terrence works for a company as a full-time delivery driver. At the end of the year, Terrence's employer issues him a Form 1099-NEC instead of a Form W-2. Terrence believes he was misclassified as an independent contractor. While he completed and filed Form SS-8 with the IRS, he has not yet received a response from the IRS by the tax return due date. Therefore, he files Form 8919, *Uncollected Social Security and Medicare Tax on Wages* with his tax return. Terrence lists the name of the employer, provides the employer's Federal Employer Identification Number, the reason he is filing, and his total alleged wages with unreported Social Security and Medicare taxes.

Worker classification is considered a "hot-button" issue for the IRS and is covered in more detail in *Book 2, Businesses.*

Advance Wages: If an employee receives advance wages, commissions, or other earnings, the employee must recognize the income in the year it is actually or constructively received. If the employee is later required to pay back a portion of the earnings, the amount would be deducted from their taxable wages at that time.

Example: Damian requests a modest salary advance of $1,300 on December 1, 2023, so he can take a two-week Christmas vacation. His employer gives him the check on December 20, 2023. Damian must recognize the income on his 2023 tax return, even though he will not actually "earn" the money until 2024, when he returns from his vacation.

Supplemental Wages

Supplemental wages are compensation paid to an employee in addition to their regular pay. These amounts are listed on the employee's Form W-2 and are taxable, just like regular wages, even if the pay is not actually for work performed. Vacation pay and sick pay are examples of supplemental wages that are taxable just like any other wage income, even though the employee has not technically "worked" for the income. Supplemental wages may also include:

- Bonuses, commissions, prizes
- Severance pay, back pay, and holiday pay
- Payment for nondeductible moving expenses

Garnished Wages

An employee may have their wages garnished for various reasons, such as when the employee owes child support, back taxes, or other debts. State and federal law require employers to comply with various income-withholding orders for child support and other court-mandated obligations. Regardless of the amounts garnished from the employee's paycheck, the full amount of gross wages must be included in his taxable wages at year-end.

Property or Services "in Lieu" of Wages

Wages paid in any form other than cash are measured by their fair market value. An employee who receives property for services performed must generally recognize the fair market value of the property when it is received as taxable income. However, if an employee receives stock or other property that is restricted, the property is not included in income until it is available to the employee without restriction.

Example: Leonard's company gives him 500 shares of restricted stock, valued at $9,000. He cannot sell or otherwise use the shares for five years. If Leonard quits his job, he forfeits the shares. He does not have to recognize the restricted stock as income in the year he receives it, because the stock is subject to substantial restrictions. Leonard will report it as taxable income when the restrictions lapse, and he gains complete control over the stock.

Another common arrangement is when colleges offer tuition reduction and/or free on-campus housing in lieu of wages to student teachers. Any portion of a grant or scholarship that is compensation for services is taxable as wages.

Example: Violet is a doctoral student attending Boston University. Violet received a grant of $32,500 to pay her tuition and on-campus housing. As a condition for receiving the scholarship, Violet must serve as a part-time teaching assistant. Of the $32,500 scholarship, $11,000 represents payment for teaching. The University gives Violet a Form W-2 showing $11,000 as wages. All the money was used to offset her tuition and course-related expenses. Assuming that all other conditions are met, $21,500 of her grant is tax-free. However, the $11,000 Violet received for teaching is taxable as wages, because it was for services that she performed.

Tip Income

Tips received by food servers, baggage handlers, hairdressers, and others for performing services are taxable income. An individual who receives $20 or more per month in tips must report the tip income to their employer. An employee who receives less than $20 per month in tips while working one job does not have to report the tip income to his employer. Tips of less than $20 per month are exempt from Social Security and Medicare taxes, but are still subject to federal income tax. [61]

In situations where an employee works more than one job, the $20 tip reporting threshold applies on a per job basis, and not on an overall basis for the employee. An employee who does not report all their tips to their employer generally must report the tips and related Social Security and Medicare taxes on Form 1040. Form 4137, *Social Security and Medicare Tax on Unreported Tip Income,* is used to compute the additional tax.

---

[61] Rev. Rul. 2012-18 (Q&A #2), 2012-26 IRB 1032

Example: Sherrie works two jobs: as an administrative assistant during the week and as a part-time bartender on the weekends. She reports $3,000 in tip income from the bartending job to her employer. Her W-2 Forms show wage income of $31,000 (administrative assistant) and $8,250 (bartender). Sherrie must report $39,250, the total amount earned at both jobs, on her Form 1040. Since she reported the tip income to her employer, her bartending tips are already included on her Form W-2 for that job.

Taxpayers who are self-employed and receive tips must include their tip income in gross receipts on Schedule C.

Example: Baltazar is a licensed hairdresser who works for a popular salon franchise, Super-Duper Cuts. He is an employee of the franchise and receives minimum wage as well as tips. He must report these tips to his employer. Baltazar also cuts hair in the evenings in his garage, offering his barbering services to friends and family. All the income he earns cutting hair at home (including tips) is treated as self-employment income and must be reported on Schedule C.

Non-cash tips (for example, concert tickets, or other items) do not have to be reported to the employer, but they must be reported and included in the taxpayer's gross income at their fair market value.

Example: Benita is a waitress at the Denton Diner, a popular restaurant. One of Benita's regular customers leaves Benita an expensive piece of jewelry, as an additional tip. Benita accepts the jewelry and plans to wear it. Benita does not have to report the noncash tip to her employer, but she must include the noncash tip (the jewelry) in her gross income.

Taxable Fringe Benefits for Employees

While the tax law does not have a specific definition for fringe benefits, the IRS considers them to be any additional cash, property, or service given to employees on top of their regular taxable wages. Employers often offer fringe benefits as part of a compensation package, with common examples being health insurance, retirement plans, and parking passes.

While most fringe benefits are not subject to taxes, there are some exceptions. These include certain entertainment expenses, which are no longer deductible for employers. This means that any entertainment provided to employees, such as tickets to sporting events, must now be included in their taxable income.[62] Some other examples of taxable fringe benefits include:

- Off-site athletic facilities and health club memberships,
- Concert and athletic event tickets,
- The value of employer-provided life insurance *over* $50,000,
- Any cash benefit in the form of a credit card or gift card (an exception applies for occasional meal money or transportation fare to allow an employee to work beyond normal hours),
- Transportation benefits exceeding the monthly maximum ($300 per month in 2023),
- Employer-provided vehicles, if they are used for personal purposes. There is an exception for qualified nonpersonal use vehicles (i.e., police cars, school buses, transit buses, etc.).

---

[62] There is a narrow exception for entertainment expenses that are directly for the benefit of employees, other than highly compensated employees, (i.e., office parties or company picnics that include all company staff).

Example: Smithville Pharmaceuticals, Inc. pays for country club memberships for all its top sales executives. Membership costs $8,000 a year per person. The executives use the country club to entertain prospective clients and investors. Even though the club membership is used frequently for business purposes, this type of fringe benefit is taxable compensation to the employees. Smithville Pharmaceuticals, Inc. must include the full amount of the club membership ($8,000) in the employee's wages, subject to income tax and payroll taxes.

Nontaxable Fringe Benefits for Employees

Many fringe benefits are not taxable and may be excluded from an employee's income. For example, the value of accident or health plan coverage provided by an employer is not included in an employee's income. The following sections cover the rules for some common types of nontaxable employee fringe benefits.

Retirement Plans

Employer contributions on behalf of their employees' qualified retirement plans are not taxable to the employees when they are made. However, when an employee receives distributions from a retirement plan, the amounts received are taxable income.

Retirement plans may also allow employees to contribute part of their pre-tax compensation to the plan. This type of contribution is called an elective deferral and is excluded from taxable compensation for income tax purposes but is subject to Social Security and Medicare taxes.[63]

Cafeteria Plans

A cafeteria plan allows employees to receive certain benefits before taxes are taken out. Employees must be given the option to choose at least one taxable benefit (like cash) and one qualified benefit (nontaxable). Some examples of qualified benefits that can be offered in a cafeteria plan include accident, dental, vision, and medical insurance (excluding Archer medical savings accounts and long-term care insurance), flexible spending accounts[64] for health and dependent care, as well as adoption assistance and dependent care assistance.

Employee contributions are typically deducted through salary reduction agreements, meaning the money is taken directly from their paychecks and deposited into an account. These contributions do not count as taxable income and are not subject to employment taxes. Employers may also extend these benefits to employees' spouses and dependents.

Flexible Spending Arrangements (FSAs)

An FSA is a form of cafeteria plan benefit that reimburses employees for expenses incurred for certain qualified benefits, such as health care and daycare expenses. The two most common types of FSA accounts are: Healthcare FSAs (HCFSA), Dependent Care FSAs (DCFSA). In 2023, employee salary reduction contributions to a Healthcare FSA are capped at $3,050. Both employer and employee may contribute to an employee's Healthcare FSA, but contributions from all sources combined must not

---

[63] The tax provisions of retirement plans are covered in detail later.
[64] An FSA is *not the same* thing as an HSA. A health savings account is always paired with a high deductible health plan, and it is an account that a taxpayer may establish and fund on his own. An FSA, on the other hand, is always offered by an employer as part of a cafeteria plan.

exceed the annual maximum. FSA benefits are subject to annual maximums and are typically subject to an annual "use-it-or-lose-it" rule, with a short (two-and-a-half-months) grace period after year-end to claim subsequent year qualifying expenses against the prior plan year remaining balance.

Typically, Healthcare FSA funds that are not spent by the employee within the plan year are forfeited back to the employer. Cafeteria plans may offer employees a two-and-a-half-month grace period after the end of the year to spend down any remaining FSA funds. Employee plans can also offer a carryover option, with the maximum amount that can be carried forward into the following year (if allowed by the employer) being 20% of the maximum available salary reduction for the year (so the maximum amount of contributions from the 2023 year that can be carried forward into 2024 is $610 ($3,050 × 20%).[65]

Separate from the Health Care FSA is the Dependent Care FSA (also known as a Dependent Care Assistance Plan), which is used to pay for dependent care. For unmarried taxpayers and married couples filing jointly, the annual limit is $5,000. For married couples filing separately, the limit is $2,500. The funds in a DCFSA can be used to pay for eligible daycare services, before or after school programs, and adult daycare for disabled dependents.

> **Example:** Ariana works for TechMedia, Inc. She has two small children, age 4 and 6, that are in daycare. TechMedia sponsors an FSA plan for its employees. Ariana opts-out of the health care FSA, but she elects to fund her DCFSA $5,000 for the 2023 plan year. Ariana spends $6,900 in daycare during the year. She may request a reimbursement of $5,000, the annual maximum. TechMedia, Inc. will properly reset the DCFSA limit to $5,000 for the next year.

> **Example:** Jace is 45, unmarried and does not have any children, but he does have a dependent parent. He works full-time and cares for his elderly mother, Ursula, who is 79 years old and has mild dementia. While Jace is at work, Ursula needs a caretaker to watch over her. Jace hires a caretaker through a caregiver support service. He pays $13,000 in 2023 for adult daycare so he can work. Jace's employer offers a DCFSA, and Jace contributes the maximum of $5,000 in 2023. Jace may request a reimbursement of $5,000, the maximum for 2023. These amounts are pre-tax, thus reducing the amount of Jace's income that is subject to taxes.

DCFSA accounts may only reimburse up to the amount the account is funded. For example, if an employee makes only $2,900 in pre-tax contributions to their dependent care FSA, and then later attempts to submit a claim for $3,000 in daycare expenses, the employee will only be reimbursed for $2,900.

> **Example:** Mila has a six-year-old son and participates in her employer's Dependent Care FSA. Each month, $400 is set aside from her paycheck and deposited into her FSA. At the end of each month, her daycare provider gives Mila a receipt, which she submits to her employer for reimbursement. Mila's employer then reimburses the funds directly from her FSA account. The money she contributes to her Dependent Care FSA is not subject to payroll tax or income tax, so she will end up paying less in taxes when she files her tax return.

---

[65] It is the employer's decision whether or not to offer a carryover <u>or</u> a grace period. Healthcare FSAs, specifically, have an additional option of allowing participants to carryover a portion of unused funds. Healthcare FSA plans can elect either the carryover <u>or</u> grace period option but not both. The specific deadline also depends on the employer's cafeteria plan year end, and how the employer decides to set up their plan.

Adoption Assistance in a Cafeteria Plan: Although uncommon, adoption assistance benefits may be offered under a cafeteria plan and paid for entirely with pre-tax salary reductions. An employee can exclude amounts paid or reimbursed by an employer under a qualified adoption assistance program (up to a maximum of $15,930 for 2023).

Highly Compensated Employees (HCEs) and Key Employees

A cafeteria plan cannot have rules that favor eligibility for highly compensated employees to participate, contribute, or benefit from a cafeteria plan. If a benefit plan favors HCEs, the value of their benefits may become taxable.

This is to discourage companies from offering excellent tax-free benefits to their top executives while ignoring the needs of lower-paid employees. Per Publication 15-B, a "highly compensated employee" is for 2023 is defined as:

- A company officer (i.e., company president, vice-president, treasurer).
- A 5% (or greater) shareholder in the current or prior year;
- An employee paid $150,000 or more for 2023,
- A spouse or close family member of one of the persons described above, regardless of salary level.

The IRS uses a process called "family attribution" in order to make the determination of who qualifies as an HCE, which means that an employee can be determined to be an HCE merely by familial relationship. An individual is attributed to interests owned by their spouse, siblings, and ancestors. For example, family attribution rules will treat the child of an owner as having the same ownership percentage.

> **Example:** Jasper is the 100% employee-shareholder of Silica Corporation. Jasper's wife and son both work for Silica corporation, but they are not stockholders. However, because family attribution rules apply, Jasper's stock is attributed to both his wife and his child, meaning they are all considered 100% owners for HCE determination purposes.

Employees that are hired in the middle of the year will not receive HCE status until the start of the *following* year, when they are eligible to collect the entirety of their salary. For example, an employee hired on June 1, 2023 would not be classified as an HCE until January 1, 2024, (regardless of their salary level).[66]"Highly compensated employees" and "key employees" have similar-sounding names, but the rules for defining Key Employees are slightly different. Employer-provided benefits also cannot favor "key employees." Publication 15-B defines "key employees" as any of the following:

- A company officer having annual pay of more than $215,000 in 2023 (in this case, the officer does not have to be an owner of the company).
- An employee who is either of the following:
  - A 5% owner of the business, or;
  - A 1% owner of the business whose annual pay is more than $150,000 in 2023.

---

[66] Corporate executives often receive extraordinary fringe benefits that are not provided to other employees. Any property or service that an executive receives in lieu of or in addition to regular taxable wages is a fringe benefit that may be subject to taxation. This is such an important issue to the IRS that they have developed an Audit Technique Guide about the subject (Executive Compensation-Fringe Benefits Audit Techniques Guide).

Although the compensation threshold is lower for HCEs than Key Employees, an employee can be classified as a key employee without having any ownership in the company.

> **Example:** Brody is a vice-president of Grainger Plastics, Inc., a manufacturing firm. Brody is not an owner of the company, and he is not related to any of the owners. His salary is $290,000 in 2023, and was $225,000 in the previous year. Brody is classified as a key employee, even though he does not have an ownership stake in the company, by virtue of his high salary and his position as a company officer.

A plan is considered to have improperly "favored" HCEs and key employees if more than 25% of all the benefits are given to those employees. If a cafeteria plan or a retirement plan fails to pass IRS non-discrimination testing, highly compensated employees and key employees may lose the tax benefits of participating in the plan. If this happens, then the plans can lose their tax-favored status, and the HCEs or key employees must include the value of these benefits as taxable compensation. These types of "corrections" often take the form of taxable distributions to plan participants.

> **Example:** Dixie Motorsports, Inc. is a small corporation with fifty-five employees. The sole shareholder of the company, Randall, sets up a cafeteria plan as well as a 401(k) retirement plan. However, he only allows his wife and his two sons to participate in the plans. The rest of the employees are not offered any type of benefits, and in fact, are never told about the plans. Later, Dixie Motorsports goes through a retirement plan audit, and the company fails discrimination testing. Randall is forced to recognize the value of his pretax benefits as taxable income. Randall's spouse and his two sons are also considered HCEs because they are Randall's family members, so they are also forced to recognize their benefits as taxable income, as well. They will be required to amend the business' tax returns as well as their individual returns to include the additional compensation.

> **Example:** McGovern Energy, Inc. is a C corporation with 300 employees, twenty-five of whom are considered highly compensated employees. McGovern Energy's cafeteria plan and its benefits are available to all full-time employees, and the benefits offered are the same for everyone, regardless of the employee's level of pay. Everyone is treated equally under the plan. Therefore, the discrimination rules do not apply, and the employees' benefits are not taxable, and fully deductible by the employer as a business expense.

Other Types of Employee Fringe Benefits

Educational Assistance: An employer can offer employees educational assistance for the cost of tuition, fees, books, supplies, and equipment. The payments may be for either undergraduate or graduate-level courses, and do not have to be work-related.

In 2023, up to $5,250 in educational assistance may be excluded per year per employee. If an employer pays more than $5,250, the excess is generally taxed as wages to the employee.[67] An employer may contribute up to $5,250 annually toward educational expenses, student loans, or a combination of both.[68] The cost of courses involving sports, games, or hobbies is not covered unless

---

[67] There is an exception for job-related education. If the education is directly job related, amounts in excess of the $5,250 limit may qualify for exclusion as a working condition fringe benefit. For instance, an accounting firm can cover the cost of courses for a staff accountant preparing business tax returns without taxing the employee, regardless of the amount.
[68] The *Consolidated Appropriations Act of 2021* extended this provision through tax year 2025.

they are related to the business or are required as part of a degree program. The cost of lodging, meals, and transportation is also not included.

Tuition Reduction Benefits: A college or other educational institution can exclude the value of a qualified undergraduate tuition reduction to an employee, his spouse, or a dependent child. A tuition reduction is "qualified" only if the taxpayer receives it from, and uses it at, an eligible educational institution. Graduate education only qualifies if it is for the education of a graduate student who performs teaching or research activities for the educational organization.

Example: Mayra is a graduate teaching assistant at Louisiana State University. As part of her employment agreement with the college, Mayra is offered a 50% tuition waiver, reducing the cost of her own graduate tuition at the school. The normal graduate tuition cost is $14,800 per year. Because of the tuition waiver, Mayra only pays $7,400. The tuition reduction is not taxable to Mayra, but any wages that she receives as compensation for student teaching would be taxable.

Employer-Provided Meals and Lodging: An employer may exclude the value of meals and lodging provided to employees if they are provided:

- On the employer's business premises, and
- For the employer's convenience.

For lodging, there is an additional rule: it must be required as a condition of employment. Lodging can be provided for the taxpayer, the taxpayer's spouse, and the taxpayer's dependents and still not be taxable to the employee. However, the exclusion from taxation does not apply if the employee can choose to receive additional pay instead of lodging.

Example: Sullivan is a project supervisor for Birchwood Construction. He is provided free lodging at remote job sites in an RV, where he is required to stay on-site for several months while the timber is cleared and the grounds are prepared for various construction projects. Sullivan's presence at the job site helps deter theft and vandalism. The value of the lodging and his meals are excluded from Sullivan's income, because it is primarily for the employer's security and convenience.

Meals may be provided to employees for the convenience of the employer on the employer's business premises for several reasons, such as when:

- Police officers and firefighters need to be on call for emergencies during the meal period.
- The nature of the business requires short meal periods.
- Eating facilities are not available in areas near the workplace, such as in the case of remote or dangerous locations.
- Meals are furnished immediately after working hours because the employee's duties prevented him from obtaining a meal during working hours.

Meals furnished to restaurant employees before, during, or after work hours are also considered furnished for the employer's convenience and are not taxable to the employee.

Example: Paramedic Transport, Inc. regularly provides meals to employees during working hours so that paramedics are available for emergency calls during the meal. The employees are not permitted to take regular lunches or eat off-site because of the nature of their employment. The value of the free meals is therefore excludable from the employees' wages, and the employer is allowed to deduct the cost of the meals as a business expense, subject to the 50% limit.

Transportation Fringe Benefits

Employers have the option to provide transportation benefits to their employees, such as transit passes, paid parking, or commuter passes (bus passes). These benefits are non-taxable for employees up to a certain amount.

However, under the Tax Cuts and Jobs Act (TCJA), employers can no longer deduct these expenses. This does not affect the tax-exempt status of transportation benefits for employees (with the notable exception of bicycle commuting benefits, which became taxable to the employee under the TCJA). Any expenses exceeding $300 per month in 2023 for transit and parking benefits will be added to the employee's taxable income as wages. It is possible for an employee to receive both parking and transit benefits in the same month.

The use of a company car for commuting purposes or other personal use is generally a taxable benefit. Thus, the value of using the vehicle for these reasons will be included in their taxable wages.

Example: Sienna was offered a lucrative new job in New York City as a computer programmer. As part of her employment contract, she negotiates a reserved parking space for her car. Her new employer agrees to pay the cost of the space at the garage across the street from her work. Monthly parking is quite expensive in New York City, and the monthly parking fee at the garage is $500. Since this amount exceeds the allowable limit for parking fringe benefits, a portion of the parking costs will be taxable to Sienna as wages. In 2023, the allowable transportation benefit for parking is $300. Therefore, an additional $200 ($500-$300 limit) would be taxable to Sienna each month as wages and must be added to her Form W-2.

Example: Bowie is employed by Eagle Hardwood, a lumber company. He drives an employer-provided pickup truck, hauling equipment on job sites and delivering lumber to customers. He also gets to take the truck home in the evenings. In 2023, Bowie drives the truck 20,000 miles, of which 4,000, or 20%, are personal miles (4,000/20,000 = 20%). The truck has an annual lease value of $4,100. Personal use is therefore valued at $820 and is included in Bowie's taxable wages, subject to all payroll taxes.

There is an exception in IRS regulations that exempts the personal use of certain types of vehicles. Qualified "nonpersonal use" vehicles, such as police or fire vehicles, school buses, and ambulances, are exempt from fringe benefit reporting, even if the vehicles are used for commuting purposes, as long as the employer requires their use for the employees to do their jobs.

Example: Martina works as a school bus driver for Garden City Elementary School. She drives a school bus, and her primary job is to transport students to and from the school during the week. She also occasionally drives longer distances for field trips. Since she is responsible for the bus and cannot leave it unattended, Martina uses the bus to drive to a local sandwich shop to buy lunch on her break. This small amount of personal use is not taxable to Martina, because a school bus is a qualified nonpersonal use vehicle, and an employee's use of a qualified nonpersonal-use vehicle is considered a nontaxable working condition benefit.

Cell Phones: Employer-provided cell phones can be excluded from an employee's income. The employer must have valid business-related reasons for providing the phone, such as the need to contact the employee during work emergencies or to communicate with clients while away from the office. However, if the phone is given solely for the purpose of creating goodwill, boosting employee morale, or attracting potential employees, its value must be added to the employee's wages.

Group-Term Life Insurance Coverage: Up to $50,000 of life insurance coverage may be provided as a nontaxable benefit to an employee. The cost of insurance coverage on policies that exceed $50,000 is a taxable benefit. If an employer provides more than $50,000 of coverage, the amount included in the taxpayer's income is reported as part of their taxable wages on their Form W-2. The taxable amount is shown separately with a "code C" in box 12 of their Form W-2.

Work-Related Moving Expense Reimbursements: Moving expenses are no longer deductible for most taxpayers, except for certain members of the armed forces. Therefore, moving expenses that are reimbursed or paid by an employer must be included in the employee's taxable income as wages.

Example: Margaret was offered a new job in another state on November 5, 2023. Her new employer offered to reimburse her moving expenses as a condition of her employment. She accepted the position and moved on December 17, 2023. Margaret submits the paperwork, and her employer reimburses all her moving expenses on December 30, 2023. Even though she submitted receipts for reimbursement, all of the amounts would be taxable to Margaret as wages. The employer may deduct the amounts as employee compensation, and all the normal payroll taxes that are applicable to regular wages would apply.

No-Additional-Cost Services: Nontaxable fringe benefits also include services provided to employees that do not impose any substantial additional cost to the employer because the employer already offers those services in the ordinary course of doing business. Employees do not need to include these no-additional-cost services in their income. Typically, no-additional-cost services are excess capacity services, such as unused airline seat tickets for airline employees or open hotel rooms for hotel employees.

Example: Momentum Airlines is an airline company that offers both domestic and international flights. Donahue is a pilot for this airline. When Donahue is not on duty, the airline allows him to fly as a passenger on their flights free of charge, as long as there are seats available. This is an example of an excess capacity service. In this case, the airline is already offering flights as part of its business, and Donahue occupying an otherwise empty seat does not incur any significant extra cost. Therefore, it qualifies as a no-additional-cost service and is a nontaxable fringe benefit for Donahue.

If an employee is provided with free or low-cost use of a health club <u>on the employer's premises</u>, the value is not included in the employee's compensation. The gym must be used primarily by employees, their spouses, and their dependent children. However, if the employer pays for a fitness program or use of a facility at an *off-site* location, the value of the program is included in the employee's compensation.

Example: Orion is employed at a software company located in downtown Los Angeles. His employer provides an optional subsidized gym membership at Iron Fitness Club, a local gym, as part of a fitness reimbursement program to promote employee health and wellbeing. Orion happily takes advantage of this benefit. However, the monthly fee for the off-site gym membership ($25) is taxable as wages, and will be reported on Orion's Form W-2. An off-site gym membership is a taxable fringe benefit.

Employee Achievement Awards: Employers may generally exclude from an employee's taxable wages the value of awards given for length-of-service or safety achievement. The tax-free amount is limited to the following:

- $400 for awards that are not qualified plan awards.
- $1,600 for qualified plan awards. A qualified plan award is one that does not discriminate in favor of highly compensated employees, and that is established under a written plan.

> **Example:** Wallace has worked for Telegraph Corp. for ten years. Telegraph Corp. makes a qualifying length-of-service award to Wallace in the form of an engraved silver watch. The cost of the watch was $575. The watch was presented to Wallace during a meaningful presentation. All the company employees are eligible to receive length-of-service awards based on their tenure with the company. The watch is deductible to Telegraph Corp. as a business expense, and the value of the watch is not taxable to Wallace.

The exclusion for employee awards does not apply to awards of cash, gift cards, lodging, stocks, bonds, or tickets to sporting events.

De Minimis (Minimal) Benefits: This is a property or service an employer provides that has so little value that accounting for it would be impractical. Examples of de minimis benefits include the following:

- Occasional personal use of a company copying machine.
- Holiday gifts with a low fair market value (such as a holiday turkey or a gift basket)
- Flowers, fruit, books or similar property provided to employees under special circumstances, such as an employee's birthday
- Beverages and snacks, such as coffee or doughnuts for employees
- Cash is not excludable as de minimis benefits unless they are for occasional meal money or transportation fare, and they <u>are not</u> given out on the basis of hours worked (for example, $1.50 per hour for each hour over 8 hours). In order to be non-taxable, the benefit must also be provided so that an employee can work an unusual, extended schedule.

> **Example:** Wayne works for Dogwood Dairy Farms as a farmhand. One day, there was an emergency on the farm where several dairy cows accidentally ingested tainted feed. The cows began to have seizures, and all the employees were forced to work overtime to stabilize the livestock and administer medicine. Dogwood Dairy Farms gives Wayne $20 in cash to purchase a meal during this unusual overtime shift. The cash can be excluded as a *de minimis* benefit because Wayne is working overtime for the benefit of his employer, and it is an unusual and infrequent situation.

> **Example:** Bennett owns Greenhaven Farms. He has 10 employees. One day, severe storms struck the area, and all of the company's crops were at risk. Bennett asks all his employees to work overtime in order to bring in crops and secure the farm buildings and fencing. During this emergency situation, Bennett gives his employees $25 in cash to purchase their lunch and dinner at a nearby deli. The amounts would be excluded from the employees' wages as a *de minimis* benefit, because the storm is an unusual and infrequent occurrence.

Employee Discounts: Employers may exclude the value of employee discounts from wages up to the following limits:

- For services, a 20% discount of the price charged to nonemployee customers.
- For merchandise, the company's gross profit percentage multiplied by the price nonemployee customers pay.

Accountable Plan Reimbursement of Employee-Business Expenses

When a company reimburses its workers for specific business-related costs, such as work travel and meals, the reimbursements are not considered taxable income if the employees meet all of the following requirements under an accountable plan:

- Have incurred the expenses while performing their duties as employees.
- Provide proper documentation for travel, meals, and lodging expenses.
- Supply evidence of their employee business expenditures, such as receipts or records.
- Return any surplus reimbursements within a reasonable timeframe.

The decision to create an accountable plan is ultimately up to the employer, not the employee. An employer is not obligated to establish an accountable plan for reimbursing employee business expenses. Furthermore, they have the freedom to choose which expenses will be covered under this plan.

Under an accountable plan, a company may give cash advances to employees. These advances must reasonably align with anticipated expenses and must be given within a reasonable timeframe. If any expenses reimbursed through this arrangement cannot be substantiated, they will be considered taxable income for the employee.

Qualifying expenses for travel are excludable from an employee's income if they are incurred for temporary travel on business away from the area of the employee's tax home. Travel expenses paid in connection with an indefinite work assignment cannot be excluded from income. Any work assignment more than one year is considered "indefinite." Reimbursement for travel expenses may cover: expenses incurred while traveling to and from the designated business location (such as airfare and mileage reimbursements), transportation costs during the trip (such as taxi fares), hotels, meals, and other related costs, and dry cleaning, laundry, and any other miscellaneous expenses during the period spent away from home on assignment.

Example: Cohen works full-time for a software company in Seattle. He flies to San Francisco for a business conference that lasts an entire week. His employer reimburses the cost of the $400 round trip flight to San Francisco as well as lodging and meals while he is attending the conference. The reimbursements for travel expenses are excluded from Cohen's income, and deductible by his employer as a business expense.

Example: Miriam runs a tax preparation business as a sole-proprietor. She advances $250 to her only employee, Nasser, so that he can become a registered notary. Nasser spends $90 on a live notary seminar, and then another $100 to take the notary exam. Nasser returns the unused funds ($60), as well as copies of his receipts to Miriam. The expenses are qualified expenses under an accountable plan, so the amounts paid are not taxable income for Nasser, and still deductible as business expenses by Miriam.

Taxation of Clergy Members

There are special rules regarding the taxation of clergy members, defined as individuals who are ordained, commissioned, or licensed by a religious body or church denomination. A clergy member's salary is reported on Form W-2 and is taxable. For services in the exercise of the ministry, members of the clergy receive a Form W-2 but do not have social security or Medicare taxes withheld. Offerings and fees received for performing marriages, baptisms, and funerals must be reported as self-employment income on Schedule C.

Housing Allowance for Clergy: A clergy member who receives a housing allowance may exclude the allowance from gross income to the extent it is used to pay the expenses of providing a home. Only taxpayers who are serving as clergy (ministers, priests, etc.) are eligible for a housing allowance.[69] The exclusion is limited to the *lesser* of the following amounts:

- The amount officially designated as a housing allowance.
- The amount actually used to provide or rent a home.
- The fair market rental value of the home (including utilities, property taxes, insurance, etc.)

The housing allowance cannot exceed reasonable pay and must be used for housing in the year it is received. Salary, other fees, and housing allowances must be included in income for purposes of determining self-employment tax.

Example: Garrison is an ordained pastor for the First Baptist Church. His church allows him to use a cottage that has a rental value of $8,000. He is paid an additional $22,000, and his church does not withhold Social Security or Medicare taxes. Garrison's income for *income tax purposes* is $22,000, but for self-employment tax purposes is $30,000 ($22,000 + $8,000 housing). Any amount of housing allowance excluded from gross income is still subject to Social Security and Medicare tax.

Example: Emanuel is an ordained minister who receives $32,000 in salary from his church. He receives an additional $4,000 for performing private marriage ceremonies. His housing allowance is $500 per month, for a total of $6,000 per year, and is excluded from his gross income. Emanuel must report the $32,000 as salary and $4,000 as self-employment income. The $6,000 housing allowance is subject to self-employment tax, but not income tax.

A clergy member may apply for an exemption from self-employment tax if he is conscientiously opposed to public insurance because of religious principles. For a clergy member or a minister to claim an exemption from SE tax, the minister must file IRS Form 4029, *Application for Exemption from Social Security and Medicare Taxes and Waiver of Benefits.* Generally, this exemption is irrevocable.

The sect or religious order must also complete part of the form. The exemption does not apply to federal income tax, only to self-employment tax. If the exemption is granted, the clergy member will not pay Social Security or Medicare taxes on his earnings, and he will not receive credit toward those benefits in retirement. If a clergy member is a member of a religious order that has taken a vow of poverty, he is exempt from paying SE tax on his earnings for qualified services. The earnings are tax-

---

[69] A minister's housing allowance is exempt from income tax under IRC §107, but it is still subject to self-employment tax. If a congregation provides housing in-kind instead of a housing allowance, the fair market rental value of the housing is also included in net earnings from self-employment.

free because they are considered the income of the religious order, rather than of the individual clergy member.[70]

Combat Pay and Veterans Benefits

Typically, military personnel's regular wages are subject to taxes. However, there are specific exceptions and rules for military personnel regarding income that is taxable. For instance, combat zone wages or "combat pay" is not considered taxable income. Hazardous duty pay is also excludable for military personnel. Enlisted personnel who serve in a combat zone for any part of a month may exclude their pay from tax. For officers, the pay is excluded up to a certain amount, depending on the branch of service.

Example: Ashton is an Air Force pilot who served in a combat zone from January 1, 2023, to November 3, 2023. He is only required to report his income for December, because all of the other income is excluded from taxation as combat-zone pay. Even though Ashton only served three days in November in a combat zone, his income for the entire month of November is excluded.

Similarly, veterans' benefits paid by the Department of Veterans Affairs to a veteran or his family are not taxable if they are for education (the GI Bill), training, disability compensation, work therapy, dependent care assistance, or other benefits or pension payments given to the veteran because of disability.

Example: Colton is a Navy Veteran who has recently enrolled in his local junior college's Automotive Technology Program. Colton can receive up to $3,500 annually as a GI education benefit. Colton's tuition is $4,000. His $3,500 GI benefit payment is made directly to his college, directly reducing his college tuition. The GI benefit is not taxable to Colton.

Medicare Waiver Payments

"Difficulty-of-care" payments, also known as Medicare waiver payments, can be excluded from a taxpayer's gross income.[71] These payments are nontaxable to the caregiver if they are for in-home-care services provided to a disabled individual who resides in the same home. The exemption applies to anyone providing care in their own home, regardless of who owns the home. It is also not necessary for the caregiver to be related to the disabled individual, although this is often the case. Qualified Medicare waiver payments may be excluded from income *only* when the care provider and the care recipient reside in the **same home.** When the care provider and the care recipient do *not* live together in the same home, the Medicare waiver payments may not be excluded from gross income.

Example: Brooke moved into her elderly mother's home to care for her. Brooke begins to receive $575 monthly payments under a state Medicare Home and Community-Based Services waiver program for supportive home care. The payments are not taxable to Brooke, because she is living in the home with her mother while providing the care. This is true even if she receives a Form W-2 or a Form 1099 for the income.

---

[70] Poverty vows only exempt priests and ministers from federal income tax if they give their earnings from third parties to the church. Payments received directly from the church are not exempt.

[71] According to IRS Notice 2014-7, payments through state Medicaid and Medicare Personal Care programs for in-home supportive care are considered "difficulty of care payments" and can be excluded from a provider's gross income. Full FAQs here: https://www.irs.gov/individuals/certain-medicaid-waiver-payments-may-be-excludable-from-income.

> **Example:** Timothy cares for his elderly uncle five days a week. Timothy eats all his meals at his uncle's home and sleeps there occasionally. Most evenings and weekends, Timothy leaves his uncle's home at 6PM and goes home to his wife and family in their separate home. Timothy receives monthly Medicare waiver payments for his uncle's care. Since Timothy has a separate home, the Medicare waiver payments are taxable to Timothy.

Taxpayers who receive these payments may choose to include them in their income for purposes of the earned income credit (EITC) or the additional child tax credit (ACTC).[72] In addition, under the SECURE Act, taxpayers can use this income to fund an IRA, but since the contributions come from amounts excluded from tax, they are treated as nondeductible contributions.

Disability Payments

There are several types of disability payments, and the taxability of the income depends on several factors. Some types of disability-related payments are given to workers that are not taxable at all. Worker's compensation is one such example. Worker's compensation should *not* be confused with disability insurance, sick pay, or unemployment compensation; it is a type of benefit that only pays workers who are injured on the job.[73]

Worker's compensation is a type of mandatory business insurance, meaning most large and mid-sized employers are required to have coverage for their employees. Worker's compensation coverage can include wage replacement as well as rehabilitation services that help injured employees return to work when they are medically able to do so. Worker's compensation is always exempt from tax.

> **Example:** Kieran is a construction worker. During the year, he is struck by falling concrete on a construction site. The concrete crushes his pelvis, causing catastrophic injuries and a long hospital stay. His employer's worker's compensation policy covers Kieran's medical costs as well as a portion of his lost wages while he is recovering from his injury. The amounts are not taxable to Kieran and do not need to be reported on his tax return.

Disability Retirement Benefits

Disability *retirement* benefits are unique. These benefits are taxable as **wages** if a taxpayer retired on disability *before* reaching the minimum retirement age. The benefit is usually based on the employee's final average earnings and their years of actual service. Once the taxpayer reaches retirement age (usually, this is age 62), the payments are no longer taxable as wages, they are taxable as pension income.

This type of disability retirement benefit is offered to most Federal government workers and U.S. Postal Service employees and is often called "FERS disability" because the disability retirement benefits are offered under the Federal Employees Retirement System (FERS).[74] To apply for this benefit, the employee's disability generally must have caused them to discontinue working.

---

[72] A reference can be found at: https://www.irs.gov/pub/irs-utl/vta-2020-03.pdf.

[73] Under worker's compensation law, an injury or illness is covered, without regard to fault, if it was sustained in the course and scope of employment, this would also include injuries sustained during work-related travel, but would not cover injuries incurred by an employee's willful criminal acts or self-injury, or intoxication from drugs or alcohol.

[74] Social Security Disability Insurance (SSDI) benefits is a separate benefit from disability retirement benefits that are offered to federal and postal service employees. Supplemental Security Income (SSI) is also different from SSDI. SSI is a non-taxable needs-based federal benefit.

Example: Sloane is a U.S. Postal Service employee. She is 50 years old and has worked for the postal service for over sixteen years, but she is still many years away from official retirement age. On January 29, 2023, Sloane sustains a life-altering spinal injury and becomes permanently disabled. She immediately applies for disability retirement under the Federal Employees Retirement System, or FERS, and is awarded disability retirement benefits. Her disability retirement benefits will be taxable as wages until she reaches retirement age (usually 62 years of age). After she reaches retirement age, the benefits will be taxable as pension income instead of wages.

Disability Insurance Benefits

A taxpayer may receive long-term disability insurance payments because of an insurance policy. Generally, long-term disability payments from an insurance policy are excluded from income if the *taxpayer* pays the premiums for the policy. If an *employer* pays the insurance premiums, the employee must report the payments as taxable income.

Disability Insurance Premiums	Taxability of Benefits
The employer pays 100%	100% taxable
The employer pays a portion, and the employee pays the balance with post-tax dollars	Partially taxable; the taxable percentage is based on the premiums paid by the employer
The employer pays a portion, and the employee pays the balance with pretax dollars	100% taxable
The employee pays 100% with post-tax dollars	Not taxable
The employee pays 100% with pre-tax dollars	100% taxable

If both an employee and the employer have paid premiums for a disability policy, only the employer's portion of the disability payments would be reported as taxable income.

Example: Robyn became disabled in 2023 and began to receive a long-term disability benefit of $4,200 a month. The original insurance policy was paid for by both her employer and herself. Before Robyn became disabled, her employer paid 80% of the disability insurance premiums. Robyn paid the remaining premium amount (20%) with post-tax dollars. In this case, because the employer paid 80% of the policy premiums, 80% of the benefits received would be taxable to Robyn. This means that $3,360 ($4,200 × 80%) would be taxable. The remaining benefits of $840 (20% × $4,200) would not be taxable since Robyn paid that portion of the insurance premium with her own post-tax dollars.

Veterans Disability Benefits

Veterans' *disability* benefits (also called *VA Disability Compensation*) are a type of disability benefit paid specifically to a veteran for disabilities that are service-connected, which means the injury or disease is linked to their military service.

Veterans' disability benefits are exempt from taxation if the veteran was terminated through separation or discharged under honorable conditions. The VA typically does not issue Form W-2, Form 1099-R, or any other tax-related document for veterans' disability benefits.

Example: Phoebe is a Navy veteran who was medically discharged after she sustained a serious injury in Iraq. She lost vision in one eye and the use of one hand due to an explosion. Since Phoebe's discharge from the Armed Forces, she has received $1,950 per month in Veterans' disability benefits. She now has a civilian job working in a factory, where she earns regular wages as an employee. Her wages are taxable, but the disability compensation remains non-taxable to Phoebe. Her veterans' disability benefits do not need to be reported on her tax return.

Note: Do not confuse "sick pay" with disability pay or disability benefits. Sick pay, or sick leave, is always taxable as wages, just like vacation pay and holiday pay.

Life Insurance Payments

Life insurance payouts generally are not taxable to a beneficiary if the payment was the result of the death of the insured. This is true even if the proceeds were paid under an accident or health insurance policy. However, interest income received on life insurance proceeds is usually taxable. Further, if a taxpayer surrenders a life insurance policy for cash, they must generally include in income any proceeds that are more than the cost of the policy. However, an exception exists for when a terminally ill person receives a viatical settlement.[75] In this case, the funds are tax-free. Sometimes, a taxpayer will choose to receive life insurance proceeds in installments rather than as a lump sum. In this case, part of the installment generally includes interest income.

If a taxpayer receives life insurance proceeds in installments (also called a life insurance annuity), they can exclude part of each installment from his income. To determine the excluded part, the amount held by the insurance company (generally the total lump sum payable at the death of the insured person) is divided by the number of installments to be paid. The taxpayer would include any amount over this excluded portion as taxable interest income.

Example: Molly's brother died in 2023, and she is the sole beneficiary of his life insurance. The face amount of the policy is $75,000. Rather than take a lump sum payment, Molly chooses to receive 120 monthly installments of $1,000 each. The excluded part of each installment is $625 ($75,000 ÷ 120), or $7,500 for an entire year. The rest of each payment, $375 a month (or $4,500 for an entire year), is taxable as interest income to Molly.

---

[75] A "viatical settlement" when the policyholder is deemed to be terminally or chronically ill and executes a "deemed sale" of their life insurance policy. As long as the taxpayer has proof from a physician that they have a life expectancy of 24 months or less, the sale of their life insurance policy is treated as a viatical settlement and is tax-free.

Unit 4: Study Questions

(Test yourself first, then check the correct answers at the end of this quiz.)

1. Orval and Rainelle are married, and both are self-employed with their own businesses. Orval owns a business that has a $9,750 net profit during the year. His wife, Rainelle, has an overall business loss of ($11,100). They both file Schedules C to report their self-employment income. Which of the following statements is correct?

A. On their joint return, they will not have to pay self-employment tax, because the losses from Rainelle's business will offset Orval's income.
B. Orval must pay self-employment tax on $9,750, regardless of his wife's income or losses.
C. They can file MFS and offset each other's self-employment tax.
D. If they choose to file separate returns, they may split the profits and losses equally between their two businesses, and also split the self-employment tax.

2. Of the following items, only _____ is not taxable income to an employee:

A. A holiday bonus.
B. Overtime pay.
C. Vacation pay.
D. A mileage reimbursement under an accountable plan.

3. Which of the following fringe benefits provided by the employer will result in taxable income to the employee?

A. An off-site gym membership subsidized by the employer.
B. A cell phone used by an employee to talk to clients while outside the office.
C. Reimbursements paid by the employers for qualified business travel expenses.
D. Occasional personal use of an office copy machine.

4. Which of the following tip income, if any, is exempt from federal income tax?

A. Tips of less than $20 per month.
B. Noncash tips.
C. Tips not reported to the employer.
D. None of the above. All tips are taxable.

5. Which of the following fringe benefits is taxable (or partially taxable) to the employee?

A. Health insurance covered 100% by the employer.
B. An employer-provided company car that is used for personal commuting.
C. Group-term life insurance coverage of $50,000.
D. Employer contributions to an employee's 401(k) plan.

6. Which of the following types of fringe benefits are normally deductible by an employer, but not taxable to the employee?

A. De minimis fringe benefit.
B. Use of an employer's apartment, vacation home, or boat for personal purposes
C. Membership in a country club or athletic facility.
D. A gift card.

7. Flavian owns a restaurant. He provides his daytime waitress, Alida, two free meals during each workday. Flavian encourages (but does not require) Alida to have her breakfast on the business premises before starting work so she can help him answer phones. She is required to have her lunch on the premises. How should Flavian treat this fringe benefit to Alida?

A. None of Alida's meals at the restaurant are taxable.
B. All of Alida's meals at the restaurant are taxable.
C. Alida's lunch is not taxable, but her breakfast is.
D. Alida's meals are taxed at a flat rate of 15%.

8. What is "adjusted gross income"?

A. The sum of all sources of taxable income that the taxpayer receives during the year, minus any allowable credits.
B. The amount of earned income a taxpayer receives during the year.
C. Another term for taxable income.
D. Gross income minus certain allowable adjustments, calculated before the standard deduction or itemized deductions are taken.

9. Self-employment income does not include:

A. The income of ministers for the performance of services such as baptisms and marriages.
B. Ordinary partnership income allocated to general partners on Schedule K-1.
C. Wages earned by a temporary employee.
D. Payments received by independent contractors.

10. Bartholomew is a naval officer who was injured while serving in a combat zone. He was later awarded Veterans Affairs (VA) disability benefits. How are these payments reported on Bartholomew's tax return?

A. 100% of the disability benefits may be excluded from income.
B. 50% of the disability benefits may be excluded from income.
C. Disability benefits may be excluded from income tax, but they are subject to self-employment tax.
D. The disability benefits are all taxable as pension income.

11. Orrin is an ordained minister in the Evangelical Church of Savannah. He owns his home, and his monthly house payment is $900. His monthly utilities total $150. The fair rental value in his neighborhood is $1,000. Orrin receives a housing allowance from his church in the amount of $950 per month. What portion of his monthly housing allowance would he include in his gross income for income tax purposes?

A. $0
B. $100
C. $150
D. $950

12. Salvador is an enlisted soldier in the U.S. Army who served in a combat zone from January 30, 2023, to September 2, 2023. He returned to the United States and received his regular duty pay for the remainder of the year. How many months of his income are taxable in 2023?

A. Zero. All the income is tax-free.
B. Three months of wages are subject to tax.
C. Four months of wages are subject to tax.
D. Twelve months of wages are subject to tax.

13. Anastasia is a sales rep who sells pharmaceutical drugs to doctor's offices on commission (she is an employee). On December 25, 2023, Anastasia receives $12,000 of income from commissions, plus an advance of $1,000 for future commissions. She also receives a $200 check for expense reimbursements from her employer after turning in her receipts as part of an accountable plan. How much taxable income should Anastasia report on her 2023 tax return?

A. $11,800
B. $12,000
C. $13,000
D. $13,200

14. Paxton worked as a flight attendant in 2023 and earned a salary of $61,000. His employer provided him with complimentary standby flights from his home in Little Rock to their hub in Charlotte, NC, which were valued at $5,000. Paxton also received advances for overnight travel expenses totaling $9,000 under an accountable plan, but only spent $6,000. He returned the unspent amount of $3,000 to his employer. Unfortunately, Paxton was injured on the job when he tripped over a bag and sprained his ankle. He received worker's compensation of $4,100 because of his injury. For tax purposes, Paxton must report what amount as part of his gross income on his personal tax return?

A. $61,000
B. $64,000
C. $65,100
D. $71,000

15. Rasheed is employed as a staff accountant by a large CPA firm. When he travels for his audit work, he submits his travel receipts for reimbursement by his firm, which has an accountable plan for its employees. Which of the following statements is correct about accountable plans?

A. The reimbursed amounts are not taxable to Rasheed.
B. Rasheed may deduct his travel expenses on his personal tax return.
C. His employer cannot deduct the travel expenses as a business expense, even though Rasheed was reimbursed in full.
D. Reimbursed expenses are taxable to the employee.

16. Debby broke her leg in a car accident and was unable to work for three months. She received an accident settlement of $13,000 from her insurance company. During this time, she also received $7,500 of sick pay from her employer. In addition, she received $5,000 from an accident disability policy she had purchased herself. How much of this income is taxable to Debby?

A. $5,000
B. $7,500
C. $12,500
D. $18,000

17. Income was constructively received in 2023 in each of the following situations *except*:

A. Wages were deposited in the taxpayer's bank account on December 26, 2023, but were not withdrawn by the taxpayer until January 8, 2024.
B. A taxpayer was informed his check for services was available on December 15, 2023. The taxpayer did not pick up the check until January 30, 2024.
C. A taxpayer received a check on December 31, 2023, but did not deposit it until January 5, 2024.
D. A taxpayer's vacation property was sold on December 28, 2023. The payment was not received by the taxpayer until January 4, 2024, when the escrow company released the funds.

18. Alphonse was the sole beneficiary of his mother's life insurance policy. His mother died on June 1, 2023. Alphonse received the following payments on December 31, 2023:

- $360,000 lump-sum death benefit from his mother's life insurance policy.
- $1,775 of interest income on the life insurance proceeds.

What is the proper treatment of these payments?

A. The $360,000 in life insurance proceeds are taxable in 2023. The interest is not taxable.
B. The life insurance proceeds and interest income are both taxable to Alphonse.
C. Only the $1,775 of interest income is taxable in 2023. The life insurance proceeds are not taxable.
D. None of these payments are taxable to Alphonse. Instead, they are taxable to his mother's estate.

19. Chandra received the following income and fringe benefits in 2023:

Form W-2 wages	$30,000
End-of-the-year bonus	$2,000
Parking pass (per month)	$90
Employer contributions to her 401(k) plan	$900
Occasional free use of a copier on the employer's premises	$15

How much income must Chandra report on her tax return?

A. $30,000
B. $32,000
C. $32,500
D. $34,480

Unit 4: Quiz Answers

1. The answer is B. Orval must pay self-employment tax on the net profits from his business, regardless of how he and Rainelle choose to file. Taxpayers cannot combine both spouses' income or loss to determine their earnings subject to SE tax. However, if a taxpayer has more than one business, he must combine the net profit or loss from each to determine the total earnings subject to SE tax.

2. The answer is D. Mileage reimbursements, if paid through an accountable plan, are not included in an employee's wages.

3. The answer is A. An off-site gym membership is not a qualified fringe benefit, so it would result in taxable income to the employee. The cell phone, reimbursements for business travel, and the occasional personal use of an office copy machine are noncash fringe benefits that are not taxable.

4. The answer is D. All tip income is subject to federal income tax, whether cash or noncash. An individual who receives less than $20 per month of tips while working one job does not have to report the tip income to their employer, but the income is still subject to income tax and must be reported on Form 1040.

5. The answer is B. An employer-provided company car would be partially taxable if it was used for personal driving. The value of the personal use of the automobile must be added to the employee's wages. These valuation rules are covered in IRS Publication 15-B, *Employer's Tax Guide to Fringe Benefits.*

6. The answer is A. A *de minimis* fringe benefit is deductible by the employer but is not taxable to the employee. The IRS defines a de minimis benefit in this way: a benefit that, considering its value and the frequency with which it is provided, is so small as to make accounting for it unreasonable or impractical. For example, a de minimis fringe benefit might include occasional snacks, coffee, or doughnuts provided in a company's break room. The items in the other choices would be taxable to the employee.

7. The answer is A. Meals furnished to Alida are not taxable because they are for the convenience of the employer. Meals that employers furnish to a restaurant employee during, immediately before, or after the employee's working hours are considered furnished for the employer's convenience. Since Alida is a waitress who works during the normal breakfast and lunch periods, Flavian can exclude from her wages the value of those meals. If Flavian allowed Alida to have meals without charge on her days off, the value of those meals would be included in her wages.

8. The answer is D. Adjusted gross income (AGI) is gross income (the sum of all income subject to taxation that the taxpayer receives during the year) minus certain allowable deductions or adjustments. AGI is calculated before the standard deduction or itemized deductions are taken.

9. The answer is C. Wage income is never considered self-employment income. The other examples listed are all types of self-employment income and subject to self-employment tax on Form 1040.

10. The answer is A. All the disability benefits can be excluded from Bartholomew's taxable income. VA disability compensation is exempt from taxation if the veteran was terminated through separation or discharged under honorable conditions. The VA does not issue Form W-2, Form 1099-R, or any other tax-related document for veterans' disability benefits.

11. The answer is A. Clergy members may exclude from gross income for *income tax* purposes, but not for *self-employment tax* purposes, the rental value of a home, or a rental allowance to the extent the allowance is used to provide a home, even if deductions are taken for home expenses paid with the allowance.

12. The answer is B. Only October through December (three months) would be taxable to Salvador. If a taxpayer serves in a combat zone as an enlisted person for *any part* of a month, all his pay received for military service that month is excluded from gross income. Since Salvador served for a few days in September, as well as January, all the income for those months is excluded as combat pay.

13. The answer is C. Anastasia's commissions must be included in gross income, as well as advance payments in anticipation of future services ($12,000 + $1,000 = $13,000). The expense reimbursements from an accountable plan ($200) would not be included in her taxable income.

14. The answer is A. Paxton only has to include his wages on his tax return ($61,000). The free flights offered on standby to airline personnel are considered no-additional-cost services and are not taxable to the employee. Reimbursements under an accountable plan and amounts paid for worker's compensation because of his injury are nontaxable. Since Paxton returned the unspent amounts to his employer, the travel reimbursements qualify under an accountable plan, and the amounts spent are not taxable to him.

15. The answer is A. The reimbursed amounts are not taxable to Rasheed. Under an accountable plan, employee reimbursements are not included in the employee's income. In this scenario, the travel expenses incurred by the employee would be deductible by Rasheed's employer as an ordinary business expense.

16. The answer is B. Only Debby's sick pay is taxable, because sick pay from an employer is always taxable as wages and is therefore included in Debby's gross income. Settlements for personal injuries from an accident are not taxable. If a taxpayer pays the full cost of an accident or disability insurance plan, the benefits for personal injury or illness are not included in income. If the employer pays the cost of an accident insurance plan, the amounts are taxable to the employee.

17. The answer is D. A taxpayer's vacation property was sold on December 28, 2023, but whose payment was in escrow until January 4, 2024, would not have constructive receipt. A taxpayer does not need physical possession of income to have constructive receipt. However, income is not considered constructively received if the taxpayer cannot access the funds because of restrictions. Since the taxpayer's control of the receipt of the funds in the escrow account was substantially limited until the transaction had closed, the taxpayer did not constructively receive the income until the following year.

18. The answer is C. Alphonse must report the interest income in the year he receives it. Only the $175 of interest income is taxable. Life insurance proceeds are not taxable to the recipient. However, any interest earned on life insurance proceeds is taxable.

19. The answer is B. Only the wages and the bonus are taxable ($30,000 + $2,000). The parking pass is a nontaxable transportation benefit, and the employer contributions are not taxable until Chandra withdraws the money from her retirement account. Chandra does not have to report the use of the copier, because it is considered a *de minimis* fringe benefit.

Unit 5: Investment Income and Expenses

For additional information, read:
Publication 550, *Investment Income and Expenses*
Instructions for Schedule B

This unit covers interest and dividend income. Taxpayers who deposit cash or invest in securities such as stocks, bonds, and mutual funds may earn income from interest, dividends, and capital appreciation. Other types of income from investments, such as capital gains resulting from *sales*, are covered later.

Interest Income

Interest is a form of income that may be earned from deposits, such as bank and money market accounts, notes receivable, and investments in instruments such as bonds. Some interest income is taxable, and some is not. Certain distributions, commonly called *dividends*, are reported as taxable interest. These include "dividends" on deposits or share accounts in cooperative banks, credit unions, domestic savings and loan associations, and mutual savings banks. A taxpayer can also have taxable interest from certificates of deposits (CDs) and other deferred interest accounts.

Interest income is generally reported to the taxpayer on Form 1099-INT by the financial institution or another payor if the amount of interest is $10 or more for the year. Even if a taxpayer does not receive Form 1099-INT from a payor, all taxable interest income must be reported. If taxable interest income exceeds $1,500, the taxpayer must report the interest on Schedule B, *Interest and Ordinary Dividends*.

Example: Trixie has three savings accounts in different banks. The total amount of interest earned from all her bank accounts is $1,950. Trixie will receive three Forms 1099-INT. She must list each payor and the amount of interest she receives from each bank on Schedule B and file it with her tax return.

Example: Zebadiah loaned his best friend Rufus $20,000 for one year at 3% interest. Rufus paid Zebadiah $600 in interest in 2023 ($20,000 × .03 = $600). Since this is a personal loan, a 1099-INT is not required to be filed by the payor. Even if Zebadiah does not get a Form 1099-INT from Rufus, he must report the interest he earned on the loan as taxable income on his Form 1040.

Gift for Opening a Bank Account: When a taxpayer receives noncash gifts or services for making deposits or opening an account in a savings institution, they may need to report the value of the gift as interest. If the deposit is less than $5,000, any gifts or services valued at more than $10 must be reported. For deposits of $5,000 or more, gifts or services valued over $20 must be reported as interest. The financial institution determines the value of the gift based on its cost.

Receiving a cash bonus for opening a new checking or credit card account is also considered taxable interest. However, rewards earned from credit and debit card purchases are typically not deemed as taxable income. For example, many major airlines have frequent flyer programs that allow passengers to accumulate miles with each flight. The IRS generally views these rewards as "rebates" and not taxable income.

The same is true for customer loyalty programs like grocery store discount cards, punch cards that provide a price reduction after a number of purchases, and discounts for opening a store credit card.[76]

> **Example:** Florent applies for a new credit card on February 1, 2023, through Express Airlines Visa. The card company offers 20,000 frequent flyer miles for spending $10,000 in the first six months. Florent makes over $10,000 in purchases between February and May and receives 20,000 bonus miles. The value of the bonus miles are not taxable to Florent.

> **Example:** Kiana earns $26,000 in wages during the year. She also earns some interest from her two savings accounts. Kiana earns $9 in interest from the first savings account and $8 in interest from the second account. Because the amounts are below the reporting threshold, she does not receive a Form 1099-INT from either bank. However, the interest is still taxable and must be reported on her tax return. She can report the interest directly on her Form 1040. She does not have to file a Schedule B, since the amount of interest is less than $1,500.

Interest Earned on a Certificate of Deposit

Interest earned on a certificate of deposit (CD) is generally taxable when the taxpayer receives it or is entitled to receive it without incurring a penalty. The interest a taxpayer *pays* on funds borrowed from a financial institution to meet the minimum deposit required for a CD, and the interest a taxpayer earns on the CD are two separate items. The taxpayer must include the total interest earned on the CD in income. If the taxpayer chooses to itemize deductions, they can deduct the interest paid as investment interest, as long as it does not exceed their net investment income, by using Form 4952, *Investment Interest Expense Deduction*.[77]

> **Example:** Tiffany wants to invest in a $50,000 six-month CD. She deposited $40,000 of her own money in a CD with a bank and borrowed an additional $10,000 from the same bank to make up the minimum deposit required to buy the six-month CD. The certificate of deposit earned $575 at maturity in 2023, but Tiffany received a net amount of $265 for the year after taking into account the $310 of interest paid to the bank. This represented the $575 Tiffany earned on the CD, minus $310 interest charged on the $10,000 loan. The bank issued Tiffany a Form 1099-INT showing the $575 interest she earned. The bank also issued Tiffany a statement showing that she paid $310 in investment interest during the year. Tiffany must include the total interest amount that she earned, $575, in her gross income for the year. She can deduct the interest expense of $310 only if she itemizes deductions on Schedule A.

Tax-Exempt Interest

Interest earned on debt obligations of state and local governments (also commonly called *muni bonds* or *municipal bonds*) is generally exempt from federal income tax but may be subject to income taxes by state and local governments. Also, even if the interest on an obligation is nontaxable, the taxpayer may need to report a capital gain or loss when the investment is sold. The taxpayer's Form(s) 1099-INT may include both taxable and tax-exempt interest. Tax-exempt interest must be reported on Form 1040, even though it is not taxable.

---

[76] IRS Announcement 2002-18 addresses frequent flyer miles and promotional card benefits.
[77] The TCJA temporarily suspends miscellaneous itemized deductions subject to 2%-of-AGI until 2026. This temporary disallowance includes the deduction for most investment expenses. Other examples include: safe deposit fees, trustee fees, and investment advisor fees. However, the TCJA did *not* repeal the deduction for investment *interest* expense. Investment *interest* expense is any interest incurred on loans used to purchase taxable investments.

Example: Travis is a software programmer who earns $109,000 in wages during the year. He also receives $2,950 in municipal bond interest. The muni bond interest was reported to him on Form 1099-INT. Travis must report his wages as well as the full amount of the muni bond interest on his tax return, but the municipal bond interest is not taxable.

If a taxpayer borrows money to buy investments that generate tax-free income, the interest is not deductible as investment interest.

Example: Antoinette borrowed $60,000 from a bank to invest in municipal bonds. Antoinette purchased the bonds and received tax-exempt interest of $1,250. She also paid $950 in interest on the loan. Since Antoinette does not have to pay tax on the municipal bond income, she cannot take the investment interest expense deduction for the interest that she paid.

Interest on U.S. Treasury Bills, Notes, and Bonds

Interest on U.S. obligations, such as U.S. Treasury bills, notes, or bonds issued by any agency of the United States, is normally taxable for federal income tax purposes and exempt from state and local income taxes. The **Series EE bond** is issued at a discount, and the difference between the purchase price and the amount received when the bonds are later redeemed (or "cashed in") is interest income.

Series I bonds are issued at face value with a maturity period of thirty years. The face value and accrued interest are payable at maturity. Individual taxpayers can generally report interest income from a Series EE or Series I savings bond either:

- When the bond matures or is redeemed (whichever occurs first), or
- Each year as the bond's redemption value increases (if the taxpayer makes an election).

However, taxpayers must use the same reporting method for all the Series EE and Series I bonds they own. When taxpayers redeem savings bonds, they should receive a Form 1099-INT from a bank or another payor.

The Education Savings Bond Program

Series EE and I savings bonds are also called "educational savings bonds." A special rule permits qualified taxpayers to exempt the interest earned upon redemption of eligible savings bonds, if they are used to pay higher education expenses in the same year. The educational expenses must be for the taxpayer, a spouse, or dependents. This exclusion is known as the *Education Savings Bond Program*. Interest earned on these bonds is usually exempt from state taxes as well.

The taxpayer must use both the principal *and* interest to pay for qualified education expenses. If the amount of savings bonds cashed during the year exceeds the amount of qualified educational expenses paid during the year, the amount of excludable interest is reduced.

To exclude interest earnings on Series EE and Series I bonds, a taxpayer must be at least twenty-four years old before the bond's issue date. Certain rules must be followed for the educational exclusion to qualify:

- The bonds must be purchased by the owner. They cannot be a gift, although the bond proceeds can be used to pay the tuition expenses of a dependent child.

- Qualified higher-education expenses must be reduced by scholarships and other tax-free benefits received and by expenses used to claim the American Opportunity and Lifetime Learning credits.
- The total interest received may be excluded only if the combined amounts of the principal and the interest received do not exceed the taxpayer's qualified higher education expenses.

Example: Sonya is 28 and a full-time college student. She redeemed several education savings bonds to pay for her college expenses. She cashed in the bonds in 2023, receiving total bond proceeds of $10,000 ($8,000 principal and $2,000 in bond interest). Sonya's qualified educational expenses were only $8,000. She used the remaining $2,000 to make a down payment on a new car. Therefore, since Sonya used only 80% of the bond proceeds for qualified expenses, she can only exclude 80% of the bond interest. The excludable portion would equal $1,600 (80% × $2,000 bond interest = $1,600). She would pay tax on the remaining $400 of bond interest.

Married taxpayers who file separately (MFS) do not qualify for the education savings bond interest exclusion. If a taxpayer cashes an education savings bond during the year and then files MFS, all the interest would be taxable, regardless of whether the taxpayer had qualifying education expenses.

Example: Isaiah is married but always files separately from his wife. In 2023, Isaiah cashed out qualified Series EE U.S. savings bonds. He received proceeds of $7,520, representing a principal of $5,000 and interest income of $2,520. Isaiah paid $11,000 of college tuition for his graduate program using the bond proceeds. Normally, Isaiah would be able to exclude all the bond interest from his taxable income. However, since he is filing MFS, all the bond interest is taxable.

In general, only tuition and fees are considered qualified expenses for the purposes of the savings bond exclusion. The costs of room and board, as well as required textbooks, are *not* eligible expenses. However, the cost of required textbooks *is* a qualified educational expense for the purposes of the Lifetime Learning Credit and the American Opportunity Credit.

The amount of qualified expenses must be further reduced by the amount of any scholarships, fellowships, employer-provided educational assistance, and other forms of tuition reduction. The exclusion is calculated and reported on Form 8815, *Exclusion of Interest from Series EE and I U.S. Savings Bonds Issued After 1989*.

Dividend Income

A dividend is a distribution of cash, stock, or other property from a corporation or a mutual fund. Most large corporations pay dividends in cash. The payor will generally use Form 1099-DIV to report dividend income to its shareholders.

If a taxpayer does not receive Form 1099-DIV from a payor, the taxpayer must still report all taxable dividend income. Generally, if a taxpayer's total dividend income is more than $1,500, it must be reported on Schedule B, *Interest and Ordinary Dividends*. Otherwise, the dividend income can be reported directly on Form 1040. In 2023, the top rate on long-term capital gains and *qualified* dividends is 20%.[78]

---

[78] Note that *short-term* capital gains, which are generated by the sale of investments held for one year or less, are taxed at the individual taxpayer's ordinary income rate. This is why the holding period is so important. We will discuss the holding period in more detail later.

This means that the maximum tax rate for qualified dividends is 20%, regardless of the taxpayer's individual tax bracket. However, many higher-income taxpayers may also be subject to the Net Investment Income Tax (NIIT) on long-term capital gains and qualified dividends (the NIIT is covered in detail later).

> **Example:** Aiden is unmarried and earned $690,000 in wages in 2023. This puts him in the highest marginal tax bracket, at 37%. Aiden also earned $120,000 in qualified dividends from various investments. His dividend income will be taxed at 20%, a much lower rate than his marginal ordinary tax rate. Also, unlike his wages, the dividends are not subject to employment taxes. However, Aiden will be subject to the Net Investment Income Tax (NIIT) on the qualified dividends because his adjusted gross income is over the threshold amount for the NIIT.

Ordinary Dividends: Ordinary dividends are corporate distributions in cash (as opposed to property or stock shares) that are paid to shareholders out of earnings and profits. Unless they are qualified dividends, they are taxed at ordinary income tax rates rather than at lower long-term capital gain rates. Ordinary dividends are reported in Box 1a of Form 1099-DIV.

Qualified Dividends: Whereas ordinary dividends are taxable as ordinary income, qualified dividends that meet certain requirements are taxed at lower capital gain rates if specific criteria are met. Short-term capital gains and ordinary dividends are taxed at ordinary income rates. The top rates for qualified dividends and long-term capital gains are as follows:

Long-term capital gains tax rates for 2023			
Filing status	**0% rate**	**15% rate**	**20% rate**
Single	Up to $44,625	$44,626 – $492,300	$492,301 and over
Married filing jointly and QSS	Up to $89,250	$89,251 – $553,850	$553,851 and over
Married filing separately	Up to $44,625	$44,626 – $276,900	$276,901 and over
Head of household	Up to $59,750	$59,751 – $523,050	$523,051 and over
Trust & Estates	Up to $3,000	$3,001 - $14,650	$14,651 and over
Other long-term gains rates			
Gain on sale of collectibles	Maximum 28%		
Unrecaptured Sec. 1250 gain	Maximum 25%		

Qualified dividends are reported to the taxpayer in Box 1b of Form 1099-DIV. In order for the dividends to qualify for these preferred tax rates, the following are the two most common requirements that must be met:

- The dividends must be paid by a U.S. corporation or qualified foreign corporation,[79] and
- The taxpayer generally must have held the stock for *more than sixty days* during the 121-day period that begins sixty days before the ex-dividend date.

---

[79] A "qualified foreign corporation" for the purposes of this rule is generally a foreign corporation whose stock is traded on a U.S. stock exchange or if a tax treaty between the U.S. and the foreign country of the corporation allows for qualified dividend status.

When figuring the holding period for qualified dividends, the taxpayer may count the number of days the stock was held, with the first day being the day after the stock was acquired (the date the taxpayer acquires the stock is not included in the holding period), and include the day the stock was sold. A longer holding period may apply for dividends paid on preferred stock. The "ex-dividend date" is the date a shareholder will no longer be entitled to receive the most recently declared dividend (typically the day following the record date). [80]

Nondividend Distributions: Distributions that are not paid out of a corporation's earnings and profits are called *nondividend* distributions. They are considered a recovery or return of capital and therefore are generally not taxable. However, these distributions reduce the taxpayer's basis in the stock of the corporation. Once the basis is reduced to zero, any additional distributions are capital gains and are taxed as such. Nondividend distributions are reported in Box 3 of Form 1099-DIV.

Money market funds: Money market funds pay dividends and are offered by nonbank financial institutions, such as mutual funds and stock brokerage houses. Generally, amounts received from money market funds should be reported as dividends, not as interest.

Stock Dividends and Stock Distributions

A stock dividend is a distribution of stock, rather than money, by a corporation to its own shareholders. A stock dividend is generally not a taxable event and does not affect the shareholder's income in the year of distribution because the shareholder is not actually receiving any money, and all shareholders increase their total number of shares pro-rata. When a stock dividend is granted, the total basis of the shareholder's stock is not affected, but the basis of individual shares is adjusted by the inclusion of the newly-issued shares.

Example: AeroSystems Corporation declares a year-end stock dividend. Sharon is a shareholder in AeroSystems, and prior to the stock dividend, she owns 100 shares. Her basis in the shares is $5,000, or $50 per share. Sharon receives a stock dividend of 100 additional shares. After the dividend, Sharon owns 200 shares. Her overall basis in the shares does not change (it is still $5,000), but her new basis in each individual share is $25 per share ($5,000/200 = $25 per share). Sharon does not have any taxable income as a result of the stock dividend.

If a shareholder has the option to receive cash *instead* of stock, the stock dividend is taxable in the year it is distributed. The recipient of the stock must include the FMV of the newly issued stock in his gross income, and that same amount is the basis of the shares received.

Example: Superjet Corporation declares a year-end stock dividend and gives its shareholders the option of receiving cash instead of stock. Therefore, the stock dividend becomes a taxable event. Before the dividend, Danton owns 1,000 shares in Superjet Corp., and his basis in the shares is $10,000, or $10 per share. Danton decides to take the stock instead of cash and receives an additional 100 shares. The FMV of the stock at the time of the distribution is $15 per share. Danton must recognize $1,500 of income ($15 FMV × 100 shares = $1,500), which also is his basis in the new shares.

---

[80] The "ex-dividend date" is the day on which a corporation's shares that are bought and sold no longer come attached with the right to receive the most recently declared dividend. This is important, because if a taxpayer purchases stock *after* its ex-dividend date, the taxpayer who bought the shares will not receive the next dividend payment. Instead, the seller of the stock receives the dividend.

Dividend Reinvestment Plans (DRIP)

A dividend reinvestment plan allows a taxpayer to use their dividends to purchase more shares of stock in a corporation instead of receiving dividends in cash. If the taxpayer uses their dividends to buy more stock at a price equal to its fair market value, the taxpayer must still report the dividends as income, as illustrated in the example below.

Example: Francesco owns 100 shares of Applied Plastics, Inc., which is currently trading at $50 a share on the open market. Through the company's dividend reinvestment plan (DRIP), Francesco buys 50 additional shares at $40 per share. He must report $500 as dividend income ($10 per share difference between FMV and purchase price multiplied by 50 shares).

Some plans also allow taxpayers to invest cash to buy shares of stock at a price less than fair market value. In this case, taxpayers must report as dividend income the difference between the cash they invest and the FMV of the stock they purchase.

Mutual Fund Distributions

A mutual fund is an investment vehicle that allows investors to pool their money to invest in stocks, bonds, and other securities. The combined holdings of stocks, bonds, or other assets the fund owns are known as its "portfolio." Mutual funds are professionally managed by a portfolio manager. Mutual funds generally distribute all of their ordinary income to shareholders by the end of the year to obtain favorable tax treatment.

A taxpayer who receives mutual fund distributions during the year will also receive Form 1099-DIV, identifying the types of distributions received. Mutual fund distributions are reported based on the character of the income source and may include ordinary dividends, qualified dividends, capital gain distributions, exempt-interest dividends, and nondividend distributions. Ordinary dividends are the most common type of distribution from a mutual fund; these dividends are taxable as ordinary income.

Capital gain distributions from a mutual fund are always treated as long-term, regardless of the actual period the mutual fund investment is held. Distributions from a mutual fund investing in tax-exempt securities are tax-exempt interest and retain their tax-exempt character for the payee. Even so, the taxpayer must report them on his tax return.

If a mutual fund or Real Estate Investment Trust (REIT) declares a dividend payable to shareholders in October, November, or December, but actually pays the dividend during January of the following year, the shareholder is considered to have received the dividend on December 31 of the prior tax year and must report the dividend in the year it was declared.

Example: Alessandro has money invested in the Great Shares Mutual Fund. The fund declared a $230 dividend on December 27, 2023. Alessandro actually *received* the dividend the following year, on January 9, 2024. Alessandro must report the dividend in 2023 and not in 2024. The dividend is taxable in the year *declared in this situation*, regardless of whether Alessandro withdraws the dividends or reinvests them.

Constructive Distributions and Constructive Dividends

Certain transactions between a corporation and its shareholders may be considered constructive distributions. In general, constructive distributions (also called "constructive dividends") are assessed under audit, and they can have very negative consequences for the company as well as to the shareholder. They may be considered dividends and, therefore taxable to the shareholders and non-deductible to the corporation. Examples of constructive distributions include:

- **Payment of personal expenses:** If a corporation pays personal expenses on behalf of an employee-shareholder, the amounts should be classified as a distribution, rather than expenses of the corporation.

- **Unreasonable compensation:** If a corporation pays an employee-shareholder an unreasonably high salary considering the services actually performed, the excessive part of the salary may be treated as a distribution.

- **Unreasonable rents:** If a corporation rents property from a shareholder and the rent is unreasonably *higher* than the shareholder would charge an unrelated party for the use of the property, the excessive part of the rent may be treated as a distribution. Conversely, if a corporation rents property to a shareholder and the rent is unreasonably low, the discounted portion of the rent could be treated as a distribution as well.

- **Cancellation of a shareholder's debt:** If a corporation cancels a shareholder's debt without repayment by the shareholder, the amount canceled may be treated as a distribution.

- **Property transfers for less than FMV:** If a corporation transfers or sells property to a shareholder for less than its FMV, the excess may be treated as a distribution.

- **Below-market or interest-free loans:** If a corporation gives a loan to a shareholder on an interest-free basis or at a rate below the applicable federal rate, the uncharged interest may be treated as a distribution.

Example: Erika's father owns 95% of Spitfire Motorsports, Inc., and she and her siblings own the remaining 5%. Erika performs administrative assistant duties part-time for the corporation and is paid a salary of $700,000 yearly. The corporation also pays for various personal expenses Erika incurs, such as monthly lease payments on her personal vehicle. The IRS would likely consider Erika's salary as unreasonably high based on the nature of her duties, meaning that a portion of the salary and the personal expenses would be reclassified as constructive distributions. If that happens, then the constructive distribution becomes taxable to Erika as a taxable dividend, and the amounts are no longer deductible by the corporation as a business expense.

Unit 5: Study Questions

(Test yourself first, then check the correct answers at the end of this quiz.)

1. Six years ago, Derrick bought a U.S. Series EE savings bond and decided to report the interest earned each year until maturity. This year, he bought *another* Series EE savings bond. How should Derrick report the interest on this new bond?

A. He must wait until the second bond matures to report all the interest earned at that time.
B. He must report the interest earned each year until maturity.
C. He can use either method to report the interest as long as he makes the election on a timely return.
D. This type of interest is now exempt from federal income tax.

2. Leonardo invested in a mutual fund during the year. The fund declared a dividend on December 20, 2023, and Leonardo received the $19 dividend distribution on January 2, 2024. He did not receive a Form 1099-DIV for the amount, and he did not withdraw the money from his mutual fund. Leonardo sold his investment in the mutual fund on January 19, 2024. Which of the following statements is correct?

A. The dividend is not taxable in 2023 because Leonardo did not withdraw the earnings.
B. The dividend is not taxable in 2023 because Leonardo did not receive a 1099-DIV.
C. The dividend is taxable and must be reported in 2023.
D. The dividend is taxable but does not have to be reported until 2024.

3. Marcelo opened a savings account at his local bank and deposited $800. The account earned $20 interest during the year. On his credit card account, Marcelo received $100 worth of cash-back reward points for charging $10,000 of purchases, which he used to pay a portion of his credit card bill. How much interest income must Marcelo report on his Form 1040?

A. $20
B. $75
C. $120
D. $900

4. Abdullah bought 100 shares of stock during the year, and the stock paid him $80 in dividends. How long must Abdullah have held stock in order for his dividend income to be considered "qualified dividends."

A. More than 30 days during the 121-day period that begins 60 days before the ex-dividend date.
B. More than 60 days during the 121-day period that begins 60 days before the ex-dividend date.
C. More than 120 days.
D. More than one year.

5. Araceli received $500 of interest from municipal bonds issued by the state of New Jersey. How should she report this on her Form 1040?

A. It must be reported on her tax return, but it is not taxable income.
B. It must be reported as interest income, and it is 100% taxable.
C. She does not have to report the bond interest.
D. She must report the interest on her state tax return, but it does not have to be reported on her federal return.

6. Bastien received a Form 1099-DIV from his brokerage firm, showing that he earned $1,200 of ordinary dividends. He received no other investment income during the year. How should this income be handled on Bastien's tax return?

A. He must report the dividend income on Schedule B, but it is not taxable.
B. He must report the dividend income on Schedule D.
C. He can report the dividend income on page one of his Form 1040, taxable as ordinary income.
D. He does not have to report the dividend income until he sells the stock from the corporations that distributed the dividends.

7. All of the following statements about dividends are correct *except*:

A. A taxpayer will pay a higher tax rate on an ordinary dividend than on a qualified dividend.
B. A taxpayer will pay a higher tax rate on a qualified dividend than on an ordinary dividend.
C. The ex-dividend date is the date a shareholder will no longer be entitled to receive the most recently declared dividend (normally right after the record date).
D. When figuring the holding period for qualified dividends, the taxpayer may count the number of days he held the stock (starting the day after the stock was acquired) and include the day he disposed of the stock.

8. Miguel deposited $4,000 of his own funds and also borrowed $12,000 from the bank to buy a nine-month certificate of deposit for $16,000. The certificate earned $375 at maturity in 2023, and Miguel received $175, which represented the $375 he earned minus $200 of interest charged on the $12,000 loan. The bank gives Miguel a Form 1099-INT showing the $375 interest he earned. The bank also issues him a statement showing that he paid $200 in interest. How should Miguel report these amounts on his tax return?

A. He should report $175 of interest income.
B. He must report $375 of interest income. The $200 of interest he paid to the bank is not deductible.
C. He should report $375 of interest income and can deduct $200 on his Schedule A (if taking itemized deductions), subject to the net investment income limit.
D. He does not have to report any income from this transaction.

9. All of the following statements about stock dividends are correct except:

A. When a stock dividend is distributed, the basis of the stockholder's existing shares is adjusted to reflect the issuance of the new shares.
B. A stock dividend occurs when a corporation distributes stock to its own shareholders.
C. A taxpayer generally recognizes income only when he sells the stock received in a stock dividend distribution.
D. A stock dividend is never taxable, even if a taxpayer has the choice to receive cash instead of stock.

10. Nondividend distributions are:

A. Considered a return of capital.
B. Never taxable.
C. Always taxable as ordinary income.
D. Always taxable as passive income.

11. Constance uses educational savings bonds to help pay her college expenses. Which of the following is a "qualified expense" for the educational savings bond exclusion?

A. College tuition
B. Room and board
C. Required textbooks
D. Student health fees

12. Which of the following dividends should be reported as interest income on a taxpayer's return?

A. Stock dividends.
B. Preferred dividends.
C. Dividends earned on deposits in credit unions.
D. Qualified dividends.

13. Kendrick is a 5% shareholder of a family-owned C corporation, Archetype Builders, Inc., where he works as a full-time architect. Archetype Builders, Inc. pays for many expenses for Kendrick's benefit. Which of the following would the IRS likely classify as a constructive distribution, and therefore taxable to Kendrick and non-deductible to the corporation?

A. Use of a company copy machine for making occasional personal copies.
B. Payment of licenses and memberships directly related to his job.
C. Dental insurance premiums paid by the corporation through a cafeteria plan.
D. Payment of Kendrick's monthly gym membership by the corporation.

Unit 5: Quiz Answers

1. The answer is B. Derrick must report the interest earned each year until maturity. Savings bond owners must use the same interest-reporting method for all the Series EE and Series I bonds they own.

2. The answer is C. Leonardo is deemed to have earned the dividends in 2023, and whether or not he received a 1099-DIV is irrelevant. Mutual fund dividends are taxable regardless of whether the taxpayer withdraws the dividends or reinvests them. Furthermore, if dividends from a mutual fund (or REIT) are declared in October, November, or December and paid no later than January of the following year, the dividends are taxable in the year declared, even though they are not paid until the following year, so Leonardo must report the earnings in 2023.

3. The answer is A. If no other interest is credited to Marcelo during the year, the Form 1099-INT he receives will show $20 of interest for the year. The IRS does not count reward points or cashback from a credit card as taxable interest income (it is treated as a rebate), so Marcelo does not have to report the $100 in reward points or pay any tax on it.

4. The answer is B. Abdullah must generally have held stock for more than 60 days during the 121-day period that begins 60 days before the ex-dividend date. The ex-dividend date is the date a shareholder will no longer be entitled to receive the most recently declared dividend.[81]

5. The answer is A. Although the interest is not taxable, Araceli must still report the income on her federal return. Interest earned on state and local bonds (municipal bonds or "muni" bonds) are generally tax-exempt at the federal level. Note that these bonds may be taxable at the state and local level, even if they are not taxable at the federal level.

6. The answer is C. Ordinary dividends are taxable as ordinary income in the year they are earned. Only amounts over $1,500 must be reported on Schedule B, so Bastien may report the $1,200 of dividend income directly on page one of his Form 1040.

7. The answer is B. Ordinary dividends are taxed at higher ordinary income rates than qualified dividends. If certain conditions are met, qualified dividends are given preferred tax treatment. Qualified dividends must have been paid by a U.S. corporation or a qualified foreign corporation, and the taxpayer generally must have held the stock for more than sixty days during the 121-day period that begins sixty days before the ex-dividend date.

8. The answer is C. Miguel must include the total amount of interest earned, $375, in his income. If he itemizes deductions on Schedule A, he can deduct $200 of interest expense, subject to the net investment income limit. He may not report the investment income and expenses on a net basis (i.e., the taxable interest income less the allowable deduction).

---

[81] When figuring the holding period for qualified dividends, the taxpayer may count the number of days he held the stock and include the day he disposed of the stock. The date the taxpayer acquires the stock is not included in the holding period. A longer holding period may apply for dividends paid on preferred stock.

9. The answer is D. If a taxpayer is given a choice between receiving cash or stock, a stock dividend is taxable in the year it is distributed.

10. The answer is A. Nondividend distributions are not paid out of a corporation's earnings and profits. They are considered a recovery or return of capital and therefore are generally not taxable. However, these distributions reduce the taxpayer's basis in the stock of the corporation. Once the basis in the stock is reduced to zero, any additional nondividend distributions are taxed as capital gains.

11. The answer is A. Constance can use the amounts to pay her college tuition, but none of the other expenses are eligible for the savings bond exclusion. The savings bond education tax exclusion permits qualified taxpayers to exclude from their gross income all or part of the interest paid upon the redemption of eligible Series EE and I Bonds. Eligible educational expenses include tuition and required fees. The costs of room and board, as well as required textbooks, are *not* eligible expenses for the educational savings bond exclusion.

12. The answer is C. The dividends earned on deposits in credit unions are reported as interest income rather than dividend income.

13. The answer is D. The payment of personal expenses (such as a gym membership, personal rent, and club dues) on behalf of an employee-shareholder is treated as a constructive distribution. In this case, the payment of his monthly gym membership is likely to be reclassified as a taxable dividend to Kendrick or a nondividend distribution, depending upon whether the corporation has earnings and profits. Answer "A" is incorrect because occasionally using a company copier is an allowable de minimis fringe benefit. Choices "B" and "C" are incorrect because dental and medical benefits, as well as the reimbursement of license fees directly related to his job, are allowable employee benefits.

Unit 6: Calculating the Basis of Assets

> **For additional information, read:**
> Publication 551, *Basis of Assets*
> Publication 544, *Sales and Other Dispositions of Assets*

A large portion of tax law revolves around taxing assets. In order to accurately calculate gains and losses from selling or disposing of an asset, it is necessary to classify the asset first. Assets can generally be categorized into two main types: **real property** and **personal property**.

"**Real property**" refers to real estate, which includes land and anything permanently attached to it. Examples of real property include: buildings, farmland, residential homes, commercial properties, rental properties, and subsurface mineral rights.

"**Personal property**" encompasses all assets that are not classified as real estate. This includes items such as furniture, equipment, vehicles, household goods, collectibles, and livestock. It also covers intangible assets like stocks, trademarks, cryptocurrency, and copyrights. The tax treatment of an asset may differ depending on whether it is intended for personal use, business purposes, or investment.

Note: It is important not to confuse the term "personal property" with "personal-use property." While "personal property" is a legal and accounting term used to describe any movable asset whether or not it is used for business purposes, "personal-use" property specifically refers to assets that are used personally by the taxpayer and not for trade, business, or investment.

Basis in General

In order to accurately determine profits and deficits, it is important to grasp the idea of "basis." The original basis of an asset is typically its purchase price. However, there may be cases where the basis is calculated based on the fair market value at the time of acquisition, rather than the cost, such as when property is inherited or gifted. The cost basis of an asset may include:

- Sales taxes charged during the purchase
- Freight-in charges and shipping fees
- Installation costs and testing fees
- Delinquent real estate taxes that are paid by the buyer of a property
- The cost of any major improvements to the property
- Legal and accounting fees for transferring an asset

Example: Ambrosio purchases a new vehicle for $15,000. The sales tax on the vehicle is $1,200. He also pays a delivery charge to have the car shipped from a dealership in another state to his home. The delivery charge is $210. Therefore, Ambrosio's basis in the vehicle is $16,410 ($15,000 + $1,200 + $210).

Example: Cassandra is a self-employed copywriter who reports her income on Schedule C. She purchases a powerful new laptop for her home office. The laptop costs $3,540 with an additional $194 for sales tax. Cassandra's basis in the computer is $3,734 ($3,540 + $194). This is also her basis for depreciation.

Certain post-acquisition costs can also increase the basis of an asset, including:

- The cost of extending utility service lines to the property and impact fees[82]
- Legal fees or court costs perfecting title to a property
- Legal fees for obtaining a decrease in an assessment levied against property to pay for local improvements; and/or zoning costs and the capitalized value of a redeemable ground rent.

Example: Titus spent $45,000 to purchase a piece of farmland. However, he is soon faced with a title dispute initiated by the former owner's ex-wife, claiming that the sale was invalid. To defend his ownership, Titus hires an attorney for $7,800. After successfully proving his rights to the land and having the lawsuit deemed frivolous, Titus's adjusted basis for the property increases to $52,800 (original cost of $45,000 plus legal fees of $7,800). It should be noted that while these legal fees are not currently tax deductible, they do contribute to the basis of the property.

Example: Calix buys a house for $120,000, which he plans to use as a personal residence. Four months after he closes the sale, he paves the driveway, which costs $9,000. Calix's adjusted basis in the home is now $129,000 ($120,000 original cost + $9,000 for major improvements).

Study Note: Understanding basis and how it is applied to various types of property is critical to your success in passing Part 1 *and* Part 2 of the EA exam. You may be expected to calculate basis in multiple scenarios.

Depreciation Deduction

Depreciation is a tax deduction that allows businesses to gradually recoup the cost of assets they use over time. This process decreases the basis of an asset over the course of several years.

The annual amount allowed for depreciation is meant to account for natural wear and tear, deterioration, or obsolescence of assets. Eventually, the asset will no longer be depreciable once its basis has been fully recovered or if it is sold or retired from service. Some types of property, such as land, cannot be depreciated, but most tangible assets like buildings, machinery, vehicles, furniture, and equipment can be depreciated.

Study Note: Depreciation is an important accounting concept, so it is tested most often on *Part 2: Businesses* of the EA exam. For Part 1 of the EA exam, test-takers must understand depreciation primarily in the context of residential rental property. Most residential rental property is depreciated over 27.5 years. Only the value of the *building* can be depreciated, *never* the land.

Dispositions and Holding Period

The length of time an asset is held determines whether any gain or loss from its sale will be considered **long-term** or **short-term.** The holding period for an asset begins the day after it is acquired and ends on the day it is sold. If an asset is sold, the difference between its initial cost and selling price may result in a taxable gain or loss. In some cases, a gain or loss may not be recognized until a later date after an asset has been disposed of or sold.

---

[82] An "impact fee" is a one-time capital charge imposed on property developers by municipalities to help fund the capital cost of the additional public services. Impact fees are added to a property's basis.

To accurately report any taxable gain or loss from the sale or disposal of an asset, a taxpayer must identify:

- Whether the asset is personal-use or used for business or investment;
- The asset's basis or adjusted basis:
  - As described above, the initial basis of an asset is usually its purchase cost, including certain ancillary charges.
  - "Adjusted basis" includes the original basis plus any increases or decreases (such as subsequent improvements, depreciation deductions, casualty losses, rebates, and insurance reimbursements).
- The asset's holding period:
  - *Short-term* property is held for one year or less.
  - *Long-term* property is held for <u>more</u> than one year (at least a year, plus a day).[83]
- The proceeds from the sale.

Example: Kenji purchased 75 silver coins as an investment on January 1, 2023. The coins cost $23 each, plus an additional sales tax of $67. Kenji's basis in the silver coins is $1,792 ([$23 × 75 coins] + $67). On November 10, 2023, Kenji sold all the coins to a collector for $1,900. His net gain is $108 ($1,900 - $1,792 basis). Kenji has a $108 short-term capital gain, because he held the coins for less than a year. The short-term gain will be taxed at his ordinary income tax rate.

Example: Denise bought 500 shares of Aberdeen Inc. stock on January 1, 2023. If Denise sells the stock the following year, right on January 1, 2024, the capital gain or loss will be **short-term**. If she sells the property on January 2, 2024, (one year *plus* one additional day) her holding period will have been *over* one year, and her capital gain or loss will be **long-term**.

Basis of Real Property (Real Estate)

The basis of real estate usually includes a number of costs in addition to the purchase price. If a taxpayer purchases real property (such as land or a building), certain fees and other expenses are automatically included in the cost basis. The transaction might include real estate taxes the *seller* owed at the time of the purchase. If delinquent real estate taxes are paid by the buyer, those amounts must be added to the property's basis.

Example: Solange sells Anthony her home for $125,000. She had fallen behind on her property tax payments, so Anthony agrees to pay $3,500 of delinquent real estate taxes as a condition of the sale. Because a taxpayer is not allowed to deduct property taxes that are not his legal responsibility, Anthony must add the property taxes paid to his basis. Anthony's basis in the home is $128,500.

If a property is constructed rather than purchased, the basis of the property includes all the expenses of construction. This includes payments to contractors, building materials, and fees for inspections. Any expenses related to *preparing* the land, such as demolition costs, must be included in the basis of the land itself, not the buildings constructed on it at a later date. If raw land is purchased on its own, the basis includes the purchase price plus any legal and recording fees, abstract fees, and land survey costs.

---

[83] Long-term capital gains are given more favorable tax treatment. Although most assets have to be held for over one year in order to be treated as "long term" an exception applies to assets acquired through inheritance, which we will cover later.

Example: Dianne pays $50,000 for an empty lot where she plans to build her dream home. She also pays $2,800 for the removal of tree stumps and $6,700 to demolish an existing concrete foundation on the lot. These costs must be added to the basis of the land, not to the basis of the future house. Therefore, Dianne's basis in the land is $59,500 ($50,000 + $2,800 + $6,700).

Settlement Costs: Generally, a taxpayer must include settlement costs for the purchase of property in his basis. The following fees are some of the closing costs that can be included in a property's basis:

- Abstract fees
- Charges for installing utilities
- Legal fees (including title search and preparation of the deed)
- Recording fees and land surveys
- Transfer taxes
- Owner's title insurance

Also included in a property's basis are any other amounts the seller legally owes that the buyer agrees to pay, such as recording or mortgage fees, charges for improvements or repairs, and sales commissions. However, a taxpayer cannot include fees incidental to getting a loan in the basis of the property financed with proceeds from the loan. Settlement costs do not include any amounts placed in escrow for the future payment of items such as taxes and insurance.

Basis Other Than Cost

The following are examples of situations in which an asset's basis is determined by something *other than* the purchase cost.

Property in Exchange for Services: When a taxpayer receives property in exchange for services, they are required to report the property's fair market value as income. This value then becomes their basis for the property. In situations where two individuals have agreed on a price for services beforehand, this agreed-upon cost can be used to determine both the amount of income and the asset's basis.

Example: Jeremy is a licensed CPA who prepares a tax return for his client, Maryanne. Maryanne loses her job and cannot pay Jeremy's bill, which totals $400. Maryanne offers Jeremy an antique vase instead of paying her invoice. The fair market value of the vase is approximately $525. Jeremy agrees to accept the vase as full payment on Maryanne's delinquent invoice. Jeremy's basis in the vase is $400, the amount of the invoice that was agreed upon beforehand by both parties.

Basis After Casualty Loss: If a taxpayer has a deductible casualty loss, the taxpayer should *increase* the basis in the property by the amount spent on repairs that restore the property to its pre-casualty condition. However, a taxpayer must decrease the basis of the property by any related insurance proceeds.

Example: Broderick paid $5,000 for a used truck several years ago. His truck was damaged in a severe hailstorm, so he spends $3,000 to repair it. He does not have insurance on the vehicle to cover storm damage, so he pays for all the repairs himself. Therefore, his new basis in the truck is $8,000 ($5,000 original cost + $3,000 restoration repairs).

Basis After Mortgage Assumption: If a taxpayer buys a property and assumes an existing mortgage on it, the taxpayer's basis includes the amount paid for the property plus the amount owed on the mortgage.[84] The basis also includes the settlement fees and closing costs paid to buy the property. However, fees and costs for obtaining a loan on the property (points) are not included in a property's basis.

Example: Sabrina's cousin, Pablo, is selling his office building because he can no longer afford the mortgage payments. Sabrina agrees to purchase the office building for $220,000 cash, and she also assumes Pablo's existing mortgage of $800,000 on the property. Therefore, Sabrina's basis in the building is $1,020,000 ($220,000 cash + $800,000 mortgage assumption).

Basis of Securities

When a taxpayer purchases securities, their basis is typically the cost of purchase plus any additional fees, such as brokers' commissions. When these securities are sold, the investment broker should provide the taxpayer with Form 1099-B, which shows the proceeds from the transaction. The IRS also receives a copy of this form. In cases where Form 1099-B does not include information about the taxpayer's basis in the sold securities, they must provide it themselves using their personal records.[85] Failure to provide evidence of basis may result in the IRS assuming it is zero.

A taxpayer may own more than one block of shares in a particular company's stock. Each block may differ from the others in its holding period (long-term or short-term), its basis, or both. When instructing a broker to sell shares, the taxpayer can specify which set, or portion of a set, they wish to sell; this is known as specific identification. Keeping accurate records is essential for using this method. However, it makes calculating the holding period and starting value of sold stock easier, and it allows the taxpayer greater control over identifying profits and/or losses when selling a portion of their investment.

If the taxpayer cannot identify a specific set at the time of sale, the shares sold are considered to be from the earliest set purchased. This technique is referred to as First In, First Out (FIFO).

The IRS requires stockbrokers and mutual fund companies to report the basis for most stock sold on Form 1099-B, *Proceeds From Broker and Barter Exchange Transactions*. The form also includes any federal income tax that has been withheld (if any). The reporting is made to investors and to the IRS.

Example: Sharleen buys two blocks of 400 shares of stock (800 shares total). She bought the first 400 shares on May 1, 2020, for $11,200 and an additional 400 shares on June 1, 2020 for $12,000. On June 20, 2023, she sells 400 shares for $11,500 without specifying which block of shares she was selling. The sold shares are therefore treated as coming from the *earliest* block purchased (those purchased on May 1, 2020). Since the basis and holding period defaults to the *original* block of shares, Sharleen realizes a long-term capital gain of $300 ($11,500 - $11,200).

---

[84] An assumable mortgage is a type of home financing where the buyer assumes responsibility for the seller's existing mortgage loan. This option may be attractive to buyers if interest rates have increased since the seller first bought the home, as they can potentially secure a lower interest rate.

[85] "Noncovered" securities are exempt from broker cost basis reporting due to several factors. For example, cost basis may be missing when the shares are acquired by gift or inheritance. In that case, the taxpayer is responsible for knowing their own stock basis.

> **Note:** You must understand how to calculate the basis of securities because this subject is frequently tested on Part 1 of the exam.

After purchasing stock, any subsequent events may result in changes to the basis per individual share. These adjustments can either increase or decrease the original basis. Examples of such events include stock dividends and stock splits. While these events are typically not taxable, a stock dividend may be subject to taxes if shareholders have the choice to receive cash or other assets instead of additional stock.

- **Stock dividends** are additional shares a company grants to its shareholders in lieu of paying cash dividends and are often nontaxable. When nontaxable, these additional shares increase the number of shares owned by an individual shareholder, so his original basis is spread over more shares, which decreases the basis per individual share. The total basis of all the shares remains the same.
- A **stock split** is similar to a stock dividend and occurs when a company issues additional shares of stock for every existing share an investor holds. Stock splits are a way for a company to lower the market price of its stock. The stock's market capitalization, however, remains the same.

For example, in a 2-for-1 stock split, a corporation issues one share of stock for every share outstanding. This decreases a shareholder's basis per individual share by half. An original basis of $200 for 100 shares becomes $200 for 200 shares in a 2-for-1 stock split. However, the total basis in the stock remains the same even though the basis per share decreases.

> **Example:** Leticia pays a total of $1,050 for 100 shares of Azure Cola, Inc., plus an additional broker's commission of $50. This means her initial cost for the 100 shares is $1,100 ($1,050 original cost + $50 broker's commission). This equals $11 per share ($1,100 ÷ 100 shares). At a later point in time, Leticia receives a stock dividend of 10 shares without any tax implications. However, her original basis of $1,100 must now be divided over 110 shares (the initial 100 shares plus the additional ten-share dividend). Her basis per share decreases to $10 ($1,100 ÷ 110).

> **Example:** Irwin buys 100 shares of Cortex Technology, Inc. for $50 per share. His cost basis is $50 × 100 shares or $5,000. Six months later, Cortex Technology, Inc. declares a 2-for-1 stock split, and Irwin receives 100 additional shares of stock. Therefore, his new basis in each individual stock is $25 = ($5,000 ÷ [100 + 100]). His total basis in the shares remains $5,000.

Stock Options

A taxpayer may purchase *options* to buy or sell securities (such as stocks or commodities) through an exchange or in the open market. With a stock option, an investor can choose to buy or sell a stock at a predetermined price. There may be a gain or loss from trading just the option itself, or the investor can exercise the option and buy or sell the underlying securities, which could result in a gain or loss from those securities.

> **Example:** Peter is a casual investor. He purchases a call option in Wellstone Manufacturing Inc., which allows him to buy company stock at $5 per share. Two weeks later, the stock's price climbs to $10 a share. Peter can use his option contract to buy that stock at a discount, or he could sell the option itself for a profit.

Companies may also offer stock options to their employees as a form of equity-based compensation. This is typically done to motivate employees, increase loyalty, and decrease employee turnover.

> **Example:** Zidan works for Worthington Corporation. On January 1, 2023, Zidan is granted 30,000 shares of incentive stock options (ISOs) with a grant price of $20 per share. These options would vest (become exercisable) over a four year period, meaning that he would have to stay at the company for at least four years in order to exercise them all. Zidan is pleased to get the options. In this way, the stock options motivate employees and lower employee turnover.

Generally, there are two types of stock options:

- Options granted under an employee stock purchase plan (ESPP) or an incentive stock option (ISO) plan are **statutory stock options.** When exercising ISOs, no taxes are due until the eventual sale of the shares. Although incentive stock options come with favorable tax treatment, they may be subject to alternative minimum tax (AMT) in the year of exercise.
- Stock options that are *not granted* under an employee stock purchase plan or an ISO plan are called **nonstatutory stock options.**[86] Generally, a taxpayer recognizes taxable wage income upon the exercise of a nonstatutory stock option. The taxable wage income is the difference between the fair market value of the stock on the exercise date and the option price and will be reflected on the employee's Form W-2.

The nature, timing, and amount of income that needs to be reported by the taxpayer depends on whether the options are **statutory** or **nonstatutory** options.

The tax advantage of a *statutory* stock option is that income is not reported when the option is granted or when it is exercised. Income is only reported once the stock is ultimately sold.

> **Note:** For Part 1 of the EA Exam, you must understand the concept of stock options from the perspective of the individual taxpayer *receiving* the options. For Part 2 of the EA Exam, you must understand stock options from the point of view of the corporation *issuing* the stock options.

> **Example:** Muscle Fitness, Inc. has an employee stock purchase plan (ESPP). The plan allows employees to purchase company stock at a discounted price. The "option price" is the lower of the stock price at the time the option is granted, or at the time the option is exercised. Annamaria is an employee of Muscle Fitness, and she decides to take advantage of the ESPP that her employer provides. Muscle Fitness deducts $5 from Annamaria's pay every week for 48 weeks (total = $240 [$5 × 48]). The value of the stock when the option was granted was $25. When Annamaria exercises her options, the FMV of the stock is $20. Annamaria receives 12 shares of Muscle Fitness stock ($240 ÷ $20). Her holding period for all 12 shares begins the day *after* the option is exercised, even though the money used to purchase the shares was deducted from her pay on many different days. Annamaria holds onto all the shares and does not plan to sell them. Her basis in each share is $20 (based on an example in Publication 525).

---

[86] Refer to Publication 525, *Taxable and Nontaxable Income* for more information on the treatment of statutory or nonstatutory stock options.

Property Transfers Incident to Divorce

When property is transferred from one spouse to another, the recipient's adjusted basis remains the same as the original owner's. Typically, there will be no tax implications for this transfer, regardless of whether it was due to divorce or not.

For property transfers related to a divorce, the transfer generally must occur within one year after the date the marriage ends. This nonrecognition rule applies even if the transfer was in exchange for cash, the release of marital rights, the assumption of liabilities, or other financial considerations.[87]

Example: Quinton and Adrienne finalized their divorce on January 23, 2023. Quinton owns a vacation home in Hawaii with a current adjusted basis of $285,000 and a fair market value of $550,000. Pursuant to their divorce agreement, Quinton agrees to transfer his ownership in the home to Adrienne. He transferred the property to Adrienne on June 1, 2023. Since the transfer was made within a year after their divorce was made final, there is no gain or loss recognized by either spouse, and no tax reporting is required. Adrienne's basis in the property is the same as Quinton's basis before the transfer: $285,000.

Example: Adelynn and Graham jointly owned an antique collector Porsche that had a basis of $50,000 and an FMV of $150,000. When they divorced in 2023, Adelynn transferred her entire interest in the automobile to Graham as part of their property settlement. Graham's basis in the vehicle is the same as their original joint basis of $50,000.

The Basis of Gifted Property

The basis of property received as a gift is determined differently than property that is purchased or inherited. The taxpayer must know the donor's adjusted basis in the property when it was gifted, its fair market value on the date of the gift, and the amount of gift tax the donor paid on it (if any). The concept of "fair market value" is important when calculating any capital gains tax liability on a gift, so it is important to know how the basis and FMV is determined.

Generally, the basis of gifted property for the donee is equal to the donor's adjusted basis. This is called a "transferred basis." For example, if a father gives his son a car and the father's basis in the car is $4,000, the basis of the vehicle remains $4,000 for the son. The holding period of the gift would also transfer to the donee.

Example: Matteo purchases a valuable collectible stamp on February 1, 2023 for $1,000. Matteo gives the stamp to his daughter, Anne, on April 1, 2023, for her 25th birthday. Anne lists the stamp online and sells it on May 1, 2023 for $1,500. Since Matteo only held the stamp for two months before giving it to Anne, and Anne only held the stamp for a month, their combined holding period is less than a year. Anne has a short-term capital gain on the stamp ($1,500 sale price - $1,000 transferred basis). Anne's gain will be taxed at ordinary income rates. She will be required to report the sale on Schedule D and Form 8949.

---

[87] A divorce, for this purpose, also includes the end of a marriage by annulment or due to violations of state laws, such as bigamy.

Example: Shira's father, Logan, gives her 50 shares of IBM stock that he purchased ten years ago. Logan originally purchased the stock for $1,800. Shira's basis in the stock, for purposes of determining gain on any future sale, is also $1,800 (this is a transferred basis). Shira is also considered to have "held" the stock for ten years, the same amount of time that her father held the stock.

However, in situations where the fair market value of the property on the date of the gift is *less* than the transferred basis, the donee's basis for *gain* is the transferred basis. However, if the donee reports a *loss* on the sale of gifted property where the fair market value of the property on the date of the gift is less than the transferred basis, the basis is the FMV of gifted property on the date of the gift.

The sale of gifted property can also result in no gain or loss. This happens when the sale proceeds are greater than the gift's FMV but less than the transferred basis in situations where the fair market value of the property on the date of the gift is less than the transferred basis.

Example: Noah's aunt, Fatima, bought 100 shares of Fairway Airlines Inc. stock when it was at $92 per share. Fatima's basis for the 100 shares is $9,200. Fatima gives the stock to Noah when it is selling at $70 and has an FMV of $7,000 (it has lowered in value). In this case, Noah has a "dual basis" in the stock. He has one basis for purposes of determining gain, and a different basis for determining a loss. Here are three separate scenarios that help illustrate how the gain or loss would be calculated when Noah sells his gifted stock:

Scenario #1: If Noah sells the stock for *more* than his aunt's basis, he will use her basis to determine his amount of gain. For example, if he sells the stock for $11,000, he will report a gain of $1,800 ($11,000 - $9,200).

Scenario #2: If Noah sells the stock for *less* than the FMV of the stock at the time of the gift ($7,000 in the example), he will use as his basis the FMV at the time of the gift to determine the amount of his loss. For example, if the stock continues to decline, and Noah eventually sells it for $4,500, he can report a loss of $2,500 ($7,000 - $4,500).

Scenario #3: If Noah sells the stock for an amount *in between* the FMV and the donor's basis, no gain or loss will be recognized. For example, if Noah sells the stock for $8,000, there will be no gain or loss on the transaction (his basis will be deemed to be $8,000, the same as his sales price).

The Basis of Inherited Property

The basis of inherited property is treated very differently for tax purposes as compared to gifts. In most cases, the basis of inherited property is the fair market value of the property on the date of the decedent's death, regardless of what the deceased person paid for the property or the adjusted basis of the property right before death. In addition, when inherited property is sold by the beneficiary, it is deemed to have a long-term holding period, regardless of how long the beneficiary held it.

When inherited property is sold by a beneficiary, the gain will be calculated based on the change in value from the date of death. This usually results in a beneficial tax situation for anyone who inherits property because the taxpayer generally gets an increased or "stepped-up" basis.

Example: When Libby's uncle, Jonathan, passed away, she inherited 300 shares of stock that he had purchased for $850 twenty years ago. At the time of his death, the shares were valued at $19,000, so that is now Roseanne's basis. This is known as a "stepped up" basis. Three months after inheriting the stock, she sells all the shares for $21,000, resulting in a long-term capital gain of $2,000 ($21,000 - $19,000). Although she held the stock for less than a year, it is inherited property and therefore qualifies for beneficial tax treatment.

However, there are cases in which this rule can work against taxpayers. Although the value of most property such as stock, collectibles, and bonds, generally increases over time, there are also instances in which a property's value drops. This creates a "stepped-down" basis.

Example: Norbert purchased a home with cash in Connecticut for $240,000. His neighborhood becomes riddled with crime, and Norbert's home declines in value. On February 3, 2023, Norbert dies. On the date of his death, the home's FMV was only $198,000. Norbert's daughter, Nikki, inherits the home. Nikki's basis in the home is $198,000. This is a "stepped-down" basis situation.

Example: Anson bought 100 shares of stock many years ago for $10,000. In 2023, Anson dies, and his daughter, Haley, inherits her father's stock. On the date of Anson's death, the value of the stock had plummeted to $5,000, meaning Haley's basis in the stock is "stepped down" for tax purposes to $5,000. The stock continues to decline, so six months later, she sells the stock for $4,000. Haley has a long-term capital loss of $1,000 ($5,000 -$4,000), the difference between her inherited basis and the selling price.

Although the basis of an estate for estate tax purposes is usually determined on the date of death, a special rule allows the personal representative of the estate to elect a different valuation date of six months after the date of death. This is known as the *alternate valuation date*. To elect the alternate valuation date, the estate's value and related estate tax must be *less* than they would have been on the date of the taxpayer's death.

If the alternate valuation date has been elected for the estate, the basis for inherited assets is normally the fair market value of the assets six months after the date of death. However, if any assets are received from the estate less than six months after the date of death, the basis in these inherited assets is the fair market value as of the date the asset was distributed to the heir. If a federal estate tax return (Form 706) is not filed for the deceased taxpayer, the basis in the beneficiary's inherited property is the FMV value at the date of death, and the alternate valuation date does not apply.

Unit 6: Study Questions

(Test yourself first, then check the correct answers at the end of this quiz.)

1. Henry bought 1,000 shares of Pharmacology Corp. stock for $4 per share and paid an additional $70 in broker's commissions. What is Henry's overall basis in the stock?

A. $1,000
B. $3,930
C. $4,000
D. $4,070

2. Claudine owns a piece of land that she purchased several years ago for $250,000. The land is now worth $750,000. During the year, she borrows $500,000 from a bank to improve the property. She uses $260,000 of the loan to demolish two existing buildings on the property and clear the land for the construction of a stockyard and horse stable, which will begin next year. What is Claudine's basis in the land after the demolition is completed?

A. $250,000
B. $460,000
C. $510,000
D. $750,000

3. Ronald owns a valuable antique painting that he purchased at auction many years ago. This year, he wants to sell the painting, but he lost all the paperwork related to the purchase. He has no records of his basis and cannot remember the price he paid. If Ronald cannot determine his basis in the painting, the IRS will deem the basis to be:

A. Zero.
B. Fair market value.
C. Actual cost.
D. Average cost.

4. Yoshiko owns two shares of common stock in Singleton Toys, Inc. She bought one share for $30 in 2017 and the other for $45 in 2018. In 2023, the corporation distributed two additional shares of common stock for each share held (a 3-for-1 stock split). Yoshiko owns six shares after the stock split. How is Yoshiko's basis allocated between these six shares?

A. All six shares now have a basis of $12.50.
B. Three shares have a basis of $10 each, and three have a basis of $15 each.
C. The shares are all valued at $45 each.
D. Three shares have a basis of zero, and three shares have a basis of $30.

5. The basis of inherited property is generally:

A. The adjusted basis to the decedent.
B. The fair market value of the property on the date of the decedent's death.
C. The purchase price that the decedent paid.
D. Determined nine months after the death of the decedent.

6. Esteban owns a landscape design business. He installs artificial turf at a client's home and bills the client $1,500 for his services. After the installation, his client, Alice, receives a foreclosure notice and is unable to pay Esteban's bill. Alice has a pedigreed Golden Retriever show dog that just had puppies. The FMV of each puppy is $1,800. Esteban loves animals and decides to take one of the puppies as full payment on Alice's delinquent bill. What is Esteban's basis in his new dog?

A. $0
B. $300
C. $1,500
D. $1,800

7. On May 3, 2023, Brigit purchased 1,000 shares of Equity Industries, Inc. for $5,100, including the broker's commission. On August 14, 2023, she sold 500 shares for $3,300. What is the adjusted basis of the stock she *sold?*

A. $2,550
B. $3,255
C. $3,300
D. $5,100

8. Which of the following statements is *correct* about the basis of assets?

A. The basis of an asset is always equal to its cost.
B. Depreciation increases the basis of an asset.
C. The basis rules are the same for assets received through inheritance as those obtained by gift.
D. The cost basis of an asset generally includes sales tax and other expenses connected with the original purchase.

9. Four years ago, Rahul paid $1,050 for 100 shares of Silverton Corporation stock, plus an additional broker's commission of $50. During the year, Rahul received ten additional shares of Silverton stock as a nontaxable stock dividend. What is the adjusted basis of Rahul's stock at the end of the year?

A. $9 per share.
B. $10 per share.
C. $11 per share.
D. $25 per share.

10. Mackenzie purchases an empty lot at auction for $50,000. She puts down $15,000 in cash and finances the remaining $35,000 with a bank loan. The lot has a $4,000 tax lien against it for unpaid property taxes, which she also agrees to pay as a condition of the sale. What is Mackenzie's basis in the lot?

A. $19,000
B. $46,000
C. $50,000
D. $54,000

11. Manish buys a work truck for $15,000 to use in his carpentry business. He pays $5,000 as a downpayment and takes out a five-year auto loan for the remaining $10,000. In addition, he pays sales taxes and delivery fees of $1,300 and spends an extra $250 for a protective bedliner. What is Manish's basis for the depreciation on the truck?

A. $6,550
B. $10,000
C. $16,300
D. $16,550

12. During the year, Kaylie bought 52 total shares of Deerfield Corporation stock for $624. That cost included a $40 broker commission. Three months later, Deerfield Corporation issued a 2-for-1 stock split. What is her basis per share after the split?

A. $6 per share.
B. $12 per share.
C. $24 per share.
D. $26 per share.

13. Which of the following is added to a property's basis instead of deducted on the tax return?

A. Casualty loss.
B. Personal property tax based on the value of a car.
C. Investment interest expense.
D. The cost of demolishing a building.

14. Which of the following is *not* added to the basis of property?

A. Legal and accounting fees for transferring the title.
B. Points on a loan.
C. Sales tax.
D. Freight-in charges.

15. Mccoy bought one share of Sugar City Media, Inc. on January 1 for $45. On December 20, the corporation distributed two new shares of common stock for each share held. After the split, Mccoy had three shares of common stock. What is Mccoy's new basis per share?

A. $5
B. $15
C. $45
D. $135

16. Flora gifted her grandson, Clifford, a residential rental property. She had purchased the property ten years ago for $120,000 and has claimed $18,000 in depreciation. The fair market value of the rental house on the day of transfer was $144,000. Assuming no gift tax was paid, what is Clifford's basis in the property?

A. $102,000
B. $120,000
C. $126,000
D. $144,000

17. What happens to the adjusted basis of a property when it is transferred from one spouse to another due to a divorce?

A. The adjusted basis increases.
B. The adjusted basis decreases.
C. The adjusted basis remains the same.
D. The adjusted basis is split according to community property rules.

18. Vladimir wishes to sell a home that he inherited from his mother in 2023. His mother paid $45,000 for the home fifteen years ago. She put a new roof on the property two years ago at the cost of $10,500. The fair market value of the home on the date of his mother's death was $120,000. An estate tax return was not required for his mother's estate, and the alternate valuation date was not elected. What is Vladimir's basis in the inherited home?

A. $34,500
B. $45,000
C. $55,500
D. $120,000

Unit 6: Quiz Answers

1. The answer is D. The broker's commissions are added to the basis. Henry's basis in the Pharmacology Corp. stock is therefore, $4,070 ([1,000 × $4] = $4,000 + $70).

2. The answer is C. Claudine's basis in the land is calculated as follows: $250,000 (cost basis) + $260,000 (demolition costs) = $510,000. The loan amount is irrelevant because the act of borrowing alone does not increase the basis; the amount spent on the improvement of the property increases its basis.

3. The answer is A. If Ronald cannot determine his basis in the painting, the IRS will treat the asset as having a zero basis. To compute gain or loss on a sale, a taxpayer must determine his basis in the property sold. If he cannot determine his basis in the property, the IRS will deem the basis to be zero.

4. The answer is B. Yoshiko's shares are now valued as follows: three with a basis of $10 each ($30 ÷ 3), and three with a basis of $15 each ($45 ÷ 3). Yoshiko received a nontaxable stock dividend, so she must divide the adjusted basis of the old stock by the number of shares of old and new stock. The basis per share after the 3-for-1 stock split is calculated by dividing the original price by 3.

5. The answer is B. The basis of inherited property is generally the FMV of the property on the date of the decedent's death, regardless of what the deceased person paid for the property or the tax basis in the property in the hands of the decedent right before death.

6. The answer is C. Esteban's basis in the pedigreed animal is $1,500. If a taxpayer receives property as payment for services, he must include the property's FMV in income, and this becomes his basis in the property. However, if the two parties agree on a cost beforehand, the IRS will usually accept the agreed-upon cost as the asset's basis.

7. The answer is A. Brigit's original basis in the total stock was $5,100, which is $5.10 per share, so her basis in the 500 shares she sold is 500 × $5.10, or $2,550.

8. The answer is D. The cost basis of an asset includes sales tax and other expenses connected with the purchase. In most situations, the basis of an asset is its cost, including any sales tax, installation costs, or brokers' commissions paid. However, there are many other times when cost cannot be used to determine basis, such as when an asset is inherited or received as a gift. None of the other answers are correct.

> **Note:** Depreciation *reduces* the basis of an asset, the basis of an inherited asset is usually based on its FMV on the date of death, the basis of an appreciated asset received as a gift is the same as the person that gave the gift (i.e. a "transferred" basis), while the basis of an asset received as a gift where the FMV at the time of the gift is less than the gift provider's basis is a dual-basis for the person receiving the gift.

9. The answer is B. Rahul's original basis per share was $11 ([$1,050 + $50 broker's commission = $1,100] ÷ 100). After the stock dividend, his $1,100 basis must be spread over 110 shares (100 original shares plus the additional 10 shares). Therefore, if Rahul's basis in the stock was $1,100 for 100 shares, the ten additional shares mean Rahul's basis per share decreased to $10 per share ($1,100 ÷ 110).

10. The answer is D. Mackenzie's basis is determined as follows: ($50,000 + $4,000 = $54,000). She cannot deduct the delinquent property taxes on her Schedule A. Any obligations of the seller assumed by the buyer increase the basis of the asset and are not currently deductible. Since Mackenzie did not owe the property taxes, but she still agreed to pay them, she must add the property tax to the basis of the property.

11. The answer is D. Manish's basis in the truck includes the cost of acquiring the property (including any taxes associated with the purchase and delivery charges) and preparing it for use (in this case, installing the bedliner). Therefore, his basis is as follows: ($15,000 + $1,300 + $250) = $16,550. Any funds that are borrowed to pay for an asset are also included in the basis.

12. The answer is A. After the stock split, Kaylie's stock basis is $6 per share. The answer is figured as follows: initial cost:

> 52 shares = $624 ($40 broker commission already included in the basis)
> 2-for-1 stock split doubles the shares to 104 total shares
> $624 (original basis) ÷ 104 total shares = **$6 per share.**

13. The answer is D. Demolition costs are not deductible. They must be added to the basis of the land on which the building was located. The costs increase the basis of the land, and not the basis of any subsequent building that may be constructed on the property at a later date.

14. The answer is B. Points related to a loan used to acquire property may be deductible in the year they are paid or amortizable over the term of the loan. Points are a type of mortgage interest. They are not added to the basis of the property.

15. The answer is B. Mccoy's basis in each share after the stock dividend is $15 ($45 ÷ 3). If a taxpayer receives a nontaxable stock dividend, they must divide the adjusted basis of the stock by the total number of shares of stock. The result is the taxpayer's basis for each share of stock.

16. The answer is A. Clifford's basis is $102,000. The basis of gifted property for the donee is generally equal to the donor's adjusted basis, which is called a "transferred basis," when its FMV exceeds the donor's basis ($120,000 minus $18,000 depreciation = $102,000) at the time of the gift. While not the case here, if the fair market value of the property on the date of the gift is *less* than the transferred basis, the donee's basis for gain is the transferred basis. However, if the donee reports a loss on the sale of gifted property when the fair market value of the property on the date of the gift is less than the transferred basis, his basis is the lower of: the transferred basis *or* the FMV of the property on the date of the gift.

17. The answer is C. The adjusted basis remains the same. When property is transferred from one spouse to another in a divorce, the receiving spouse's basis in the property remains the same. Typically, there will be no tax implications for this type of transfer.

18. The answer is D. Vladimir's basis in the home is $120,000, the FMV on the date of his mother's death. Heirs can generally use a stepped-up basis for inherited property, regardless of what the deceased person actually paid for the asset. The improvements that his mother made while she was still alive are also irrelevant in Vladimir's basis calculation. The basis of inherited property is generally the FMV of the property on the date of the decedent's death.

Unit 7: Capital Gains and Losses

For additional information, read:
Publication 550, *Investment Income and Expenses*
Publication 523, *Selling Your Home*
Publication 544, *Sales and Other Dispositions of Assets*

Capital Assets

In the previous chapter, we covered assets in a general sense. This chapter will delve into capital gains and losses, which occur when a taxpayer sells or disposes of their capital assets. Personal or investment items are often considered "capital assets," meaning that any net gains from their sale may be subject to more favorable tax rates for capital gains.

The specific rate depends on factors such as how long the asset was held, what type of asset it is, and the taxpayer's income bracket. Some examples of common individual-owned capital assets include a primary residence or vacation home, furniture, vehicles, boats, antiques and collectibles,[88] stocks, bonds, mutual funds (excluding those held by professional securities dealers), and cryptocurrency or virtual currency.[89]

Losses from the sale of *personal-use* property, such as a main home, a vacation home, personal-use furniture, or jewelry, are not deductible. However, *gains* from the sale of personal-use assets usually are taxable, subject to certain exclusions.

Example: Sanjay owns a station wagon that he uses to commute to work and run errands. He purchased the station wagon four years ago for $24,000. This year, he decides to buy a new vehicle, so he sells his station wagon to a private party for $13,000 in cash. Sanjay does not have to report the sale, and he cannot claim a loss from the sale since it is his personal-use vehicle.

Example: Judith collects antique coins as a hobby. She is not a professional coin dealer. Ten years ago, Judith purchased an antique Roman coin at an estate sale for $50. In 2023, she was offered $6,000 for the coin, and she promptly sells it for the offered price. Judith has a taxable capital gain of $5,950 that she must report on her tax return. Since she held the coin for more than one year, she may be eligible for favorable capital gains rates if her applicable tax rate on ordinary income happens to be greater than 28%.

How to Report the Sale of Capital Assets

Most people possess multiple assets, such as investments (stocks and bonds) and other valuable items like collectibles, primary residences, or vacation homes. The profit or loss for each asset is calculated individually, and the tax consequences vary depending on the type of asset sold. For capital assets, gains and losses are typically reported using two forms: Schedule D, *Capital Gains and Losses*, and Form 8949, *Sales and Other Dispositions of Capital Assets*.[90]

---

[88] Antiques and collectibles (such as artwork and coin collections), while normally capital assets for nondealers, have special tax rates applicable if they are sold at a gain and held greater than a year prior to sale. The tax rate on long-term capital gains on antiques and collectibles is taxed at the individual's ordinary tax rate, but at a maximum rate of 28%.

[89] IRS Notice 2014-21 states that, for federal tax purposes, virtual currency is treated as property.

[90] Capital assets include homes (such as personal residences and vacation homes), stocks, vehicles, coins, artwork, and other collectibles. In the case of individuals, a "capital asset" is typically anything the taxpayer owns for personal or investment purposes.

Schedule D is used to report gain or loss on the sale of investment property and most capital gain (or loss) transactions. The taxpayer may also have to complete Form 8949, *Sales and Other Dispositions of Capital Assets.* Form 8949 reports specific details about each sale the taxpayer makes during the year. Form 8949 is used to report the following:

- The sale or exchange of capital assets
- Gains from involuntary conversions (other than from casualty or theft)
- Nonbusiness bad debts and
- Worthless securities
- The election to defer capital gain invested in a qualified opportunity fund (QOF) and the disposition of interests in QOFs.

There are two parts to Form 8949. The first part is for short-term assets, and the second part is for long-term assets. This form must be filed along with Schedule D, which contains the summary of all capital gains and losses.

Example: Maura received both a Form 1099-S and a Form 1099-B in 2023. The 1099-S was for the sale of farmland, and the 1099-B was for the sale of stock. Maura also sold some cryptocurrency, but she did not receive an information statement for the sale. Maura should report all these transactions on Form 8949. The totals will be transferred to Schedule D, where all her capital transactions will be summarized and "netted" for the year.

Example: On August 1, 2023, Guadalupe received a collectible model train as a gift from her uncle, who originally purchased the train for $1,300 on January 1, 2023. Two months later, a collector offers Guadalupe $1,500 for the train, and Guadalupe decides to sell it. On her tax return, she reports $200 of short-term capital gain from the sale ($1,500 - $1,300) on Form 8949 and Schedule D. Since the train was held less than a year (adding up the time her uncle owned it and Guadalupe owned it), the gain will be short-term and taxed at ordinary income tax rates.

Certain sales and dispositions can be reported on Schedule D without also reporting them on Form 8949. This is only possible if the taxpayer received a Form 1099-B that reports the basis to the IRS and does not include any nondeductible wash sale losses. Additionally, no adjustments need to be made to the basis or type of gain or loss reported on Form 1099-B, or to their overall gain or loss.

Noncapital Assets

Assets held for business-use or created by a taxpayer for purposes of earning revenue (copyrights, inventory, etc.) are considered *noncapital* assets. The following assets are *noncapital* assets:

- Inventory or any similar property held for sale to customers
- Depreciable property used in a business, even if it is fully depreciated
- Real property used in a trade or business, such as a commercial building or a rental
- *Self-produced* copyrights, transcripts, manuscripts, photographs, or artistic compositions
- Accounts receivable or notes receivable acquired by a business
- Stocks and bonds held by stockbrokers and professional securities dealers
- Business supplies
- Commodities and derivative financial instruments

Gains and losses from the sale of business assets are typically reported on Form 4797, *Sales of Business Property*, and in the case of individual taxpayers, the amounts flow through to Form 1040, Schedule D, *Capital Gains and Losses.* However, the sale of the inventory is reported as ordinary income on the Schedule C (or Schedule F) and not as a sale of an asset on the Form 4797.

Example: Nolan is the sole proprietor of a fitness club. He reports his income and loss on Schedule C. In 2023, he sells several used treadmills in order to make room for new gym equipment. Since the used equipment was business property, Nolan reports the sales on Form 4797. Also, during the year, Nolan sells some stock at a substantial profit. He is a casual investor and not a professional stockbroker, so he must report his capital gains on Schedule D and Form 8949.

Example: Lester is a farmer who reports his earnings and expenses on Schedule F. In 2023, he sells a used farm tractor at a loss. The tractor is a noncapital asset, and the sale must be reported on Form 4797, *Sales of Business Property.* In addition, Lester also sells 7,000 bushels of wheat that he grew on his farm. Since the wheat is considered a farm product, it is classified as inventory. Any income from the sale of farm products grown and sold by a farmer must be reported on line 2 of Schedule F. This income will be subject to both income tax and self-employment tax.

Example: Gerald is a self-employed author who has written several popular children's books. During the year, he sells one of his copyrights to a large publisher. Since Gerald is the creator of the copyright, it is a noncapital asset in his hands. The copyright is not eligible for capital gains treatment, and Gerald will owe ordinary income tax on the sale. He must use Form 4797 to report the sale of the copyright. Also, during the year, Gerald sells his vacation home at a substantial loss. Gerald never rented the home and it was only used for family vacations. His vacation home is a capital asset, but since it is also *personal-use* property, he cannot deduct the loss.

Unlike capital assets, the costs of many noncapital assets may be deducted as business expenses when they are sold, and losses are generally fully deductible. Depending on the circumstances, a gain or loss on a sale or trade of property used in a trade or business may be treated as either capital or ordinary (this topic is covered in more detail in Book 2, Businesses).

Holding Period (Short-Term or Long-Term)

When a taxpayer disposes of investment property, such as stocks and bonds, the holding period affects the tax treatment. This is important because long-term capital gains are taxed at lower rates than short-term gains. If a taxpayer holds investment property for more than one year, any capital gain or loss is **long-term** capital gain or loss. If a taxpayer holds investment property for one year or less, any capital gain or loss is **short-term** capital gain or loss.

Long-term = <u>more</u> than one year (at least a year and a day)

Short-term = one year or less

To calculate the holding period of investment property, one must start counting on the day *after* they acquire the property and end on the day they sell it. The date of the sale is included in the holding period.

Example: Leesa bought 50 shares of XYZ stock on February 2, 2023, for $10,000. She sells all the shares on February 2, 2024, for $20,500. She held the stock for <u>exactly one year</u>. Since Leesa's holding period is not *more* than one year, she has a *short-term* capital gain of $10,500. The short-term gain is taxed at ordinary income tax rates. If Leesa had waited just a few more days to sell the stock, she would have received long-term capital gain treatment, and the gain would have been taxed at a lower rate.

Example: Zoran bought 100 shares of ABC stock on January 1, 2023, for $1,200. To determine his holding period, Zoran must start counting his holding period on January 2, 2023 (the day *after* the purchase). He sells all the stock on January 5, 2024, for $2,850. Zoran's holding period exceeds one year, and therefore, he will recognize a long-term capital gain of $1,650 in 2024, the year in which he actually sold the stock ($2,850 - $1,200).

Stock shares acquired because of a nontaxable stock dividend or stock-split[91] have the same holding period as the original shares owned.

Example: Five years ago, Cagney bought 500 shares of Stellar, Inc. stock for $1,500. On June 6, 2023, Stellar, Inc. distributes a 2% nontaxable stock dividend (10 additional shares). Three days later, Cagney sells all his Stellar, Inc. stock for $2,300. Although Cagney owned the 10 shares he received as a nontaxable stock dividend for only three days, a long-term holding period applies to all of his shares. Because he bought the stock for $1,500 and then sold it for $2,300 more than a year later, Cagney has a long-term capital gain of $800 on the sale of the 510 shares.

The holding period for a gift is treated differently than the holding period for purchased property. If a taxpayer receives a gift of property, their holding period normally includes the donor's holding period. This concept is known as "tacking on" the holding period.

Example: Eugenia gives her nephew, Dustin, an acre of land. At the time of the gift, the land had an FMV of $23,000. Eugenia's adjusted basis in the land was $22,000. Gena only held the land for six months prior to making the gift. Dustin holds the land for another seven months. Neither held the property for over a year. Regardless, Dustin may "tack on" his holding period to his aunt's holding period. Therefore, if Dustin were to sell the property, he would have a long-term capital gain or loss, because jointly they held the property for 13 months, which is more than one year.

When a taxpayer acquires property through inheritance, it is automatically classified as long-term property. This means that even if a person sells their inherited property shortly after receiving it, the holding period for tax purposes will still be considered long-term. This rule applies regardless of the actual length of time the beneficiary or the decedent held the asset.

Example: Nella inherited a vacation home from her father, who died on February 10, 2023. The fair market value of the house was $210,000 on the date of her father's death. Nella immediately puts the house up for sale. On August 30, 2023, the house is sold for $215,000. Nella has a long-term capital gain of $5,000 on the sale. All the gain is treated as long-term, even though she held the property for only a few months, because inherited property is always treated as long-term.

---

[91] A stock split is when a corporation increases the number of its outstanding shares, generally to boost a stock's liquidity. A stock split revalues the price per share and increases the total number of shares by the issuance of additional shares to existing shareholders.

Example: Madeline purchased five gold bars as an investment on January 3, 2023, paying $10,300. Six months later, on July 3, 2023, Madeline dies, and her only son, Ezra, inherits her entire estate. On the date of Madeline's death, the gold bars were valued at $10,500. Ezra holds the gold bars for one more month, and then sells them to a pawn shop for $9,500. Ezra has a $1,000 long-term capital loss. The loss is treated as long-term, because inherited property is always treated as long-term, even if the decedent or the beneficiary does not hold the property for a year.

Determining Capital Gain or Loss

A taxpayer determines gain or loss on a sale or trade of stock or property by comparing the amount realized with the adjusted basis of the property. A disposition of stock and the related income or loss must always be reported in the year of the sale, regardless of when the taxpayer actually receives the proceeds.

Example: When Madden receives his Form 1099-B, it shows that he sold 600 shares of Centrex, Inc. on September 25, 2023 for a net sales price of $1,200. He had purchased the stock six years earlier for $1,455. As a result, Madden will report a capital loss of $255 on Schedule D.

Capital losses are *netted* against any capital gains that may be generated in the same year. A taxpayer can deduct up to $3,000 ($1,500 for MFS) of *net* capital losses against ordinary income in a tax year. Unused losses above this limit are carried over to subsequent years.

Example: Lucas purchased 100 shares of stock three years ago for $16,000. His stock declines in value, and he sells all the shares in 2023 for $9,000, generating a $7,000 long-term capital loss on the sale. He also earned $60,000 of wages during the year. He can claim $3,000 of his long-term capital loss against his ordinary income, thereby lowering his gross income to $57,000 ($60,000 - $3,000). The remainder of the long-term capital loss ($4,000) must be carried forward to the following year.

Carryover losses are combined with gains and losses that occur in the next year. A taxpayer first nets short-term capital gains and losses (including carryover losses) against each other, and then long-term capital gains and losses (including carryover losses) against each other. The results are then *netted* against each other, if applicable.

Any net capital losses carried over retain their character as either long-term or short-term and are reported on Schedule D. Thus, a long-term capital loss carried over to the next tax year will reduce that year's long-term capital gains before it reduces that year's short-term capital gains.

A net capital loss can be carried over indefinitely during the taxpayer's life. However, once a taxpayer dies, the capital losses not used on the final return cannot be carried over to a beneficiary or an heir. Capital losses always belong to the decedent. Any capital loss carryovers that are not used on the taxpayer's final return are lost forever.

Example: Ethan has $13,000 of capital losses from the sale of cryptocurrency in 2023. On December 20, 2023, Ethan dies. His executor may claim the capital losses on Ethan's final individual tax return, up to the allowable limit. However, any unused capital losses cannot be carried over to a future year, because Ethan is dead. The losses do not transfer to Ethan's estate or to his heirs.

Digital assets, such as cryptocurrencies and nonfungible tokens (NFTs), are typically treated as property and their sale or disposition generally results in capital gain or loss. Exchanging one digital asset for another is generally treated as a disposition and is a fully taxable event.

Example: On April 30, 2023, Kaito exchanged $63,000 of Bitcoin for $63,000 of Ethereum. The Bitcoin was purchased in 2018 for $7,800. Kaito has a long-term capital gain of $55,200 on the exchange. Also, on May 10, 2023, Kaito sells Litecoin for $3,820. Kaito had purchased Litecoin (another type of cryptocurrency) on February 10, 2023, for $9,660 cash (purchased and sold in the same year). Kaito, therefore, has a $5,840 short-term capital loss on the sale of Litecoin. His losses and gains are "netted" for the year. Kaito will report a net long-term capital gain of $49,360.

Digital Asset	Basis	Sale or Exchange Price	Gain or (Loss)
Bitcoin	$7,800	$63,000	Long-term gain: $55,200
Litecoin	$9,660	$3,820	Short-term loss: ($5,840)
Kaito's Net Capital Gain:			**$49,360**

Special rules apply to married couples. Married taxpayers are at a disadvantage when deducting capital losses. On a joint return, the net capital loss deduction limit is still $3,000, which is the same limit for unmarried taxpayers. And MFS filers only get half of that limit (a $1,500 capital loss limit can be offset against other income).

Example: Ariana purchased 100 shares of BMC, Inc. stock two years ago for $6,800. The stock declines in value, and she sells all her BMC shares on December 20, 2023, for $4,000, resulting in a $2,800 capital loss. She is married, but files separately from her husband. Ariana has $52,000 in wages for the year. Since she is filing MFS, Ariana can only claim $1,500 of her long-term capital loss against her ordinary income, thereby lowering her gross income to $50,500 ($52,000 - $1,500). The remainder of the long-term capital loss ($1,300) must be carried forward to the following tax year.

Example: Monique and Jerrod are married and live in Florida, a non-community property state. They keep their income separate and plan to file separate returns (MFS). In 2023, Monique sells some stock that she owns and incurs a ($5,000) capital loss. Jerrod also sells some stock and has a $12,500 capital gain. Monique can only claim ($1,500) of her loss on her tax return because she is filing MFS. Jerrod cannot use any of Monique's losses on his return, because they are filing separate returns. Jerrod must pay tax on his entire capital gain on his separate tax return. If they had instead chosen to file *jointly*, then their capital losses would have "offset" each other, which would have reduced the amount of their taxable gain to $7,500 ($12,500 Jerrod's capital gain - $5,000 Monique's capital loss).

Capital Gains from Mutual Funds

A mutual fund is a regulated investment company generally created by pooling funds of investors to allow them to take advantage of a diversity of investments and professional management. Two different types of transactions may result in taxable capital gains reporting by a taxpayer who invests in mutual funds. First, profits resulting from investments made by the fund itself are reported to its own shareholders as capital gain distributions on Form 1099-DIV. The capital gain distributions are always taxed at long-term capital gains tax rates, without regard to how long a taxpayer has owned shares in the mutual fund.

If a taxpayer disposes of shares that represent all or a portion of his investment in the mutual fund itself, a Form 1099-B will be issued. The taxable gain or loss that results from the sale or exchange of the taxpayer's shares in the mutual fund is reported on Form 1040, Schedule D. Brokers are now required to include the basis of mutual funds on Form 1099-B.

Wash Sales

A "wash sale" occurs when an investor sells a security to claim a capital loss, only to repurchase it again very soon thereafter. A taxpayer cannot deduct a loss on the sale of an investment if a substantially identical investment is purchased within 30 days *before* or *after* the sale.[92] A wash sale is considered to have occurred when a taxpayer sells a security at a loss and, within 30 days:

- Buys the identical security,
- Acquires a "substantially identical" security in a taxable trade, or
- Acquires a contract or option to buy the identical security.

If a taxpayer's loss is disallowed because of the wash sale rules, he must add the disallowed loss to the basis of the new stock or securities. The result is an increase in the taxpayer's basis in the new stock or securities.

This adjustment postpones the loss deduction until the later disposition of the new stock or securities. These rules apply only to stocks and securities.[93] It is considered a wash sale if a taxpayer sells stock and the taxpayer's spouse then repurchases identical stock within 30 days, even if the couple chooses to file separate tax returns.

> **Example:** Malcolm sells 800 shares of Quanta Corporation stock on December 4, 2023, resulting in a loss of $3,200. He immediately regrets selling the stock, so on January 2, 2024, (less than a month later) he repurchases 800 shares of Quanta stock through his online trading account. Because of the wash sale rules, all of the $3,200 loss is disallowed. He must add the disallowed loss to the basis of the newly purchased shares. He cannot take the disallowed loss until he finally sells the repurchased shares at some later time.

In situations where only a portion of the stock is repurchased during the applicable wash sale period, only the percentage of the shares repurchased will be used to determine the amount of the disallowed loss.

> **Example:** Ayami sells 1,000 shares of Hampstead Corporation stock on July 4, 2023, resulting in a loss of $5,000. She regrets selling all of her stock, and less than a month later, on August 1, 2023, she repurchases 200 shares of Hampstead stock on the open market. Because of the IRS wash sale rules, 20% of the $5,000 realized loss, $1,000, is disallowed, but the remaining $4,000 loss may be recognized.

---

[92] The "wash sale" period is technically 61 days long, from 30 days *before* the date of the sale to 30 days *after*.
[93] Wash sales are governed by §1091 of the Internal Revenue Code. At the time of this book's printing, the wash sale rules in §1091 do not apply to cryptocurrency or any other type of digital asset. Bitcoin and other cryptocurrencies are currently classified as property, not securities, by the IRS. The wash sale rules also do not apply to commodity futures contracts and foreign currency trading.

The wash sale rules do not apply to professional securities dealers or stockbrokers.[94]

> **Example:** Melville is a full-time securities dealer with professional trader status. His sole business consists of trading in securities. He properly made a mark-to-market election (Sec. 475 election) several years ago. Melville trades stocks and bonds all year, for himself as well as his clients. He manages dozens of investment accounts. His trades are not subject to the wash sale rules. Melville's losses from the sales of stocks and other securities are treated as ordinary losses, and his gains are treated as ordinary income, as well. He would report his business activity on Schedule C.

For purposes of the wash sale rules, securities of one corporation are not considered identical to securities of another corporation. This means that a person can sell shares in one corporation and then purchase shares in a different corporation, and this will not trigger a wash sale. Similarly, preferred stock of a corporation is not considered identical to the common stock of the same corporation.

> **Example:** Oswald is not a professional securities dealer, but he owns stock in many different companies. On February 1, 2023, Oswald sells 200 shares of common stock in Frontline Manufacturing, Inc. for a $2,300 loss. A month later, on March 1, Oswald purchases 200 shares of preferred stock in the same company. Common stock and preferred stock are not considered "substantially identical" securities, so these transactions are not subject to the wash sale rules. Oswald is permitted to recognize the $2,300 capital loss in 2023.

Home Sale Gain or Loss

The rules for selling a primary residence are beneficial for taxpayers. Typically, selling a home does not result in a taxable gain. However, there are specific guidelines for when a taxpayer sells their main residence. We will discuss these rules in more detail in the chapter on nonrecognition property transactions. For now, we will focus on how to calculate a home's basis. The following are used to determine the basis and the gain (or loss) on a home sale:

- Selling price
- Amount realized
- Basis
- Adjusted basis

Selling Price: The total selling price for a main home includes all forms of payment received by the taxpayer, such as cash, notes, mortgages, or other debts assumed by the buyer. The fair market value of any additional property or services given to the seller also contributes to the selling price. Typically, Form 1099-S, *Proceeds from Real Estate Transactions,* is used to report real estate sales proceeds. If this form is not received, taxpayers must rely on sale documents like the HUD-1 and other records.

Amount Realized: The "amount realized" is calculated by subtracting selling expenses from the sales price. Expenses can include: realtor's commissions, advertising fees, legal fees, and loan charges paid by the seller, such as points.

---

[94] Professional securities dealers report their business expenses on Schedule C (Form 1040). Per IRS Revenue Procedure 99-17, in order to claim ordinary gains and loss treatment on the sale of securities, a professional securities dealer must make the mark-to-market election (a Sec. 475(f) election) by the original due date (not including extensions) of the tax return for the year prior to the year for which the election becomes effective.

Basis in a Home: The basis of a residence is determined by how the owner of the home acquired the property. For instance, if an individual purchases a home, their basis would be the cost of the home. If an individual constructs a home, their basis would be the building expenses plus the cost of the land. In cases where an individual inherits a property, their basis would typically be its fair market value on the date of the previous owner's death or on the later alternate valuation date selected by the representative for the estate. And if an individual receives a home as a gift, their basis would typically be the donor's adjusted basis at the time of the gift.

Adjusted Basis: The adjusted basis is the taxpayer's basis in the home increased or decreased by certain amounts. Increases include additions or improvements to the home that have a useful life of more than one year. Repairs that simply maintain a home in good condition are not considered improvements and should not be added to the basis of the property. Decreases to basis include deductible casualty losses, credits, and product rebates.[95]

The formula for figuring adjusted basis:
Basis + Increases - Decreases = Adjusted Basis
Example: Raphael purchased his home ten years ago for $125,000. In 2023, he added another bathroom and an outdoor pool to the property at a cost of $25,000. Raphael's adjusted basis in his home after these improvements is $150,000 ($125,000 purchase price + $25,000 improvements).

If the amount realized on the sale of a home is *less* than the adjusted basis, the difference is a nondeductible loss. If the amount realized is *more* than the adjusted basis of the property, the difference is a gain (but not always a *taxable* gain).

As we will cover later, the taxpayer may be able to exclude all or part of the gain. If not excluded, and the taxpayer owns a home for one year or less, the gain is reported as a short-term capital gain. If the taxpayer owns the home for more than one year, the gain is reported as a long-term capital gain.

> **Example:** Misty is 49 years old and unmarried. She sells her main home for $350,000. She purchased the home ten years ago for $50,000 and has lived in it continuously since then. She pays $4,000 in realtor's fees to sell the home. Her amount realized in the sale is $346,000 ($350,000 - $4,000 = $346,000). Her basis is subtracted from her amount realized to figure her gain: ($346,000 - $50,000 basis) = $296,000.

Related Party Transaction Rules

Special regulations are in place for transactions between related parties. If a taxpayer sells an asset to a family member or a business they own, they may not qualify for the full benefits of capital gains tax rates and may be limited in deducting their losses. These rules were established to prevent the transfer of assets between related persons or entities for the purpose of claiming improper losses.

In general, a loss on the sale of property between related parties is not deductible. When the property is later sold to an unrelated party by the original party buyer, a *gain* is recognized by the related party buyer only to the extent it is more than the disallowed loss to the original party seller.

---

[95] Depreciation reduces the basis of business assets, such as rental property or commercial buildings. Depreciation is never taken on personal-use property, such as a primary residence.

However, if the property is later sold at a *loss* by the original party buyer, the loss that was disallowed to the related party cannot be recognized.

> **Example:** On February 2, 2023, Roxie purchases 10 shares of stock from her father, Eugene, for $8,600. Eugene's basis in the stock is $11,000, which means he sold the stock to his daughter at a loss, but Eugene cannot claim that loss on his tax return because it was a related-party sale. The stock continues to decline in value, and Roxie eventually sells the stock on the open market for $6,900 on December 10, 2023. Her recognized loss is $1,700 (her $8,600 basis - $6,900 sales price). Roxie cannot deduct the loss that was disallowed to her father.

In the case of a related party transaction, if a taxpayer sells *multiple* pieces of property and some are at a gain while others are at a loss, the gains will generally be taxable while the losses cannot be used to offset the gains.

More Than "50% Control" Rule: If a taxpayer has majority control (**more than** 50%) of a corporation, partnership, or other business entity, any property transactions between the taxpayer and the business are subject to related party transaction rules. This means that if a taxpayer sells or trades property at a loss (except in the complete liquidation of a corporation), the loss cannot be deducted if the transaction involves any of the following related parties:

- Immediate family members, such as a spouse, siblings, and direct ancestors (e.g., parents, grandparents), and lineal descendants (i.e., grandchildren). For purposes of this rule, the following are not considered related parties: uncles, aunts, nephews, nieces, cousins, step-children, step-parents, in-laws, and ex-spouses.
- Partnership, corporation, or other business entity that is controlled by the taxpayer. "Control" is defined as having "more than 50%" ownership in the entity. This also includes ownership by other family members.
- A tax-exempt organization that is controlled by the taxpayer or a member of their family.
- A closely-related trust, or business entities controlled by the same owners.

> **Example:** Selma buys 300 shares of stock from her brother, Spencer, for $7,600. Spencer's cost basis in the stock is $10,000. Spencer cannot deduct the loss of $2,400 because of the related party transaction rules. Later, Selma sells the same stock on the open market for $10,500, realizing a gain of $2,900. Selma's reportable gain is $500 (the $2,900 gain minus the $2,400 loss that was not previously allowed to her brother).

> **Example:** Irene sells 100 shares of stock to her step-brother, Saul, for $5,000. She originally paid $8,000 for the stock, so she recognizes a $3,000 capital loss on the transaction. Since her stepbrother is not considered a "related party" for IRS purposes, she is allowed to claim the full loss on her tax return.

Installment Sales

An installment sale is a type of financing arrangement. It is essentially a seller-financed purchase of a capital asset in which at least one payment is expected to be received after the tax year in which the sale occurs. The most common type of installment sale is the sale of business real estate (i.e., farmland, rental properties, office buildings). Other common installment sales include the sale of a small business, and the sale of intangibles (such as a patent, client list, trademark, or a website).

Installment sales are reported on Form 6252, *Installment Sale Income*, which is attached to the taxpayer's Form 1040. A taxpayer may also be required to complete Schedule D or Form 4797, depending on the type of asset that is being sold.

Example: Tammy is a successful enrolled agent who is retiring in 2023. She decides to sell her tax business to Palmer. Tammy will sell her existing client list, her office furniture, and her existing website to Palmer for an agreed contract price of $375,000. Tammy agrees to carry the note, and Palmer will make annual payments to Tammy over three years, starting in 2023. This is an installment sale.

Example: Cooper owns a valuable website domain that he bought several years ago as an investment. A potential buyer contacts him and offers a price of $1 million for the domain. Cooper originally bought the domain for $600,000. Cooper will recognize a gross profit of $400,000 which means his gross profit percentage is 40% on the sale ($400,000/$1 million = 40%). The buyer strikes a deal with Cooper where he can make annual installment payments over the next 6 years. This is an installment sale.

If a taxpayer sells property and receives payments over multiple years, the seller may use the installment method to defer tax by only reporting a portion of the gain as each installment is received. The installment sale method is the *default* method in this situation, unless the taxpayer *elects* to report all gain in the year of sale. If a seller "elects out" of the installment method, the seller must report all the gain in the year of the sale. If applicable, any depreciation recapture must also be recognized in full in the year of the sale. Each payment received on an installment sale typically consists of the following three parts:

- Interest income
- Return of the adjusted basis in the property
- Gain on the sale (determined by applying the gross profit percentage to the amount of the payment received minus the interest portion)

Each year the seller receives a payment, they must report the interest income and the portion of the payments that relate to their gain on the sale. A taxpayer's gain, or gross profit, is the amount by which the selling price exceeds the adjusted basis in the property sold. A gross profit percentage is calculated by dividing the gross profit from the sale by the selling price. The seller does not get taxed on the portion that is the return of their basis in the property.

Example: Marisol owns a parcel of timberland that she inherited from her grandfather. Her basis in the timberland is $40,000. She sells the land for $100,000 to an unrelated person in a private-party sale. Rather than involve a bank, Marisol agrees to carry the buyer's note. This way, she can earn some interest on the sale, and her gains will be spread out over several years, lessening the tax impact. Her overall gross profit on the sale is $60,000 ($100,000 sale price - $40,000 basis) for a gross profit percentage of 60%. She receives a $20,000 down payment and the buyer's note for $80,000 at the time of the sale. In 2023, Marisol must report a $12,000 gain allocated from the down payment she received. The note provides for four annual payments of $20,000 each, *plus* 8% interest, starting in January, 2023. Exclusive of the interest income, she must report $12,000 of her installment gain for each $20,000 payment received ($20,000 × .60 = $12,000). [Based on an example in Publication 537, *Installment Sales*].

The selling price includes the cash and any other property to be received from the buyer, any existing mortgage or debt the buyer pays or assumes, and any selling expenses the buyer pays. However, if the buyer assumes or pays off an existing mortgage on the property, the calculation of gross profit percentage is affected. The mortgage assumption is considered a recovery of basis in the year of sale and is subtracted before calculating the gross profit percentage, except to the extent that it exceeds the adjusted basis of the property for installment sale purposes.

In contrast, if the property is sold to a buyer who holds a mortgage on it and the mortgage is canceled rather than assumed, the cancellation is treated as a payment received in the year of the sale and is not subtracted in calculating the gross profit percentage.

If installment payments are made according to a schedule other than what was originally agreed, income is recognized according to the actual payments received. However, if the parties subsequently agree to adjust the selling price, the gross profit percentage must be recalculated, and income from future installments must be recognized based upon the adjusted gross profit.

Sometimes, a taxpayer may choose to elect out of the installment method on purpose. This is especially true if they anticipate their future tax rates to be higher.

Example: Pablo sells an acre of farmland to Marissa, an unrelated person. The sale price of the land is $100,000 and Pablo's basis in the farmland is $20,000. Marissa will make equal payments to Pablo over five years. This is an installment sale. Pablo's marginal tax rate in 2023 is relatively low, but he recently got a high-paying job, so he expects his tax rate in future years to be much higher. Pablo decides to elect out of the installment method, and reports all the gain from the sale in 2023, even though he has not received all the payments yet. In this way, he expects to save substantially on his taxes in future years.

The installment method cannot be used for publicly-traded securities, such as stocks and bonds that are traded on an established securities market (i.e., NASDAQ or the New York Stock Exchange). A taxpayer must report the gain on the sale of securities in the year of the sale regardless of whether the proceeds are received in the following year. However, stock in a private company, such as a small corporation that is being sold to a private buyer, can qualify for the installment method.

Example: Jorge owns 500 shares of Roca-Cola stock, which he sells at a $7,000 gain on December 29, 2023, through his online brokerage account. The proceeds of the sale were not deposited into his bank account until January 3, 2024. Jorge must report the gain on the sale of the stock on his 2023 tax return, *not* his 2024 return. He cannot delay reporting the gain, and the sale is not an installment sale.

The installment sale rules also <u>do not</u> apply to property that is <u>sold at a loss</u>, or to the sale of inventory.

Example: Preston owns a pawn shop, where he sells a variety of collectibles, toys, and jewelry. All of the items that Preston has in his showroom are inventory, and available for sale to the public. He sells a group of paintings to a collector for $200,000 in 2023. Preston allows the buyer to make payments over the course of three years. The sale is not an installment sale, because the paintings are inventory in his shop.

Installment sales to related persons are permitted. However, if a taxpayer sells a property to a related person who then sells or disposes of the property within two years of the original sale, the seller will lose the benefit of installment sale reporting (although there are exceptions to this rule for involuntary conversions or death of the original seller or buyer).

> **Example:** Lorne sells a plot of farmland to his daughter, Mindy. The sale price is $25,000, and Lorne realizes a profit on the sale of $10,000 (he paid $15,000 for the land). Mindy agrees to pay in five installments of $5,000. A year later, Mindy decides she no longer wants the land, and she sells the land to another, unrelated person. Lorne must report the entire profit of $10,000 on the sale, even though he may not have received all the installment payments. The installment sale method is disallowed on the related-party sale because the property was disposed of during the two-year holding period.

Special Rules for Worthless Securities

A loss from worthless securities receives special tax treatment.[96] A taxpayer may choose to "abandon" a security that has lost its entire value in order to take advantage of the loss for tax purposes rather than retaining ownership. Stocks, stock rights, and bonds (other than those held for sale by a securities dealer) that became worthless during the tax year are treated as though they were sold for zero dollars on the last day of the tax year.

Unlike other losses, a taxpayer is allowed to amend a tax return for up to seven years in order to claim a loss from worthless securities. This is more than double the usual three-year statute of limitations for amending returns.

To "abandon" a worthless security, a taxpayer must permanently surrender all rights to it and receive no consideration in exchange. Taxpayers should report worthless securities on Form 8949 and indicate as a worthless security deduction by writing "WORTHLESS" in the applicable column of Form 8949.

> **Example:** Leandro owns 500 shares of Crossroad Corporation stock. The company files for bankruptcy, and the bankruptcy court extinguishes all rights of the former shareholders. Leandro learns of the bankruptcy court's decision on December 20, 2023. Rather than wait for a formal notice from the court, he chooses to abandon all his Crossroad securities, knowing that his shares are essentially worthless. He takes a capital loss on his 2023 tax return, reflecting the value of his worthless shares as "zero."

> **Example:** Gerri owns 2,000 shares of DMX Manufacturing, Inc. She purchased the stock five years ago for $7,500. In 2023, the company files for bankruptcy, and Gerri's stock becomes worthless. She chooses to abandon the securities to take a tax deduction in 2023. Then she reports the valueless stock on Form 8949 and treats the abandonment as a sale. For the sale date, she puts December 31, 2023, and she lists her proceeds as $0. She now has a long-term capital loss of ($7,500) that she can use to offset other taxable income.

---

[96] On January 13, 2023, the IRS Office of Chief Counsel published Memorandum 202302011 stating that a taxpayer that owns cryptocurrency that has substantially declined in value cannot deduct a cryptocurrency loss under section 165 due to worthlessness of the cryptocurrency.

Note: Once a corporation has been delisted from a stock exchange as a result of bankruptcy, the stockholder will usually have the option to fill out a worthless securities processing request. Some brokerage firms will purchase worthless stock for a nominal amount (such as a penny), to provide closure and an official sale date to the customer on their brokerage statement.[97]

Special Rules for Sec. 1244 Small Business Stock

Section 1244 stock is a special type of investment that is subject to beneficial tax treatment. If a taxpayer's stock qualifies as Section 1244 stock, and sells that stock for a loss, up to $50,000 of the loss ($100,000 if MFJ) may be treated as an ordinary loss instead of a capital loss. The benefit of this provision is that the loss is not subject to the $3,000 "loss limitation" that normally applies to capital losses. Section 1244 stock means stock in a domestic corporation if:

- At the time such stock is issued, such corporation was a "small business corporation" (discussed below),
- Such stock was issued by the corporation for money or other property, and
- The corporation, during the five year period preceding the loss year, derived more than 50 percent of its aggregate gross receipts from sources other than royalties, rents, dividends, interests, annuities, and sales or exchanges of stocks or securities.

A corporation is a "small business corporation" only for purposes of Section 1244 stock if the aggregate amount of money and other property received by the corporation for stock, as a contribution to capital, and as paid-in surplus, does not exceed $1,000,000.

Note that only the original shareholders of the stock of the corporation while it was still a small business corporation are allowed to take advantage of the ordinary loss provisions of Section 1244 (i.e., if an original shareholder sells or transfers the stock to another taxpayer, Section 1244 status of the stock does not carry over to the other party).

Example: Marigold is one of the original founding shareholders in Acorn Energy Corp, Inc. a small, domestic C Corporation. She sold 20 shares in Acorn Energy Corp, Inc., which qualified as Section 1244 stock. She sold the stock for $35,000, and her basis in the 20 shares was $50,000. Her only other income for the year was $95,000 in wages. Marigold can deduct the entire ($15,000) loss as an ordinary loss on her tax return, and not as a capital loss. She can deduct the full amount of the loss, because it is not limited to the normal $3,000 "loss limit" that applies to normal capital losses.

---

[97] "Worthless securities" are stocks or bonds that have a market value of zero. A taxpayer may treat worthless securities as though they were sold or exchanged on the last day of the tax year.

Unit 7: Study Questions

(Test yourself first, then check the correct answers at the end of this quiz.)

1. Caleb bought ten shares of Atomic Corporation stock on January 1, 2023. He sold all the shares for a $7,000 loss on December 31, 2023. He has no other capital gains or losses. He also has $20,000 of wage income during the year. How must Caleb treat this transaction on his tax return?

A. He can deduct the $7,000 as a long-term capital loss on his return.
B. He can deduct the $7,000 as a short-term capital loss on his return.
C. He can deduct $3,000 as a short-term capital loss to offset his wage income on his return. The remaining amount, $4,000, must be carried over to future tax years.
D. He cannot deduct any of the capital loss; it must be carried over to future tax years.

2. Simeon owns 100% of the stock in TOP Corporation. Gerald owns 100% of the stock in DAB Corporation. In 2023, TOP Corporation sold used manufacturing equipment to DAB Corporation at a $52,000 loss. Simeon and Gerald are stepbrothers. Concerning the related party transaction loss rules, how should this transaction between Simeon and Gerald be handled?

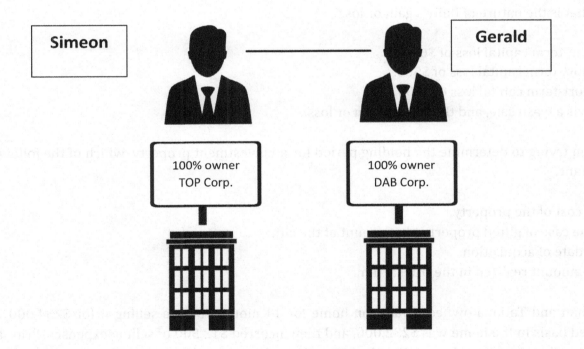

A. Any losses on the sale of property between the corporations would be disallowed, and the transaction would be treated as a constructive dividend to Simeon.
B. The related party transaction rules do not apply to their corporations, but they would apply individually to Simeon and Gerald, resulting in taxable income to each of them.
C. The related party transaction rules apply individually to Simeon and Gerald, but not to their corporations.
D. The related party transaction rules do not apply in this scenario.

3. Which of the following losses is deductible?

A. A loss on the sale of a primary residence.
B. A loss on the sale of a vacation home.
C. A loss on the sale of rental property.
D. A loss on the sale of a personal-use mobile home.

4. Marsha bought 100 shares of stock two years ago. She sold all the stock on February 10, 2023. Marsha's original cost for the stock was $10,110 plus an additional $35 in broker's fees. When she sold the stock, she received gross proceeds of $8,859. What is the net gain (or loss) from this transaction?

A. $1,286 long-term capital loss.
B. $1,286 short-term capital gain.
C. $1,251 long-term capital loss.
D. $1,251 long-term capital gain.

5. Rajiv bought 100 shares of stock on February 1, 2022, when the share price was $26. He sold the stock for $20 a share on February 1, 2023 (exactly one year later). How should this trade be reported, and what is the nature of Rajiv's gain or loss?

A. A long-term capital loss of $600.
B. A short-term capital loss of $500.
C. A short-term capital loss of $600.
D. This is a wash sale, and there is no gain or loss.

6. When trying to determine the holding period for an investment property, which of the following is important?

A. The cost of the property.
B. In the case of gifted property, the amount of the gift.
C. The date of acquisition.
D. The amount realized in the transaction.

7. Roshan and Tatiana owned a vacation home for 14 months before selling it for $254,000. Their adjusted basis in the home was $232,000, and they incurred $12,500 of selling expenses. Prior to the sale, they did not rent the home. What is the nature and amount of their gain?

A. $22,000 long-term capital gain.
B. $9,500 long-term capital gain.
C. $9,500 short-term capital gain.
D. $34,500 long-term capital gain.

8. What is the maximum number of years a taxpayer can carry over an unused capital loss?

A. One year.
B. Two years.
C. Five years.
D. Indefinitely.

9. Melissa purchased 1,000 shares of Sunshine Foods, Inc. stock five years ago at $10 per share. She sold 900 shares on January 15, 2023, at $9 per share, resulting in a $900 loss. Melissa's husband, Singh, purchased 900 shares of Sunshine Foods Inc. stock on February 10, 2023. Singh and Melissa keep their finances separate and will file separate tax returns. Which of the following statements is correct?

A. Melissa can deduct the $900 capital loss on her tax return.
B. Melissa has a wash sale, and her loss is not deductible.
C. Singh can deduct the loss on his separate tax return.
D. None of the above.

10. Nikhil's adjusted basis in 500 shares of Medico Corporation was $2,550. He owned the shares for six months. If he sells all 500 shares for $3,300, what is the resulting gain or loss?

A. $750 short-term gain.
B. $700 short-term gain.
C. $750 long-term gain.
D. $750 long-term loss.

11. Tahir purchased 100 shares in Foresthill Mutual Fund on June 1, 2023, for $750. He also received a capital gain distribution of $120 in 2023, but he did not sell his shares in the mutual fund during the year. The $120 was reported to him on Form 1099-DIV. How should this be reported on his tax return?

A. He must reduce his stock's basis by $120.
B. He must report the $120 as interest income.
C. He must report the $120 as a long-term capital gain.
D. He must report the $120 as a short-term capital gain.

12. Rishi purchased his main home five years ago for $150,000. He sold it at a loss, for $115,000 in 2023. Which of the following statements is correct?

A. If he itemizes deductions, Rishi can claim a loss of $35,000 on his tax return.
B. Rishi can claim a loss of $3,000 but must carry over the remainder to future years until the loss is completely deducted.
C. Rishi can claim a loss of $35,000 because the home sale was an involuntary conversion.
D. Rishi cannot claim a loss for the sale of his home.

13. Consuela is unmarried. She purchased 1,000 shares of Hometown Mutual Fund on February 15, 2019, for $15 per share. On April 30, 2023, she sold all her shares for $3.75 per share. She also earned $49,000 of wages in 2023. She has no other transactions during the year. How should the mutual fund sale be reported on her tax return?

A. She has a capital loss of $11,250 that she can deduct against her wage income.
B. She must carry over all the losses to a future tax year to offset future capital gains.
C. She can deduct a $3,000 capital loss on her tax return, and the remainder of the losses will carry forward to subsequent years.
D. She can deduct a $1,500 capital loss on her tax return, and the remainder of the losses will carry forward to subsequent years.

14. Colin purchased 100 shares of Entertainment Media, Inc. stock for $1,000 on January 3, 2023. He sold these shares for $750 on December 22, 2023. Colin has seller's remorse, and on January 19, 2024, he repurchases 100 shares of Entertainment Media for $800. Which of the following statements is correct?

A. Colin can report a $250 capital loss in 2023.
B. Colin can report a taxable loss in 2024.
C. Colin cannot deduct his stock loss of $250 and must add the disallowed loss to his basis.
D. Colin can deduct the loss as an adjustment to income in 2024.

15. Two years ago, Sunil purchased 100 units of Ethereum, a cryptocurrency, for $9,000. On March 5, 2023, he exchanged all 100 units of Ethereum for 3.47826 units of Bitcoin, another cryptocurrency, worth $160,000 on the date of exchange. What gain, if any, must Sunil report in 2023?

A. $151,000 long-term capital gain
B. $151,000 short-term capital gain
C. $151,000 long-term capital loss
D. Sunil has no gain or loss from the exchange.

16. Noah bought two blocks of Acme Corporation stock. Each block was 400 shares. He purchased the first block on May 30, 2021, for $1,200 and the second block on June 8, 2023, for $1,600. On July 12, 2023, he needed money to fix his car, so he sold 400 shares for $1,500 but did not specify which block of stocks he sold. Noah's stock sale results in a:

A. Long-term loss of $100.
B. Long-term gain of $300.
C. Short-term loss of $100.
D. Short-term gain of $300.

Unit 7: Quiz Answers

1. The answer is C. Caleb has a short-term capital loss because he did not hold the stock for over one year (he needed to hold the stock at least a year and an additional day). He can deduct $3,000 of the loss, netting it against his wage income. The remaining amount ($4,000) must be carried over to future tax years.

2. The answer is D. The related party transaction rules do not apply in this scenario. Related party transaction rules are designed to prevent improper deductions between two parties joined by a special relationship. However, the related party transaction rules do not apply to stepsiblings, so there are no related party issues between Simeon and Gerald or their corporations. Related party transaction rules do not apply to uncles, aunts, nieces, nephews, cousins, stepchildren, stepsiblings, stepparents, or in-laws.

3. The answer is C. Losses on the sale of personal-use property, including a loss on the sale of a primary residence or a vacation home, are not deductible. Only losses associated with business property and investment property (such as stocks and bonds or rental property) are deductible.

4. The answer is A. The answer is calculated as follows: The original basis is increased by the broker's commission. Therefore, Marsha's adjusted basis is $10,145 ($10,110 + $35). The gross proceeds from the sale are $8,859, which is subtracted from the basis, resulting in a long-term capital loss of $1,286 ($8,859 - $10,145) because she held the stock for more than one year.

5. The answer is C. Rajiv has a short-term capital loss of $600 = (100 shares × $26) - (100 shares × $20) that would be reported in the year of sale. Rajiv's holding period was not *more* than one year, which means that the loss must be treated as short-term.

6. The answer is C. To determine the holding period, a taxpayer must begin counting on the day *after* the acquisition date. If a taxpayer's holding period is not more than one year, the taxpayer will have a short-term gain or loss. The amount realized in the transaction has no bearing on the holding period.

7. The answer is B. The sale of a second home is a taxable event in the event of a gain. Since Roshan and Tatiana owned the property for longer than one year, their gain is long-term. The gain is calculated as follows:

Sale price	$254,000
Minus selling expenses	(12,500)
Net proceeds	241,500
Minus adjusted basis in the property	(232,000)
Taxable gain on the sale	**$9,500**

8. The answer is D. Unused capital losses may be carried over indefinitely until they are utilized. There is no limit to how many years an individual taxpayer can claim the losses. However, capital losses do not transfer to an estate or surviving spouse after the taxpayer has died.

9. The answer is B. Melissa's capital loss is disallowed. Melissa has a wash sale because her spouse repurchased identical securities within 30 days. It does not matter if they file separate returns. If a taxpayer sells the stock and her spouse then repurchases identical stock within 30 days, the taxpayer has a wash sale. The fact that the taxpayers file MFS is irrelevant—the wash sale rules still apply, even if the taxpayers file separate returns.

10. The answer is A. The sales price is $750 more than the adjusted basis of the shares. The gain is short-term since Nikhil did not own the shares for more than one year.

11. The answer is C. Tahir must report the $120 as a long-term capital gain. Mutual funds frequently distribute capital gains to shareholders. Capital gain distributions for mutual funds are *always* taxed as long-term capital gains, no matter how long a taxpayer has actually held the mutual fund shares.

12. The answer is D. Rishi cannot claim a loss for the sale of his home. Losses on the sale of personal-use property, including a personal residence, are never deductible. If the house had been a rental property, however, the loss would have been deductible and reported on Form 4797 and Schedule D.

13. The answer is C. Consuela cannot deduct all her capital losses in the current year. However, she is allowed to claim a $3,000 capital loss on her 2023 tax return. The remainder of the loss ($8,250) will carry forward indefinitely to subsequent years until they are fully exhausted.

14. The answer is C. Because Colin bought shares in the same corporation within 30 days of its sale at a loss, this is considered a "wash sale," and he cannot deduct his loss of $250 on the sale. Instead, he must add the disallowed loss to the cost of the newly purchased stock.

15. The answer is A. Sunil has a $151,000 ($160,000 - $9,000) long-term capital gain from this transaction. The gain is long-term because he held the cryptocurrency (Ethereum) for more than one year before exchanging it. The exchange of one cryptocurrency for another is treated as a sale.

16. The answer is B. Noah realized a long-term gain of $300 because the basis and holding period would automatically default to the oldest block of shares, which he purchased in 2021 (over a year ago). The "FIFO method" is used if the taxpayer cannot or does not specifically identify the shares sold.

Unit 8: Nonrecognition Property Transactions

> **For additional information, read:**
> Publication 544, *Sales and Other Dispositions of Assets*
> Publication 523, *Selling Your Home*

When a taxpayer sells or exchanges property, the resulting gains may fall into one of three categories: nontaxable, partially taxable, or deferred. The three most common examples of nonrecognition transactions are:

- **Selling a primary residence** (excluded gain under Section 121)
- **Like-kind exchanges** (nontaxable/deferred exchange under Section 1031)
- **Involuntary conversions** (exchange under Section 1033)

Note: On Part 1 of the EA Exam, you will primarily be tested on selling a main home, converting personal-use property involuntarily, and exchanging residential rental properties as like-kind properties. Part 2 of the EA Exam, you will be tested on nonrecognition property transactions exclusively involving business property.

Sale of Main Home (Section 121 Exclusion)

When selling their primary residence, taxpayers can often exclude the gain from selling their primary residence. For those who are unmarried or Married Filing Separately, up to $250,000 of gain can be excluded. Joint filers have a higher exclusion amount of $500,000. Additionally, special rules apply for taxpayers whose spouses have passed away.[98]

If the entire profit is excluded, it is not necessary to report the sale unless a Form 1099-S is received for the proceeds. If a portion of the gain is taxable, the sale must be reported on Schedule D and Form 8949. Any profit earned from selling a home that is not considered the taxpayer's primary residence must be reported as taxable income.

The Section 121 exclusion only pertains to a taxpayer's primary residence and does not apply to rental properties, vacation homes, or secondary residences. A taxpayer's main home is considered to be the place where they reside for the majority of the year, and it does not have to be a typical house. This could include a variety of living arrangements such as a houseboat, mobile home, cooperative apartment, or condominium. The key criteria for a property to be classified as a home includes having sleeping quarters, a kitchen, and bathroom facilities.

Example: Parker resides in a house located in Phoenix, Arizona, as his primary residence. In addition, he has a lake cottage in Lake Tahoe, Nevada, that he only uses during the summer months. Parker decides to sell the vacation cottage, resulting in a $220,000 capital gain. Unfortunately, he cannot exclude this gain from income tax since the cottage is not his main residence. As a result, he will be responsible for paying taxes on the entire gain.

---

[98] There is a special rule for surviving spouses, even if they cannot file as a qualified surviving spouse. If a spouse passes away, and all the requirements (to be discussed later) were in place for the gain exclusion on their primary residence at the time of death of their spouse, the surviving spouse can exclude up to $500,000 of gain if the widow(er) sells the house within **two years** of their spouse's death, regardless of their filing status in the year of sale, as long as they remain unmarried at the time of the sale. IRC section 121(b)(4).

Example: Mickie owns a duplex and resides in one unit while allowing her brother, Harry, to live in the other unit rent-free. She bought the property for $200,000 ten years ago. During the year, Mickie sells the duplex for $340,000, a gain of $140,000. Since only half of the duplex counts as her main home, Mickie may exclude only half of the gain ($70,000). She must report the other $70,000 as a long-term capital gain on her individual return.

Eligibility Requirements for Section 121

To be eligible for the Section 121 exclusion, a taxpayer must:

- Have sold their main home
- Meet "ownership and use" tests
- Not have excluded gain in the two years prior to the current sale of a home (although there are exceptions when the primary reason for selling the home residence was a change of employment, health, or unforeseen circumstances, covered later).

Example: Paula is retired and lives in Miami, Florida. On January 1, 2023, Paula purchased a new home in Tampa, Florida. On January 15, 2023, (two weeks later) Paula sells her old home in Miami at a $40,000 gain. She had owned and lived in the Miami home for four years. She can exclude all the gain on the sale of the Miami home. Paula moves into the Tampa home, but she hates her new neighborhood and decides to sell the home just a few months later. On October 1, 2023, Paula sells the Tampa home. She has a $6,000 profit on the sale. The sale was not due to a change in place of employment or health, Paula just sold the home because she hated the neighborhood. Because Paula had excluded gain on the sale of another home within the two-year period, she cannot exclude the gain on the sale of the Tampa residence. The entire gain is taxable as a short-term capital gain.

Ownership Test and Use Test

The IRS figures the ownership and use tests *separately*, and the time periods do not have to be continuous. During the five-year period ending on the date of the sale, the taxpayer must have:

- Owned the home for at least two years (the **ownership** test), and
- Lived in the home as their main home for at least two years (the **use** test).

A taxpayer meets both tests if the taxpayer *owned* and *lived* in the property as their main home for either 24 full months or 730 days (365 × 2) during the five-year period. The required two years of ownership and use do not have to be continuous. Further, ownership and use tests can be met during different two-year periods.

Example: Evelyn bought her home on February 1, 2020. She lived there continuously for 2 years and 11 months. She moves out on January 2, 2023, and starts advertising the home online as a rental. Evelyn does not have any luck finding a good tenant, and eventually decides that she does not want to rent the property anymore. December 30, 2023, approximately one year later, she sells the home at a gain. Even though Evelyn moved out of the house for a year, she qualifies for the Section 121 exclusion because she personally <u>owned and used</u> the home for at least two years during the five-year lookback period before the sale.

Example: Mabel bought a house on September 1, 2018. After living there for ten months, she moved in with her boyfriend and left her house vacant. They later broke up, and Mabel moved back into her own house in 2021. She lived there for an additional 16 months until she sold it on September 1, 2023. Mabel meets the ownership and use tests because, during the five-year period ending on the date of sale, she owned the house for five years and lived in the house a total of 26 months—both more than the required 24-month (2-year) requirements.

Example: Briella, who is 25 years old and unmarried, has always resided in her parents' house since birth. In January of 2023, she purchased her childhood home from her parents. Her parents had retired and moved to a different state. Briella remained in the house until December. However, she ultimately sells the property on December 26, 2023 because she wanted a larger residence. Despite living in the house as her primary residence for over two years, Briella does not qualify for the Section 121 exclusion. Although she *lived* in the house for more than two years, she did not actually *own* it for two years (it was owned by her parents, not her). Therefore, she fails to meet both the ownership and use requirements and will be required to pay taxes on any gains she made from the sale.

To satisfy the "use" requirement, the taxpayer must physically occupy the home. However, brief, temporary absences, are still considered periods of use, even if the property is rented during that time. Examples of short absences include short vacations and seasonal trips. However, longer breaks, such as a one-year sabbatical, do not count towards the period of use.

Example: Alannah is a college professor who teaches Medieval history. She purchases and moves into her home on June 1, 2021. On June 1, 2022, (exactly one year later) she moves abroad for a one-year sabbatical to study ancient manuscripts in Germany. On August 1, 2023, she returns to the U.S. from her sabbatical, and on September 1, 2023, (one month later) she sells the house because she wants to move into a smaller apartment. Even though she *owned* the home for over two years, the year-long sabbatical is not considered a short, temporary absence. She is not entitled to take the Section 121 exclusion because she did not satisfy the "*use* requirement."

Example: Sophie lived in and owned a house in Miami, Florida as her main residence for many years, from 2014 until the end of 2018. On December 1, 2018, Sophie gets a job overseas and permanently relocates to Australia. Sophie's daughter, Tamera, moves into the Miami house and lives there rent-free until it is eventually sold on November 31, 2023. Sophie cannot exclude any of the profit from the sale of the house because she did not use the property as her primary residence for at least two of the five years prior to the sale. As a result, Sophie will be subject to paying long-term capital gains tax on all the profits from the sale.

Example: Juanita bought her home on February 1, 2021. Each year, Juanita leaves her home for a two-month summer vacation in Ecuador to visit her family. Juanita sells her house on June 1, 2023. She owned and lived in the home for over two years, so she can exclude up to $250,000 of gain. Her vacations are considered brief and temporary absences, which still count towards her overall period of use for the property.

Remember, the periods of "use" and the periods of "ownership" do not need to be concurrent or consecutive, so long as the total duration of "ownership and use" adds up to two years.

Example: On January 2, 2020, Cillian began living in an apartment in New York, which he rented from a landlord. The apartment complex was later converted to condominiums, and Cillian purchased his unit on June 1, 2021. In 2023, Cillian's daughter invites her father to visit her in Hawaii, where she owns a beach house. Cillian loves Hawaii and the beach house, and his daughter invites him to stay and live with her. On January 2, 2023, he moves permanently into his daughter's home. Cillian does not return to his New York condo, and on August 1, 2023, while still living in his daughter's home, Cillian sells his condo. He can exclude all the gain on the sale because he meets the ownership and use tests. His five-year "lookback" period is the five year period before August 1, 2023 (**five years** *before* the date he actually *sells* the condo). He *owned* the condo from June 1, 2021, until August 1, 2023 (more than two years). He *lived* there from January 2, 2020 until January 2, 2023 (more than two years), so he would qualify to exclude all the gain, even though his ownership and use periods do not always overlap.

Different Rules for Married Homeowners

The ownership and use tests are applied differently to married homeowners. Married homeowners can exclude gain of up to $500,000 if they meet all the following conditions:

- They file a joint return.
- Either spouse meets the ownership test (only one is required to own the home).
- Both spouses meet the use test.
- Neither spouse has excluded gain in the two years before the current sale of the home.

If the requirements are not met, the couple will not be able to claim the full $500,000 exclusion for married couples. However, if only one spouse qualifies, that spouse may still be eligible for a separate exclusion of up to $250,000.

Example: Irene owns her home and has lived in it continuously for the last seven years. She meets Julien and marries him on September 1, 2023. They move in together, but Julien doesn't like Irene's house, and he convinces her to sell it a few months later. Irene sells the home on December 10, 2023, and has $350,000 of gain on the sale. Irene meets the ownership and use tests, but Julien does not meet the use test because he only lived in the house for a few months. Irene can exclude up to $250,000 of gain on her 2023 tax return, whether she files MFJ or MFS. Julien cannot exclude any of the gain. The $500,000 exclusion for joint returns does not apply.

Example: Hubert owns a home that he has lived in continuously for a decade. On June 1, 2019, he marries Jasmine, she moves into Hubert's home, and they both live in the house together until December 9, 2023, when the house is sold. Hubert meets the ownership test and the use test. Jasmine does not own the home because Hubert is listed as the sole owner of the property and the only one listed on the deed. However, she meets the "use test" because she lived in the home for at least two years with her husband. Therefore, on a jointly filed return, they can claim the maximum $500,000 exclusion.

Legally married spouses are eligible for the maximum $500,000 exclusion from gain on their jointly filed returns. If an *unmarried* couple owns and lives in a house together, and later gets married, the $500,000 exclusion applies if they file a joint return. If the couple files separate returns, each spouse would figure their exclusion separately on their own return.

Example: Mavis and Santiago have lived together for a decade, but only got married a year ago. In 2023, they sell the house they had co-owned and lived in together for 10 years. They are both listed as co-owners on the deed, even though they were not married when they bought the home. They purchased the house for $210,000 and sold it for $785,000, which means they have a profit of $575,000. Mavis and Santiago may claim the maximum $500,000 exclusion for married couples when they file jointly in 2023. Even if they chose to file separate returns, each one would be eligible for a $250,000 exclusion on their separate MFS return, because they both owned the home and used it as their primary residence for the requisite 2 years. The remaining $75,000 of gain ($575,000 profit - $500,000 exclusion) is taxable as a long-term capital gain. They would have to recognize the gain whether they file jointly or separately.

A special rule for the holding period applies to a home that is transferred by a spouse in a divorce. The receiving spouse is considered to have *owned* the home during any period of time that the transferor owned it. However, the receiving spouse must still satisfy the two out of five-year *use* test on their own to qualify for the entire exclusion. This is a tax-free transfer of property "incident to a divorce" (a Section 1041 transfer).

Example: Theodore buys a home for $400,000 on January 2, 2018. Approximately two years later, Theodore meets Kayla, and they get married on February 1, 2020. Kayla moves in with Theodore, but the home's ownership remains in Theodore's name only. They start having marital difficulties a few years later, and Kayla moves out on March 1, 2023. Six months later, they get divorced. As part of their divorce settlement, Theodore transfers complete ownership of the house to Kayla. Theodore's basis also transfers to Kayla. The home reminds Kayla of unhappy times, so on December 25, 2023, she sells the home for $475,000, making a $75,000 profit on the sale. Kayla keeps the entire proceeds from the sale for herself. She is entitled to the Section 121 exclusion, because IRS regulations treat Kayla as having owned the home during the time Theodore owned it. The time Kayla occupied the home as her principal residence prior to and after the divorce will count toward the two-year "use" test. She meets both tests, so she may exclude the entire $75,000 gain on her tax return.

Unrelated Individuals: An unmarried couple who own a home and live together may take the $250,000 exclusion individually on their separate returns if they meet the use and ownership tests. This would also be the case if it was any type of cohabiting partners. Whether or not they are related to each other is irrelevant, although many times siblings will cohabitate and own a home together.

Example: Shawn and Alan are retired Navy buddies. Both are unmarried. Shawn and Alan decide to purchase a home together for $135,000. They both own and live in the home together for three years. In 2023, they both get married to new partners. Shawn and Alan decide to sell the home, and on May 1, 2023, the home sells for $245,000, generating a $110,000 overall gain. Each one received $55,000 ($110,000 gain ÷ 2 owners). The title company that handled the sale sent Shawn and Alan a 1099-S reporting the gross sales price of the home. Since they received a 1099-S, Shawn and Alan should report the sale on their individual tax returns, but the gain is not taxable, because they meet the ownership and use tests, and each would qualify for the full $250,000 Section 121 exclusion on their individual returns.

Example: Harper and Carolyn are sisters. They are both retired and widowed, and decided to purchase a home for $220,000 and live together. They live together in the home for six years, before selling the home on December 1, 2023 for $600,000. Together, they have $380,000 in gain ($600,000 - $220,000 basis). The ownership and use tests apply to them individually, and each one would qualify to exclude up to $250,000 for her portion of the sale on her individual return. This means that all their gain can be excluded.

Deceased Spouses: In the case of a deceased spouse, the surviving spouse is treated as if they owned and lived in the home during any period that the deceased spouse did. This means that the surviving spouse may exclude up to $500,000 of gain from the sale of the home, even if it occurs within two years after the death of the deceased spouse (as long as the surviving spouse did not remarry before the sale). Essentially, the holding period for the deceased spouse is transferred to the surviving spouse, allowing them to benefit from the full exclusion for married couples.

Example: Rosalee has owned and lived in her own home for six years. She marries Caspian on February 1, 2023, and he moves into the home with her. Rosalee dies suddenly seven months later, and Caspian inherits the home. Caspian does not remarry. Caspian decides to sell the home on December 1, 2023. Even though he did not own or live in the house for two years, he meets the requirements for Section 121 because his period of ownership and use includes the period that Rosalee owned and used the property before her death. Caspian may exclude up to $500,000 of the gain under the special rule that applies to deceased spouses.

Military Personnel Exception: Members of the armed forces are often required to move and might have difficulty meeting the tests for ownership and use within the five-year period prior to the sale of a home. The five-year period can be suspended for up to ten years for U.S. military[99] as well as for Foreign Service personnel, U.S. Peace Corps workers, and intelligence officers that are on official extended duty. This offers taxpayers a greater chance to fulfill the two-year residency requirement, even if they or their spouse did not physically reside in the home for the standard five-year timeframe that applies to other taxpayers.

Example: Ensign Smith is a U.S. naval officer. He is single and owns his home. Ensign Smith bought and moved into his home on January 2, 2015. He lived in it as his main home for 2½ years. For the following 6 years, he did not live in the home because he was on qualified official extended duty with the U.S. Navy. He did not return to the home during that time and lived overseas. Ensign Smith sold his home for a $125,000 gain on December 26, 2023. To meet the use test, he may suspend the normal 5-year test period for the time he was on qualifying official extended duty. This means that Ensign Smith can disregard the 6 years that he lived abroad when he is calculating his period of "ownership and use." He meets the "ownership and use" tests because he owned and lived in the home for at least 2 years. Ensign Smith may exclude all the gain from the sale on his individual tax return.

Disability Exception: There is an exception to the use test if, during the five-year period before the sale of the home, a taxpayer becomes physically or mentally disabled. They must have owned and lived in the home for at least one year. However, a taxpayer is considered to have "lived in the home"

---

[99] This includes members of the U.S. Army, Navy, Air Force, Marine Corps, etc.

during any time that they are forced to live in a licensed facility, including a nursing home. The taxpayer must still meet the two-year ownership test.

> **Example:** Marylou, age 72, retired and bought a new home in Florida on January 13, 2021. She moved into her home and lived in the home continuously for 12 months, but then she fell and broke her hip. Marylou cannot walk, and the doctor says that her condition is unlikely to improve, so she is forced to move into her daughter's home. Marylou's disability prevents her from returning to her own home, and on July 20, 2023, while still living in her daughter's home, Marylou sells her house, making a $40,000 gain on the sale. Marylou can exclude all the gain on the sale of her home because she owned the home for over 2 years, and she lived in the home at least a year before becoming disabled.

Rules for Reduced Exclusions

A taxpayer who owned and used a home for less than two years (and therefore does not meet the ownership and use tests) or who has used the home sale exclusion within the prior two-year period, may still be eligible for a "reduced" exclusion if they meet one of the following three exceptions:

- **Work-Related Move:** This safe harbor applies if a new job is at least 50 miles farther from the old home than was the former place of employment. If there was no former place of employment, the distance between the new place of employment and the old home must be at least 50 miles. Other circumstances may qualify as related to a job change even if the safe harbor is not met based on the facts and circumstances.
- **Health-Related Move:** The health safe harbor applies if a doctor recommends a change of residence for reasons of health of the taxpayer, a spouse, a child, or certain other related persons. The related person does not have to be a dependent for the reduced exclusion to apply. Other circumstances may qualify as related to health even if the safe harbor is not met based on the facts and circumstances.
- **Unforeseeable Events:** The "unforeseen circumstances" safe harbors include the following:
  - Death, divorce, or legal separation,
  - Unemployment,
  - Multiple births resulting from the same pregnancy,
  - Damage to the residence resulting from a disaster, an act of war, or terrorism; and
  - Involuntary conversion of the property or condemnation.
  - Other situations may qualify as unforeseen circumstances.

The reduced exclusion amount equals the full $250,000 (or $500,000) multiplied by a fraction. The numerator is the *shorter* of:

- The period the taxpayer owned and used the home as a principal residence during the five-year period ending on the sale date, or
- The period between the last sale for which the taxpayer claimed the exclusion and the sale date for the home currently being sold.

The denominator is two years or the equivalent in months or days. Thus, the amount of the reduced exclusion is figured by multiplying the full exclusion amount by the number of days or months the taxpayer owned and used the property and dividing by either 730 days or 24 months.

Example: Katherine is unmarried. She bought her principal residence for $340,000 in San Diego, CA on January 1, 2023. Nine months later, she loses her high-paying job and could no longer afford the mortgage payments. She sells the house for $600,000 on December 31, 2023. She has a $260,000 gain ($600,000 sale price - $340,000 basis). She owned and lived in the house exactly one year (365 days) before selling it. Even though she only occupied the house for a year, she qualifies for the reduced exclusion because she became unemployed. Katherine can exclude $125,000 of the gain ($250,000 × [365 ÷ 730]). The remainder of the gain would be taxable and cannot be excluded.

Example: On January 5, 2023, Thane, who is single, purchases a home in Mississippi and uses it as his principal residence. A few months later, Thane's employer transfers his job to Alaska. Thane moves to Alaska to begin working his new position. On July 5, 2023, (exactly six months later), Thane sells his Mississippi home, generating $60,000 in gain. He qualifies for a reduced exclusion due to his job relocation. He may exclude up to a maximum of $62,500 ($250,000 maximum exclusion × 6/24 months) of the gain on the sale. Since his gain on the sale is *less* than $62,500, then he does not have a taxable gain.

Land Sales: If a taxpayer sells the land on which their main home is located but not the house itself, the gain is not excludible. Similarly, the sale of a vacant plot of land with no house on it does not qualify for the Section 121 exclusion.

Example: Bernarda purchased an empty lot three years ago for $90,000, planning to build her dream home. Construction was delayed, and her house was never completed. In December 2023, Bernarda sells the land for $150,000. She owned the land for more than a year, so she has $60,000 of long-term capital gain. None of the gain can be excluded from income because there is no residence on the property. Section 121 only applies to actual homes, not to an empty lot.

In certain cases, a taxpayer may be able to exclude the gain from selling a vacant lot that is connected to their primary residence. This exclusion can only be applied if the vacant land was used in connection with the main home and the sale occurs within two years before or after selling the home. The land must have been directly adjacent to the home and must have been owned and used as part of the home, not for any business purposes. In terms of tax treatment, both the sale of the land and the sale of the home are considered one transaction for the purpose of applying this exclusion.

Example: Gregory bought a property with 10 acres, which included a house that he uses as his main residence. After living there for five years, Gregory sells eight acres of land on February 1, 2023, earning a profit of $100,000. Ten months later, on December 1, 2023, he sells the remaining two acres and the house, earning an additional gain of $140,000 from the sale. Since the first sale occurred within two years of selling the dwelling unit, it is also considered a sale of his primary residence. As a result, Gregory can exclude up to $250,000 of gain from both sales, effectively eliminating any taxable gain ($100,000 + $140,000 = $240,000).

Homes Used Partially for Business

If a taxpayer's home was used partially for business purposes or as a rental property, the gain is reported on Form 4797, *Sales of Business Property.* If a taxpayer claimed depreciation deductions for using their home as a rental property or for other business purposes, they cannot exclude the portion of the gain equivalent to the amount of depreciation deducted.[100] Section 121 only applies to the personal portion of a home.

In addition, under IRC section 121(b)(5), an additional rule applies for properties that are converted *from* a non-qualifying use (for example, as a rental) *to* a qualifying use (i.e., as a personal residence). In these situations, generally time of the non-qualifying use of the property is compared to the total time the property was owned by the taxpayer prior to sale. This ratio is then applied to the realized gain on the sale of the property to determine (exclusive of any depreciation deductions that may have been taken on the property prior to the date of sale) the amount of the gain that can potentially be excluded under IRC section 121.

Example: Asami purchased a single family residence on January 1, 2018 and immediately rents it out to tenants, and she continues to do so through December 31, 2020. On January 1, 2021, Asami no longer has tenants, so she decides to move into the home as her personal residence. On January 1, 2023 she sells the property at a $290,000 gain. Looking back at the uses of the property up to the date of sale, there were three years of non-qualifying use (from January 1, 2018 through December 31, 2020 as a rental) and two years of qualifying use (January 1, 2021 through December 31, 2022 as her primary residence) of the property. As such, three-fifths of the property's use leading up the sale was for non-qualifying purposes, therefore three-fifths (60%) of the realized $290,000 is not eligible for the Section 121 exclusion (i.e., $174,000). The remaining $116,000 of the realized gain (not including any applicable depreciation) can be excluded under Section 121. Note that any depreciation applicable on the property during its time as a rental would be subtracted from the $116,000 excludable portion of the gain noted above, resulting in a slightly lower amount of the gain that can be excluded under Section 121.

Another common scenario is when a taxpayer has a home office for their business activities, and they depreciate the home office and then later sell the home at a gain. The amount of straight-line depreciation claimed in prior years is considered as "unrecaptured §1250 gain" up to the amount of recognized gain.

"Unrecaptured §1250 gain" is *technically* long-term capital gain, with a special maximum rate of 25%. This only applies to the sale of depreciable real estate, and not other types of business assets, like machinery or equipment.

Example: Georgiana owns her home in San Antonio, Texas, and has lived in it continuously for several years. She is a personal injury attorney that works exclusively out of a home office. She has a qualified home office for which she deducts all relevant business expenses, including straight-line depreciation, for five years. In 2023, Georgiana sells her main home at a gain. Since the home is her primary residence, the sale qualifies for the section 121 exclusion, but the depreciation that she claimed on her home office is classified as "unrecaptured section 1250 gain," and will be subject to a maximum capital gains rate of 25%. She would report the uncaptured Section 1250 gains on Form 4797, then transfer that total to Schedule D.

---

[100] A unique tax rate applies to capital gains on the sale of real property for which a taxpayer has previously claimed depreciation. Unrecaptured section 1250 gain is an income tax provision that provides that gain attributable to the depreciation will be subject to a maximum 25% unrecaptured Section 1250 gain tax rate.

Like-Kind Exchanges (Section 1031 Exchange)

A Section 1031 like-kind exchange takes place when a taxpayer trades one qualifying real property for another. In this type of exchange, any gain is considered *postponed*.

The most straightforward type of Section 1031 exchange involves a **simultaneous swap** of two properties. The other type of exchange is called a "**deferred exchange**." A deferred exchange allows a taxpayer to sell their property and then acquire one or more replacement properties at a later date. Deferred exchanges offer more flexibility but are more complex, and they also require a qualified intermediary, or QI. It's important to note that like-kind exchanges only apply to real estate exchanges; any exchange of personal property will be treated as a non-cash sale and will not qualify for nonrecognition treatment. Currently, the following types of real property may qualify for like-kind treatment:

- Land, and improvements to land (such as buildings, concrete parking lots, foundations),
- Unsevered natural products of land, (such as natural mineral deposits, mines, and wells)
- Water and air space superjacent to land,
- Certain intangible interests in real property (such as leaseholds and options), and
- Property that is real property under state or local law.

The most common type of section 1031 exchange is a swap of one rental property for another. However, taxpayers may exchange different types of real property, including buildings, farmland, timberland, even undeveloped land. To qualify for nonrecognition treatment, the exchange must meet all the following conditions:

- The property must be held for investment or business-use. Property held for personal use, such as a personal residence, does not qualify.
- The property must NOT be "held primarily for sale" (such as real estate held as inventory by a real estate dealer).
- There must be an actual exchange of two or more assets or properties (the exchange of *property* for *cash* is always treated as a sale, not an exchange).
- In instances when a property is transferred in exchange for like-kind property to be received later (known as a "deferred exchange"), the property to be received must be identified in writing (or actually received) within 45 days after the date of transfer of the property given up.
- For most exchanges, a "qualified intermediary" must be procured to facilitate the exchange using escrow accounts. This type of qualified intermediary (sometimes also known as an exchange accommodator or facilitator) promises to return the proceeds of the exchange to the transferor of the property.[101]

Deadlines: The replacement property in a section 1031 exchange **must** be received by the earlier of:

- The 180th day after the date on which the property was given up was transferred, or
- The due date, including extensions, of the tax return for the year in which the transfer of that property occurs. The IRS is very strict about these deadlines.

---

[101] Only in a "simultaneous" 1031 exchange (a two-party swap) is a qualified intermediary not needed. That occurs only when the exchange is processed on the same day and there is no delayed exchange.

Taxpayers report like-kind exchanges on Form 8824, *Like-Kind Exchanges*. The taxpayer must calculate and keep track of their basis in the new property they acquired in an exchange.

In general, any exchange of any real property generally qualifies as like-kind, regardless of how each property is used or whether each property is improved or unimproved. For instance, the exchange of an office building for farmland would qualify, as would the exchange of an apartment complex for an office building.

Nonqualifying Exchanges: Personal-use realty is not eligible for a like-kind exchange. So, the exchange of a personal residence for another personal residence does not qualify, nor would an exchange of a personal residence for an apartment building. This prohibition would also apply to a vacation home.

The exchange of property within the United States for similar property *outside* the United States also would not be a qualifying exchange. Foreign real estate is not eligible for nonrecognition treatment. And remember, inventory is *never* eligible for like-kind treatment.

> **Example:** Lawrence is a professional real estate developer. Lawrence purchases large tracts of land and then sells the subdivided lots for later development. All the lots he purchases are available for sale to customers. In this case, Lawrence is a professional real estate dealer: to him, the land is inventory. Lawrence cannot use section 1031 to escape recognition of gain on the transfer or sale of his land lots.

> **Example:** Maddie is a full-time house-flipper. She buys distressed properties at auction, fixes them up, and then re-sells them, usually within six months of purchase. She does not rent them out or live in the properties while they are being rehabbed. In 2023, she has five houses that are in the process of being flipped. Once the current restorations are complete, Maddie intends to re-sell the homes to future buyers. The properties are treated as inventory. Therefore, none of the properties would be eligible for a section 1031 exchange.

Taxable Exchanges: If a taxpayer receives property in exchange for other property that does not meet the like-kind exchange rules, he may need to recognize gain if the fair market value of the property received is greater than the adjusted basis of the property given up. His basis in the property received is generally its FMV at the time of the exchange.

> **Example:** Cassidy exchanges a residential rental in Hawaii with an adjusted basis of $100,000 with a residential rental property in Cancun, Mexico. The Cancun property has a fair market value of $145,000. The exchange of foreign realty for real property in the United States does not qualify for section 1031 treatment. Instead, the transaction is treated as a taxable sale. Since the exchange does not qualify for nonrecognition treatment, Cassidy must recognize $45,000 of taxable income on the transaction. Her basis in the Cancun property is $145,000, which would be the same treatment if the property had been purchased with cash.

Cash Boot and Mortgage Boot

Although the Internal Revenue Code itself does not use the term "boot," it is frequently used to describe cash or other property added to an exchange to compensate for a difference in the values of properties traded. A taxpayer must generally not receive "boot" in an exchange, in order for the exchange to be completely tax-free.

This does not mean that the exchange is not valid, but the taxpayer who receives boot may have to recognize taxable gain to the extent of the cash and the FMV of unlike property received, but the recognized gain when boot is received is still limited to the realized gain on the exchange. The amount considered boot would also be reduced by any qualified costs paid in connection with the transaction.

> **Example:** Glenn exchanges a residential rental property for a parcel of farmland in a section 1031 exchange. The relinquished rental property has an FMV of $60,000 and an adjusted basis of $30,000. The farmland Glenn receives has an FMV of $50,000, and he also receives $10,000 of cash as part of the exchange. Glenn, therefore, has a realized gain of $30,000 on the exchange (combined value of $60,000 received minus his basis of $30,000 in the rental he exchanged). He is required to pay tax and recognize gain on only $10,000, the cash (boot) received in the exchange. The remaining $20,000 of gain is deferred until he disposes of the farmland at a later date.

In situations when there is a realized loss on a section 1031 exchange, and the taxpayer receives boot, none of the loss is recognized. However, the deferred loss is added to the basis of the contributed like-kind property given to the other party to determine the basis of the like-kind property received.

Boot can be given, as well as received, in a like-kind exchange. If cash is given to the other party in a like-kind exchange, none of the realized gain (or loss) will be recognized. However, if <u>noncash boot</u> is given to the other party, then gain (or loss) will be recognized based on the difference between the non-cash boot's fair market value and adjusted basis at the time of the exchange.

> **Example:** Alice exchanges her commercial building for another commercial property. Her commercial building is worth more than the building she is receiving. So as part of the deal, she also receives a valuable antique gold coin valued at $15,000 from the other party. Since the gold coin is not "like-kind" property, this constitutes non-cash boot to Alice.

> **Example:** Kaden wants to exchange his office building for a commercial warehouse. His office building has a fair market value of $209,000 and an adjusted basis of $150,000. The warehouse has a fair market value of $200,000. Since the warehouse is worth less, and Kaden's office building is worth more, the owner of the warehouse offers Kaden a forklift as part of the exchange. Kaden accepts the forklift, which is valued at $21,000. Although the exchange still qualifies as a section 1031 exchange, Kaden must recognize $21,000 (the FMV of the forklift) on his return because it is *boot*, and "unlike" property (i.e., not qualifying real estate).[102]

When an exchange involves property that is subject to a liability (such as an existing mortgage), the assumption of the liability is treated as if it was a transfer of cash and thus considered boot by the party who is relieved of the liability. Sometimes this is called "mortgage boot" or "debt reduction boot."

On the other hand, if a party assumes a mortgage from the other party, it is treated as cash boot given to the other party. If each property in an exchange is transferred subject to a liability, a taxpayer is treated as having received boot only if they are relieved of a greater liability than the liability they assume. When there is mortgage boot and cash boot in the same transaction, the mortgage boot paid does not offset any "cash boot" received. Net cash boot received is *always* taxable if there is a realized gain on the exchange.

---

[102] Scenarios based on examples illustrated in Publication 544, *Sales and Other Dispositions of Assets.*

Basis of Property Received in a Like-Kind Exchange

The basis of property received in a section 1031 exchange is the basis of the property given up with some adjustments. Gain is only *deferred*, not forgiven, in a like-kind exchange.

> **Example:** Cossette owns a residential rental property with a FMV of $355,000 an adjusted basis of $270,000. In 2023, she trades her rental property for a commercial parking lot with an FMV of $360,000. The properties were very close in terms of fair market value, so no cash was exchanged, and it was a straight exchange of properties. Cossette's basis in the parking lot is $270,000, which is the same as the adjusted basis of the rental property she gave up in the exchange. In other words, Cossette's basis remained the same.

If a taxpayer trades property and *also* pays money as part of the exchange, the basis of the property received is the basis of the property given up, increased by any additional money paid.

> **Example:** Charlie owns a parcel of timberland with a fair market value of $70,000. His basis in the timberland is $30,000 (this is how much he paid for the land ten years ago). He wants to exchange the timberland for a parcel of farmland in another state. The farmland has a FMV of approximately $75,000, so it is more valuable than his timberland. Charlie agrees to pay the owner of the farmland an additional $4,000 in cash to complete the transaction. Charlie's basis in the new farmland is $34,000—his original $30,000 basis in the timberland he gave up, *plus* the additional $4,000 cash he paid out-of-pocket to acquire the farmland.

If a taxpayer receives boot in connection with an exchange and recognizes gain, the basis of the like-kind property received is equal to the basis of the like-kind property given up *plus* the amount of gain recognized, plus the basis of any boot given, *minus* the fair market value of any boot received, minus any loss recognized. The basis of any non-cash boot received is its fair market value. The taxpayer may reduce the amount of recognized gain by any exchange expenses (closing costs) paid.

> **Example:** Joshua owns a tract of woodland with an adjusted basis of $80,000 and a current fair market value of $110,000. Joshua wants to exchange the woodland for a small office building with an FMV of $100,000. Since Joshua's woodland is worth more than the office building, the seller of the office building offers Joshua $10,000 in cash to complete the exchange. Joshua must recognize gain to the extent of the cash boot he received. However, Joshua also pays $5,000 in legal fees and other related closing costs in order to complete the exchange. Joshua's recognized (taxable) gain is only $5,000, figured as follows: (cash boot received $10,000 - $5,000 exchange expenses paid = $5,000 in recognized gain).[103]

> **Example:** Elaine owns a retail office building with a basis of $500,000 and a current fair market value of $750,000. Rowan owns a strip mall with a fair market value of $900,000. Elaine and Rowan agree to exchange properties. Since Rowan's property is worth considerably more, Elaine pays Rowan $150,000 in cash to complete the exchange, which is the difference in the property's fair market values. Once the 1031 exchange is complete, Elaine's basis in the strip mall would be $650,000 ($150,000 cash she paid to Rowan, plus the $500,000 adjusted basis in her old property).[104]

---

[103] Example based on scenario in Publication 544, *Sales and Other Dispositions of Assets.*
[104] Example based on scenario in Publication 551, *Basis of Assets.*

Like-Kind Exchanges Between Related Parties

Like-kind exchanges are permitted between related parties. However, if either party disposes of the property within two years after a 1031 exchange, the exchange is disqualified from nonrecognition treatment; any gain or loss that was deferred in the original transaction must be recognized in the year the disposition occurs. For purposes of this rule, a "related person" includes a close family member (i.e., spouse, sibling, parent, or child). It also includes a corporation or partnership in which a taxpayer holds ownership or interests of *more than* 50%. This mandatory two-year holding period rule does not apply:

- If one of the parties involved in the exchange subsequently dies;
- If the property is subsequently converted in an involuntary exchange (such as a fire);
- If it can be established to the satisfaction of the IRS that the exchange and subsequent disposition were not done mainly for tax avoidance purposes.

The IRS closely scrutinizes exchanges between related parties because they can be used by taxpayers to evade taxes on gains. Taxpayers must file Form 8824 for the two years following the year of a related party exchange.

Involuntary Conversions (Section 1033 Exchanges)

An involuntary conversion refers to a situation where a taxpayer's property is lost, damaged, or destroyed, and the taxpayer receives a payment as a result. This can occur due to a casualty, disaster, theft, or condemnation. Sometimes, a taxpayer can have a taxable gain from an involuntary conversion. This usually happens when a taxpayer's insurance reimbursement exceeds their basis in the property.

Involuntary conversions are also called "involuntary exchanges." Involuntary conversions can occur with business property, investment property, as well as personal-use property, but the rules differ for each. Gain or loss from an involuntary conversion is usually recognized for tax purposes unless the property is a main home (covered later). A taxpayer reports the gain or deducts the loss in the year the gain or loss is realized. However, an involuntary conversion does not automatically result in a taxable event, even if the insurance reimbursement exceeds the taxpayer's basis.

Under section 1033, a taxpayer can elect to *defer* reporting the gain from an involuntary conversion if they reinvest the proceeds in similar property. In other words, the gain on an involuntary conversion can be deferred until a later, *taxable* sale occurs. Unlike a 1031 exchange, replacing the converted property with property purchased from a related party does not qualify for nonrecognition treatment.

Example: Vernon owns an office building. A catastrophic fire destroyed his building on January 3, 2023. He had purchased the building five years ago for $150,000. The depreciation deductions he had taken were $78,000, so the building had an adjusted basis of $72,000. Vernon received a $120,000 insurance payout on May 3, 2023, realizing a gain of $48,000 ($120,000 insurance payment - adjusted basis of $72,000). Vernon immediately spends $100,000 of the insurance payment to purchase a replacement property. He uses the rest of the insurance money to go on vacation to Hawaii. Since $100,000 of the $120,000 insurance payment was used to buy replacement property, his taxable gain under the rules for involuntary conversions is limited to the remaining $20,000 insurance payment. His taxable gain on the involuntary conversion is limited to $20,000.

Longer Replacement Period: While a section 1031 exchange only has a 180-day exchange period, a section 1033 exchange has a much longer time for completion. The replacement period for an involuntary conversion generally ends two years after the end of the first tax year in which any part of the gain is realized. There is no requirement under Section 1033 that a qualified intermediary be employed to hold the escrow funds or conversion proceeds.

Property Type	Replacement Period
Most property except those noted below; the two-year replacement period also includes personal homes.	Two years
Real property (real estate) that is held for investment or business use, such as residential rentals and office buildings	Three years
Sale of livestock due to weather-related conditions	Four years
Main home in a federally declared disaster area	Four to five years, depending on IRS guidance

Real property that is held for investment or used in a trade or business is allowed a three-year replacement period. The replacement period is four years for livestock that is involuntarily converted because of weather-related conditions. Typically, any new animals bought must be used for the same purpose as the ones that were sold due to weather-related circumstances. For example, dairy cows must be replaced with new dairy cows.

If a taxpayer's main home is damaged or destroyed and is in a federally declared disaster area, the replacement period is four years, but sometimes can even be extended to five years, depending on the severity of the disaster.[105]

Example: Webster runs a farming business as a sole proprietor, and reports his income and loss on Schedule F. On July 1, 2023, an explosion destroyed a grain silo on his land. He had originally purchased the grain silo for $300,000, and depreciated it down to zero using section 179. Webster's insurance company reimburses him $300,000 for the entire loss on October 26, 2023. Webster is not required to report the gain on his tax return if he reinvests all of the insurance proceeds in a new grain silo. He has until December 31, **2025** (the end of the *second* year after the gain was realized) to replace the grain silo using the insurance proceeds.

If a taxpayer reinvests in replacement property similar to the converted property, the replacement property's basis is the same as the converted property's basis on the date of the conversion, subject to certain adjustments.

The basis is **decreased** by any loss a taxpayer recognizes on the involuntary conversion, or any money a taxpayer receives that they do not spend on similar property. The basis is **increased** by any gain a taxpayer recognizes on the involuntary conversion and any additional costs of acquiring the replacement property.

---

[105] A five-year replacement period has been applied to certain extreme disaster areas. The IRS will usually announce an extended replacement period in a news release or other official guidance.

Example: A cyclone tears through Genevieve's rental condo, leaving it in ruins. The condo had an adjusted basis of $49,000, but Genevieve's insurance company gives her a $175,000 insurance settlement, which was the fair market value of the property before it was destroyed. Nine months later, Genevieve uses all of the insurance proceeds to purchase a replacement rental property for $175,000 and also pays $3,000 in legal fees to a real estate attorney transfer the title. Her gain on the involuntary conversion is $126,000 ($175,000 insurance settlement minus her $49,000 basis). However, Genevieve does not have to recognize any *taxable* gain because she reinvested all the insurance proceeds in a similar property. The basis of her new property becomes $52,000 ($49,000 + $3,000), reflecting both her original basis and the additional legal fees she incurred during the acquisition of the replacement property.

Example: Reuben owns a rental fourplex in Texas with a basis of $250,000. He receives an insurance settlement of $400,000 after the building is destroyed by a tornado. Six months later, Reuben purchases another apartment building in Texas for $380,000. His realized gain on the involuntary conversion is $150,000 ($400,000 insurance payout - $250,000 basis). He must recognize $20,000 of gain because he received an insurance payment of $400,000 but only spent $380,000 on a replacement property ($400,000 - $380,000). His basis in the new property is $250,000, which is calculated as the cost of the new property minus the deferred gain ($380,000 - $130,000 = $250,000). If Reuben had used all the insurance proceeds and reinvested it all in the new property, he would not have to report any taxable gain.

Condemnations and Eminent Domain

A "condemnation" is a specific type of involuntary conversion that involves the legal process of taking private property for public use. If a building poses a threat to public safety or health, it may also be condemned by the government. This process is sometimes referred to as "eminent domain." It is considered a *forced sale*, where the owner is essentially selling their property to the government or another party.

Eminent domain gives the government the power to take private property in exchange for compensation. A condemnation can be initiated by a state or local government or by a private organization with the authority to seize property. In most cases, the owner will receive some form of payment or compensation for their property that is being taken.

Example: A local government informs Zavier that his farmland is being condemned to create a public highway. Although Zavier does not want to sell his farmland, the government forces the sale and issues a condemnation award to Zavier, paying him the property's fair market value of $400,000. Zavier's original basis in the farmland was $80,000, because he bought the land many years ago. Zavier is frustrated by his government and decides not to purchase replacement farmland. Therefore, he has a taxable event, and he must recognize $320,000 as taxable income ($400,000 - $80,000 = $320,000). However, if Zavier were to purchase replacement property with the condemnation award, he would have a nontaxable section 1033 exchange. He has up to three years to decide if he wants to reinvest the proceeds.

Amounts taken out of a condemnation award to pay debts on the property are considered paid to the taxpayer and are included in the amount of the award.

Example: Kenton owns ten acres of farmland, which he uses to grow wheat and corn. He bought the land several years ago, and still owes a mortgage on the property. The state condemned Kenton's farm and the surrounding land in order to build a light rail system. Kenton tries to fight the condemnation, but he loses his case in court. The court award was set at $200,000. The state paid him only $148,000 because it paid $50,000 to his mortgage company and $2,000 in accrued real estate taxes that were delinquent on the property. Kenton is considered to have received the entire $200,000 as a condemnation award.

The deadlines for replacing condemned property are the same as other qualified section 1033 exchanges.

Example: Hammond owns a strip mall which he rents out to commercial tenants. On March 12, 2023, the building was condemned by the county in order to build a public skatepark. Hammond decides not to fight the condemnation, and the strip mall is torn down a few months later, and he receives his condemnation award from the government on November 30, 2023. Since the strip mall is business-related real estate, Hammond has three full years to reinvest the proceeds in a similar property. He has until December 31, **2026**, to replace the condemned strip mall with a similar building (**three years** from the *end* of the year in which he received the condemnation award). As long as he buys a similar business property within the next three years with the proceeds, he will not have to recognize any of the gain or report it on his return.

Condemnation or Destruction of a Main Home

If a taxpayer's main home is condemned or destroyed, the taxpayer can generally exclude the gain as if they had sold the home under the section 121 exclusion. This includes homes that are seized or disposed of under the "threat of condemnation." In the case of a condemnation, the property owner must be aware of the threat and must reasonably believe that a condemnation is likely to occur.

If the taxpayer's main home is eligible for a section 121 exclusion, single filers can exclude up to $250,000 of the gain and joint filers up to $500,000.

Example: Sharla has owned and lived in her home for seven years. On January 3, 2023, a local government informed Sharla that it wished to acquire her home and surrounding land in order to create a public park. This is a condemnation of private property for public use. After the local government took legal action to condemn her property, Sharla went to court to keep her home. The court decided in favor of the government. The governmental agency takes possession of Sharla's home, and Sharla receives a $355,000 condemnation award from the government on December 27, 2023. Her basis in the home is $153,000. Even if she decides not to reinvest the proceeds of the condemnation award, Sharla will not have a taxable gain, because the gain would have been excludable under section 121 if she had *voluntarily* sold the home ($355,000 award - $153,000 basis = $202,000 non-taxable capital gain).

Any *excess* gains above these amounts may be potentially deferred under section 1033 if the taxpayer reinvests all the proceeds in another, similar property. In order to qualify for deferral, the taxpayer's use of the replacement property must be substantially the same as the replaced property. In other words, a home must be replaced with another home (see example, next).

Example: On February 8, 2023, a fire destroys Claudia's main home. She bought the home ten years ago for $80,000. Claudia's insurance company pays Claudia $400,000 for the house, which was the fair market value of the home when it was destroyed. Claudia realizes a gain of $320,000 ($400,000 insurance proceeds - $80,000 basis). Claudia decides to downsize, and on August 27, 2023, she purchases a smaller condo at the cost of $100,000. Because the destruction of her old house is treated as a "sale" for purposes of section 121, Claudia may exclude $250,000 of the realized gain from her gross income. For purposes of section 1033, the amount "realized" is then treated as being $150,000 ($400,000 insurance proceeds - $250,000 section 121 exclusion) and the gain realized is $70,000 ($150,000 amount realized - $80,000 basis). Claudia elects under section 1033 to recognize only $50,000 of the gain ($150,000 amount realized - $100,000 cost of new house). The remaining $20,000 of gain is deferred and Claudia's basis in the new house is $80,000 ($100,000 cost - $20,000 gain not recognized).[106]

---

[106] The examples in this section are modified from IRS Final Regulations, *Exclusion of Gain from Sale or Exchange of a Principal Residence,* [TD 9030]. RIN 1545-AX28. https://www.irs.gov/pub/irs-regs/td9030.pdf.

Unit 8: Study Questions

(Test yourself first, then check the correct answers at the end of this quiz.)

1. Which form might be received by a taxpayer who has sold their primary residence?

A. Form 1099-MISC
B. Form 8949
C. Schedule D
D. Form 1099-S

2. Alistair and Gabrielle are married and file jointly. They sold their primary residence in Los Angeles after living in it for 292 days because Gabrielle gave birth to triplets, and they needed a larger place to live. They originally bought their home for $585,000 and sold it for $845,000. The total gain on the sale of their home is $260,000. Since they lived there for less than two years but meet one of the exceptions, what is the actual amount of their *reduced* exclusion? (Two years = 730 days.)

A. $60,000
B. $200,000
C. $260,000
D. $500,000

3. Which of the following is NOT considered a primary residence under Section 121 exclusion?

A. A houseboat where the taxpayer resides for the majority of the year.
B. A mobile home where the taxpayer resides for the majority of the year.
C. A rental property with kitchen, bathroom, and cooking facilities.
D. A cooperative apartment where the taxpayer resides for the majority of the year.

4. Which of the following transactions does *not* qualify for a Section 1031 like-kind exchange?

A. An exchange of a commercial building in Chicago for empty farmland in Nebraska.
B. An exchange of an apartment building in Delaware for a factory building in Alaska.
C. An exchange of a residential rental for an undeveloped lot of land.
D. An exchange of a home developer's inventory for a house flipper's housing inventory.

5. Clayton trades a commercial building with an adjusted basis of $84,000 for an industrial tractor with a fair market value of $97,000. Clayton plans to use the tractor in his farming business. What is the basis of the tractor, and how much taxable gain, if any, must Clayton report?

A. $0 gain; $97,000 basis.
B. $0 gain; $13,000 basis.
C. $13,000 gain; $84,000 basis.
D. $13,000 gain; $97,000 basis.

6. Elvis bought a house for $189,000 on July 1, 2019. He lived there continuously for 13 months and then moved in with his girlfriend. They later separated, and Elvis moved back into his own house and lived there for an additional 12 months until he sold it on June 1, 2023, for $220,000. What is the amount and nature of his taxable gain?

A. $0.
B. $31,000 long-term capital gain.
C. $31,000 short-term capital gain.
D. $30,000 long-term capital gain.

7. Magnus and Grace were married on January 12, 2015. They purchased their first home together on March 30, 2015, for $150,000. On February 2, 2023, Magnus and Grace legally separate. The court grants Grace sole ownership of the home as part of their divorce settlement. The divorce became final on August 10, 2023, and the fair market value of the home was $370,000 when sole ownership was transferred to Grace. She sells the house on December 23, 2023, for $480,000 and keeps all the proceeds for herself. What is Grace's taxable gain in this transaction?

A. $0
B. $80,000
C. $120,000
D. $210,000

8. A fire destroyed Bryant's main home on July 15, 2023. On November 23, 2023, he received an insurance reimbursement, which exceeds his basis in the home. Rather than recognizing any gain, Bryant wants to replace the home, but at the end of the year, he still has not found a property that he likes yet. What is the *latest* date that Bryant can purchase a replacement home to defer all the gain from his insurance reimbursement?

A. July 15, 2024
B. August 23, 2025
C. December 31, 2025
D. This scenario does not qualify for nonrecognition treatment.

9. Mitchell and Kaylie are married and file jointly. They live in Texas and have owned and used their house as their main home for 15 months. Mitchell got a job transfer to work in Washington, so the couple is forced to move and sell their home. What is the maximum amount they can exclude from income under the rules regarding a reduced exclusion?

A. $156,250
B. $250,000
C. $312,500
D. $500,000

10. Grady exchanges his residential rental property with an adjusted basis of $50,000 and an FMV of $80,000 for 10 acres of undeveloped land with an FMV of $80,000. He plans to hold the land as an investment. What is Grady's basis in the land after this Section 1031 exchange?

A. $50,000
B. $70,000
C. $80,000
D. This is not a qualifying like-kind exchange.

11. Lenora had several unfortunate events happen to her during the year. Which of the following would not be an acceptable "unforeseen circumstance" for Lenora to take a reduced exclusion on the sale of her primary residence?

A. Her home is condemned by the city.
B. Moving to another state to be closer to her grandchildren.
C. A legal separation that will lead to a divorce.
D. Serious illness of a close family member who she must go care for.

12. Isaiah has lived in and owned his home for 15 months. He decides to move in with his girlfriend, so he sells his home for $285,000. His adjusted basis in the home is $160,000. What is the amount and nature of his taxable gain on the sale?

A. $0
B. $35,000 long-term capital gain.
C. $125,000 long-term capital gain.
D. $125,000 short-term capital gain.

13. Fleur is single and bought her first home ten years ago for $350,000. She lived continuously in the house until she sold it in 2023 for $620,000. Which of the following statements is correct?

A. She may exclude $250,000 of the gain and report the remainder as a long-term capital gain.
B. She may exclude the entire gain. No amount needs to be reported.
C. She may not exclude any of the gain.
D. She may exclude $250,000 of gain. The remaining amount must be reported as ordinary income.

14. Hoshiko and her husband are married, but they live apart in separate homes. They are not legally separated. Hoshiko plans to sell her main home this year. She will file Married Filing Separately. What is the maximum exclusion that she can claim on her MFS return?

A. $0
B. $125,000
C. $250,000
D. $500,000

15. Geoff is a self-employed therapist. He sold his main home in 2023 at a $29,000 gain. He meets the "ownership and use" tests to exclude the gain from his income. However, he used one bedroom of the home as a business office for the last two years, to meet clients in his home. His records show he claimed $3,000 of depreciation for a qualified home office, taking the deduction on his Schedule C. What is Geoff's taxable gain on the sale, if any?

A. $0
B. $1,000
C. $2,000
D. $3,000

16. Annalise is unmarried. During the year, she sold her primary residence in Utah and moved to Florida. She had purchased her house in 2018 for $200,000, and she sold it in 2023 for $550,000, net of selling expenses. During the time she lived in the house, she paid $25,000 for major improvements (a new pool) and $15,000 for general repairs. Assuming that Annalise utilizes the maximum available exclusion, what amount would she report as a taxable capital gain?

A. $0
B. $60,000
C. $75,000
D. $100,000

17. Griffon is a qualified farmer. He trades a plot of pasture land (adjusted basis $300,000, FMV $665,000) for land with an existing almond orchard (FMV $725,000). His pastureland is not as valuable as the almond orchard property, so Griffon pays $60,000 of cash to complete the exchange. What is his basis in the orchard property after the exchange is completed?

A. $325,000
B. $360,000
C. $690,000
D. $725,000

Unit 8: Quiz Answers

1. The answer is D. The Form 1099-S is used to report the gross proceeds from the sale of real estate. If the entire profit is excluded, it is not necessary to report the sale unless a Form 1099-S is received for the proceeds.

2. The answer is B. Alistair and Gabrielle are allowed to claim a *reduced* exclusion of $200,000 (292/730 multiplied by the $500,000 maximum exclusion available for married taxpayers). The remaining $60,000 would be taxed as long-term capital gain and would be reported on Schedule D. This scenario qualifies for the reduced exclusion because multiple births from the same pregnancy is considered an unforeseen circumstance.

3. The answer is C. A rental property would not qualify for the exclusion. The Section 121 exclusion only pertains to a taxpayer's primary residence and does not apply to rental properties, vacation homes, or secondary residences.

4. The answer is D. Inventory never qualifies for like-kind exchange treatment, regardless of whether it is real property or not. The property in a Section 1031 exchange must NOT be held "primarily for sale." Generally, real property exchanges will qualify for like-kind treatment, even though the properties themselves might be dissimilar, so the other exchanges would be permissible.

5. The answer is D. This is not an acceptable like-kind exchange, so the entire transaction is treated as a sale. This is a taxable exchange of property that is not similar, or "unlike" property. Therefore, this is treated like a taxable barter, and the entire $13,000 gain ($97,000-$84,000) is taxable. Clayton's basis in the tractor would be $97,000.

6. The answer is A. Elvis has no taxable gain because the sale qualifies for an exclusion. This sale qualifies for Section 121 treatment. Elvis meets the "ownership and use" tests because, during the five-year period ending on the date of sale, he owned the house for over three years and lived in it for a total of 25 months (over two years). The gain is not taxable and does not need to be reported.

7. The answer is B. Grace meets the ownership and use tests, and the basis in the property remains the same. Property transfers related to a divorce are generally nontaxable, and the FMV of the property at the time of the divorce has no bearing on the taxable outcome of the later sale. Since she owned the property for longer than one year, the taxable portion of Grace's gain would be reported as a long-term capital gain. The gain is calculated as follows:

Sales price	$480,000
Her basis in the home	($150,000)
Total realized gain	$330,000
Section 121 exclusion	($250,000)
Long-Term Capital Gain (taxable)	**$80,000**

8. The answer is C. This is an involuntary conversion of a primary residence. Bryant must acquire qualifying replacement property by December 31, 2025 (*two* years from the *end* of the tax year during which any part of his gain is realized.) Since Bryant received the reimbursement check in 2023, he has two years from December 31, 2023 (the end of the year that he actually received the check), to acquire replacement property. Different types of property have different replacement periods. For example, if Bryant's main home had been destroyed in a federally declared disaster area, he would have four years to replace the property.

9. The answer is C. A reduced exclusion is available, even though Mitchell and Kaylie did not live in the home for two full years. They qualify for a reduced exclusion because they are moving for a change in Mitchell's employment. Their maximum reduced exclusion is $312,500 ($500,000 × [15 months/24 months]). This would be the maximum that they could exclude on the sale. A reduced exclusion applies when the premature sale is primarily due to a move for employment in a new location.

10. The answer is A. This is a qualifying 1031 exchange, so Grady's basis in the land is the same as the basis of the property given up: $50,000. IRC Section 1031 does not limit "like-kind" property to certain types of real estate. Any real property held for productive use in a trade or business *or* for investment can be considered "like-kind" property.

11. The answer is B. Lenora's move to be closer to her grandchildren would not qualify. All of the following events would be qualifying events to claim a reduced exclusion from a premature sale:

- A divorce or legal separation.
- A pregnancy resulting in multiple births.
- The home is sold after being seized, involuntarily converted, or condemned.
- A move due to a new job or new employment (or unemployment).
- Certain health reasons related to care for the taxpayer, a spouse, a child, or certain other related persons.

If any of these exceptions apply, the taxpayer may figure a reduced exclusion based on the number of days he owned and lived in the residence.

12. The answer is C. Isaiah's gain is $125,000, the result of subtracting the adjusted basis in the home from the amount realized ($285,000 - $160,000 = $125,000). Since he does not meet the ownership or use tests or qualify for a reduced exclusion, he cannot exclude any of his gains under Section 121 (because he has not lived in the house for two out of the last five years, and the reason why he moved was not an "unforeseen circumstance"). He owned the property for more than a year, so the gain is taxed as a long-term capital gain.

13. The answer is A. As a single taxpayer, Fleur may exclude a maximum gain amount of $250,000 from the sale of her home. Her gain is $270,000 ($620,000 - $350,000). Her taxable gain is $20,000 ($270,000 gain - $250,000 exclusion), which must be reported as a long-term capital gain.

14. The answer is C. Hoshiko may be able to exclude up to $250,000 of gain on her separate tax return. Unmarried taxpayers or those filing separately can exclude up to a maximum of $250,000 of gain from selling their primary residence.

15. The answer is D. Geoff can exclude $26,000 ($29,000 - $3,000) of his gain. He has a taxable gain of $3,000. He must report the $3,000 of prior depreciation as unrecaptured §1250 gain (taxed at a maximum 25% capital gains rate). Since Geoff took depreciation deductions on his home for business purposes, he cannot exclude the part of the gain equal to any depreciation allowed as a deduction.

16. The answer is C. Annalise's adjusted basis in the house would be $225,000, the total of her original purchase price of $200,000 added to the $25,000 improvements. The cost of general repairs would not be considered in determining her adjusted basis. Therefore, her overall gain on the sale would be $325,000, or the excess of her net proceeds over her adjusted basis. Since she meets the requirements for "ownership and use" of the house, she qualifies for the maximum exclusion of $250,000 available to single taxpayers, and the taxable portion of her gain would be $75,000.

Net proceeds of the sale	$550,000
Less: The purchase price of the house	($200,000)
Less: Cost of improvements	(25,000)
[Total adjusted basis]	[225,000]
Gain on sale	325,000
Exclusion for a single taxpayer	(250,000)
Taxable long-term gain	**$75,000**

17. The answer is B. Griffon's basis in the orchard property is $360,000: the $300,000 basis of his relinquished pastureland plus the additional $60,000 cash he paid.

Unit 9: Rental and Royalty Income

For additional information, read:
Publication 527, *Residential Rental Property (Including Rental of Vacation Homes)*
Publication 946, *How to Depreciate Property*

Rental income refers to any payment received for the use or occupancy of physical property. Examples of rental activities include residential rentals, transient lodging at hotels and motels, commercial rentals, and personal property rentals such as car rentals or machinery rentals. Taxpayers must report all rental income as part of their gross income, and the way in which rental activities are reported may differ depending on the specific type of rental activity involved.

Royalty income is a form of income received for the use of another person's property. This type of income can come from patents, copyrights, or the use of natural resources like timberland, oil and gas wells, or a copper mine. Generally, rental and royalty activities are declared on Schedule E (Form 1040), though there are some exceptions to this rule.

Example: Faris owns a residential duplex. He has two long-term tenants, one on each side of the duplex. He is not a real estate professional. He manages the rental property himself and does many of the repairs and general maintenance. The rental income Faris receives from his tenants is taxable and would be reported on Schedule E, *Supplemental Income and Loss*. The income is subject to income tax, but not self-employment tax.

Example: Madeline owns 200 acres of forestland that she inherited from her grandfather. She leases the forestland to a lumber company that harvests and processes the timber. Madeline receives quarterly payments under a contract agreement with the timber company based on the value of the timber taken from her property during the year. At the end of the year, the timber company provides Madeline with a Form 1099-MISC reporting the payments as "royalties" in Box 2. Madeline reports the royalty payments received as royalty income on Schedule E, *Supplemental Income and Loss*.

Rental Income Defined

Rental property owners are eligible to deduct various expenses related to the management, preservation, and upkeep of their properties. These expenses may include:

- Interest on mortgage payments and property taxes
- Maintenance, lawn care, repairs, and cleaning services
- Expenses for advertising vacancies
- Utilities that are covered by the homeowner (such as sewer or trash)
- Insurance premiums for home, liability, and natural disaster coverage
- Depreciation

Advance Rent: Taxpayers must report rental income when it is constructively received (i.e., available without restrictions). This includes advance rent, which is any amount received before the period that it covers. Thus, a taxpayer must include advance rent in income in the year they receive it, regardless of the period covered or the accounting method used, unless the amounts are subject to restrictions.

Example: Hiraku rents out a duplex. On December 20, 2023, his tenant Cynthia pays two months of rent in advance, in cash, for January 2024 and February 2024 because she is going to Europe on an extended vacation. Hiraku cannot delay reporting the rental income. He must report all the advance rent as taxable income in 2023 (when he received it).

Example: Calvin owns a residential rental property. His tenant, Angelique, is planning to go overseas for four months. On December 31, 2023, she gives Calvin four checks for the rent of January 2024 through April 2024, but she post-dates all the checks. Since the post-dated checks are dated for a future date, Calvin cannot deposit them until 2024. The checks are subject to "substantial restrictions," so he does not have constructive receipt of the income until he actually deposits the checks in the months in which they are payable. He does not have to recognize the advance rental payments until 2024, when he can legally deposit the checks.

Lease Cancellation: If a tenant pays to cancel a lease, the amount received for the lease cancellation is classified as rental income. The payment is included in the year received regardless of the taxpayer's accounting method.

Example: Frawley owns a commercial office building in downtown Chicago. One of Frawley's tenants, a medical doctor, wants to break his lease. The doctor plans to move to another state due to a divorce. Frawley agrees to terminate the lease if the doctor pays an early termination fee equal to two months' rent. The doctor agrees, and pays Frawley $4,000 to terminate the lease on his medical office. Frawley must include the lease termination fee in his rental income on Schedule E.

Refundable Security Deposits: When a tenant pays a refundable security deposit upon renting a property, the money is not considered income for the landlord at that time. However, if the property owner keeps some or all of the security deposit because the tenant did not live up to the terms of the lease or because they damaged the property, then the deposit amount retained is recognized as income in the year it is forfeited by the tenant.

Example: Benjamin owns a residential rental. He signs a lease to rent his residential rental to Shelly, his new tenant. Benjamin receives $750 for the first month's rent and a $500 refundable security deposit from Shelly. Benjamin must include $750 in his rental income, but the refundable security deposit would not be reported, unless and until it was later forfeited by Shelly on account of damages to his property.

Insurance Premiums Paid in Advance: If a taxpayer operates on a cash-basis and they pay an insurance premium that covers <u>multiple years</u>, they can only deduct the portion of the payment that applies to the current year. It is not possible to deduct the entire premium in the year it was paid, if the policy is paid multiple years in advance.

Local Benefit Taxes: In most cases, a property owner cannot deduct charges for local taxes that increase the value of a rental property, such as assessments for streets, sidewalks, or water and sewer systems. These charges are capital expenditures that must be added to the basis of the property. Only taxes to maintain or repair such infrastructure, or interest charges related to financing its construction, can be deducted.

Property or Services in Lieu of Rent: If a landlord receives property or services as payment for rent instead of cash, the fair market value must be recognized as rental income. If the tenant and landlord agree in advance to a price, the agreed-upon price is deemed the fair market value unless there is evidence to the contrary.

> **Example:** Loretta owns an apartment complex with five separate units. One of Loretta's tenants, Maloney, is a professional chimney sweep. Maloney offers to clean all of Loretta's chimneys in her apartment building instead of paying three months' rent in cash. Loretta accepts Maloney's offer. Loretta must recognize income for the amount Maloney would have paid for three months' rent. However, Loretta can deduct that same amount as a business expense for the maintenance of the property.

If a tenant pays expenses on behalf of the landlord, the landlord must recognize the payments as rental income. However, the property owner can also deduct the expenses as rental expenses.

> **Example:** Woodrow owns a residential rental property that he manages himself. While he is out of town on vacation, a pipe bursts inside the rental property and starts flooding the garage. Woodrow's tenant, James, contacts an emergency plumber, pays for the necessary repairs, and deducts the repair bill from his rent payment. Woodrow should include both the net amount of the rent payment and the amount James paid for the utility bills and the repairs as rental income. Woodrow can also deduct the cost of the repair as a rental expense.

> **Example:** Savannah owns an apartment building in New York. The furnace in the apartment building breaks down in the middle of the night. Temperatures are below freezing, so Savannah's tenant, Diego, pays for the emergency repairs out-of-pocket and deducts the furnace repair bill from his rent payment. Savannah must recognize as rental income both the actual amount of rent received in cash from Diego and the amount he paid for the repairs. Savannah can also deduct the cost of the furnace repair as a rental expense.

Vacant Rental Property

A property owner cannot claim a "loss" of rental income for any period of time when the property remains unoccupied. However, if the owner is putting in effort to attract tenants and make the property available for rent, they can still deduct necessary expenses as soon as the property is deemed "available" for renting, regardless of whether or not a tenant is found immediately. In other words, if the property is *available* for rent, the owner can deduct expenses, including depreciation, even if the property is unoccupied.

> **Example:** Finnegan purchased a rental property and made the property available for rent on February 1, 2023, by advertising it in the local newspaper. Finnegan immediately started accepting rental applications and found a tenant who moved in on June 1, 2023. Even though the rental property was unoccupied from February until June, Finnegan can still deduct the mortgage interest and other expenses related to the property during that period, because the property was available, ready, and advertised for rent.

Sometimes a rental property will stand vacant for other reasons. For example, if a landlord must make repairs after a tenant moves out, the owner may still depreciate the rental property during the time it is not available for rent. This is assuming the rental property had already been placed in service as a rental.[107]

Example: Artie owns a residential rental that he has rented continuously for over a decade. In January 2023, he evicts his tenant for non-payment. Artie's tenant vandalizes the property before leaving in the middle of the night. When Artie finally visits the property, he discovers that it will need extensive repairs, which may take over six months to fix. The home will be uninhabitable until the repairs are completed. Artie may continue to claim the expenses on the property, including depreciation, while the repairs are being made. This is considered "idle property."

The rules are different, however, if the owner makes rental property repairs *before* actually placing the property into service. In this case, the repairs must be capitalized and included in the property's basis. The owner can only deduct expenses once the property is placed into service for the production of rental income.[108]

Example: Janessa purchased a rental property in Montana on November 1, 2023. The cost of the home was $145,000. She spends another $12,000 on repairs before actually placing the property into service on January 20, 2024 (the following year), when she begins advertising it for rent. She cannot deduct any of the expenses in 2023, including any mortgage interest or repairs, because the rental was not placed into service until the following year. Instead, those costs would be added to the property's basis. She could begin depreciating the property and deducting expenses in 2024, the year in which she actually placed the property into service.

Depreciation of Rental Property

A landlord can start claiming deductions for the depreciation of a rental property once it is put into use for generating income. A rental property is considered to be "put into use" when it is prepared and available for rent. Depreciation stops when the landlord has either fully recuperated their cost or basis, or when the property is no longer in use, whichever comes first. There are three main factors that determine how much depreciation a landlord can deduct: the property's basis, the recovery period for the property, and the depreciation method used.

Most residential rentals are depreciated over 27.5 years. For example, a residential rental home with a cost basis of $137,500 would generate depreciation of $5,000 per year ($137,500/27.5 years) over most of the years of its depreciable life. Nonresidential buildings are generally depreciated over 39 years, with a half-month's worth of depreciation allowed for the first and last month of the depreciable life of the property (i.e., the mid-month convention). An example of a nonresidential rental would be an office complex, where the offices are rented to business tenants, but nobody lives or sleeps in the building. The cost of land is never depreciated because land does not wear out, become obsolete, or get used up.

---

[107] See IRS Publication 527, *Residential Rental Property*, under the subheading "Idle Property."
[108] In order to deduct costs as expenses rather than having to capitalize them, the rental unit must be placed into service, i.e., it must be ready and available for rent (IRS Reg. § 1.263(a)-2(d)(1)).

Example: Stanislav owns a strip mall as well as an apartment complex. The strip mall is rented to commercial tenants, mostly retail shops. The apartment complex is occupied by month-to-month (residential) tenants, mostly families. The strip mall would be depreciated over 39 years. The apartment complex would be depreciated over 27.5 years.

Example: Mason purchased a rental tri-plex on January 1, 2023, for $395,000. The assessed value of the building is $275,000 and the assessed value of the land is $120,000. It is a residential rental so a MACRS class life of 27.5 years is used. Using straight-line depreciation, the yearly depreciation amount is calculated as follows: $275,000/27.5 years = $10,000 depreciation expense per year just on the building (the land is not depreciable). Mason would report the rental activity on Schedule E (Form 1040).

Example: In 2023, Bernice buys a residential rental property for $200,000 and immediately places it into service as a rental. The most recent property tax assessment made by the county assessor's office is out of date, and it places the value of the home at only $160,000 (which is less than what she actually paid), so she obtains a private appraisal of the property. The private appraisal comes in at a total value of $210,000, so Bernice knows she got a good deal on the purchase of the home. Per the appraisal, 85% of the appraised value of the property ($178,500) was attributable to the home and 15% ($31,500) was attributable to the land. In order to figure out her basis for depreciation, Bernice can allocate 85% of the purchase price to the house and 15% of the purchase price to the land. Therefore, the basis of the house is $170,000 (85% of $200,000) and her basis in the land is $30,000 (15% of $200,000). Bernice may use $170,000 as her basis for depreciation on the property.

Converting a Home to Rental Use: Sometimes, taxpayers will convert their personal residence to a rental property. If a taxpayer converts a personal home to rental use at any time other than the beginning of a tax year, the owner must divide the expenses between rental use and personal use. Only the portion of expenses for the period when the property was used or held as a rental can be deducted as rental expenses.

When converting a property to rental use, it will be considered "placed in service" on the date of conversion. Additionally, if a taxpayer converts a personal home into a rental property, the basis for depreciation will be **the lesser of** the fair market value or their adjusted basis on the date of conversion.

Example: Albert bought his home for $180,000 five years ago. On the date he bought the house, the land was assessed at $30,000 and the home was valued at $150,000. But on January 30, 2023, Albert decided to turn his home into a rental property. However, a recent crime wave has caused real estate values in the area to drop significantly. As a result, the county assessor's office now estimates the Fair Market Value (FMV) of the property to be $130,000, with $20,000 being for the land and $110,000 for the house. The basis for depreciation of the house is the FMV on the date of conversion ($110,000) because it is *less* than Albert's allocated cost when he purchased the property five years ago ($150,000). Albert must use $110,000 as his basis to calculate depreciation on the converted rental, which is reported on Schedule E, *Supplemental Income and Loss*. The cost of land cannot be depreciated, so only the home's value is included in the calculation.

Section 179 Rules for Certain Types of Rental Property

In 2023, the maximum Section 179 deduction is $1,160,000. In the past, a landlord could not claim the Section 179 deduction for any property that was used to produce rental income. This prohibition included *any* rental assets (such as furniture and appliances) as well as capital improvements, such as HVAC systems.

The Tax Cuts and Jobs Act expanded the Section 179 deduction to certain types of tangible personal property that is used predominantly to furnish lodging. This new provision includes lodging facilities, such as dormitories, hostels, drug treatment centers, or similar facilities where sleeping accommodations are provided. As always, Section 179 is elective and can be taken on new or used property. The TCJA also expanded the definition of "eligible property" to include certain expenditures for *nonresidential* buildings: including roofs, heating, ventilating, and air conditioning (HVAC) equipment, fire protection and alarm systems, and security systems. Nonresidential commercial property includes office buildings, medical centers, hotels, and malls.

Example: Isaac owns a medical office building that he rents out exclusively to medical and dental professionals. It generates $325,000 of taxable income (before any Section 179 deduction). During the year, Isaac spends $17,525 on a new HVAC system for the building. He also installs a new alarm system, which cost $16,750. Isaac may choose to deduct the entire cost of the equipment by taking the Section 179 election on his tax return. He does not need to depreciate the HVAC system or the alarm system over their useful lives.

Example: Imogen owns the Bamboo Hostel in New Orleans. The hostel offers inexpensive, short-term rentals to guests. Daily breakfast and clean linens are provided. During the year, Imogen invests in a new air conditioning system, which costs $19,700. Her hostel is classified as a *nonresidential* business property, so she is permitted to take Section 179 to deduct full cost of the air conditioning system in the current year.

Example: Hassan owns a residential duplex that he rents out to month-to-month tenants. During the year, Hassan spends $25,900 on a new roof for the duplex. He cannot deduct the cost of the roof, or take Section 179 for the cost, because it is a *residential* rental. Hassan must capitalize and depreciate the entire cost of the roof as an improvement.

All types of rental properties can produce revenue for their owners, although the tax treatment of the revenue varies on several different factors.

Mixed-Use Buildings: Special rules apply to "mixed-use" buildings. Under current IRS rules, if 80% or more of the annual gross rental income from a mixed-use building is generated from the residential rental apartments, the entire building and its structural components will be classified as a residential rental property.[109] This also means that if 80% of the income generated is from residential rentals, then the entire building and improvements are depreciated over 27.5 years. If the building does *not* meet the 80% test, the entire building and improvements are depreciated over 39 years.

---

[109] This rule for "mixed-use" properties does *not* include a unit in a hotel, motel, inn, or other establishment where the units are rented on a transient basis. These types of properties are classified as "transient occupancy" residential structures, and are treated as commercial properties by default.

Example: Benny purchases a building in historic downtown Sacramento, California. He renovates the building into a mixed-use development consisting of two distinct sections. The upstairs contains 4 residential rental apartments, and the bottom of the building is a retail space rented out to two commercial tenants: a coffee shop and a clothing retailer. 30% of Benny's rental income is from the upstairs residential apartments. The remaining 70% of the revenue comes from the commercial tenants (the downstairs coffee shop and clothing store). In this scenario, the entire building would be treated as *nonresidential* (commercial) property. Benny would depreciate the entire building over 39 years. Later in the year, Benny spends $14,000 to install sprinklers and a new fire protection system. Since the building is treated as nonresidential commercial property, he may use Section 179 to expense the entire cost of the upgrades.

Repairs vs. Improvements to Rental Property

Taxpayers often misunderstand when an expense qualifies as a **repair** or an **improvement**. A taxpayer can expense the cost of repairs to rental property but cannot currently expense the cost of substantial improvements.[110] The IRS defines repairs and improvements in the IRS' tangible property regulations. These are a complex set of provisions governing repairs and capitalization that affect all taxpayers who use tangible property in their businesses.

Unless the improvement qualifies for accelerated depreciation, a property owner must typically recover the cost of an improvement by taking depreciation deductions over the asset's applicable recovery period.

A **repair** generally keeps an asset or property in good working condition but does not add to the value of the asset or substantially prolong its life. Repainting a rental, fixing leaks, and replacing broken windows are examples of repairs that are fully deductible in the year they are paid or incurred.

Improvements are major expenditures that go beyond normal repairs. This can include adding a bedroom or completely replacing the plumbing system, and in most cases, these improvements must be depreciated over time. An "improvement" is defined as anything that results in the **betterment** of a property, **restoration** of a property, or **adaptation** of a property to a new or different use.

Repairs (Currently Expensed)	Improvements (Capitalized and Depreciated)
Painting a room	Adding a room addition or extra bathroom
Fixing a broken window	Replacing all the windows on a property
Replacing a few broken roof tiles	Replacing the entire roof
Power washing a driveway	Repaving or installing an entirely new driveway
Repairing broken appliances	Replacing all the plumbing
Fixing a broken garage door	Construction of a swimming pool

---

[110] Sometimes, the IRS will use the different terms to mean the same thing, such as "betterment of a property" instead of "improvement." These are keywords that the IRS may use interchangeably on the exam.

For the EA exam, most of the specific details of these regulations will likely not be tested. However, you should have a general understanding of the concept that a rental property owner or business owner may recover the costs of property either through current deductions or through periodic depreciation deductions for items required to be capitalized.

Example: Odette owns a residential rental property which she manages herself. In 2023, she spent $18,000 to replace all the plumbing, $9,540 to re-pave the entire driveway, and $575 to repair a couple of broken gutters. Only the gutter repair ($575) can be expensed on her tax return. The costs of the new plumbing and the new driveway must be capitalized and depreciated over time.

The capitalized cost of an improvement is depreciated separately from the original cost of the asset or property that is being improved.

Example #1: Quaid owns a rental property. A baseball broke a window, so he replaced it with an upgraded model, an insulated double-pane window that helps control heating and cooling costs. Even though this window is a substantial upgrade from the previous one, it is still considered a repair, because the old window was broken and needed to be replaced. If Quaid were to replace all the windows in the house, the upgrade would be considered an "improvement," rather than a repair, and he would be required to capitalize the cost and claim depreciation deductions over a period of years.

Example #2: Later in the same year, Quaid also replaces the house's septic tank at a total cost of $19,500. This is considered a substantial improvement, and the cost of the septic tank must be depreciated over time, rather than deducted against current income.

Under the **de minimis safe harbor rule** of the tangible property regulations,[111] the taxpayer can elect to expense tangible property costing no more than $2,500 per invoice or item in the year they are used or consumed. The de minimis safe harbor election does not apply to inventory or to the purchase of land, but can apply to land improvements, such as: livestock fencing, driveways, walkways, retaining walls, and outdoor lighting.

Example: Kenneth owns a residential rental property. During the year, Kenneth replaces the linoleum flooring in the bathroom and the kitchen. His friend is the installer, and gives him a discount on the price. The total cost for installation and materials is $2,100 and is clearly listed on the invoice. Kenneth may deduct this cost as a repair or as supplies, because the total invoice amount is less than $2,500, which is under the safe harbor rule. Kenneth should attach a statement claiming the *"Section 1.263(a)-1(f) de minimis safe harbor election"* to his timely filed federal tax return.

Example: Annie is age 75 and owns 50 acres of pastureland that she rents to local farmers for a flat cash amount. During the year, Annie pays to have a barbed wire fence installed around the property. The barbed wire fence is a land improvement, which typically must be capitalized and depreciated. However, the fencing company gives Annie a generous senior discount, and the invoice cost for the entire job ends up being $2,475, which is just under the de minimis safe harbor. Annie makes the election and deducts the entire cost of the fence as an expense on Schedule E.

---

[111] The tangible property regulations are covered in greater detail in **Book 2, *Businesses*.** For Part 1 of the exam, you may have to know how these regulations apply to rental property or sole proprietors.

There is also an *additional* **safe harbor election for small taxpayers** (SHST) that applies to landlords who own rental properties. Landlords can use the SHST only if the total amount paid during the year for repairs, improvements, and similar expenses for a building does not exceed the *lesser* of (1) $10,000 or (2) 2% of the unadjusted basis of the building. The SHST applies only to buildings with an unadjusted basis of $1 million or less (not including the cost of the land).

Example: Mubarak is a landlord who owns a small office building. Mubarak's office building has an unadjusted basis of $800,000. He wants to upgrade the outdoor lighting system to energy-efficient lights. Under the safe harbor election for small taxpayers (SHST) the annual expense limit for Mubarak's building is the lesser of $10,000 or 2% of the building's unadjusted basis. The cost of the lighting project is $6,500, well below the safe harbor threshold. Mubarak makes the SHST election by attaching a statement to his income tax return for the year. Doing so will allow him to deduct the entire cost of the lighting upgrade as a current expense on Schedule E.

Deductible Rental Losses

The tax treatment of rental income depends on several factors: whether a property owner is a real estate professional or actively participates in managing a property; whether there is any personal use of the rental property, and if so, whether the dwelling is considered a home; and whether the rental activity is for "carried on" for profit. In general, a trade or business activity is considered a passive activity if the taxpayer does not *materially participate* in it, and rental activities are *generally* considered passive activities regardless of the participation of the owners. The deductibility of losses from passive activities is limited, and a taxpayer usually cannot deduct losses from passive activities to offset other nonpassive income (such as wages, or self-employment).

Note: Property owners that provide "substantial services" may be classified as self-employed, and their rental activities classified as business activities on Schedule C, rather than rental activities on Schedule E. The IRS defines "substantial services" as: regular cleaning, changing linen and towels, and/or daily maid service (such as the services a guest might receive at a hotel or a motel). In this case, the rental income and expenses, including interest and taxes, would be reported on Schedule C and subject to self-employment tax. Motel and hotel owners are covered in more detail later in the chapter.

Generally, losses from passive activities that exceed income from passive activities in the same year are disallowed. The disallowed losses are carried forward to the next taxable year and can be used to offset future income from passive activities. There is a special "$25,000 exception" to this rule, however, for rental real estate activities.

Special $25,000 "Loss Allowance" for Real Estate Rental Activities

If a landlord is actively involved in managing their rental properties, they may be eligible to deduct up to $25,000 of losses from their nonpassive income. It is important to distinguish that active participation does not require the same level of involvement as material participation.

Note: "Active participation" is not the same standard as "material participation." Material participation is a much higher standard. For example, the owner of a rental property will generally be treated as *actively* participating if they make management decisions such as deciding rental contracts, approving repairs, and other similar management decisions.

To be considered "actively participating" in a rental activity, a property owner must own at least 10% of the rental property and must make management decisions in a significant and bona fide way, such as approving new tenants and establishing the rental terms. Active participation can also include participation by the property owner's spouse.

> **Example:** Basil owns a residential rental property in Los Angeles, California. He lives in Los Angeles and has a regular full-time job as a teacher. Basil actively manages his rental by choosing his own tenants, hiring contractors to do any required repairs, and personally collecting the rent. Basil is not a real estate professional, but he is *actively participating* in his rental activity.

However, if the IRS determines a taxpayer has not actively participated, rental losses are not currently deductible, and the taxpayer would not be eligible for the special $25,000 loss allowance.

> **Example:** Camelia owns a rental condo in Hawaii. She lives and works in Nevada. Camelia hired a management company to manage the property and screen new tenants. The management company handles all the repairs and collects the rent. The management company charges a fee for its services and then remits the net proceeds to Camelia monthly. It has been several years since Camelia has even visited the property. Camelia is not actively participating in this rental activity. In 2023, she has $43,000 in rental income from the property, but her expenses are $51,000, which means she had a net rental loss of ($8,000). Since she is not actively participating in the rental activity, she is not eligible for the special loss allowance. In 2023, she has $75,000 in wages and no other income. Since she does not have any other passive income to offset, she must carry over her $8,000 passive rental losses to a future tax year.

This special loss allowance is subject to an income phaseout. The full $25,000 loss allowance is available for taxpayers, whether single or MFJ, whose modified adjusted gross income (MAGI) is $100,000 or less.

> **Definition: MAGI** is a taxpayer's adjusted gross income with certain deductions added back in. These may include IRA contributions, rental losses, student loan interest, and qualified tuition expenses, among others. A taxpayer's MAGI is used as a basis for determining whether he qualifies for certain tax deductions.

If a taxpayer is married and files a separate return, but lived apart from their spouse for the entire tax year, the taxpayer's special allowance for rental losses cannot exceed $12,500; and this $12,500 allowance would only be available if the taxpayer's MAGI is $50,000 or less. However, if the taxpayer *lives* with their spouse at any time during the year and is filing MFS, the taxpayer cannot use any passive rental losses to offset nonpassive income.

> **Example:** Camden and Brenda are married and live together, but they choose to file separate returns. They do not live in a community property state and keep all their income and assets separate. Camden owns a residential rental as his sole property. Camden actively participates in the rental activity by choosing his own tenants and making repairs to the property as necessary. In 2023, he earned $68,000 in wages. His rental activity has an overall loss of ($14,800). Because he files separately, but lived with his wife during the year, Camden cannot deduct any of the rental losses from his nonpassive income (his wages). His entire rental loss must be carried forward to future years.

Example: Mustafa and Fatima are married, but have lived apart for several years. They file separate tax returns. Mustafa owns a residential rental that he manages himself. Mustafa's wages for the year were $42,000, and he had no other taxable income. Mustafa incurred a ($6,000) loss on his rental property. Even though he files MFS, he is allowed to take the full rental loss because (1) he did not live with his wife at any time during the year, (2) his MAGI was under $50,000, and (3) his rental losses were less than $12,500 (one-half of the "special allowance"). After deducting his allowable rental losses from his wages, his adjusted gross income would be reduced down to $36,000 ($42,000 wages - $6,000 allowable rental loss).

Only passive rental activities qualify for this "special loss allowance," and not other types of passive activities. Furthermore, certain taxpayers do not qualify for the special loss allowance. The following taxpayers are not allowed to claim the special loss allowance:

- A limited partner in a business activity,
- A property owner who has less than 10% ownership in a rental activity,
- A trust or corporation (The $25,000 special allowance is available only to natural persons, although disregarded grantor trusts are permitted.)

Example: Callum is a 5% minority-interest partner in Crestview Rentals, LLC, a partnership that owns a 50-unit apartment complex in Texas. The other investors in the apartment building are unrelated to Callum. The complex is managed by a professional management company. Callum has little or no involvement in the rental activity. Since Callum does not own at least 10% of the activity, he cannot be treated as "actively participating" in the rental. If the rental has losses for the year, Callum will not be able to offset his active income with those losses. Instead, the losses would have to be carried to future years to offset future passive income.

Rental losses that cannot be deducted due to the limitations described above can be carried forward indefinitely and used in subsequent years, subject to the same limitations.

Example: Kamal works as a full-time grocery store manager and earns $80,000 in wages per year. He also owns two residential rental properties, but he is not a real estate professional. He manages the properties himself and personally collects the rents. Whenever repairs are needed, he hires contractors to complete them. Kamal should report his rental income and losses on Schedule E. His rental income is considered passive activity income, and it is not subject to self-employment tax. He is also eligible for the $25,000 loss allowance if his rentals have losses for the year.

Example: Hamid and Emeline are married and file jointly. They own a residential rental duplex that they manage themselves together. They have combined wages of $98,000 and a rental loss on the duplex of ($26,800). Because they meet both the active participation and the MAGI tests, they are allowed to deduct $25,000 of the rental loss as an offset to their nonpassive income (their wages). The remaining amount over the $25,000 limit ($1,800) that cannot be deducted in the current year is carried forward and may potentially be used in the following year.

If a taxpayer's MAGI is more than $100,000, the "loss allowance" decreases by $1 for every $2 above the threshold. If their MAGI reaches $150,000 or higher (or $75,000 if filing separately when married), the full $25,000 allowance is phased out and any losses must be carried over to future years.

Example: Ernesto and Fabiola file jointly and have MAGI of $140,000. They have $25,000 of losses from the residential rental property that they actively manage. Because they actively manage the property, they potentially qualify to deduct up to $25,000 of losses against their nonpassive income. However, because their joint income is over $100,000, they are subject to a phaseout. Therefore, Ernesto and Fabiola's deduction for rental losses is reduced by $20,000 (0.5 × [$140,000 - $100,000]). They can deduct $5,000 ($25,000 - $20,000) against their nonpassive income. The additional $20,000 of losses is carried forward to the following year.

Suspended losses can also be released when the taxpayer's income goes below the applicable thresholds, or also when the property is disposed of in a fully taxable sale.

Example: Guillermo owns a rental property in San Diego. He actively participates in the rental activity by choosing all his own tenants and collecting the rents himself. In the prior tax year, he incurred ($9,000) in net losses on his rental. Guillermo's modified adjusted gross income was $175,000 for the year. Because of his income threshold, all of Guillermo's rental losses were suspended, and he was not allowed to deduct any rental losses. In 2023, Guillermo incurred an additional ($5,000) in losses from his rental activity. However, he also switched jobs in the middle of the year, and now his salary is lower. In 2023, Guillermo's adjusted gross income is $89,000, so his rental losses are now permissible. His suspended rental losses from the prior year ($9,000) and his current-year losses ($5,000) will be allowed on his 2023 tax return, for a total loss of ($14,000) on Schedule E. This loss will offset his wages, and give him a lower tax liability in 2023.

Renting Only Part of Property

In the case of a taxpayer who only rents a portion of a property, they must allocate specific expenses between the part used for rental purposes and the part used for personal use, essentially treating the property as two separate units. Any costs related to the rental portion can be claimed as rental expenses on Schedule E. This would include a percentage of the home's expenses that normally are nondeductible personal expenses, such as painting the outside of a house. If an expense applies to both rental use and personal use, such as a heating bill for the entire house, the landlord must divide the expense between the two. The two most common methods for dividing such expenses are based on either (1) the number of rooms in the house, or, (2) the square footage of the house.

Example: Dustin rents out a single bedroom in his house, which measures 12 × 15 feet, or 180 square feet. The total area of his entire house is 1,800 square feet. As a landlord, Dustin can deduct 10% of any expense that is divided between rental use and personal use. However, any expense solely for the rental portion can be fully deducted. During the year, Dustin spends $525 to replace the wallpaper in the rented bedroom; he does not replace the rest of the wallpaper in the house. This cost of the new wallpaper can be fully deducted, because it was solely allocatable to the rental portion. Additionally, Dustin's heating bills for the whole house come out to $900 for the year, but only $90 ($900 × 10%) can be deducted as a rental expense. The remaining $810 is a personal expense and cannot be deducted by Dustin.

A common scenario involves a duplex where the landlord resides in one unit while renting out the other. In this situation, certain costs such as mortgage interest and property taxes must be divided in order to determine which apply to the rental portion and which are personal expenses.

> **Example:** Marisa owns a duplex with two units of the same size. She lives on one side and rents out the other. Marisa paid $12,000 of mortgage interest and $4,000 of real estate taxes for the entire property. Marisa can deduct $6,000 of mortgage interest and $2,000 of real estate taxes on Schedule E (half of these costs). She can claim the other $6,000 of mortgage interest and $2,000 of real estate taxes attributable to her personal use on Schedule A as itemized deductions.

If a taxpayer has partial ownership of a rental property, they can deduct expenses proportionate to their share of ownership.

> **Example:** Adrian and Carleen are first cousins. They are joint owners of a rental property in Lake Tahoe that they inherited from their grandfather. They rent out the property to long-term tenants, and manage it themselves. Each owns a 50% interest in the house, and they hold the title to the home personally, not through an LLC or a trust. Adrian and Carleen divide the income and expenses 50-50, and each reports their respective share on their individual returns on Schedule E.

Personal Use of Dwelling Unit

When a person owns a residence, whether it is their main home or a second home, and they use it for both personal and rental purposes, they must allocate expenses accordingly. If a family member lives in the property without paying rent, this counts as personal use.

Rental expenses generally will be no more than a taxpayer's total expenses multiplied by the following fraction: the denominator is the total number of days the dwelling is used, and the numerator is the total number of days actually rented at a fair rental price. Any day where a fair rental price was charged counts as a day of rental use.

> **Example:** Pamela owns a vacation home in Florida, that she rented for 90 days in January, February, and March. The rest of the year, her son lived in the home rent-free. Pamela can deduct the rental expenses, including mortgage interest and real estate taxes on Schedule E only for those 90 days that the property was rented at fair rental value. However, she can deduct expenses, the mortgage interest and real estate taxes for the other 275 days of the year on her Schedule A.

Partial Rental Activity (with a Profit Motive)

If a taxpayer uses a property for both personal and rental purposes, the way expenses are handled depends on if their personal use qualifies as usage of a "residence." The home is considered a "residence" if the owner uses the property for personal purposes during the year for more than the greater of (1) fourteen days, or (2) 10% of the total days it is rented at a fair rental price. Personal use includes when a member of the taxpayer's family stays in the property without paying rent, anyone else staying at the property for less than the fair rental price, or any day that the property is donated to a charitable organization.

If the property is (1) deemed to be a personal residence, (2) the rental activity is a "partial rental activity" and (3) the owner's rental expenses exceed rental income, then the owner cannot use the excess expenses to offset income from other sources. However, excess deductions may be carried forward to the next year and treated as rental expenses for the same property, subject to the same limits.

Example: Ronnie lives primarily in Washington, but he also owns a condominium in Florida. He uses his Florida condo as a personal residence for four months out of each year, during the winter. He rents it out to tenants for the rest of the year. He has a profit motive in the rental activity. Ronnie's total rental income is $9,000 in 2023, and his rental expenses are $10,000 (during the months it was available for rent). Ronnie cannot deduct the full $10,000 of rental expenses, because the condominium is not strictly a rental. It is also a personal home that he used for several months. Ronnie can carry over the remaining ($1,000) in disallowed losses and deduct that amount from future rental income on the condominium. He would report the rental activity on Schedule E.

Any day the owner of the property spends working on repairs and maintaining the property is not counted as "personal use," even if the owner's family is also staying at the property.

Example: Zachariah lives in San Diego, California, and owns a residential rental property in Boulder, Colorado. Typically, Zachariah rents out the Boulder property all year round, however, in 2023, Zachariah decides to visit the property while it is unoccupied between tenants. He spends a month there, working on repairs and renovations such as replacing the carpet and painting the exterior. As his main purpose for staying at the property was to perform necessary maintenance and upkeep, these days do not count as personal use. Therefore, all the rental expenses associated with the property can be claimed as usual on Schedule E.

Not-for-Profit Rentals and Below-Market Rentals

If a taxpayer does not rent their property with the intention of making a profit, they cannot claim any rental expenses that exceed their rental income. In the case of a "not-for-profit" rental, the rental income is not reported on Schedule E, and the taxpayer cannot deduct a loss. Any unused expenses on a "not-for-profit" rental cannot be carried forward to the following year.

When a taxpayer rents below fair market price, such as rental to a close family member, the taxpayer would be considered to be renting "not-for-profit." Below-market rentals to a family member or another related party is the most common type of "not-for-profit" rental. Not-for-profit rental income is reported on Form 1040 as "other income."

If the taxpayer itemizes deductions, they can deduct the mortgage interest and real estate taxes (subject to the limitations on the deductibility of state and local taxes) on the appropriate lines of Schedule A (Form 1040).

Example: Alessandra rents her second home to her grandson, Boris, for $500 per month, which is much less than fair market value (fair rental value in her city would be $2,500 per month). There is no profit on the rental, because Alessandra's rental expenses exceed the income generated by the property. Since the rental activity does not have a profit motive, Alessandra should report the rental income on Form 1040, Schedule 1, Line 8j as "activity not engaged in for profit income." The mortgage interest and property taxes[112] are deductible on Alessandra's Schedule A, just like they would be for any other second home. She would not use Schedule E to deduct the losses or claim any deductions.

---

[112] Because of changes in the Tax Cuts and Jobs Act, property taxes (along with other state and local taxes) for non-business and non-rental activities are generally subject to an overall deduction limit of $10,000 ($5,000 for those that file MFS). This will be covered in more detail in Unit 12.

Minimal Rental Use (15-Day Rule)

If a taxpayer rents a main home or vacation home that is considered a "residence" for fewer than 15 days a year, the taxpayer does not have to recognize any of the income as taxable. This is called the "15-day rule," or "minimal rental use." While the rental income is not taxable, the homeowner also cannot deduct any expenses related to the rental of the property during this period. This includes costs such as maintenance, utilities, insurance, and repairs.

Example: Estelle owns a condo on the Gulf Coast, which is her personal residence. She lives in the home and does not have another residence. While she was away visiting her sister, she rented her condo for 11 days, using an online hosting service, charging $100 per day for a total of $1,100. She also had $320 of rental expenses during that time, because her renters broke a bathroom window that she had to get replaced. Estelle does not report any of the income or expenses, based on the exception for minimal rental use.

Example: Jonah lives in Phoenix, Arizona. In 2023, the World Series was held in Arizona, and Jonah's home is within walking distance of the ballpark. Jonah took this opportunity to rent his home during the series to make some extra cash. He advertised his home for rent online and rented the home during the World Series. During that time, he slept on his friend's couch in a neighboring city. He rented his personal home for 7 days, charging $350 per night, for a total of $2,450 in rental income. Since the rental period is fewer than 15 days, it is considered minimal rental use. He does not have to report any of the income. He also cannot deduct any expenses related to the rental.

Example: Ezekiel rented out his Miami beach house for 10 days to a New York family in 2023, earning $7,000. This is not taxable income and he does not need to report it on his tax return due to the "15-day rule." During the 10 days the family stayed at his beach house, Ezekiel incurred some expenses related to the rental. Ezekiel spent $290 on a cleaning service to tidy up before and after their stay. This expense is non-deductible. If Ezekiel were to rent the beach house out for more than 15 days in the future, he would need to report and deduct rental income and expenses accordingly.

Special Rules for Real Estate Professionals

For a taxpayer to be considered a "real estate professional," they must meet certain criteria. If they do qualify, any losses from rental real estate activities where they actively participate are not classified as passive and can be deducted in full. However, if they do not meet the requirements for material participation, any rental losses are typically classified as passive and can only be deducted up to $25,000 according to the previously outlined passive activity rules. [113]

To be classified as a real estate professional, a taxpayer must provide more than one-half of their total personal services in real property trades or businesses in which they materially participate, **and** perform more than 750 hours of services during the tax year in real property business activities, which includes: property development, renovation, construction, acquisition, conversion, rental, operation,

---

[113] The determination of whether someone is a "real estate professional" is based on a number of factors. In general, a taxpayer qualifies as a real estate professional if (1) they perform more than 750 hours of services during the taxable year in real property trades or businesses in which they materially participate, and (2) more than one-half of the total personal services performed in trades or businesses by the taxpayer during the year are performed in real property trades or businesses in which the taxpayer materially participates.

management, leasing, or brokerage services. The taxpayer must own **more than 5 percent** of any activity for it to be considered under the real estate professional rules.

If a taxpayer is married and files jointly, one spouse must meet the 750-hour test and more than one-half of personal services test with their own hours alone; however, for determining whether that taxpayer materially participated, the spouse's participation hours are considered.

Example: Hoshi spends 800 hours a year repairing, maintaining, and dealing with tenants at her five apartment complexes, which she owns. Every spring, she also works part-time in her father's accounting firm to help him through the busy season. She works 500 hours total at her father's accounting firm. Because Hoshi (1) spends more than 750 hours materially participating in real estate, and (2) the 800 hours of real estate services is more than half of the 1,300 hours of total time she spends on both real estate and accounting services for the year, she is classified as a real estate professional. As such, if she generates a tax loss in her rentals for the year, she will be able to deduct the losses on her return without any limitations.

In most instances, even if a taxpayer is a real estate professional, but they only provide basic services to tenants, such as trash collection, the owner would report rental income and expenses on Schedule E, Form 1040, and the rental income would not be subject to self-employment tax.

Example: Sofia, who is unmarried, is a self-employed real estate agent. She also owns four residential rental properties, all of which she manages herself. She also materially participates in each of the rental activities, as she is the only one doing any work for them. Sofia works more than 2,000 hours per year (40 hours a week), working in her real estate business and managing the rental properties that she owns. She meets both hours tests for real estate professional status and can deduct any losses from the rentals against non-passive income. She will report her rental activities on Schedule E, and her realtor's commissions on Schedule C.

In contrast, owners of property who provide "substantial services" to the renter, such as maid cleaning and housekeeping services, are generally required to report revenue and expenses related to the property on Schedule C, *Profit or Loss from Business,* and any net profit is subject to self-employment tax. The most common examples of property owners who report their rental activities on Schedule C, instead of Schedule E, are hotel and motel operators (covered next).

Hotels, Motels, and Bed and Breakfasts

Operators of hotels, motels, boarding houses, and bed and breakfasts must report their rental income on Schedule C, not Schedule E. If the property is rented on a transient basis, and if the owner provides "substantial services" to the tenant, such as daily maid service, laundry service, or regular breakfast service, the property owner should report the rental income and expenses on Schedule C (Form 1040), *Profit or Loss from Business*, rather than Schedule E.

Example: Hattie owns a small, 10-unit motel near downtown Cincinnati. The hotel does not offer long-term rentals, and Hattie's hotel license only permits guests to stay a maximum of 30 days or less. Her hotel offers full maid service, cleaning, and breakfast daily. Since Hattie provides "significant services" as the motel owner, the income and expenses would be reported on her Schedule C.

Example: Chilton owns a camping resort in the Rocky Mountains called "Chilton's Wilderness Retreat." It has rustic cabins that attract tourists from all over the United States. Chilton provides substantial services to his guests, including daily housekeeping, continental breakfast, hiking and sightseeing activities, and transportation. Chilton reports his income and expenses on Schedule C, due to the substantial services he provides to his guests.

In some cases, renting out part of a house can be classified for tax purposes as the equivalent of running a bed-and-breakfast. The facts and circumstances of each situation must be considered to determine if the taxpayer is providing "substantial services" to a tenant.

Example: Moriah lives in a popular tourist area in Palm Springs, CA. She has a small granny cottage behind her home. Moriah listed her granny cottage on a popular website for vacation rentals, Airweb. She used Airweb to rent her cottage 140 days last year to several guests. She provides daily cleaning service, continental breakfast service, and fresh towels and linens, just like a hotel would. Even though she is not a real estate professional, Moriah would report the rental income and related expenses on Schedule C, not Schedule E, because she is providing a short-term rental and "substantial services" to her tenants.

Personal Property Rentals

The rental of personal property (such as vehicles, equipment, or formal wear) is not reported on Schedule E. Instead, it is reported on Schedule C, if the activity is a trade or business. Taxpayers who are "not in the business" of renting personal property but still have a profit motive, should report their income on line 8l and expenses on line 24b of Schedule 1 (Form 1040). For example, if a taxpayer only rents out their boat occasionally to friends and family, this would be a personal property rental that may not rise to the level of a "trade or business."

Note: Personal property is not the same as "personal-use" property that a taxpayer uses for personal purposes. "Personal property" is an accounting term that is used to describe any tangible asset other than real estate. In civil law, personal property is sometimes called "movable property." Examples of personal property include appliances, furniture, vehicles, and collectibles. The distinguishing factor between personal property and real property is that personal property is movable, while real property, such as land or buildings, remains in one location.

Note that the IRS publications do not specifically address the treatment of personal property rentals, nor do they define at which point a personal property rental activity becomes a "trade or business." Advance payments for renting personal property must be reported in the year received.

Example: Ralph owns an RV that he rents out sporadically during the summertime to family and friends. He rents his RV for $39 a day, which covers his costs as well as generates a small profit for him. He does not advertise and only rents to people he knows. His rental activity does not rise to the level of a trade or business, but he does have a profit motive in the activity. He should report his rental income on line 8 of Schedule 1 (Form 1040), and any expenses associated with the personal property rental activities may be entered as an adjustment to income on Schedule 1, Line 24b. The expenses would be limited to his income from the activity.

> **Example:** Laurel owns Sunbelt Party Rentals, LLC which rents out catering equipment, pop-up tents, and tables for weddings and other celebrations. Laurel has a profit motive in the activity and works in the business full-time, all year round. She should report her personal property rental activity on Schedule C, not Schedule E.

Royalty Income

Like rental income, royalties are typically reported on Schedule E of the taxpayer's return, not subject to self-employment tax. However, if the taxpayer is actively involved in the production or maintenance of the property generating the royalties, they might be considered self-employment income and could be subject to self-employment tax (explained next).

Natural resource royalties are paid for the extraction of natural resources, like timber, oil, gas, and minerals. The owner of the land or mineral rights typically receives a royalty based on the value of the resource extracted. Royalties from copyrights on literary, musical, or artistic works are usually paid to a taxpayer for the right to use a creator's work over a specified period of time. Royalties can also be based on the number of units sold. For example, an author might receive a royalty for each book sold, or a musician might receive a royalty for each song streamed or downloaded. Royalty payments are always reported to the taxpayer on Form 1099-MISC. A business is required to issue Form 1099-MISC, *Miscellaneous Income,* to each person that has been paid at least $10 of royalties for the year.

> **Example:** Corey owns 200 acres of farmland. In 2023, natural gas deposits were discovered on his property. Corey negotiates a contract with an energy company that wishes to extract the natural gas from his land. The contract stipulates that he will receive 12% of the revenue generated by the gas extracted from his property. During the year, Corey receives $98,000 in royalties from the energy company. The amounts were reported as royalties to Corey on Form 1099-MISC, and he will report this income on his Schedule E, Form 1040. The royalties are not subject to self-employment tax, and Corey is not considered to be self-employed.

Special rules apply to *self-employed* writers, musicians, and inventors. These taxpayers must report their royalty income on Schedule C, *Profit or Loss from Business*, and the income is also subject to self-employment tax. This is because their personal efforts created the property. As stated in earlier chapters, a copyright or trademark in the hands of its creator is not a capital asset.

> **Example:** Tilda is a self-employed writer of a popular series of children's books. She receives royalties from her publisher based on the number of books she sells during the year. In 2023, Tilda's most popular children's book, *The Pretty Butterfly*, was optioned for a cartoon movie, and Tilda received a large sum from the movie studio to license her book's copyright to them. Tilda must report all her income, including the book royalties, as business income on her Schedule C.

> **Example:** Phillip is a multi-talented musician who composes, performs, and produces his own jazz music. He has a contract with an online music distribution company that compensates him based on the number of streams and downloads of his songs. As a self-employed musician, Phillip's earnings from royalties are considered self-employment income. The income must be reported on Schedule C of his tax return and is subject to self-employment taxes.

Example: Lorelai is a professional photographer. All throughout the year, she visits movie premieres and takes thousands of photos of popular celebrities, then sells them on several online stock photo websites. Her celebrity photographs are licensed by media outlets worldwide. She earned $92,000 in royalties during the year. Since she is self-employed, and the photographs were taken by her, she must report these photography royalties as business income on Schedule C, *not* Schedule E.

In the event that the creator of an intellectual property asset passes away, and the asset is passed down to a beneficiary through inheritance, it is classified as a capital asset for the beneficiary. Any income earned by the beneficiary on this asset will no longer be subject to self-employment tax.

Example: Iggy Jones was an author who always reported his earnings on Schedule C. In 2023, Iggy Jones dies, leaving his daughter Hazel as the sole heir of his estate. One of Iggy's best-selling works was an instructional handbook on survival techniques. After her father's death, Hazel licenses the copyrighted material to various educational institutions and publishers. As she did not create the copyright herself (it was inherited from her father), any royalty income she receives will be reported on Schedule E. This income is taxable to Hazel, but it is not subject to self-employment tax since she did not create the copyright herself.

Unit 9: Study Questions

(Test yourself first, then check the correct answers at the end of this quiz.)

1. Which of the following costs related to rental property should normally be classified as a capital improvement and depreciated rather than being expensed currently?

A. Building a new outdoor deck.
B. Repairing a broken toilet.
C. Painting the family room.
D. Patching a hole in the wall.

2. In 2023, Gaston and Brittany moved from California to Florida. They decided to rent their old house in California instead of selling it. They had purchased the home two years ago for $500,000 and had paid $80,000 for various capital improvements over the years. The purchase price of $500,000 was attributable to fair market values of $100,000 for the land and $400,000 for the house. Their new tenant paid a refundable security deposit of $6,000 and moved in on July 1, 2023. The FMV of the property on July 1 was $525,000, comprised of $105,000 for the land and $420,000 for the house. The tenant then paid rent of $3,000 each month from July through December of 2023. Gaston and Brittany incurred the following expenses related to the house for the entire year:

- Mortgage interest: $10,000
- Property taxes: $10,000
- Casualty insurance: $1,000

In addition, they paid $500 for repairs during December, when a bathroom pipe broke. Exclusive of depreciation expense, what was Gaston and Brittany's taxable rental income?

A. $1,500
B. $7,000
C. $7,250
D. $13,000

3. Zachariah lived in his home until the end of September. Then his employer transferred his job overseas and Zachariah began renting out his residence on October 1, 2023. The property is rented at fair rental value. The total amount of Zachariah's mortgage interest for the entire tax year was $2,400 and his property taxes were $600 for the year. How much of Zachariah's mortgage interest and property taxes should be reported on his Schedule E?

A. $600 in interest and $150 in property taxes
B. $1,800 in interest and $450 in property taxes
C. $2,000 in interest and $500 in property taxes
D. None of it

4. Antoine and Ludivina are physically separated and have lived apart for three years. They file separate tax returns (MFS). They own a rental property jointly; actively participate in the rental activity, and share income and losses equally. The rental property had ($30,000) of losses during the year, mostly due to accidental damage that was done by a tenant. Antoine has wage income of $48,000. He has no other items of income or loss. What is the maximum amount of rental losses that Antoine can claim on his *separate* return?

A. $0
B. $12,500
C. $15,000
D. $25,000

5. Treyton owns a commercial building. He signs a three-year lease with a business tenant who wishes to rent the building. Treyton offers a substantial discount to the tenant if payment is made in advance. The tenant agrees, and in December 2023, Treyton receives $12,000 for the entire first year's rent and $12,000 as rent for the last year of the lease. He also receives a $1,500 security deposit that is refundable at the end of the lease. How much rental income must Treyton include in his tax return?

A. $1,500
B. $12,000
C. $24,000
D. $25,500

6. Annika converted her primary residence to rental use during the year. Her original cost was $189,000, of which $13,200 was allocated to the land, and $175,800 was to the house. The property's value has gone down since its purchase, and on the date of the conversion to a rental property, the property had a fair market value of $158,000, of which $11,000 was allocable to the land and $147,000 to the house. What is Annika's basis for depreciation on Schedule E?

A. $147,000
B. $158,000
C. $175,800
D. $189,000

7. Miley's home is used exclusively as her residence all year, except for 13 days. During this time, Miley rents her home to alumni while the local college has its homecoming celebration. She made $3,000 of rental income and had $200 of rental expenses during this 13-day period. Which of the following statements is correct?

A. Miley must recognize $3,000 of rental income, and deduct the $200 in expenses on Schedule E.
B. Miley can exclude only $2,700 of the rental income.
C. Miley can deduct her expenses when she reports her rental income on Schedule E.
D. All of the rental income may be excluded.

8. Kenia is unmarried and earns $40,000 of wages and $2,000 of passive activity income from a limited partnership. These are her only sources of income for the year. She also has ($3,500) in passive activity *losses* from a rental real estate activity in which she actively participated. Which of the following statements is correct?

A. The first $2,000 of her $3,500 passive loss offsets her passive income. She can deduct the remaining $1,500 loss to reduce taxation of her wages.
B. She cannot deduct the passive loss to reduce taxation of her wages.
C. She cannot offset the rental loss against the passive income from the partnership because it is not the same type of passive activity.
D. She must carry over her loss to the subsequent tax year.

9. Kyung-Hu owns a residential rental home. Last year, she paid $968 to repair a broken window. The cost of the labor was $468, and the cost of the replacement window was $500. She replaced the broken window with a premium energy-saving window. What is the correct treatment of this expense?

A. She cannot deduct the cost since it was an improvement; she must add it to the basis of the property.
B. She can deduct $468 as a rental expense on Schedule E (the labor cost). The cost of the actual window ($500) must be capitalized and depreciated.
C. She can deduct the entire $968 as a rental expense on Schedule E.
D. She can deduct $968 on Schedule A as an itemized deduction.

10. Asher decides to convert his primary residence into a rental property. He moves out of his home on May 1, 2023, and starts advertising and renting it a month later, on June 1, 2023. The property rents immediately, and his first tenant moves in right away. Asher paid $12,000 of mortgage interest for the entire year. He itemizes his deductions. How should Asher report his mortgage interest expense?

A. Report the entire $12,000 on Schedule E.
B. Report the entire $12,000 on Schedule A.
C. Report $7,000 on Schedule E as interest expense and $5,000 on Schedule A as mortgage interest.
D. Report $8,000 on Schedule E as interest expense and $4,000 on Schedule A as mortgage interest.

11. Habib owns a residential rental property that he actively manages himself. He collects rental income of $20,600 during the year. The rental expenses total $17,000. In addition, there is $11,000 of depreciation. Habib earns $90,000 in wages during the year, and has no other activity for the year. He files as single. What is his *allowable* rental loss on Schedule E?

A. $0, all his losses must be carried forward.
B. $7,400
C. $10,600
D. $28,000

12. Which of the following describes depreciation?

A. A business expense that applies only to rental properties.
B. An improvement to an asset that must be capitalized.
C. A common type of accounting method used by most partnerships.
D. A tax deduction that allows a business to recover the cost basis of an asset over time.

13. Pamela ordered an HVAC unit for her rental property on November 30, 2022. It was delivered on December 28, 2022, and was installed and ready for use on January 2, 2023. She paid for the unit using a credit card and paid off the card on February 3, 2023. On which date would the HVAC unit be considered "placed in service" for depreciation purposes?

A. November 15, 2022
B. December 28, 2022
C. January 2, 2023
D. February 3, 2023

14. Abdul owns a commercial office building that he manages himself. In 2023, he incurred the following expenditures in connection with the rental property. Which of these must be capitalized and depreciated over time?

A. New HVAC system
B. A material expansion of the building
C. Fixing a crack in the driveway
D. New alarm system

15. Which type of royalty income would be considered self-employment income?

A. Royalties received by an author from book sales.
B. Royalties received by a landowner from oil extraction on their land.
C. Royalties received by a land owner for timber cut on their land.
D. Royalties received by an heir from an inherited copyright.

16. Alexander owns a small car rental company in Boca Raton, Florida, a popular vacation spot. He owns nine vehicles and rents them out to tourists. He works full-time in the business, and has a profit motive in the activity, which is taxed as a sole proprietorship. How should this rental income be reported on his tax return?

A. The rental income should be reported on Schedule C.
B. The rental income should be reported on Schedule E.
C. The rental income should be reported as "other income" on Schedule 1.
D. The rental income should be reported on Form 4835.

17. What is the definition of "personal property" for tax purposes?

A. Personal assets of an individual taxpayer.
B. Real property owned by a business or individual.
C. Assets that are moveable and tangible, whether owned by a business or an individual.
D. Real property owned by a business taxpayer.

18. Khalil is a motel owner who rents out rooms for short periods and provides daily maid service and continental breakfast service to his tenants. Which form should he use to report his rental income?

A. Schedule 1
B. Schedule B
C. Schedule C
D. Schedule E

Unit 9: Quiz Answers

1. The answer is A. The building of the new deck on a rental property would normally be considered a depreciable improvement. The other choices are repairs and may be deducted as current expenses.

2. The answer is B. Gaston and Brittany must report six months of rental income at $3,000 per month, or $18,000, but the refundable security deposit of $6,000 is not recognized as income. They can deduct 50% (6/12 months) of the amounts incurred for mortgage interest, property taxes, and casualty insurance, or $10,500, plus the $500 repair that was incurred while the house was rented. Thus, their reportable net rental income before considering depreciation would be $7,000. The calculations are as follows:

Taxable rental income	
Six months of rent (at $3,000 per month)	$18,000
Minus deductible expenses:	
Mortgage interest (for six months)	5,000
Property taxes (for six months)	5,000
Casualty insurance (for six months)	500
Repair costs	500
Expenses before depreciation	(11,000)
Rental income before depreciation	**$7,000**

3. The answer is A. Zachariah would report nine months (January–September) of mortgage interest and property taxes as itemized deductions on Schedule A, that is, $1,800 and $450, and the other three months (October–December, when the house was rented) as expenses on Schedule E, that is, $600 and $150 (this question is based on an example in Publication 4491).

4. The answer is B. Antoine is allowed to claim a maximum of $12,500 of losses on his separately filed return. If a taxpayer actively participated in a passive rental real estate activity that produced a loss, he can deduct the loss to offset his nonpassive income, up to $25,000. However, married persons filing separate returns who <u>lived apart</u> during the year are each allowed a maximum of $12,500 for losses from passive real estate activities. Married persons who file separate returns but lived together during the year are not allowed to take losses on rental real estate activity. Instead, the losses are suspended and must be carried over until the property produces income, or the property is disposed of.

5. The answer is C. Treyton must report $24,000 in rental income in the first year. He must recognize all the advance rent as income in the year of receipt. The security deposit does not have to be recognized as income because it is refundable to the tenant at the termination of the lease period.

6. The answer is A. Annika's basis for depreciation on the house is its fair market value on the date of the conversion ($147,000) because the FMV on the date of conversion is less than the amount of her original cost that was allocable to the house ($175,800). When a taxpayer converts property held for personal use to rental use (for example, the rental of a former home), the basis for depreciation will be the *lesser* of fair market value or the adjusted basis on the date of conversion.

7. The answer is D. All the rental income may be excluded under the "15-day rule." Miley's home is primarily for personal use, and a rental period of fewer than 15 days is disregarded, which means the IRS does not consider it a rental. The rental income is not taxable, but the rental expenses (such as utilities or maintenance costs) are also not deductible.

8. The answer is A. Kenia can use $2,000 of her rental loss to offset the passive activity income from the limited partnership. The remaining $1,500 loss can be offset against her $40,000 of wages. Since her income is below $100,000, Kenia can potentially deduct up to $25,000 per year of losses for rental real estate activities in which she actively participates. This special allowance is an exception to the general rule disallowing losses in excess of income from passive activities against nonpassive income.

9. The answer is C. Kyung-Hu may deduct the entire $968 as a rental expense on Schedule E. Generally, the expenses of renting a property, such as maintenance, insurance, taxes, and interest, can be deducted from rental income. This cost is a repair, not an improvement, because the window was already broken. If *all* the windows had been replaced with energy-efficient windows, the cost would have been considered an improvement and added to the property's basis.

10. The answer is C. Asher can report $7,000 on Schedule E as interest expense and $5,000 on Schedule A as mortgage interest. He must allocate his expenses between personal use and rental use, so he can deduct seven-twelfths (7 months/12 months) of his mortgage interest as a rental expense. When figuring his allowable depreciation, he should treat the property as placed in service on June 1.

11. The answer is B. Habib has a net loss on his rental of $7,400 ($20,600 - $28,000 [$17,000 in expenses + $11,000 of depreciation]). The loss is permitted because he actively participates in the activity, and his income is below the threshold for the "special loss allowance." He can deduct the $7,400 rental loss from his nonpassive income (i.e., his wages).

12. The answer is D. Depreciation is an income tax deduction that allows a business to recover the cost or basis of property it uses over time. It is an annual allowance for the wear and tear, deterioration, or obsolescence of assets.

13. The answer is C. Depreciation begins on the placed-in-service date when an asset becomes ready and available for first use. Typically, the placed-in-service date and the purchase date are the same, but that is not always the case. Since Pamela did not have the HVAC unit installed and ready for use until January 2, 2023, she must wait until 2023 to begin depreciating the unit. The fact that the unit was paid for with a credit card is irrelevant (it is treated the same as if it was paid by check or cash).

14. The answer is B. An expansion of the building is a capital improvement that must be capitalized and depreciated over time. An "improvement" is any change that increases the value of a property, extends its useful life, or modifies it for a different purpose. Choice "C" is not correct because fixing a crack in the driveway can be expensed as a repair. Choices "A" and "D" are incorrect because some improvements made to nonresidential buildings, such as fire suppression systems, alarms and security systems, and HVAC and roofing, are eligible for immediate expensing under Section 179.

15. The answer is A. Royalties received by an author from book sales could be considered self-employment income if the author is actively involved in creating the work and is self-employed. Answer "B" and "C" are incorrect, because royalties from oil extraction or timber are typically considered unearned income and are not subject to self-employment tax. Answer "D" is incorrect, because royalties earned on an inherited copyright would not be subject to self-employment tax.

16. The answer is A. Alexander's income should be reported on Schedule C. Renting personal property, like equipment, machinery, tools, or vehicles, should be reported as either Schedule C income or "other income" depending on if the income is business or nonbusiness income. Since Alexander runs the business with a profit motive, it is business income (and not income from a hobby activity).

17. The answer is C. In a broad definition, "personal property" includes any asset other than real estate. Personal property is *movable*, unlike land and buildings that remain in one location. "Personal property" should not be confused with "personal-use" property that a taxpayer uses for personal purposes rather than for business purposes.

18. The answer is C. Khalil is a motel owner offering short-term rentals on a transient basis, so he should report his rental income on Schedule C, Profit or Loss from Business.

Unit 10: Other Taxable Income

> **For additional information, read:**
> Publication 525, *Taxable and Nontaxable Income*
> Publication 4681, *Canceled Debts, Foreclosures, Repossessions, and Abandonments*
> Publication 4345, *Settlements—Taxability*

This chapter covers various other types of taxable income. Any income that does not have a designated line on the Form 1040 is typically recorded on Schedule 1, *Additional Income and Adjustments to Income*. Schedule 1 allows for reporting of various types of miscellaneous income, including taxable alimony, unemployment compensation, jury duty pay, and gambling winnings.

Taxable Recoveries

A "recovery" is a return of an amount a taxpayer deducted or took a credit for in an earlier year. The most common recoveries are state tax refunds, medical reimbursements, and rebates of deductions that were previously reported on Schedule A. Taxpayers must include a recovery in income in the year they receive it, but only to the extent the deduction or credit reduced income tax in the prior year. Income tax refunds from state and local governments are only taxable if the taxpayer itemized deductions in the year they overpaid those taxes and only to the extent the amount paid in the previous year reduced their tax liability. The entity issuing the refund will provide a Form 1099-G, *Certain Government Payments,* to the taxpayer and send a copy to the Internal Revenue Service by January 31st.

> **Example:** Corby lives in California. He claimed the standard deduction on his prior-year federal tax return. In 2023, he received a California state tax refund of $700 for state income taxes that he overpaid in the prior year. The state tax refund is not taxable in 2023, because Corby received no federal tax benefit from his state tax payments because he did not itemize his deductions in the previous year. In other words, since he did not deduct his state income taxes in the prior year, he does not have to report his state tax refund as taxable in the current year.

Federal income tax refunds (i.e., IRS tax refunds) are not included in a taxpayer's income because they are never allowed as a deduction.

Taxable Alimony Received

The Tax Cuts and Jobs Act changed the treatment of alimony starting in 2019, making it nondeductible to the payor and nontaxable to the recipient. Divorce and separation agreements entered into before 2019 are "grandfathered," so there will continue to be alimony deductions and taxable alimony income for individuals with divorce agreements that were finalized prior to 2019. The payor does not have to itemize to deduct alimony payments made (for divorce decrees that are grandfathered). In contrast, child support is never taxable income to the receiver and not deductible by the payor because it is viewed as a payment a parent makes simply to support their own child.

For a payment to qualify as alimony:

- The divorce agreement may not include a clause indicating that the payment is something else (such as repayment of a loan).
- The payor must have no liability to make any payment after the death of the former spouse.

Not all payments that are made to an ex-spouse qualify as alimony. Alimony does *not* include:

- Payments that are a former spouse's share of income from community property
- Payments to keep up the payor's property, or free use of the payor's property
- Noncash property settlements, and any payment made other than in cash
- Any payments made to an ex-spouse when the divorce was finalized in 2019 or later years.

Also, if alimony payments continue after the death of the receiving spouse, the payments will not be considered alimony for federal tax purposes.

> **Example:** On February 20, 2023, Connie and Derrick divorced. According to the terms of their divorce decree, Derrick is obligated to pay Connie $1,000 monthly in alimony and an additional $1,200 per month for child support. These payments are not deductible by Derrick and are not taxable to Connie.

> **Example:** Beck and Patsy divorced in 2017. As a result, their divorce decree is considered "grandfathered," and the pre-TCJA rules apply. Their divorce decree requires Beck to pay Patsy $200 per month as child support and $150 per month as alimony. Beck makes all his child support and alimony payments on time. Therefore, in 2023, he can deduct $1,800 ($150 × 12 months) as alimony paid, and Patsy must report $1,800 as alimony received as taxable income. The amount paid as child support, $2,400 ($200 × 12) is not deductible by Beck and is not reported as income by Patsy.

If an alimony payment is subject to reduction based on a contingency relating to a child (e.g., attaining a certain age, marrying, or going to college), the amount subject to a reduction is treated as child support, not alimony, for tax purposes.

This is regardless of what the divorce decree states, or whether or not the contingency is likely to occur.

> **Example:** Khalil and Reema's divorce became final in 2017. Khalil agrees to pay Reema $4,000 in alimony per month ($48,000 per year), but their divorce agreement specifies that the alimony payments will be reduced by $3,000 a month (down to $1,000 a month) once their only child, Taavi, reaches the age of 18. Since this is clearly a "contingency related to a child," only $1,000 of the monthly payments are actually considered "alimony" for federal tax purposes. In 2023, Reema pays a tax attorney to carefully review her divorce decree, and he notifies her about the contingency in her decree. Reema decides to report only $12,000 as taxable alimony ($1,000 × 12 months). Khalil, on the other hand, reports the full $48,000 as alimony paid, deducting the amounts from his taxable income. Both of their returns are subsequently audited. Reema shows the IRS auditor the contingency in her divorce decree, and the auditor agrees with her. Reema will only be taxed on $12,000 of alimony, and Khalil will have his return adjusted by the IRS, reducing the amount of alimony paid that he is permitted to deduct.

If a "grandfathered" divorce decree is later modified, and expressly invokes the new treatment, then the alimony receives the new treatment.

If a divorce agreement specifies payments of *both* alimony *and* child support and only partial payments are made by the payor, the partial payments are considered child support until all the child support obligations are fully paid. Any additional amounts paid are then treated as alimony.

Example: Dayna and Clemente legally divorced in 2017. Their divorce decree is "grandfathered," and the pre-TCJA rules apply. Their divorce decree requires Clemente pay Dayna $2,000 a month ($24,000 [$2,000 × 12] a year) as child support and $1,500 a month ($18,000 [$1,500 × 12] a year) as alimony. Clemente falls behind on his payments and pays only $36,000 during the year. In this case, the first $24,000 paid is considered child support and only the remaining amount of $12,000 ($36,000 - $24,000) is considered alimony. Clemente can deduct $12,000 as alimony paid. Dayna must report $12,000 as alimony income received.

Note: Property settlements are simply a division of property and are not treated as alimony. In general, property transferred to an ex-spouse as part of a divorce proceeding is not a taxable event.

Example: Brooklynn and Galvin file for divorce. As part of their divorce agreement, Brooklynn must transfer a portion of her 401(k) account to Galvin. The transfer is properly outlined in their divorce settlement agreement, and a QDRO[114] is issued by the court. On October 1, 2023, their divorce becomes final. Two days later, the retirement plan transfer is completed, and $105,000 is transferred directly from Brooklynn's 401(k) to Galvin's retirement account. The transfer is considered a division of marital assets and is not subject to the 10% early withdrawal penalty.

Payments made to a third party can be considered alimony in some cases. For example, if, under the terms of a divorce agreement, a husband is required to pay the medical bills of his ex-wife, a cash payment to the hospital can count as alimony.

However, these additional payments *must* be made based on their written divorce or separation agreement in order to be classified as alimony.

Government Benefits

Most government welfare benefits, including food stamps, heating assistance programs, and poverty assistance from state or local agencies are exempt from federal taxation. Worker's compensation is a form of insurance that provides wage replacement and medical benefits to workers who are injured on the job. Worker's compensation is not subject to federal income tax.

In contrast, unemployment compensation is taxable. Unemployment compensation is a type of government benefit that is paid to workers who have lost their jobs. It is intended to replace wages that would have been subject to tax if the individual had not lost their job. Therefore, individuals receiving unemployment compensation must report it as taxable income on their federal tax return.

Example: Haima was laid off from her job in 2023. She received $300 a week of unemployment compensation for 26 weeks. When she was unable to find another job, she began receiving benefits from her state's WIC program, which provided vouchers for food for her and her toddler. The unemployment compensation would be taxable income, but the welfare (WIC) benefits would not be taxable income.

---

[114] Both employer plans and IRA funds can be awarded to a spouse in a divorce, but to split an ERISA-qualified plan, (such as a 401(k)) a qualified domestic relations order is required. A QDRO (Qualified Domestic Relations Order) is a court judgment or court order that is used to legally assign company-provided benefits to an alternate payee, typically as part of divorce or marital separation proceedings. An ex-spouse (or spouse, if legally separated and not yet divorced) may roll over tax-free all or part of a distribution from a qualified retirement plan that they received under a QDRO.

Social Security Income

Social Security is a type of government benefit that applies to individuals who have earned enough Social Security credits and are at least 62 years of age.[115] Social Security income is reported to taxpayers on Form SSA-1099, *Social Security Benefit Statement*.

The portion of benefits that are taxable depends on the taxpayer's income and filing status. To determine the taxability of Social Security benefits, a taxpayer must compare the base threshold amount for their filing status with the total of:

- One-half of their Social Security benefits, plus
- All of the taxpayer's other income, **including** tax-exempt interest.

If the sum is less than the base amount for their filing status, none of the Social Security is taxable. If the sum is more than the base amount for their filing status, a percentage of the Social Security may be taxable. The taxable portion of Social Security benefits is never more than 85%.

Base Amounts for Calculating Taxability of Social Security	
Married filing jointly	$32,000
Single, HOH, QSS, or MFS (and lived apart from their spouse all year)	$25,000
MFS (if lived with spouse at any time during the year)	$0

Spouses who file jointly must combine their incomes and Social Security benefits when figuring the taxable portion of their benefits, even if one spouse did not receive any benefits.

Example: George and Mabel are both 67 years old. They file jointly, and both received Social Security benefits during the year, but they also have income from other sources. At the end of the year, George received a Form SSA-1099 showing net benefits of $7,500. Mabel received a Form SSA-1099 showing net benefits of $3,500. George also received wages of $20,000 and taxable interest income of $500. He did not have any tax-exempt interest.	
1. Total Social Security benefits	$11,000
2. Enter one-half of Social Security (× 50%)	$5,500
3. Enter taxable interest and wages	$20,500
4. Sum ($5,500 + $20,500)	**$26,000**
George and Mabel's benefits are not taxable because the total above is not more than the base amount ($32,000) for married filing jointly.	

---

[115] Social Security benefits include monthly retirement, survivor and disability benefits. They don't include supplemental security income (SSI) payments, which aren't taxable. SSI payments are monthly payments to adults and children with a permanent disability or blindness who have income and resources below specific financial limits.

Other Types of Income

Income that does not have a designated line on Form 1040 is typically classified as "other income." Other income must be reported on Schedule 1 of Form 1040. Examples of "other income" include gambling winnings, cancellation of debt income, hobby income, certain types of court awards, lottery winnings and other prizes, and taxable distributions from a Coverdell education savings account or qualified tuition program if they exceed the qualified higher education expenses for a designated beneficiary. It is important to note that all taxable income must be reported, regardless if they receive a document from the payor reporting the amount paid.

Gambling Winnings

Gambling income may include winnings from lotteries, raffles, horse races, and casinos. Gambling winnings will typically be reported to a taxpayer on Form W-2G, *Certain Gambling Winnings*. A taxpayer must report and pay tax on all gambling winnings, regardless of whether the taxpayer receives a Form W-2G. Gambling losses are deductible on Schedule A as a miscellaneous itemized deduction, but the deduction is limited to the amount of gambling winnings for the year.

Example: Eva had $11,000 of gambling winnings and ($23,000) of gambling losses during the taxable year. Her itemized deduction for gambling losses cannot exceed $11,000, the amount of her winnings. To claim the deduction for her losses, Eva must itemize and list her gambling losses on Schedule A, Form 1040. If Eva does not itemize, she will not be able to deduct any of her gambling losses.

Note: The Tax Cuts and Jobs Act changed the definition of "gambling losses." In prior years, professional gamblers who filed on Schedule C were able to generate an NOL from their wagering activities. The TCJA modified the limit on gambling losses so that all deductions for expenses incurred in carrying out gambling activities, not just direct gambling losses, are limited to the extent of gambling winnings. For example, an individual who is a professional gambler can include expenses traveling to and from a casino as gambling losses as an offset against any gambling winnings, but cannot use the expenses to generate a loss on Schedule C.[116]

The taxpayer must keep an accurate diary or similar record of gambling winnings and losses, along with tickets, receipts, canceled checks, and other documentation. The taxpayer is not required to include these supporting records with their tax return, but they should be retained in case of an audit.

Cancellation of Debt Income

When a taxpayer's debt is canceled or forgiven, they may be required to report the amount of forgiven debt as part of their gross income. This can create confusion for taxpayers since the canceled debt may occur in a year when no cash was received. In cases where a property is surrendered or repossessed, like in a foreclosure, the taxpayer may assume that relinquishing the property means they are no longer responsible for the debt. However, this is not always true and tax implications must still be considered. If a lender cancels a debt and issues Form 1099-C, *Cancellation of Debt*, the lender will indicate on the form if the borrower was personally liable for repayment of the debt. The tax impact depends on the type of debt, and whether the loan is *recourse* or *nonrecourse*. Canceled debt income

---

[116] The TCJA modified IRC Sect. 165(d) to provide that all deductions for expenses incurred in carrying out gambling and wagering activities are limited to the extent of gambling winnings. This is a temporary provision that ends after tax year 2025.

may include any indebtedness for which a taxpayer is personally liable, or which attaches to the taxpayer's property, such as an auto loan, home mortgage, or home equity loan.

A **recourse debt** holds the borrower personally liable. All other debt is considered **nonrecourse**.[117] Whether a debt is recourse or nonrecourse may vary from state to state, depending on state law. If a lender forecloses on property subject to a recourse debt and cancels the portion of the debt in excess of the FMV of the property, the canceled portion is treated as taxable income.

This amount must be included in gross income unless it qualifies for an exception or an exclusion. Most home mortgages are "nonrecourse loans." This means that if the borrower defaults, the lender can seize the home, but cannot seek out the borrower for any further compensation, even if the FMV of the home does not cover the remaining loan balance. In other words, if a mortgage is **nonrecourse** and the borrower does not retain the home (after a foreclosure by a lender), the borrower does not have to recognize the cancellation of debt as income.

If the taxpayer abandons property that secures a debt for which the taxpayer is not personally liable (a nonrecourse loan), the abandonment is treated as a sale or exchange. However, there is a deemed sales price based on the amount of the nonrecourse loan at the time of the abandonment, foreclosure or short sale.

Example: Denny lost his home to foreclosure because he got fired from his job and could no longer make his mortgage payments. At the time of the foreclosure, Denny owed a balance of $170,000 to his mortgage lender, and the fair market value of the home was $140,000 (the home had gone down in value). Denny's mortgage is a nonrecourse loan. Denny moves out, abandoning the property, and the bank forecloses on the home a few months later. Denny is not personally liable for the debt (since it is a nonrecourse loan). The abandonment and subsequent foreclosure are treated as a disposition (for tax purposes), and the "selling price" would be $170,000, which is the balance of his loan. Even if Denny later receives a Form 1099-C from the bank, the debt cancellation is not a taxable event.

Note: A "nonrecourse" loan does not allow the lender to pursue anything other than the collateral to collect the debt. For example, if a borrower defaults on a nonrecourse home loan, the bank can only foreclose on the home. The bank cannot take further legal action to collect the money owed on the debt.

Example: Edith borrows $10,000 on her credit card in order to take a vacation. She takes her vacation and then defaults on the balance after paying back only $2,000. She has the ability to pay back the loan, but chooses not to. The credit card company writes off the remaining balance of the loan instead of legally pursuing Edith for the credit card balance. Therefore, there is a cancellation of debt of $8,000, which is taxable income to Edith, unless an exclusion applies.

If the original debt is a *nonbusiness* debt, the canceled debt amount is reported as "other income" on line 8c of Schedule 1, Form 1040. If a personal asset such as a home or a vehicle is repossessed, the taxpayer may have to report two transactions: (1) the cancellation of debt income, and (2) gain or loss on the sale or repossession, generally equal to the difference between the FMV of the property at the time of the foreclosure and the taxpayer's adjusted basis in the property.

---

[117] There is no taxable income from a canceled debt if it is intended as a gift (for example, if a taxpayer owes his parents money, but they choose to forgive the debt).

Remember, a repossession or foreclosure is treated as a "sale" for tax purposes, so a gain or loss must be computed. Any loss related to a personal-use asset would be nondeductible.

> **Example:** Zeus lost his personal yacht to repossession because he could no longer afford to make his payments. At the time of the repossession, he owed a balance of $190,000 to the lender, and the FMV of the yacht was $130,000 (it had declined in value). Zeus is personally liable for the debt (it is a recourse loan), so the repossession of the yacht is treated as a sale. The "selling price" from the repossession is $130,000, and Zeus must recognize $60,000 in debt forgiveness income ($190,000 outstanding debt - $130,000 FMV).

Nontaxable Canceled Debt

Even if a loan is a recourse loan, there are certain scenarios where the resulting canceled debt is still not subject to taxation.

There are several circumstances in which canceled debt is not taxable, even if the loan is recourse. Federal law has established exceptions that allow for exclusion of canceled debt from income or deem it nontaxable, depending on the type of debt, or financial situation of the taxpayer. The most common **exclusions** to canceled debt income are:

- Bankruptcy or insolvency
- Cancellation of qualified farm indebtedness, or qualified real property business indebtedness
- Cancellation of student loan debt
- Cancellation of qualified principal residence indebtedness[118]

If a taxpayer can exclude their canceled debt under any of the situations listed above, they must attach Form 982, *Reduction of Tax Attributes Due to Discharge of Indebtedness* to their individual return and check the appropriate box that applies to them.

Bankruptcy: Debts discharged through bankruptcy court in a Title 11 bankruptcy case (generally, Chapters 7 and 13) are not taxable. Some common types of debt that can be discharged in bankruptcy are credit card debt, personal loans, and medical debts. The taxpayer must attach Form 982, *Reduction of Tax Attributes Due to Discharge of Indebtedness*, to their federal income tax return to exclude any debt canceled in bankruptcy.

> **Example:** Max had a severe auto accident a few years ago in which he was at fault. He was badly injured and incurred large medical debts totaling $1.5 million. He was also sued by the other driver and incurred legal bills due to the lawsuit. On the advice of his attorney, Max decides to file for bankruptcy. Max's only major asset is his teacher's pension, which is protected by state law. The entire $1.5 million in debt is discharged by the bankruptcy court. The canceled debt is not taxable to Max.

Insolvency: It is a condition in which the fair market value of all assets is less than one's liabilities. A taxpayer is legally insolvent when total debts exceed the value of their total assets immediately prior to the discharge of their debt. If a taxpayer is insolvent when their debt is canceled, the canceled debt is not taxable, <u>but only to the extent of the insolvency</u>. For this purpose, the taxpayer's assets include the value of everything they own, including pensions and retirement accounts.

---

[118] Qualified real property business indebtedness is debt incurred in connection with, real property used in a trade or business.

Extended example: Rocio owns a vacation condo in Hawaii. She has a HELOC (home equity loan) on the property which she financed through a mortgage lender. The proceeds of the HELOC were not used to acquire or substantially improve the condo, instead, she used the HELOC to pay off credit cards. Rocio becomes ill and defaults on the HELOC. The HELOC is a recourse loan, and she is personally liable for all the debt. Rocio's mortgage lender forecloses on the condo when the loan balance was $280,000 and the fair market value of the condo is only $260,000. Rocio later receives a 1099-C from the lender for $20,000 of canceled debt. Since the property is a vacation home, and not her main home, all the canceled debt is potentially taxable. Rocio believes that she may qualify for an exclusion under the insolvency provisions. She prepares an insolvency worksheet, totaling up her assets and liabilities at the time of the cancellation.

Rocio's Insolvency Determination Worksheet			
Assets (FMV)		**Liabilities**	
Condo FMV	$160,000	Mortgage on condo	$180,000
Vehicles FMV	$5,000	Vehicle loans	$25,000
Bank accounts	$1,000	Credit card debt	$10,000
Traditional IRA	$60,000	Hospital bills	$40,000
Furniture	$2,000	Outstanding student loan	$13,000
Clothing	$600	Real estate taxes owed	$8,000
Total assets	**$228,600**	**Total Liabilities**	**$276,000**
Total assets minus total liabilities = ($47,400). Rocio's liabilities exceed her assets; therefore, she is insolvent, and the amount of her insolvency exceeds the canceled debt, so her canceled debt is not taxable.[119]			

Note that the amount of a taxpayer's insolvency is sometimes expressed as a negative net worth.

Example: Lucy had $5,000 of credit card debt, which she could not afford to pay. The credit card company decided to cancel the entire $5,000 balance. She received a Form 1099-C from her credit card company showing canceled debt of $5,000. Immediately before the cancellation, Lucy's total debts were $15,000, and the fair market value of her total assets was $12,000. Therefore, at the time the debt was canceled, Lucy was insolvent to the extent of $3,000 ($15,000 total liabilities minus $12,000 FMV of her total assets). Lucy can only exclude $3,000 of the canceled debt from income; the remaining $2,000 is taxable. Lucy must report the amount of debt forgiven on her return and the excluded amount by completing Form 982, *Reduction of Tax Attributes Due to Discharge of Indebtedness.*

Primary Residence Debt Cancellations

Normally, when a bank forecloses on a home and sells it for less than the borrower's outstanding mortgage, the bank forgives the unpaid mortgage debt. The canceled debt may be taxable to the homeowner. However, a taxpayer may exclude canceled debt if the cancellation of the mortgage occurs on a taxpayer's principal residence. This is true even if the mortgage debt is a **recourse debt.**[120] "Qualified principal residence indebtedness" or QPRI, is a mortgage secured by a taxpayer's principal

---

[119] This example and table are based on an insolvency example in IRS Publication 4491.
[120] Under the *Mortgage Forgiveness Debt Relief Act*, mortgage debt on a primary residence that was forgiven was excluded from taxable income. This provision was set to expire, but was extended until 2025.

residence that was taken out to *buy, build, or substantially improve* that residence and may also include debt from refinancing.[121] QPRI cannot be more than the cost of the home (plus improvements).

To exclude QPRI, the taxpayer must report the amount of debt forgiven by completing Form 982, *Reduction of Tax Attributes Due to Discharge of Indebtedness*. The maximum amount of qualified principal residence debt that can be discharged tax-free in 2023 is $750,000 ($375,000 for married individuals filing separately). The QPRI exclusion *only* applies to a main home: it does *not* apply to second homes, raw land, rental properties, or vacation homes.[122]

Example: Alan refinanced his mortgage two years ago, and his primary residence is now subject to a $320,000 *recourse* mortgage. Alan gets sick and stops making his payments. Alan's mortgage lender forecloses on the home on January 10, 2023 and Alan moves out. The residence is later sold by the bank for $280,000 on May 20, 2023. Alan has $40,000 of canceled debt income from the discharge of indebtedness. All of the mortgage debt was qualified principal residence indebtedness. Therefore, he can claim the qualified principal residence *exclusion* by filing Form 982 with his individual tax return.

Example: Maxim used a lender to finance the purchase of an empty lot for $175,000. He had plans to build a house on the land, but unfortunately lost his job and was unable to keep up with the loan payments. As a result, he defaulted on the loan and the bank took back the property. Eventually, they were able to sell it for $130,000. The remaining balance of $45,000 was forgiven by the lender. Maxim has a valuable 401(k) that he refuses to touch, so he was not insolvent or in bankruptcy at the time the debt was forgiven. Since the canceled debt does not meet any exclusions, Maxim is required to report it as taxable income. This is because the qualified principal residence indebtedness exclusion only applies to primary residences, and in this case, Maxim's property was an empty lot rather than a home.

Remember, even if the canceled debt does not qualify under the *qualified principal residence indebtedness* exclusion, canceled mortgage debt does not have to be included in taxable income if the debt was canceled in a bankruptcy case or while the taxpayer was insolvent (up to the amount of the insolvency of the taxpayer right before the debt cancellation).

Example: Irving's vacation condo in Hawaii is subject to a $320,000 *recourse* mortgage. Irving loses his job and stops making payments on the loan. Irving's mortgage lender forecloses on the home on January 20, 2023, when the fair market value of the home was $280,000. The residence has declined in value because a serious construction defect was discovered. The home is later auctioned off by the bank for $280,000. Irving has $40,000 of canceled debt from the discharge of indebtedness because the mortgage was $40,000 more than the property's fair market value at the time of the foreclosure. The home was not his main home, so the canceled debt is not QPRI, or "qualified principal residence indebtedness." However, right before the foreclosure, Irving was insolvent – with the amount of all his debts (including this mortgage, his auto loan and credit card debts) equaling $400,000. The value of all his assets was $350,000 at that time – resulting in an insolvency amount of $50,000. Since the $40,000 canceled debt is less than the $50,000 extent of his insolvency, the forgiven debt is not taxable. Irving can exclude the forgiven debt by completing Form 982, *Reduction of Tax Attributes Due to Discharge of Indebtedness*, and marking the box to report his insolvency.

---

[121] QPRI can include debt resulting from the refinancing of debt if that debt was incurred to acquire, construct, or substantially improve a principal residence.
[122] The lender is required to report the amount of the canceled debt to the taxpayer a Form 1099-C, Cancellation of Debt.

Cancellation of Student Loans

Special rules apply to canceled student loans. The American Rescue Plan Act (ARPA) allows exclusion from taxation on most student loans forgiven through tax year 2025. This includes all federal student loans and certain private loans and institutional loans.[123]

> **Example:** Pascal takes out a student loan of $32,500 and uses it to pay his college tuition and textbooks. He is personally responsible for the loan. On February 1, 2023, Pascal becomes disabled in a car accident. The student loan is forgiven by the lender on December 1, 2023. The forgiven debt is not taxable to Pascal on his tax return, regardless of whether he receives a 1099-C or not.

Qualified Farm Indebtedness: If a taxpayer incurred the canceled debt in a farming business, it is generally not considered taxable income.

Canceled Debt that is Otherwise Deductible: If a taxpayer uses the cash method of accounting, they should not recognize canceled debt income if payment of the debt would have otherwise been a deductible expense.

> **Example:** Alexa is a self-employed interior designer. A CPA firm agrees to file her business tax return and bill her later. Alexa receives $2,200 of tax preparation and bookkeeping services for her business on credit. Later, Alexa loses a major design account and has trouble paying her debts, so her CPA forgives the amount she owes. Alexa does not include the canceled debt in her gross income because payment of the debt would have been deductible as a business expense had it been paid.

Hobby Income

A "hobby" is an activity that is usually done for enjoyment or leisure, rather than for financial gain. Even if it occasionally brings in some income, a hobby is not considered a business because it is not carried on to make a profit. Any income earned from a hobby must be reported on Form 1040, Schedule 1 and is taxable.

If expenses related to the hobby exceed the income generated, taxpayers will have a loss from the activity. However, this loss cannot be deducted from other forms of income. Although expenses for a hobby are not deductible, one benefit is that hobby income is not subject to self-employment tax.

The determination of whether an activity is being carried out for profit depends on individual circumstances and can be subjective. To provide some clarity, Sec. 183(d) offers a safe harbor provision stating that if certain criteria are met, the activity will be presumed as a for-profit endeavor. Under the IRS safe harbor test, an activity is presumed to be operated for profit if it generates a profit at least three out of last five years, including the current year. The safe harbor is two out of the last seven years for activities involving horse breeding or racing.

The use of hobby expenses to offset hobby-related income is not permitted. The Tax Cuts and Jobs Act repealed most miscellaneous itemized deductions, including the deduction for hobby-related expenses on Schedule A.

---

[123] The American Rescue Plan Act (ARPA) exempted federal student loan forgiveness from gross income through 2025 (IRC Section 108(f)(5)). The IRS advises that Form 1099-C, Cancellation of Debt, should not be filed for student loans covered by this expanded forgiveness under the American Rescue Plan Act. Note that student loan forgiveness may still be taxable at the state level.

However, a taxpayer with hobby income is still allowed to deduct cost of goods sold (COGS), as a reduction of the hobby's taxable gross income, in order to arrive at taxable income.[124]

> **Example:** Stefan works full time as a bank manager. He also buys and breeds aquarium fish as a hobby. Twice a year, he travels to the International Exotic Fish convention to showcase and sell some of his exotic aquarium fish. Although he occasionally makes a profit from this hobby, it is mainly a source of enjoyment for him. Stefan has no plans to stop attending the conventions, regardless of how much money he makes. Therefore, any income he earns is considered hobby income. His expenses are not deductible, (such as the cost of his travel), but his income from selling the fish is taxable. Stefan is permitted to deduct the cost of goods sold (i.e., the cost of the fish he sells to customers) to calculate his hobby-related income.

Taxation of Court Awards and Damages

The tax treatment of court awards varies, based on the origin of the legal claim. Court awards for compensation for lost wages or profits are generally taxable as ordinary income, as are punitive damages. Interest payments on any settlement award are also taxable. Compensatory damages for personal physical injury or physical sickness are not taxable, whether they are from a legal settlement or an actual court award.

Damages received for emotional distress due to "physical injury or sickness" are treated the same way as damages for physical injury or sickness, so they are not included in income. However, if the plaintiff's emotional distress is *not* due to a physical injury (for example, an employment lawsuit in which a taxpayer suffers emotional distress for injury to reputation), the proceeds are taxable, except for any damages received for medical care that are directly related to that emotional distress. "Emotional distress" can include physical symptoms such as headaches, depression, insomnia, and stomach disorders.

> **Example:** Sheila won a court award for emotional distress caused by unlawful discrimination. The emotional distress resulted in her hospitalization for a nervous breakdown. The court awarded Sheila damages of $100,000, including $30,000 to refund the cost of her medical care for the nervous breakdown. In this case, $70,000 ($100,000 - $30,000) would be considered a taxable court award. The $30,000 awarded to reimburse her medical care would not be taxable to Sheila.

> **Example:** Terrill was injured in a car accident. Both his legs were broken, and he suffered other serious physical injuries. He received an insurance settlement for his injuries totaling $950,000. The settlement is nontaxable because it is payment for a physical injury. He does not have to report the amounts on his tax return.

Punitive damages are *always taxable,* even if the punitive damages were received in a settlement for personal physical injuries or physical sickness. Punitive damages are legal damages awarded by a jury or a court in order to "punish" the defendant for outrageous or malicious conduct. Punitive damages should be reported as "Other Income" on Schedule 1 (Form 1040).[125]

---

[124] Treasury Regulation Section 1.183-1(e) states that a taxpayer may determine gross income from <u>any activity</u> by subtracting the cost of goods sold (COGS) from the gross receipts so long as he consistently does so and follows generally accepted methods of accounting in determining such gross income.
[125] Refer to IRS Publication 4345, *Settlements—Taxability,* for more information on the tax treatment of court settlements.

Example: Aileen purchases a new car; a sporty sedan called the "Flinto." She enjoys the vehicle and drives it to and from work every day. After about six months of ownership, she has a small fender-bender on a residential street. During the accident, her car's gas tank mysteriously explodes. Aileen manages to escape the burning vehicle, but she experiences third-degree burns on her right arm and leg from the blast. Aileen later discovers that the "Flinto" has a serious design flaw, and the manufacturer of the car knew about it, but refused to issue a recall. She decides to sue the manufacturer of the car in a civil action. The case goes to trial, and the jury awards Aileen $2 million in compensatory damages for her injuries, but also an additional $15 million in punitive damages, which was designed to punish the manufacturer for its conduct. The $2 million in compensatory damages would not be taxable to Aileen, as it was payment for her physical injuries. The $15 million in punitive damages would be taxable as "other income" on Schedule 1 of her Form 1040.

Civil damages, restitution, or other monetary awards that the taxpayer received as compensation for wrongful incarceration are not taxable.

Example: Ryan was wrongfully convicted of murder and later released after spending almost 15 years in prison. Ryan was awarded $50,000 per year of wrongful imprisonment. None of the award is taxable income to Ryan.

No tax deduction is allowed for any settlement, payout, or attorney fees related to sexual harassment or sexual abuse if the payments are subject to a nondisclosure agreement.

Example: Arsenio is a self-employed therapist who files on Schedule C. Arsenio has several employees who work in his office. On January 4, 2023, Arsenio's full-time secretary, Keira, sues him for sexual harassment. Rather than risk a public lawsuit that might damage his reputation, Arsenio settles with Keira, coming to a confidential settlement with Keira and her attorney. The settlement was $25,000, and their settlement agreement was subject to a nondisclosure clause. Arsenio also incurred $5,000 in legal fees for his attorney to negotiate the settlement. Arsenio cannot deduct the settlement or his related legal fees as a business expense. However, Keira is required to report the full amount of the settlement as taxable income on her individual return.

Prizes and Awards

Prizes and awards are taxable and are reported as "other income" on Line 8i of Schedule 1 of Form 1040. If the prize or award is in the form of property rather than cash, the fair market value of the property is treated as the taxable amount. The winner may avoid taxation of the award by rejecting the prize. The taxpayer may also avoid taxation by having the payor directly transfer the prize to a charity or other nonprofit organization.

Example: A national education association chooses Paulo, a college instructor, as its teacher of the year. He is awarded $3,000, but he does not accept the prize. Paulo directs the association to give all his winnings to a charitable college scholarship fund, instead. Paulo never receives a check or has control over the funds; therefore, the award is not taxable to him.

Employee awards for safety, length-of-service, or achievements are generally not taxable to the employee unless they exceed specified limits. These types of awards are treated as fringe benefits, and are covered in detail in Book 2, *Businesses*. Employee fringe benefits are commonly tested on Part 2 of the EA exam.

Tax-Free Educational Assistance

Many types of educational assistance are tax-free if they meet certain requirements. Tax-free educational assistance includes scholarships, Pell Grants, and employer-provided educational assistance. Qualifying educational assistance plans (Qualified EAPs) provided under an employer's qualified educational assistance program, also include the payments of tuition and fees, as well as *student loans,* up to an annual maximum of $5,250 in 2023.[126]

Example: Deloft Accountancy, Inc. is an accounting firm. The company offers an educational assistance program to its employees as a fringe benefit. As part of the plan, the company reimburses costs for tuition, fees, and books for college and university classes. Gregory is a junior auditor working for Deloft Accountancy. In 2023, he incurs $6,300 in educational expenses. He submits copies of his tuition statements and receipts for his books to his employer. The company reimburses Gregory for $5,250 worth of his expenses (the annual maximum). The reimbursed amounts are not taxable to Gregory, and fully deductible by the company. However, if Gregory is eligible for an education credit (such as the American Opportunity Tax Credit), he is required to reduce the amounts of his qualified educational expenses by the amounts that were reimbursed by his employer.

Scholarships and Fellowships: A scholarship is an amount paid to an undergraduate or graduate student to pursue a college degree. A fellowship is an amount paid to an individual to pursue research. A scholarship or fellowship may be excluded from income only if:

- The taxpayer is a degree candidate at an eligible educational institution
- The amounts do not exceed qualified educational expenses.
- It is not designated for other purposes, such as room and board.
- It does not represent payment for teaching, research, or other personal services.

Qualified educational expenses include: tuition, required fees, and course-related expenses such as books and required equipment. An athletic scholarship is tax-free only if it meets the requirements described above.

Example: Marybeth is a graduate student at a private university. She received a total scholarship of $30,000. Under the scholarship's terms, she must work part-time as a teaching assistant. From the $30,000 scholarship, she receives $14,500 for teaching, which is reported to her as wages on Form W-2 by the university. The remaining amount, $15,500, was applied directly to her tuition costs. She had qualified educational expenses of $20,000 for tuition, fees, and course-related books. Marybeth may exclude $15,500 of the scholarship funds from income, but the $14,500 she earned as a teaching assistant is taxable as wages and must be included on her individual tax return.

Pell Grants: A Pell Grant is a need-based grant that is treated as a scholarship for tax purposes. It is tax-free to the extent it is used for qualified educational expenses during the specified grant period.

Payment to Service Academy Cadets or Midshipmen: An appointment to a United States military academy is not a scholarship or fellowship. Cadets and midshipmen receive free tuition and

---

[126] The Coronavirus Aid, Relief, and Economic Security Act (CARES Act) added student loan repayments to the types of payments that are eligible for this exclusion. This provision was extended through 2025.

room and board, which is nontaxable. However, they may also receive government pay while attending the military academy; these amounts are taxable income.

Veterans' Educational Benefits: Veterans' benefits (VA benefits) for education are tax-free if administered by the Department of Veterans Affairs. Payments from all GI Bill programs are tax-free. This is true for the servicemember, as well as dependents or surviving spouses of servicemembers who die in the line of duty.

Example: Reggie served in Afghanistan as a medic and Blackhawk pilot. He has since returned to college full-time. He is studying chemistry and he is a degree candidate. Reggie receives two education benefits under the GI bill: a $1,200 monthly basic housing allowance and $3,500 tuition paid directly to his college. Neither of these benefits is taxable to Reggie, and he is not required to report them on his tax return. However, if Reggie wants to claim educational tax credits based on his education expenses, he will need to subtract his GI education benefit payments from his qualifying educational expenses.

Qualified Tuition Programs

Qualifying Tuition Programs, also known as QTPs and Section 529 plans, are established and maintained by states or educational institutions. These plans allow a taxpayer to contribute to an account that will be used to pay future education expenses, usually for a beneficiary such as a child. A Section 529 plan functions somewhat like a Roth IRA account: the amounts contributed to a Section 529 plan are not deductible for federal tax purposes,[127] but the earnings grow tax-free. A beneficiary may be anyone the taxpayer designates: himself, a child, a grandchild, or an unrelated person; the donor and beneficiary do not need to be related to one another.

Contributions to a Section 529 are treated as gifts for tax purposes, which means that a donor can contribute up to $17,000 in 2023, per beneficiary, without incurring any gift tax or having to file a gift tax return. The amounts contributed to a 529 are also removed from the calculation of a donor's gross estate (this is why 529 plans are frequently used for estate planning purposes).

Unlike a Coverdell ESA, (covered in the next section), a 529 plan does not impose age limits or income limits to contribute. Distributions from a 529 plan are reported on Form 1099-Q. The part of a distribution representing the amount paid or contributed to the plan (the taxpayer's basis) is not taxable when funds are withdrawn.

The beneficiary also generally is not taxed on any earnings distributed from a 529 plan if the total distribution does not exceed a student's qualified education expenses (after reduction of the latter by other tax-free education assistance received during the year).

"Qualified expenses" include tuition, fees, books, computer equipment, and software, and room and board for any time the beneficiary is enrolled in school. The definition of "qualified higher education expenses" for 529 accounts also includes the purchases of computer equipment and technology, such as required computer software for a college course.

---

[127] 529 savings plans are named after Section 529 of the Internal Revenue Code. They include prepaid tuition plans and savings plans and, more recently, 529A or "ABLE Accounts" that offer tax-deferred incentives to help pay for disability-related expenses. Although there is no federal tax deduction for contributions to a 529 plan, some individual states do allow a deduction for contributions. This can be a factor when taxpayers are deciding between different types of educational savings accounts.

Eligible institutions include: accredited colleges, universities, vocational schools, and postsecondary educational institutions. Section 529 plans also allow distributions (not exceeding $10,000) for tuition expenses incurred in connection with the enrollment at any public, private or religious elementary or secondary (K-12) school. This means that Section 529 plans can be used for private elementary schools, middle schools, and high schools.

The SECURE Act 1.0 expanded Section 529 plans to permit tax-free distributions to pay for fees and equipment required for a qualifying apprenticeship program. Examples of acceptable apprenticeship programs can include: electrical certification, dental assistants, welders, and pipefitters. 529 plans can also be used to pay off student loans (up to $10,000 lifetime) for the designated beneficiary, or a sibling of the designated beneficiary.

If the total distribution is greater than a student's adjusted qualified expenses, an allocable portion of the earnings is taxable. In this type of taxable distribution, an additional excise tax of 10% generally applies to the taxable amount that must be included in income.

Any amount distributed from a 529 plan is not taxable if it is rolled over to another 529 plan for the use of the same beneficiary or for a member of the beneficiary's family.[128] If the distribution is being done as an indirect rollover, the amount distributed must be rolled over to another educational account within 60 days after the date of distribution.

> **Example:** Bernardo still had $3,000 left in his 529 plan after he graduates from college. He wants to help his younger sister, Angelina, who was still a senior in high school. She also plans to go to college. He distributed the entire amount that was left in his 529 plan, and within 60 days after the distribution, Bernardo contributed all the money to his sister's 529 plan. As a qualified rollover, the distribution was not taxable to him or his sister. Instead of taking a distribution, Bernardo could also have instructed the trustee of his 529 account to change the name of the beneficiary on his existing account to his sister's name.

Coverdell Education Savings Accounts (ESA)

A Coverdell ESA is a self-directed, tax-advantaged investment account for higher education. Formerly called "Education IRAs," these plans were named after the late Senator Paul Coverdell, who was their primary backer. A Coverdell is structured as a custodial account set up to pay qualified elementary, secondary, or higher education expenses for a designated beneficiary.

Contributions to a Coverdell ESA are not tax-deductible, but amounts deposited in the account grow tax-free until they are later distributed. The funds withdrawn from a Coverdell are tax-free when used for qualifying educational purposes.

Coverdell ESAs have income and age limits, but they offer more flexibility in investing. Coverdell accounts are self-directed, which means that there are a variety of investment options available, whereas 529 plans are limited to the state's selected investment options. In order to contribute to a Coverdell ESA, the contributor's MAGI in 2023 is subject to an income phaseout range of $95,000 to $110,000, or $190,000 to $220,000 for couples who are married filing jointly.

---

[128] The SECURE Act 2.0 added a provision that will permit rollovers from a Section 529 account into a Roth IRA, but this provision does not become effective until 2024.

All contributions must be in cash, not property or stock, and must be made by the due date of the contributor's tax return, not including extensions. So, for example, if a parent wanted to set up a Coverdell account for their child in 2023, the parent would have until April 15, 2024, to set up the account and fund it.

Coverdell accounts have age limits. Contributions to a Coverdell must be made before the beneficiary reaches age 18, and the use of the account must be made by age 30, unless the beneficiary is special needs (in which case there are no age limitations). If there is a balance in the ESA when the beneficiary reaches age 30, it must be distributed within 30 days of turning 30 (or within 30 days after the death, if the beneficiary dies before their thirtieth birthday). The beneficiary may transfer the ESA to another beneficiary (such as a younger sibling or another family member) to avoid the tax.

Example: Arjun was awarded a full scholarship to Stanford University. He enrolled in college when he was 18 and had a Coverdell ESA with a balance of $52,000 that was set up by his parents when he was a baby. Since his tuition was already paid by a scholarship, Arjun only used the Coverdell to pay for his textbooks, required equipment, and lab fees. Arjun graduated from college 4 years later and had only used a total of $14,000 from his ESA. Rather than withdrawing the remaining money in the account and paying a 10% penalty, Arjun transferred the Coverdell to his younger sister, who is 17 and still in high school. His sister can use the remaining amounts in the Coverdell ESA for her own future college expenses. His sister will have until age 30 to use the funds for her own college expenses.

If the beneficiary is special needs, the Coverdell account can continue in existence (without transfer to another beneficiary) even after the beneficiary turns 30.

Example: Hallie has a Coverdell education savings account that her parents set up for her when she was a child. Hallie has autism and is considered disabled. She is enrolled in a special college program for students with diagnosed learning disabilities. This year, Hallie turned 30 years of age. She is not required to withdraw or transfer the amounts in her Coverdell because she is special-needs.

There is no limit to the *number* of Coverdell accounts that can be established for a beneficiary; however, the total contribution to all accounts on behalf of a beneficiary cannot exceed $2,000 per year, no matter how many accounts are established. However, if a taxpayer wants to do some year-end tax planning, they can set up a Coverdell as late as the filing deadline, and contribute $2,000 for 2023 up until April 15, 2024 (the individual filing deadline), and then another $2,000 for 2024.

All contributions that exceed $2,000 for a single beneficiary per year will be treated as excess contributions. There is a 6% excise tax if the excess contributions and earnings on them are not withdrawn from the child's accounts by May 31 of the following tax year. This excise tax will apply to each year that the excess remains in the account. Any earnings withdrawn as part of a corrective distribution are taxable in the year of the excess contribution, even if the corrective distribution occurs in the following year.

Example: Three Coverdell ESAs were set up for Kendra when she was born: one by her parents, one by her grandparents, and one by her favorite uncle. In 2023, her grandparents contribute $1,500 to Kendra's account. The most her parents and uncle can contribute is a combined $500, because the maximum contribution per year for a single beneficiary is $2,000.

The penalty for excess contributions is imposed on the beneficiary of the account (usually a minor child), and not on the person who overcontributed to the account. The excise tax must be reported on the child's income tax return, using IRS Form 5329, *Additional Taxes on Qualified Plans (Including IRAs) and Other Tax-Favored Accounts*. This rule seems contrary to common sense, but the penalty is imposed on the child, not the child's parents, or the contributor of the excess funds.

The beneficiary of a Coverdell account can receive distributions to pay qualified education expenses that are tax-free if the amount of the distributions does not exceed the beneficiary's adjusted qualified education expenses.

If a distribution does exceed the beneficiary's qualified education expenses, a portion of the earnings is taxable and is reported as "other income" on Schedule 1 of Form 1040. In addition, a penalty tax of 10% applies to distributions that are not used for qualifying educational expenses.[129] Exceptions to the penalty include death or disability of the beneficiary.

> **Example:** Evaline is 21 years old. She enrolled in college for the first time on January 6, 2023. Evaline's parents set up a Coverdell account for her when she was a child. Her parents contributed a total of $9,000 to Evaline's Coverdell over the years, and now her account is worth $10,000. Evaline withdraws the entire amount from the Coverdell account and then promptly drops out of college without paying any of her tuition. Instead, spends the withdrawn funds on a vacation to Cabo San Lucas. Ten percent of the balance on the account is earnings, so $1,000 of the distribution is taxable. In addition, Evaline will owe a 10% penalty on the $1,000 taxable portion of the distribution, because she did not have any qualifying education expenses.

> **Example:** Oliver is 24 years old. He is the beneficiary of a Coverdell ESA that was set up for him by his parents when he was a child. There is $19,000 in the Coverdell account at the beginning of the year. Oliver signs up for an automotive certificate program at his local community college. The tuition and books for the program costs $13,700. Oliver withdraws $13,700 from the Coverdell account, intending to use the amounts to pay for his tuition. However, a few days before his semester is about to begin, Oliver gets into a serious auto accident and becomes disabled. He never uses the distribution to pay for tuition. Instead, he uses the money to help pay his medical bills. He receives a Form 1099-Q reporting the distribution, which he will use to report the taxable portion of his withdrawal (the earnings). However, the distribution will not be subject to a 10% penalty, because he became disabled during the year.

There is no law that prevents a taxpayer from contributing to both a Coverdell and a 529 for the same beneficiary, so a taxpayer could potentially set up a Coverdell and a Section 529 for the same child, and the earnings would grow tax-free in both accounts.

If a beneficiary receives distributions from both a 529 plan and a Coverdell ESA in the same year, and the total distributions exceed the beneficiary's adjusted qualified education expenses for that year, the educational expenses must be allocated between the distributions from each account.

---

[129] The beneficiary may also avoid this 10% penalty by rolling over the full balance to another Coverdell ESA for another family member, such as a sibling. (IRS Tax Tip 2003-38).

Miscellaneous Other Income

Other types of income that are taxable to the recipient and reported on Schedule 1 (Form 1040) include the following (this list is not exhaustive):

- Union strike benefits,
- Jury duty pay (when it is not turned over to the employer and deducted as an adjustment to income),
- Alaska Permanent Fund dividends
- Fees paid by an estate to a personal representative/executor,[130]
- Gifts or gratuities received by a host or hostess of a party or event where sales are made.

Example: Shirley is 72 years old and retired. She supports herself primarily with her Social Security income. In 2023, she receives a jury duty summons. She is chosen for the jury, and she is paid $40 a day for serving ten days on a jury trial. Shirley was also reimbursed by the court for reasonable transportation expenses and parking fees. The $400 she earned for jury duty is taxable and must be reported on Line 8h of Schedule 1 of her Form 1040. The reimbursement for transportation and parking fees is not taxable and does not have to be reported on her return.

Example: Ethan is the executor of his grandmother's estate. His grandmother died on January 29, 2023. Her estate includes several rental properties that must be managed after her death. Ethan is not an attorney or professional executor, but he did agree to manage his grandmother's estate. Ethan pays bills, hires an accountant to file the estate's tax returns, and manages his late grandmother's rental properties until they can be sold. His grandmother's final will stipulates that the executor should receive 4% of the income generated by the estate, as well as reimbursement for all estate-related business expenses. In 2023, Ethan receives $9,500 in executor fees, which he reports as other income on his Form 1040 (Line 8z of Schedule 1).

Example: Johanna hosts a cooking party for 15 of her friends, which includes a live demonstration by a Pampered Chef consultant. At the end of the evening, the women order $2,000 worth of Pampered Chef cookware and other merchandise from the consultant. Johanna receives a gift of $115 of cookware for hosting the party, which she must report as income at its fair market value.

---

[130] Executor fees are considered taxable income to the recipient. Executors of an estate will typically receive some type of compensation for their work on the estate. Many U.S. states have a specific set of statutory rates (based on the value of the estate) that can be paid to an executor of an estate as listed in their probate codes. We will cover estates more extensively in a later unit.

Table: Taxable vs. Nontaxable Income	
Taxable Income	**Nontaxable Income (or Variable)**
Wages, salaries, tips, bonuses, vacation pay, severance pay, commissions	Most employer-provided fringe benefits
Interest on bank and money market accounts	Interest on state and local bonds (muni bonds)
Gains from sales of property, stocks, bonds, etc.	Life insurance proceeds
Fees paid to an estate's executor	Gifts and inheritances
Alimony (pre-2019 divorce decrees)	Alimony (post-2019 divorces) and child support
Social Security benefits (above the base amount and limited to 85% of benefits)	Welfare payments, food stamps, other forms of public assistance
Court awards for punitive damages, sexual harassment claims, and lost wages	Compensation or court awards for physical injury or illness, and awards for wrongful incarceration
Unemployment compensation; strike benefits	Worker's compensation due to an on-the-job injury
Barter and hobby income	Combat pay, G.I. Bill, certain veteran's benefits
Distributions from Coverdell savings accounts or qualified tuition programs that are not used for educational expenses	Scholarships, Pell grants, employer-provided educational assistance
Cancellation of debt income (unless excludable)	Canceled qualified principal residence indebtedness, canceled debt while in bankruptcy, or insolvency, canceled student loans.
Gambling winnings; most prizes and awards	Certain employee awards for safety, achievement, or service

Unit 10: Study Questions

(Test yourself first, then check the correct answers at the end of this quiz.)

1. Which of the following would be considered taxable income to the recipient?

A. Life insurance proceeds paid to a beneficiary.
B. Unemployment compensation.
C. Alimony received from a divorce finalized in 2021.
D. Welfare benefits.

2. Lucian, age 70, experiences age-related discrimination on his job and sues his company. After he files the lawsuit, he is physically attacked by the company owner, who breaks Lucian's arm. The court awards Lucian the following amounts:

- $4,000 for emotional distress attributable to the age discrimination lawsuit.
- $10,000 for loss of wages attributable to the age discrimination lawsuit.
- $35,000 for physical injury related to the assault.
- $16,000 reimbursement for medical expenses related to the assault

How much of this award is taxable to Lucian?

A. $4,000
B. $10,000
C. $14,000
D. $49,000

3. Emmy had $9,000 of gambling winnings from slot machine play during the year. She also incurred $15,000 of gambling losses. How should these transactions be reported on her tax return?

A. The $9,000 of winnings are reported as income, and the $15,000 of losses are reported as an adjustment to income on Schedule 1.
B. The $9,000 of winnings are reported as income, and the $15,000 of losses are reported as an itemized deduction on Schedule A.
C. The $9,000 of winnings are reported as income, and $9,000 of losses are reported as an itemized deduction on Schedule A.
D. The $9,000 of winnings are reported as income, but the gambling losses are not deductible.

4. Which of the following types of debt would not be classified as qualified principal residence indebtedness, for the purposes of the QPRI exclusion?

A. A home equity loan incurred to install an outdoor pool in a principal residence.
B. Secured debt on a residence that a taxpayer's dependent parent lives in. The taxpayer lives in his own home, but pays the mortgage and all the expenses on his parent's home.
C. A secured loan on a main home that was used to replace the roof on the residence.
D. A mortgage used to purchase land on which the taxpayer's main home was eventually built.

5. Latrice and Jackson's divorce decree requires Jackson to pay Latrice $250 per month of child support and $1,500 per month of alimony. Their divorce was final on January 13, 2023. Jackson makes all his child support and alimony payments on time during the year. How much of these payments is Latrice required to report as taxable income on her 2023 return?

A. $0
B. $1,500
C. $18,000
D. $21,000

6. Barton, age 64, is unmarried and retired. He earned the following income in 2023. To determine if any of his Social Security is taxable, Barton should compare how much of his income to the $25,000 base amount?

Part-time job	$8,000
Bank interest	5,000
Social Security	11,000
Taxable pension	6,000
Total	**$30,000**

A. $11,000
B. $19,000
C. $24,500
D. $30,000

7. Sheldon received Social Security in 2023 totaling $11,720. Sheldon also liquidated all his stock and moved into senior housing during the year. He received $350,500 of taxable income from the stock sale. What is the maximum *taxable* amount of Sheldon's Social Security benefits?

A. $0
B. $5,860
C. $9,962
D. $11,720

8. Bianca was discharged from her liability to repay $9,000 of credit card debt. The lender reported the discharged debt on Form 1099-C. Immediately prior to the debt cancellation, Bianca had liabilities of $15,000, and the fair market value of her assets was $2,000. What portion of the canceled debt must Bianca include in income?

A. $0
B. $3,000
C. $7,000
D. $9,000

9. Marcello received $32,000 of wages in 2023. He also won a prize from his homeowner's association for developing a new water conservation plan. The prize was free landscaping service for a year, valued at $600. Marcello also received $7,000 in child support and $2,000 in alimony from his ex-wife, whom he divorced in 2017. Marcello has sole custody of his children. What is Marcello's gross income (before deductions and adjustments) for 2023?

A. $32,000
B. $32,600
C. $34,600
D. $39,600

10. Armando received a $15,000 personal loan from his credit union but stopped making payments. The credit union determined that the legal fees to collect might be higher than the amount Armando owed, so it canceled the remaining amount of $5,000 due on the loan. Armando did not file for bankruptcy, nor is he insolvent. How much income must he include from the debt cancellation?

A. $0
B. $5,000
C. $10,000
D. $15,000

11. Archer is a former National Football League cornerback. In 2023, he is awarded a sizable settlement in a class-action lawsuit for concussion injuries for physical pain and suffering. The settlement will be paid in installments over a period of ten years. How should Archer report the damages he is awarded on his income tax return?

A. He must include the entire amount of his settlement in gross income for the year.
B. He must include in his gross income only the portion of the settlement paid to him each year when it is received.
C. He must report the settlement on his tax return, but it is not taxable income.
D. He may exclude the payments from his gross income.

12. Karly is trying to get her finances in order. During the year, she negotiated a settlement with her credit card company, to which she owed a delinquent debt. She owed $10,000 on her credit card. As part of the negotiation, the credit card company agreed to accept a $2,500 settlement as payment in full. Karly was not insolvent and not in bankruptcy when the debt was canceled. What amount should be reported as "other income" on Karly's Form 1040 (Schedule 1)?

A. $0
B. $2,500
C. $7,500
D. $10,000

13. Velma is 16 years old. She has two Coverdell accounts. One was set up by her grandparents, and the other was set up by her mother. Velma received $3,200 in total contributions in her Coverdell accounts in 2023: $1,500 from her grandparents, and $1,700 deposited by her mother. Which of the following statements is true?

A. The Coverdell contributions are deductible and can remain in the accounts until Velma reaches 30 years of age.
B. Velma has an excess contribution of $1,200. The excess contribution must be withdrawn, or it will be subject to an excise tax.
C. Velma may withdraw the funds penalty-free and invest the amounts in a Roth IRA.
D. Velma has an excess contribution of $200. She can transfer this excess contribution to an IRA account.

14. Verona legally divorced from her husband in 2017. In 2023, she received all the income listed below. What is her *taxable* income?

Source	Amounts
Wages	$13,000
Interest income	15
Child support	6,000
Alimony	2,000
Inheritance	10,000
Worker's compensation	1,000
Lottery winnings	5,000

A. $13,015
B. $18,015
C. $20,015
D. $30,015

15. In which of the following instances is canceled debt not excluded from income?

A. Mortgage debt of a vacation home where the borrower is not insolvent or in bankruptcy.
B. Qualified farm indebtedness.
C. Medical debt discharged in bankruptcy.
D. Student loans discharged after death.

16. Which of the following is never taxable to the recipient?

A. Gambling winnings.
B. Hobby income.
C. Social Security income.
D. A settlement for wrongful incarceration.

17. Ginny had the following income and losses in 2023:

Source	Amounts
Wages	$14,000
Interest income	125
Gambling winnings	1,000
Gambling losses	(2,000)
Discrimination lawsuit settlement	10,000
Child support payments	9,000
Food stamp benefits	5,000

How much gross income must Ginny report on her tax return?

A. $14,125
B. $15,125
C. $25,125
D. $39,000

18. Avery and Samantha are married and file jointly. They received the following income during the year. How much income should be reported on their joint return?

- W-2 income for Samantha for wages of $40,000.
- 1099-MISC for Samantha for $2,000, the value of a prize trip she won to the Bahamas. She is planning to take the trip in the following year.
- Court settlement of $10,000 paid to Avery from a car accident for injuries he suffered.
- $4,000 child support for Samantha's son from a previous marriage.

A. $40,000
B. $42,000
C. $46,000
D. $52,000

Unit 10: Quiz Answers

1. The answer is B. Unemployment compensation is taxable income. None of the other amounts would be taxable to the recipient.

2. The answer is C. Lucian must report $14,000 in taxable income. The amounts for loss of wages and emotional distress are taxable as ordinary income ($4,000 + $10,000 = $14,000). Damages for emotional distress that is not due to physical injury or sickness are usually taxable (as in this case where the distress was attributed to the job discrimination and lawsuit). The damages awarded for physical injury are not taxable.

3. The answer is C. Emmy must report $9,000 of her winnings as taxable income, and $9,000 of the losses are reported on Schedule A as an itemized deduction. The amount of losses deducted may not exceed gambling winnings.

4. The answer is B. Secured debt on a residence that a taxpayer's dependent parent lives in would not qualify as QPRI, because the qualified principal residence indebtedness exclusion only applies to a taxpayer's main home (not a parent's home, a vacation home, or rental property). A "principal residence" is generally the home where the taxpayer lives most of the time. A taxpayer can have only one principal residence at a time.

5. The answer is A. Since the divorce decree was finalized in 2023, none of the alimony is deductible by Jackson, and the alimony is not reported as income by Latrice.

6. The answer is C. Barton does not have to pay tax on his Social Security. In order to figure out the taxable portion of Social Security, the taxpayer's total income, including tax-exempt interest, must be compared to the base amount for his filing status, which is $25,000. The amount of income that should be compared to the $25,000 base amount is calculated as follows:

Part-time job	$8,000
Interest	5,000
½ of Social Security	5,500
Taxable pension	6,000
Total	$24,500

His income plus one-half of Social Security is less than the applicable base amount ($25,000). However, he is still required to file a tax return, because his overall income exceeds the minimum filing requirement.

7. The answer is C. The maximum amount that is ever taxable on net Social Security benefits is 85%, which in Sheldon's case is (11,720 × 85% = 9,962).

259

8. The answer is A. Bianca does not have any taxable canceled debt. The amount of Bianca's assets immediately prior to the debt cancellation exceeded the amount of debt that was discharged. The entire amount of the debt cancellation can be excluded from income, due to her insolvency. She should still report the canceled debt by filing Form 982, and checking the box for "insolvency." The canceled debt will not be taxable.

Liabilities	$15,000
The fair market value of assets	(2,000)
Amount of insolvency	13,000
Amount of debt cancellation that is not taxable	**$9,000**

9. The answer is C. The wages and the prize are both reportable as taxable income. Child support is not taxable to the receiver, nor deductible by the payor. The alimony is taxable to Marcello and deductible by his ex-wife, since the divorce decree was finalized *before* 2019, when the TCJA alimony changes took effect. The answer is calculated as follows: ($32,000 + $600 + $2,000) = $34,600.

10. The answer is B. Armando's inability to pay his debt is not a result of bankruptcy or insolvency, so he must include the full amount of the canceled debt ($5,000) in his gross income.

11. The answer is D. Gross income does not include damages received due to physical injuries or sickness, regardless of whether the damages are paid as lump sums or as periodic payments. Archer may exclude all the payments from gross income.

12. The answer is C. Karly would report $7,500 in canceled debt income ($10,000 - $2,500) on her Form 1040 (Schedule 1).

13. The answer is B. Velma has an excess contribution of $1,200. The excess contribution must be withdrawn, or it will be subject to an excise tax of 6%, plus an additional 6% on any interest or profits derived from the excess contribution. This tax will apply to each year that the excess remains in the account. The maximum contribution to a Coverdell is $2,000 per year per beneficiary, regardless of how many accounts the beneficiary has. Any *earnings* withdrawn as part of a corrective distribution are taxable in the year of the excess contribution, even if the corrective distribution occurs in the following year (note that the rules for excess contributions do not apply to 529 plans, there is no limit that can be contributed to a 529, although there may be gift tax considerations if the amounts contributed exceed annual gift limits).

14. The answer is C. Verona must report $20,015 in taxable income. The wages, interest, alimony (because her divorce was finalized <u>before 2019</u>), and lottery winnings are taxable income ($13,000 + $15 + $2,000 + $5,000 = $20,015). Child support, inheritances, and worker's compensation are non-taxable income.

Note: Do *not* confuse worker's compensation with unemployment compensation. Worker's compensation is NOT taxable, while unemployment compensation is taxable.

15. The answer is A. Foreclosure of a vacation property does not qualify for the exclusion of canceled debt income. Canceled mortgage debt related to second homes and vacation homes does not qualify (unless the taxpayer has filed bankruptcy or is insolvent).

16. The answer is D. A settlement for wrongful incarceration would not be taxable to the recipient. All of the other items are taxable (or may be taxable).

17. The answer is C. Ginny must report her wages, interest income, gambling income, and settlement from a discrimination lawsuit ($14,000 + $125 + $1,000 + $10,000 = $25,125). The child support payments and the food stamp benefits are not taxable. The gambling losses do not affect the inclusion of the gambling income within gross income. However, if Ginny chooses to itemize deductions, her gambling losses may be deducted on Schedule A to the extent of her gambling income. If Ginny does not itemize, the gambling losses are not deductible.

18. The answer is B. The answer is $42,000 ($40,000 wages + $2,000 prize). Samantha must recognize the prize even though she has not taken the trip because she had constructive receipt of the winnings. The accident settlement and child support payments are not taxable.

Unit 11: Adjustments to Gross Income

For additional information, read:
Publication 504, *Divorced or Separated Individuals*
Publication 970, *Tax Benefits for Education*
Publication 590-A, *Contributions to Individual Retirement Arrangements*

"Adjustments to income" refers to deductions that can be made before calculating taxable income, thus reducing the amount of tax owed. These adjustments are reported on Form 1040, Schedule 1, *Additional Income and Adjustments to Income.*

Adjustments are taken before AGI is calculated; they are often called "above-the-line" deductions. Adjustments are subtracted from gross income to arrive at adjusted gross income (AGI), whereas itemized deductions and the standard deduction are subtracted from AGI. Adjustments are beneficial because they directly reduce taxable income, and may increase a taxpayer's eligibility for certain credits and deductions. Unlike other deductions, adjustments are not added back when calculating the alternative minimum tax.

Common Adjustments to Gross Income

There are many types of adjustments to gross income, and we will cover the most common ones in this unit. These are the adjustments listed in the order they are reported on the 2023 version of the Schedule 1, Form 1040:

- Line 11: Qualified educator expenses
- Line 12: Certain business expenses of Armed Forces reservists, performing artists, and fee-basis government officials.
- Line 13: Health savings account deduction (HSA deduction).
- Line 14: Moving expenses for members of the Armed Forces.
- Line 15: Deductible part of self-employment tax.
- Line 16: Self-employed SEP-IRA, SIMPLE, and qualified plans
- Line 17: Self-employed health insurance deduction
- Line 18: Penalty for early withdrawal of savings
- Line 19: Alimony paid (the form requires the amount paid, recipient's SSN, and the date of the original divorce or separation agreement)
- Line 20: Traditional IRA deduction
- Line 21: Student loan interest deduction
- Line 22: Reserved for future use (no deduction listed on this line of the form)
- Line 23: Archer MSA deduction
- Line 24: Other adjustments
  - a) Jury duty pay remitted to an employer
  - b) Deductible expenses related to the rental of personal property
  - c) Nontaxable amount of the value of Olympic and Paralympic medals
  - d) Reforestation amortization and expenses
  - e) Repayment of supplemental unemployment benefits
  - f) Contributions to section 501(c)(18)(D) pension plans

- o g) Contributions by certain chaplains to section 403(b) plans
- o h) Attorney fees for actions involving unlawful discrimination claims
- o i) Attorney fees paid in connection with an IRS whistleblower award
- o j) Housing deduction from Form 2555
- o k) Excess deductions of section 67(e) expenses from Schedule K-1 (Form 1041)
- o z) Other (write in) adjustments.

Line 11: Qualified educator expenses

This is sometimes called the "Teacher Credit" or the "Educator Expense Deduction." An eligible educator is allowed to deduct up to $300 of unreimbursed expenses in 2023. If both taxpayers are teachers, the couple may deduct up to a maximum of $600 on a joint return. Any expenses that exceed these limits cannot be deducted as unreimbursed employee business expenses on Schedule A.

Qualified expenses include books, supplies, computer equipment (including related software and services), other equipment, and supplementary materials used in the classroom. Professional development expenses are also allowed.

Since this is an adjustment to income, teachers can deduct these expenses even if they do not itemize deductions. For courses in health and physical education, expenses are deductible only if they are related to athletics. Nonathletic supplies for physical education, and expenses related to health courses do not qualify for this deduction. Materials used for homeschooling also cannot be deducted.

An eligible educator must work at least 900 hours a school year in a school that provides elementary or secondary education (K-12). College instructors do not qualify. For the purposes of this credit, an "educator" may include a teacher, counselor, principal, classroom aide, or a school coach.

Example: Donnie is a part-time biology teacher at an elementary school. He spent $185 on qualified expenses for his students to use in the classroom. During the tax year, he worked 550 hours at the school. Because Donnie does not have enough hours of documented employment as an educator during the tax year, he cannot deduct any of his unreimbursed educator expenses. The required minimum is 900 hours during the school year.

Example: Gayle is a fifth-grade art teacher who worked 1,600 hours during the tax year. She spent $262 on supplies for her students. Of that amount, $212 was for educational design software for her students to use in the classroom. The remaining $50 went towards supplies for a unit on reproductive health. Only the $212 spent on educational software is considered a qualified educator expense and can be deducted on Gayle's tax return.

Note that the following items for the year *reduce* the amount of qualifying educator expenses used to determine the amount of the final deduction amount:

- Non-taxable U.S. series EE and I savings bond interest income reportable on Form 8815;
- Nontaxable qualified tuition program earnings or distributions;
- Any nontaxable distribution of Coverdell education savings account earnings; and
- Any reimbursements received from an employer for qualifying educator expenses that were not reported as taxable income on Form W-2.

Line 12: Certain business expenses of reservists, performing artists, and fee-basis government officials

Although most employee-related business expenses are no longer deductible, work-related expenses for reservists, performing artists, and fee-basis government officials are still permitted.[131] Form 2106, *Employee Business Expenses*, is used to calculate the deduction.

This adjustment applies only to reservists[132] (members of the reserve component of the Armed Forces of the United States, National Guard, etc.), qualified performing artists; and state or local government officials who are compensated on a fee basis (examples may include a town mayor, county commissioner, justice of the peace, local registrars).

With regards to deductible expenses for reservists, Armed Forces Reservists are able to claim a deduction for amounts attributable to travel more than 100 miles away from their home. The travel must be reserve-related in order to be deductible.

Example: Wilfred is an Army reservist. He also has a regular full-time job in addition to his job as a reservist. Wilfred's drill location is 200 miles away from his home, where he normally reports for reserve drills and official meetings. He trains one weekend a month plus an additional two weeks per year. Wilfred is allowed to deduct the mileage and other travel expenses related to his reservist duties on Form 2106. The amounts are then transferred to Schedule 1, Form 1040, and claimed as an adjustment to income.

Line 13: Health savings account deduction

A high deductible health plan (HDHP) can be combined with a health savings account (HSA), allowing the taxpayer to pay for medical expenses on a tax-preferred basis. The HSA contributions are deductible as an adjustment to income on Form 1040.

Before a taxpayer can contribute to an HSA, the taxpayer must *first* be enrolled in a high-deductible health plan (HDHP). Once the HSA is set up, the taxpayer can take tax-free withdrawals from the HSA to pay for his qualifying medical expenses. An HSA must be established *exclusively* to pay medical expenses for the taxpayer, a spouse, and/or their dependents. HSA accounts are usually set up with a bank, an insurance company, or through an employer. To qualify for an HSA, the taxpayer:

- Must not be enrolled in Medicare,
- Cannot be claimed as a dependent on anyone else's tax return,
- Must be covered under a high deductible health plan and have no other health coverage, other than for a specific disease or illness; a fixed amount for a certain time period of hospitalization; or liabilities incurred under worker's compensation laws or tort liabilities.

An employee and his employer are both allowed to contribute to the employee's HSA in the same year. If an employer makes an HSA contribution on behalf of an employee, it is excluded from the employee's income and is not subject to income or payroll taxes.

---

[131] An employee with impairment-related work expenses is also still allowed to deduct employee business expenses, if the expenses are directly related to their work and disability.
[132] These deductions for travel-related expenses are not available for active-duty service members, only reservists.

2023 HSA and HDHP Limits	
HSA Contribution maximum	Self-only: $3,850, Family: $7,750
HDHP minimum deductible	Self-only: $1,500, Family: $3,000
HDHP maximum out-of-pocket amounts (not including insurance premiums)	Self-only: $7,500, Family: $15,000
HSA catch-up contributions (age 55 or older)	$1,000

HSA holders who are age 55 and older get to contribute an extra $1,000, beyond the regular limits (as detailed in the chart), as a catch-up contribution. Any excess contributions over these limits are subject to a 6% penalty. Any amount the employer puts into the employee's HSA counts toward the employee's contribution maximum for the year.

Example: Otto is 32 years old and married with children. His employer provides a health care HSA and a high-deductible health plan that covers Otto's entire family. Otto's employer adds $1,500 to his HSA account during the year. Otto may contribute up to $6,250 ($1,500 + $6,250 = $7,750 limit in 2023) more to his HSA account if he wishes. The amounts that Otto contributes to his own HSA would be deductible as an adjustment to income, and he is able to withdraw the amounts tax-free, as long as he uses the amounts to pay for qualified medical expenses.

Allowable medical expenses refer to those that would typically qualify for the medical expense deduction. However, there are some differences between what is considered a qualified medical expense for an HSA (Health Savings Account). Due to a provision in the CARES Act, "qualified medical expenses" for an HSA also include over-the-counter medications without a prescription, (such as aspirin) as well as menstrual products.

While funds from an HSA can be withdrawn at any time, withdrawals not used for qualifying medical expenses are subject to income tax and may also incur a 20% penalty, *except* when a taxpayer reaches the age of 65, becomes permanently disabled, or dies.

Example: Fred is age 66, unmarried, and has an HSA through his employer. In 2023, he has no qualifying medical expenses for the year, but his car breaks down, and he doesn't have the funds to repair it. Fred withdraws $2,000 from his HSA to pay for the car repairs. Since he did not use the funds to pay for qualifying medical expenses, the entire withdrawal is subject to income tax. However, Fred avoids the 20% additional penalty tax because he is over 65.

A taxpayer will receive annual Form 5498-SA from their HSA trustee showing the amount of contributions for the year. The deduction for an HSA is reported on Form 8889, *Health Savings Accounts*. To claim the HSA deduction for a particular year, the HSA contributions must be made on or before that year's tax filing date (without extensions, so by April 15, 2024, for the 2023 tax year).

Note: Do *not* confuse an HSA (Health Savings Account) with a Healthcare FSA (Flexible Spending Arrangement). The two are *not the same thing*. Although both types of accounts are used to pay medical expenses on a pre-tax basis, there are significant differences between an HSA and a Healthcare FSA. An HSA is *always* paired with a high-deductible health plan, and the funds in the HSA belong to the participant, not the employer. Unlike an FSA, funds in an HSA <u>do not expire</u> from year-to-year.

Line 14: Moving Expenses for Members of the Armed Forces

The Tax Cuts and Jobs Act suspended the moving expense deduction for most taxpayers through 2025, except for those in the Armed Forces who are moving under military orders or a permanent change of station. A member of the armed forces can also deduct the costs of moving their spouse, dependents, pets, and household goods. Any expenses already reimbursed by the government cannot be claimed as a deduction.

For 2023, the standard mileage rate for moving expenses is 22 cents per mile. To calculate qualifying moving expenses, Armed Forces personnel must use Form 3903, *Moving Expenses.*

Example: Catarina is a U.S. Army medic. In 2023, she is transferred from Fort Rucker Army Base in Alabama to the Tripler Army Medical Center in Hawaii. She is offered a relocation reimbursement by the Army that covers most of her moving expenses. The only costs that the Army would not cover were the transport costs for her pets. She pays $1,200 to a pet relocation service in Hawaii to process the transportation of her pets on a private airline, as well as to board her pets for the quarantine period required by the state of Hawaii. The cost of transporting pets is a deductible moving expense, and Catarina is eligible to deduct any out-of-pocket moving expenses related to household goods and personal effects, including pets, because she is an employee of the U.S. Armed Forces. She files Form 3903, *Moving Expenses*, and correctly deducts the $1,200 that she paid to transport her pets.

If a taxpayer is not a U.S. service member, and an employer reimburses their moving expenses, the reimbursement is taxable to the employee as wages. Employers who reimburse employees for their moving expenses must now include the reimbursements on the employee's Form W-2, and the entire amount is subject to payroll tax.

Example: Cedric was offered a job at Highland Engineering, Inc. on February 2, 2023. He agreed to accept the offer if the company paid all his moving expenses. The cost of his professional movers was $9,600, which the company paid. Highland Engineering also reimbursed Cedric $7,500 for temporary storage fees and other travel expenses. The total reimbursement was $17,100. Because moving expenses are no longer a deductible expense, the entire $17,100 is taxable as wages, and must be included on Cedric's Form W-2. The amount is deductible to Highland Engineering, but it is categorized as a wage expense and subject to payroll taxes.

Line 15: Deductible Part of Self-Employment Tax

A self-employed taxpayer can subtract from income 50% of their self-employment tax, equal to the amount of Social Security and Medicare taxes that an employer normally pays for an employee, which is excluded from an employee's income. The deduction is figured on Schedule SE. The self-employment tax rate is a percentage of your net income from self-employment.

The rate for self-employment tax is 15.3% which is a combination of 12.4% Social Security tax and 2.9% Medicare tax.[133] It's calculated from 92.35% of self-employment net income. A self-employed taxpayer cannot deduct one-half of the Additional Medicare Tax on earned income.[134]

---

[133] Employees and their employers typically "split" the amounts for Social Security tax and Medicare tax. Each pays 7.65% (the employer pays 7.65%, and the employee also pays 7.65%). But self-employed individuals are responsible for both halves, resulting in the full 15.3% self-employment tax.
[134] The Additional Medicare Tax and other provisions of the Affordable Care Act are covered later.

Line 16: Self-employed SEP, SIMPLE, and qualified plans

When taxpayers are self-employed, they have access to many of the same kinds of retirement plans that are utilized by larger employers. Self-employed individuals can deduct contributions to the following types of retirement plans:

- **Simplified Employee Pension (SEP) plans**
- **Savings Incentive Match Plan for Employees (SIMPLE) plans**
- **Qualified plans, such as a 401(k)**

A self-employed taxpayer must have qualifying income to contribute to their own plan.[135] This means that their business must show a profit. However, a self-employed business owner does not need to show a profit on Schedule C in order to contribute to a retirement plan for their employees.

Example: Rakeem is a self-employed kickboxing instructor. He has a full-time receptionist named Dayanara who works in his training gym. In 2023, Rakeem makes a large fitness equipment purchase. The fitness equipment qualifies for Section 179 and bonus depreciation. Rakeem claims Section 179 depreciation on all the equipment and reduces his taxable income to zero for the year. He cannot contribute to his own retirement plan because he has no taxable income on his Schedule C. However, Rakeem is still allowed to contribute to Dayanara's retirement plan. This is true even if there is a loss on his Schedule C.

Line 17: Self-employed health insurance deduction

A self-employed taxpayer may be able to deduct 100% of their health insurance premiums as an adjustment to income (as long as the business has profits for the year). Premiums paid by the taxpayer for a spouse and dependents under age 27 are also deductible. The deduction is limited to the net profits from the business. The taxpayer must either:

- Be self-employed and have a net profit for the year,
- Be a partner in a partnership with net earnings from self-employment, or
- Have received wages from an S corporation in which the taxpayer was a more-than-2% shareholder.

Long-term care insurance and Medicare premiums are also considered health insurance for purposes of this deduction.

Example: Breton is unmarried and runs his own business as a refrigerator repairman. During the year, he paid health insurance premiums of $3,000 ($250 per month). After deducting all his business expenses, his Schedule C shows a profit of $15,500. He may deduct the full $3,000 in health insurance as an adjustment to income on Schedule 1 (Form 1040).

If a self-employed individual (or their spouse, if filing jointly) has the option to join an employer-sponsored and subsidized health insurance plan, they are not eligible for the self-employed health insurance deduction, even if they decline to enroll in the employer's plan.[136]

---

[135] SEP, SIMPLE, and qualified retirement plans are primarily tested on the businesses section of the EA exam (Part 2), so they are covered in much more detail in Book 2, Businesses.

[136] For self-employed individuals filing a Schedule C or F, a health insurance policy can be either in the name of the business or in the name of the individual.

> **Example:** Heather and Jeremy are married. Jeremy is a self-employed carpenter and pays for his own individual insurance policy. Heather works for a grocery store as a cashier. Jeremy was eligible to participate in a subsidized health plan through his wife's employer, but Jeremy declined the coverage because he didn't want to switch doctors. Jeremy cannot take a deduction for the health insurance premiums that he paid because he declined to participate in his wife's employer-sponsored coverage.

Line 18: Penalty for early withdrawal of savings

If a taxpayer withdraws money from a certificate of deposit (CD) or other time-deposit savings account prior to maturity, they usually incur a penalty for early withdrawal. This penalty is charged by the bank or other financial institution and withheld from a taxpayer's proceeds.

Taxpayers can take an adjustment to income for early withdrawal penalties. The penalties are reported on a taxpayer's Form 1099-INT, *Interest Income*, or on Form 1099-OID, *Original Issue Discount*, which lists interest income as well as the penalty amount.

> **Example:** On January 4, 2023, Nikita invested in a $45,000 one-year certificate of deposit through her credit union. Later that year, she had an unexpected medical expense and had to liquidate the CD early. She paid a penalty of $450. Nikita can claim the entire penalty ($450) as an adjustment to income on Schedule 1 of Form 1040. She can take the deduction for the early withdrawal penalty even if she did not have any interest income for the year.

> **Note:** Do not be confused by this concept! Only the penalty for early withdrawal from a timed deposit (a certificate of deposit) is tax-deductible. The penalty for early withdrawal from an IRA or a retirement plan is never deductible.

Line 19: Alimony paid

By definition, alimony is a payment to a former spouse under a divorce or separation instrument. Sometimes these payments are called "spousal support" or "separate maintenance." The payments must be made in cash, but they do not have to be made directly to the ex-spouse. For example, payments made on behalf of the ex-spouse for expenses such as medical bills and other expenses can also qualify as alimony.

While alimony paid on divorces finalized since 2019 is not deductible, if the divorce decree was finalized *before* 2019, alimony paid is normally an adjustment to income for the payor on Line 19a of Schedule 1. In order to deduct alimony paid, the payor's Form 1040, Schedule 1 requires the amount paid, the recipient's SSN, and the date of the original divorce or separation agreement.

On the other side, alimony *received* on pre-2019 divorces is taxable income to the payee, which is claimed on Schedule 1 (Line 2a) of Form 1040.

> **Example:** Farrah and Esteban were legally divorced on November 10, 2018. Farrah is a wealthy actress, and their divorce settlement requires that Farrah must pay her ex-husband $58,000 a year in alimony. Since their divorce was finalized before 2019, it is considered "grandfathered," and all the alimony is deductible by Farrah and taxable to Esteban.

> **Example:** Elizabeth and Archibald's divorce decree was finalized on May 3, 2023. Their divorce agreement requires that Archibald must pay his ex-wife $12,000 a year in alimony, as well as $19,000 a year in child support. Also, per their divorce agreement, Archibald also must pay Elizabeth's ongoing medical insurance costs. Archibald cannot deduct any of these payments as alimony, because their divorce was finalized in 2023.

Voluntary payments that are not required by a divorce decree or separation instrument do not qualify as alimony.

> **Example:** Finnigan and Annabella legally divorced in 2018. Under the terms of their divorce, Finnigan must pay his ex-wife $12,600 per year in alimony ($1,050 per month). Finnigan also pays $10,000 a year for Annabella's medical insurance, because that is required as part of their divorce settlement. As a personal favor, he also makes $2,400 in auto loan payments on her car, so she can keep steady employment. Since his divorce was final before 2019, Finnigan can claim $22,600 ($12,600 +$10,000) as alimony paid, and claim the amounts as an adjustment to income on his Form 1040. Annabella must also report these amounts as taxable alimony on her return. However, Finnigan cannot deduct the auto payments as alimony because they are not required by the divorce agreement. Those voluntary payments would be treated as a gift.

Line 20: Traditional IRA deduction

An individual retirement arrangement (IRA) offers tax advantages for setting aside money for retirement. Most taxpayers can claim a deduction for the amounts contributed to a traditional IRA. Only amounts contributed to a *traditional* IRA are deductible. Amounts that do *not* qualify for the IRA deduction include:

- Contributions to a Roth IRA,
- Contributions to a traditional IRA that are nondeductible because the taxpayer and/or spouse is covered by an employer-sponsored retirement plan and modified adjusted gross income (MAGI) exceeds certain limits,
- Contributions that apply to the previous tax year,
- Rollover contributions.

Individuals who are not covered by a retirement plan at work may fully deduct contributions made to a traditional IRA. However, for those already covered by another retirement plan at work, the deduction for their IRA contributions may be reduced above certain income thresholds. The rules regarding IRA contributions, distributions, and rollovers are covered in detail later, in a dedicated unit for retirement plans.

Line 21: Student Loan Interest Deduction

The interest paid on a qualified student loan may be deductible. A qualified student loan refers to a loan used solely for paying qualified higher-education expenses for the taxpayer, their spouse, or their dependents. To claim the deduction, the taxpayer must have personally paid the interest on a qualified student loan and cannot be claimed as a dependent on someone else's tax return. Additionally, married couples who file separate tax returns are not eligible for this deduction.

Example: Sharon and Winston are married, but choose to file separate returns. They both have qualified student loans, and both are paying interest. Sharon pays $2,100 in student loan interest on her loan, and Winston pays $3,000 in interest on his student loan. Sharon and Winston decided to file separate returns in 2023. Neither one of them can take a deduction for student loan interest, because they are filing separate tax returns (MFS).

In order for student loan interest to qualify, the student must have been enrolled in a higher education program leading to a degree, certificate, or other recognized educational credential. A student who used the loan for other purposes does not qualify.

The maximum deduction for student loan interest in 2023 is $2,500. The student loan interest deduction limit is per *return*, not per *student*. For example, if a taxpayer has three children and pays $2,000 in student loan interest for each of them, their maximum deduction is still only $2,500 per year. A phaseout applies to higher-income taxpayers. This deduction is subject to income limitations and begins to phase out for taxpayers with MAGI between $75,000 – $90,000 ($155,000 – $185,000 for joint filers) in 2023.

Example: Tasha is an unmarried physician with a modified adjusted gross income of $209,000. She paid $5,400 of student loan interest in 2023. Due to her high income, she cannot deduct any of her student loan interest as an adjustment to income.

Example: Rudy graduated from a technical college where he was enrolled full-time in a certificate program for Electrical Technology. Rudy is single and earned $48,000 in wages during the year. He had no other income. Rudy paid $1,250 in student loan interest in 2023. He may take the student loan interest deduction and deduct all the interest that he paid as an adjustment to income.

A student loan is not eligible if it is from certain related persons (such as family members or related corporations, partnerships, or trusts). Loans from an employer plan also do not qualify. Qualifying higher-education expenses include the costs of attending an eligible educational institution, including graduate schools, such as:

- Tuition and fees,
- Room and board,
- Books, supplies, and required equipment, and other necessary school-related expenses.

The amounts for qualified expenses must be reduced by the amounts of tax-free items used to pay them, such as tax-free scholarships and fellowships, veterans' educational assistance benefits, or any other nontaxable payments (except gifts or inheritances) that are received for educational expenses. Lenders are required to send the taxpayer Form 1098-E, *Student Loan Interest*, when the amount of student loan interest paid exceeds $600 or more.

Line 22 and Line 23

Line 22 is reserved for future use (there is no deduction listed on that line). Line 23 is the deduction for contributions to Archer MSA accounts. Archer MSA accounts are an older type of tax-advantaged medical savings account available to self-employed taxpayers and employees of small businesses with fifty or fewer employees. New Archer MSAs are no longer available, but grandfathered plans still exist. Archer MSA accounts are not listed on the EA exam content outlines for 2023.

Line 24: Other Adjustments

The last lines of Schedule 1, Form 1040 are used for other miscellaneous adjustments and writing-in more obscure deductions. Although these deductions are not frequently seen, they are still available. A taxpayer does not need to itemize in order to deduct these amounts. These "other adjustments" are covered in more detail in the instructions for Form 1040.

An example of one of these "uncommon" adjustments is the deduction for legal costs from unlawful discrimination claims. A taxpayer may deduct, as an adjustment to income on Schedule 1 (Form 1040), attorney fees and court costs for legal claims involving a claim of unlawful discrimination. This includes job-related discrimination on account of race, sex, religion, age, or disability as well as other federal, state, and local legal actions related to the employment relationship. However, the amount the taxpayer can deduct is limited to the amount of the judgment or settlement the taxpayer includes in income for the tax year. In 2023, the deductible legal fees will be reported on line 24(h) of Schedule 1.

Example: Francine, age 62, sues her employer for age discrimination after she discovers an incriminating email from her supervisor, stating that the company was planning to fire Francine because she was "too old" and they could hire a younger worker for less money. She makes a copy of the email and gives it to her lawyer, who immediately files suit. Rather than face an expensive trial, Francine's employer agrees to settle the suit. The total settlement amount is $800,000, and Francine's employment lawyer charges a 40% contingency fee, which is typical for her type of legal claim. Francine must report the full amount of the settlement as income, but she is allowed to take a deduction for the legal fees she paid to her attorney, which are $320,000 ($800,000 × 40%).

Unit 11: Study Questions

(Test yourself first, then check the correct answers at the end of this quiz.)

1. Deborah was a self-employed chicken farmer in 2023. She files Schedule F to report her income and loss. She incurred a self-employment tax of $4,896 on her Schedule SE. Which of the following statements is correct?

A. She can deduct 100% of the self-employment tax as an adjustment to income on Form 1040.
B. She can deduct 50% of the self-employment tax as an adjustment to income on Form 1040.
C. She can deduct 50% of the self-employment tax as a business expense on Schedule F.
D. She cannot deduct the self-employment tax.

2. Jasmine is a part-time teacher at an elementary school. She spends $350 on qualified expenses for her art students and $75 on materials for a reproductive health course she teaches. She worked 600 hours as an educator during the tax year. How much can she deduct in educator expenses as an adjustment to income?

A. $0
B. $250
C. $300
D. $375

3. Chuck and Aurora are married and file jointly. Chuck is self-employed, and his net profit from his Schedule C business was $50,000 in 2023. The couple pays $700 per month for Chuck's self-employed health insurance coverage. Aurora was a homemaker until she started working for a construction company in February. Aurora and Chuck became eligible to participate in her employer's subsidized health plan on March 1, 2023, but they did not want to switch doctors or insurance plans, so Aurora declined her employer's coverage. Which of the following statements is correct?

A. They can deduct $700 for both January and February, and $350 per month for each of the last ten months of the year, as self-employed health insurance premiums on Chuck's Schedule C.
B. They can deduct $1,400 in self-employed health insurance premiums, which is for January and February, the two months they were not eligible to participate in an employer plan.
C. They can deduct 100% of their health insurance premiums because they declined the employer coverage.
D. They can deduct 50% of their health insurance premiums on Chuck's Schedule C.

4. All of the following statements are correct about the qualified educator expense deduction except:

A. A high school counselor may qualify.
B. A part-time teacher may qualify.
C. A school principal may qualify.
D. A college instructor may qualify.

5. An adjustment to income is considered the most beneficial type of deduction because:

A. It favors taxpayers who choose to itemize their deductions.
B. It is simpler to figure out than other deductions.
C. Adjustments to income directly reduce adjusted gross income.
D. There is no significant difference between an adjustment to income and other tax deductions.

6. Gabin and Keyah have a MAGI of $75,000. They are married and file a joint return. Four years ago, they took out a loan so their daughter, Miranda, could earn an associate's degree at a local junior college. Miranda is 22 and is still their dependent. In 2023, they paid $3,800 of student loan interest on Miranda's student loan. How much student loan interest can Gabin and Keyah deduct on their tax return?

A. $0
B. $1,000
C. $2,500
D. $3,800

7. Georgina was offered a management position in another state on May 30, 2023. She accepts the position, and her new employer reimburses her $4,550 for her moving expenses. Georgina submitted all the proper receipts to her new employer. How should this reimbursement be treated for tax purposes?

A. The employer can reimburse Georgina on a pre-tax basis.
B. The expense is nontaxable as long as Georgina's employer gives her a gift card.
C. The reimbursement is tax-exempt because it is a qualified moving expense.
D. Because this is a reimbursement of a nondeductible expense, it is treated as taxable wages and must be included on Georgina's Form W-2.

8. Sherry is 31 and has an HSA. She became permanently disabled during the year due to a serious automobile accident. Sherry withdraws all the money from her HSA, but does not incur any out-of-pocket medical expenses, because she became eligible for Emergency Medicaid and Medicaid covered her medical expenses. Instead, she used the HSA funds to pay off other debts. Which of the following statements is correct?

A. She may withdraw money from her HSA for nonmedical expenses, but the withdrawals will be subject to income tax and also an additional penalty of 20%.
B. She may not take nonmedical distributions from her account.
C. She may withdraw money from her HSA for nonmedical expenses. The withdrawals will be subject to income tax but will not be subject to a penalty.
D. She must be at least 65 to take nonmedical distributions from an HSA.

9. Marshall lost his job last year and withdrew money from a number of bank and investment accounts. He paid the following penalties:

Penalty for early withdrawal from a certificate of deposit (CD)	$140
Penalty for early withdrawal from a traditional IRA	200
Late penalty for not paying his credit card on time	50

What amount can Marshall deduct as an adjustment to income on his Form 1040?

A. $0
B. $140
C. $200
D. $250

10. Bruce accidentally makes an excess contribution to his HSA by contributing over the maximum allowable amount. What is the *penalty* on excess contributions if Bruce does not timely withdraw the overcontribution?

A. No penalty
B. 6% penalty
C. 10% penalty
D. 20% penalty

11. Two full-time teachers who are married and file jointly can deduct a maximum of _____ in qualified educator expenses in 2023:

A. $0
B. $250
C. $300
D. $600

12. Rick and Linda's divorce was finalized in 2017. Under the legal terms of his divorce decree, Rick must pay the medical expenses of his ex-wife, Linda. In January 2023, Rick sends a check totaling $4,000 directly to Mercy General Hospital to pay for Linda's emergency surgery. Which of the following statements is correct?

A. Linda must include the $4,000 as taxable alimony on her individual tax return.
B. This payment does not qualify as alimony, but Rick can claim a deduction for the medical expenses on his return.
C. Linda must include the $4,000 as income on her return, but Rick cannot deduct the expense as alimony because it was paid to a third party.
D. None of the above

13. Zander is a college instructor at Chico State University in California. In 2023, he paid $400 for materials and supplies that he used in the classroom. He also paid $210 in parking fees to park across the street from the university when the faculty lot was full. What amount of qualifying expenses does he have for purposes of the educator expense deduction?

A. $0
B. $300
C. $400
D. $610

14. Graciela, age 41, had an HSA account set up with her employer that had $4,000 in the account at the end of the year. She quit her job in June and withdrew all the funds from her HSA. She had no qualifying medical expenses during 2023. Instead, she used the funds to buy a used car. What is the consequence of this action?

A. Nothing; taxpayers are allowed to withdraw from their HSA accounts at any time.
B. Her withdrawal is prohibited and will result in a forfeiture of the funds.
C. Graciela must pay income tax and a 20% penalty on the withdrawal.
D. Graciela must pay income tax and a 6% penalty on the withdrawal.

15. Obadiah paid $22,000 of alimony to his ex-wife in 2023. His divorce became final in 2017, and the alimony payments are required by the terms of his divorce decree. Which of the following statements is correct?

A. He can deduct alimony paid as an adjustment to income.
B. The deduction for alimony is entered on Schedule B.
C. He can deduct alimony only if he itemizes deductions on his tax return.
D. He cannot deduct the alimony.

16. Blythe and Cardan are married and file jointly. Both are full-time high school teachers. Blythe spent $495 on books and supplies for her chemistry students. Cardan teaches art education, and he spent $310 on paints and canvas for his class. All of the supplies they purchased are qualifying supplies. What is the maximum amount for educator expenses they can deduct on their 2023 tax return?

A. $300
B. $500
C. $600
D. $805

Unit 11: Quiz Answers

1. The answer is B. Deborah can deduct 50% of the self-employment tax she paid as an adjustment to income on Schedule 1 of her Form 1040.

2. The answer is A. Because Jasmine worked only 600 hours as an educator during the tax year, she cannot deduct her educator expenses as an adjustment to income. A teacher must have at least 900 hours of qualified employment during the school year to take this deduction as an adjustment to income.

3. The answer is B. Chuck and Aurora can deduct only $1,400 ($700 × two months) of self-employed health insurance for the months that they were ineligible to participate in an employer plan. No deduction is allowed for self-employed health insurance for any month that the taxpayer has the *option* to participate in an employer-sponsored and subsidized plan. This is true even if the taxpayer declines the coverage. A self-employed taxpayer can deduct 100% of health insurance premiums as an adjustment to income, but only if neither he nor his spouse was eligible to participate in an employer's health plan.

4. The answer is D. College instructors do not qualify. An eligible educator must work 900 hours a year in a school that provides elementary or secondary education (K-12). Part-time teachers qualify if they meet the yearly teachers' requirement for hours worked. The term educator includes instructors, counselors, principals, and aides.

5. The answer is C. Adjustments are deducted from gross income to derive adjusted gross income (AGI). The amount of a taxpayer's AGI is important, as it can affect his eligibility for certain deductions and the amounts that taxpayers can claim.

6. The answer is C. Gabin and Keyah's maximum deduction for student loan interest is $2,500. The deduction is limited to the lesser of $2,500 or the amount of interest actually paid. It doesn't matter how many qualifying student loans there are; the maximum is $2,500 **per tax return** (not per taxpayer or per student).

7. The answer is D. The moving expense reimbursement must be reported as wages on Georgina's Form W-2. If an employer pays or reimburses moving expenses, the amounts are treated as taxable compensation to the employee. The only exception to this rule is for moving expenses reimbursed by the government on behalf of U.S. Armed Forces personnel.

8. The answer is C. Withdrawals for nonmedical expenses from an HSA are allowed but are subject to income tax. Nonmedical distributions are also subject to an additional penalty tax of 20%, except when the taxpayer has turned 65, become disabled, or died. Sherry has become permanently disabled, so her HSA withdrawals are not subject to a 10% penalty, but the withdrawals will still be subject to income tax, because she did not use the funds to pay for medical expenses.

9. The answer is B. Marshall can only deduct the $140 early withdrawal penalty from the CD. Early withdrawal penalties are deductible if made from a time deposit account, such as a certificate of deposit. The other types of penalties are not deductible.

10. The answer is B. Bruce will have to pay a 6% excise penalty if he does not properly correct the overcontribution. A 6% penalty applies to excess contributions to a health savings account.

11. The answer is D. On a jointly filed tax return, if both taxpayers are teachers, they both may take the qualified educator expense deduction, up to a maximum of $600 in 2023 ($300 each).

12. The answer is A. This payment qualifies as alimony, and Linda must include the $4,000 as taxable alimony income on her return. Since their divorce was finalized prior to 2019, the payment may be treated as alimony for tax purposes because the payments of Linda's medical expenses are a condition of their divorce agreement. Payments to a third party on behalf of an ex-spouse under the terms of a divorce instrument can be alimony if they qualify. These include payments for a spouse's medical expenses, housing costs (rent and utilities), taxes, and tuition. The payments are treated by the ex-spouse as if they were received directly and included as income.

13. The answer is A. Zander cannot deduct any of his expenses. The educator expense deduction is only available for K-12 educators. College instructors do not qualify.

14. The answer is C. Graciela must pay income tax and a 20% penalty on the withdrawal. Withdrawals from an HSA for non-eligible expenses are allowed, but the withdrawal is subject to a 20% penalty, in addition to regular income tax. Exceptions to the penalty exist for taxpayers age 65 or over, and death or disability of the HSA owner. Graciela is under 65 and does not qualify for any of the exceptions, so she will be forced to pay income tax as well as the penalty on the entire withdrawal.

15. The answer is A. Obadiah can deduct alimony paid as an adjustment to income, because his divorce was final before the 2019 tax year and is therefore considered "grandfathered." He does not need to itemize his deductions in order to take the deduction. He must file Form 1040 and enter the amount of alimony paid as an adjustment to income on Schedule 1.

16. The answer is C. The most that Blythe and Cardan can deduct is $600 ($300 + $300). Because they are married and filing jointly, and both are teachers, they can count up to $300 in qualifying expenses each.

Unit 12: Standard Deduction and Itemized Deductions

For additional information, read:
Publication 502, Medical and Dental Expenses
Publication 529, Miscellaneous Deductions
Publication 936, Home Mortgage Interest Deduction
Publication 526, Charitable Contributions

The Tax Cuts and Jobs Act (TCJA) made sweeping changes to the standard deduction and itemized deductions. The standard deduction nearly doubled after the enactment of the TCJA. As a result, fewer taxpayers now choose to itemize. Many itemized deductions have been suspended or restricted through 2025. The TCJA also temporarily removed the so-called "Pease limitation" on itemized deductions, which means that itemized deductions will not be phased out at higher income levels through 2025.

Generally, taxpayers may choose either to claim a standard deduction amount or to itemize deductions. Depending on the option selected, either the applicable standard deduction amount or the taxpayer's total itemized deductions is subtracted from adjusted gross income. The choice should be based on which option results in a lower tax liability.

The Standard Deduction

The standard deduction is a specific dollar amount that reduces the amount of income on which a taxpayer is taxed. Using the standard deduction eliminates the need for a taxpayer to itemize his actual allowable deductions, such as medical expenses, charitable contributions, or state and local taxes. The standard deduction amounts are based on a taxpayer's filing status and are adjusted every year for inflation. The standard deduction amounts for the 2023 tax year are as follows:

Filing Status	2023 Standard Deduction
Single or MFS	$13,850
Head of Household	$20,800
Married Filing Jointly or QSS	$27,700
Dependent Standard Deduction	$1,250[137]

Additional Standard Deduction

An *additional* standard deduction is available to taxpayers who, at the end of the year, are:

- 65 or older, and/or
- Blind or partially blind.

The standard deduction is $1,500 higher for joint filers who are over 65 and/or blind, and $1,850 higher for unmarried taxpayers (Single and head of household).

---

[137] A dependent's standard deduction for 2023 is limited to the greater of: (1) $1,250, or (2) their earned income plus $400 (but the total can't be more than the basic standard deduction for their filing status).

A taxpayer who is *both* blind and 65 or older may take the basic standard deduction, as well as additional standard deduction amounts for <u>both</u> age <u>and</u> blindness. For filing purposes, a taxpayer is considered to be age 65 in the tax year 2023 if they were 65 on December 31, 2023, or if they turned 65 on January 1, 2024.

Additional Standard Deduction Amounts–2023	
Taxpayers who are age 65 and/or blind	
Filing Status	Additional Amount Allowable
Single, HOH	$1,850
MFS, MFJ, QSS	$1,500

The additional amount for *blindness* is allowed if the taxpayer is blind on the last day of the year, even if the taxpayer was not blind the rest of the year. In order to qualify, the taxpayer must obtain a statement from an eye doctor stating that their vision cannot be corrected to better than 20/200 with eyeglasses or that their peripheral vision is limited to 20 degrees.

Example: Thane, an unmarried taxpayer, is age 40 and legally blind. His vision cannot be corrected with glasses. He would be entitled to a basic standard deduction plus an *additional* standard deduction for his blindness. This means that his standard deduction amount would be $15,700 in 2023 ($13,850 + $1,850).

Example: Larry, age 67, and Priscilla, age 60, are married and file jointly. They do not plan to itemize their deductions. Because they file jointly, their base standard deduction is $27,700 in 2023. Larry is over 65, so he can claim an *additional* standard deduction amount of $1,500. Therefore, the total standard deduction in 2023 is ($27,700 + $1,500) = $29,200.

Example: Angelo, age 65, and Allegra, age 50, are married and always file jointly. Allegra is blind. They decide not to itemize their deductions. Since Angelo is over the age of 65, and Allegra is blind, they get two *additional* standard deductions in 2023 ($27,700 + $1,500 + $1,500) = $30,700.

Example: Jensen is 83 years old and unmarried. He became legally blind during the year due to a serious infection in both eyes. Jensen is entitled to the regular standard deduction for single filers ($13,850) *plus two* additional standard deductions. One for being over the age of 65 *and* blind (2 × $1,850). In 2023, his standard deduction is $17,550 ($13,850 + $1,850 + $1,850).

The standard deduction for a deceased taxpayer is the same as if the taxpayer had lived the entire year, with one exception: if a taxpayer dies *before* their 65th birthday, the higher standard deduction for being 65 does not apply.

Example: Octavio was 64 and unmarried when he died on November 6, 2023. He would have been 65 if he had lived to reach his birthday on December 18, 2023. He does not qualify for a higher standard deduction because he died before his 65th birthday, even though it would have happened during the tax year. His standard deduction is $13,850 on his final income tax return, which must be filed by his executor on or before the filing deadline.

Standard Deduction for Dependents

In 2023, the standard deduction for dependents is limited to the greater of: (1) $1,250, or (2) their earned income plus $400 (but the total cannot be more than the basic standard deduction for their filing status). The standard deduction amount can be higher if the dependent happens to be 65 or older and/or blind. If a dependent must file an income tax return but cannot file due to age or any other reason, the parent, guardian, or other legally responsible person, must file the return for the child. If a child cannot sign their own return, the parent or guardian must sign the child's name followed by the words: "By (*parent's signature*), parent for minor child."

Example: Rosanna is 17 years old and single. She is a high school student who is also legally blind. Rosanna's parents can claim her as a dependent. Rosanna's grandfather gifted her investments several years ago, so she has interest income of $1,300 as well as wages of $4,900 from a part-time job in 2023. She has no itemized deductions. Rosanna uses the standard deduction worksheet for dependents in Publication 501 to calculate her standard deduction. She enters her wages of $4,900 on line 1a. She adds lines 1 and 2 and enters $5,300 on line 3. On line 5, she enters $5,300, the larger of lines 3 and 4. Because she is single, Rosanna enters $13,850 on line 6. She enters $5,300 on line 7a. This is the smaller of the amounts on lines 5 and 6. Because she is blind, she enters $1,850 on line 7b. She then adds the amounts on lines 7a and 7b and enters her standard deduction of $7,150 on line 7c. (Based on an example in Publication 501).

Table 8. **Standard Deduction Worksheet for Dependents**

Use this worksheet only if someone else can claim you (or your spouse if filing jointly) as a dependent.

Keep for Your Records

Check the correct number of boxes below. Then go to the worksheet.

You: **ROSANNA** — Born before January 2, 1959 ☐ — Blind ☒
Your spouse: — Born before January 2, 1959 ☐ — Blind ☐

Total number of boxes you checked: **1**

1.	Enter your earned income (defined below). If none, enter -0-.	$4,900
2.	Additional amount.	$400
3.	Add lines 1 and 2.	$5,300
4.	Minimum standard deduction.	$1,250
5.	Enter the larger of line 3 or line 4.	$5,300
6.	Enter the amount shown below for your filing status. • Single or Married filing separately—$13,850 • Married filing jointly—$27,700 • Head of household—$20,800	$13,850
7.	**Standard deduction.**	
a.	Enter the smaller of line 5 or line 6. If born after January 1, 1959, and not blind, stop here. This is your standard deduction. Otherwise, go on to line 7b.	$5,300
b.	If born before January 2, 1959, or blind, multiply $1,850 ($1,500 if married) by the number in the box above.	$1,850
c.	Add lines 7a and 7b. This is your standard deduction for 2023.	$7,150

Earned income includes wages, salaries, tips, professional fees, and other compensation received for personal services you performed. It also includes any taxable scholarship or fellowship grant.

Itemized Deductions

Itemized deductions may be taken *in lieu* of the standard deduction; they allow taxpayers to reduce their taxable income based on specific personal expenses. In most cases, taxpayers may choose whether to claim itemized deductions or the standard deduction, depending on which is more beneficial. However, the following taxpayers are *required* to itemize, and cannot take the standard deduction:

- **MFS filers whose spouses itemize:** If both spouses are filing MFS, and one spouse itemizes, the other spouse also must itemize (or else deduct $0 as a standard deduction). As such, in lieu of a $0 standard deduction, they both must itemize.[138]
- **Nonresident Aliens:** If the taxpayer is a nonresident alien or dual-status alien filing Form 1040-NR (who is not married to a U.S. citizen or resident, and electing to be treated as a U.S. resident).
- **Short tax year:** If the taxpayer files a tax return for a period of less than twelve months due to a change in accounting methods (this scenario would be *extremely rare* for an individual taxpayer).

Itemized deductions are reported on Schedule A, Form 1040. Nonresident aliens can also claim a limited amount of itemized deductions on Schedule A, Form 1040-NR. We will review the specific requirements for various itemized deductions next.

Medical and Dental Expenses

Medical and dental expenses (other than self-employed health insurance premiums) are deductible only if a taxpayer itemizes deductions. Qualifying medical expenses include the costs of diagnosis, cure, mitigation, treatment, or prevention of disease, and the costs of medical (but not cosmetic) treatments. Qualifying expenses must be primarily to alleviate or prevent a physical or mental defect or illness. This does not include expenses that are merely beneficial to general health, such as vitamins, spa treatments, gym memberships, or vacations. The IRS defined qualifying costs as:

- Medically necessary equipment, supplies, and diagnostic devices,
- Dental and vision care,
- Transportation to obtain medical care,
- Qualified health insurance and long-term care insurance.

Deductible medical expenses include:

- Fees paid to doctors, in-patient hospital care or nursing home services, including the cost of meals and lodging charged by the hospital or nursing home, acupuncture treatments, lactation supplies (breastfeeding supplies).
- Treatment centers for alcohol or drug addiction, participation in smoking-cessation programs, and prescription drugs to alleviate nicotine withdrawal, weight-loss programs prescribed by a physician (but not diet food items, such as weight-loss shakes).
- Insulin and prescription drugs (but prescription drugs brought in or shipped from a different country are generally not deductible),

---

[138] This rule only applies when *both* spouses are filing MFS. If one spouse is MFS, but the other spouse qualifies for HOH filing status (Head of Household), then the spouses are not forced to itemize, and they may choose the standard deduction if they wish.

- Admission and transportation to a medical conference relating to a chronic disease (but the costs of meals and lodging while attending the conference are not deductible),
- Veterinary care when it relates to the care of animals trained to assist persons who are visually impaired, hearing-impaired, or disabled.

Example: Carnell is a Gulf War Veteran. Carnell is recovering from severe post-traumatic stress disorder. He also has frequent seizures related to a head injury sustained during combat. Carnell's physician recommends that he obtain a service dog to help him with his recovery. The doctor gives Carnell a written physician's statement explaining the recommendation. With the help of a Veteran's support group, Carnell obtains a trained service dog. The dog's veterinary costs are deductible medical expenses on Carnell's individual tax return.

A taxpayer may only deduct medical expenses they *paid* during the year, regardless of when the services were provided.[139] Qualified medical expenses include expenses paid for the taxpayer, their spouse, and their dependents. The dependent must generally have been a dependent at the time the medical services were provided or at the time the expenses were paid. However, there is an exception to this rule for children of divorced or separated parents. A parent can also deduct medical expenses paid on behalf of an adopted child, even before the adoption becomes final.

Note: If a child of divorced or separated parents is claimed as a dependent on either parent's return, each parent can deduct medical expenses they individually paid for the child. This is true even if the other parent claims the child's dependency exemption. Basically, it does not matter which parent claims the child—the medical expenses are deductible for the parent who pays them.

Example: Bernard and Cindy are divorced. Their 10-year-old son, Michael, lives primarily with Cindy, who claims him as a dependent on her tax return. Cindy deducts Michael's annual medical and dental bills, including orthodontia expenses for his braces. However, in September, Michael falls on the playground and fractures his arm. The out-of-pocket expenses for Michael's broken arm are $15,400. Michael's father, Bernard, pays for the emergency room visit and all the expenses related to his son's injury. Therefore, Bernard can deduct the expenses on Schedule A, even if he does not claim his son as a dependent.

A taxpayer can deduct medical expenses paid for a dependent parent. All the standard rules for a dependency exemption apply, so the dependent parent does not have to live with the taxpayer to qualify.

Example: Lorelei is 45 years old and unmarried, filing as head of household. She claims her father, Uriel, age 86, as a dependent on her tax return. Lorelei is responsible for all of her father's out-of-pocket medical expenses and provides him with financial support. Although he does not live with her, Uriel is considered a dependent on Lorelei's tax return. She can deduct the medical expenses she paid for him as an itemized deduction, as long as they exceed the 7.5% threshold of her adjusted gross income.

Taxpayers can deduct only the amount of unreimbursed medical expenses that exceed 7.5% of adjusted gross income (AGI).

---

[139] An exception to this rule exists for deceased taxpayers (covered later).

Example: Renea incurred medical expenses of $8,000 in 2023. Her AGI was $70,000. She plans to itemize her deductions. She can deduct the amount in excess of the 7.5% AGI floor ($70,000 × 7.5% = $5,250). This means that she may claim a deduction of $2,750 for medical expenses on Schedule A ($8,000 medical expenses - $5,250 7.5% AGI floor).

Example: Hattie, age 53, had unreimbursed medical expenses totaling $2,500 in 2023. Her AGI was $40,000. Hattie cannot deduct any of her medical expenses on Schedule A because they are not more than 7.5% of her AGI ($40,000 × 7.5% = $3,000).

Example: Garrison, age 46, paid $12,000 in out-of-pocket expenses for knee surgery in 2023. His AGI was $100,000. The amount of medical expenses in excess of $7,500 (AGI of $100,000 × 7.5%), or $4,500, is allowed as an itemized deduction on Schedule A.

Medical Insurance: When a taxpayer receives insurance reimbursement for medical expenses, they cannot deduct those amounts. Only insurance premiums paid with *after-tax* dollars for medical and long-term care insurance can be considered as qualifying medical expenses. Medical expenses reimbursed out of a health savings account (HSA) are not deductible, but contributions to HSAs may be deducted as an adjustment to gross income, and withdrawals from an HSA are tax-free as long as they are used to pay for qualifying medical costs.

Note: The cost of an employee's annual health care coverage is typically reported on Form W-2. The amount includes the portions paid by both the employer and the employee. Although this amount is reported on Form W-2, it does not mean the amount is taxable; it is for informational purposes only.

Long-Term Care Premiums: A taxpayer may include amounts paid for qualified long-term care services and insurance premiums in his medical expense deductions. Long-term care services include necessary diagnostic, preventive, therapeutic, rehabilitative, maintenance, and personal care services that are required by a chronically ill individual and provided under a plan of care by a licensed doctor.

The deductibility of costs of qualified long-term care premiums is limited by the age of the taxpayer. The expenses generally cannot include costs that would be reimbursed under Medicare. In 2023, the amounts paid for long-term care premiums up to the amounts shown below can be included as medical expenses on Schedule A. The limits are per person, not per tax return.

Taxpayer's Age At End of Tax Year	Deductible Limit
40 or less	$480
41 to 50	$890
51 to 60	$1,790
61 to 70	$4,770
71 or more	$5,960

Other Medical Expenses: If a taxpayer or a dependent is in a nursing home, and the primary reason for being there is medically related, the entire cost, including meals and lodging, is a medical expense. A taxpayer can deduct any legal fees necessary to authorize treatment for mental illness. However, legal fees for the management of a guardianship estate or for conducting the affairs of a person being treated are not deductible as medical expenses.

Medical Expenses of Deceased Taxpayers: In addition to expenses paid before a taxpayer's death, a deceased taxpayer's executor (or personal representative) can elect to treat medical expenses paid by the estate within one year after his death as if the taxpayer had paid when the medical services were provided. In other words, an executor can elect to treat medical expenses as if they were paid at the time they were incurred, even if the expenses are paid the year *after* the taxpayer's death.[140]

> **Example:** Harrison had heart surgery on November 3, 2023, and incurred over $20,000 of medical bills. The surgery did not go well, and when he died on December 20, 2023, his medical bills had not yet been paid. The executor of Harrison's estate is his adult son, Dominic. Dominic pays his late father's outstanding medical bills on March 3, 2024. As the executor, Dominic may elect to deduct Harrison's final medical expenses on his father's 2023 individual return (Harrison's final tax return), even though the medical expenses were not paid until 2024. This special election *only* applies to deceased taxpayers.

Cosmetic Surgery: Cosmetic surgery is only deductible if it is used to correct a defect or disease. A cosmetic procedure simply for the enhancement of someone's physical appearance is not a deductible medical expense.

> **Example:** Delia undergoes a mastectomy to remove her breasts as part of treatment for breast cancer. A cosmetic surgeon later reconstructs her breasts to correct the deformity that is directly related to cancer. The cost of her cosmetic surgery is deductible as a medical expense because the surgery corrects an earlier defect or disease.

Medically Related Transportation, Meals, and Lodging: Vehicle mileage may be deducted if transportation is for medical reasons, such as trips to and from doctors' appointments. If a taxpayer uses his own car for medical transportation, he can deduct actual out-of-pocket expenses for gas and other expenses, or he can deduct the standard mileage rate for medical expenses. In 2023, the medical mileage rate is 22 cents per mile.

A taxpayer can also deduct the costs of taxis, buses, trains, planes, or ambulances, as well as tolls and parking fees. A taxpayer can deduct the cost of meals and lodging at a hospital or similar institution if the principal reason for being there is to receive medical care. The amount for lodging cannot be more than $50 for each night for each person, although the taxpayer can include lodging for a person traveling with the person receiving the medical care, up to $100. The cost of meals is not included.

> **Example:** Andrew is 12 years old and has severe allergies. Andrew's father, Harlan, accompanies his son to a medical facility in a neighboring state so he can receive treatment from an allergy specialist. Harlan books a hotel room across the street from the hospital, where they stay for one week while Andrew is receiving outpatient medical treatment and blood tests. The cost of lodging at the hotel is $110 per night. Harlan may deduct up to $100 per night as a medical expense.[141]

---

[140] If this election is made by the executor, the medical expenses cannot be claimed as a deduction for Federal estate tax purposes as well (no double-dipping).
[141] Based on an example in Publication 502, Medical and Dental Expenses.

Capital Improvements for Medical Reasons: Capital improvements such as home improvements are usually not deductible. However, a home improvement may qualify as a deductible expense if its main purpose is to provide medical care to the taxpayer (or to family members). The amount that can be deducted for capital improvements is limited to the difference between the cost of the improvements and the corresponding rise in the home's fair market value. Home improvements that qualify as deductible medical expenses may include:

- Wheelchair ramps
- Lowering of kitchen cabinets
- Railings and support bars
- Elevators
- Special lift equipment

Tenants can deduct the entire cost of disability-related improvements, even if they are not the owners of the property.

> **Example:** Elliott, age 61, has a serious heart condition. He cannot easily climb stairs or get into a bathtub. On his doctor's advice, Elliott pays for the installation of a special sit-in bathtub and a stairlift in his rented home. Elliott does not own the property, and his landlord did not pay any of the costs. Elliott can deduct the entire amount that he spent on these devices (bathtub and stairlift) as a medical expense, subject to the 7.5% threshold.

State and Local Income Taxes (SALT)

Taxpayers can deduct certain taxes if they itemize deductions. In order to be deductible, a tax must have been imposed on the taxpayer and paid by the taxpayer during the tax year. Deductible taxes include:

- State, local, and foreign income taxes,[142]
- State and local sales taxes,
- Real estate taxes (but not for foreign real estate),
- Personal property taxes (such as the portion of DMV fees based on the value of the car).

The Tax Cuts and Jobs Act instituted a temporary cap on state and local taxes (also called the "SALT cap"). This deduction is capped at $10,000 ($5,000 for MFS filers) until 2025.

State and Local Taxes: Taxpayers are allowed to deduct either *sales/use* taxes or state and local *income* taxes, depending on which provides the larger deduction, but not both. Income taxes paid include taxes withheld from salaries and wages, amounts paid for prior years, and estimated tax payments.

Real Estate Taxes: State and local real estate taxes, based on the assessed value of the taxpayer's real property (such as a house or land), are deductible. If the taxes are paid from a mortgage escrow account, the taxpayer can deduct only the amount actually paid out of the escrow account during the year to the taxing authority.

---

[142] Foreign *income* taxes are not subject to the "SALT" cap. These taxes are still deductible in full. Also, taxes incurred in a trade or business, or for the production of income, (on Schedules C, E, and/or F), are not subject to the SALT cap.

Some real estate taxes are not deductible, including taxes imposed to finance improvements of property, such as assessments for streets, sidewalks, and sewer lines. In addition, itemized charges for services and homeowner's association fees are not deductible.

Example: Minnie makes the following payments in 2023: state income tax, $2,000; real estate taxes on her main home, $900; local benefit tax for maintaining the sewer system, $75; and homeowner's association fees of $550. Her total deductible taxes are $2,900 ($2,000 + $900 = $2,900). The $75 local benefit tax and the $550 homeowner's association fee are not deductible.

Real estate taxes paid on *foreign* real property are nondeductible on Schedule A; however, they may be deducted as an expense in other situations, such as the rental of foreign real property.

Escrow accounts: If a portion of the taxpayer's monthly mortgage payment goes into an escrow account, and periodically the lender pays the real estate taxes out of the account to the local government, the taxpayer is only allowed to deduct the amount that was actually paid out of the escrow account during the year to the taxing authority.

Personal Property Taxes (including DMV Fees): Personal property taxes for individuals are deductible if they are:

- Charged on personal property, including cars, motorcycles and boats;
- Based on the value of the property; and
- Charged on a yearly basis, even if collected more than once a year.

Example: Debbie receives an annual registration notice for her automobile from the California Department of Motor Vehicles. The DMV bill is broken down as follows:

> Registration: $25
> Vehicle license fee: $58
> Weight fee: $32
> County fee: $13
> Owner responsibility fee: $15

The notice states that the vehicle license fee is based on the car's value. Only the vehicle license fee is tax deductible on Schedule A.

As mentioned previously, the Tax Cuts and Jobs Act eliminated the deduction for foreign *real estate* taxes on personal homes. These taxes are no longer deductible on Schedule A as an itemized deduction. However, foreign *income* taxes are still deductible on Schedule A.

Foreign income taxes are also *not subject* to the SALT cap. Foreign income tax is listed on line 6, of Schedule A, under "Other Taxes."

Example: Hideo is a U.S. citizen who lives and works in Japan. He earns $178,000 in wages working for an international investment firm. He owns a home in Japan, which is his primary residence. During the year, he pays $3,600 in foreign property taxes on his home. These amounts are not deductible, because the home is considered foreign real estate. Hideo also pays $29,000 in foreign income taxes to Japan. The foreign income taxes are fully deductible on Schedule A and not subject to the SALT cap.

Example: Zahra lives and works in New York, which has a high cost of living. She earns $195,000 in wages per year. Zahra paid $14,000 in property taxes on her NY condo, and $11,900 in NY state income taxes. The state income tax was automatically withheld from her wages. She also owned a vacation home in Rio de Janeiro, Brazil. She paid $4,000 in foreign real estate taxes on her vacation home. The foreign real estate taxes are not deductible at all, and the other taxes are limited because of the SALT cap. The maximum deduction that she can take for the taxes she paid on Schedule A is $10,000.

Foreign Income Taxes: Generally, a taxpayer can choose between claiming the Foreign Tax Credit or claiming an itemized deduction on Schedule A for income taxes paid to a foreign country, depending on which option results in the lowest tax. The rules regarding which foreign taxes qualify for either the credit or the deduction are covered later. Foreign *income* taxes are not subject to the "SALT cap."

Deductible Interest

Taxpayers are allowed to deduct certain types of interest. Qualified interest payments are deductible as itemized deductions on Form 1040, Schedule A. Deductible interest includes:

- Home mortgage interest,
- Late fees on a mortgage loan,
- Points on a mortgage loan,
- Investment interest expense.

Home Mortgage Interest

A taxpayer is allowed to deduct the mortgage interest related to a primary residence and a second home. The loan must be secured by the taxpayer's home, in order for the interest to be deductible. The loan may be a mortgage, a second mortgage, a home equity loan, or a line of credit.

The maximum amount of qualified acquisition Indebtedness secured by a qualified primary or secondary residence to allow a full deduction for home mortgage interest is $750,000 in 2023 ($375,000 for MFS).[143]

Interest paid on debt related to a primary and secondary residence is only tax deductible if the proceeds from the loan were used to acquire, build, or significantly enhance the main home. For instance, if a taxpayer takes out a $250,000 home equity line of credit and uses all of it towards improving their home, the entire amount would qualify for the mortgage interest deduction. This dollar limit also applies to construction debt, such as home renovations.

Example: Peggy is single and purchased her first home on March 4, 2023, for $450,000. A month after she purchases the home, she takes out an additional $28,000 home equity line of credit to install an inground swimming pool. The pool is completed on August 30, 2023. This is considered a capital improvement to the home. The interest Peggy incurs on the mortgage, as well as the home equity line, is deductible as mortgage interest on Schedule A, because the loan proceeds were used to "acquire, build, or substantially improve" her home.

---

[143] If the home was purchased on or before December 15, 2017, the qualified acquisition indebtedness limit is "grandfathered" at a higher limit of $1 million ($500,000 MFS).

Example: Donatella takes out a $30,000 home equity loan in 2023 to help pay off her credit cards. She uses the entire proceeds of the loan to pay off all her credit card debt. This home equity line is secured by her residence, but the interest is not deductible, because the home equity loan was not used to "acquire, build, or substantially improve" her primary residence.

Example: Jeannette is single and owns her home. She has an existing mortgage totaling $475,000. Jeannette wants to expand the size of her home, so she applies for a home equity line of credit to finance new home improvements. She decides to add an extra bedroom, a new bathroom, and she installs a pool in the backyard. The new bedroom addition cost $66,000, the new bathroom cost $22,000, and the new pool cost $29,000, for a total cost of $117,000. Since the home equity loan was used entirely to improve the property, and her total mortgage debt does not exceed $750,000, all the mortgage interest is deductible on Schedule A.

A vacant piece of land is not eligible for the mortgage interest deduction. However, if a taxpayer constructs a house that meets the requirements of a qualified home once it is ready to be lived in, they can deduct mortgage interest for a period of up to 24 months from when construction begins.

Example: Spencer owns an empty lot, which he inherited from his grandfather. He plans to build his dream home on the lot. He borrows $175,000 from the bank and begins construction on February 1, 2023. Spencer can treat the home under construction as a qualified home once the construction has started. At that point, the interest he pays may qualify as deductible mortgage interest.[144]

Late fees and pre-payment penalties incurred on a mortgage loan are also deductible as mortgage interest on Schedule A.

Example: Fergus owns his home and pays his mortgage monthly. During the year, he falls behind on his mortgage payments and sends in his house payment late on two occasions. The mortgage company charges Fergus a $35 fee for each late payment. The late fees are deductible as mortgage interest on Schedule A.

A second home can include any other residence a taxpayer owns and treats as a home, but the taxpayer does not have to actually use the second home during the year to deduct the mortgage interest paid on the related loan.

Note: Although a taxpayer can potentially deduct real estate taxes on more than two properties, a taxpayer cannot deduct mortgage interest on more than two personal homes.

Example: Ellery owns three homes. None of the homes are rental properties. He has a $150,000 mortgage on his main home in Boise, ID, where he lives most of the time. He also has a $75,000 mortgage on a beach cottage in North Carolina and a $90,000 mortgage on a ski condo in Utah. Ellery can deduct the mortgage interest on his main home and on the ski condo, but he cannot deduct the mortgage interest on the beach cottage because the deduction is limited to two homes. He is allowed to deduct the property taxes on all three homes. However, the property taxes are subject to the $10,000 SALT cap.

---

[144]Some interest may be deductible on a construction loan once construction begins. A taxpayer can treat a home under construction as a qualified home for a period of up to 24 months, but only if it becomes their qualified home at the time it's ready for occupancy. Construction loans are covered in detail in Publication 936, Home Mortgage Interest Deduction.

Mortgage Insurance Premiums (PMI)

The itemized deduction for mortgage insurance premiums has expired. Taxpayers can no longer claim the deduction for 2023 and going forward.[145] Mortgage insurance premiums paid during the year are reported to the taxpayer on Form 1098, *Mortgage Interest Statement,* by the bank or financial institution that received the payments.

Points and Prepaid Mortgage Interest

Points are interest charges a borrower pays up-front to obtain a loan. Points generally represent prepaid interest a borrower pays at closing to obtain a lower interest rate. Points may also be called loan origination fees, including VA and FHA fees, maximum loan charges, premium charges, loan discount points, or prepaid interest. Loan fees paid for specific services, such as home appraisal fees, document preparation fees, or notary fees are not interest and are not deductible. In order to deduct points, the following requirements must be met:

- The mortgage must be secured by the taxpayer's main home, and the mortgage must have been used to buy, build, or improve the home.
- The points must not be an excessive or unusual amount.
- The points paid must not be more than the amount of unborrowed funds.
- The points must be computed as a percentage of the loan principal, and they must be listed on the settlement statement (the HUD-1).

If all these requirements are met, the taxpayer can deduct points in connection with the acquisition or construction of the home either in the year paid or over the life of the loan. Tax law treats "purchase" mortgage points differently from "refinance" mortgage points. Points paid to refinance a mortgage are generally not fully deductible in the year paid and must be deducted over the life of the loan unless the proceeds are used to improve a main home. A second home or vacation home would not qualify for this exception.

> **Example:** Tammy refinanced her home mortgage on January 10, 2023, in order to get a lower interest rate than the rate she currently had. She paid $1,500 in points for a 15-year refinance of her existing home mortgage. She is entitled to deduct only $100 per year on her Schedule A ($1,500 ÷ 15 years, the life of the loan).

Investment Interest Expense

The Tax Cuts and Jobs Act suspended all the miscellaneous itemized deductions subject to the 2%-of-AGI floor, including the deduction for investment expenses such as safe deposit fees, trustee fees, and investment advisor fees. However, the TCJA did *not* suspend the deduction for investment *interest* expense.

Investment interest expense is defined as any interest paid on loans used to purchase taxable investments. A common example of this is margin interest, where investors borrow funds from brokerage houses, also known as margin accounts, to purchase stocks and bonds without needing to invest the full cash amount.

---

[145]The deduction for PMI was extended as part of the Taxpayer Certainty and Disaster Relief Tax Act. It is currently expired in 2023, unless Congress decides to retroactively extend the deduction again.

Example: Anton likes to invest in stocks using his online brokerage account. He applies for a margin-approved brokerage account in order to buy more stock. At the beginning of the year, Anton has $100,000 in cash and stocks in his existing brokerage account. His brokerage firm approves him for a 20% margin loan. This means that Anton can purchase an additional $20,000 worth of marginable stock. The extra $20,000 is granted to him in the form of a margin loan, for which he will have to pay interest. The interest would be potentially deductible on Schedule A as a miscellaneous itemized deduction (subject to limitations, as detailed below).

If a taxpayer takes out a loan to purchase investment property, such as stocks, the interest paid on that loan can be considered as investment interest expense and may be eligible for deduction. The deductible amount is limited to the net investment income earned in a given year, but any unused portion can be carried over to the following year.

Example: Thurston borrows money from a bank to buy $30,000 worth of short-term corporate bonds. The bonds mature during the year, and Thurston makes $900 of investment interest income. He also has $510 in investment interest expense, which he paid on the loan originally taken out to buy the bonds. Thurston must report the full amount of $900 as investment interest income. He can deduct the $510 of investment interest expense on Schedule A.

Example: Sully borrows money from a brokerage firm to buy $8,500 worth of stock as an investment. During the year, the stock loses value, and he does not sell them. He has no other investment income. Sully paid $326 of interest expense on the loan he used to buy the stock. He may not take a deduction for the investment interest expense because he has no investment income, but he may carry over to the next tax year the investment interest expense he could not deduct.

The deductible amount of investment interest expense and any disallowed amount that may be carried over to the following year are calculated on Form 4952, *Investment Interest Expense Deduction.* A taxpayer cannot deduct interest related to passive activities or incurred to produce tax-exempt income (such as state and local bonds that generate tax-exempt interest income) as investment interest expense.

Example: Melvin borrowed $15,000 to purchase municipal bonds in 2023. The tax-free municipal bonds yield 5% in interest income, and Melvin paid 3% in investment interest expense on the loan. Since muni bond interest is exempt from federal tax, Melvin cannot deduct any of the interest he paid on the loan.

Nondeductible Interest and Investment Expenses: The following expenses <u>cannot</u> be deducted as investment interest:

- Interest on personal loans, such as car loans
- Fees for credit cards and finance charges for nonbusiness credit card purchases
- Loan fees for services needed to get a loan
- Interest on debt the taxpayer is not legally obligated to pay
- Service charges (such as monthly account fees, ATM fees, and foreign transaction fees).
- Interest to purchase or carry tax-exempt securities
- Late payment charges paid to a public utility
- Expenses relating to stockholders' meetings or investment-related seminars

- Interest expenses from single-premium life insurance and annuity contracts
- Interest incurred from borrowing against a life insurance policy
- Fines and penalties paid to any government entity for violations of the law

> **Example:** Tyler and Magdalena file a joint return. During the year, they paid:
> 1. $3,180 of home mortgage interest reported to them on Form 1098
> 2. $400 of interest paid on personal credit card expenses
> 3. $1,500 for an appraisal fee on their personal residence
> 4. $2,000 of interest on a personal car loan
> 5. $45 late fee for paying their electricity bill one month late
>
> Tyler and Magdalena can deduct only their home mortgage interest ($3,180). None of the other costs are allowable as a tax deduction.

Charitable Contributions

The rules for charitable contributions have recently changed. For the tax years 2023 and 2024, individuals can deduct up to 60% of their adjusted gross income in cash contributions. Different AGI limits apply to contributions of *property* (covered next). A donation can only be deducted in the year it was actually made. A donation charged to a credit card before the end of 2023 counts for 2023, even if the credit card bill is not paid until the following year. Similarly, a check sent in 2023 will count towards deductions for 2023, even if it is not cashed until the following year by the charity.

Contribution Limits

In 2023, taxpayers can elect to deduct cash contributions up to 60% of adjusted gross income. The 60%-of-AGI limit applies to *cash contributions only*—not real estate, not stocks, not furniture, or any other type of noncash donations.[146]

A *property* contribution may be limited to 50%, 30%, or 20% of AGI, depending on the type of property donated and the type of organization the donor gives it to. In 2023, there are four major AGI limits:

- **The 60% limit**: In 2023, a 60%-of-AGI limit applies to *cash* contributions to a public charity, specifically, 501(c)(3) organizations. These are called "qualified cash contributions." Contributions of noncash property do not qualify for this limit.
- **The 50% limit**: This limit applies to most *noncash* contributions to public charities. Examples of noncash contributions include furniture, clothing, and housewares. This limit also applies to gifts of inventory and depreciable property, such as machinery and vehicles. This limit also applies to most conservation easements.[147]
- **The 30% limit**: This limit applies to donations of most appreciated capital gain property (property that would have resulted in a long-term capital gain if sold instead of donated) where

---

[146] Cash contributions include those paid by cash, check, electronic funds transfer, debit card, credit card, payroll deduction, or a transfer of a gift card redeemable for cash.
[147] A conservation easement, also called a qualified conservation contribution (QCC) are subject to unique rules. This is the contribution of real property to a qualified organization exclusively for conservation purposes. For qualified farmers or ranchers, a conservation easement can be as high as 100% of their AGI (under IRC 170(b)(1)(E)(iv)).

the donor can claim the FMV as a deduction. Common examples include stock, cryptocurrency, land, or other real estate that has appreciated in value.[148]

- **The 20% limit**: This limit applies specifically to gifts of appreciated capital gain property to most private nonoperating foundations and certain other non-public charities.

Charitable contributions cannot generate a net operating loss. Excess contributions that exceed a taxpayer's AGI may be carried over and deducted over a 5-year period. Carryovers are subject to the same percentage limits in the year to which they are carried.

> **Example:** Trinidad donated $6,800 in cash to his church during the year. He also donated several large pieces of furniture to Goodwill. The furniture had a fair market value of $500. The cash contribution would be limited to 60% of his AGI, while the property donation to Goodwill would be limited to 50% of his AGI. Trinidad's AGI is $42,000, and he plans to itemize his deductions. His donations would not be limited; he could deduct the amounts in full on Schedule A.

Be aware that a 50% limit applies to most *noncash* charitable contributions, only *cash donations* are subject to the higher 60%-of-AGI limit. The 60%-of-AGI contribution limit applies to cash contributions made to 501(c)(3) charities, including:

- Churches, mosques, synagogues, and similar religious organizations,
- Hospitals, and most schools and colleges,
- State or federal government entities,
- Nonprofits organized solely for charitable, religious, educational, scientific, or literary purposes or for the prevention of cruelty to children or animals,
- Organizations that foster youth sports, or national or international amateur sports competitions (examples include: Little League Baseball, the Olympics, Special Olympics, and the Paralympic Games).

A taxpayer's deductible contributions to certain other types of nonprofit organizations are limited to either 30% or 20% of AGI. The **30% limit** applies to organizations that include the following:

- Certain private nonoperating foundations,[149]
- Veterans' organizations and fraternal benefit societies (such as the Knights of Columbus, Odd Fellows, and the Shriners),
- Nonprofit cemeteries.

In addition, a separate **30% limit** applies in the following cases:

- Gifts for use by the charitable organization (such as the donation of a vehicle the organization uses for itself),
- Gifts of appreciated capital gain property.

The **20% limit** applies to contributions of capital gain property to organizations subject to the 30% limit (such as most private nonoperating foundations).

---

[148] In addition to appreciated capital gain property, ordinary income property donated to most private nonoperating foundations fall under this AGI limit as well

[149] A private nonoperating foundation grants money to other charitable organizations. Private foundations usually are established with funds from a single source, such as a single wealthy family or corporate money.

Example: Cooper's income for the year is $40,000, all of which comes from his wages. He decided to donate 100 shares of appreciated stock with a current value of $11,000 to the Knights of Columbus, a fraternal benefit society, which is a 30%-of-AGI limit organization. However, because the gift is in the form of appreciated property, there is an additional restriction - only 20% of AGI can be deducted based on the nature of the organization. Therefore, Cooper's deduction is limited to $8,000 (20% × $40,000 = $8,000), and the remaining amount of $3,000 will need to be carried over to future years ($11,000 - $8,000 = $3,000 carryover).

To the extent a taxpayer's deductions for contributions are limited; they may be carried over to subsequent years. The carryover period is generally limited to five years. Any carryover amounts that cannot be deducted within five years due to AGI limits are lost.

Any contributions made by the taxpayer and carried over to future years retain their original character. For example, contributions made to a 30% organization continue to be subject to the 30%-of-AGI limit in future years.

Example: Regina's adjusted gross income is $50,000 for the year. In March, she gave her church a plot of land with a fair market value of $28,000 and a basis of $22,000 that she held for more than five years. Regina has a qualified appraisal for the property. Regina did not make any other charitable gifts during the year. Regina's allowable charitable contribution for the land would be its fair market value of $28,000. Although the church is a 501(c)(3) organization, the land donation is a gift of appreciated property, which means that Regina's deduction is limited to 30% of her AGI. Her current-year deduction for the land is limited to $15,000 (30% × $50,000 AGI). The unused part of the contribution ($13,000) can be carried over to future years. In addition, Regina does not pay capital gains tax on the $6,000 of appreciation built into the land.

Qualified Charitable Gifts

In most cases, a donor may claim a deduction for the fair market value of a property. Donated clothing, furniture, or household items must be in usable condition. No deduction is allowed for items that are in poor or unusable condition. Deductible contributions may include:

- Unreimbursed expenses that relate directly to the services the taxpayer provided for the organization.
- The amount of a contribution in excess of the fair market value of items received, such as merchandise and tickets to a charity ball.
- Transportation expenses, including bus fare, parking fees, tolls, and either the actual cost of gas and oil or a standard mileage deduction of 14 cents per mile in 2023.

Volunteer Expenses: Volunteer hours cannot be assigned a monetary value for tax purposes. However, individuals can claim deductions for any out-of-pocket expenses related to their volunteer work for eligible organizations.

A taxpayer can deduct expenses incurred while traveling to perform services for a charitable organization only if there is no significant element of personal pleasure in the travel. However, a deduction will not be denied simply because the taxpayer enjoys providing the services.

Example: Maya is an attorney who donates time to her local homeless shelter for its legal needs. In 2023, she spent ten hours drafting legal documents for the shelter, which is a qualified charitable organization. She also had $200 of out-of-pocket expenses because she purchased several boxes of printer paper for the shelter's administrative office. The paper was delivered directly to the shelter for its use. Maya can take a charitable deduction for $200, the amount she spent on behalf of the shelter. She cannot deduct the value of her time.

Example: Odessa regularly volunteers at her local animal shelter, a qualified animal rescue organization. She uses her own car to travel to and from the shelter. She is not reimbursed for mileage. Odessa also fosters kittens on behalf of the shelter. She pays for cat food for the foster kittens and other supplies out-of-pocket. She receives an annual statement from the animal shelter substantiating her donations. Odessa can deduct her mileage and her unreimbursed expenses as a charitable contribution but cannot deduct the value of her time.

Qualified Charitable Distributions (QCDs)

Donors age 70½ or older may also donate up to $100,000 per tax year directly from a traditional IRA. This is called a "Qualified Charitable Distribution" or QCD. If a taxpayer is already taking RMDs, they can also choose to make a QCD in lieu of taking an annual required minimum distribution (RMD) from their IRA. If a taxpayer makes a QCD, the amount of the distribution from a traditional IRA will not be included in taxable income. However, the taxpayer will not be able to claim a charitable deduction for the amounts given via the QCD to a qualified charity (QCDs are covered in more detail later).

Nonqualifying Organizations

Not all nonprofit organizations qualify as "charitable" organizations for donors to claim tax deductions. An organization may qualify for nonprofit status so that its own activities are not subject to income tax, but this designation does not automatically provide qualification for purposes of deductible contributions. The following are examples of gifts that do not qualify as deductible charitable contributions:

- Gifts to civic leagues, social and sports clubs, and Chambers of Commerce,
- Gifts to political groups, candidates, or political organizations,
- Gifts to homeowner's associations,
- Donations made directly to individuals,
- The cost of raffle, bingo, or lottery tickets, even if the raffle is part of a qualified organization's fundraiser,
- Dues paid to country clubs or similar groups,
- Dues to labor unions,
- Blood donated to a blood bank or to the Red Cross (although the mileage incurred to donate blood may be deductible),
- Any part of a contribution that benefits the taxpayer, such as the FMV of a meal eaten at a charity dinner.

Donors who purchase items at a charity auction may claim a charitable contribution deduction only for the excess of the purchase price paid for an item over its fair market value.

Example: Chavo goes to a nonprofit hospital fundraiser that includes a bingo game. Chavo spends $200 on bingo cards but does not win anything. Even though the $200 went directly to the hospital, the cost of the bingo game is not considered a charitable gift (because it is a wagering activity).

Example: Tonya participates in a charity auction for her church. All the auction proceeds go to the church. She bids on a $100 gift certificate to a popular restaurant in town. She pays $135 for the gift certificate. The FMV for the gift certificate is $100, so her qualifying donation is $35 ($135 amount paid - $100 FMV of the certificate).

Example: Scarlett paid the Sacramento Chamber of Commerce a $30 entry fee to run in a half marathon it was sponsoring on behalf of a cancer-related charity. The Chamber is not a qualifying charitable organization, so none of Scarlett's entry fee is tax-deductible as a charitable contribution. If the race had been organized by the charity itself, part of her entry fee might have been deductible.

Substantiation Requirements for Charitable Gifts

Those who claim deductions for charitable contributions must adhere to strict recordkeeping requirements. These guidelines include recordkeeping and substantiation rules for donors, as well as disclosure and reporting requirements for the charities themselves. Here are the basic rules for ALL charitable gifts:

- At a minimum, the donor must have at least a bank record **or** a written receipt (or written acknowledgment) from a charity for **any** cash contribution before the donor can claim a charitable deduction.
- For single contributions of $250 or more, the donor must obtain a written receipt from the charity before claiming a charitable deduction.

Rules for Cash Donations

Cash Donations of LESS than $250: Cash contributions include those paid by cash, check, debit card, credit card, or payroll deduction. If the value of an individual donation is *less* than $250, the taxpayer must keep a reliable written record, such as the following:

- A bank, credit union, or credit card statement that shows the name of the qualified organization, the date of the contribution, and the amount of the contribution
- A receipt (or a letter or other written communication) from the qualified organization showing its name, the date of the contribution, and the amount of the contribution
- For payroll deductions, a pay stub, or Form W-2, plus a pledge card or other document showing the name of the qualified organization
- For text donations, a telephone bill, as long as it shows the name of the qualified organization, the date of the contribution, and the amount given

Donors should not attach an acknowledgment or a receipt to their tax return, but must retain copies to substantiate their contributions.

Example: Langley donates $25 per month to the Humane Society. Langley always pays by check, and he keeps the canceled check as a record of his contribution. This is a valid method of recordkeeping for donations under $250. He does not need to have an additional receipt from the organization to substantiate his deduction.

Example: Sandy donates $125 a month to her local public library, a qualified 501(c)(3) organization. She sends her donation via credit card, on the library's website, then saves a copy of the credit card transaction details in her records. At the end of the year, she has made a total of $1,200 in donations to the library. Since each of her *individual* donations were less than $250, and she has a record of each one, she has complied with the substantiation requirements for her donations.

Cash Donations of $250 or <u>MORE</u>: For cash donations of $250 or more, the donor must have a receipt or a written acknowledgment from the organization that includes:

- The amount of cash the taxpayer contributed,
- The date of the contribution,
- Whether the qualified organization gave any goods or services as a result of the contribution (other than certain token items and membership benefits). The absence of this simple statement by a charity has led to court cases in which major cash contributions have been challenged, and in some cases, disallowed.
- If applicable, a description and a good faith estimate of the value of goods or services provided by the organization as a result of the contribution (if applicable).

A single, annual statement from the charitable organization may be used to substantiate multiple contributions. These are also commonly called "donor acknowledgment letters." There is no specific IRS form for the acknowledgment.

Example: Trudy donates $300 a month to her local Baseball Little League, which is a qualified 501(c)(3) charity. Sometimes she pays with cash, and sometimes with a check. She does not keep a record of her individual gifts, but at the end of the year, the Little League mails out an annual donor acknowledgment letter, listing all her donations, including the dates and specific amounts she contributed during the year, and stating she received no goods or services for the donations. The annual statement will suffice to substantiate Trudy's deduction.

Rules for Noncash Donations (Gifts of Property)

Noncash Contributions of Less than $250: For each noncash contribution of less than $250, the taxpayer must obtain a receipt from the receiving organization and keep a list of the items donated.

Example: Weston generously gave away twenty of his shirts to Goodwill. As a responsible donor, he made sure to keep track of the items he donated and received a receipt from the organization upon dropping off his clothing. In Weston's town, the thrift shop values dress shirts at approximately $5 each. Based on this valuation, Weston has made a charitable contribution of $100 (20 shirts × $5 fair market value per shirt). He must keep the Goodwill receipt, but he does not need to attach it to his tax return. He may claim $100 as a charitable deduction on Schedule A without any additional documentation.

Noncash Donations between $250 and $500: For each contribution of at least $250, but not exceeding $500, the donor must have the same documentation for noncash contributions less than $250. In addition, the organization's written acknowledgment must definitively state whether the taxpayer received any goods or services in return and included a description and a good faith estimate of the fair market value of any such items.

Noncash Donations Over $500: If a taxpayer's total deduction for all noncash contributions for the year is more than $500, the donor must also file Form 8283, *Noncash Charitable Contributions,* and attach this form to their individual tax return.

> **Example:** Amelia donated a significant amount of property to her church this year for its annual rummage sale. All the proceeds from the rummage sale go to the church. Amelia estimates that she donated $950 worth of clothing, housewares, and other furniture. Amelia received an acknowledgment letter from her church. Since her noncash donations exceed $500, Amelia would need to file a Form 8283 and include the name and address of the donee organization (her church) and description of the items she donated on the form.

Noncash Donations Over $5,000: If any single donation or a group of similar items is valued at more than $5,000, a qualified appraiser is required to make a written appraisal of the donated property. The donor must also complete Form 8283, Section B, and attach the form to their tax return. The donor generally does not have to attach the appraisal itself but must retain a copy for their records. However, if the donation includes artwork valued at more than $20,000 or any other property valued at more than $500,000, the appraisal itself must be submitted along with the tax return.[150]

> **Example:** Michelle has an AGI of $125,000. She decides to donate a plot of farmland to her church, a qualified 501(c)(3) organization. The land is worth over $5,000, so Michelle hires a qualified appraiser to give her a written appraisal for the property before she donates it. The appraiser values the land at $18,000. She also requests a receipt for the donation from her church. When she files her tax return, she claims a charitable deduction of $18,000 on her Schedule A. She also attaches Form 8283 to her return. She is not required to attach the actual appraisal, but she must keep a copy of it for her records. Michelle has complied with all the recordkeeping requirements for her property donation.

> **Example:** Ratcliffe is a wealthy industrialist who likes to donate to many different causes. In 2023, he donates 100,000 shares of Ford Motor Co. stock to the Special Olympics, a qualifying 501(c)(3) nonprofit organization. The value of the stock on the date of the donation is $1,150,000. Since the stock is from a publicly-traded corporation, Ratcliffe does not need to obtain a qualified appraisal. He will still be required to obtain an acknowledgment letter from the organization, as well as attach Form 8283 to his tax return.

Special Rules for Donated Vehicles

Different guidelines are in place for donating vehicles, such as boats and airplanes. If the donor claims a deduction of over $500, they can only deduct the smaller of (1) the total earnings from the charity's sale of the vehicle, or (2) the fair market value of the vehicle on the donation date.

The charitable organization should provide Form 1098-C, *Contributions of Motor Vehicles, Boats, and Airplanes,* which shows the gross proceeds from the sale of the vehicle donated. If the taxpayer does not attach Form 1098-C, the maximum deduction that can be taken for the donation is $500.

---

[150] Per Publication 526, a qualified appraisal is not required for contributions of certain inventory, publicly traded securities, or certain intellectual property. See Regulations section 1.170A-16(e)(2). Also, if the taxpayer is required to obtain a qualified appraisal, they cannot take a deduction for the cost of the appraisal itself (per Publication 526). On January 13, 2023, the IRS released guidance stating that a charitable contribution of cryptocurrency in excess of $5,000 requires obtaining a qualified appraisal. In Chief Counsel Advice 202302012, the IRS stated that cryptocurrency fails to fall into any category of property exempted from the qualified appraisal rules of §170(f)(11)(c).

Example: Porter donates his used motorcycle to his church fundraiser. According to Blue Book values, the FMV of the motorcycle is $3,500 on the date he makes his donation. The church sells the motorcycle 60 days later at a fundraising auction for $2,700 and sends Porter a Form 1098-C. He can deduct only $2,700 on his Schedule A (the smaller of the FMV or the gross proceeds from the sale) and must attach a copy of Form 1098-C to his tax return.

Two exceptions apply to the rules regarding vehicle donations:

- If the charity keeps the vehicle for its own use, the donor can generally deduct the vehicle's FMV, or
- If the charity subsequently gives the vehicle directly to a needy person, the donor can generally deduct the vehicle's FMV.

Example: Quincy owns a used minivan that is still in good working condition. He donates the minivan to Meals-on-Wheels, a 501(c)(3) charity that delivers hot meals to disabled people and homebound seniors. The organization uses the minivan to deliver meals to needy individuals. The FMV of the minivan is $4,900 on the date of Quincy's donation. Since the vehicle was put into direct use by the charity, Quincy may deduct the FMV of the vehicle, as long as he obtains a contemporaneous written acknowledgment that the charity kept the vehicle for its own use. The deduction is subject to a 30%-of-AGI limit, and Quincy will be required to attach Form 8283 to his return.

Special Rules for Conservation Easements

Conservation easements are used for land conservation purposes by restricting the future use of the land in order to protect its conservation values. There are specific regulations that apply to these donations. Unlike other appreciated property, conservation easements are not limited to 30% of adjusted gross income. The charitable deduction allowed for conservation easements is generally limited to 50% of adjusted gross income, but can be as high as 100% for qualified farmers or ranchers. Also, the carryforward period for a donor to take tax deductions for a conservation agreement is fifteen years, rather than the usual five years for other types of charitable gifts.

Example: Daryl decides to give a permanent easement of his property to The Nature Conservancy, a qualifying 501(c)(3) organization. Daryl's property is 500 acres of wetlands, and his intent is to preserve the area for fishing and wildlife in perpetuity. Daryl purchased the land twenty years ago for $1,000,000. The land has appreciated in value. Daryl obtains a qualified appraisal of the easement, stating that the easement has a current fair market value of $1,400,000. In 2023, Daryl's AGI is $400,000. Because of the special threshold that applies to conservation easements, Daryl will be able to take a charitable deduction of up to 50% of his $400,000 AGI. Therefore, his $1,400,000 gift permits a deduction of $200,000 ($400,000 AGI × 50% = $200,000) in 2023. He will have a charitable contribution carryforward of $1,200,000 that he can use in future years to offset his taxable income. The carryforward is valid for fifteen years, rather than the usual five.

Personal Casualty and Theft Losses

The Tax Cuts and Jobs Act suspended the itemized deduction for most *nonbusiness* casualty and theft losses through tax year 2025. Only personal losses derived from federally declared disaster areas are deductible. Taxpayers who incur disaster-related casualty losses can deduct their losses for the year in which the loss occurred, or if elected, in the year *prior* to the year of the loss.[151] Electing to claim a loss in a prior tax year allows affected taxpayers in a disaster area to quickly obtain the tax benefits associated with the deduction without having to wait up to a year from the casualty event before filing their returns to claim the deduction.

Personal casualty and theft losses attributable to a federally declared disaster (FEMA disaster) are subject to a $100-per-casualty and 10%-of-adjusted gross income (AGI) limit. These limitations only apply to personal casualty losses.

> **Example:** Eleanor lives in Florida. On August 29, 2023, Hurricane Idalia hit the state. The resulting storms and flooding destroyed Eleanor's home and car. The county where Eleanor lived was designated a federal disaster area. Eleanor immediately files a claim with her insurance company. Eleanor assumed that her insurance would recover the full amount of her losses. Her insurance claim was settled several months later, on January 2, 2024 (the following year), but Eleanor's insurance company reimbursed her for only a small portion of her losses. The IRS deems the "disaster year" to be 2024 (not 2023, when the actual hurricane occurred), because that is when it became certain that Eleanor would not be fully reimbursed by her insurance company. Eleanor can either deduct the unreimbursed loss in 2024, or make an election to deduct the losses on her 2023 tax return.[152]

The casualty loss deduction on a personal-use asset is the *lesser* of (1) the decrease in the fair market value of the property (before and after the casualty event) or (2) the taxpayer's adjusted basis in the property at the time of the casualty event. Casualty losses of investment property are treated differently, and covered in the next section. Business casualty losses are covered in more detail in Part 2, *Businesses*.

Miscellaneous Itemized Deductions

The Tax Cuts and Jobs Act suspended miscellaneous itemized deductions subject to the 2%-of-AGI floor through 2025, including most unreimbursed employee business expenses. There are still some miscellaneous itemized deductions that a taxpayer can deduct on Schedule A. These are less commonly seen, but some of them are still tested on the EA exam. Miscellaneous itemized deductions that are still deductible in 2023 include:

- The amortizable premium on taxable bonds,
- Casualty and theft losses from "income-producing" or "investment" property,
- Losses from Ponzi-type investment schemes,
- Federal estate tax on income "in respect of a decedent" (IRD),
- Gambling losses to the extent of gambling winnings,
- Impairment-related work expenses of persons with disabilities,
- Excess deductions of an estate or trust in the entity's final tax year,
- Repayments of more than $3,000 under a claim of right,
- Unrecovered investment in an annuity.

---

[151]IRC section 165(i) allows a special election to deduct losses occurring in a federally declared disaster area in the tax year immediately preceding the tax year the loss occurred.

[152] Scenario modified directly from an example in IRS Instructions for Form 4684, Casualties and Thefts.

The amortizable premium on taxable bonds: If the amount a taxpayer pays for a bond is greater than its stated principal amount, the excess is called a bond premium. Annual amortization of the premium is treated as a miscellaneous itemized deduction.

Casualty or theft losses from investment property or "income-producing" property: A taxpayer can deduct a casualty or theft loss as a miscellaneous itemized deduction if the damaged or stolen property was income-producing property (meaning property held for investment, such as gold coins, silver coins, artwork, and vacant lots). The taxpayer must report the loss on Form 4684, *Casualties and Thefts,* Section B.

Example: Stewart purchased a plot of coastal land as an investment. He had planned to build a tourist campground on the site. On June 1, 2023, a severe storm hit the area, and the bluffs were badly damaged. Two weeks later, his land completely collapsed into the sea. Stewart neglected to purchase any insurance on the property, so his loss was not covered. Stewart's loss of valuable waterfront property is a deductible casualty loss, because it was purchased for investment. He would report the loss on Form 4684, Section B, Part I, for the loss of his investment property.

Losses from Ponzi investment schemes: Victims of fraudulent investment schemes can claim a theft loss deduction if certain conditions apply. Under IRS rules, an investor who is a victim of a Ponzi scheme is entitled to deduct Ponzi losses as a *theft* loss, instead of a *capital* loss from an investment. Ponzi scheme losses are not limited to the $3,000 annual limit that applies to other capital losses. As a result, Ponzi scheme losses may be offset against ordinary income, including wages, self-employment income, etc. with no limit. Ponzi scheme losses are deducted on Form 4684, Section C, *Theft Loss Deduction for Ponzi-Type Investment Scheme.*

Example: Celeste is a potential investor. She is looking for a financial advisor to help her invest. Bernie holds himself out to the public as an investment advisor and securities broker. In 2023, Celeste is persuaded to invest with Bernie. She opens an investment account with Bernie and contributed $100,000 to the account and provided Bernie with a power of attorney to use the funds to purchase and sell securities on her behalf. Unbeknownst to Celeste, Bernie only invests a small amount of her funds and embezzles the rest into his own personal accounts. Later, it is discovered that Bernie's purported investment advisory and brokerage activity was, in fact, a fraudulent investment arrangement known as a "Ponzi" scheme. Bernie is convicted of securities fraud and sentenced to prison. Celeste is only able to recover $5,000 of her original $100,000 investment. Therefore, Celeste has a $95,000 deductible Ponzi loss. She would report the loss on Schedule A as an itemized deduction, and the losses are not limited.

Federal Estate tax on income in respect of a decedent: Income in respect of a decedent (IRD) is income owed to a decedent at the time of death. If a decedent's estate has paid federal estate taxes on IRD assets, a beneficiary may be able to claim an IRD tax deduction. IRD is covered more extensively later, in the chapter that covers estate taxes.

Gambling losses to the extent of gambling winnings: The full amount of a taxpayer's gambling winnings must be reported on Form 1040. Gambling *losses* are deducted on Schedule A, up to the total amount of gambling winnings. Taxpayers must have kept a written record of their losses. Gambling losses in excess of winnings are not deductible.

Example: Akeem likes to gamble at his local casino. In 2023, he wins $6,200 playing slot machines, but has $9,500 in gambling losses. He does not keep track of his daily wins and losses. He is required to report the full amount of the winnings on Form 1040. His deduction for gambling losses is limited to $6,200 on Schedule A. He cannot write off the remaining $3,300 in losses. He also cannot carry the losses forward to future years. If Akeem chooses not to itemize his deductions, then none of his gambling losses would be deductible.

Impairment-related work expenses for disabled workers: These are expenses that enable a disabled person to work, such as special equipment or attendant care services at his workplace. Impairment-related work expenses must be incurred in connection with the taxpayer's place of work, or necessary for the taxpayer to be able to work.

In most cases, a disabled taxpayer would be able to deduct these expenses either as (1) medical expenses or (2) miscellaneous itemized deductions. Taxpayers can generally choose the method that will give them the best tax result.

Example: Farida has a serious visual disability, macular degeneration. She requires a large screen magnifier to see well enough to perform her work. Farida purchased her own screen magnifier for $650. Farida's employer is a very small company and did not reimburse the cost. Farida plans to itemize, and she deducts the full cost of the screen magnifier as a miscellaneous itemized deduction on Schedule A, without any income limitations.

Repayments of more than $3,000 under a claim of right: On occasion, a taxpayer may have to repay income that was included on a previous year's tax return because at the time the taxpayer received it, they thought they had an unrestricted right to it. This is a "repayment under claim of right" under IRC section 1341. A "claim of right" occurs when a taxpayer reports income in one year, but then must repay that income back in a future tax year. An example could be when a taxpayer has to repay the unemployment benefits or wages that they received in a prior year. If the amount of the repayment is more than $3,000, the taxpayer can elect to take a deduction or credit in the year the amounts are repaid. If the amount repaid was $3,000 or less, claim of right under IRC 1341 does not apply. [153]

Example: Truman is a college professor at a private university. Truman quits his job on November 31, 2023; the day before he receives his year-end bonus. Truman received his Form W-2 from the university and files his 2023 tax return on February 1, 2024, like he usually does. On February 15, 2024, Truman is informed by the university's payroll department that he was overpaid $6,500 in wages in 2023. He was not eligible for the year-end bonus because he quit before the end of the year. Rather than risk a bad employment reference, Truman fully repays the $6,500 requested by the University on April 30, 2024. Truman would not amend his 2023 tax return. Instead, he is allowed to take an itemized deduction for the $6,500 repayment as an itemized deduction on his 2024 return (the following year), because that is the year he repaid his employer. Alternatively, if it results in a larger tax benefit, Truman can elect to take a tax credit under IRC section 1341 on Schedule 3 based on the tax rate(s) applied on the income in 2023, because the amount of the repayment exceeds $3,000.

[153] If the amounts repaid were self-employment income, the taxpayer can deduct the repayment as an expense directly on the Schedule C or Schedule F. Detailed examples can be found in Publication 525, *Taxable and Nontaxable Income.*

> **Example:** Fritz is 65 and receives Social Security. In 2023, the Social Security Administration (SSA) sends Fritz a Notice of Overpayment. Due to a computation error, Fritz must repay $750 in overpaid Social Security benefits that he received and included in his gross income in the prior year. He pays the full $750 back to the Social Security Administration in 2023, but since his repayment was less than $3,000, the repayment is not deductible by Fritz.

Excess Deductions of an Estate or Trust: If, in its final tax year, an estate or trust has more deductions than gross income, the beneficiary can claim the excess deductions on their individual tax return, depending on the type of deduction.

These excess deductions are listed on the Schedule K-1 form, which is included in the estate or trust's final tax return. Each beneficiary receives a copy of the Schedule K-1 and uses it to report the deductions on their personal Form 1040.

The character of these deductions remains unchanged and they are reported as adjustments to gross income on Schedule 1 (Form 1040), or itemized deductions on Schedule A (Form 1040). Trusts and Estates are covered in greater detail in Part 2, *Businesses*.

Itemized Deductions for Nonresident Aliens on Form 1040NR

Specific limitations on deductions apply to nonresident aliens who are required to file Form 1040NR. Nonresident aliens cannot claim the standard deduction. Further, except for certain allowable itemized deductions, they can claim deductions only to the extent they are connected with income related to their U.S. trade or business. The following itemized deductions are allowed:

- State and local income taxes,
- Qualifying charitable contributions to U.S. nonprofit organizations
- Casualty and theft losses in a presidentially declared disaster area, and
- Some miscellaneous itemized deductions.

Nonresident aliens filing Form 1040-NR cannot take an itemized deduction for mortgage interest, and most other itemized deductions are restricted to them. Similar restrictions apply to dual-status taxpayers. There are special exceptions in the law for tax treaty partners, but the IRS will not test on any specific tax treaties with other nations.

> **Example:** Ishaan is a renowned international scholar teaching at Gonzaga University in Washington on a J-1 Visa. He is permitted to work on campus for the university because he is doing research under a university grant program. Ishaan earns $77,000 working for the University in 2023. He is FICA-exempt and only had federal and state income taxes withheld. During the year, Ishaan made a charitable gift of $900 in cash to the university's scholarship program, which is a qualifying donation. Ishaan cannot take the standard deduction, because he is a nonresident alien. However, he is allowed to itemize his deductions. He files Form 1040-NR, and claims an itemized deduction of $900 for the charitable gift that he made, as well as for the state income taxes withheld from his paychecks during the year.

Nondeductible Expenses

The IRS has a lengthy list of expenses that individual taxpayers cannot deduct.[154] These are just a sample of personal expenses the IRS lists as nondeductible:

- Lunch with coworkers or meals while working late
- Country club dues, athletic club fees, and gym memberships
- Home repairs, insurance, and rent
- Losses from the sale of a home, furniture, or a personal car
- Brokers' commissions
- Burial or funeral expenses, including the cost of cemetery lots
- Fees and licenses, such as car license or registration costs (except certain portions that may be considered deductible property taxes), marriage licenses, and dog tags
- Fines and penalties for breaking the law, such as parking tickets
- Life and disability insurance premiums
- Investment-related seminars
- Lost or misplaced cash or property
- Political contributions
- Expenses of attending stockholders' meetings
- Voluntary unemployment benefit fund contributions
- Adoption expenses (although a taxpayer may be able to claim an adoption credit)
- Travel expenses for another individual
- Interest on a credit card used for personal expenses
- Expenses of earning or collecting tax-exempt income

---

[154] A basic rule is that most personal, living, or family expenses are not deductible.

Unit 12: Study Questions

(Test yourself first, then check the correct answers at the end of this quiz.)

1. Byrne is a visiting foreign professor from Ireland who is teaching at a U.S. university on a J-1 visa. He is classified as a nonresident alien for tax purposes and will file Form 1040-NR. Which of the following is Byrne potentially allowed to claim on his income tax return?

A. Disability insurance premiums.
B. A charitable gift of $150 to the American Cancer Society.
C. Mortgage interest on his main home.
D. The standard deduction.

2. Which of the following taxpayers must itemize their deductions?

A. Mindy, who files a joint return with her disabled husband.
B. Leslie, who is unmarried, claims two dependents, and files Form 1040.
C. Pearl, whose itemized deductions are more than the standard deduction.
D. Gabriel, whose wife Melinda files a separate return and itemizes her deductions.

3. Which of the following taxes can taxpayers deduct on Schedule A?

A. Foreign sales taxes.
B. Foreign income taxes.
C. Excise taxes on alcohol and tobacco.
D. Foreign real estate taxes.

4. Landon is deaf. He purchased a special device to use at his workplace so he can identify when his phone rings. He paid for the device out-of-pocket, and his employer did not reimburse him. How should Landon report this on his tax return?

A. Landon can claim the purchase as an itemized deduction on Schedule A.
B. Landon can deduct the purchase as an adjustment to income.
C. Landon cannot deduct the purchase because he is not totally disabled.
D. Landon cannot deduct the purchase because he is not self-employed.

5. Which of the following home improvements cannot be deducted as a medical expense?

A. The cost of installing stairlifts for a disabled individual.
B. The cost of lowering cabinets to accommodate a disability.
C. The cost of making doorways wider to accommodate a wheelchair.
D. An elevator that costs $15,000, but adds $20,000 to the value of the home.

6. Hakeem owns three personal homes. None of them are rental properties. He has an AGI of $128,000 in 2023. His primary residence is in Chicago, where he works. He also owns a mountain cabin in Lake Tahoe and a small condo in Las Vegas, which he uses several times a year. Hakeem did not use the mountain cabin, and it sat empty all year. He pays property tax and mortgage interest on all three properties.

Home Location	Mortgage Interest	Property Tax
Main home in Chicago	$18,500	$7,500
Cabin in Tahoe	$5,200	$2,800
Condo in Las Vegas	$4,500	$1,950

All the mortgage debt is qualifying acquisition debt. Based on the information above, which of the following statements is correct?

A. Hakeem may claim a mortgage interest deduction of $18,500 and a property tax deduction of $7,500 on Schedule A.
B. Hakeem may claim a mortgage interest deduction of $23,700 and a property tax deduction of $10,300 on Schedule E.
C. Hakeem may claim a mortgage interest deduction of $28,200 and a property tax deduction of $12,250 on Schedule A.
D. Hakeem may claim an allowable mortgage interest deduction of $23,700 and a property tax deduction of $10,000 on Schedule A.

7. Zachary is a volunteer delegate for the United Methodist Church. He spent three days attending his church's annual conference. He spent $250 on a plane ticket to the meeting and $25 on materials for the meeting. In the evening, Zachary went to the theater with two other meeting attendees. He spent $50 on theater tickets. The church did not reimburse Zachary for any of his costs. How much can he deduct as a charitable expense?

A. $0
B. $250
C. $275
D. $325

8. Emelie donates $430 in cash to her church. Which of the following is required on the receipt to substantiate the donation correctly for IRS recordkeeping requirements?

A. The reason for the contribution.
B. Emelie's home address.
C. The amount of the donation.
D. Emelie's method of payment.

9. Which of the following can taxpayers deduct on Schedule A?

A. Local sales taxes.
B. Fines for speeding.
C. Social Security taxes.
D. Homeowners' association fees.

10. Which of the following taxpayers is required to itemize deductions and cannot take the standard deduction?

A. Tawana, who has one dependent child.
B. Vernice, who wants to deduct the alimony she paid to her ex-husband.
C. Leslie, whose itemized deductions are more than the standard deduction.
D. Qiang, who is a nonresident alien.

11. Alejandra had the following medical expenses in 2023:

- Botox injections for wrinkles: $6,000.
- Treatment for a broken leg: $9,000 (of which $8,000 was reimbursed by insurance).
- Doctor-prescribed back brace: $1,900.
- Child care while in the hospital: $200.

What is her medical expense deduction *before* the limitation based on the 7.5%-of-AGI threshold?

A. $1,900
B. $2,900
C. $7,900
D. $8,900

12. For a tax to be deductible in 2023, all the following must be correct except:

A. The tax must be imposed during the tax year.
B. The taxpayer must be legally liable for the tax.
C. The tax must be paid during the tax year.
D. The tax must be paid by the taxpayer.

13. Herschel and Angeline will both file "married filing separate" tax returns in 2023. Herschel plans to claim itemized deductions on Schedule A; therefore, what must Angeline do?

A. They will have to file jointly.
B. Angeline must take the standard deduction.
C. Angeline must either itemize her deductions or claim zero as her standard deduction.
D. Angeline may choose to itemize or take the standard deduction.

14. All of the following factors determine the amount of a taxpayer's standard deduction *except:*

A. The taxpayer's filing status.
B. The taxpayer's adjusted gross income.
C. Whether the taxpayer is 65 or older, or blind.
D. Whether the taxpayer can be claimed as a dependent.

15. Yoshiko is single and has the following income and expenses:

Form W-2 wages	$70,000
Interest income received from a CD	3,000
Mortgage interest on a primary residence (acquisition debt of $400,000)	(24,000)
Investment interest expense	(5,000)
Personal credit card interest	(3,400)
Car loan interest on her personal vehicle	(1,200)
Late fees incurred on her mortgage	(50)

She plans to itemize this year. What is her total allowable deduction for interest expense on her Schedule A?

A. $24,000
B. $27,000
C. $27,050
D. $32,400

16. Kiara bought her car seven years ago for $15,000. A used car guide shows the vehicle is currently worth approximately $5,000. Kiara's cousin, Buckley, offered her $4,500 for the car a week ago, but she declined to sell it to him. Instead, she decides to donate her used car to a qualified charity. At the end of the year, she receives a Form 1098-C from the charity showing the car was sold at auction for $1,900. How much is Kiara's allowable charitable deduction on Schedule A?

A. $1,900
B. $4,500
C. $5,000
D. $15,000

17. Oscar donated a leather coat to a thrift store operated by his church. He paid $450 for the coat three years ago. Similar coats in the thrift store sell for $50. What is Oscar's charitable deduction?

A. $0
B. $50
C. $400
D. $450

18. Leandra's adjusted gross income was $75,000 in 2023. She incurred the following expenses:

Homeowners' association dues	$1,000
Fine from homeowner's association for violation of bylaws	100
Mortgage interest on her main home (acquisition debt of $350,000)	9,000
Property taxes on her main home	2,800
Political contributions to the Green Party	250
Unreimbursed orthodontic fees for a tooth extraction	1,200

Based on the information provided, what is the amount of expenses she can deduct as an itemized deduction on Schedule A?

A. $11,800
B. $12,250
C. $13,450
D. $14,450

19. Which of the following taxes is not deductible on Schedule A?

A. Property taxes paid on a vacation home located in Hawaii.
B. Income taxes on foreign income, paid to a foreign country.
C. Property taxes based on a vehicle's value (a portion of DMV fees).
D. Property taxes paid on a vacation home in France.

20. Isaac's main home was damaged by a hurricane, and his county was later deemed a federal disaster area. He incurred $90,000 worth of flood damage to his home, but $80,000 was reimbursed by his homeowner's insurance. His basis in the home was $200,000 at the time of the hurricane. Isaac's employer had a disaster relief fund for its employees. Isaac received $4,000 from the fund and spent the entire amount on repairs to his home. What is Isaac's casualty loss (before the calculation of any limitations)?

A. $0
B. $4,000
C. $6,000
D. $10,000

21. Lamar donates to his church multiple times during the year. Which one of the donations listed below will require a qualified appraisal before the contribution can be deducted on his return?

A. A cash donation of $12,000.
B. A donation of antique furniture valued at $6,500.
C. A donation of publicly-traded stock with a fair market value of $12,500.
D. A donation of an old motorcycle valued at $450.

22. Bowen donated to all of the following nonprofit organizations in 2023. What is his allowable deduction for charitable gifts on Schedule A?

Organization	Amount
Methodist church	$100
County animal shelter	120
Salvation Army	75
American Red Cross	25
Republican party	50
Chamber of Commerce	300
Total contributions	$670

A. $220
B. $320
C. $520
D. $670

23. Angie and Sheldon, both age 41, file a joint return and claim their two children as dependents. They have adjusted gross income of $125,000. In 2023, the family accumulated $12,120 of unreimbursed medical and dental expenses that included the following:

Prescription medications filled in the U.S.	$6,500
Prescription medications ordered and shipped from another country	1,320
Prescription contacts lenses for Angie	500
Teeth whitening procedure by Angie's dentist and custom bleach trays	2,600
Prescribed smoking cessation program for Sheldon	1,200

What amount can they deduct for their medical expenses?

A. $0
B. $6,500
C. $8,200
D. $9,375

24. All of the following miscellaneous itemized deductions are allowable in 2023 except:

A. Impairment-related work expenses of persons with disabilities.
B. Federal estate tax on income in respect of a decedent.
C. Gambling losses to the extent of gambling winnings.
D. Union dues.

25. Yamir is unmarried and files as head of household. During the year, he paid:

Mortgage interest on his main home (acquisition debt of $300,000)	$5,000
Credit card interest	600
Auto loan interest	4,000
Loan interest on an empty lot that was purchased to build a second home	3,000
Interest on a payday loan	1,000

What amount can they report as deductible mortgage interest?

A. $5,000
B. $6,000
C. $8,000
D. $8,600

Unit 12: Quiz Answers

1. The answer is B. Byrne is allowed to deduct the charitable gift to a U.S. charity on his Form 1040-NR. Nonresident aliens are limited as to the types of itemized deductions they can claim. Among other restrictions, they are not allowed to claim the deduction for mortgage interest. Answer "D" is incorrect because nonresident aliens cannot claim the standard deduction.

2. The answer is D. Gabriel is not allowed to claim the standard deduction. A married taxpayer who files separately (MFS) and whose spouse itemizes deductions must either itemize his deductions (or claim "zero" as their standard deduction).

3. The answer is B. Only the foreign <u>income</u> taxes are deductible. Taxpayers can deduct foreign income tax on Schedule A as an itemized deduction. Foreign income taxes are not subject to the SALT cap.

4. The answer is A. Landon can claim the expenses for the special device as an impairment-related work expense. If a taxpayer has a physical or mental disability that limits employment, he can deduct the expense as a miscellaneous itemized deduction on Schedule A.

5. The answer is D. The deduction for capital improvements is limited to the excess of the actual cost of the improvements over the increase in the fair market value of the home. Since the increase in the fair market value of the home exceeds the cost of the elevator, none of the costs can be deducted as a medical expense.

6. The answer is D. Hakeem may claim an allowable mortgage interest deduction of $23,700 and a property tax deduction of $10,000 on Schedule A. The mortgage interest and property tax on both his main home in Chicago and the mountain cabin are deductible (assuming the ceiling on qualifying mortgage debt is not an issue). The mortgage interest on the third home is not deductible. The property tax on all the homes is *potentially* deductible, but the deduction is limited to $10,000 by the SALT cap in 2023. The mortgage interest on a second home is deductible, even if Hakeem did not use the home during the year. The answer is calculated as follows:

Home Location	Mortgage Interest	Property Tax
Main home in Chicago	$18,500	$7,500
Cabin in Tahoe	$5,200	$2,800
Condo in Las Vegas	3rd home Not Deductible	$1,950
Totals *before* limitations	$23,700	$12,250
Allowable deduction	**$23,700**	**$10,000 (SALT limit)**

7. The answer is C. Zachary's charitable contribution is $275 ($250 plane ticket + $25 materials = $275). He can claim his travel and meeting expenses as charitable contributions because they are directly related to his charitable activities. However, he cannot claim the cost of the evening at the theater, as that is a personal entertainment expense.

8. The answer is C. Emelie can claim a deduction for a contribution of $250 or more only if she has a receipt or acknowledgment from a qualified organization. The receipt must include:

- The amount of cash contributed.
- Whether the qualified organization gave the taxpayer any goods or services in return.
- If applicable, a description and good faith estimate of the value of any goods or services provided in return by the organization.

A receipt must also show the date of the donation and the name of the organization that was paid.

9. The answer is A. A taxpayer has the option of claiming sales taxes as an itemized deduction on Schedule A instead of claiming state and local income taxes. A taxpayer cannot claim both. The other expenses listed are not deductible on Schedule A.

10. The answer is D. Qiang cannot use the standard deduction. A nonresident or dual-status alien (who is not married to a U.S. citizen or resident, and electing to be treated as a U.S. resident for tax purposes) must itemize deductions. The other taxpayers listed are not required to itemize their deductions but may elect to do so if they wish.

11. The answer is B. Alejandra's medical expense deduction (before any AGI limitations) is $2,900 ($1,900 + $1,000). The childcare cost is not deductible, even though it was incurred while she was obtaining medical care. The amount reimbursed by insurance is not deductible. Most cosmetic procedures are not deductible, unless they are specifically to correct a disease or defect, so the Botox injections for wrinkles are not deductible.

12. The answer is A. Taxpayers can deduct taxes imposed during a *prior* year, as long as the taxes were *paid* during the current tax year.

13. The answer is C. Since they are both filing MFS, Angeline is forced to either (1) itemize her deductions or (2) claim "zero" as her standard deduction. A taxpayer whose spouse itemizes deductions must either itemize deductions or claim zero as the standard deduction. This only applies in situations when both taxpayers are filing MFS. If one spouse qualifies for Head of Household filing status, then neither spouse would be forced to itemize.

14. The answer is B. The standard deduction amount is based on the taxpayer's filing and dependent status, and whether the taxpayer is blind or at least 65 years old. It is not based on a taxpayer's income.

15. The answer is C. Yoshiko's allowable deduction is $27,050. The answer is calculated as follows: $24,000 + $3,000 + $50 = $27,050. The deduction for investment interest expense is *limited* to her net investment income of $3,000. The excess amount of interest expense of $2,000 ($5,000 - $3,000) must be carried over to the next tax year and may be used to offset investment income in future tax years. Late fees paid on a qualifying home mortgage are deductible as mortgage interest on Schedule A. The credit card interest and interest paid on her car loan are not deductible.

16. The answer is A. Kiara can deduct $1,900 for her donation. She is allowed to take the <u>lesser of</u> (1) the car's FMV or (2) the amount for which the charity sold the car. Since the charity sold the car for only $1,900, that is the amount of her allowable deduction, regardless of any other estimates of its value.

17. The answer is B. Oscar's donation is limited to $50. Generally, the FMV of used clothing and household goods is far less than the original cost. The IRS permits taxpayers to deduct the fair market value of clothing and household goods that are in "good" condition. For used clothing, a taxpayer may claim a deduction of the price that a buyer typically would pay in a thrift shop for those items.

18. The answer is A. Leandra can only deduct her mortgage interest and her property taxes. Neither the homeowner's association dues, nor the fine, or political contribution are deductible. Although the orthodontic fees for the tooth extraction are a qualified medical expense, the amounts are less than 7.5% of her AGI, so she cannot deduct her medical costs, either. The answer is figured as follows:

Homeowners' association dues	NO
Fine from homeowner's association for violation of bylaws	NO
Mortgage interest on her main home	9,000
Property taxes on her main home	2,800
Political contributions to the Green Party	NO
Unreimbursed orthodontic fees for a tooth extraction	NO
Total allowable deductions on Schedule A	$11,800

19. The answer is D. Property taxes paid on a personal-use home in France are not deductible. The deduction for foreign real property taxes is no longer allowed.

20. The answer is C. Isaac's casualty loss is $6,000. Isaac must reduce his ($90,000) loss by the $80,000 insurance proceeds and the $4,000 he received from his employer.

21. The answer is B. The antique furniture donation would require an appraisal, because the value of this property donation exceeds $5,000. Lamar must also complete Form 8283 and attach it to his tax return. The IRS requires a taxpayer to obtain a written appraisal by a qualified appraiser for most *noncash* contributions of $5,000 or more. Lamar must retain a copy of the appraisal for his own records. Answer "A" is incorrect because a cash donation does not require an appraisal. Answer "C" is incorrect because the donation of publicly-traded stock or other securities does not require an appraisal. Answer "D" is incorrect because a donation of a vehicle valued at less than $500 does not require an appraisal or any other type of documentation beyond a written acknowledgment from the organization.

22. The answer is B. The contributions to the political organization and the Chamber of Commerce are not deductible on Schedule A. Bowen's allowable deduction is calculated as follows: $100 + $120 + $75 + $25 = $320.

23. The answer is A. Angie and Sheldon cannot deduct any of their medical expenses. In 2023, only the medical expenses that exceed 7.5% of the taxpayer's AGI are deductible. The total of Angie and Sheldon's *qualifying* medical expenses, $8,200, is less than $9,375 ($125,000 × 7.5%). Of the items listed, only the smoking cessation program, the contact lenses, and the prescription medications filled in the United States are qualified medical expenses. Prescription medications shipped from other countries are ineligible. The teeth whitening procedure would be considered a cosmetic enhancement and would not be a qualified medical expense, whether performed by a dentist or not.

24. The answer is D. Union dues are not deductible as a miscellaneous itemized deduction. All of the other expenses would be deductible on Schedule A.

25. The answer is A. Only Yamir's home mortgage interest ($5,000) is potentially deductible as interest on Schedule A. The other types of interest are all personal interest, which is not deductible. Interest paid on an empty plot of land is not deductible as mortgage interest. Only the interest secured by an actual home (not land) is deductible as mortgage interest.

Unit 13: Individual Tax Credits

> **For additional information, read:**
> Schedule 8812 instructions
> Publication 503, *Child and Dependent Care Expenses*
> Publication 596, *Earned Income Credit*
> Publication 970, *Tax Benefits for Education*

A tax credit directly reduces a taxpayer's liability on a dollar-for-dollar basis, which means it is usually more valuable than a tax deduction of the same dollar amount that only reduces the amount of taxable income. Various types of tax credits are either *refundable* or *nonrefundable*.

Nonrefundable Tax Credits

A *nonrefundable* tax credit reduces a taxpayer's liability for the year to zero but not beyond that, so any remaining credit is not refunded to the taxpayer. The most common nonrefundable tax credits available in 2023 are:

- Child and Dependent Care Credit
- Adoption Credit
- American Opportunity Tax Credit (although the AOTC has a refundable component)
- Lifetime Learning Credit
- Retirement Savings Contributions Credit or, the "Saver's Credit"
- The Credit for Other Dependents (ODC)
- Child Tax Credit (CTC) (the CTC also has a refundable component)
- Foreign Tax Credit (covered later)

Refundable Tax Credits

A *refundable* tax credit can reduce a taxpayer's liability to zero and also generate a refund to the taxpayer for the amount by which the credit exceeds the amount of tax he would otherwise owe. Refundable tax credits include the following:

- Additional Child Tax Credit (ACTC)
- The Earned Income Tax Credit (EITC)
- Premium Tax Credit (related to the Affordable Care Act, covered later in chapter 14)
- American Opportunity Tax Credit (partially refundable)
- Credit for excess Social Security and RRTA tax withheld

Stringent due diligence requirements apply to tax preparers who prepare returns claiming the Earned Income Tax Credit, the Child Tax Credit, and the American Opportunity Tax Credit. Due diligence requirements also apply to the determination of Head of Household filing status. Tax preparers must complete Form 8867, *Paid Preparer's Due Diligence Checklist,* for each EITC, CTC/ACTC, or AOTC claim they prepare.[155]

The American Opportunity Tax Credit, Additional Child Tax Credit, Child Tax Credit, Credit for Other Dependents, and the Earned Income Tax Credit require the taxpayer, spouse, and qualifying child

---

[155] Due diligence for tax preparers is covered in more detail in Book 3, Representation.

to have a valid taxpayer identification number (TIN) assigned on or before the due date (or extended due date) of the return.

In the past, a taxpayer was allowed to amend their return to claim these credits retroactively after a valid taxpayer identification number was issued, but this is no longer permitted. This includes the filing of an original return past the due date (including extensions) if the taxpayer failed to timely file.

Example: Blanca is an immigrant from Cuba currently residing in the U.S. She is in the process of adjusting her residency status via the Cuban Adjustment Act, which allows her to apply for permanent residency and a green card. Blanca filed her 2023 tax return early, on February 1, 2024, using her ITIN. She does not file an extension. Three months later, on May 1, 2024, Blanca's application for U.S. residency is granted, and she receives a Social Security number (SSN). Her income level would allow her to claim EITC, but she cannot amend her 2023 return and claim EITC, because she did not receive her Social Security number by the due date of her tax return, and she did not file an extension. The IRS would prohibit Blanca from retroactively claiming the EITC by amending her return. If she did attempt to file a retroactive claim, her claim would be denied.

Example: Samir and Noor are married and file jointly. Samir and Noor are lawfully present in the United States as visiting scholars, but they are not U.S. residents. Both Samir and Noor apply for permanent residency on January 1, 2023, and expect to receive their Social Security Numbers soon. On April 1, 2023, Samir and Noor are granted conditional permanent residency in the United States. They receive valid green cards and Social Security numbers. Samir and Noor file their tax return on April 10, 2023, using their newly-assigned SSNs. They will be eligible for all the refundable credits, (assuming they otherwise qualify), because they had valid SSNs before the due date of their tax return.

Child and Dependent Care Credit (CDCTC)

The Child and Dependent Care Credit (CDCTC) is not refundable in 2023. This credit allows a taxpayer a credit for a percentage of child care expenses for children under age 13 and/or for disabled dependents of any age.

This is a credit for childcare expenses that allow taxpayers to work or to seek work. If a taxpayer receives a reimbursement under a flexible spending account, the amount is treated as being pretax, and the taxpayer must deduct the reimbursed amount from their qualified expenses to determine the allowable credit.

For tax year 2023, the maximum amount of care expenses used to calculate the credit is $3,000 for one qualifying dependent, or $6,000 for two or more qualifying dependents.

Example: Zane and Shari both work full time and file jointly. They have two children, a daughter who is four years old, and a son that is two years old. Zane and Shari incur $5,000 of daycare expenses for their daughter and $4,600 for their son. Their total child care expenses are $9,600 for the year. The maximum amount of qualifying expenses they can use to figure the credit is $6,000, even though their actual expenses exceed that amount.

The amount of the credit ranges between 20% to 35% of qualified expenses, with the maximum credit being 35% of a taxpayer's qualifying daycare expenses.

2023 Credit Rate based on AGI (from the Form 2441 Instructions)

Taxpayer's AGI	Credit Percentage	Taxpayer's AGI	Credit Percentage	Taxpayer's AGI	Credit Percentage
$0—15,000	.35	$25,000—27,000	.29	$37,000—39,000	.23
15,000—17,000	.34	27,000—29,000	.28	39,000—41,000	.22
17,000—19,000	.33	29,000—31,000	.27	41,000—43,000	.21
19,000—21,000	.32	31,000—33,000	.26	43,000—No limit	.20
21,000—23,000	.31	33,000—35,000	.25		
23,000—25,000	.30	35,000—37,000	.24		

Example: Dina and Joseph are married and file jointly. They have one child, Abel, who is 7 years old. Dina and Joseph both work, so Abel attends after-school daycare. His parents spend $3,200 on daycare during the year. The maximum amount of daycare expenses that can be used to calculate the credit is $3,000. Dina and Joseph's joint AGI is $69,000 in 2023. Based on their AGI, they can claim a 20% Child and Dependent Care Credit, which results in a $600 credit ($3,000 qualifying daycare expenses × 20% credit rate = $600).

Qualifying expenses: The following kinds of expenses qualify for the credit.

- **Preschool education:** Preschool or other programs *below* the level of kindergarten. Expenses for enrolling in kindergarten or higher grades are not qualifying expenses.

- **After-school care:** Daycare services provided before or after school hours. Childcare expenses during the summer and throughout the year may also be considered qualifying if they are necessary to allow parents to work.

- **Disabled care:** Adult daycare or assistance services for a disabled dependent or a disabled spouse of any age who is unable to care for themselves.[156]

- **Transportation costs:** Expenses incurred by the care provider to transport an eligible person to and from their place of care.

- **Fees and deposits:** Any payments made to a daycare or preschool for the purpose of securing childcare services.

- **Household services:** Any services performed by a full-time nanny or in-home care aide that benefit and protect an eligible person.

Example: Marina is unmarried and files as head of household. Marina claims her elderly mother, Rosa, as her dependent. Rosa has mild dementia and is disabled, so she must be in an adult daycare. Marina pays $12,000 per year for Rosa to be in an adult daycare. Marina may claim the Child and Dependent Care Credit because Rosa is her dependent, and she is disabled and incapable of self-care. Marina earns $75,000 in wages in 2023, and has no other income for the year. Based on Marina's AGI, she can claim a $600 Child and Dependent Care Credit ($3,000 maximum daycare expenses × 20% credit rate).

---

[156] With regards to supportive care for disabled individuals, disabled persons who cannot dress, clean, or feed themselves because of physical or mental problems are qualifying individuals. This also includes persons who must have constant attention to prevent them from injuring themselves or others.

> **Example:** Cheng and Jingyi are married and file jointly. Cheng works full time. His wife, Jingyi, does not work, because she is disabled. Cheng and Jingyi have one 6-year-old daughter, who is in elementary school. Cheng pays for after-school care for his daughter, and picks her up at school when he is finished with his workday. The cost of the after-school care would be a qualifying expense for the Child and Daycare Credit, even though Cheng's wife is not working, because Jingyi is disabled.

Eligibility tests: A taxpayer must pass **five** eligibility tests to qualify for the child and dependent care credit (CDCTC):

- **Qualifying person test**
- **Earned income test**
- **Work-related expense test**
- **Joint return test**
- **Provider identification test**

In 2023, a taxpayer may qualify for the CDCTC, even if filing MFS, if they meet certain requirements.

Test #1: Qualifying Person Test

For purposes of the Child and Dependent Care Credit, a "qualifying person" is:

- A dependent child *under* the age of 13 (at the time the care was provided),
- A spouse who is physically or mentally disabled,
- Any other disabled dependent who is incapable of self-care,
- A disabled person that the taxpayer *could* claim as a dependent except the disabled person had gross income of $4,700 or more in 2023 (IRC Section 21(b)(1)(B)).

> **Example:** Conrad is an architect who works full-time. Conrad's wife, Dacia, is permanently disabled. The couple has an 8-year old daughter named Kaylani. Conrad hires an in-home caregiver to look after his disabled wife and his daughter. Both Dacia and Kaylani are qualifying persons for the Child and Dependent Care Credit.

Test #2: Earned Income Test

If a taxpayer is married, both spouses must have "earned income" during the year to qualify for this credit. This generally means both spouses must work (if filing a joint return). In the event one spouse does not work, for purposes of this test the taxpayer's spouse is *treated* as having earned income for any month they are:

- A full-time student, or
- Disabled.

For any month that a spouse has no actual earned income, but has "deemed earned income" because they were a full-time student or disabled, the amount of "deemed" earned income by the nonworking spouse is $250 per month if the couple has one qualifying dependent, or $500 per month if the taxpayer has two or more dependents.[157]

---

[157] If a spouse dies during the year, the deceased spouse's earned income is not taken into consideration when determining the eligibility for this credit. This is true even if a joint return is filed with the deceased spouse. See Treas. Reg. Sect. 1.21-2(b)(2).

Example: Theresa and Jordan are married and have one 5-year-old son named Timmy. Timmy is in daycare. Jordan works full-time for an accounting firm. Theresa attended college full-time from January 1 to June 30. She was unemployed during the summer and did not attend school for the rest of the year, but Timmy continued to stay in daycare, so Theresa could volunteer at her church. Theresa is treated as having "deemed earned income" only for the six months she attended school full-time. In other words, they are allowed to take the dependent care credit in the months that Theresa was attending school. The daycare expenses that were incurred when Theresa was not in school or working would not be qualifying expenses for the purposes of the credit.

The amount of qualifying daycare expenses used to figure the credit cannot be more than the taxpayer's earned income for the year (if unmarried at the end of the year), or the smaller of the spouse's earned income for the year, if married.

Example: Kenny and Selena are married and have one 3-year-old daughter named Poppy. Poppy is in daycare. The parents spend $4,000 on daycare during the year so both can work. Selena works full-time as a cashier at a retail store. She earns $40,000 in wages during the year. Kenny is self-employed as a graphic designer. His business does poorly during the year, and he has an overall loss on his Schedule C. Since Kenny does not have any earned income (his business shows a loss), then they cannot claim the Child and Dependent Care Credit.

Example: Tanner and Ursula are a married couple who file their taxes jointly. They have a 7-year-old son and spend $5,750 on daycare expenses for the year. Tanner's annual wages are $49,000, while Ursula only makes $2,000 from a part-time job. Neither of them received any dependent care assistance from their employers. When calculating their Child and Dependent Care Credit, they can only consider the *lesser* of Tanner's earned income or Ursula's earned income. Since Ursula's earnings were only $2,000, it sets the limit for what can be counted as qualifying expenses towards this credit.

Test #3: Work-Related Expense Test

Child and dependent care expenses must be "work-related" to qualify for this credit, meaning a taxpayer must be working (or actively searching for work). An exception exists for spouses who are disabled or full-time students. In addition, any daycare expenses incurred so that a spouse may do volunteer work or so that a married couple can go on a "date night" do not qualify.

Example: Nikita is a stay-at-home mom who volunteers several hours a week for a local suicide hotline. Her husband works full-time as a custodian. They pay a babysitter to stay with their daughter during the hours Nikita volunteers. The couple does not qualify for the credit because the babysitting expense is not "work-related." Since Nikita does not have a job, is not disabled, and is not a full-time student, their child care expenses are ineligible for the credit.

Example: Maureen's four-year-old son attends a daycare center while she works three days a week. The daycare charges $150 for three days a week and $250 for five days a week. Sometimes Maureen pays the extra money so she can run errands or go to the doctor on her days off. This extra charge is not a qualifying expense. Maureen's deductible expenses are limited to $150 a week, the amount of her work-related daycare expenses.

Nonqualifying expenses: Examples of child care expenses that do *not* qualify for the credit include:

- Tuition for children in kindergarten and above (i.e., private elementary school costs),
- Summer school or tutoring programs,
- The cost of sending a child to an overnight camp (but *day camps* generally do qualify),
- The cost of transportation not provided by a daycare provider,
- A forfeited deposit to a daycare center (since it is not for care and therefore not a work-related expense).

Example: Archie's 7-year-old son, Kanyon, attends a private elementary school, which costs $300 a week. In addition to paying for school tuition, Archie pays an extra weekly fee of $100 for after-school daycare so he can be at work during his scheduled hours. Archie can count the cost of the after-school daycare program when figuring the child care credit, but cannot count the cost of private school tuition.

Example: Lorie is divorced and has custody of her 12-year-old daughter, Bree. In August, Lorie spends $2,000 to send Bree to an overnight camp (sleepaway camp) for two weeks. She also sends Bree to a Girl Scout day camp for a week in July. The cost of the Girl Scout camp is $750. Lorie may only count the $750 toward the credit because the cost of sending a child to an overnight camp is not considered a qualifying child care expense. Next year, when Bree turns 13, she will no longer be a qualifying child under the rules for this credit, (unless the child is disabled).

Example: Dominga takes her three-year-old son, Abram, to a nursery school that provides daily lunch and activities as part of its program, which costs $800 per month. The meals are included in the overall cost of care, and they are considered incidental and not itemized on her monthly bill. Dominga can count the total cost of the daycare when she figures her daycare credit.

The Child and Dependent Care Credit does not apply to child care payments made to a family member who is the taxpayer's own dependent under 19 years old, or any other dependent listed on their tax return.

Example: Garrison, age 30, pays his 60-year-old mother, Bettie, $300 per month to watch his 5-year-old son. Bettie watches her grandson while Garrison is at work. Normally, the $300 Garrison pays his mother would be a qualifying childcare expense. However, in 2023, Garrison claims his mother as a dependent on his tax return, along with his 5-year-old son. Since Garrison is claiming his mother as a dependent, the payments made to her for childcare are not qualifying expenses for the purposes of the Child and Dependent Care Credit.

Taxpayers may combine costs for multiple dependents. For example, if a taxpayer pays daycare expenses for three qualifying children, the annual limit on qualifying expenses does not need to be divided equally among them.

Example: Darby has three children, all under the age of 13. His qualifying daycare expenses are $2,300 for his first child; $1,900 for his second child; and $900 for his third child. Darby can use the total amount, $5,100, when figuring his credit.

In the case of divorced or separated taxpayers, only the **custodial parent** of the child is allowed to claim the Child and Dependent Care Credit.

Test #4: Joint Return Test

The joint return test specifies that married couples who wish to take the Child and Dependent Care credit *generally* must file jointly. Recently modified rules apply to married taxpayers who file separate returns. If a taxpayer's filing status is married filing separately, and *all* of the following apply, the taxpayer is still permitted to claim the daycare credit on Form 2441.

- The taxpayer lived apart from their spouse during the last 6 months of 2023.
- The taxpayer's home was the qualifying person's home for more than half of 2023.
- The taxpayer paid more than half of the cost of keeping up the home for the year.

Example: Mirabella physically separated from her husband on March 9, 2023. She has not filed for divorce or legal separation yet. She does not have any children. Mirabella's AGI is $95,000. Mirabella maintains a home for herself and Sebastian, who is her disabled father. Sebastian is 72 years old and permanently disabled, so Mirabella pays $9,000 for a home-health aide to come in and take care of her father while she is working. Sebastian has $5,100 in interest income, so Mirabella cannot claim him as a dependent (his gross income is greater than $4,700, the 2023 gross income threshold for qualifying relatives). Because Mirabella is not able to claim her father as a dependent and she is still legally married as of the end of the year, she also cannot use the head of household filing status. Mirabella's filing status is married filing separately, but Sebastian is a qualifying person for the Child and Dependent Care Credit. Because of the following facts, Mirabella is able to claim the credit for the dependent care expenses she incurred for her father, even though her filing status is married filing separately.[158]

Test #5: Provider Identification Test

To qualify for this credit, taxpayers must include the name, address, and identification number of the caregiver or organization who provided care for their child or dependent. If a daycare provider refuses to provide their tax ID information, the taxpayer can still claim the credit by reporting whatever information they have (such as the provider's name and address) and attaching a statement to Form 2441 explaining the situation.

However, foreign daycare providers are exempt from this requirement as they do not need a U.S. taxpayer ID.

Example: Edwin is a widowed U.S. citizen. He is working overseas in Saudi Arabia on a multi-year contract for an international accountancy firm. Edwin worked in Saudi Arabia for the entire taxable year. Edwin has one 11-year-old daughter named Sadie. Edwin pays a full-time nanny to watch his daughter, Sadie, while he is working. Since all the care was provided in a foreign country, the nanny is not required to have a U.S. tax ID, and Edwin is still allowed to claim the Child and Dependent Care Credit. When Edwin files his individual return, the tax software will automatically enter "LAFCP" (Living Abroad, Foreign Care Provider) in the space for the care provider's taxpayer identification number.

---

[158] Example based on scenario in the Form 2441 instructions.

Child Tax Credit and Additional Child Tax Credit

Note: It is important to note that the Child Tax Credit (CTC) is entirely distinct from the Child and Dependent Care Credit. These are two separate credits, so be careful not to mix them up!

The rules in 2023 for the Child Tax Credit and the Additional Child Tax Credit (ACTC) are as follows:

- The *nonrefundable* Child Tax Credit is $2,000 per qualifying child
- The *refundable* Additional Child Tax Credit is a maximum of $1,600 per qualifying child.
- The AGI phaseout for the Child Tax Credit is $200,000 ($400,000 for joint filers). If income exceeds the limit, the credit will decrease by $50 for every $1,000 that the AGI exceeds the limit.
- The child must have a valid Social Security number to qualify. ITINs and ATINs are not sufficient.

Example: Joshua and Anika are married and file jointly. They have one 10-year old child. Joshua has wages of $195,000. Anika does not work, but she has various profitable investments. Anika has interest and dividend income of $300,000. Their joint AGI is $495,000. They are not eligible to take the Child Tax Credit, because their joint AGI is above the phaseout threshold for joint filers ($400,000 is the phaseout).

Example: Eduardo files as head of household and has two minor children, ages 5 and 7. Both children qualify for the Child Tax Credit. His MAGI is $79,000, and after figuring his itemized deductions, his remaining tax liability is $4,680. Eduardo is eligible to take the full credit of $2,000 per child ($2,000 × 2 children = $4,000) because his MAGI is less than $200,000 and his tax liability is greater than $4,000. The credit will eliminate most of his remaining tax liability.

Taxpayers with income below certain threshold amounts can claim the Child Tax Credit for each qualifying child *under* the age of 17. In order to qualify for the Child Tax Credit, the taxpayer must have "earned income," such as wages or income from self-employment.

Note: Unlike the Child and Dependent Care Credit or Earned Income Credit, the Child Tax Credit is not affected by a child's disability. The main factor in determining a dependent's eligibility for the credit is the child's age.

A taxpayer whose tax liability is zero cannot take the Child Tax Credit because there is no tax to reduce. In addition, the Child Tax Credit is limited to the amounts of regular income tax and any alternative minimum tax owed. However, a taxpayer with zero tax liability may be able to take the *Additional* Child Tax Credit, (which is covered in the next section).

Qualifying Child for the Child Tax Credit: To be eligible to claim the Child Tax Credit, the taxpayer must have at least one qualifying child, and the child must meet the following tests:

- **Age Test:** The child must have been *younger* than 17 on December 31.
- **Relationship Test:** The child must be the taxpayer's child, stepchild, foster child, sibling, step-sibling, half-sibling, or a descendant of any of them. For example, a qualifying child could include grandchildren, nieces, and nephews. Adopted children always qualify as the taxpayer's own child.
- **Support Test:** The child must not provide more than half of their own support.

- **Dependency Test:** To receive the child tax credit, the taxpayer must claim the child as a dependent. If a noncustodial parent is eligible to claim the child as a dependent and meets all other qualifications, then they may claim the child tax credit for their child.
- **Joint Return Test:** The child cannot file a joint return for the year unless the only reason they are filing is to claim a refund, and otherwise the child would not have a tax liability.
- **Citizenship Test:** The child must be a U.S. citizen or U.S. resident alien with a valid Social Security Number. An ITIN or ATIN is not acceptable.
- **Residency Test:** In most cases, the child must have lived with the taxpayer for more than half of the year (over six months). Exceptions exist for temporary absences and children who are born or die within the year.[159]

Example: Viviana is unmarried and has a 16-year-old son, named Cesar. Viviana and Cesar do not have Social Security numbers, but both of them are U.S. residents for tax purposes. They both have valid ITINs. Viviana cannot claim the Child Tax Credit for Cesar, because a child must have an SSN that is valid for employment in order to qualify.
Example: William is unmarried and files head of household. William's son, Elijah, is a full-time student who turned 17 on the last day of the year: December 31, 2023. William and Elijah are both U.S. citizens and have valid Social Security numbers. Elijah is William's qualifying child. However, Elijah is not a qualifying person for the Child Tax Credit because he was not *under* age 17 at the end of the year.
Example: Lissette's adopted son, Myron, is 14. His adoption was finalized on November 1, 2023, but before that date, he lived with Lissette all year as her foster child. Myron is a U.S. citizen. Lissette provided all her son's support. Myron is a qualifying child for the Child Tax Credit because he was under age 17 at the end of the tax year; he meets the relationship requirement; he lived with Lissette for more than six months of the year, and he did not provide more than half of his own support.
Example: Victoria is a legal U.S. resident (a green card holder) and she has a valid Social Security number. Her two nieces, Rosalie, age 15, and Juana, age 16 live with Victoria all year long. The children do not have valid Social Security numbers, they only have ITINs. Victoria can claim her nieces as dependents, but she cannot claim the Child Tax Credit for either of them, because they do not have valid SSNs. She may be able to claim the Credit for Other Dependents for her nieces, instead.
Example: Adam and Esme recently emigrated to the U.S. They are married and plan to file jointly. They have two dependent children under the age of 10. Adam became a green card holder the prior year. He works full time and has a valid Social Security Number. Esme and the children have applied for permanent residency but their application is still pending with U.S. immigration (USCIS). As of January 1, 2024, Esme and the children only have ITINs. If Adam and Esme attempt to file their return early, they will not be able claim the Child Tax Credit, because Esme and the children do not have valid SSNs. Adam and Esme should consider extending their return. If Esme and the children receive valid Social Security numbers before the extended due date, they will qualify to claim the Child Tax Credit.

---

[159] Temporary absences include: school, vacation, medical care, military service, or incarceration in a juvenile facility. There are special rules for children of divorced or separated parents, as well as children of parents who never married. In some cases, the noncustodial parent may be entitled to claim the child as a dependent and thus the Child Tax Credit. In addition, there is an exception for an infant who is born during the tax year.

Additional Child Tax Credit (ACTC)

The Additional Child Tax Credit is the refundable component of the Child Tax Credit. In order to claim the Additional Child Tax Credit, a taxpayer must be able to claim the Child Tax Credit, even if the taxpayer does not qualify for full refundability.

Example: Mendel and Jada file jointly and have two children who qualify for the Child Tax Credit. Their MAGI is $47,000, and their tax liability is $954. They can offset the $954 in tax using the Child Tax Credit, reducing their tax to zero. Since their tax liability is zero, Mendel and Jada cannot claim the maximum Child Tax Credit of $2,000 per child, but they may be eligible for the Additional Child Tax Credit, which is a refundable credit.

Unlike the nonrefundable Child Tax Credit, the *Additional* Child Tax Credit is refundable, and it can produce a refund even if the taxpayer does not owe any tax. The additional child tax credit allows eligible taxpayers to claim up to $1,600 for each qualifying child in 2023. The ACTC is based on the *lesser* of:

- 15% of the taxpayer's taxable earned income that is over $2,500 or,
- The amount of unused Child Tax Credit (caused when the tax liability is less than the allowed Child Tax Credit)

Example: Maisie files as head of household and claims her 12-year-old daughter, Ruby, and her 9-year old son, Daniel, as dependents on her return. Maisie and her children are U.S. citizens and have valid Social Security numbers. Maisie's only income is from wages, from a part time job where she earns $19,900. She does not owe any income tax, because the standard deduction for her filing status exceeds her wages. Since she does not owe any income tax, she is not eligible for the *nonrefundable* Child Tax Credit. However, she is eligible for the *refundable*, Additional Child Tax Credit, which can produce a refund even if Maisie does not owe any tax. The maximum ACTC she can receive is $1,600 per child in 2023. Since she has two qualifying children, she would be eligible for a maximum credit of $3,200 ($1,600 × 2 children).

Note: A special rule that applies to the ACTC, but not to the CTC, states that a taxpayer that claims the foreign earned income exclusion, the foreign housing exclusion, or the foreign housing deduction on Form 2555, cannot claim the *refundable* Additional Child Tax Credit, but they can still qualify for a *nonrefundable* Child Tax Credit (up to the amount of income tax that they owe).

Schedule 8812 is used for figuring and reporting the Additional Child Tax Credit as well as the Child Tax Credit and the Credit for Other Dependents.

Credit for Other Dependents (ODC)

The $500 "Credit for Other Dependents" or "Other Dependent Credit" (ODC) applies to dependents who do not qualify for the Child Tax Credit, such as children who are over the age threshold or other dependents (such as elderly parents).

Taxpayers cannot claim the ODC credit for themselves or a spouse; in other words, the credit is only available for dependents who are listed on the return. The dependent must be a U.S citizen, U.S. national, or U.S. resident.

The AGI phaseout for the Credit for Other Dependents begins at $200,000 for unmarried taxpayers in 2023 and $400,000 for joint filers, with the credit being reduced by $50 for each $1,000 (or a portion thereof) above these thresholds

Example: Finlay and Hazel file a joint return and they both have valid SSNs. They have two qualifying dependents. Amber is their 22-year-old daughter. Amber is a full-time student, she has an SSN, and she meets the qualifying child test. Finlay's mother, Esther, is 75 years old, has a valid SSN, and meets the "qualifying relative" test. Amber and Esther are not qualifying dependents for the Child Tax Credit, because they are both over the age of 17, but they are qualifying dependents for the Credit for Other Dependents.

Example: Rosario's AGI in 2023 is $62,000. She financially supports her elderly father, Orlando, who is age 79, and her disabled cousin, Pedro, who is age 16. Orlando and Pedro live with Rosario in her home all year, and neither one has any taxable income. Rosario cannot claim the Child Tax Credit for Orlando, because Orlando is her father and over the age threshold for the Child Tax Credit. Pedro is not a qualifying child for the Child Tax Credit, because he is Rosario's cousin, which is not a qualifying relationship. Pedro and Orlando are both Rosario's **qualifying relatives**, and she can claim a $500 ODC for both of them.

To claim the Credit for Other Dependents, the dependent must have a valid identification number (ATIN, ITIN, or SSN) by the due date of the return (including extensions).

Adoption Credit

In 2023, a nonrefundable credit of up to $15,950 per child can be taken for qualified expenses paid to adopt a child. An eligible child must be under the age of 18 years of age, or physically or mentally disabled (regardless of age). Taxpayers who file MFS cannot claim the adoption credit.

For a special needs child, the maximum credit amount is allowed even if the taxpayer does not have any adoption expenses. If an employee receives employer-provided adoption benefits that are excluded from income, the employee may still be able to take the Adoption Credit. However, the exclusion and the credit cannot be claimed for the same expenses (i.e., no double-dipping allowed).

Unlike most other tax credits, the adoption credit has the same phaseout range for all filing statuses. The MAGI phaseout range in 2023 starts at $239,230 and ends at $279,230 for all filing statuses. If a taxpayer's MAGI is higher than $279,230 in 2023, they cannot claim the adoption credit. Although the adoption credit is nonrefundable, any unused credit may be carried forward for up to five years. Qualified adoption expenses must be directly related to the adoption of the child. Qualifying expenses may include:

- Attorney fees, adoption fees and court costs,
- Travel expenses related to the adoption, including meals and lodging,
- Costs of an unsuccessful adoption of a U.S. citizen or U.S. national,
- Re-adoption expenses to adopt a foreign child.

Unsuccessful Adoptions: A taxpayer who has attempted to adopt a child in the U.S. and been unsuccessful is still eligible for the adoption credit. Eligible expenses may include those related to unsuccessful attempts to adopt as well as an adoption attempt that is ultimately successful. However, if the eligible child is from a foreign country, the taxpayer cannot take the credit or exclusion unless the adoption becomes final. A foreign child is defined as a child who was not a citizen or resident of the United States at the time the adoption effort began. The credit is claimed on Form 8839, *Qualified Adoption Expenses*. Qualified expenses do *not* include: any illegal adoption expenses, any surrogate parenting arrangement, or the adoption of a spouse's child.

Example: Tabitha and Edison are married and file jointly. This year, Tabitha takes the necessary legal steps to adopt Layla, Edison's 16-year-old daughter from his previous marriage. The total cost for the adoption is $7,600, but unfortunately, none of these expenses can be deducted on their tax return. This is because the costs associated with adopting a spouse's child do not count as qualifying expenses for the purpose of the adoption credit.

Special Needs Adoptions

A taxpayer can claim the full credit for a special needs child regardless of actual expenses paid or incurred. For the purposes of this rule, a special-needs child must be a United States citizen or U.S. resident when the adoption begins.[160] Further, one of the following must apply:

- The state has determined the child cannot (or should not) be returned to the parents' home, or,
- The state has determined the child will not be adopted unless assistance is provided to the adoptive parents.

In making the determination about special needs, a state may take into account the following factors: a child's ethnic background and age; whether the child is a member of a minority or sibling group; and whether they have a physical, mental, or emotional handicap. The child does not have to be disabled for the child to qualify as "special needs."

Example: Olympia adopts two special-needs children from the U.S. foster care system in 2023. She incurs only $2,100 in adoption expenses; however, because both children are considered special needs, Olympia is allowed an adoption credit of $31,900 ($15,950 × 2 children).

Example: Esther is 62 and is employed full-time as an accountant, earning $159,000 per year. Three of her nieces were put into the U.S. foster care system because their mother (Esther's sister) was arrested and later incarcerated. Esther adopts her three nieces from foster care, and the government paid all the legal fees. All three children were considered endangered and receive monthly adoption assistance benefits from the government and thus are considered special needs. Esther is below the income limits for the credit, so she can claim the full adoption credit of $15,950 per child for a total of $47,850 in 2023. Any unused credit can be carried forward for 5 years.

Example: In 2023, Andrew and Noreen finalize the adoption of a disabled child from China. They pay $7,500 in expenses for the adoption, but they are only eligible to claim these actual expenses as a tax credit. Despite their child's disability, foreign adoptions do not qualify as special needs adoptions, for the purposes of the adoption credit. Their income tax liability for the year is $6,000 so the adoption credit will reduce their tax liability in 2023 to zero. They can carry forward any unused adoption credit ($1,500 carryover) for up to five years.

---

[160] With regards to foreign children, if the child is not a U.S. citizen or U.S. resident, they are not considered to be "special needs" for purposes of the adoption credit.

The Timing of the Payment: Adoption expenses are generally includible for the credit in the year the adoption becomes final, with a few exceptions.

- **Domestic adoptions:** With the adoption of a domestic child, qualified expenses paid before the year in which the adoption becomes final may be claimed in the year after the expenses were paid. This rule applies even if the adoption is unsuccessful.
- **Foreign adoptions:** For a foreign adoption, expenses paid before or during the adoptive process are only includible for the credit once the adoption actually becomes final.
- **Post-adoption expenses:** Any additional expenses paid after an adoption becomes final (for example, additional legal fees related to the adoption) are included in the tax credit calculation in the year paid, regardless of whether the adoption was foreign or domestic.

Example #1 (domestic adoption): Alicia is going through the process of adopting a 3-year-old child named Lorena from the U.S. foster system. The child is a U.S. citizen and was legally placed in her home. Alicia's AGI is $89,000 for the year. The adoption process takes 3 years. Alicia pays legal fees related to the adoption of $3,000 in 2022, $4,200 in 2023, and $5,000 in 2024. On February 1, 2024, Lorena's adoption becomes final. The $3,000 of expenses she paid in 2022 are includible for the credit in 2023 (the year after the year the costs were incurred) and may be claimed towards the credit on Alicia's 2023 tax return. Since the adoption became final in 2024, Alicia can claim both the $4,200 she paid in 2023 and the $5,000 she paid in 2024 as a credit on her 2024 tax return.

Example #2 (foreign adoption): Veronica and Charles are attempting to adopt a foreign child named Manuel, who is 4 years old and a citizen of Colombia. The couple pays qualified adoption expenses of $4,000 in 2022, $6,000 in 2023, and $2,000 in 2024. On January 27, 2024, the adoption becomes final. Veronica and Charles may claim all $12,000 in qualified adoption expenses ($4,000 paid in 2022, $6,000 paid in 2023, and $2,000 in 2024) on their 2024 tax return, because it is a foreign adoption, and 2024 is the year in which the adoption became final.[161]

Education Credits

Two education credits are available based on qualified expenses a taxpayer pays for post-secondary education:

- **American Opportunity Tax Credit (also called the AOC or AOTC)**
- **Lifetime Learning Credit**

There are general guidelines that apply to both types of credits, as well as specific rules for each one. A taxpayer can receive education credits for themselves, their spouse, and any dependents who attended an eligible educational institution during the previous tax year.

Eligible institutions include colleges, universities, vocational schools, and community colleges. Payments made in advance for an academic term beginning within the first three months of the next calendar year can also be claimed.

---

[161] Examples modified from scenarios in IRS Tax Topic 607, Adoption Credit at: https://www.irs.gov/taxtopics/tc607.

Example: Fahad is 25 years old and single. On December 28, 2023, he prepaid $2,800 for his college tuition for the spring semester that begins on January 9, 2024. Fahad can use the $2,800 of educational expenses towards an education credit on his 2023 return (in the year he actually *paid* the costs), even though he will not start college until 2024.

Education credits are not available to those who: can be claimed as a dependent on another person's tax return, file separately as married individuals (MFS), or have an income that exceeds the phaseout limits. In 2023, these limits are between $80,000 and $90,000 for unmarried individuals, and $160,000 and $180,000 for married couples who file jointly. Additionally, individuals with a nonresident alien spouse are not eligible for education credits.[162]

Example: Natalia, age 52, has a 21-year-old son named Raul who is a college student. Natalia and Raul do not have enough money to pay for Raul's college tuition. As a gift, Raul's grandmother pays his $4,500 in tuition costs directly to the college. For purposes of claiming an education credit, either Natalia or Raul can be treated as receiving the gifted money, and paying for the qualified tuition and related expenses. If Natalia claims Raul as a dependent, she can claim an education credit. Alternatively, if Raul's mother does not claim him as a dependent, he can claim the credit.[163]

A taxpayer cannot claim both the American Opportunity Credit and the Lifetime Learning Credit for the *same* student in one year. However, if a taxpayer incurs education expenses for *multiple* students, the taxpayer may be eligible to take the American Opportunity Credit for one student and the Lifetime Learning Credit for another student on the same tax return.

Example: Armando is 49 and pays college expenses for himself and his dependent daughter, Sarah, age 18. Armando is attending graduate school to earn his doctorate degree. Armando qualifies for the Lifetime Learning Credit. Sarah is an undergraduate student in her first year of college. She qualifies for the American Opportunity Credit. Armando can take both credits on his tax return for each eligible student—Sarah and himself.

Form 8863, *Education Credits,* is used to figure and claim both education credits. Qualified education expenses include: tuition and related fees, required textbooks and other course materials required as a condition of enrollment. Any course involving sports, games, or hobbies is not a qualifying expense *unless* the course is part of the student's degree program (or if taken to improve job skills, in the case of the Lifetime Learning Credit).

Qualified education expenses must be reduced by the amount of any tax-free educational assistance received, such as Pell grants, tax-free portions of scholarships, and employer-provided educational assistance.

Example: Casper is age 26 and an Air Force veteran who receives the GI Bill. His total college tuition and textbooks cost $8,900 for the year. He receives $4,000 of his GI Bill to help cover his tuition. He also receives a gift of $1,900 from his mother to help pay for his textbooks. Casper's qualified higher education expenses for the purposes of calculating an education credit are $4,900 ($8,900 - $4,000) because his veterans' assistance benefits must be subtracted. The gift from his mother does not have to be subtracted.

---

[162] This rule does not apply if the nonresident spouse elects to be treated as a U.S. resident alien for tax purposes.
[163] Example from Publication 4491, under the section for "education expenses."

Certain college expenses cannot be used to claim an education credit, such as: the cost of room and board (even if on-campus housing is required by the college), medical fees (including student health fees), insurance expenses, transportation costs (like bus fare or on-campus parking fees), and any other personal, living, or family expenses. Tuition expenses are reported to the student on Form 1098-T, *Tuition Statement*, issued by the school.

Example: Blakely is an undergraduate student attending Chico State University in California. She received Form 1098-T, *Tuition Statement*. It shows that her tuition was $8,100 and that she received a $1,500 tax-free scholarship. She also paid an additional $800 for required textbooks, which was not reported on the Form 1098-T. Blakely's maximum qualifying expenses for an education credit is $7,400 ([$8,100 + $800] - $1,500 scholarship).

Example: Everly is 27 years old and single. She is a graduate student attending Fayetteville State University, NC. She paid $9,200 for tuition and $7,000 for room and board at the university. She was awarded a $5,000 tax-free tuition scholarship. She also applied for a $4,000 student loan. To qualify for an education credit, she must first subtract the tax-free scholarship from her tuition, her only qualified expense. Everly has $4,200 of qualified educational expenses ($9,200 tuition - $5,000 scholarship). The student loan is not considered in this calculation, because it must be paid back.

American Opportunity Tax Credit (AOTC)

The American Opportunity Tax Credit (also referred to as the AOTC or AOC) allows taxpayers to claim a maximum credit of up to $2,500 for each eligible student. The credit covers 100% of the first $2,000 and 25% of the second $2,000 of eligible expenses per student. Qualified expenses include tuition and required fees, books, supplies, equipment, and other *required* course materials (but *not* room and board or student health fees).

Example: Efren is a junior in college studying to be a mechanic. He pays $6,500 in tuition to his college. This year, in addition to tuition, he pays a $550 fee to the school for the rental of the automotive equipment he is required to use in his training program. Efren's equipment rental fee is also a qualified education expense.

The American Opportunity Tax Credit has a refundable portion. Up to 40% of the credit can be refunded, allowing taxpayers to receive a maximum of $1,000 even if they do not owe any tax. To qualify for the AOTC, students must meet these requirements:

- **Degree requirement:** The student must be enrolled in a program that leads to a degree, certificate, or other recognized educational credential. Taking classes merely for recreation or personal interest will not qualify.
- **Minimum course load:** The student must be enrolled at least half-time for at least one academic period beginning in the tax year.
- **No felony drug conviction:** The student cannot have any felony convictions for possessing or distributing a controlled substance.
- **Four years of postsecondary education:** The credit can be claimed only for expenses related to a student's post-secondary education and only for a maximum of four years.

Example: Celeste has not yet completed her first bachelor's degree, but it took her five years to get all the credits she needed to graduate. She expects to graduate with her bachelor's degree on December 19, 2023. Celeste properly claimed the American Opportunity Tax Credit in 2019, 2020, 2021, and 2022. Since the credit has already been claimed for the first four years of her undergraduate education, she cannot claim the AOTC on her 2023 return. She may be able to claim the nonrefundable Lifetime Learning Credit for the tuition costs that she incurred in 2023.

For 2023, the AOTC phases for unmarried taxpayers with MAGIs between $80,000 and $90,000 ($160,000 and $180,000 for MFJ). Taxpayers who file MFS cannot claim the credit.

Example: Bella, age 26, and Callen, age 33, are married and always file jointly. Bella is a full-time student working towards her first bachelor's degree. Bella incurs $13,000 in qualifying tuition expenses during the year. Callen works full time and has $220,000 of taxable income. Their joint AGI is over $180,000, so they cannot claim the American Opportunity Credit. They are phased-out because of their high income level.

Note: Taxpayers claiming the American Opportunity Credit must have a valid taxpayer identification number by the due date of the tax return (including extensions). Further, the student claimed for the credit must also have a valid identification number by the due date (including extensions). Taxpayers *cannot* file an amended return to claim the credit for a year that the taxpayer and/or student did not originally have a valid identification number by the return due date.

If a student does not meet all the conditions for the American Opportunity Tax Credit, the student may still qualify to take the Lifetime Learning Credit.

Lifetime Learning Credit

The Lifetime Learning Credit is a nonrefundable tax credit of 20% of qualified tuition, fees, and any amounts paid directly to the educational institution for required books, supplies, and equipment, up to $10,000, paid during the tax year. The maximum credit is $2,000 per *tax return,* not *per student.* A family's maximum credit is the same regardless of the number of qualified students. The Lifetime Learning Credit is phased out at $80,000-$90,000 for unmarried filers and $160,000–$180,000 for joint filers. Taxpayers who file Married Filing Separately cannot take the credit. The requirements for the Lifetime Learning Credit differ from those for the AOTC as follows:

- **No degree or workload requirement:** There are no specific degree or workload requirements for eligibility. Part-time students can also qualify, and non-degree courses are eligible. A student who is taking a course merely to enhance their job skills is eligible.

- **All levels of postsecondary education:** A student may be an undergraduate, graduate, or professional degree candidate. The courses can also be just for professional development.

- **An unlimited number of years:** There is no limit on the number of years for which the credit can be claimed for each student.

- **Felony drug convictions permissible:** A student can be convicted for a felony drug conviction and still qualify.

Example: Brent attends Creek Community College after spending twelve months in prison for a felony cocaine conviction. He paid $4,400 for the course of study, which included tuition, equipment, and books required for the course. The school requires that students pay for books and equipment when registering for courses. The entire $4,400 is an eligible education expense under the Lifetime Learning Credit. Although he meets all the other requirements for the American Opportunity Credit, Brent does not qualify for the AOTC because he has a felony drug conviction. He may claim the Lifetime Learning Credit instead.

Example: Karina works full-time as a paralegal at a lawyer's office. She takes a few night courses at a local junior college. Some of the courses are not for credit, but she is taking them to advance her career. She is not pursuing a degree. The education expenses may qualify for the Lifetime Learning Credit, but not for the American Opportunity Credit, because the Lifetime Learning Credit does not have a degree requirement.

Earned Income Tax Credit (EITC)

The Earned Income Tax Credit (EITC), also commonly known as the Earned Income Credit (EIC), is a refundable tax credit for lower-income people who work and have earned income and adjusted gross income under certain thresholds. Taxpayers who claim EITC must have valid Social Security numbers by the due date of the return (including extensions).[164] Refunds for taxpayers claiming the EIC will not be issued prior to February 15.

There are strict rules[165] and income guidelines for the EITC. To claim the EITC, a taxpayer must meet all of the following tests:

- Have a Social Security number that is valid for employment.
- Have "earned income" from wages, combat pay, or self-employment, etc.
- Investment income must also be $11,000 or less for the year for 2023 (this figure is now indexed for inflation every year). Investment income includes: interest payments, dividends, capital gains and passive rental income.
- Not be claimed as a dependent by another taxpayer,
- Be a U.S. citizen or legal resident all year (a nonresident alien married to a U.S. citizen or resident alien filing jointly can still qualify under some narrow circumstances).
- Cannot file Form 2555 (related to the foreign earned income exclusion).

Example: Amadeo is a U.S. citizen with a valid Social Security number. He claims his 18-year old daughter, Cassandra, as his dependent. His daughter is a full time student and a qualifying child for EITC. Amadeo also qualifies for head of household filing status. In 2023, he received $39,500 in interest and dividends for the year. Amadeo does not work, and he relies on his investments as his main source of income. Amadeo would not qualify for the EITC because he does not have any earned income. Also, his investment income exceeds the maximum limits set for the EITC.

---

[164] Taxpayers cannot file an amended return to *retroactively* claim EIC for any year in which they did not have a valid Social Security number by the due date of the return (including extensions).

[165] Among the EITC rules is a requirement that practitioners make reasonable inquiries to determine that the information the taxpayer is giving is correct. We cover the due diligence for the EITC, CTC, and other credits in Book 3, *Representation*.

Earned Income and AGI Limits

The amount of the credit varies based on a taxpayer's earnings and how many children are claimed as dependents on the return. Both a taxpayer's earned income and their AGI must be *less* than the following limits:

2023 Income limits for EITC		
Children Claimed	**Maximum AGI (MFJ filers)**	**Maximum AGI (All other filing statuses)**
Zero ("childless EITC")	$24,210	$17,640
One	$53,120	$46,560
Two	$59,478	$52,918
Three or more	$63,398	$56,838

2023 maximum amount of the EITC:

- No qualifying children (i.e., the "childless EITC"): $600
- 1 qualifying child: $3,995
- 2 qualifying children: $6,604
- 3 or more qualifying children: $7,430
- Taxpayers whose investment income is more than $11,000 in 2023 cannot claim EITC.

Example: Seren and Gilroy are married and their joint AGI is $59,900 in 2023. Normally, they would not qualify for EITC because of their income level. However, Seren becomes pregnant at the beginning of the year, and gives birth to triplets on December 30, 2023. Now Seren and Gilroy have 3 children. They qualify to claim EITC in 2023, because their AGI is now below the threshold for taxpayers with *three or more* qualifying children.

Example: Chelsea is unmarried and age 32. She has one 7-year-old child and files as head of household. She earns $14,900 in wages during 2023. Her wages would normally qualify her for the Earned Income Tax Credit, but she also has $11,450 of investment income during the year, from a rental property that she inherited from her grandmother. A taxpayer with $11,000 or more of investment income in 2023 does not qualify for the EITC, regardless of their earnings, so Chelsea would not qualify for EITC.

Qualifying Income for the EITC: Only "earned" income, such as: wages, tips, combat pay, union strike benefits, and net earnings from self-employment qualifies for the EITC. For EITC purposes, "earned income" does not include the following income:

- Social Security benefits, Supplemental Security Income (SSI), or welfare payments,
- Alimony (even if taxable to the recipient) or child support,
- Pensions or annuities,[166]
- Unemployment benefits,
- Inmate wages, including work release programs,
- Income from investments, passive rental activities, or other passive sources.

---

[166] Although uncommon, some disability retirement benefits qualify as earned income to claim the EITC.

Income that is excluded from tax is generally not considered earned income for the EITC. Nontaxable combat pay and qualified Medicare waiver payments are a notable exception. A taxpayer can choose to include this nontaxable pay in their earned income if it gives them a better tax result.

> **Example:** Roshan and Mandy are married and file jointly. They are both age 27. Mandy does not work; she stays home and takes care of their 2-year old daughter. Roshan is active-duty military, and served in a combat zone the entire year. He earned $36,900, which can all be excluded as combat pay. They have no other income. Military personnel have the option of treating excludable combat pay as earned income for purposes of the EITC. Roshan and Mandy elect to file a return, claiming their daughter, and treating Roshan's nontaxable combat pay as earned income to qualify for the Earned Income Tax Credit. In addition to the EITC, they will also qualify for the refundable Additional Child Tax Credit. This will produce a nice refund for them.

Qualifying Children for EITC Purposes

The definition of a "qualifying child" for purposes of the EITC is stricter than it is for being able to claim someone as a dependent. The taxpayer's qualifying child must meet <u>all</u> the following tests:

- **Relationship test**
- **Age test**
- **Joint return test**
- **Residency test**

Relationship Test: The child must be related to the taxpayer in one of the following ways:

- Son, daughter, stepchild, eligible foster child, adopted child, or descendant of any of them (for example, a grandchild), or
- Brother, sister, half-brother, half-sister, stepbrother, stepsister, or descendant of any of them (for example, a niece or nephew).

> **Example:** Ronan is 37 and financially supports his younger sister, Genevieve, who is age 16 and still in high school. Ronan has taken care of his sister since their parents died three years ago. She lives with him all year. Ronan earns $31,900 in wages. Ronan can file as head of household, and Genevieve is Ronan's qualifying child. He is eligible for the Earned Income Tax Credit.

> **Example:** Barbara's niece, Aimee, is 22 and attending college full time. Aimee lives with Barbara all year. Barbara made $30,400 in wages in 2023 and is filing as Head of Household. She is claiming Aimee as her dependent. Aimee meets the rules for a qualifying child. Barbara can claim the EITC.

Any qualifying child listed on Schedule EIC also must have a valid SSN. An ITIN or an ATIN is not sufficient for EITC purposes, although in some situations, the parents may still qualify for EITC even if their child does not have an SSN.

> **Note:** Taxpayers who have valid Social Security numbers can claim the EITC, even if their children do not have SSNs. In this instance, they would get the smaller credit available to taxpayers without children (the "childless EITC"). In the past, these filers did not qualify for the credit.

Example: Lupita is a legal U.S. resident with a valid green card. She has an SSN that is valid for employment. She earned $14,900 in wages in 2023. Lupita's nephew, Mateo, is 18 years old and has lived with his aunt all year. Mateo is a citizen of Mexico and does not have a valid SSN, but he does qualify as a U.S. resident for tax purposes, because he meets the substantial presence test. Mateo has lived with his aunt continuously since his parents died two years ago, but he only has an ITIN. Lupita may claim Mateo as a dependent on her tax return, and also claim the EITC for herself. Lupita will qualify for the smaller "childless EITC," because Mateo is not a qualifying child for EITC purposes.

A foster child can also be an eligible child for EITC purposes. The child must be placed in the taxpayer's home by an authorized placement agency or by the courts in order to be eligible.

Age Test: To qualify for the EITC, the child must be:

- Age 18 or younger,
- A full-time student, age 23 or younger, or
- Any age, if permanently disabled.

In addition, a qualifying child must be younger than the taxpayer claiming them, *unless* the child (dependent) is permanently disabled.

Example: Harriet, 40 years old, has never been married and made $40,400 in wages for the year. Her brother Chester, who is 50 and also unmarried, has lived with her since their parents passed away a decade ago. Chester has Down's syndrome and earns $9,100 working in a sheltered workshop for disabled workers. This income does not count towards Chester's gross income when determining dependency. Despite being older than Harriet, and due to his disability, Chester is Harriet's qualifying child (not qualifying relative). Harriet can claim Chester as her dependent and file as head of household. She is eligible for EITC.

Joint Return Test: The qualifying child (dependent) cannot file a joint return with a spouse, except to claim a refund.

Example: Todd and Sophie are both 18 years old and got married right out of high school. They both live with Clara, Todd's mother. Clara supports the young couple and they live in her home. Todd only had $3,010 of wage income from a part-time job. Neither Todd or Sophie are required to file a tax return. Taxes were taken out of Todd's wages, so Todd and Sophie file a joint return only to get a refund of the income taxes withheld. The exception to the joint return test applies, so Clara may claim her son and daughter-in-law as her qualifying children, if all the other tests are met.

Residency Test: The child must have <u>lived with</u> the taxpayer in the United States for more than half the year (although there are exceptions to this test for temporary absences).[167] Only a custodial parent can claim the EITC (or, in the case of another family member that claims the child, the child must have lived with that family member for more than half the year). A child who was born or died during the year would meet the residency test for the entire year if the child lived with the taxpayer the time the child was alive.

---

[167] For purposes of the EITC, U.S. military personnel stationed outside the United States on extended active duty are considered to live in the U.S. during that duty period, so their children meet the residency test. There are also exceptions for temporary absences, including: college attendance, vacations, military service, and detention in a juvenile facility.

Example: Catherine gave birth to a baby girl on March 3, 2023. The infant was born sickly and died two months later. The child is still a qualifying child for purposes of the EITC because she meets the other tests for age and relationship.

Example: Cassidy has one son, named Kiernan, who is age 18 and attending college full-time in another state. Cassidy provides all her son's financial support and pays for his tuition. Kiernan lives in the on-campus dorms and only comes home for the holidays. Cassidy can claim Kiernan as her qualifying child, and file as head of household. He meets the residency test for EITC purposes because college attendance is considered a temporary absence.

"**Childless EITC**": A taxpayer with a qualifying child can claim the EITC without any age limitations, but a taxpayer *without* a child can only claim the EITC if all of the following tests are met:

- Must be between the age of 25 and 65. On a joint return, only one spouse must meet the age requirement.
- Must not qualify as a dependent of another person,
- Must live in the United States for more than half the year,
- Cannot file Form 2555 (related to the foreign earned income exclusion).[168]

Example: Cornelius is 23 years old. He moved out of his parents' home three years ago, and now lives in his own apartment. He is unmarried and provides all his own financial support. He is not a student and has no dependents. In 2023, Cornelius earns $16,000 in wages working in a restaurant. He has no other income. Even though his income is below the threshold to claim EITC, Cornelius is not eligible for the credit because he is under the age of 25, and therefore does not meet the age requirement for the "childless EITC."

Example: Ruth and Alfred are married and file jointly. They do not have any dependents. Alfred is 67 and Ruth is 60 years old. Ruth works as a church secretary in 2023, earning $16,500 in wages. Alfred has a small amount of Social Security income, $3,900, in 2023. All of Ruth's and Alfred's children are grown up and they do not have any dependents. Based on their joint AGI, Ruth and Alfred are eligible for the "childless EITC" in 2023. If all other rules are met, they would qualify for the EITC, because for a couple filing a joint return, only one taxpayer has to meet the age requirement, and Ruth is under the age of 65, so they qualify.

EITC Fraud and Penalties: If the IRS audits a taxpayer's return and disallows all or part of the EITC, the taxpayer:

- Must pay back the amount in error with interest,
- May need to file Form 8862, *Information to Claim Earned Income Credit after Disallowance*,
- Cannot claim the EITC for the next <u>two years</u> if the IRS determines the error is because of reckless or intentional disregard of the rules, or
- Cannot claim the EITC for the next <u>ten years</u> if the IRS determines the error is because of fraud.

---

[168] The mere act of *earning* foreign income would not automatically disqualify a taxpayer from claiming EITC. A taxpayer who elects not to exclude foreign income from their gross income may still be eligible for the EITC.

Retirement Savings Contributions Credit (Saver's Credit)

The credit is 10%–50% of eligible contributions to IRAs and other qualifying retirement plans up to a maximum credit of $1,000 ($2,000 MFJ), depending on a taxpayer's adjusted gross income. Eligible contributions must be made to an IRA or an employer-sponsored retirement plan.[169]

ABLE account designated beneficiaries may be eligible to claim the Saver's Credit for a percentage of their contributions. The amount of the credit is the eligible contribution multiplied by the applicable credit rate, which is based on filing status and AGI.

> **Note:** On past exams, the IRS has referred to this credit as either the "Retirement Savings Contributions Credit" or the "Saver's Credit." Either term may be used on the EA exam, since both terms are currently used on the IRS website as well as IRS publications. Do not be confused by this—they are the same credit.

To be eligible for this credit, the taxpayer must fulfill all the following requirements:

1. Be at least age 18 or older;
2. Not be a full-time student; and
3. Not claimed as a dependent on another person's return.

The income limitations in 2023 are as follows:

2023 Retirement Savings Contribution Credit Phaseouts			
Credit Rate	MFJ	HOH	Single, QSS, MFS
50% of the contribution	AGI not more than $43,500	AGI not more than $32,625	AGI not more than $21,750
20% of the contribution	$43,501- $47,500	$32,626 - $35,625	$21,751 - $23,750
10% of the contribution	$47,501 - $73,000	$35,626 - $54,750	$23,751 - $36,500
No Credit Allowed	more than $73,000	more than $54,750	more than $36,500

Most workers who contribute to traditional IRAs already deduct all or part of their contributions. The Saver's Credit is *in addition* to these deductions. In essence, a taxpayer could potentially deduct their contribution to a traditional IRA, and then also receive the Saver's Credit in the same year.

> **Example:** Paisley works at a restaurant. She is married and earned $41,000 in 2023. Paisley's spouse, David, is disabled and did not have any earnings. Paisley contributed $2,000 to her IRA for 2023. After deducting her traditional IRA contribution, the adjusted gross income shown on her joint return is $39,000. Paisley may claim the maximum 50% Saver's Credit of $1,000 for her $2,000 IRA contribution on her 2023 tax return.

> **Example:** Alonzo is 24 and earns $39,500 during the year. He is single and contributes $3,000 to his 401(k) plan at work. Alonzo is not eligible for the credit because his income exceeds the threshold limit for single filers.

---

[169] Eligible contributions include those to both traditional IRAs and Roth IRAs, elective deferrals to 401(k) or other qualified employer-sponsored retirement plans, and voluntary employee contributions to other qualified retirement plans.

Example: Edith works at a grocery store. She is married and earned $36,000 in wages during 2023. Edith's husband, Anthony is on a religious sabbatical and didn't have any earnings for the year. Edith contributed $1,000 to her traditional IRA in 2023. After deducting her IRA contribution, the adjusted gross income shown on their joint return is $35,000. Edith may claim a 50% Retirement Savings Contribution Credit, or $500, for her $1,000 IRA contribution.

Example: Rory works as a cashier at a retail store. He is married and earned $31,000 in wages during the year. Rory's wife, Natasha, has a part-time job at a pet food store. She earned $8,000 in wages. Their combined wage income is $39,000 ($31,000 + $8,000) *before* making any IRA contributions. Rory contributes $1,000 to his traditional IRA for 2023, and Natasha contributes $1,000 to her IRA. After deducting their IRA contributions, their adjusted gross income is $37,000 ($39,000 wages - $2,000 IRA contributions). Rory and Natasha may claim a 50% Saver's Credit ($2,000 contributions × 50% = $1,000 credit). Their allowable credit is $1,000 on their jointly-filed return.

However, when figuring the credit, taxpayers generally must subtract the amount of *distributions* received from their retirement plans:

- In the two years before the year the credit is claimed;
- The year the credit is claimed; and
- The period after the end of the credit year but before the due date, including extensions, for filing the return for the credit year.

Also, note that foreign income cannot be included in the taxpayer's adjusted gross income for the purposes of calculating this credit. This credit is claimed on Form 8880, *Credit for Qualified Retirement Savings Contributions*.

Credit for Excess Social Security and RRTA Tax Withheld

This credit is for workers who overpay their tax for Social Security, which usually happens when an employee is working two jobs, and both employers withhold Social Security tax. Each year, a limit is set as to how much Social Security tax an individual should have withheld from his earnings.

If the taxpayer's withholding for Social Security tax exceeds the annual maximum, the taxpayer can request a refund of the excess amount (the maximum earnings subject to Social Security tax is $160,200 in 2023). This also applies to overpaid Railroad Retirement taxes. This credit is fully refundable. If a *single* employer overwithheld too much social security (or RRTA tax), that is the employer's error and the employer should adjust the excess for the employee.

Example: Zachary is a medical doctor. In 2023, he works for two different hospitals as an employee. His first employer pays him $120,000 in wages during the year. The second hospital pays him $50,000. His total wages were $170,000, and the entire amount was subject to Social Security tax, because each of his employers is required by law to withhold Social Security tax from the entire amount. His total wages for the year exceed the 2023 Social Security contribution limit of $160,200. When Zachary files his tax return, his overpayment of Social Security tax is calculated automatically by his software, by adding up the combined Social Security tax withheld from all his wages. He will receive a credit for any overwithheld amounts.

If a *single* employer refuses to refund the over-collection, the employee can file a claim for refund using Form 843, *Claim for Refund and Request for Abatement.*

Example: Grover works for a large corporation. He typically earns a $175,000 salary. In the middle of the year, he is transferred to a new location, and the human resources department accidentally registers him as a new employee, rather than a transferred employee. As a result, Grover gets two Form W-2's from the same employer. Both his W-2 forms show withheld Social Security taxes. He doesn't notice the issue until late April, and when he contacts his employer for a refund of the excess FICA taxes withheld, the company refuses to correct the issue, saying that it is too late. Since Grover's employer would not correct the error, he can file Form 843 with the IRS to claim a refund, along with copies of his two Form W-2s.

Unit 13: Study Questions

(Test yourself first; then check the correct answers at the end of this quiz.)

1. Which of the following individuals would be a qualifying child for the Child Tax Credit?

A. A 17-year-old dependent who is a full-time student.
B. A six-year-old nephew who lived with the taxpayer for nine months.
C. A step-brother who is 21 years old and disabled.
D. A foster child who has lived with the taxpayer for four months.

2. Orlando is a senior in college studying to be an optometrist. Which of the following expenses is a qualifying expense for the American Opportunity Tax Credit?

A. Mandatory equipment rental
B. Student health fees
C. Room and board
D. A physical education course unrelated to his program

3. Lizzie adopted two children from Korea. Both foreign adoptions became final in 2023. She incurred $42,000 in legal, travel, and agency fees. How much can Lizzie claim in 2023 as an adoption credit?

A. $0
B. $15,950
C. $31,900
D. $42,000

4. Karen has three children, ages 10, 18, and 19. All the children live with her, are full-time students, and claimed as dependents on her tax return. Karen's AGI is $165,000 in 2023 and she files as head of household. Her tax liability before the application of any credits is $8,900. What is the maximum Child Tax Credit she can claim on her 2023 tax return?

A. $0
B. $2,000
C. $4,000
D. $6,000

5. Which of the following expenses is not a qualified expense for purposes of the Adoption Credit?

A. Court costs.
B. Re-adoption expenses to adopt a foreign child.
C. Attorney fees for a surrogate arrangement.
D. Travel expenses.

6. Sienna is 30 and unmarried. Sienna earned $22,900 in wages in 2023. She also has qualified dividends of $4,750. She contributed $1,000 into her traditional IRA during the year. She has a valid Social Security number. She does not have any dependents and no other income for the year. Which of the following credits may she qualify for in 2023?

A. Earned Income Tax Credit
B. Child Tax Credit
C. Credit for Other Dependents
D. Retirement Savings Contribution Credit

7. In 2023, Sebastian and Hannah adopt a special-needs infant from a private adoption agency in another state. The child is a U.S. citizen with a valid SSN. Their adoption expenses are $7,000, and their travel expenses related to the adoption are $1,200, which was the cost of their flights. What is their maximum Adoption Credit?

A. $0
B. $7,000
C. $8,200
D. $15,950

8. All of the listed expenses are eligible for the Lifetime Learning Credit except:

A. Required books.
B. Childcare in order to attend class.
C. Tuition.
D. Required fees.

9. William is 53 and unmarried. William's half-brother, Felix, turned 16 on June 30, 2023. Felix lived with William all year, and he is a U.S. citizen. William claimed Felix as a dependent on his return. Which of the following statements is correct?

A. Felix is a qualifying child for the Child Tax Credit.
B. Felix is not a qualifying child for the Child Tax Credit, because he is a sibling.
C. Felix is not a qualifying child for the Child Tax Credit because siblings do not qualify.
D. Felix only qualifies for the Child Tax Credit if he is a full-time student.

10. The American Opportunity Credit has a maximum credit of up to _____.

A. $2,000 credit per eligible student.
B. $2,500 credit per eligible student.
C. $2,500 credit per tax return.
D. $4,000 credit per eligible student.

11. Rocco has three kids in college. They are all his dependents:

- Patricia, age 22, a college sophomore working on her first bachelor's degree.
- Marico, age 19, a college freshman working on his first bachelor's degree.
- Kasha, age 23, a graduate student, working on her first master's degree. Kasha had a four-year bachelor's degree from the same college.

Based on the above scenario, what is the maximum amount of American Opportunity Tax Credits (AOTC) Rocco can claim on his tax return?

A. $2,500
B. $4,500
C. $5,000
D. $7,500

12. Danika and Ralph are divorced. They have one child together, Amelie, age 15, who lives with Danika. Amelie is a full-time student at a private high school. All are U.S. citizens and have SSNs. Together, Danika and Ralph provide more than half of Amelie's support, including $10,000 in tuition expenses for Amelie's private school. Danika's AGI is $31,000, and Ralph's AGI is $39,000. Ralph is the noncustodial parent, but Danika signs Form 8332, giving Ralph the right to claim Amelie on his tax return. Based on this information, which credit might Ralph qualify for if he claims his daughter as a dependent?

A. Child Tax Credit
B. Adoption Credit.
C. Earned Income Tax Credit.
D. American Opportunity Credit.

13. Edwin is a bookkeeper working for a construction firm as an employee. He takes an accounting course at the local community college to improve his bookkeeping skills. Edwin is not a degree candidate. Which educational credit does he qualify for?

A. American Opportunity Credit
B. College Saver's Credit
C. Lifetime Learning Credit
D. General Education Credit

14 Aaron pays for daycare costs for the following individuals so he can work. Each is a qualifying individual for purposes of the Child and Dependent Care Credit *except*:

A. Aaron's wife, Lilly, who is completely disabled.
B. Aaron's son, Cameron, age 14, who is a student, and not disabled.
C. Aaron's nephew, Andy, age 10, who is also his dependent.
D. Aaron's mother, Polly, who is 72, and is permanently disabled.

15. Donald is 50 and widowed. Four people live with Donald. Donald provides all of their financial support, and all of them qualify as Donald's dependents.

- Tania, who is 17 years old and Donald's niece. Tania has an ITIN.
- Chester, who is Donald's 85-year old father. Chester has an SSN and is disabled.
- Dwight, who is Donald's 22-year-old step-son, who has an SSN and attends college full time.
- Dawn, who is Donald's 18-year-old cousin. Dawn has an SSN and is still in high school.

Which of them are qualifying children for Earned Income Tax Credit purposes?

A. Tania
B. Chester
C. Dwight
D. Dawn

16. Zahir has two children who are attending graduate school. His wife, Elmeria, also attends a graduate program at a local university. Zahir and his wife file jointly. What is the maximum amount of the Lifetime Learning Credit that Zahir and Elmeria can claim on their joint return?

A. $2,000
B. $2,500
C. $4,000
D. $6,000

17. Which of the following education tax benefits listed below is partially refundable?

A. Coverdell Education Savings Account
B. American Opportunity Credit
C. Lifetime Learning Credit
D. Student Loan Interest Deduction

18. For purposes of the EITC, which of the following types of income is considered "earned" income?

A. Taxable alimony
B. Interest and dividends
C. Capital gains
D. Household employee income

19. Which of the following individuals is eligible for the American Opportunity Tax Credit?

A. Garrett, who is enrolled full-time as a graduate student pursuing a master's degree in biology.
B. Lucy, who is taking a ceramics class at a community college for fun.
C. Willie, a full-time undergraduate student, who was convicted of a felony for selling cocaine.
D. Bethany, a college freshman pursuing an undergraduate degree in computer science, and who attended classes half-time the entire school year.

20. Which Schedule is required to calculate the Additional Child Tax Credit?

A. Schedule 8812
B. Schedule EIC
C. Schedule 8862
D. Schedule J

21. Generally, which is most beneficial to taxpayers when it comes to reducing income tax liability: a nonrefundable credit, a refundable credit, or a deduction?

A. A nonrefundable tax credit.
B. A refundable tax credit.
C. A tax deduction.
D. All are equally beneficial in reducing income tax liability.

22. All of the following are qualified expenses for purposes of the Child and Dependent Care Credit except:

A. $500 payment to a grandparent for child care while the taxpayer is employed.
B. $300 payment to a daycare center while the taxpayer is looking for employment.
C. $500 child care expense while the taxpayer obtains emergency medical care.
D. $600 adult daycare expense for a disabled spouse while the taxpayer works.

23. Wynona is 25 and attends college full-time, pursuing an undergraduate degree in architecture. Because she changed majors in her junior year, she is now in her fifth year of college. She received a $4,000 Pell grant for 2023, and her parents have claimed the American Opportunity Credit for Wynona the past four years. Wynona earned $19,000 working on campus and will file her own return as "single" in 2023. What amount can she claim for the AOTC in 2023 based upon the following expenses?

Tuition	$15,000
Room and board	$12,000
Required Student Health Fees	$1,000

A. $0
B. $2,000
C. $2,500
D. $11,000

24. Which of the following credits is not refundable in 2023?

A. Earned Income Tax Credit.
B. Additional Child Tax Credit.
C. The Child and Dependent Care Credit.
D. American Opportunity Credit.

25. Orrin was audited in 2023, and the IRS determined that he claimed the Earned Income Tax Credit erroneously due to reckless disregard of the EITC rules. For how many years is Orrin prohibited from claiming the EITC?

A. None
B. Two years
C. Five years
D. Ten years

26. Stephen files as head of household. He has three children, ages 8, 10, and 18. All the children lived with Stephen all year long, and all have valid Social Security numbers. All of Stephen's income for the year is from wages, and his modified AGI is $190,000. Based on this information, what is the maximum Child Tax Credit that Stephen can claim on his return?

A. $0, his AGI is too high.
B. $2,000
C. $4,000
D. $6,000

27. What should an employee do if a single employer overwithheld too much Social Security tax from their wages?

A. The employee should request that the employer adjust the excess.
B. The employee should claim the excess amount paid as an itemized deduction.
C. The employee should ignore it as it's the government's responsibility.
D. The employee should report it to the Social Security Administration.

Unit 13: Quiz Answers

1. The answer is B. A nephew who lived with the taxpayer for nine months may qualify for the Child Tax Credit. Answers "A" and "C" are both incorrect because the children are not <u>under</u> the age of 17. Answer "D" is incorrect because the foster child only lived with the taxpayer for four months, so the foster child did not meet the residency test.

2. The answer is A. Because Orlando's equipment rental fee is mandatory, it is considered a qualified expense. For AOTC purposes, "qualified education expenses" do not include insurance or medical expenses (such as student health fees), room and board, transportation, or similar personal, living, or family expenses, or any course of instruction or other education involving sports, games, or hobbies, unless the course is part of the student's degree program.

3. The answer is C. Lizzie can claim a maximum adoption credit of $31,900 in 2023 ($15,950 per child). Note that the adoption credit is not refundable, but any amount that she cannot use in the current year may be carried forward up to 5 years.

4. The answer is B. Karen can claim $2,000 as a Child Tax Credit for one child (the credit is $2,000 per qualifying child <u>under</u> the age of 17). In 2023, Karen only has one qualifying child (the 10-year-old), because children who are <u>17 or older</u> are not qualifying children for purposes of the Child Tax Credit.

5. The answer is C. Expenses related to a surrogate arrangement are not a qualified adoption expense. Qualified adoption expenses are expenses directly related to the legal adoption of an eligible child. These expenses include adoption fees, court costs, attorney fees, travel expenses (including amounts spent for meals and lodging) while away from home, and re-adoption expenses to adopt a foreign child.

6. The answer is D. She may qualify for the Retirement Savings Contribution Credit (also called the Saver's Credit). Sienna does not qualify for the Earned Income Tax Credit because her income exceeds the AGI threshold for her filing status in 2023. She does not qualify for the Child Tax Credit or Credit for Other Dependents because she does not have a qualifying dependent.

7. The answer is D. Sebastian and Hannah can take the full Adoption Credit of $15,950 in 2023 because they adopted a special needs child. Under a special rule for taxpayers who adopt special needs children, the maximum Adoption Credit is allowed, even if the taxpayer has a lesser amount of adoption expenses. These special rules apply to private adoptions, as well as adoptions from public agencies like the U.S. foster care system, as long as the child is a U.S. citizen or U.S. resident. Foreign children aren't considered to have "special needs" for purposes of this rule.

8. The answer is B. Childcare is not a qualifying education expense, even if the childcare is offered on-campus. For purposes of the Lifetime Learning Credit, qualified education expenses are tuition and certain related expenses required for enrollment or attendance at an eligible educational institution.

9. The answer is A. Felix is a qualifying child for the Child Tax Credit because he was *under* age 17 at the end of the year. Siblings can be qualifying children for purposes of this credit, and half-siblings are treated the same as full siblings for tax purposes.

10. The answer is B. The American Opportunity Tax Credit is worth up to $2,500 per eligible student. The maximum credit equals 100% of the first $2,000 and 25% of the next $2,000 of qualified expenses.

11. The answer is C. The American Opportunity Tax Credit is worth up to $2,500 *per qualifying student.* Rocco can potentially claim $5,000 in AOC credits on his tax return ($2,500 each for Patricia and Marico). Patricia and Marico would be qualifying students for AOC purposes because they are working on their first undergraduate degree. Kasha would not qualify, because she is working on a graduate degree after having completed a four-year undergraduate degree. The American Opportunity Credit is only available for four years of postsecondary school. Kasha's educational expenses may be eligible for the Lifetime Learning Credit, however.

12. The answer is A. Ralph, the noncustodial parent, can claim the Child Tax Credit if Danika signs Form 8332. He cannot claim the Earned Income Tax Credit because he is not the custodial parent. He cannot claim the Adoption Credit because the Adoption Credit is only for qualified adoption expenses. He cannot claim the American Opportunity Credit, because the credit only applies to expenses incurred for postsecondary education (i.e., college expenses, not private school tuition for K-12 students, and Amelie is a high school student).

13. The answer is C. Edwin qualifies for the Lifetime Learning Credit. He does not qualify for the American Opportunity Credit because he is not a degree candidate and because his course does not meet the requirements. The "College Saver's Credit" and the "General Education Credit" do not exist.

14. The answer is B. Aaron's son, Cameron, does not qualify because he is over the age limit for the credit. To qualify for the Child and Dependent Care Credit, the dependent must be *under* the age of 13 (unless the person is disabled).

15. The answer is C. Only Dwight would be a qualifying child for EITC. Tania does not qualify because she only has an ITIN, not a Social Security number. Chester would not qualify because he is Donald's parent, and cannot be a qualifying child, regardless of his disability. Dawn would not qualify because she is Donald's cousin, and that is not a qualifying relationship.

16. The answer is A. Zahir and Elmeria can claim a maximum credit of $2,000 on their joint tax return. The Lifetime Learning Credit is allowed for 20% of the first $10,000 of qualified tuition and fees paid during the year. The credit is per tax return, not *per student*, so only a maximum of $2,000 can be claimed each year, no matter how many qualifying students a taxpayer may have.

17. The answer is B. The American Opportunity Credit (AOTC) is the only answer that is a refundable tax credit. Up to 40% of the American Opportunity Tax Credit is refundable, meaning that the taxpayer can receive a refund even if they have zero tax liability.

18. The answer is D. Household employee income is considered earned income because it is a type of wages. Alimony, capital gains, interest and dividends are not considered earned income for purposes of the EITC.

19. The answer is D. Bethany is eligible for the American Opportunity Tax Credit because she is pursuing a degree and is enrolled at least half-time for at least one academic period during the year. Answer "A" is incorrect, because graduate students do not qualify. The AOTC is a credit for qualified education expenses paid for an eligible student only for the first <u>four years</u> of higher education. Answer "B" is incorrect because courses that do not lead to a degree, certificate, or other recognized credential do not qualify for the AOTC. Answer "C" is incorrect because students with felony drug convictions are ineligible for this credit.

20. The answer is A. Schedule 8812 is used to calculate the Child Tax Credit as well as the Additional Child Tax Credit.

21. The answer is B. A refundable credit is generally more valuable in reducing tax liability. Refundable credits, such as the Earned Income Tax Credit, are not limited by an individual's tax liability. The taxpayer can receive a refund even with zero tax liability.

22. The answer is C. Childcare costs to obtain medical care are not a deductible expense. Deductible costs must be "work-related" and for a child under 13, a disabled dependent, or a disabled spouse of any age. Childcare costs incurred so that the taxpayer can volunteer, obtain medical care, run errands, or do other personal businesses do not qualify.

23. The answer is A. Wynona does not qualify for the AOTC because she is in her fifth year of college, and her parents have already claimed the credit for her in the prior four years. It is irrelevant that she will be filing her own return this year, the credit has already been claimed for her first four years of college. If she had been eligible for the credit, she would have had $11,000 of qualifying expenses. Room and board and student health fees are not qualifying expenses for the AOTC, and the qualifying tuition cost must be reduced by any tax-free scholarships, such as the Pell grant. The AOC is a maximum credit of $2,500 per student (100% of the first $2,000 of eligible expenses and 25% of the next $2,000). Wynona may use her education expenses to calculate the Lifetime Learning Credit, instead.

24. The answer is C. The Child and Dependent Care Credit is not refundable in 2023, meaning it can reduce a taxpayer's income tax to zero, but will not produce a refund beyond that. All the other credits listed are refundable or have a refundable component.

25. The answer is B. Orrin cannot claim the EITC for two tax years. There are restrictions on EITC claims by taxpayers for whom a previous claim was denied or reduced due to any reason other than a math or clerical error. If a taxpayer was determined to have claimed the EITC due to reckless or intentional disregard of the EITC rules, he cannot claim the EITC for two tax years. If the error was due to fraud, the taxpayer cannot claim the EITC for ten tax years.

26. The answer is C. Since two of his children are under the age of 17, and his AGI is under the limit of $200,000 for non-joint-return filers, Stephen is eligible to take a Child Tax Credit of $4,000 on his return ($2,000 × 2 children).

27. The answer is A. The employee should request that their employer adjust the excess. If a single employer overwithheld too much social security (or RRTA tax), that is the employer's error and the employer should adjust the excess for the employee. If a single employer *refuses* to refund the over-collection, the employee can file a claim for refund using Form 843, Claim for Refund and Request for Abatement.

Unit 14: The ACA and the Premium Tax Credit

For additional information, read:
Publication 5187, *Health Care Law: What's New for Individuals and Families*
Publication 974, *Premium Tax Credit (PTC)*

The Affordable Care Act (ACA)[170] is a comprehensive health care reform law first enacted in March 2010. The Affordable Care Act tax provisions are administered by the IRS. The Tax Cuts and Jobs Act permanently eliminated the penalty under the Affordable Care Act's individual mandate (i.e., the penalty for an individual for failing to have health insurance).[171]

However, even though the individual healthcare penalty has been reduced to $0, most of the other Marketplace provisions are still active. Taxpayers can still purchase health insurance through the Marketplace and receive the Premium Tax Credit (PTC), which is designed to cover a percentage of their health insurance costs. This credit is essentially a subsidy.

Taxpayers can receive the Premium Tax Credit <u>in advance</u> to lower their monthly insurance payments when they enroll in a Marketplace plan. The amount of Advance Premium Tax Credit (APTC) received by consumers is based on their estimated annual household income.

However, if taxpayers underestimate their annual income and receive more APTC than they are eligible for, they will have to repay all or some of the credit when filing their federal tax return for that year. This repayment amount is referred to as "excess APTC" and is the difference between the taxpayer's advance credit payments and the premium tax credit they are entitled to for that year. For 2023, the repayment caps range from $350 to $3,000, depending on the taxpayer's income and filing status.

2023 Repayment Caps for APTC		
Income (as % of the federal poverty line)	Single Filers	All other filing statuses
Under 200%	$350	$700
200%-299%	$900	$1,800
300%-399%	$1,500	$3,000
400% and above	No cap (full repayment)	No cap (full repayment)

The Inflation Reduction Act extended larger PTCs to qualifying households in 2023, and through the 2025 plan year. The law extends eligibility to taxpayers with household income above 400% of the federal poverty line and lowers premium contribution percentage at all levels of household income.

The two taxes that were instituted to help fund the ACA are the **Additional Medicare Tax** and the **Net Investment Income Tax**. Both of these taxes will be covered in this unit.

---

[170] The actual name of the health care law is the "Patient Protection and Affordable Care Act," often shortened to the Affordable Care Act, or ACA.
[171] Some states have their own individual health insurance mandate, requiring taxpayers to have health coverage or pay a fee with the state.

Note: In this book, we will cover the ACA from the individual taxpayer's perspective. The ACA from the *employer's* perspective is covered in detail in Book 2, *Businesses*. All of the employer-shared responsibility provisions remain in place, which means that employers with 50 employees or more must offer qualifying health coverage to their employees or face the prospect of severe excise penalties.

Premium Tax Credit

The Premium Tax Credit is a refundable federal tax credit to help eligible taxpayers pay for health insurance premiums. The credit is based on a taxpayer's income and is only available for taxpayers who purchased their insurance through a federal or state healthcare exchange. There are two ways to get the Premium Tax Credit:

1. If the taxpayer qualifies for *advance* payments of the Premium Tax Credit, they can choose to have the amounts paid directly to the insurance provider to help cover their monthly insurance premiums. This is also called the "Advance Premium Tax Credit" (APTC) because the taxpayers receive the credit in *advance* to lower their monthly health insurance premiums.

2. The taxpayer can choose to pay full price for their insurance through the Marketplace, then receive the PTC as a refundable credit on their individual tax return.

The amount of the Premium Tax Credit is based on a sliding scale, so the higher the household income, the lower the amount of the credit.

Note: The Premium Tax Credit is *only available* to taxpayers who purchase their insurance from the federal exchange (i.e., the "Healthcare Marketplace");[172] it is *not* available to taxpayers who obtain insurance through their employer, or purchase their health insurance directly from an insurance provider.

To be eligible for a Premium Tax Credit or the Advance Premium Tax Credit, a taxpayer must generally meet all of the following requirements:

- Purchase health insurance through the Healthcare Marketplace,
- Be a U.S. citizen or legal U.S. resident,
- Be unable to get coverage from an employer or the government (i.e., cannot be enrolled in Medicare, Tricare, Medical, or Medicaid),
- Not be claimed as a dependent on anyone else's tax return,
- If married, the couple must generally file a joint tax return.[173] Taxpayers who file separate returns will not qualify for the credit, although there are some exceptions.
- The taxpayer must meet certain household income requirements. For purposes of the Premium Tax Credit, a taxpayer's household income is the total of the taxpayer's modified adjusted gross income (MAGI), the taxpayer's spouse's MAGI (if filing jointly), and the MAGI of all dependents that are required to file a federal income tax return.

---

[172] The Health Insurance Marketplace, also called simply the Marketplace, is the place where you will find information about private health insurance options, purchase health insurance, and obtain help with premiums and out-of-pocket costs if you are eligible. The Department of Health and Human Services (HHS) administers the requirements for the Healthcare Marketplace.

[173] In the case of married taxpayers who file separately (MFS), certain eligibility exceptions exist for victims of domestic abuse or spousal abandonment.

Example: Ambrose and Vidalia are married and file jointly. They have two dependent children. Vidalia works part-time and does not receive health insurance through her employer. Ambrose was unemployed at the beginning of 2023 before starting a new job on April 20, 2023. His employer-sponsored health insurance started on May 1, 2023. From January through April, the family purchased health insurance through the Marketplace. Ambrose and Vidalia can claim the Premium Tax Credit for the four months that they had Marketplace coverage, assuming they meet the income guidelines.

If a worker voluntarily enrolls in an employer-sponsored plan, (including retiree coverage or COBRA coverage), the worker is not eligible for the premium tax credit, even if the employer plan is unaffordable or fails to provide minimum value. However, the taxpayer may be eligible for a premium tax credit for coverage of another member of the family who enrolls in Marketplace coverage, if that family member is not enrolled in an employer plan.

Example: Shelly is single and 32 years old. She works for a small hardware store that does not offer health coverage, so she obtains her health insurance through the Marketplace. On June 1, 2023, Shelly started a new job with a bank. The bank offers Shelly full health coverage, including medical and dental. Shelly enrolled in her new employer's coverage at the end of June, but she forgot about her Marketplace policy and did not cancel it. For June through December, Shelly is enrolled in her employer plan as well as her Marketplace plan at the same time. Since Shelly enrolled in an employer-sponsored plan, she is not eligible for the PTC for her Marketplace coverage for the months of June through December.

Example: Weston is 45, unmarried, and has one 25-year-old daughter named Debbie. Debbie is a full-time student and has no income, so Weston claims her as a dependent. Weston is self-employed at the beginning of the year, and he has a Marketplace policy for himself and his daughter Debbie. On May 5, 2023, Weston gets a full-time job working for a construction firm. The firm offers health insurance to Weston, but not to his 25-year-old daughter. Weston cancels *his* Marketplace policy, but he does *not* cancel his daughter's Marketplace coverage. Weston's income for 2023 is 300% of FPL. He is eligible for a premium tax credit for the months he was self-employed and did not have employer coverage for himself. Weston also qualifies for a credit for the full year of his daughter's coverage, because she is not enrolled in his employer's plan and is not eligible for any other health insurance.

Advance Premium Tax Credit and Repayments

When a taxpayer first applies for a Marketplace plan, the amount of the credit is estimated using information the taxpayer provides about family size and projected household income. Since it can be difficult to know exactly how much income a taxpayer will earn in any given year, and family circumstances can change during the year, the actual amount of the credit can vary from the estimated amount.

Note: A taxpayer who received Advance Premium Tax Credit (APTC) payments *must* file a tax return, to reconcile the advance credit payments with the actual Premium Tax Credit earned. This is called "reconciling" the advance payments of the Premium Tax Credit and the actual Premium Tax Credit the taxpayer actually qualifies for based on their annual income. The calculation for this reconciliation can be found on Form 8962, *Premium Tax Credit.* If an individual received advance payments and files their taxes electronically without including Form 8962, the IRS will reject their return.

At the end of the year, if the taxpayer has taken more Premium Tax Credit in advance than they are due based on their final income, the taxpayer may have to pay back the excess when they file their federal tax return. If the taxpayer has taken less than they qualify for, they will get the difference back as a refundable credit when they file their tax return.

Example: Mariano is a self-employed individual whose income varies greatly from year to year. Upon enrolling in a state exchange health insurance plan, he estimated his earnings for the upcoming year based on his previous year's income. Based on his estimated income, he was eligible for the Premium Tax Credit, which he chose to receive as advance credit payments. However, Mariano's business did much better than he expected in 2023, resulting in a higher income than the prior year and disqualifying him from the Premium Tax Credit. He must reconcile the amounts received through advance credits using Form 8962, where he discovers that he received $4,000 in excess advance premium tax credits that he must repay. As he does not qualify for the credit, this amount is added to his overall tax liability.

If a taxpayer fails to file a tax return to reconcile advance payments of the premium tax credit on Form 8962, the taxpayer could be prevented from applying for Marketplace premium tax credits in the following calendar year.

Changes in family size due to marriage, death, divorce, birth, or adoption can affect the amount of the credit. A taxpayer is supposed to report changes in circumstances to the Marketplace so the amount of the advance credit payments can be recalculated during the year. A taxpayer should also report changes in eligibility for government-sponsored or employer-sponsored health coverage, a move to a new address, an increase or decrease in the number of dependents, and other factors that may affect eligibility for the Premium Tax Credit. Although the IRS is restricted in its ability to collect the pre-2018 shared responsibility payment, the agency may use full collection actions, including levies and liens, against a taxpayer who does not repay excess advance premium tax credits.

Note: Remember, the Premium Tax Credit is a *refundable credit*. If the amount of the credit is more than the amount of the tax liability of the return, a taxpayer may receive the difference as a refund. If no tax is owed, a taxpayer can receive the full amount of the credit as a refund.

Example: Adelaide was enrolled in a qualified health plan through the Marketplace. She turned 65 on July 1, 2023, and became eligible for Medicare. Adelaide applied for Medicare in September and became eligible to receive Medicare benefits beginning on December 1, 2023. Adelaide can get the Premium Tax Credit for her healthcare coverage that she received from January through November. Beginning in December, Adelaide cannot get the Premium Tax Credit for her coverage in the qualified health plan, because she is enrolled in Medicare. She should cancel her Marketplace coverage as soon as possible.

Important Forms

The IRS has created a group of forms to help handle the employer reporting requirements of the ACA. Taxpayers who are covered by health insurance will most likely receive one of the forms listed below. Taxpayers must use the information from these statements when preparing their taxes. The forms are provided to different groups of people.

- **Form 1095-A**, *Health Insurance Marketplace Statement:* This form is for individuals who enroll in Marketplace coverage. This form reports basic information about the insurance company that issued the taxpayer's policy, the exchange where they are enrolled, and it documents the taxpayer's coverage for each month.
- **Form 1095-B**, *Health Coverage:* This is for employees or taxpayers whose insurance comes from a source other than the Marketplace.
- **Form 1095-C**, *Employer-Provided Health Insurance Offer and Coverage*: Individuals who work for applicable large employers will typically get this form (employees will also get this form if they enroll in self-insured coverage provided by an applicable large employer).

Some taxpayers will receive multiple forms in the same year. For example, if a taxpayer purchased health insurance through the Healthcare Marketplace at the beginning of the year, and then started a new job in the middle of the year that offered health coverage, the taxpayer may receive a Form 1095-A from the Marketplace, as well as Forms 1095-B or 1095-C.

Example: At the start of the year, Ghalib was a self-employed bookkeeper who had purchased his health insurance through the Healthcare Marketplace. In June he was offered a full-time position at a law firm that provided group health insurance after 30 days. He eagerly signed up for his employer-provided coverage and cancelled his individual Marketplace policy immediately thereafter. When tax season arrives, Ghalib received two forms: a 1095-A for the months he had Marketplace insurance and a 1095-C for the insurance from his employer.

Net Investment Income Tax (NIIT)

One of the many taxes imposed by the Affordable Care Act is the 3.8% Net Investment Income Tax (NIIT). This tax may apply to individuals, estates, and trusts. For individuals, a 3.8% tax is imposed on the lesser of: the individual's net investment income for the year, or any excess of the individual's modified adjusted gross income for the tax year over the following thresholds:

Filing Status	Threshold Amounts
MFJ or QSS	$250,000
MFS	$125,000
Single or HOH	$200,000

These threshold amounts are not indexed for inflation.

Example: Lamar is single and earned a salary of $175,000 during the year. He also had $19,000 of income from dividends, for a total MAGI of $194,000. This amount is less than the $200,000 threshold for single filers, so it doesn't matter how much investment income Lamar has, he is not subject to the Net Investment Income Tax.

Example: Irfan is married to Mahira, and they file jointly. Irfan earns $210,000 in wages during the year. Mahira, his wife, does not work, but she is an avid collector of antique jewelry. In 2023, she sells an antique gold brooch online for a hefty $45,000 profit. The couple's joint AGI is $255,000 ($210,000 wages + $45,000 capital gains from the sale of the collectible). This is $5,000 above the threshold for their filing status ($250,000 for MFJ). They will owe the NIIT on the excess ($5,000 × 3.8% = $190), since $5,000 is less than their net investment income ($45,000) for the year.

The NIIT is imposed only on U.S. citizens and U.S. resident aliens. Nonresident aliens are not subject to the NIIT, even if they have U.S. source investment income.[174] Investment income that is subject to the tax includes:

- Interest income, unless it is tax-exempt, (like municipal bonds),
- Dividends and capital gains,
- Rental and royalty income (if passive),
- Nonqualified annuities,
- Income from trading of financial instruments or commodities,
- Income from businesses that are passive activities for the taxpayer (such as passive income or rental income from a limited partnership interest).

To the extent that gains are not otherwise offset by capital losses, the following are common examples of income that is included in computing a taxpayer's net investment income:

- Capital gains from the sale of stocks, bonds, and mutual funds,
- Capital gain distributions from mutual funds,
- Gains from the sale of real estate, collectibles, or other capital assets,
- Gains from the sale of interests in partnerships and S corporations, to the extent the partner or shareholder was a passive owner.

Net investment income **does not** include earned income or pension income. The NIIT does not apply to: wages, self-employment income, Social Security benefits, veterans' benefits, unemployment compensation, taxable alimony payments, or distributions from IRAs or certain qualified retirement plans.

Example: Adara is single and earned a salary of $175,000 in 2023. She also received $80,000 of dividend income, for a total MAGI of $255,000, which exceeds the threshold for single filers by $55,000. The NIIT is based on the *lesser* of $55,000 (the amount by which her MAGI exceeds the threshold for single filers) or $80,000 (her total "net investment income"). Adara owes NIIT $2,090 ($55,000 × 3.8% = $2,090).

Example: Wahid is unmarried. In 2023, he earns $180,000 of self-employment income, and $99,000 in passive income from a limited partnership interest. He also has ($9,000) in losses from a residential rental for the year. The rental loss is netted against the passive partnership income, and Wahid's modified adjusted gross income is $270,000 ($180,000 + [$99,000 - $9,000]). His income exceeds the threshold for his filing status by $70,000. His Net Investment Income (NII) is $90,000. The Net Investment Income Tax is based on the *lesser* of (1) $70,000 (the amount that Wahid's MAGI exceeds the $200,000 threshold for single filers) or (2) $90,000 (his investment income). Wahid will owe NIIT of $2,660 ($70,000 × 3.8%).

The NIIT does not apply to any gains or investment income that is excluded from gross income for regular income tax purposes. For example, municipal bond interest is exempt from federal tax, so it is not included in the calculation for the NIIT.

---

[174] A dual-status alien, who is a resident of the United States for part of the year and a nonresident alien for the other part of the year, is subject to the NIIT only with respect to the portion of the year during which the individual is a United States resident. The threshold amount is not reduced or prorated for a dual-status resident.

Example: Tavish is age 34 and claims his 64-year-old mother, Penelope, as his dependent parent. Tavish qualifies to file as head of household. In 2023, Tavish has $395,000 of wage income and $40,000 of interest income. All his interest income is from municipal bonds. Although his total income is $435,000 for the year, he is not subject to the NIIT, because all his investment income is from tax-exempt municipal bonds.

Net investment income also does not include any gain on the sale of a personal residence that is excluded from gross income (such as the Section 121 exclusion on the sale of a main home).

Example: Deborah is single. She earns $45,000 in wages during the year. In 2023, she sells her main home that she has owned and lived in for the last 10 years. The sale price was $1 million, and Deborah's cost basis in the home was $600,000. She is allowed to exclude $250,000 of the gain under section 121.

$1,000,000 sales price - $600,000 basis = $400,000 realized gain

$400,000 - $250,000 section 121 exclusion = $150,000 *recognized* gain

$45,000 wages + $150,000 recognized gain = **$195,000 MAGI**

After subtracting her allowable exclusions, her modified adjusted gross income is $195,000, which is below the threshold amount of $200,000, so she does not owe any Net Investment Income Tax.

A gain from the sale of a second home, rental property, or a vacation home would not be eligible for section 121 exclusion and therefore, would be subject to the NIIT.

Example: Brandon and Christine are married and file jointly. Brandon earns $75,000 in wages for the year, and Christine does not work or have any earned income. In 2023, Brandon and Christine also have $225,000 of capital gains from the sale of their vacation home. None of the gain from the sale of the home can be excluded from income. After adding in the wages from Brandon's job, their joint modified adjusted gross income is $300,000 ($75,000 wages + $225,000 in capital gains). Their MAGI exceeds the threshold amount by $50,000 (the threshold is $250,000 for joint filers). Brandon and Christine are subject to NIIT on the *lesser* of $225,000 (their Net Investment Income) or $50,000 (the amount of their modified adjusted gross income that exceeds the $250,000 MFJ threshold). Brandon and Christine owe Net Investment Income Tax of $1,900 ($50,000 × 3.8%).

Example: Ruskin is unmarried and earns $180,000 in wages. He also earned $90,000 in capital gains from the sale of a plot of land. Ruskin's modified adjusted gross income is $270,000 ($180,000 + $90,000). Ruskin's modified adjusted gross income exceeds the threshold of $200,000, so he will owe Net Investment Income Tax. Ruskin's investment income is $90,000 for the year (the capital gains). His NIIT is based on the *lesser* of $70,000 (the amount that Ruskin's modified adjusted gross income exceeds the $200,000 threshold) or $90,000 (his investment income). Ruskin owes NIIT of $2,660 ($70,000 × 3.8%).

Investment interest *expense* can be deducted to determine gross investment income, which is used to arrive at net investment income. The NIIT is subject to estimated tax provisions, so taxpayers may need to adjust their withholding or estimated payments to avoid underpayment penalties. Individuals, estates, and trusts must compute the tax on Form 8960, *Net Investment Tax.*

Example: Aster, a single filer, typically earns approximately $200,000 in wages during the year. Wages are not subject to the NIIT. However, he plans to sell a large block of cryptocurrency during the year, and he knows that his normal withholding will not cover the additional tax from the cryptocurrency sale. Aster can request that his employer increase his withholding by filling out a new Form W-4, *Employee's Withholding Certificate.* This way, additional taxes will be taken out with each paycheck. Aster can also choose to make estimated payments directly to the IRS to cover the additional taxes that he anticipates to owe.

Additional Medicare Tax

The Additional Medicare Tax was also legislated to help fund the Affordable Care Act, and has been in effect since 2013. The tax only applies to *earned* income, like wages. The Additional Medicare Tax is withheld at a rate of 0.9% and computed on Form 8959, *Additional Medicare Tax.* The tax is assessed only on earned income in excess of the following thresholds:

Filing Status	Threshold Amounts
MFJ	$250,000
MFS	$125,000
Single, HOH, or QSS	$200,000

Filing status determines the threshold amount, and these thresholds are not adjusted for inflation. A taxpayer's earned income (including wages, taxable fringe benefits, bonuses, tips, commissions, and self-employment income) that is subject to regular Medicare tax is also subject to the Additional Medicare Tax to the extent it exceeds the applicable threshold amount for their filing status.

Unlike regular Medicare taxes, there is no "employer share" of the Additional Medicare Tax. Self-employed taxpayers also cannot deduct one-half of the 0.9% Additional Medicare Tax. It is imposed entirely on the employee (or the self-employed taxpayer). An employer is required to withhold the Additional Medicare Tax if an employee is paid more than $200,000, regardless of an employee's filing status or whether the employee has wages paid by another employer. The Additional Medicare Tax applies, even if the amounts are not withheld from a taxpayer's wages.

Example: Montgomery and Lucy are married and file jointly. Montgomery earned $120,000 of salary working as a physician and Lucy earned $190,000 working as a scientist. Neither of their employers withhold amounts for the Additional Medicare Tax, because neither earned wages above $200,000. However, their combined earned income is $310,000, which exceeds the $250,000 threshold for joint filers by $60,000. Montgomery and Lucy will owe $540 of Additional Medicare Tax on their income tax return ($60,000 × 0.9% = $540). They must calculate the tax and attach Form 8959, *Additional Medicare Tax*, to their tax return.

Example: Vivian is single. She earns $350,000 in wages during the year, all from one employer. The additional 0.9% tax will be calculated on her earnings above $200,000. This means that $150,000 will be subject to Additional Medicare Tax ($350,000 wages - $200,000 threshold amount). She will pay $1,350 in Additional Medicare Tax on her tax return ($150,000 × 0.9% = $1,350). This additional tax will be withheld from Vivian's wages automatically by her employer.

Example: Sasha is unmarried with one dependent son. She files as head of household. She earns $130,000 in self-employment income from an online business, and $23,000 in wages during the year. Sasha is not liable for the Additional Medicare Tax because her combined self-employment income and wages is $153,000, which is less than the $200,000 threshold for her filing status.

For couples who are married and file a joint return, they must combine all their wages, compensation, or self-employment income to figure the amount of tax.

Extended Example #1: David is single and earned $145,000 in wages in 2023. Because his earnings are below the $200,000 threshold for single filers, his company did not withhold any amount for the Additional Medicare Tax. He also had $85,000 of self-employment income from a side job as a web designer. David's total earned income is $230,000, so he will be required to pay Additional Medicare Tax on the $30,000 of earned income that exceeds the $200,000 threshold. David will owe $270 in Additional Medicare Tax on his income tax return ($30,000 × 0.9% = $270). He must calculate the tax and attach Form 8959, *Additional Medicare Tax*, to his tax return.

Extended Example #2: David gets married on December 31, 2023, to Patty, who only earned $7,000 in wages during the year. Because they are married as of the last day of the year and file jointly, their threshold for the Additional Medicare Tax is now $250,000. Their combined earned income is now $237,000, which is below the $250,000 threshold for MFJ. David and Patty do not owe the Additional Medicare Tax.

If an employer withholds amounts for a married employee who earns *more* than $200,000, but the combined earnings of the employee and their spouse are *less* than the $250,000 MFJ threshold, the taxpayers can apply the overpayment against any other type of tax that may be owed on their joint tax return.

Example: Herman and Katherine are married and file jointly. Herman makes $225,000 in wages during the year. Herman's employer is required by law to withhold the Additional Medicare Tax on Herman's wages (because he earns more than the $200,000 threshold for when mandatory withholding becomes necessary). Katherine has a small part-time job at a local church. She only earns $8,000 in wages. When they file their joint return, their combined wages total $233,000, which is under the threshold amount for joint filers. They do not owe any Additional Medicare Tax. This means that the Additional Medicare Tax that was withheld on Herman's paycheck will be treated as an overpayment on their individual return, and will be applied as an automatic credit against any other taxes they might owe for the year.

Unit 14: Study Questions

(Test yourself first, then check the correct answers at the end of this quiz.)

1. Adrienne and Konnor are married and file jointly. Adrienne has $133,000 of self-employment income. Konnor earned $184,000 in wages. Compute the amount of their Additional Medicare Tax, if any.

A. $0
B. $603
C. $1,053
D. $2,853

2. Which of the following taxpayers would be subject to the Additional Medicare Tax?

A. Nasir, who files as head of household and has $180,000 in wages and $50,000 in interest income.
B. Kerrie, who is single and earned $196,000 in wages.
C. Lizzie, who files separately from her husband and earned $140,000 in wages.
D. Adley, who is a qualifying widower and has $200,000 in wages.

3. Which of the following would not be subject to the net investment income tax (NIIT)?

A. An estate of a deceased taxpayer.
B. A nonresident alien.
C. A trust.
D. An individual with only rental income.

4. The Premium Tax Credit is:

A. A refundable credit.
B. A nonrefundable credit.
C. Available to all taxpayers with Marketplace insurance.
D. Available to all taxpayers with any health insurance.

5. Terry and Myriam are married but choose to file separately because of Terry's past-due child support. Their household income for 2023 is at 200% of the federal poverty line. They enroll in the federal Marketplace for health coverage. Which of the following statements is correct?

A. They are not eligible for the Premium Tax Credit because their income is too high.
B. They will owe a shared responsibility payment.
C. They are not eligible for the Premium Tax Credit because of their filing status.
D. They are eligible for the Advance Premium Tax Credit.

6. Which of the following individuals would be eligible for the Premium Tax Credit, assuming they meet the applicable income guidelines?

A. Bowie, who had minimum essential coverage through his employer.
B. Zhavia, who was enrolled for two months through the federal Marketplace.
C. Imran, who received Medicaid coverage for twelve months of the year.
D. Peyton, who is a full-time U.S. military officer.

7. The Additional Medicare Tax is:

A. 0.9% on a taxpayer's earned income above a certain threshold.
B. 3.8% on a taxpayer's earned income above a certain threshold.
C. 0.9% on a taxpayer's investment income above a certain threshold.
D. 3.8% on a taxpayer's investment income above a certain threshold.

8. Which form is used to reconcile the Premium Tax Credit?

A. Form 1095-B
B. Form 1095-C
C. Form 8832
D. Form 8962

9. Emilee files single. She has the following income in 2023:

- $50,000 in capital gains from the sale of stock.
- $40,000 in passive royalty income.
- $20,000 in municipal bond interest.
- $170,000 of self-employment income.

Calculate her net investment income tax, if any.

A. $0
B. $2,280
C. $3,420
D. $4,180

10. How can a taxpayer receive advance payments of the Premium Tax Credit?

A. When a taxpayer applies for health insurance on the Marketplace.
B. When a taxpayer receives Medicare or Medicaid.
C. When a taxpayer receives an offer of coverage from a private employer.
D. When a taxpayer applies for travel insurance through a private insurer.

11. Kyong enrolled in the Federal Marketplace for 2023 to obtain health insurance. She estimated her household income for the year, qualified for the Premium Tax Credit, and her expected credit paid in advance to her insurance company. What must Kyong do when she files her income tax return?

A. She must repay half of the credit that she received in advance.
B. She will not owe any additional tax but may be eligible for a larger amount of the credit.
C. She must reconcile the advance premium tax credit payments with the actual Premium Tax Credit that she calculates on Form 8962. Any excess amount will be counted as household income and used to project her credit for the next year.
D. She must reconcile the advance premium tax credit payments with the actual Premium Tax Credit she calculates on Form 8962. She may receive a refund, or she may have to repay any excess advance premium tax credit payments, depending on her individual situation.

12. Herman gets his health insurance from the Healthcare Marketplace and receives advanced Premium Tax credit payments during the year to help pay for his health insurance premiums. He has a filing requirement, but he does not file his tax return on time, or reconcile his Premium Tax Credit. What are the consequences of this?

A. Herman could be prevented from receiving the Premium Tax Credit in the future.
B. Herman can no longer obtain insurance from the Marketplace.
C. Herman can be assessed an excise tax totaling 100% of his healthcare premiums.
D. There are no consequences.

Unit 14: Quiz Answers

1. The answer is B. Adrienne and Konnor are required to pay the Additional Medicare Tax. Their combined income is $317,000, exceeding the threshold of $250,000 by $67,000. As a result, their Additional Medicare Tax amounts to $603 ($67,000 × 0.9%).

2. The answer is C. Lizzie will have to pay the Additional Medicare Tax since she files her taxes as "Married Filing Separately" and received more than $125,000 in earned income. This means that she will owe an extra 0.9% tax on the amount of her earned income that exceeds $125,000, which in this case is $15,000 ($15,000 × .009 = $135 Additional Medicare Tax).

3. The answer is B. A nonresident alien would not be subject to the net investment income tax (NIIT). The net investment income tax applies to individuals, estates, and trusts. Only U.S. citizens and U.S. residents are subject to the tax.

4. The answer is A. The Premium Tax Credit is refundable, meaning that a taxpayer may be able to receive the full amount of credit as a refund, assuming he has no other tax liability. The PTC is available only to a taxpayer, his spouse, or his dependents who had health coverage through a federal or state exchange (i.e., the Healthcare Marketplace) for all or part of the year.

5. The answer is C. Terry and Myriam are not eligible for the Premium Tax Credit because they file separate returns. Unless one of a limited number of exceptions applies,[175] a married couple cannot claim the Premium Tax Credit unless they file jointly.

6. The answer is B. Zhavia would be the only taxpayer who would be eligible, because she is the only one who had coverage from the Marketplace. Answer "A" is incorrect, because a taxpayer enrolled in an employer-sponsored plan is not eligible for the Premium Tax Credit. Answers "C" and "D" are incorrect, because a taxpayer who receives coverage through Medicaid, Medicare, or other government health plans, such as military (Tricare) coverage *outside* of the Marketplace is not eligible for the PTC.

7. The answer is A. The Additional Medicare Tax applies to 0.9% of a taxpayer's **earned** income above a threshold based on his filing status. For single, head of household, and qualifying surviving spouses, the threshold is $200,000. For married couples filing jointly, the amount is $250,000. For married couples filing separately, the amount is $125,000.

8. The answer is D. Form 8962, Premium Tax Credit, is used to calculate the PTC and reconcile advance payments of the credit. Taxpayers who receive advance payments of the Premium Tax Credit are required to file a tax return and reconcile the payments on Form 8962; this is regardless of the taxpayer's income level.

---

[175] If a taxpayer is MFS and is eligible for relief from the requirement to file MFJ because of spousal abuse or abandonment, there is a special box on Form 8962 that should be checked.

9. The answer is B. Emilee's modified adjusted gross income is $260,000 (170,000 + $50,000 + $40,000). The municipal bond interest is not included in the calculation, because it is tax-exempt. Emilee's modified adjusted gross income exceeds the threshold of $200,000 for single taxpayers by $60,000. Her net investment income is $90,000 ($50,000 + $40,000). Her NIIT is based on the *lesser* of $60,000 (the amount that Emilee's modified adjusted gross income exceeds the $200,000 threshold) or $90,000 (Emilee's Net Investment Income). Emilee owes NIIT of $2,280 ($60,000 × 3.8%).

10. The answer is A. A taxpayer can only receive the APTC if they obtain health insurance through the Marketplace. The credit is essentially a "subsidy" to help a taxpayer obtain health insurance.

11. The answer is D. Kyong must do a monthly calculation to determine the actual amount of her PTC, which must then be reconciled with the advance premium tax credits paid to her insurer to lower her premium payments. Kyong must enter the amount of any excess advance premium tax credit payments made on her behalf on her return and normally repay the excess. Any taxpayer who claims the Premium Tax Credit (whether advance credit payments were made or not) must file a tax return and include Form 8962, *Premium Tax Credit* (PTC). If there were no excess advance premium tax credit payments and the amount of the PTC is more than the amount of her tax liability, she may receive the difference as a refund.

12. The answer is A. If Herman does not file a tax return and reconcile his advance payments of the premium tax credit on Form 8962, he could be prevented from applying for Marketplace premium tax credits in the following calendar year.

Unit 15: Additional Taxes and Credits

More Reading:
Publication 54, *Tax Guide for U.S. Citizens and Resident Aliens Abroad*
Publication 926, *Household Employer's Tax Guide*
Publication 514, *Foreign Tax Credit for Individuals*
Tax Topic 556, *Alternative Minimum Tax*
Form 5405, *Repayment of the First-Time Homebuyer Credit (Instructions)*

In this unit, we cover a variety of other taxes and credits, including the taxation and reporting of foreign income, the "nanny tax," and the "kiddie tax." We start with a look at the Alternative Minimum Tax (AMT).

Alternative Minimum Tax

The Alternative Minimum Tax (AMT) gives an alternative set of rules to calculate an individual's taxable income. For this reason, the AMT is sometimes called a "parallel tax" system. Congress adopted the AMT in 1969 in an attempt to ensure that individuals and corporations paid at least a minimum amount of tax. What this translates into, is that for some higher-income taxpayers, some deductions can be disallowed, and certain types of income that might be tax-exempt under the normal income tax system (like municipal bond interest) may be subject to income tax under the AMT regime. The Tax Cuts and Jobs Act made a number of significant changes to the individual AMT. First, the AMT exemption was increased substantially and is now indexed for inflation every year. The AMT exemption amounts in 2023 are as follows:

Filing status	2023 AMT exemption amount	AMT exemption phaseout begins
Single or HOH	$81,300	$578,150
MFJ or QSS	$126,500	$1,156,300
MFS	$63,250	$ 578,150

This means that taxpayers who have Alternative Minimum Taxable Income (AMTI) below the exemption threshold will not be subject to AMT, regardless of how many tax deductions or credits they may have. AMT exemption amounts are reduced 25 cents for every dollar the taxpayer's AMTI exceeds the phaseout thresholds listed above. Certain situations may "trigger" the AMT tax. Some scenarios when a taxpayer may have to pay the AMT tax include:

- Having a high income coupled with high itemized deductions,
- The exercise of incentive stock options,
- A large sale of capital assets that results in long-term capital gains,
- Tax-exempt interest from private activity bonds.

Individual taxpayers compute AMT on Form 6251, *Alternative Minimum Tax—Individuals.* As described in the preceding units, federal tax law provides special treatment for certain types of income and allows deductions and credits for certain types of expenses. These tax benefits can significantly reduce the regular income tax liabilities for some taxpayers.

AMT "Tax Preference" Items

The AMT limits the extent to which deductions and credits can be used to reduce the total amount of income tax paid by higher-income taxpayers. These are called "tax preference" items. When calculating the AMT, many common items considered in the computation of the regular income tax liability are either adjusted downward or eliminated entirely.

Because of the Tax Cuts and Jobs Act, fewer AMT adjustments are required through the end of 2025 as compared to before the changes made by the TCJA. For taxpayers who itemize, only state and local taxes and foreign income taxes need to be adjusted when figuring alternative minimum taxable income. In addition, the following tax preference items may also be eliminated when calculating the AMT:

- Depletion
- Excess intangible drilling costs
- Interest on private activity bonds
- Accelerated depreciation on property placed in service before 1987
- Exclusion of gain on qualified small business stock (QSBS)

Example: Florence is unmarried and files single. She earns high wages as a physician. She also has investments in a copper mine, for which she receives royalties every year. Florence had taxable income before exemptions of $600,000. She also reported $65,000 in depletion deductions from the copper mine on Schedule E. Florence's AMTI is computed by taking her taxable income before exemptions of $600,000, and *adding back* the preference item of $65,000 in depletion to arrive at AMTI of $665,000.

The AMT is the excess of the tentative minimum tax over the regular income tax. Thus, the AMT is owed only if the tentative minimum tax is greater than the regular tax. In general, the tentative minimum tax is computed by:

1. Starting with AGI minus itemized deductions, if any, for regular tax purposes,
2. Eliminating or reducing certain adjustments and preferences (the exclusions, deductions, and credits that are allowed in computing the regular tax, such as those mentioned above), to derive alternative minimum taxable income (AMTI),
3. Subtracting the AMT exemption amount,
4. Multiplying the amount computed in (3) by the applicable AMT rate, and
5. Subtracting the AMT Foreign Tax Credit.

The AMT exemption in step 3 is an amount that is deducted from alternative minimum taxable income before calculating the tentative minimum tax. Most tax preparation software will automatically compute whether a taxpayer owes the AMT. Taxpayers who received or claimed any of the following items in the tax year, are required to complete, (but may not necessarily need to file), Form 6251, *Alternative Minimum Tax, Individuals, Estates, and Trusts*:

- Accelerated depreciation
- Stock received through incentive stock options that were not sold in the same year
- Tax-exempt interest from private activity bonds
- Intangible drilling, circulation, research, experimental, or mining costs

- Amortization of pollution-control facilities or depletion
- Income (or loss) from tax-shelter farm activities or passive activities.

Credit for Prior Year Minimum Tax

A nonrefundable credit may be available to individuals, estates, and trusts for alternative minimum tax paid in prior years to the extent that a taxpayer's regular tax in the current year is greater than their tentative minimum tax. If applicable, the credit is calculated on Form 8801, *Credit for Prior Year Minimum Tax-Individuals, Estates, and Trusts*.

The AMT is caused by two types of adjustments and preferences: "exclusion" items and "deferral" items. Exclusion items are those that affect only a single tax year and therefore cause a permanent difference between regular taxable income and alternative minimum taxable income (AMTI).

For individual taxpayers, an example of an "exclusion item" is the deduction for state and local income taxes. These taxes are never deductible for AMT purposes, and they are added back into AGI in the calculation of AMTI in the year they are paid. Deferral items are adjustment and preference items, such as depreciation, that affect more than one tax year.

Because they affect the difference between regular taxable income and AMTI in multiple tax years, they generally do not cause a permanent difference in taxable income over time. The minimum tax credit is allowed only for the portion of AMT caused by deferral items, which may generate a credit for future years.

> **Note:** A taxpayer can only claim the AMT credit in a year when they do not have to pay AMT. In other words, even though the AMT *credit* is triggered by the payment of the alternative minimum tax, the credit is a regular tax credit and a taxpayer cannot use it to offset alternative minimum tax.

> **Example:** Brandon and Stacy are married and file jointly. They are high-income earners, but also have high itemized deductions on Schedule A. They had an AMT liability in the previous year because their taxable income exceeded $1.9 million after they exercised some incentive stock options. They use Form 8801 to calculate how much of their AMT was related to that and other deferral items and discover they have a $112,000 AMT credit. They can use their AMT tax credit to reduce their regular tax, but they cannot reduce it below the tentative minimum tax amount. Any unused AMT credit balance can be carried forward to be used in a future year.

Kiddie Tax on Investment Income

Years ago, wealthy families could transfer investments to their minor children and save tax dollars because the investment income would be taxed at the children's lower rates. Congress closed this tax loophole, and now investment income earned by dependent children may be taxed at the parent's rate. This law became known as the "kiddie tax."

The kiddie tax never applies to earned income (such as wages or self-employment income); it applies only to *unearned* income and investment income, such as interest, dividends, and capital gains distributions. The kiddie tax also applies to unemployment income. Part of a child's investment income *may* be subject to the kiddie tax if:

- The child's investment income is more than $2,500 (in 2023);

- The child is (1) a dependent under age 18, (2) under the age of 19 and does not provide more than half of their support with their own earned income, or (3) a full-time college student under age 24 and does not provide more than half of their support with their own earned income;
- The child is required to file a tax return for the tax year; and
- At least one of the child's parents was alive at the end of the year (if both of the child's parents are deceased, then the kiddie tax does <u>not</u> apply, regardless of how much unearned income the child has).

Remember, the kiddie tax *only* applies when a dependent child's investment income exceeds $2,500 in 2023. The first $1,250 in investment income is tax-free; the second $1,250 is taxed at the child's marginal rate. If this unearned income threshold ($2,500 in 2023) is not exceeded, then the kiddie tax does not apply. If this threshold is exceeded, only the child's *unearned* income in excess of the threshold is subject to the kiddie tax. All the child's investment income in excess of $2,500 is then taxed at the parent's tax rate. There are two ways to report the kiddie tax.

- **Child's return:** The child can file their own return, and report the tax by attaching Form 8615, *Tax for Certain Children Who Have Unearned Income*, to their Form 1040. This is the most common method.
- **Parent's return:** Or, the parents can report their child's unearned income on Form 8814, *Parent's Election to Report Child's Interest and Dividends*, on their Form 1040, rather than having the child file a separate return. To use this method, the child can only have income from interest, dividends, or capital gain distributions. If the child's gross income is $12,500 or more in 2023, the Form 8814 cannot be used, and the child must file their own return to report the income that way.

A child's investment income may also be subject to the net investment income tax, which is calculated using only the child's income. However, the NIIT applies only if the child's net investment income exceeds the $200,000 threshold for single filers (this scenario would be very rare, and would only apply if a dependent child had *more* than $200,000 in taxable income).

Example: Rochelle is 16 years old. Both of her parents died in a car accident three years ago, and she inherited several valuable investments from them. Rochelle lives with her grandmother, Pearl, all year. Pearl has sole custody of her granddaughter and claims her as a dependent. Rochelle has $17,600 in investment income in 2023. Most of this income goes into a college savings account for Rochelle. Rochelle is not subject to the kiddie tax rules because both of her parents are deceased (i.e., she does not have a living parent). In this case, Rochelle's income would not be subject to the kiddie tax, even if Pearl claims her granddaughter as a dependent. Rochelle must file her own tax return, but none of her income is subject to the kiddie tax.

Example: Marcus and Renee have a 16-year-old son named Tony. In 2023, Tony has $2,900 of interest income from a CD his grandfather gave him. Tony does not have any other taxable income. The first $1,250 of investment income is not taxable. The next $1,250 is taxed at the 10% income tax rate (which is the child's marginal rate). The remainder, $400, is subject to the kiddie tax. Tony may choose to file his own tax return and attach Form 8615, or Tony's parents can choose to report their son's income on their joint return by attaching Form 8814.

Example: Contessa has a 17-year-old son named Xander. Contessa files as head of household and claims her son as a dependent. Xander earns $9,300 in wages at a part-time job. He also has an additional $5,000 in capital gains from the sale of a collectible toy, which he sold at a tidy profit to a private collector. Xander must file his own tax return and attach Form 8615. Contessa cannot use Form 8814, because Xander has a mix of wages and investment income, plus the total amount of his income exceeds the $12,500 maximum threshold to use the Form 8814 in 2023.

Note: The kiddie tax does not apply to a child who is married and files a joint return with their spouse. This applies whether the child is a minor, under age 19, or a full-time college student under age 24.

Example: At 19 years old, Angelica is a full-time college student who relies on her parents for financial support. She received $3,950 in qualified dividends from a mutual fund gifted by her grandfather when she graduated high school. Because she would normally be claimed as a dependent by her parents, her investment income would be subject to the kiddie tax. However, during the year, Angelica meets Harrison, age 26, in one of her college classes. They fall in love and get married on December 15, 2023. She will file a joint tax return with her new husband. As a result, she is no longer considered a dependent and is not subject to the kiddie tax.

First-Time Homebuyer Credit Repayment

First-time homebuyers who claimed a special tax credit in 2008[176] are required to repay a portion of the funds received over a 15-year period. The First-Time Homebuyer Credit took the form of a loan in 2008, and there are still taxpayers who are repaying that loan on their tax returns (2025 will be the final year for taxpayers who claimed this credit and are still paying it back).

For example, a homebuyer who claimed the maximum credit of $7,500 must repay $500 per year as an additional tax. In 2023, the repayment amount is entered on Schedule 2, line 10, of the Form 1040.

Example: Melinda purchased her home in 2008 and claimed the full amount of the First-Time Homebuyer Credit. She still lives in the home and continues to use it as her main residence. She is required to pay back her credit in equal yearly installments of $500 over a period of 15 years. When she files her tax return, the repayment is listed on her Form 1040 (Schedule 2, Line 10) as an additional tax.

A taxpayer who claimed the credit and sells the home (or who no longer maintains it as their primary residence, including a conversion to rental property) must complete Form 5405, *Repayment of the First-Time Homebuyer Credit.*[177]

In the case of a sale (including through abandonment or foreclosure), the taxpayer must repay the credit with the tax return for the tax year in which the sale is completed. The following are exceptions to the repayment rule:

---

[176] The credit was optional and applied to first time home purchases after April 8, 2008, and before July 1, 2009. The repayments began in 2010 and have a 15 year repayment period.

[177] The repayment is limited to the amount of gain on the sale if the sale is to an unrelated taxpayer. A similar, $8,000 credit was also available in 2009 and 2010 but did not have to be repaid. A taxpayer who purchased his home and received the credit in either 2009 or 2010 did not have to repay the credit unless the home was sold within a three-year period following the purchase.

- **Involuntary conversion:** If the home is destroyed or condemned, and the taxpayer does not acquire a new home within the 2-year replacement period, the repayment owed with the taxpayer's return for the year in which the 2-year period ends is limited to the gain on the disposition. The amount of the credit in excess of the gain doesn't have to be repaid. If the taxpayer does not have a gain on the involuntary conversion, they do not have to repay any of the credit, unless they sold the home under threat of condemnation to a related party.
- **Transfers incident to divorce:** If the home was transferred to a spouse (or ex-spouse as part of a divorce settlement), the spouse who received the home is responsible for repaying the credit (regardless of which spouse purchased the home) if none of the other exceptions apply.
- **The person who claimed the credit dies:** If a person who claimed the credit dies, repayment of the remaining balance of the credit is not required unless the credit was claimed on a joint return. If the credit was claimed on a joint return, then the surviving spouse is required to continue repaying their half of the credit if none of the other exceptions apply.

Example: Giuliana and Arturo purchased a home together in 2008, and claimed the full amount of the First-Time Homebuyer Credit. They use the home as their primary residence. On December 1, 2023, Arturo dies. Giuliana is required to continue repaying her half of the credit, but Arturo's portion of the credit does not have to be repaid (it is considered forgiven).

Nanny Tax (Tax on Household Employees)

When a taxpayer employs household workers, they are responsible for paying employment taxes. This is commonly known as the "nanny tax" or tax on household employees. A worker is classified as an employee if the taxpayer has control over what work is done and how it is done, whether the work is full-time or part-time. Some examples of household employees include babysitters, housekeepers, private nurses, yard workers, and chauffeurs.

Example: Vance hires Sally as full-time nanny, to care for his two toddlers while he is at work. Sally also does housework in his home. Vance sets Sally's schedule and gives specific directions about household and childcare duties. Vance also provides all the equipment and supplies Sally needs to do her work. Sally is Vance's household employee and subject to the nanny tax rules. Vance must file a Schedule H.

However, self-employed individuals such as daycare providers who care for multiple children from different families in their own home are not considered household employees.

Example: Yelena runs a licensed daycare in her own home. Yelena cares for seven children from different families in her home. Draco brings his 5-year-old son to Yelena's daycare and pays $600 per month for ongoing daycare. Yelena is not Draco's household employee, because she operates her own daycare business.

Example: Wagner hires Jorge to do weekly yard maintenance and cut his grass. Jorge runs his own lawn care business called Gonzalez Landscaping Services, and he provides gardening services to many other commercial and residential clients. Jorge advertises his business online and in the local newspaper. Jorge provides his own tools and supplies. Jorge is self-employed and not considered Wagner's household employee.

If a taxpayer pays a household employee cash wages (including amounts paid by check, money order, etc.) of $2,600 or more in 2023, the employer must normally withhold the employee's share of Social Security and Medicare taxes and remit them along with the employer's matching share, for a total of 15.3%. If the wages paid to an employee during the year are less than this threshold, no Social Security or Medicare taxes are owed.

A taxpayer who withholds tax for a household employee must file Schedule H, *Household Employment Taxes,* with their Form 1040. The employer will need to request an employer identification number (EIN) to file Schedule H. The employer also must file Form W-2, Wage and Tax Statement, and furnish a copy of the form to the employee (unless wages paid were less than $2,600 for 2023 and no Federal income taxes were withheld).

> **Note:** An employer is not required to withhold *income* tax from a household employee's wages. However, income tax may be withheld at the employee's request. Even if the employer is not required to pay FICA (Social Security and Medicare) taxes, the employee's wages may be subject to income tax.

> **Example:** Randall is a widowed single taxpayer with infant twin boys. Randall hires Hilda to take care of his twin boys while he is at work. Hilda usually works Monday through Friday, 9 AM to 6 PM. She is an experienced nanny, and she also cleans Randall's home during the day. Hilda is a household employee. Randall pays Hilda $33,000 in wages during the year. He is required to file Schedule H with his Form 1040. He must also file a Form W-2 to report the wages he paid to Hilda, and provide her with a copy of her W-2.

An employer of household employees may need to increase the federal income tax withheld from their earnings, or make estimated tax payments to avoid an estimated tax penalty resulting from their liability for employment taxes in connection with household employees, (as shown on Schedule H). The taxpayer has several options. The employer can:

- Increase federal income tax withheld by giving their employer a new Form W-4;
- Increase their federal income tax withheld by giving the payor of their Social Security or pension a new Form W4-P, *Withholding Certificate for Pension or Annuity Payments;*
- Make estimated tax payments by filing Form 1040-ES, *Estimated Tax for Individuals.*

Estimated taxes must be withheld or paid as the tax liability is incurred, so employers cannot wait until they file their tax return (and Schedule H) to pay household taxes owed. Wages paid to a taxpayer's spouse, parent, or child under the age of 21 are exempt from the nanny tax rules. In that case, the taxpayer would not have to withhold FICA tax.

> **Example:** Geraldine hires her own mother, Enola, to take care of her children during the week. In this case, since Geraldine has hired her mother, the payments are exempt from the nanny tax rules. No Social Security and Medicare taxes will be owed by either Geraldine or her mother. No Federal Unemployment Tax (FUTA) would be owed. However, Enola would owe income tax on the amounts that she earned, and she would need to report the income on her individual tax return.

A taxpayer cannot claim a household employee as a dependent, even if the employee lives with the taxpayer all year long.

Section 199A Qualified Business Income Deduction

This provision, also known as the "Section 199A Deduction" or the "QBI deduction," allows a deduction of up to 20% of qualified business income for owners of some businesses. The deduction is available, regardless of whether an individual itemizes their deductions on Schedule A or takes the standard deduction. This deduction expires after 2025, unless Congress decides to extend it.

The deduction only applies to individuals and estates/trusts who own interests in businesses taxed as sole proprietorships, partnerships, or S corporations.

Income earned by a C corporation is not eligible for the 199A deduction for its shareholders. The deduction allows eligible taxpayers to deduct up to 20% of their qualified business income on their own 1040 (or, in the case of an estate or trust, Form 1041), subject to an overall deduction limit of 20% of taxable income (less any net long-term capital gains, qualified dividends and any QBI deduction for the year).

QBI Deduction: Modified Taxable Income Threshold Amounts

For taxpayers with taxable income that exceeds the threshold amounts, the deduction is subject to two limitations: (1) the type of trade or business and (2) the amount of W-2 wages paid by the qualified trade or business and the unadjusted basis immediately after acquisition (UBIA) of qualified property held by the trade or business. The modified taxable income thresholds are indexed for inflation. In 2023, the modified taxable income threshold amounts are as follows:

- **Married Filing Joint: $364,200-$464,200**
- **All other filing statuses: $182,100-$232,100**

Example: Samira is married and files jointly with her husband, Larry. They take the standard deduction for the year. Samira operates a medical billing service as a sole proprietor. Her business has one employee, a secretary who is paid $50,000 during the year. The business has no significant assets. After figuring her allowable deductions, Samira's business generates $200,000 of net qualified business income. Larry earns $15,000 in wages during the year. Larry and Samira's modified taxable income (before applying the QBI deduction) is $187,300 ($215,000 adjusted gross income minus the $27,700 standard deduction for MFJ filers in 2023). Samira is entitled to a QBI deduction of $40,000 ($200,000 net qualified business income × 20% QBI deduction) on their joint tax return. The wage and UBIA limitations do not apply because Samira and Larry's joint modified taxable income is less than $364,200 in 2023.

The Section 199A deduction only applies to domestic income (U.S. business activities only). Only taxable income is counted. A taxpayer's "QBI component" is generally 20% of the taxpayer's QBI from qualifying trades or businesses. QBI is the net amount of qualified items of income, gain, deduction and loss from any qualified trade or business.

Only items included in taxable income are counted. In addition, the items must be effectively connected with a U.S. trade or business. In other words, the business income *must* be generated by domestic business activity. Items such as capital gains and losses, certain dividends and interest income are excluded.

"Qualified Business Income," or QBI, does <u>not</u> include:

- Employee wages, (except wages earned by a statutory employee),
- Reasonable compensation, (i.e., salary, wages) earned by a shareholder-employee of an S corporation;
- Any guaranteed payment from a partnership for services rendered with respect to the trade or business;
- Investment income; such as capital gains or interest and dividend income,
- Hobby income,
- Non-taxable income, (such as municipal bond interest)
- Rental real estate income where the real estate activity does not rise to the level of a trade/business. This **does not** mean that the taxpayer has to be a "real estate professional" in order to get the QBI deduction. The rental of real property may constitute a trade or business, even if the rental activity is reported on Schedule E.

> **Example:** Warren operates three businesses as a sole proprietor. One is a cupcake bakery with $10,000 in taxable income. The second business is a farming business that has a ($4,000) loss for the year. The third business is a fishing tour company that operates in Cancun, Mexico. The tour company has $20,000 in profits. Since the tour company is not a domestic business, that particular income is not QBI. Based on this information, Warren's §199A deduction is based on the Schedule C net income from the bakery and farming businesses of $6,000, ($10,000 - $4,000).

The QBI deduction is claimed by individuals, so S corporations and partnerships cannot take the deduction at the entity level. However, all S corporations and partnerships report each shareholder's or partner's share of QBI on Schedule K-1, so the shareholders or partners may potentially claim the 199A deduction on their individual tax returns. [178]

> **Note:** The determination of whether a business qualifies for the 199A QBI deduction occurs at the *entity* level. The deduction then "flows through" to the individual owners to be claimed on the taxpayer's individual returns. The QBI deduction is listed on the official Prometric test specs, so you may see a question on this topic on either Part 1 or Part 2 of the exam. The QBI deduction is covered in more detail from a business' perspective in Book 2, *Businesses.*

Eligible individuals may also be entitled to a special deduction of up to 20% of their combined qualified real estate investment trust (REIT) dividends and qualified publicly traded partnership (PTP) income. The total Section 199A deduction is the lesser of:

- 20% of qualified business income plus 20% of their qualified real estate investment trust (REIT) dividends and qualified publicly traded partnership (PTP) income, or
- 20% of taxable income (before any QBI deduction) minus any net long-term capital gains and qualified dividends.

---

[178] The rules to determine whether or not real estate rental activity rises to the level of a trade/business is complex. However, to help partially alleviate this issue, the IRS issued guidance that provides a safe harbor where a real estate rental activity will be treated as a trade/business. In addition to other requirements, the safe harbor provides for trade/business status when a taxpayer (either themselves, through employees or independent contractors) provides at least 250 hours of qualifying services in the activity for at least three of the past five years (including the current tax year), or 250 hours every year if the activity has been operated for less than four years. A number of additional rules apply when a taxpayer owns and rents multiple properties.

An overall qualified business loss results in no QBI deduction for the taxable year. The loss carries over to subsequent years and reduces the section 199A deduction for QBI in the following years.

Foreign Earned Income Exclusion

All income of U.S. citizens and U.S. resident aliens is subject to tax by the United States, regardless of where the individual lives and even if the income is earned outside the United States. "Foreign earned income" is income received for *services* performed in a foreign country while the taxpayer's tax home is also in a foreign country. It does not matter whether the income is paid by a U.S. employer or a foreign employer. The tax home of the taxpayer (where the taxpayer resides) is the main determining factor.

Example: Candice is a U.S. citizen living in Canada. She is legally present in Canada, but works online for a U.S. company. She has lived continuously in Canada for the last five years, only coming back to the U.S. on sporadic short visits of less than a few days. Her tax home is in Canada, and therefore, her income is considered "foreign earned income." The *taxpayer's* tax home is what matters, not the physical location of the employer.

The exclusion does not apply to investment income, such as dividends, interest, or passive income from rental activities. It also does not apply to pension or retirement income. If a taxpayer is eligible for the foreign-earned income exclusion, their foreign income up to a certain threshold is not taxed. For 2023, the maximum foreign-earned income exclusion is $120,000. For married couples, the exclusion is applied on a *per spouse* basis, whether filing MFS or MFJ. In other words, if married taxpayers file jointly (or separately) and both individuals live and work abroad, each can claim the foreign earned income exclusion, for a total exclusion amount of $240,000 in 2023.

Example: Sophia and Abe are married and live abroad. In 2023, they were both living and employed in Peru for the entire taxable year. Sophia earned $82,000 and Abe earned $96,000. Each qualifies for the foreign earned income exclusion, and they can exclude all their wages from federal income tax. Each spouse must file their own Form 2555, whether they file MFJ or MFS.

Example: Donnie and Sherri are a married couple, both 55 years old. They have chosen to make Belize their permanent home and live there year-round. Donnie is self-employed and works online as a financial planner, earning $150,000 in self-employment income. Sherri is a teacher, and she also works online for a tutoring company, tutoring students in English. Sherri earns $35,000 in wages. While Sherri can exclude her entire wage earnings, Donnie can only exclude $120,000 of his self-employment income, because that is the maximum foreign earned income exclusion per individual in 2023. Both Donnie and Sherri must individually file Form 2555, regardless of whether they file jointly or separately.

The foreign earned income exclusion is *not* automatic. Eligible taxpayers must file a U.S. income tax return each year, with a Form 2555 attached, if they wish to claim the exclusion. All of the normal filing thresholds for U.S. taxpayers apply, regardless of where the taxpayer works or resides. If the election is made to exclude foreign earned income, the election remains in effect for subsequent years, unless it is formally revoked. However, it is not necessary to affirmatively revoke the election if the taxpayer does not have any foreign earned income for the year. For example, if the taxpayer lived overseas and had foreign earned income in the prior year, but returned to the United States in 2023 and did not have any foreign earned income in 2023, then the taxpayer does not need to revoke the election.

Example: Wayne is a U.S. citizen who lives and works in Serbia. He has lived continuously in Serbia for several years, working as a consultant for a multinational company. He earns $70,000 in foreign wages in 2023. He also has additional interest income of $37,000, which is from a CD that he has invested in a U.S. bank. His $70,000 foreign wages can be excluded from taxable income, but the interest income cannot be excluded using the foreign earned income exclusion.

A taxpayer must be either a U.S. citizen or a legal resident alien of the United States[179] who has foreign earned income, a foreign tax home, and passes one of two tests to claim the exclusion:

- **Bona Fide Residence Test:** A U.S. citizen or U.S. resident alien who is a bona fide resident of a foreign country for an uninterrupted period that includes an entire tax year.

- **The Physical Presence Test:** A U.S. citizen or U.S. resident alien who is physically present[180] in a foreign country or countries for at least **330 full days** during twelve consecutive months. A taxpayer may qualify under the physical presence test, and the income may span a period of multiple tax years. If so, the taxpayer must prorate the foreign earned income exclusion based on the number of days spent in a foreign country.

Note: The foreign earned income exclusion generally does not apply to the wages and salaries of members of the Armed Forces and government employees of the United States. In addition, citizens or residents of the U.S. working in a combat zone as civilian contract workers may qualify as having a tax home in a foreign country, even if the taxpayer retains a residence in the U.S.[181]

Foreign Housing Exclusion or Deduction

In addition to the foreign earned income exclusion, a taxpayer can claim an exclusion (or a deduction) for foreign housing costs.

The foreign housing *exclusion* applies only to amounts paid by an employer, while the foreign housing *deduction* applies only to amounts paid with self-employment earnings. Qualified housing expenses include reasonable expenses paid for housing in a foreign country. Only housing expenses for the part of the year that the taxpayer actually qualified for the foreign earned income exclusion are considered. Housing expenses do not include the cost of meals, or expenses that are lavish or extravagant. The foreign housing exclusion and/or deduction will reduce regular income tax, but will not reduce self-employment tax (for taxpayers who are self-employed).

Example: Wilmer is a U.S. citizen who lived in Ecuador all of 2023 and was employed by a foreign company as an advertising representative. He lived rent-free in an apartment provided by his employer. Wilmer received a salary of $95,000, and the fair rental value of his housing was $12,000, for a total of $107,000. He qualifies for the foreign earned income exclusion as well as the foreign housing exclusion. He can exclude all his income using Form 2555.

---

[179] Nonresident aliens do not qualify for the foreign earned income exclusion.
[180] The physical presence test, within the meaning of Internal Revenue Code section 7701(b)(1)(A), is based only on how long a person stays in a foreign country or countries. This test does not depend on the kind of residence established, a person's intentions about returning to the United States, or the nature and purpose of a person's stay abroad.
[181] The Bipartisan Budget Act changed the tax home requirement for certain eligible taxpayers, specifically contractors or employees of contractors supporting the U.S. Armed Forces in designated combat zones, who may now qualify for the foreign earned income exclusion.

> **Example:** Claire is a well-known American artist that lives and works in Bogota, Columbia. She runs her art gallery in Columbia and qualifies for the foreign earned income exclusion. Her gross income is $95,000, her business deductions total $27,000, making her net profit $68,000 on Schedule C. She can use the foreign earned income exclusion to exclude all her business income from income tax, but she must still pay self-employment tax on all her net profits.

The Foreign Tax Credit and Foreign Income Taxes

Generally, income taxes paid to a foreign country can be deducted as an itemized deduction on Schedule A or as a credit against U.S. income tax. A taxpayer can *choose* between a foreign tax deduction or a foreign tax credit; they can use whichever one results in the lowest tax. The foreign tax credit *usually* produces a better tax result, but not always. We will talk mainly about the foreign tax credit in this chapter.

U.S. citizens and U.S. resident aliens are eligible for the Foreign Tax Credit, which is designed to relieve taxpayers of the double taxation burden that occurs when their foreign source income is taxed by both the U.S. and a foreign country.[182] Nonresident aliens are not eligible for this credit. Four tests must be met to qualify for the credit:

- The tax must be imposed on the taxpayer.
- The taxpayer must have paid the tax.
- The tax must be a legal and actual foreign tax liability.
- The tax must be an income tax (not an excise tax, sales tax, etc.).

Although taxpayers can choose between taking the deduction or the credit for all foreign taxes paid, in most cases, it is to their advantage to take the Foreign Tax Credit, since a credit directly reduces tax liability. Taxpayers cannot claim the Foreign Tax Credit for taxes paid on any income that has already been excluded using the foreign earned income exclusion or the foreign housing exclusion.

Unlike the foreign earned income exclusion, which applies only to income that is earned while a taxpayer is living and working abroad, the Foreign Tax Credit applies to any type of foreign income, including investment income. Foreign tax paid may be reported to the taxpayer by a financial institution on Form 1099-INT or Form 1099-DIV.

If the amount of foreign tax that the taxpayers incur is small, then taxpayers can claim the credit directly on Schedule 3 if, among other conditions, all foreign income is specified passive income, reported on an information return (such as a 1099-DIV or 1099-INT) and total taxes paid do not exceed $300 ($600 MFJ).

> **Example:** Josephine and Walter are age 65 married, and file jointly. They both receive Social Security, as well as other pension income. They own a number of foreign stocks, and their Form 1099-DIV for the year shows foreign tax paid of $590. They have no other foreign income. The couple is not required to complete Form 1116 because their foreign taxes are less than $600 on their joint return. They can take a foreign tax credit of $590 directly on their Form 1040.

---

[182] For foreign tax credit purposes, a "foreign country" includes: any foreign country, its political subdivisions, and U.S. possessions. U.S. possessions include Puerto Rico and American Samoa.

If the foreign tax paid exceeds $300 ($600 MFJ), a taxpayer must file Form 1116, *Foreign Tax Credit*, in order to claim the foreign tax credit. Certain taxes do not qualify for the Foreign Tax Credit, including interest or penalties paid to a foreign country, taxes imposed by countries involved with international terrorism, and taxes on foreign oil or gas extraction income.

Note: Individuals claim the Foreign Tax *deduction* on Schedule A (Form 1040) as an itemized deduction. The Foreign Tax *Credit* is claimed on Form 1116, *Foreign Tax Credit.* A taxpayer cannot claim both—the deduction and the tax credit—on the same return, but may alternate years, taking a credit in one year and a deduction in the next year, choosing whichever one gives them a better tax result.

A taxpayer is allowed to switch between claiming the Foreign Tax Credit or an itemized deduction for foreign tax paid. If a taxpayer claimed an itemized deduction for a prior year for qualified foreign taxes, the taxpayer can also switch to claiming a credit by filing an amended return within ten years from the original due date of the return. This type of amended return has a much longer statute period than normal amended returns.

Note: Per IRS Publication 514, the foreign tax credit does not apply to any tax paid to Iran, North Korea, Sudan, or Syria. These countries are currently sanctioned by the U.S.

Example: Arshad is a U.S. citizen. He lived and worked in Iran until August, when he was transferred to Greece. Arshad paid taxes to each country on the wages earned in that country. Arshad cannot claim a foreign tax credit for the income taxes he paid in Iran. Because the income he earned in Iran is a disallowed category of foreign income, he must fill out a separate Form 1116 for that income. Further, he cannot take a foreign tax credit for the taxes paid on the income earned in Iran, but all his worldwide income is still taxable by the United States.

Unit 15: Study Questions

(Test yourself first, then check the correct answers at the end of this quiz.)

1. In 2023, at which threshold does an employer have to withhold and pay Social Security and Medicare taxes for a household employee?

A. When the taxpayer pays a household employee $400 or more of wages.
B. When the taxpayer pays a household employee $600 or more of wages.
C. When the taxpayer pays a household employee $2,600 or more of wages.
D. When the taxpayer pays a household employee $12,550 or more of wages.

2. Leopoldo is an entrepreneur with an ownership stake in several businesses. He earns income from many sources. Which of the following activities *cannot* produce a QBI deduction for Leopoldo on his individual Form 1040?

A. A rental activity reported on Schedule E
B. Dividends paid to Leopoldo by a C corporation
C. Income earned from a limited partnership interest.
D. Pass-through income from his ownership in an S corporation.

3. Colton is 22, a full-time college student, and is claimed as a dependent on his parents' tax return. He has a part-time job at a local mall. Colton has $210 of dividend income in 2023. What is the maximum amount of wages Colton can earn in 2023 without triggering the kiddie tax?

A. $1,250
B. $2,500
C. $13,850
D. Unlimited - the kiddie tax is not applicable.

4. Which of the following statements is *correct* regarding the Foreign Tax Credit?

A. The Foreign Tax Credit is a refundable credit.
B. The Foreign Tax Credit is available to U.S. citizens and nonresident aliens.
C. Taxpayers may choose to deduct foreign taxes paid, in lieu of the Foreign Tax Credit.
D. Taxpayers can claim both a deduction and a tax credit for foreign taxes paid to different countries.

5. All of the following statements are correct about the alternative minimum tax *except*:

A. Congress passed the alternative minimum tax to ensure that individuals who benefit from certain exclusions, deductions, or credits pay at least a minimum amount of tax.
B. The tentative minimum tax is figured in addition to a taxpayer's regular tax.
C. The AMT is the excess of the tentative minimum tax over the regular tax.
D. The AMT is permanently indexed for inflation.

6. Charlotte is a U.S. citizen who lives and works in France, which is her tax home. She does not maintain a residence in the U.S., although she does own a residential rental property in Florida, which is currently rented and produces rental income. She received the following income:

- Rental income earned on the Florida rental: $12,000
- Dividend income earned on investments: $500
- Municipal bond interest: $2,000
- Wages earned in France: $90,000

Charlotte wants to take the foreign earned income exclusion on her individual tax return. What is the total amount of qualifying foreign-earned income that Charlotte can report on her Form 2555?

A. $90,000
B. $92,500
C. $99,200
D. $102,100

7. Which of the following taxpayers would not be eligible for the Credit for the Prior Year Minimum Tax by filing Form 8801?

A. An S corporation
B. A trust
C. A decedent's estate
D. An individual

8. Jabbar is a tax preparer. Upon reviewing a new client's prior-year tax return, Jabbar sees taxes paid for the first-time homebuyer credit repayment. Jabbar should ask the taxpayer all of the following questions *except:*

A. What was the total amount of the original credit received?
B. How much of the original credit was repaid on the prior year's returns?
C. Was the entire credit used towards the purchase of their main home?
D. Are the taxpayers still using the home that generated the credit as their main home?

9. The Foreign Tax Credit applies to:

A. Taxpayers who have paid foreign taxes to a foreign country on foreign-sourced income and are subject to U.S. tax on the same income.
B. Taxpayers who have paid U.S. taxes while living and working abroad.
C. Taxpayers who have paid U.S. taxes while living and working abroad and who are subject to U.S. tax on their worldwide income.
D. Nonresident aliens who have paid foreign taxes to a foreign country on foreign-sourced income and are subject to U.S. tax on the same income.

10. Usman and Alyssa filed their 2008 return as Married Filing Jointly and claimed $7,500 for the first-time homebuyer credit. The couple used their home as a primary residence. In 2023, Usman and Alyssa converted the home into a rental property. What, if any, is the tax obligation of this couple, regarding the first-time homebuyer credit?

A. Since they used the home at least 2 of the last 5 years, there is no requirement to repay.
B. They must pro-rate the credit received over 15 years and repay 50% of the original credit.
C. They must reduce their basis in the property by 50% of the unpaid balance of the credit.
D. They must repay the entire unpaid balance of the credit in the current year.

11. Sasha and Anton are married and file jointly. Both are U.S. citizens who live and work in Poland, which is their tax home. They received the following income in 2023:

- Foreign wages Sasha earned in Poland: $129,000
- Foreign wages Anton earned in Poland: $90,000
- Dividend income Anton earned on his investments: $11,800

Sasha and Anton both qualify to take the foreign earned income exclusion on their joint tax return. What is the total amount of qualifying foreign-earned income that Sasha and Anton can exclude in 2023?

A. $112,000
B. $202,000
C. $210,000
D. $240,000

12. Evelyn hired a part-time nanny to work in her home. She paid the nanny $1,950 of wages in 2023 before firing her for being constantly late. No Federal payroll or income taxes were withheld from the nanny's paychecks. Which of the following statements is correct?

A. Evelyn is not required to issue a Form W-2 to the nanny and does not have to report or pay Social Security and Medicare taxes on the nanny's wages.
B. The income is not taxable to the nanny.
C. No reporting is required by either party if the wages are paid in cash.
D. Evelyn can deduct the nanny's wages as a business expense on Schedule C.

Unit 15: Quiz Answers

1. The answer is C. In 2023, the nanny tax applies when a taxpayer pays a household employee $2,600 or more of wages during the year.

2. The answer is B. Dividends paid by a C corporation would not be eligible for the QBI deduction. The "Section 199A Deduction" or the "QBI deduction," allows a deduction of up to 20% of qualified business income for owners of passthrough businesses. A C corporation is not a passthrough entity, so any income earned or later distributed by a C corporation is not eligible for the 199A deduction for its shareholders.

3. The answer is D. Colton's wage income will never be subject to the kiddie tax. The kiddie tax *only* applies to investment income, never to wages or other types of "earned income." Since Colton's dividend income is way below the kiddie tax threshold, he will not be subject to the kiddie tax no matter how much he earns in wages.

4. The answer is C. Taxpayers can claim an itemized deduction for foreign taxes paid on Schedule A. They may choose either the deduction or the credit, whichever gives them the lowest tax. Taxpayers cannot claim both the deduction and a tax credit on the same return.

5. The answer is B. The tentative minimum tax is calculated separately from the regular tax (it is *not* figured *in addition* to the taxpayer's regular tax). The AMT is owed only if the tentative minimum tax is *greater* than the regular tax.

6. The answer is A. Charlotte has $104,500 of *gross* income, but only her wages ($90,000) would qualify for the foreign-earned income exclusion. U.S. citizens and U.S. resident aliens who live abroad are taxed on their worldwide income. However, they may qualify to exclude a portion of their foreign earnings (up to $120,000 for 2023). A qualifying individual with qualifying income may elect to exclude foreign-earned income, and this exclusion applies only if a tax return is filed and the income is reported. The municipal bond interest would be nontaxable, so the only income that would potentially be subject to income tax in this scenario would be the $12,000 in rental income and $500 in dividends.

7. The answer is A. Only individuals, estates, and trusts are eligible to claim the Credit for the Prior Year Minimum Tax by filing Form 8801. The AMT credit is calculated differently for corporations, which use a different form and set of instructions to determine whether they are eligible for the credit.

8. The answer is C. Jabbar does not need to ask if the entire credit was used to purchase their main home. From the instructions for Form 5405: To properly complete Form 5405, all of the questions should be asked *except* for the use of the proceeds of the credit. There was no stipulation as to how the credit would be used when the first-time homebuyer received it. (This question is modified from an EA exam question that was released by the IRS).

9. The answer is A. The Foreign Tax Credit applies to taxpayers who have paid *foreign income* taxes to a foreign country on foreign-sourced income and are subject to U.S. tax on the same income.

10. The answer is D. Usman and Alyssa must pay the entire unpaid balance of the entire credit in 2023, the year they made the rental conversion.

11. The answer is C. The maximum foreign-earned income exclusion is $120,000 in 2023. This amount is applied *per taxpayer*. Sasha's earned income exceeded the exclusion amount. She can exclude up to $120,000 in 2023. Anton's *earned* income is $90,000, so that is the most he can exclude. His dividends do not figure into the calculation. The maximum excluded income on their joint return would, therefore be ($120,000 + $90,000) = $210,000. Each spouse would file their own, separate Form 2555, and attach it to their Form 1040 to take the deduction.

12. The answer is A. Evelyn is not required to issue a Form W-2 to her nanny as less than $2,600 in wages were paid and no Federal income taxes were withheld. In addition, Evelyn does not have to report or pay Social Security and Medicare taxes on the nanny's wages. If an employer pays a household employee cash wages of *less than* $2,600 in 2023, the employer is not required to report or pay Social Security and Medicare taxes on that employee's wages. Regardless of whether Form W-2 is issued, the nanny must report the income on Form 1040.

Unit 16: Individual Retirement Accounts

More Reading:
Publication 590-A, *Contributions to Individual Retirement Arrangements*
About Publication 590-B, *Distributions from Individual Retirement Arrangements*
Publication 575, *Pension and Annuity Income*
Publication 560, *Retirement Plans for Small Business*

There are a variety of retirement accounts individuals can establish for themselves and retirement plans that can be established by employers and self-employed individuals.

In this unit, we primarily cover traditional individual retirement arrangements (traditional IRAs) and Roth IRAs, as they are tested heavily on Part 1 of the EA exam. We will also briefly address other types of retirement plans.

Note: The **SECURE Act 2.0** was signed into law as part of the Consolidated Appropriations Act of 2023. SECURE 2.0 includes many provisions affecting retirement savings plans which are intended to build upon the SECURE (Setting Every Community Up for Retirement Enhancement) Act of 2019 ("SECURE 1.0"). SECURE 2.0 includes changes that affect both employers and employees. Most of the changes in SECURE 2.0 apply to 2023 and going forward.

Form 1099-R, *Distributions from Pensions, Annuities, Retirement or Profit-Sharing Plans, IRAs, Insurance Contracts, etc.*, is used to report distributions of $10 or more from a retirement plan or an IRA. In addition, Form 1099-R will reflect a "code G" in Box 7 for any eligible rollover distribution from a qualified retirement plan that is directly rolled over to an IRA.

Traditional IRA: Amounts in a traditional IRA, including contributions and earnings, are generally not taxed until they are distributed. Typically, a taxpayer can deduct their traditional IRA contributions as an adjustment to gross income. However, the deduction is phased out at higher income levels, when the taxpayer (or the taxpayer's spouse) is also covered by a workplace retirement plan.

Roth IRA: Contributions to a Roth IRA are made with after-tax income and are never deductible. In contrast to a traditional IRA, withdrawals from a Roth IRA are generally not taxed. Unlike traditional IRAs, Roth IRAs do not require participants to start taking minimum distributions at a certain age. Income limits apply in determining who is eligible to participate in a Roth IRA. However, there is no income limit for taxpayers who wish to convert their traditional IRA to a Roth. This process is known as a "Roth conversion" and involves paying taxes on the converted amount.

IRA Contribution Limits

IRA accounts cannot be held jointly. This means that each person must have their own IRA account, but in the case of married spouses that file jointly, only one spouse must have qualified compensation. The limits for contributions to an IRA in 2023 are the *lesser* of (1) qualifying taxable compensation (as described next) or (2) **$6,500** per taxpayer (**$7,500** if age 50 or older).

For those who file as MFJ, under the spousal IRA rules (discussed later), each spouse can potentially contribute up to these limits for a total maximum contribution (for both spouses) of **$13,000** (or **$15,000** if *both* spouses are age 50 or older).

This yearly IRA contribution limit does not apply to:

- Rollover contributions[183] (rolling over from one IRA account to another)
- Qualified reservist repayments[184]
- <u>Repayments</u> of qualified disaster distributions (QDDs)[185] and Coronavirus-Related Distributions (CRDs). Repayments are reported on Form 8915-F.

Example: Oleg, age 51, received a qualified coronavirus-related distribution from his traditional IRA in the amount of $90,000 on September 30, 2020. Oleg elected to recognize all the income from the IRA distribution on his 2020 tax return. Since it was a qualified coronavirus-related distribution, the amount was not subject to a penalty, but it was subject to income tax, which he paid when he filed his return. Oleg later regrets withdrawing the money out of his IRA, and wants to pay it back. On May 3, 2023, Oleg makes a qualified repayment of $45,000. In 2023, he reports the entire $45,000 as a repayment on Form 8915-F, *Qualified Disaster Retirement Plan Distributions and Repayments,* which he attaches to an amended tax return (Form 1040-X) for the 2020 tax year, to reduce the amount of income originally reported by $45,000. The repayment is permitted because it was made within the 3-year period for repayment.

Note: Do not confuse a "qualified disaster distribution" or a "coronavirus-related distribution" with other types of emergency retirement distributions. These were generally allowable distributions of up to $100,000 from certain retirement plans for *specific* disasters. Unlike most distributions, taxpayers can choose to recognize the income ratably over three years, and taxpayers can also choose to repay a qualified disaster distribution over a three-year period. The repayments are treated as a trustee-to-trustee transfer.

Traditional IRA Rules

To make contributions to a traditional IRA, the taxpayer must have qualified taxable compensation, such as wages, salaries, commissions, tips, bonuses, or self-employment income. This also includes *taxable* alimony (but not child support), allowing individuals who rely on alimony for financial support to save for retirement through an IRA. This allows taxpayers to build retirement savings in IRAs even if they rely on alimony income for support.

Nontaxable combat pay also qualifies as compensation for this purpose. Also, difficulty-of-care payments (also called "qualified Medicare waiver payments") to home healthcare workers, are considered "qualifying compensation" for IRA contribution purposes. The SECURE Act 1.0 expanded the definition of "qualifying compensation" to include certain taxable stipends and non-tuition fellowship payments received by graduate students.

---

[183] Indirect rollovers are limited to one rollover per year, but trustee-to-trustee rollovers are not limited.

[184] If a taxpayer was a reservist in the Armed Forces and was called to active duty, the taxpayer can contribute (repay) any IRA amounts equal to any qualified reservist distributions received. The taxpayer can make these repayment contributions even if the payments would cause the total yearly contributions to exceed the general limit on IRA contributions.

[185] The Secure Act 2.0 includes a retroactive provision which includes permanent relief for those impacted by federal disasters. This provision allows penalty-free disaster distributions of up to $22,000 from a retirement plan per participant. This change is retroactive and applies to FEMA disasters occurring on or after January 26, 2021 and moving forward. Taxpayers can choose to recontribute those amounts back into their retirement accounts within three years. Do not confuse Qualified Disaster Distributions (QDDs) with Coronavirus-Related Distributions (CRDs), which ended on December 30, 2020. A Qualified Disaster Distribution is only available FEMA disasters that are non-COVID related. The last year that "qualified disaster distributions" could be made was in 2021, but taxpayers can still choose to *repay* these withdrawals in 2023. A disaster repayment is not considered a "rollover" and the "once-a-year" rollover limits do not apply.

Example: Charlton is an Army medic serving in a combat zone for all of 2023. He earns $43,000 in wages. Although none of his combat pay is taxable, it is still considered qualifying compensation for purposes of an IRA contribution. He is allowed to contribute to a Roth or traditional IRA if he wishes.

Example: Sandra is 45, and divorced her ex-husband in 2016. Her divorce decree is "grandfathered" and her alimony is taxable. She receives $5,000 a month in alimony, ($60,000 per year) which she properly reports on her tax return. She does not have any other sources of income. Sandra is allowed to contribute to a traditional IRA or Roth IRA if she chooses.

In prior years, there were age limits to contribute to a traditional IRA, but the age limits were abolished by the SECURE Act 1.0. Anyone with qualifying compensation, regardless of age, may now contribute to a traditional IRA.

If either the taxpayer or their spouse is covered by an employer plan and their taxable income is too high, their deductible IRA contribution will be phased out. However, as long as a taxpayer has qualifying compensation, they may contribute to a traditional IRA (although they may not be able to *deduct* the contribution).

Note: If the taxpayer (or their spouse, if they are married) *does not* participate in a retirement plan at work, a traditional IRA contribution is <u>fully deductible</u> up to their allowable contribution limit.

"Compensation" for purposes of contributing to an IRA does *not* include:

- Child support or *nontaxable* alimony,
- Passive rental income,
- Dividend and interest income,
- Pension or annuity income,
- Deferred compensation,
- Prize winnings or gambling income,
- Items that are excluded from income, such as certain foreign earned income and excludable foreign housing costs (except for nontaxable combat pay and qualified Medicare waiver payments).

Example: Leroy is single and 67 years old. He received $14,000 of rental income from a residential rental and $13,000 in Social Security income during the year. All his rental income is passive, from long-term residential tenants. The rental income and the retirement income are not qualifying compensation for IRA purposes. Since he does not have any earned income, Leroy is not permitted to contribute to a Roth IRA or a traditional IRA.

Example: Connie is 17 years old and has a part-time job working in a retail shop. She is claimed as a dependent on her parents' tax return. She earns $4,350 in wages during 2023. She also has $2,050 in dividend income. Connie may contribute to an IRA in 2023 because she has qualifying earned income (her wages). Her IRA contribution would be limited to $4,350, the amount of her wages. The investment income is not qualifying compensation for IRA purposes. Connie would be allowed to take a deduction for her IRA contribution on her individual tax return, even if she is claimed as a dependent by her parents.

Example: Dalton is 54 and wants to contribute to a traditional IRA. He received $15,000 of capital gains from the sale of stock; $18,000 of interest income; and $3,950 of wages from a part-time job. The capital gains and interest income are not qualifying compensation for the purposes of determining his IRA contribution. Therefore, the maximum he can contribute to a traditional IRA or a Roth IRA is $3,950; the amount of his wages.

Roth IRA Rules

Roth IRAs and traditional IRAs have many differences, but they are both used for retirement planning. Unlike a traditional IRA, none of the contributions to a Roth IRA are deductible, but qualified distributions are generally tax-free at the time of withdrawal. The major differences between a Roth IRA and a traditional IRA are as follows:

- Contributions to a Roth IRA are not deductible by the taxpayer, and participation in an employer plan has no effect on the taxpayer's contribution limits.
- Roth IRA owners are not required to make minimum distributions during their lifetime. Distributions only become required after the owner's death.
- Roth IRA contributions can be made at any age.
- Income limits apply, which means high-income earners may be prohibited from contributing to a Roth IRA.

Whether or not a taxpayer can make a Roth IRA contribution depends on filing status and modified adjusted gross income (MAGI). The following income limits apply to Roth IRAs:

Filing Status	2023 Roth IRA Phaseout Ranges
Single, HOH, MFS (did not live with spouse)	$138,000–$153,000
MFJ and QSS filers	$218,000–$228,000
MFS (lived with spouse)	$0–$10,000

In general, a taxpayer cannot contribute to a Roth IRA if their income is above the full phaseout figures shown above. However, a "backdoor" Roth IRA is still possible in 2023. This is accomplished when a taxpayer (1) opens a traditional IRA, (2) makes a non-deductible IRA contribution, and then (3) converts the funds to a Roth in the same year. We will cover IRA conversions in more detail later.

If married taxpayers choose to file separately, they must consider only their own qualifying compensation for IRA contribution purposes, whether they contribute to a Roth or a traditional IRA.[186]

Example: Falco is 35, works full-time, and earned $55,000 in wages during the year. His wife, Danielle, is 34 and earned only $3,650 working a small part-time job. Although they are married, they choose to file separate returns. Therefore, Danielle is limited to a $3,650 IRA contribution, the amount of her qualifying compensation. Falco may contribute the full $6,500 (the limit for his age) to his own IRA account.

---

[186] Other than the exceptions for married couples who file jointly, a taxpayer can never contribute more than their earned income for the year. Minors who want to start contributing to an IRA must abide by limits based on their own income, not the income of their parents.

IRAs cannot be owned jointly. Therefore, each spouse must have their *own* IRA account. However, a married couple filing jointly may contribute to each of their IRA accounts, even if only one taxpayer has qualifying compensation. This is called a "spousal IRA contribution."

> **Example:** Derrick, 49, and Elaine, 51, are married and file jointly. Derrick works as a paramedic and makes $76,000 per year. Elaine is a homemaker and has no taxable income. Even though Elaine has no qualifying compensation, Elaine may contribute to an IRA account because her husband has enough earned income to allow her to make a spousal contribution. Their combined maximum contribution for 2023 is $14,000. Derrick may contribute $6,500 to his IRA, and Elaine may contribute $7,500 to her IRA because she is over 50 years old. This special rule for "spousal contributions" only applies if Derrick and Elaine file jointly.

Contributions can be made to a traditional IRA at any time on or before the due date of the return (*not* including extensions). For the 2023 tax year, this means that a taxpayer may make an IRA contribution up until April 15, 2024. Filing an extension does not give a taxpayer additional time to contribute to an IRA.

This makes an IRA contribution a rare opportunity for late-stage tax planning because it can occur after the tax year has already ended. A taxpayer can even file their return, claiming a traditional IRA contribution before the contribution is actually made. However, if a traditional IRA contribution is reported on the taxpayer's return, but the contribution is not *actually made* by the deadline, the taxpayer must file an amended return.

> **Example:** Inigo is age 62 and earns $56,000 in wages during the year. He files his 2023 tax return early, on February 28, 2024, and deducts a $7,500 traditional IRA contribution, the maximum that he can contribute for his age. Inigo may wait as late as April 15, 2024, the due date of the return, to actually make his IRA contribution. If Inigo forgets to make his IRA contribution by the deadline, he will be forced to amend his tax return.

If a taxpayer's only qualifying compensation for the year is from self-employment and the self-employment activity generates a loss for that year, they would not be able to contribute to an IRA. However, if the taxpayer has wages *in addition* to self-employment income, a loss from self-employment would not be subtracted from the wages when figuring total "qualifying" compensation income for purposes of determining his IRA contribution.

> **Example:** Florence, age 42, has a profitable rental property netting $23,000 in passive income. She also works part-time at a library earning $10,000 in wages. On weekends, she's self-employed as a wedding photographer but had a net loss of ($5,400) on her Schedule C business this year. Her earned income for 2023 is only $4,600 ($10,000 wages - $5,400 loss from self-employment), but her "qualifying compensation" for purposes of an IRA contribution remains at $10,000; the amount of her wages. Thus, Florence can contribute the full amount of $6,500 to her IRA, assuming she has enough available funds to do so.

For married taxpayers filing a joint return, the combined IRA contributions cannot exceed their combined qualifying compensation.

Example: Cuthbert and Jacqueline are a 60-year-old married couple who typically file their taxes jointly. This year, Cuthbert has made $53,000 in passive income from his commercial rental property while Jacqueline earned $28,000 in qualified dividends and an additional $8,000 from a part-time job. These are the only sources of income for the year. Only Jacqueline's wages count as "qualifying compensation" for purposes of an IRA contribution. Together, they can contribute up to $8,000 to their IRAs if they file jointly. One of them can contribute up to the maximum annual amount of $7,500 in 2023 (for their age), while the other can contribute the remaining $500 (equal to Jacqueline's remaining qualifying compensation). Alternatively, they could divide the $8,000 equally between their respective IRAs ($4,000 each) or split it in any other way they choose. However, regardless of how they split their contributions, their total combined contributions cannot exceed $8,000.

Deductibility of Traditional IRA Contributions

The deductibility of a traditional IRA contribution is based on income, filing status, and whether the taxpayer (or their spouse) is covered by an employer retirement plan at work. Any taxpayer with qualifying compensation is permitted to contribute to a traditional IRA, regardless of whether they are covered by an employer retirement plan; *however*, the *deductibility* of the contribution may be limited. This only applies to *traditional* IRA contributions, because Roth IRA contributions are never tax-deductible.

If a taxpayer exceeds the income limits for making a fully deductible contribution to a traditional IRA, the excess portion can still be made as a nondeductible or after-tax contribution. If a taxpayer makes nondeductible contributions to a traditional IRA, the taxpayer must file Form 8606, *Nondeductible IRAs.* Form 8606 reflects a taxpayer's cumulative nondeductible contributions, which is the taxpayer's "basis in the IRA."

If a taxpayer does not report nondeductible contributions properly, all future withdrawals from the IRA may be taxable unless the taxpayer can prove, with satisfactory evidence, that nondeductible contributions were made. Regardless of whether a portion of the contribution is nondeductible, the related earnings will grow on a tax-deferred basis. If neither the taxpayer (or spouse) is *not covered* by an employer plan, there is *no limitation* on the deductibility of their traditional IRA contributions.

Example: Cressida is single and earned $135,000 in wages in 2023. She is covered by a 401(k) retirement plan at work. She contributes the annual maximum to her workplace 401(k), but she also wants to contribute to a traditional IRA. She is phased out for the deduction because her MAGI exceeds the threshold for single filers covered by an employer plan. If she contributes to a traditional IRA in 2023, she must file Form 8606 to report her nondeductible contribution. She is still allowed to *contribute* to a traditional IRA, but the amounts would not be deductible on her Form 1040. Cressida is responsible for keeping track of her own IRA's basis, so she should keep copies of her Forms 8606 indefinitely.

Note: Remember, if *neither* spouse is covered by an employer-sponsored retirement plan, their IRA contributions are fully deductible on Form 1040 as an adjustment to income. However, if either a taxpayer or his spouse, (or both,) is covered by (i.e., participates in) an employer retirement plan, the tax-deductible contribution to a traditional IRA may be phased out.

Taxpayers that are covered by an employer retirement plan are phased out at the following levels of modified adjusted gross income (MAGI):

2023 Phaseouts when the Taxpayer (or Spouse) is Covered by an Employer Plan		
Filing Status	MAGI Range	Allowable Deduction
Single, HOH, MFS (did not live with spouse*)	$73,000 or less	full deduction
	more than $73,000 but less than $83,000	partial deduction
	$83,000 or more	No deduction
MFJ (for the covered spouse*), QSS	$116,000 or less	full deduction
	More than $116,000 but less than $136,000	partial deduction
	$136,000 or more	No deduction
MFS (lived with spouse*)	$0- $10,000	A partial deduction
	$10,000 or more	No deduction

If *neither* spouse is a participant in an employer retirement plan, their traditional IRA contributions are fully deductible.

*Note #1: If the taxpayer files MFS but did not live with their spouse at any time during the year, their IRA deduction is determined under the "single" filing status.

*Note #2: If filing as MFJ and only one spouse is covered by a retirement plan, for the non-covered spouse, in 2023, a full deduction is allowed at MAGI of $218,000 or less; a partial deduction for more than $218,000 but less than $228,000; and no deduction at $228,000 or more (see detailed charts in Publication 590-A).

Remember, taxpayers can always have a traditional IRA *whether or not* they are covered by another retirement plan. However, they may not be able to *deduct* all of their traditional IRA contributions if they are also covered by an employer plan.

Example: Leif and Araceli are both age 39, married, and file jointly. Leif is a member of the U.S. House of Representatives and covered by a retirement plan at work. Araceli is not covered by a workplace retirement plan, because she is self-employed. Leif's salary for the year is $239,000. Araceli earned $45,000 in taxable self-employment income. Araceli makes a maximum $6,500 contribution to her traditional IRA in 2023. Since Leif is covered by a retirement plan at his work, and their joint AGI exceeds the phaseout threshold, (The phaseout is $228,000 or more in 2023 if one spouse is covered by a retirement plan at work) Araceli's IRA contribution is not deductible. She is still allowed to make a nondeductible contribution, and the earnings in her IRA account will grow tax-free. Araceli must file Form 8606, *Nondeductible IRAs*, to report her nondeductible contribution.

Example: Henrietta, 59, is employed full-time as a manager for a family-owned restaurant. Her husband, Kirk, 62, is a full-time welder. Neither of them has retirement plans through their jobs, but They both have traditional IRAs that they contribute to every year. Their joint AGI in 2023 is $145,000. They can each deduct up to $7,500 each as an IRA contribution since they are over 50 years old. This deduction is not limited and can be claimed on their joint tax return as an adjustment to income.

Married taxpayers who file MFS generally have a much lower phaseout range than those with any other filing status. However, if a taxpayer files a separate return but did *not* live with their spouse at <u>any time</u> during the year, the taxpayer is treated as "single" for IRA contribution purposes.

Example: Stefano, age 43, and his wife Emmy are not divorced, but they have lived in separate homes for the past two years. In 2023, Stefano earned $41,000 in wages during the year and files as MFS. Stefano is covered by a 401(k) at work, but he has a traditional IRA, also. He is nevertheless allowed to deduct his full IRA contribution of $6,500. This is because he did not live with his spouse during the year, and therefore is not subject to the lower IRA phaseout limits that normally apply to MFS filers.

Example: Adeline and Brixton are married and live together. Adeline has a 401(k) through her job, so she is covered by a workplace retirement plan. Adeline wants to save for her retirement, so she usually makes contributions to a traditional IRA in *addition* to contributing to her workplace 401(k). Adaline's IRA contribution is normally deductible. However, Brixton gets angry at Adeline and refuses to file a joint return with her this year. Adeline is forced to file MFS. She earns only $32,000 in wages, but she cannot *deduct* her IRA contribution because she is filing MFS, and earned more than $10,000 while living with her husband, while also being covered by a retirement plan at work.

Splitting IRA Contributions Between Multiple Accounts

A person may have IRA accounts with multiple financial institutions and may split their annual contributions between accounts; their aggregate contributions for the year are subject to the limits described above. In other words, an individual may own and deposit into multiple IRA accounts, as long as they do not contribute more than the annual limit. Further, a taxpayer may choose to split contributions between a traditional IRA and a Roth IRA; again, their combined contributions are subject to the maximum annual contribution limits outlined before.

Example: Josue is 62. He has a traditional IRA through his credit union and a Roth IRA through an online investment firm. Josue wants to contribute to both accounts. Josue earns $50,000 in wages. He can contribute to both of his retirement accounts, but the combined contributions for 2023 cannot exceed $7,500, the annual maximum for his age (he is allowed a catch-up contribution because he is over 50). Josue decides to contribute $3,500 to his Roth IRA and $4,000 to his traditional IRA.

Example: Gaspar is age 48, earns $5,200 in wages and $45,000 in passive rental income. He does not have any other earnings during the year. His maximum IRA contribution is limited to $5,200 (the amount of his earned income). Gaspar decides to split his IRA contributions between a traditional IRA and a Roth IRA. He contributes $4,200 to a traditional IRA and $1,000 to a Roth IRA. The most Gaspar will be able to deduct as an adjustment to income is the $4,200 contribution to his traditional IRA. Roth IRA contributions are never deductible.

Example: Inez, 28, has $13,000 of gambling income and no other income in 2023. Inez marries Wilmer on August 15, 2023. Wilmer is age 32 and has wages of $74,000. He plans to contribute $6,500 to his traditional IRA. If Wilmer and Inez file jointly, each can contribute $6,500 to a traditional IRA. Inez, who has no qualifying compensation, can use Wilmer's compensation, reduced by the amount of his IRA contribution ($74,000 - $6,500 = $67,500), to determine her maximum contribution to a traditional IRA.

IRA Distributions

Distributions from a **traditional IRA** are generally taxable in the year they are received, subject to the following exceptions:

- Rollovers to another retirement plan (other than conversions to a Roth IRA),
- Qualified charitable distributions directly to a qualified charity (must be a trustee-to-trustee transfer),
- Tax-free withdrawal of contributions (made in the same year),
- Distributions of nondeductible contributions.

Qualified Distributions from a Roth

The rules are different for Roth IRA distributions. Distributions from a Roth IRA may be completely tax-free and penalty-free if they are "qualified" distributions. In order to be a "qualified" distribution, the distribution must satisfy a five-year waiting period, and the taxpayer must be at least 59½, although there are exceptions for disability or death of the IRA owner. A taxpayer can withdraw their regular Roth IRA contributions (their basis, but not the earnings) at any time and at any age with no penalty or tax. Taxpayers over 59½ who have held their Roth accounts for at least five years can withdraw contributions and earnings with no tax or penalty. However, withdrawing *earnings* before age 59½ may result in a 10% early withdrawal penalty, unless an exception applies. Penalty exceptions include death or disability of the IRA owner, and are covered in more detail in the next section.

Example: Walker is 71 and has held his Roth IRA for over fifteen years. He withdraws $9,000 from his Roth account during the year. The entire withdrawal is tax free and penalty free, because he is over the age of 59½, and he has held the Roth for more than five years.

Example: Hetta is age 49 and has owned her Roth IRA for fifteen years. In 2023, Hetta dies. The Roth IRA passes to her adult son, Trevor, who is age 26 and her closest living relative. The Roth IRA includes $86,000 from Hetta's contributions over the years, and $14,000 of accumulated investment earnings. Trevor withdraws the entire balance of the inherited Roth IRA as a distribution. The entire amount is tax-free to Trevor, because (1) his mother, Hetta, had held the Roth IRA for more than five years, and (2) the distribution was made by a beneficiary (Trevor) after the death of the original IRA owner.

Early Withdrawal Penalties and Exceptions

IRAs are owned and controlled by their owners. This means that a taxpayer may withdraw funds at any time from their traditional IRA account, regardless of age and for any reason; however, there may be serious tax consequences if distributions are made early. Distributions before age 59½ may be subject to an extra 10% excise tax, in addition to income tax. There are several exceptions to the general rule for early distributions. An individual may not have to pay the additional 10% tax in the following situations:

- To the extent the taxpayer has unreimbursed medical expenses that exceed 7.5% of AGI,
- To cover the cost of medical insurance while the taxpayer is unemployed,
- The IRA owner becomes permanently disabled or dies,
- The distributions are not more than qualified higher education expenses,
- The distributions are used to buy, build, or rebuild a first home (up to $10,000),

- The distributions are used to pay the IRS due to a levy,
- Made as part of a series of substantially equal periodic payments,
- The distributions are made to a qualified reservist (an individual called up to active duty),
- Qualified disaster distributions, or QDDs.
- Qualified birth and adoption distributions (maximum $5,000 per child, per parent, made within one year of the date of birth or adoption) and terminal illness distributions (for distributions made on or after December 29, 2022).[187]

Even though these distributions will not be subject to the 10% penalty, they will be subject to income tax at the taxpayer's normal rates. Distributions that are properly rolled over into another retirement plan or account (other than conversions to a Roth IRA) are not subject to either income tax or the 10% additional penalty. Taxpayers should use Form 5329 to report penalty exceptions.

Example: Ethan, age 32, and Enya, age 29, are married and file jointly. Enya gave birth to twins on May 3, 2023. Ethan withdraws $10,000 from his traditional IRA a week later. Enya does not own a retirement account. Ethan's entire $10,000 distribution is a qualified birth distribution. Ethan should report the SSN of his twins on his 2023 tax return, and check the exception that applies. Ethan's IRA distribution will be subject to income tax, but is not subject to a 10% early withdrawal penalty.

Example: On January 2, 2023, Oksana, age 39, takes a $8,000 distribution from her traditional IRA account in order to buy a car. She does not meet any of the exceptions to the 10% additional penalty tax, so the $8,000 is an early distribution and is subject to a penalty. Oksana must include the $8,000 in her gross income and pay income tax on the full amount. In addition, she must pay a 10% penalty tax of $800 (10% × $8,000). This penalty will be added to her overall tax liability.

Required Minimum Distributions (RMDs) from Traditional IRAs

Roth IRA accounts do not require minimum distributions during a taxpayer's lifetime, but traditional IRA accounts do. A person cannot keep funds in a traditional IRA account indefinitely. The SECURE Act 1.0, which was passed in 2019, raised the required minimum distribution (RMD) age from 70½ to 72, for taxpayers who reached age 70½ in 2020 or later, and allowed traditional IRA owners to keep making contributions indefinitely. The Secure Act 2.0 pushed RMDs back even further, from age 72 to age 73 in 2023 (and to age 75 in 2033).

These are permanent changes that became effective in 2023. The Secure Act 2.0 also reduces the penalty tax for failure to take RMDs from 50% to 25%. If the failure is corrected in a timely manner (within two years), the penalty is reduced to 10%. This penalty reduction also applies starting in 2023. The *first* RMD distribution can be delayed until April 1 of the year *following* the year the taxpayer turns 73. The distribution for each subsequent year must be made by December 31. The amount of each RMD is based on IRS tables.[188] Failure to take a required RMD can result in an excise penalty equal to 25% of the amount that the taxpayer should have withdrawn but did not.

---

[187] These distributions may be repaid within three years from the day after the distribution was received; this is a new provision under the SECURE 2.0 Act.

[188] Beginning in 2023, the SECURE 2.0 Act raised the age that taxpayers must begin taking RMDs to age 73. If a taxpayer reaches age 72 in 2023, the required beginning date for their first RMD is April 1, 2025, (for 2024). IRS Notice 2023-23 directs financial institutions to notify IRA owners no later than April 28, 2023, that no RMD is required for 2023. An RMD is calculated by dividing the balance of the IRA account by a life expectancy factor that the IRS publishes in tables within Publication 590-B, *Distributions from Individual Retirement Arrangements (IRAs)*.

Example: Shoshana has a traditional IRA that she has contributed to for many years. Shoshana turned 73 on December 1, 2023. Her first RMD is not due until April 1 of the year *after* she turns age 73. She must take her *first* RMD (for 2023) on or before April 1, 2024, and her second RMD (for 2024) by December 31, 2024. Many times, people will forget to take their required RMDs. Previously, the penalty tax was 50% for RMDs that were not withdrawn in time. Now, effective in 2023, that amount is reduced to 25%. If Shoshana forgets to take her required RMD, but corrects her mistake within two years, her RMD penalty will shrink down to 10%. If Shoshana fails to correct the failed RMD within two years, she will be subject to a 25% penalty. Shoshana would file Form 5329, *Additional Taxes on Qualified Plans*, to report the excise tax that applies because of her failure to take the RMD.

Note that these RMD rules do not apply to Roth IRAs, because Roth IRAs do not require withdrawals until after the death of the owner.

Qualified Charitable Distributions (QCD)

A taxpayer who is 70½ or older may choose to make a qualified charitable distribution (QCD)[189] of up to $100,000 from a traditional IRA to qualified charitable organizations and exclude that amount from income. QCD amounts count toward a taxpayer's RMD, if the taxpayer is required to take an RMD, but cannot be claimed as a charitable deduction. In order to qualify, the funds must come out of the taxpayer's IRA by the deadline for minimum distributions (generally December 31). If a taxpayer is filing jointly, the other spouse can also take a QCD up to $100,000.[190]

Charitable distributions are reported on Form 1099-R for the calendar year the distribution is made. The IRA trustee must make the distribution <u>directly</u> to the qualified charity; the taxpayer cannot request a distribution and then donate the money later.

Example: Guadalupe is 77, and she has been taking RMDs from her IRA for many years. Her required minimum distribution is $9,400 in 2023. Guadalupe always donates a large portion of her income to her local Methodist church. Instead of taking an RMD, Guadalupe directs her IRA trustee to make a QCD directly to her church, which is a qualifying 501(c)3 charity. Her IRA trustee transfers a $10,000 qualified charitable distribution from Guadalupe's traditional IRA account directly to her church's bank account on March 31, 2023. In this way, she is able to fulfill her RMD requirement for the year, as well as contribute to her church tax-free. The distribution is not taxable to her, because she never has constructive receipt of the funds. Guadalupe cannot deduct the contribution on Schedule A, because the amounts she donated are already pre-tax.

If a taxpayer over age 70½ makes deductible traditional IRA *contributions*, that taxpayer must later recapture those deducted amounts by reducing any potential qualified charitable distribution made in later years by including those in the taxpayer's taxable income (no double-dipping!). This is not just for the year of the contribution—the effect is cumulative and carries forward.

---

[189] The PATH Act made the QCD election permanent. Although the SECURE ACT 1.0 raised the RMD age, the SECURE Act 1.0 did not change the Qualified Charitable Distribution (QCD) rules. This means that a taxpayer who is 70½ may make a QCD as well as any future tax years. Employer-sponsored plans (like 401(k) plans) cannot make QCDs, but the participant could potentially rollover the funds into an IRA and then make a QCD from the IRA once the rollover is complete.

[190] Beginning in tax year 2024, the $100,000 cap on the QCD amount is indexed for inflation, under the SECURE Act 2.0. For 2024, the annual QCD limit will increase to $105,000.

> **Example:** Norma turned 75 in 2023. She works full-time at the Clydesdale Foundation, a 501(c)(3) horse rescue organization. She loves her job working with horses, and doesn't plan to retire. She still contributes to her traditional IRA every year, and has always deducted the amounts on her tax return. She wants to make a QCD directly to the Clydesdale Foundation. Her QCD exclusion must be reduced by all the contributions she made over the age of 70½.

A taxpayer could potentially make a QCD from a Roth IRA, but there would generally be no tax advantage to doing so, since the amounts in Roth IRAs have already been taxed, and qualified distributions are normally tax-free anyway.[191]

IRA Rollover Rules

A "rollover" is a transfer from one retirement plan to another retirement plan. If executed properly, most rollovers are nontaxable events. A taxpayer can make only one *indirect* rollover from an IRA to another IRA in any twelve-month period. However, trustee-to-trustee transfers between IRAs are not limited, and rollovers from a traditional IRA to a Roth IRA are not limited.

With a **direct rollover**, the funds from the taxpayer's current retirement account are transferred directly to a new retirement plan. This is also called a "trustee-to-trustee" transfer. With an **indirect rollover,** it is up to the employee to redeposit the funds into the new IRA or another qualifying retirement account within the mandatory 60-day period to avoid penalty.[192]

60-Day-Rule: If a taxpayer receives an IRA distribution and wishes to make a nontaxable rollover, they must complete the rollover transaction by the 60th day following the day he receives the distribution. The "60-day rollover rule" applies to **indirect rollovers** of a qualified retirement account, such as an IRA or 401(k). A taxpayer that properly completes an indirect rollover will not owe any interest or penalties as long as all the funds are redeposited into another qualified retirement account within 60 days.

It is not uncommon for employees to roll funds from one retirement plan to another, especially after a job change. When employees leave a job that had an existing retirement plan, the employee will often roll over their existing plan (such as an employer's 401k) into a traditional IRA.

An "indirect" rollover of a retirement account may be requested when an employee changes jobs or leaves a job to start their own business, but does not want to share information with a former employer. Indirect rollovers are limited to one rollover per year. With an indirect rollover, the employer generally withholds 20% of the amount that is pending transfer in order to pay the taxes due.

This withholding is mandatory, even if the taxpayer later intends to roll all the funds over into another retirement account. If the taxpayer does roll it over and wants to defer tax on the entire taxable portion, he will be forced to add funds from other sources equal to the amount of tax withheld. This money is returned as a tax credit for the year when the rollover process is completed.

---

[191] However, if the Roth IRA has not been held for five years, a QCD from the Roth IRA could prevent earnings of the IRA to be subject to taxable income, as compared to a regular distribution from the Roth IRA that has not been in existence for at least five years.

[192] Revenue Procedure 2016-47 allows eligible taxpayers to request for a waiver of the 60-day rollover limit and avoid early distribution taxes. Taxpayers submit the self-certification to their plan administrator or an IRA trustee (NOT to the IRS). In the past, taxpayers who failed to meet the rollover time limit could only obtain a waiver by requesting a private letter ruling from the IRS.

Example: Lucy, age 31, requested a $10,000 distribution from her traditional IRA on January 3, 2023, intending to buy a new car. Her IRA trustee properly withholds $2,000 from the distribution. Thirty days after receiving the money, Lucy talks to her accountant, who informs Lucy that she will be subject to a substantial early withdrawal penalty. Lucy regrets the distribution, and wishes to recontribute the amounts. If she decides to rollover the full $10,000, she must contribute $2,000 from her own savings, and she must complete the rollover within 60 days. On March 2, 2023 (58 days later), Lucy recontributes $10,000 to a traditional IRA, treating it as an indirect rollover. She made the contribution by the 60-day deadline, so on her tax return for the year, she may report $10,000 as a nontaxable rollover and $2,000 as taxes paid. She will not owe a penalty, and will not owe tax on the amounts.

Example: Sheldon quits his old job on September 1, 2023. On October 14, 2023, Sheldon begins a new job, which happens to be with a competitor of his old employer. He has an existing retirement account at his old employer. He decides to transfer the balance of his IRA account to his new employer's retirement plan. Rather than disclose any information about his new workplace to his former boss, Sheldon decides to receive a direct distribution from his IRA of $60,000 in cash. The IRA custodian is required to apply federal income tax withholding to a traditional IRA distribution. Because this was an indirect rollover, Sheldon was forced to replace the amounts that were withheld with his own savings. On October 30, 2023, Sheldon deposits the entire amount of $60,000 into his new employer's retirement plan, making up the difference with his own funds. Because the transaction is completed within 60 days, it is completely non-taxable, and any withheld amounts can be claimed when he files his 2024 tax return. The total rollover must be reported on Form 1040, by including "Rollover" next to Line 4b, with -0- listed on Line 4b.

Note: In order to avoid this mandatory 20% withholding, a taxpayer may request a "direct rollover" (also called a "trustee-to-trustee" transfer). The distribution is then made directly from the custodian or trustee for the employer-sponsored plan to the custodian for the employee's IRA or his new employer's retirement plan. Under this option, the 20% mandatory withholding does not apply. Unlike indirect rollovers, direct rollovers are not limited to one rollover per year.

If a taxpayer sells the distributed property (such as stocks or bonds distributed from an IRA) and rolls over all the proceeds into another traditional IRA or qualified retirement plan within the required time frame, no gain or loss is recognized. The sale proceeds (including any increase in value) are treated as part of the distribution and are not included in the taxpayer's gross income.

In the case of a rollover distribution, if a taxpayer is given both *property* and *cash*, they have the option to roll over any portion of the property or cash, or a combination of both. It is also possible for them to sell the property and utilize the proceeds in a traditional IRA. However, it is not permitted for them to keep the property and replace the received funds with their own.

Example: Arturo is 60 and has a 401(k) at his current job. At the end of the year, he decides to quit his position and transfer his retirement funds elsewhere. He receives a distribution from his employer's 401(k) plan of $20,000 cash and $30,000 of stock. He decides to keep the distributed stock and puts it in a taxable brokerage account. He will owe income tax on this amount, but not a 10% penalty because he is over 59½. He can still roll over the $20,000 cash received into a traditional (rollover) IRA, but he cannot substitute an additional $30,000 in cash in place of the stock and treat this amount as if it had also been rolled over.

Distributions from Inherited IRAs

Anyone can inherit an IRA, but inherited IRAs are subject to special rules. Following the death of an IRA owner, the IRA usually passes to a beneficiary. The SECURE Act 1.0 made major changes to the treatment of inherited retirement plans. The SECURE Act 1.0 changes apply to both traditional IRAs and Roth IRAs.[193]

Required minimum distributions apply once an IRA account owner dies. This applies to Roth and traditional IRAs. In the year of the account owner's death, the RMD should be taken as normal (as if the taxpayer had lived). If the RMD had been taken by the deceased IRA owner while alive, then the beneficiary(ies) of the IRA must take the RMD by the end of the year of death in order to avoid the 25-percent required RMD penalty. For the year following the owner's death, the RMD will depend on the identity of the designated beneficiary.

> **Note:** Before the SECURE Act 1.0, beneficiaries of inherited IRAs could choose a "lump sum" withdrawal or stretch the withdrawal of required minimum distributions over their life expectancy. The SECURE Act 1.0 abolished "stretch IRAs" for most non-spousal beneficiaries. In most cases, the inherited IRA must now be fully distributed to the beneficiary within 10 years after the original owner passes away.[194] When the SECURE Act 1.0 was passed, it was believed that the 10-year rule did not require annual RMDs, as long as the entire account was distributed before the end of the 10-year term. On February 23, 2022, the IRS issued proposed regulations that beneficiaries subject to the 10-year rule also will be subject to RMDs for years 1–9 <u>if the beneficiary inherited the account from someone who had already begun taking their RMDs</u>. Due to confusion created by these proposed regulations, the Internal Revenue Service issued transition relief in Notice 2022-53 and Notice 2023-54, waiving the penalty for 2021, 2022, and 2023 for RMD failures committed by designated beneficiaries.

For most beneficiaries, there are no required minimum distributions during the ten years. However, all the amounts must be distributed from the inherited account by the end of the tenth year *following* the year of the original owner's death. If a beneficiary does not distribute the balance of the account by the end of the tenth year following the year of death, a default 25% excise tax will apply to any amount left in the account that is not distributed.

Under the SECURE Act 1.0, there are two classifications of designated beneficiaries for an IRA. The Act distinguishes between "Eligible Designated Beneficiaries" (EDBs) and other beneficiaries who inherit an account or IRA. An "Eligible Designated Beneficiary" includes:

- A surviving spouse,
- A disabled or chronically ill individual,
- A minor child of the IRA owner (but **not** a grandchild), or
- An individual who is not more than 10 years younger than the account owner.

Spousal Beneficiary: Surviving spouses have the most choices and flexibility. Surviving spouses have the same options they had before the SECURE Act 1.0. A surviving spouse can elect to treat the IRA as their own by (1) changing the ownership designation or (2) rolling over the IRA balance to their

---

[193] An Inherited IRA is also sometimes called a "Beneficiary IRA." This is a retirement account that is opened by the beneficiary of an IRA when the original owner of the IRA has died.

[194] Beneficiaries who inherited IRAs *before* 2020 are grandfathered, and may still utilize the previous stretch IRA rules.

own IRA account. A surviving spouse can also choose to take distributions over their own life expectancy if desired.

> **Example:** Mariella, 42, and Kazim, 53, are married. Mariella dies in 2023, and at the time of her death, she has $83,000 in her traditional IRA account. Kazim is still working, and does not plan to retire for many years. Therefore, he chooses to roll over the entire $83,000 into his own IRA account. As a spousal beneficiary of his deceased wife's IRA, he can do this, thereby avoiding taxation on the income until he starts taking distributions.

> **Example:** Claudio, age 74, and Nanette, age 61, are married. Both spouses have traditional IRA accounts, and Claudio has already started taking RMDs from his traditional IRA. On February 1, 2023, Claudio dies, and Nanette inherits her husband's IRA account. Rather than take a distribution from her late husband's account, Nanette decides to do a spousal rollover of the entire account balance into her own IRA. The rollover is not a taxable event, and Nanette is not required to take any minimum distributions from the account until she reaches the required age for her own RMDs.

Other Eligible Designated Beneficiaries (non-spouses): Other eligible designated beneficiaries may take their distributions over their own life expectancy. However, minor children must still take remaining distributions within 10 years of reaching the age of majority. In other words, the 10-year payout "clock" will begin to run when the minor reaches the age of 18. This means that a minor child must distribute all the assets in an inherited IRA on or before turning 28 years of age.

> **Example:** Shakira is age 49 and widowed. Five years ago, Shakira's husband died and she chose to rollover his entire traditional IRA into her own IRA account. She was permitted to do this because she was a spousal beneficiary. On May 30, 2023, Shakira dies. She has one son, Robby, who is 16 years old. Robby inherits his deceased mother's IRA. Robby is a minor, and qualifies as a "designated beneficiary." His 10-year "payout clock" starts when he turns 18 years of age. He does not have to take any distributions from the inherited IRA now, he can choose to wait and allow the funds in the account to grow until his 18th birthday. When he does start taking distributions, the distributions will be subject to income tax, but not an early withdrawal penalty (regardless of age) because it is an inherited IRA.

> **Example:** Bruno is 38 and unmarried. On February 28, 2023, Bruno dies. The beneficiary of Bruno's IRA is his permanently disabled sister, Megan, who is 26 at the time of her brother's death. Since Megan is a disabled beneficiary, she is allowed to "stretch" the inherited IRA, taking distributions and stretching the tax liability over her lifetime.

Any other beneficiary: For any other beneficiaries, the account balance must generally be fully distributed by the 10-year period after the death of the IRA owner. This 10-year rule also applies to beneficiaries that are entities (trusts, estates, charities, and other organizations).

> **Example:** Crystal, age 65, was unmarried and had no children, died on May 30, 2023. At the time of her death, Crystal had a traditional IRA worth $200,000. The beneficiary of her IRA is her brother, Ozzie, age 42. Ozzie is not disabled. Ozzie can choose to distribute the IRA as a lump sum, or he has 10 years to distribute the balance and pay the tax. No matter what type of distribution he chooses, the amounts he withdraws from the inherited IRA will be subject to income tax. However, the 10% early withdrawal penalty is waived for a beneficiary of an IRA when the original IRA owner has died, (regardless of how old the beneficiary is).

Roth IRA Conversions

A rollover from a traditional IRA to a Roth IRA is more commonly called a "Roth conversion," but it is still a type of rollover. A Roth conversion will result in taxation of any previously untaxed amounts in the traditional IRA that were rolled over into a Roth IRA.

Roth conversions are used frequently as a tax strategy. In the past, taxpayers in higher income brackets were unable to contribute to a Roth IRA. They were also unable to convert from a traditional IRA to a Roth IRA. The IRS rules changed several years ago, and there is no longer an income threshold on Roth IRA conversions. High-income taxpayers can convert a traditional IRA to a Roth as long as they pay the appropriate tax on the conversion. This is frequently called a "backdoor Roth" or "backdoor conversion."

There is no 10% early withdrawal penalty on a Roth conversion, but if a taxpayer wishes to convert a traditional IRA to a Roth IRA, they are required to pay income taxes on the amount of pretax (deductible) contributions converted, as well as the growth in value resulting from earnings on those contributions.

After the funds are converted to a Roth IRA, distributions of conversion amounts are not subject to tax (because tax was paid upon conversion); however, to avoid the 10% penalty, a taxpayer must keep the converted amounts within the Roth IRA for at least 5 years.

Example: Geniece is 40 years old. She converted her entire traditional IRA to a Roth IRA in 2023. The traditional IRA has a balance of $150,000. The entire balance represents deductible contributions and earnings that have not previously been taxed. She reports the amount of the balance that was converted to a Roth IRA as taxable income on her 2023 tax return. The conversion is not subject to a penalty, regardless of Geniece's age.

Roth conversions are reported on Form 8606, *Nondeductible IRAs*. An *inherited* traditional IRA is generally not eligible to be converted to a Roth IRA unless it is inherited directly from a spouse. Non-spousal beneficiaries (for example, a child who inherits a traditional IRA from a deceased parent) are not allowed to convert an inherited IRA to a Roth IRA.

Example: Carson is age 42 and unmarried. Carson's 70-year-old mother died on June 1, 2023. Carson inherited her traditional IRA. He wants to convert the IRA to a Roth, but he is not allowed to do so because the IRA was not inherited from a spouse. He will be required to distribute the amounts in a lump sum, or create a beneficiary IRA in order to distribute the funds within 10 years.

Example: Jolene is age 60, and married to Fred, age 71. Fred dies in 2023, leaving his entire traditional IRA account to Jolene. Jolene does not want to start taking distributions from the inherited IRA, because she is still several years from retirement. She does want to convert the IRA to a Roth, so the amounts can grow tax free. Because she is a spousal beneficiary, Jolene can choose to assume ownership of the inherited IRA, and can then convert the funds to a Roth IRA.

Excise Tax on Overcontributions

If a taxpayer accidentally contributes more to an IRA than is allowed for the year, the excess contribution is subject to a 6% excise tax. However, the IRS will allow a taxpayer to correct an excess contribution if certain rules are followed.

If a taxpayer makes an IRA contribution that exceeds the annual maximum (or qualifying compensation), the excess contribution and all related earnings must be withdrawn from the IRA before the due date (*including* extensions) of the tax return for that year. If a taxpayer corrects the excess contribution by this deadline, the 6% penalty will apply only to the amounts earned on the excess contribution.

The taxpayer must also report the earnings on the excess contribution as taxable income for the year in which the withdrawal is made. If the overcontribution is not withdrawn, the taxpayer must pay a 6% excise tax, and this tax will apply for every year that the overcontribution remains in the account. However, this excise tax can never exceed 6% of the value of the taxpayer's IRA at the end of the tax year.

Note: A taxpayer cannot apply an excess contribution to an earlier year even if the taxpayer contributed less than the maximum amount allowable for an earlier year. However, the taxpayer is allowed to apply an excess contribution to a *later* year if the contributions for that later year are less than the maximum allowable for that year. This is a permitted type of recharacterization.

IRA Recharacterizations

In the past, a taxpayer was able to "undo" or reverse a rollover or conversion of one type of IRA to a different type of IRA through a *recharacterization.* Essentially, by recharacterizing an IRA, it is as if the conversion or rollover never occurred. The Tax Cuts and Jobs Act eliminates the option to recharacterize, or "unwind" an earlier Roth conversion. This means that a Roth IRA conversion cannot be reversed.

Example: On June 1, 2023, Lawrence converts his entire traditional IRA to a Roth IRA. However, the investments in his Roth IRA perform poorly, and his account loses value after the conversion. Lawrence wants to go back and change his mind. However, since he converted his traditional IRA to a Roth, the conversion is permanent. He cannot undo the conversion.

Some types of recharacterizations are still permitted. For example, a recharacterization is allowed for fixing certain mistakes. A taxpayer can use the recharacterization rules to fix an invalid contribution or an invalid rollover, for example. When a taxpayer accidentally makes an overcontribution to a traditional IRA or Roth IRA, they can also choose to either recharacterize the contribution or withdraw it, otherwise a 6% excise tax will apply.

Example: Armin is age 50 and unmarried. He earns $40,000 from his technician job at a hotel. He does not have a retirement plan at work, so he has always contributed to a Roth IRA. On May 1, 2023, Armin makes a $7,500 contribution to his Roth IRA for the 2023 tax year. In December, he sells a large block of cryptocurrency at a large gain, which raises his 2023 MAGI to $290,000, which is in excess of the maximum income thresholds to be eligible to contribute to a Roth, making the entire $7,500 an excess contribution. By the time he discovers his error, it is February 5, 2024 (the following year). Armin corrects his mistake by moving the entire contribution into a traditional IRA by making a trustee-to-trustee transfer. This is not a "rollover." It is a *recharacterization*. Armin has recharacterized the prohibited Roth IRA contribution into a traditional IRA, which is permitted. He will be able to deduct the traditional IRA contribution, as well as avoid the 6% excise tax that would have otherwise applied to his earlier (improper) Roth contribution.

Prohibited Transactions

A prohibited transaction is the "improper use" of an IRA by the owner, a beneficiary, or a disqualified person (typically a fiduciary or family member). Prohibited transactions related to an IRA include:

- Using an IRA as security or collateral for a loan,
- Buying property for personal use with IRA funds (for example, using IRA funds to buy a vacation home the IRA owner will use),
- Borrowing money from the IRA (i.e., there is no such thing as an "IRA loan," although some types of retirement plans do allow borrowing, traditional IRAs <u>do not</u>) [195]
- Selling, leasing, or exchanging property to the IRA account,
- Accepting unreasonable compensation for managing IRA assets,
- Granting account fiduciaries to obtain, use, or borrow against account assets for their own gain,
- Transferring plan assets, lending money, or providing goods and services to "disqualified persons," usually a close family member, or a business that a close family member owns and controls.

For the purposes of the prohibited transaction rules, "family members" include the taxpayer's spouse, parents, grandparents, children, and grandchildren and spouses of the taxpayer's children and grandchildren. Family members do not include: in-laws, cousins, friends, aunts, uncles, siblings, and stepsiblings. Although occurrences of prohibited transactions are rare, the consequences can be catastrophic. If a prohibited transaction occurs at any time during the year, normally, the account ceases to be treated as an IRA, and its assets are treated as if having been wholly distributed on the first day of the year.

However, in situations where an IRA account, or a portion of an IRA account, is used as security for a loan, only the amount used as security for the loan is treated as a distribution from the IRA as of the first day of the year that the loan was made, but the IRA continues to exist.

If the total fair market value as of that date is more than the taxpayer's basis in the IRA, the excess amount is reportable as taxable income. It may also be subject to the additional 10% penalty on early distributions.

> **Example:** Zamir, age 40, has a self-directed IRA account. The fair market value of Zamir's traditional IRA was $300,000 as of January 1, 2023. He had previously made $200,000 of nondeductible contributions to his IRA, so that was his basis in the account. On January 10, 2023, Zamir borrows $150,000 from his IRA to purchase a vacation home for himself. This is a prohibited transaction, and Zamir's entire IRA account will no longer be treated as an IRA from the date of the withdrawal. Since the FMV of the IRA on the first day of the year, $300,000, is greater than Zamir's basis ($200,000) the excess amount of $100,000 must be reported as taxable income. Zamir would also be subject to the additional 10% penalty on the entire amount, for withdrawing funds before the age of 59½.

---

[195] Do not confuse the borrowing restrictions for traditional IRAs and other types of retirement accounts. Loans are not permitted from IRAs or from other IRA-based plans such as SEP-IRAs and SIMPLE IRA plans. Loans are only possible from qualified plans, such as: 401(k) plans or 403(b) plans, and from governmental plans. Qualified retirement plans are covered in detail in *Book 2, Businesses.*

Note: Prohibited transactions are rare occurrences, and they generally only occur when a taxpayer has a "self-directed" IRA. A self-directed IRA is a type of account that offers a taxpayer the ability to use his retirement funds to make almost any type of investment without requiring a financial institution or another custodian.

Prohibited IRA Investments

Almost any type of investment is permissible inside an IRA, including stocks, bonds, mutual funds and even rental real estate. However, there are some investments that are prohibited. For example, the law does not permit IRA funds to be invested in life insurance contracts or collectibles. If the taxpayer invests in any of these prohibited investments using IRA funds, it is treated as a prohibited transaction. The following investments are prohibited:

- Collectibles such as: artwork, jewelry, antiques, porcelain, fine wines, baseball cards, uncut gemstones, and comic books,
- Most precious metals or coins, although there is a narrow exception for investments in gold and silver coins minted by the U.S. Treasury Department.[196]
- S corporation stock,
- Life insurance contracts,
- Real estate held for personal use (real property can be held in an IRA as long as the investments are not in the taxpayer's personal name, and not used for personal use, such as a vacation home used by the taxpayer, a spouse, ancestor, lineal descendant and any spouse of a lineal descendant).[197]

Example: Wheeler is 52 and has $500,000 in his traditional IRA. In early 2023 he purchases a rental property within his IRA as an investment property, and lists it as a short-term rental online. The rental is in a popular tourist zone, and a few weeks later, Wheeler's daughter, Maryanne, uses the property to spend a week-long vacation. Even if she pays for her stay, this is considered "self-dealing" and is a prohibited transaction. For Wheeler, the IRA is deemed immediately disqualified as of 2023 (the year in which the prohibited transaction occurred). The entire amount of the IRA is deemed distributed in 2023, and an early withdrawal penalty of 10% would also apply to the entire amount of the IRA.

Example: Donna has a Checkbook IRA, which is a self-directed IRA that she controls. On January 30, 2023, Donna purchased $374,000 of U.S. gold coins with IRA funds. The coins were shipped directly to Donna's home, in a package addressed to her. She stored the coins in her safe, alongside her personal jewelry. Donna's tax return is later selected for audit. The Tax Court deemed that Donna received a taxable distribution when she took physical possession of the coins, and had "co-mingled" the coins with other assets by putting them in her personal safe. An owner of a self-directed IRA may not take actual possession of IRA assets. The court treated the amount used to purchase the coins as a distribution and imposed accuracy-related penalties. (Based on Tax Court case: *McNulty v. Commissioner*).

---

[196] Investments in certain gold, silver, palladium, and platinum bullion are permitted.
[197] For the purposes of the prohibited transactions rule, family members would include parents, children, grandchildren, and the spouses of children or grandchildren. Siblings, cousins, aunts and uncles, or step-children are not disqualified persons.

Retirement Plans for Businesses

Retirement plans for businesses include Simplified Employee Pension (SEP-IRA) plans, Savings Incentive Match Plan for Employees (SIMPLE) plans, and qualified plans. The term "qualified" refers to certain IRS requirements that the employer must adhere to in order to obtain a retirement plan's tax-favored status. SEP and SIMPLE plans must also meet certain requirements but are much less complex than those that apply to qualified plans.

> **Study Note:** Business retirement plans are covered in greater detail, and from the *employer's* perspective, in *Book 2: Businesses*, as much of the related information is tested on Part 2 of the EA exam. In Part 1 of the exam, you will need to understand the employ**ee's** perspective regarding retirement plans. For Part 2, you must understand retirement plans from the employ**er's** perspective.

If retirement plans are structured and administered properly, businesses can deduct contributions they make on behalf of their employees or, if self-employed, themselves. Both the contributions and the earnings are generally tax-free until distribution. Further, some plans also allow employees to make contributions, most commonly in pretax dollars (so that a portion of their salaries are not taxed until the amounts are later distributed to them by the plan).

SEP-IRA Plans: SEPs provide a simplified method for employers to make contributions to a retirement plan for themselves and their employees. Instead of setting up a profit-sharing plan with a trust, an employer can adopt a SEP agreement and make contributions directly to individual SEP-IRA accounts (similar to a traditional IRA as described previously) for themselves and each eligible employee. In a SEP plan, only the employer makes contributions; employees are not allowed to contribute.[198] If an individual is self-employed and earns income from their business, they can establish and fund a SEP plan.

SIMPLE Plans: An employer can generally set up a SIMPLE plan if the business has 100 or fewer employees. Under a SIMPLE plan, employees can choose to make salary reduction contributions rather than receiving these amounts as part of their regular pay. An employer is allowed to contribute matching contributions or non-elective contributions.

A SIMPLE plan can be structured in one of two ways: as a SIMPLE IRA (again, similar to traditional IRAs as described previously) or as a SIMPLE 401(k) plan (similar to the qualified 401(k) plans described below).

Qualified Retirement Plans

There are two basic kinds of qualified retirement plans: **defined contribution** plans and **defined benefit** plans, and different rules apply to each. An employer is allowed to have more than one type of qualified plan, but contributions cannot exceed annual limits.

All qualified plans are subject to federal regulation under the Employee Retirement Income Security Act (ERISA). The federal government does not require an employer to establish a retirement plan, but it provides minimum federal standards for qualified plans.

---

[198] There are some older, grandfathered SEP plans that were set up before 1997, called SARSEPs, that permit employees to make contributions through employee salary reductions. These were discontinued after 1996, but some grandfathered plans still exist.

Defined Contribution Plans

A defined contribution plan provides an individual account for each participant in the plan depending upon how the plan is structured. It provides benefits to each participant based on the amounts contributed to the participant's account, along with subsequent investment income or losses, and, in some instances, allocations of forfeitures among participant accounts.

The participants, the employer, or both may contribute to the individual participant accounts. Examples of defined contribution plans include profit-sharing plans, 401(k) plans, 403(b) plans, and 457 plans. Depending upon how a qualified plan is structured, salary reduction/elective deferral contributions are employee contributions based on a percentage of the employee's compensation and are generally made on a pretax basis.

This limitation applies to the aggregate amounts of contributions to any qualified plans, SEPs, and SIMPLE plans in which the individual participates during the year. However, the contribution cannot exceed the amount of the employee's compensation. Depending on the individual plan, the employer may provide matching contributions for employees who make elective deferrals.

> **Example:** Spencer earns $80,000 per year as a full-time insurance adjuster. He participates in his company's profit-sharing 401(k) plan. He contributes 3% of his pretax wages to the plan in 2023, or $2,400 ($80,000 × .03). Spencer's employer also contributes a matching 3% to his individual 401(k) account.

Distributions: Distributions to participants may be made either on a periodic basis, such as annuity payments or as a lump sum. As is the case with distributions from traditional IRA accounts (as well as SEP and SIMPLE plans), distributions generally are not permitted prior to when the participant retires or otherwise terminates employment, dies, becomes disabled, or reaches age 59½. Earlier distributions are generally subject to an additional 10% penalty tax.

> **Note:** For purposes of the net investment income tax (NIIT), net investment income does not include distributions from a qualified retirement plan, such as a 401(k), or from traditional or Roth IRAs. However, these distributions are taken into account when determining the modified adjusted gross income threshold.

In 2023, required minimum distributions (RMDs) from defined contribution plans[199] must generally begin by April 1 of the year *following* the calendar year when the taxpayer retires, or the year in which the taxpayer reaches age 73, whichever comes later.[200]

> **Example:** In 2023, Norman retires at age 67 after working for three decades at an automobile manufacturing plant. His employer offers a 401(k), a defined contribution plan, in which Norman participates. Norman chooses to begin taking distributions from his 401(k) plan in the same year he retires. The distributions would be taxed as retirement income on his individual tax return. The amounts will be subject to income tax.

---

[199] Defined contribution plans include 401(k) plans, profit-sharing, and 403(b) plans.
[200] The Secure Act 2.0 increases this age limit effective January 1, 2023, the threshold age that determines when individuals must begin taking required minimum distributions (RMDs) from traditional IRAs and workplace retirement plans increases from 72 to 73. This means that individuals born in 1951 must receive their first required minimum distribution by April 1, 2025.

Defined Benefit Plans

A defined benefit plan, often called a traditional pension plan, promises a specified benefit amount or annuity for each participant after retirement. Benefits are typically based on formulas that consider the participant's years of service with the employer and his earnings history. The federal government and most state and local governments provide defined benefit plans for their employees. The benefits promised by many defined benefit plans are protected by federal insurance. Contributions to a defined benefit plan are not optional.

Contributions are typically based on actuarial calculations that estimate the amounts necessary to pay benefits in the future. Defined benefit plans are still commonly offered to federal and government workers; however, fewer and fewer private companies offer defined benefit plans because they are costly to administer and inflexible.

Example: Garrison has been a police officer in Boulder, Colorado for many years. Garrison has a defined-benefit pension through his employer. Colorado has a statewide Defined Benefit Plan that covers all full-time firefighters and law enforcement officers. Garrison retires at age 62 with a pension of $82,000. He will receive a monthly retirement benefit that is payable until his death.

Loans and Distributions from Qualified Plans

Unlike traditional IRAs and Roth IRAs, where withdrawals are permitted at any time, distributions from qualified plans are generally restricted by the employer. This means that an employee <u>cannot</u> withdraw from the qualified plan whenever they choose, (like one can from a traditional IRA or Roth IRA). Generally, distributions of elective deferrals cannot be made until one of the following occurs:

- The taxpayer dies, becomes disabled, or has a severance from employment.
- The plan terminates, and no successor-defined contribution plan is established or maintained by the employer (this may happen when a business dissolves or files for bankruptcy)
- The taxpayer reaches age 59½, or the taxpayer incurs significant financial hardship.

Some limited borrowing from *qualified plans* is allowed. Loans are not dependent upon hardship, but some plans may provide for loans as well as hardship withdrawals (although the plan is not required to do so).[201] If a loan is not repaid according to the specified payment terms, it may be considered a taxable distribution. This may happen if a participant terminates employment with the employer that sponsors the plan.[202]

Example: Ember, age 60, borrowed $40,000 from her 401(k) plan at work in order to pay some emergency expenses. She paid the balance of the loan down to $22,000 before quitting her job and defaulting on the remaining part of the loan. Ember will be treated as having taken out $22,000 from her 401(k) plan in the year of the default. She will not owe an early withdrawal penalty because she is over 59½, but she must include the $22,000 "deemed distribution" in her taxable income for the year.

---

[201] Note that these special rules for plan loans do not apply to IRAs, because loans are never permitted from an IRA. If an owner of an IRA borrows from the IRA, this is a prohibited transaction, and the value of the entire IRA is included in the owner's income (less any potential tax basis in the IRA).
[202] Most qualified plans offer employees the ability to borrow from their own retirement account and repay that amount with interest to their own retirement account. IRS regulations permit qualified plans to offer loans to plan participants, but the plan is not *required* to.

Example: Ophelia participates in her 401(k) at her work. Her employer's 401(k) plan allows for participant loans. Ophelia has a vested account balance of $100,000 in her 401(k). In 2023, Ophelia has an unexpected dental emergency and must have 4 root canals done in the same month. Her health insurance does not include dental coverage, so she has to pay for the root canals herself. Ophelia requests a plan loan from her 401(k) of $20,000 to be paid in 20 installments. The loan is not treated as a distribution, and is not taxable to Ophelia, as long as she satisfies the plan loan rules and makes her payments on time.

Hardship Distributions

A 401(k) plan may allow participants to receive hardship distributions because of an immediate and heavy financial need, such as sudden medical or funeral expenses. Hardship distributions are limited to the amount of the employee's elective deferrals and generally do not include any income earned on the deferred amounts.

The drawback to hardship distributions is that the amounts withdrawn can be subject to income tax as well as an early withdrawal penalty. The amount of the distribution may also include withholding to pay taxes or penalties anticipated to result from the distribution.

Note: Some types of retirement plans provide for hardship distributions. These include 401(k) plans, 403(b) plans, and 457(b) plans, which are employer retirement plans that may permit hardship distributions. A **"hardship distribution"** is not the same as a **"disaster distribution."** A qualified disaster distribution gets special tax treatment and is only available to taxpayers who have incurred losses or hardship in a presidentially declared disaster area (i.e., a FEMA disaster area). Hardship distributions are not eligible for repayment, but qualified disaster distributions *can* be repaid. Any disaster relief withdrawal will *not be taxable* if it is recontributed to the account within three years of the date of distribution.

Example: Damara is 37 years old. Her home is in foreclosure, and she is in immediate danger of being evicted. Her employer's 401(k) plan does not allow participant loans, but does allow for hardship distributions. Damara requests a $15,000 hardship distribution from her 401(k), which is granted. Since she is under age 59½, Damara would likely have to pay the 10% early distribution penalty, as well as income tax on the amounts withdrawn.

Traditional IRA vs. Roth IRA Comparison

Issue	Traditional IRA	Roth IRA
Age limit	No age limit in 2023 for contributions.	No age limit for contributions
2023 Contribution limits	The lesser of $6,500 (or $7,500 if age 50 or older by the end of the year) and qualifying compensation.	Same
Deductibility of contributions	Generally deductible.	Contributions to a Roth IRA are never deductible.
Filing requirements	No filing requirement unless nondeductible contributions are made. Nondeductible contributions must be reported on Form 8606.	Filing requirement related to a conversion of a traditional IRA to a Roth IRA. None related to contributions made directly to a Roth IRA.
Mandatory distributions	RMDs by April 1 of the year following the year a taxpayer reaches age 73 (in 2023)	There are no required distributions unless the IRA owner dies.
How distributions are taxed	Distributions from a traditional IRA are generally taxed as ordinary income.	Qualified distributions from a Roth IRA are generally not taxed.
Income limits	Anyone with qualifying compensation can contribute. Phaseout of deductibility is based upon AGI if the taxpayer and/or spouse are covered by an employer plan.	There are income limits for contributions, but "backdoor" conversions of a traditional IRA to a Roth IRA are still permissible.

Unit 16: Study Questions

(Test yourself first, then check the correct answers at the end of this quiz.)

1. Damon, age 50, is unmarried and permanently disabled with Down's syndrome. Damon is claimed as a dependent by his sister, Betty, who he lives with, and provides the majority of his financial support. Damon earns $5,500 in wages during 2023 working in a sheltered workshop. He also receives $500 of interest income and a $4,000 in gambling income from a scratch off ticket that his sister gave him for his birthday. What is his maximum IRA contribution in 2023?

A. $0
B. $5,500
C. $6,500
D. $7,500

2. Lainey e-files her 2023 tax return early, on February 27, 2024. She wants to take a tax deduction for a $6,500 IRA contribution on her return. Assuming that she does so, what is the latest date that she can make a traditional IRA contribution for the 2023 tax year?

A. April 15, 2024
B. February 27, 2024 (the same day she files her return)
C. December 31, 2023
D. October 15, 2024 (with a valid extension)

3. Elizabeth and Aaron are both age 61, married, and lived together all year. They both work, and each has a traditional IRA. Aaron is mostly retired, and Elizabeth still works full-time. In 2023, Aaron earned $4,200 of wages from working at a hardware store on the weekends. He also received $28,000 of pension income. Elizabeth earned $52,000 in wages. They prefer to file separately. If they file MFS, what is the maximum that Aaron can contribute to his IRA?

A. $1,000
B. $4,200
C. $5,500
D. $6,500

4. Shari switched jobs in the middle of the year. She received a total distribution of $120,000 in 2023 from her former employer's retirement plan, intending to roll it over into a new IRA. Instead of doing a direct transfer, the trustee screws up the paperwork and sends Shari a paper check. How long does she have to complete the indirect rollover to avoid income tax and penalties on the distribution?

A. 30 days from distribution.
B. 60 days from distribution.
C. December 31 of that tax year.
D. Until the unextended due date of her tax return.

5. Vadik, age 42, has a traditional IRA account. He wants to convert his traditional IRA to a Roth IRA. Which of the following statements is *correct*?

A. Vadik can convert his traditional IRA to a Roth IRA and the transaction is tax-free.
B. Vadik can rollover his traditional IRA to a Roth IRA only if his income is under $150,000.
C. Vadik cannot convert his traditional IRA to a Roth IRA because he is under 59½ years of age.
D. Vadik can convert his traditional IRA to a Roth IRA. Income tax must be paid on the conversion.

6. Melissa, age 41, and William, age 47, are married and file jointly. Both are self-employed and report their business income on Schedule C. William's Schedule C business has $9,900 in profits during the year. His wife, Melissa, has a loss of ($5,100) on her Schedule C. Melissa also earned $4,000 in wages from a part-time seasonal job. They also co-own a residential rental property that they manage together. The rental property earned $58,000 in passive income during the year. What is their maximum allowable IRA contribution for 2023?

A. William can contribute $6,500, and Melissa can contribute $6,500.
B. William can contribute $6,500, and Melissa can contribute $4,000.
C. William can contribute $6,000, and Melissa cannot contribute.
D. William can contribute $7,500, and Melissa can contribute $4,000.

7. Alfred is 42 and unmarried. He earned $47,000 in wages during the year. He has a Roth IRA and a traditional IRA with two different financial institutions. On December 15, 2023, he contributed $2,500 to his Roth IRA. He also wants to contribute to his traditional IRA account. What is the maximum he can contribute to a traditional IRA for 2023?

A. $0
B. $3,500
C. $4,000
D. $4,500

8. An "excess" contribution to an IRA is subject to an excise tax. What is the applicable excise tax rate?

A. 3%
B. 6%
C. 10%
D. 50%

9. Which of the following distributions from a traditional IRA is subject to an additional 10% penalty?

A. Distributions made prior to age 59½.
B. Distributions made after age 70½.
C. Distributions made to a beneficiary after the IRA owner's death.
D. Distributions made due to an IRS levy.

10. Kristina, 48, is a full-time graduate student with $1,250 of wages. She marries Ruslan, 50, during the year. Ruslan has taxable wages of $66,000 in 2023. What is the maximum they can contribute to their traditional IRA accounts in 2023 if they file jointly?

A. Kristina and Ruslan can both contribute a maximum of $6,500
B. Kristina can contribute $1,250, and Ruslan can contribute $7,500
C. Kristina can contribute $1,250, and Ruslan can contribute $6,500
D. Kristina can contribute $6,500, and Ruslan can contribute $7,500

11. Ernesto, age 73, and Susie, age 49, are married and file jointly. In 2023, Ernesto earned wages of $55,000, and Susie earned $4,100. If they file jointly, how much can they contribute to their traditional IRAs for 2023?

A. Susie and Ernesto can each contribute $6,500 to their respective IRA accounts.
B. Susie and Ernesto can each contribute $7,500 to their respective IRA accounts.
C. Susie can contribute $6,500. Ernesto can contribute $7,500.
D. Susie can contribute $4,100. Ernesto cannot make an IRA contribution because he is 73.

12. Steven, age 36 and single, is in the Marines. He has the following income in 2023:

Nontaxable combat pay	$30,500
Regular wages	$2,100
Interest income	$4,600

What is the maximum amount that Steven can contribute to a traditional IRA?

A. $2,100
B. $4,600
C. $6,500
D. $7,500

13. Nichelle is single, age 63, and has the following taxable income in 2023:

Annuity income	$15,600
Form W-2 wages	$5,300
Interest income	$2,800
Passive rental income from a residential rental	$26,000

What is the maximum amount that Nichelle can contribute to her traditional IRA in 2023?

A. $3,000
B. $5,300
C. $6,5000
D. $7,500

14. At which age does the owner of a Roth IRA have to begin taking required minimum distributions?

A. Never required
B. At age 70½
C. At age 73
D. 75

15. Gwendolyn, age 38, is single and has no dependents. She contributes $6,500 to a traditional IRA, and she also participates in her employer's 401(k) plan. She has a modified adjusted gross income of $239,000 in 2023. Which of the following is correct regarding her IRA contribution?

A. It is fully deductible.
B. It is partially deductible.
C. It is not deductible.
D. The entire contribution is disallowed, and is subject to a 6% excise tax.

16. For the purposes of the prohibited transaction rules, which of the following would not be considered a disqualified person?

A. The spouse of the IRA owner.
B. The daughter of the IRA owner.
C. The sibling of the IRA owner.
D. The parent of the IRA owner.

17. Margaret is age 17 and single. She is claimed as a dependent by her parents. Margaret has income totaling $2,500 for the year. The income she received consists of $1,600 earned from a part time job and $900 in interest income from investments gifted to her by her grandparents. Margaret's parents earn $125,000 in wages. What is the maximum amount of money that she can contribute to a traditional IRA?

A. $0
B. $1,600
C. $2,500
D. $6,500

Unit 16: Quiz Answers

1. The answer is B. Damon's IRA contribution for 2023 is limited to $5,500, the total amount of his wages. The interest income and the gambling income are not qualifying compensation for IRA purposes. Dependents of any age can contribute to an IRA as long as they have earned income.

2. The answer is A. Lainey is allowed to make her retirement contribution at any time during the year up to the due date of her tax return, *not including* extensions. IRA contributions for 2023 must be made by April 15, 2024 (the due date for 2024 returns). This is true even if Lainey files her return early. However, If Lainey forgets to make her IRA contribution by the deadline, and she has already filed her return, she will be forced to amend her tax return.

3. The answer is B. Since Aaron is married and lived with his wife during the year but is filing separately, he can contribute no more than $4,200, the amount of his qualifying compensation for IRA purposes. The pension income is not qualifying compensation for the purposes of contributing to an IRA.

4. The answer is B. Shari has 60 days to complete the indirect rollover to the retirement plan of her choice. If she does not complete the rollover within 60 days, the entire distribution is subject to income tax in 2023.

5. The answer is D. Vadik may convert his traditional IRA to a Roth IRA, but he will owe income tax on the conversion. If he wishes to convert all or a portion of his traditional IRA to a Roth IRA, he is required to pay income taxes on the amount of pretax (deductible) contributions converted, as well as the growth in value resulting from earnings on those contributions. After the funds are converted to a Roth IRA, additional earnings are tax-free, and distributions are generally not subject to tax. However, penalties apply if he withdraws from the Roth IRA within five years of the conversion. The conversion is reported on Form 8606, *Nondeductible IRAs*.

6. The answer is A. On a jointly filed return, they are both allowed to contribute and deduct the maximum allowable for their age bracket ($6,500 each in 2023). The rental income is not qualifying compensation for IRA purposes, but William and Melissa may use their combined self-employment income to figure their maximum allowable IRA contribution. Even though Melissa's business had a net operating loss for the year, she is not required to "offset" her Schedule C losses from her wages when determining her "allowable" IRA contribution. The answer is figured as follows:

William: $9,900 self-employment income + Melissa: $4,000 wages
= $13,900 in total "qualifying compensation"

If they file jointly, they can each contribute $6,500 to a traditional IRA for themselves ($6,500 ×2 = $13,000, which is less than the amount of their qualifying compensation).

7. The answer is C. Assuming Alfred has sufficient qualifying compensation; he could contribute $4,000 to his traditional IRA ($2,500 + $4,000 = $6,500). The 2023 maximum for contributions to *all types* of IRAs is $6,500 per individual (for taxpayers under the age of 50). Individuals are allowed to have different types of IRA accounts, but the maximum contribution limits apply to their total contributions for the year.

8. The answer is B. A 6% excise tax applies to excess contributions. The taxpayer will not have to pay the 6% tax on the excess contribution if the excess contribution and any earnings are withdrawn by the due date of his return, *including* extensions. If a taxpayer corrects the excess contribution in time, the 6% penalty will apply only to the earnings on the excess contribution.

9. The answer is A. Distributions made *prior* to age 59½ are subject to a 10% early withdrawal penalty, (if no exception applies). Some exceptions that allow early distributions from an IRA, as well as from qualified retirement plans, include the following:

- Distributions made to a beneficiary after death.
- Distributions made because of permanent disability.
- Distributions to the extent of medical expenses (medical expenses that exceed 7.5%-of-AGI), whether or not the taxpayer itemizes deductions for the year.
- Distributions made due to an IRS levy.
- Qualified disaster distributions.

The distributions listed above are not subject to the 10% early withdrawal penalty.

10. The answer is D. As long as they file jointly, Kristina can contribute $6,500, and Ruslan can contribute $7,500 (his contribution limit is higher because he is age 50). Even though Kristina only has $1,250 of qualifying compensation, she can use her husband's compensation to determine her maximum contribution because they are filing a joint return.

11. The answer is C. If they file jointly, Susie can contribute $6,500 in 2023 (she is under 50 years of age). Ernesto can contribute $7,500 because he is over the age of 50. The SECURE Act eliminated the age limit for making contributions to a traditional IRA, so taxpayers of any age can contribute to a traditional IRA as long as they have qualifying compensation.

12. The answer is C. Steven may contribute $6,500 in 2023, the maximum contribution allowed for his age, because a taxpayer may *elect* to treat nontaxable combat pay as qualifying compensation for IRA purposes. The interest income is not considered qualifying compensation, but his wages exceed the maximum contribution amount, so he is still allowed to make the maximum contribution for the year.

13. The answer is B. Nichelle's maximum contribution for 2023 is $5,300. Only her wage income qualifies as "compensation" for the purposes of an IRA contribution. The annuity income, rental income, and interest income do not qualify.

14. The answer is A. Unlike traditional IRAs, Roth IRAs do not require withdrawals until after the death of the owner. This is why Roth IRAs are used frequently as an estate-planning tool.

15. The answer is C. Gwendolyn can make a traditional IRA contribution, but she cannot *deduct* her IRA contribution. Contributions to a traditional IRA who participates in an employer-sponsored retirement plan are allowed, but their deductibility is phased out at higher income thresholds (these thresholds are in the chapter). When a taxpayer's MAGI reaches a certain threshold, the taxpayer's traditional IRA contribution is not deductible (if they are covered by a workplace plan). If Gwendolyn makes *nondeductible* contributions to her traditional IRA, she must attach Form 8606, *Nondeductible IRAs*, to her tax return.

16. The answer is C. A sibling would not be considered a disqualified person. A "prohibited transaction" under the Internal Revenue Code (IRC) is a transaction prohibited by law between a retirement plan and a disqualified person. A disqualified person is any member of the IRA owner's immediate family, spouses, ancestors, and direct lineal descendants, and spouses of those descendants. The IRS does not consider siblings, cousins, aunts and uncles, or stepchildren as disqualified persons for the purposes of this rule.

17. The answer is B. Margaret can contribute to a traditional IRA, but the amount of her contribution is limited to her qualifying compensation for the year, which is $1,600 in wages that she earned herself. She would be allowed to take a deduction for her IRA contribution on her individual tax return, even if she is claimed as a dependent by her parents. Minors may contribute to their own IRAs, but they must abide by limits based on their *own* income, *not* the income of their parents.

Unit 17: Foreign Financial Reporting

> **More Reading:**
> *Instructions for FinCEN Form 114*
> *Instructions for Form 3520*
> **Publication 5569,** *Report of Foreign Bank & Financial Accounts (FBAR) Reference Guide*
> **Beneficial Ownership Information Reporting Rule Fact Sheet**

In this chapter, we will discuss foreign financial reporting requirements for U.S. taxpayers. The *Bank Secrecy Act (BSA)* is the law that imposes reporting requirements on foreign financial accounts. The *Foreign Account Tax Compliance Act (FATCA)* is the law that mandates the reporting of foreign financial assets. The subject of foreign financial reporting is extremely complex, and the IRS continues to issue guidance on how taxpayers and tax professionals should approach this difficult topic.

Note: Congress passed the Corporate Transparency Act ("CTA") on January 1, 2021, but the requirements to report beneficial ownership information (BOI) did not go into effect until January 1, 2024. Certain entities created or registered to do business in the United States will be required to disclose personal information about their beneficial owners to the FinCEN, unless they are specifically exempt from this requirement. Note that the current EA exam specifications do <u>not</u> include these new BOI requirements.

A person who holds a foreign financial account may have a reporting obligation even when the account produces no taxable income, and even if the person does not have an individual income tax filing requirement. The definition of a "United States person" for foreign financial reporting purposes includes U.S. citizens, U.S. nationals, U.S. residents, and U.S. entities. Generally, nonresident aliens are not obligated to file FBARs. However, exceptions may occur if the nonresident chooses to be treated as a resident for tax purposes or elects to file a joint tax return with a U.S. citizen or resident.

Example: Trendy International, Inc., is a Florida C corporation that conducts business operations in Spain. The corporation has foreign bank accounts in Spain with account balances in excess of $10,000 during the year. Eliza is a U.S. citizen and is the sole shareholder of Trendy International. She has signature authority over all the foreign accounts. Therefore, Eliza and Trendy International must file FBARs, because both have a financial interest in, or authority over, a foreign financial account.

There are several different forms[203] used for reporting foreign bank accounts, foreign assets, and foreign gifts. These are:

- **FBAR,** Form 114, Report of Foreign Bank and Financial Accounts
- **Form 8938,** Statement of Specified Foreign Financial Assets
- **Schedule B,** Interest and Ordinary Dividends (Part III)
- **Form 3520,** Annual Return to Report Transactions with Foreign Trusts and Receipt of Certain Foreign Gifts
- **Form 5471,** Information Return of U.S. Persons With Respect to Certain Foreign Corporations

---

[203] This list is not comprehensive. It only includes the most commonly used forms for foreign-financial reporting and those that are listed on the Prometric test specifications for Part 1 of the EA exam. There are additional forms, such as Form 8865, *Return of U.S. Persons with Respect to Certain Foreign Partnerships,* which is used to declare interest in a foreign partnership.

Federal law requires that U.S. persons report all worldwide income, including income from foreign trusts and foreign bank accounts. In many cases, these taxpayers need to complete Schedule B and attach it to their tax return. Certain taxpayers may also have to fill out and attach Form 8938, *Statement of Foreign Financial Assets*. Form 3520 is used to report certain foreign gifts and bequests, as well as certain transactions with foreign trusts. Schedule B, Form 3520, and Form 8938 are all filed with the Internal Revenue Service. The FBAR filing requirement, however, is a separate filing requirement than filing a regular tax return. FBARs are not filed with the IRS; these forms are filed directly with the Financial Crimes Enforcement Network (FinCEN), which is a division of the U.S. Treasury Department. Generally, records of accounts required to be reported on the FBAR should be kept a minimum of five years from the due date of the report, which is the year *following* the calendar year being reported.

FBAR Enforcement Authority

The term "FBAR" refers to Form 114, *Report of Foreign Bank and Financial Accounts*. The FBAR is a reporting requirement and does not directly impact tax liability. In 2003, the Department of the U.S. Treasury delegated FBAR enforcement authority to the Internal Revenue Service (IRS). This means that the IRS does not process the FBAR filings, but the IRS is responsible for FBAR *enforcement*. With regard to FBAR filings, the IRS is responsible for:

- Investigating possible civil violations,
- Assessing and collecting civil penalties, and
- Issuing administrative rulings.

The FBAR must be filed electronically and is only available online through the BSA E-Filing System.[204] The FBAR form itself is not considered part of the taxpayer's individual tax return, but disclosure of ownership of any foreign account or an FBAR filing requirement is required on Form 1040, Schedule B, Part III. A U.S. taxpayer is required to file an FBAR if:

- The person had a financial interest in, or *signature authority* over, at least one financial account located outside of the United States, and
- The *aggregate* value of all foreign financial accounts exceeded $10,000 (U.S. dollars) at any time during the calendar year reported.[205] This threshold is the same for every filing status.[206]

Example: Erma is 24 years old and a citizen of Switzerland. She is a legal U.S. resident (a green-card holder). She lives with her fiancé in the United States, but she also frequently travels to her home country and maintains a bank account in Switzerland with an average balance of $40,000. Erma does not work because her father is wealthy and he supports her financially. Even though Erma has no taxable income and does not have to file an income tax return, she is required by law to file an FBAR to report this foreign account.

---

[204] The "BSA E-Filing System" is an official U.S. Treasury website and is used for online filing of FBAR returns. The website also supports electronic filing of Bank Secrecy Act (BSA) forms through a secure network.

[205] Accounts are converted to U.S. currency based on the exchange rate as of the *end* of the calendar year, applied to the highest balance in the account during the year, even if the highest balance in the foreign account (in U.S. dollars) was sometime before the end of the year.

[206] Currently, the Report of Foreign Bank and Financial Accounts (FBAR) regulations do not define a foreign account holding virtual currency as a type of reportable account, but FinCEN intends to propose regulations regarding reports of foreign financial accounts (FBAR) to include virtual currency as a type of reportable account (FinCEN Notice 2020-2).

Example: Gustavo is a U.S. citizen who has a bank account in Mexico. This is the only foreign account that he has. In prior years, the highest value of his Mexican bank account totaled approximately $7,500 in equivalent U.S. dollars. Therefore, Gustavo did not have an FBAR requirement. However, in 2023, Gustavo decides that he wants to build a vacation home in Mexico. He transfers $29,000 to his Mexican bank account on January 17, 2023, to begin construction on his new residence. Although he later withdraws all the funds, he is still required to file an FBAR, because the aggregate value of his foreign accounts reached $10,000 in 2023. However, he is not required to file Form 8938 (to be discussed later) because the value of his foreign assets is below the reporting threshold for Form 8938.

When filing an FBAR, taxpayers must, "reasonably figure and report the greatest value of currency or assets in their accounts during the calendar year." For example, a foreign financial account located in Japan would typically be valued in yen. The owner of the account must first determine the maximum value of the account in yen. Then, convert the maximum value of the account into U.S. dollars.

The IRS defines "signature authority" as the authority of an individual or individuals to control the disposition of assets held in a foreign financial account by direct communication with the bank or other financial institution. In other words, FBAR reporting requirements are not determined by ownership of the funds. "Foreign financial accounts" include the following types of accounts:

- Foreign bank accounts, including savings accounts, checking accounts, and time deposits,
- Foreign securities accounts such as brokerage accounts and securities derivatives or other financial instruments accounts, commodity futures or stock options accounts,
- Insurance policies with a cash value (such as a whole life insurance policy),
- Foreign mutual funds or similar pooled funds (i.e., a fund that is available to the general public with a regular net asset value determination and regular redemptions),
- Any other accounts maintained in a foreign financial institution or with a person performing the services of a financial institution.

The FBAR is due by April 15th of the year following the year in which the account holder meets the $10,000 threshold. However, FinCEN grants filers an automatic extension to October 15 to file the FBAR. There is no requirement or form to request this extension. This threshold is the same for every filing status. Whether or not an account produces income does not affect the requirement to file an FBAR. Tax treaties with the United States do not affect FBAR filing obligations. Also, if the IRS issues a release for extensions of filing due to a disaster situation, do not assume that the FBAR filing deadlines are extended, as well. FBAR filing extensions are rare, even for disaster situations.

Note: U.S. law requires taxpayers to file a Report of Foreign Bank and Financial Accounts (FBAR) if they meet a threshold of $10,000 in a foreign bank account at **any time** during the calendar year. This includes all accounts that the taxpayer may own or have any financial interest in—this includes signature authority, power of attorney, or custodianship.

Example: Carlos, a U.S. citizen, co-owns a foreign bank account in Costa Rica with his mother, Juliana, who is a Costa Rican citizen. The highest value in the account was $16,000 USD in 2023. Half of the income in the account belongs to Juliana, and the account does not produce any interest income. Carlos is required to file an FBAR. He must report the full value of the account.

Example: Alcott is a permanent legal resident of the United States (i.e., a green card holder). Alcott is a citizen of the United Kingdom, which has a favorable tax treaty with the U.S. Under the U.S.-UK tax treaty, Alcott can be treated as a "tax resident" of the United Kingdom, and he elects to be taxed as a resident of the United Kingdom. Alcott is still considered a "U.S. person" for FBAR purposes. This is because tax treaties with the United States do not affect FBAR filing obligations.

There is no minimum age requirement for filing an FBAR. The requirement includes minor children, as well. If a child holds $10,000 in a foreign financial account, even if the account is not earning revenues, the child will be required to file their own FBAR. This is true even if the child would otherwise not have a U.S. filing requirement. If a child cannot file their own FBAR for any reason, such as age, the child's parent, guardian, or another legally responsible person must file and sign it for the child.

Example: Gideon is six years old. He is a U.S. citizen. Gideon's grandmother, Aurelia, is a citizen of Italy. Aurelia sets up a savings account for her grandson in an Italian bank, and deposits 50,000 Euros into the account. Aurelia then names Gideon as the co-owner of the account. Using current currency conversion rates, the account balance is worth approximately $56,300 U.S. dollars. Gideon is required to file an FBAR to report the existence and value of the account, even if he does not withdraw the funds or personally receive any of the proceeds from the account.

Example: Russell is a U.S. citizen. Russell's parents are citizens of Canada and live in Canada. Russell has signature authority on his elderly parents' accounts in Canada, but he has never written a check or made any withdrawals from his parents' bank account. The bank account balance reaches $10,000 USD for the first time in 2023. Russell is required to file an FBAR. Whether or not his signature authority is ever exercised on the Canadian account is irrelevant to the FBAR filing requirement.

U.S. partnerships, corporations, estates, and trusts that meet the $10,000 threshold are also required to file an FBAR. The federal tax treatment of an entity does *not* determine whether the entity has an FBAR filing requirement. For example, an entity that is disregarded for purposes of Title 26 of the United States Code must file an FBAR, if otherwise required to do so. Similarly, a trust for which the trust income, deductions, or credits are taken into account by another person for purposes of Title 26 of the United States Code must file an FBAR, if otherwise required to do so.

Spouses and Jointly-Owned Accounts

Spouses do not need to file separate FBARs if they complete and sign Form 114a, *Record of Authorization to Electronically File FBARs*, and:

- All reportable financial accounts of the nonfiling spouse are jointly owned with the filing spouse, and,
- The filing spouse reports all accounts jointly-owned with the nonfiling spouse on a timely-filed FBAR.

Otherwise, both spouses must file separate FBARs, and each spouse must report the entire value of the jointly-owned accounts. The e-filing system will not allow both spouses' signatures on the same electronic form – only the filing spouse signs in the system. Taxpayers don't submit Form 114a with the FBAR, but they must keep it for their records.

Example: Reuben and Joana are married and file joint income tax returns. They are both U.S. citizens, and they live in the United States. Reuben has a foreign bank account in France, where his parents live. Joana has a bank account in Portugal, where she also has family. Reuben's account has $6,000 in equivalent U.S. dollars. Joana has $14,000 in her foreign account. They each own their foreign bank accounts separately (they are not jointly held). Joana must file an FBAR. Reuben does not have to file an FBAR. This is true whether they choose to file their income tax returns separately or jointly.

FBAR Penalties

The Treasury Department reports that FBAR filings have surged in recent years, with current filings exceeding one million per year. The consequences of failure to timely file an FBAR can be extremely severe. According to the Taxpayer Advocate's 2023 Purple Book,[207] the maximum FBAR penalty is among the harshest civil penalties the government may impose.

The most common FBAR reporting mistake is simply failing to file. For "non-willful" FBAR violations, a civil penalty of up to $10,000 per return (adjusted for inflation) can be imposed. For 2023 the maximum "non-willful" failure to file penalty is $15,611.[208]

Note: For the purposes of the "non-willful" civil penalty, on February 28, 2023, in a 5-4 decision, the United States Supreme Court ruled that this penalty applies *per FBAR report*—not for each reportable foreign account.[209] Therefore, even if an individual has multiple reportable foreign bank accounts with a "non-willful" FBAR violation, only one civil penalty can be imposed on the taxpayer for the year. Prior to this decision, there was a split in the lower courts about whether the non-willful civil penalty could be imposed per FBAR report or for each reportable foreign account.

A "willful" failure could result in the *greater* of $100,000 (this penalty is adjusted for inflation, so for 2023 it is $156,107) or 50% of the balance in an unreported foreign account per year, for up to six years.

For example, if an account holder maintains a balance of $25,000 in a foreign account that they willfully fail to report for many years, the IRS may impose a penalty of over $100,000 per year and may go back six years, producing an aggregate statutory maximum penalty of over $600,000.

In addition to the above-mentioned civil penalties for "willful" failures, criminal penalties can also be imposed. Criminal penalties may include a fine of up to $250,000 and five years in prison (in most situations) for willfully *failing to file* an FBAR report, and up to $10,000 and five years in prison for knowingly and willfully *filing a false* FBAR report.[210]

Note: The potential penalties for *willful* failure to file an FBAR are huge. These penalties can include criminal prosecution as well as severe monetary civil penalties.

---

[207] In 2023, the National Taxpayer Advocate recommended in its annual Purple Book that Congress clarify that the IRS must prove a violation was "willful" without relying on the instructions to Schedule B or the failure to check the box on Schedule B before imposing a willful FBAR penalty and must do so by clear and convincing evidence; the standard typically required in fraud cases.
[208] Per 31 USC 5321(a)(5) adjusted for inflation by 31 CFR § 1010.821(b).
[209] Bitner v. U.S. (No. 21-1195).
[210] View a list of FBAR penalties with the currently adjusted inflation amounts here, on the IRS website:
https://www.irs.gov/businesses/small-businesses-self-employed/report-of-foreign-bank-and-financial-accounts-fbar.

Example: Harold Kahn had two bank accounts in Switzerland. He failed to report the funds in his foreign bank accounts, on the FBAR. The total in both accounts was over $8 million. The U.S. government determined it was a willful failure to file the FBAR, and assessed a willful nonfiling penalty of $4 million, which was equal to 50% of Harold's aggregate account balances. Harold Kahn died soon after this penalty was assessed, and the Estate of Harold Kahn was forced to litigate, with Harold's two sons as co-executor of the estate. The government went after the estate for the penalty, and the penalty was affirmed (United States v. Kahn, No. 19-3920).

FBAR penalties for inadvertent or "non-willful" failure to file are limited. In most cases, the total penalty amount for all years under examination will be limited to 50% of the highest aggregate balance of all unreported foreign financial accounts during the years under examination. The guidance also establishes procedures and documentation requirements for IRS examiners conducting examinations related to FBAR penalties.

The IRS will normally not impose a penalty for the failure to file a delinquent FBAR if a taxpayer properly reports on the Federal income tax return, and paid all tax on, the income from the foreign financial accounts reported on the delinquent FBAR, if they have not previously been contacted regarding an income tax audit or a request for delinquent returns for the year for which the delinquent FBAR was submitted.

Foreign Financial Accounts

For FBAR purposes, a "foreign financial account" is a financial account located *outside* of the United States. An account is considered "foreign" for FBAR purposes of if it has a geographical location outside of the United States.

A foreign financial account also includes a commodity futures or stock options account, an insurance policy with a cash value (such as a whole life insurance policy), an annuity policy with a cash value, and shares in a foreign mutual fund or similar pooled fund (i.e., a fund that is available to the public with a regular net asset value determination and regular redemptions). The following accounts are not classified as "foreign financial accounts":

- Foreign financial accounts owned by a governmental entity,
- Foreign financial accounts owned by an international financial institution,
- Foreign financial accounts maintained on a United States military banking facility (for example, a banking institution on a U.S. military base).

An owner or beneficiary of an IRA or another qualified retirement plan is also not required to report a foreign financial account that is held in the retirement plan.

Example: Grady is a casual investor who directly holds shares of a U.S. mutual fund. The mutual fund invests in foreign stocks as well as domestic stocks. Since the foreign stocks are held in a U.S.-based mutual fund, Grady does not need to report his ownership in the mutual fund or the holdings of the mutual fund. The mutual fund itself would be responsible for any foreign financial reporting that was required.

Note: A safe deposit box at a foreign financial institution is not considered a "financial account" for tax reporting purposes. However, under the FBAR rules, if gold, bullion, or foreign currency is held inside a foreign financial institution, it is subject to FBAR reporting. Specified foreign financial assets do not include gold, bullion, or currency *held directly* by the taxpayer.

Example: Virgil is a U.S. citizen who lives in Columbia. Virgil collects gold and silver coins as a hobby. He keeps the coins in a wall safe inside his home. He does not trust banks, so he does not have a foreign bank account. He keeps all his cash inside the wall safe, too. Virgil does not have an FBAR filing requirement.

Form 3520: Reporting Foreign Gifts and Bequests

U.S. individuals who received large gifts or bequests from certain foreign persons may be required to file Form 3520, *Annual Return to Report Transactions with Foreign Trusts and Receipt of Certain Foreign Gifts.* Form 3520 is due at the same time as the U.S. person's income tax return (including extensions) but is filed separately from the income tax return.

A foreign person is defined as a nonresident alien individual or a foreign corporation, partnership, or estate. In 2023, a U.S. person must file Form 3520, *Annual Return to Report Transactions with Foreign Trusts and Receipt of Certain Foreign Gifts,* if they receive gifts or bequests valued at more than $100,000 from a nonresident alien individual or foreign estate. A taxpayer must aggregate gifts received from related parties.

Form 3520 is considered an "information return," not a tax return, and no taxes are assessed on this form, because foreign gifts or bequests are not subject to U.S. income tax.

Example: Alyssa is a U.S. citizen who has many relatives living in Canada. In 2023, Alyssa received $60,000 from her Canadian grandfather and $52,000 from her Canadian brother. Alyssa must report the gifts because the total is more than $100,000 in a single year from related parties. These gifts are not taxable to Alyssa, but she is required to report them in Part IV of Form 3520.

Failure to file a required Form 3520 can result in steep penalties. The penalty is equal to 5% of the amount of the foreign gift or bequest for each month for which the failure to report continues (not to exceed a total of 25%). However, no penalty applies if the failure to report was due to reasonable cause and not willful neglect. The taxpayer is required to report a gift or bequest on Form 3520 when they constructively receive it.

Note: A "foreign gift" to a U.S. person does not include amounts paid for qualified tuition or medical payments made on behalf of the U.S. person. These types of gifts do not have a reporting requirement, regardless of the amounts, if the payments are made directly to the institutions.

Example: Jason is a U.S. citizen attending University of Chicago in the United States. His aunt, Sedona, is a citizen of Australia. Sedona is very wealthy and she offers to pay all her nephew's tuition. She makes a $108,000 payment directly to Jason's college, covering the entire cost of his tuition and on-campus housing. There are no filing requirements for this foreign gift, and neither Jason nor his aunt have to file gift tax returns or a Form 3520.

Example: Percy is a legal U.S. resident (green card holder) who lives and works in California. Percy's grandmother, Claudette, is a French citizen. On January 30, 2023, Claudette dies and leaves Percy a large inheritance of $250,000. After his grandmother's estate is settled by the executor in France, Percy receives the inheritance via wire transfer on June 10, 2023. Since Percy constructively received the funds in 2023, his Form 3520 is due on April 15, 2024 (the filing due date for 2023 individual tax returns). The funds are not taxable to Percy, but the inheritance must be reported, since it is a bequest from a foreign estate over the reporting threshold.

Form 8938: Statement of Specified Foreign Financial Assets

Generally, taxpayers who hold "specified foreign financial assets" must also file Form 8938, *Statement of Specified Foreign Financial Assets,* with their tax returns if the amount of their assets exceeds certain thresholds. This is a separate filing requirement in addition to the FBAR filing requirements. Form 8938 requires the taxpayer to provide detailed financial information about their foreign accounts. Specified foreign assets include (this is not an exhaustive list):

- Foreign stock or foreign securities (not held in a U.S. brokerage account),
- Financial accounts maintained by a foreign financial institution,
- Foreign pensions or deferred compensation plans,[211]
- Interests in a foreign estate,
- A partnership interest in a foreign partnership;
- Any interest in a foreign-issued insurance contract or annuity with a cash-surrender value.

Example: Jocelyn, a U.S. citizen, has an uncle who is a Greek citizen. In 2023, her uncle died, and Jocelyn inherited $200,000 in foreign bearer bonds from her uncle. The bonds are held outside of a regular bank account. Jocelyn is required to report the value of the bonds on Form 8938, even if she did not cash the bonds out. Jocelyn must also report the inheritance on Form 3520.

Example: Edward, a U.S. citizen, purchased securities of a Swiss corporation through a securities brokerage firm located in New York. Edward is not required to report his Swiss securities on an FBAR or on a Form 8938, because he purchased the securities through a brokerage institution located in the United States.

Failure to report foreign financial assets on Form 8938 on a timely filed return (including extensions) may result in a penalty of $10,000. If a taxpayer does not file Form 8938 and later receives a written notice from the IRS about the lack of filing, the taxpayer has 90 days after the mailing of the IRS letter to file Form 8938 to avoid additional penalties.

If the taxpayer does not file within that 90-day period, an *additional* $10,000 penalty may apply to each 30-day period (or a portion thereof) that Form 8938 is not filed after the 90-day deadline (up to a maximum of $50,000 of *additional* late filing penalties—resulting in a total late filing penalty assessment of $60,000). Further, underpayments of tax attributable to non-disclosed foreign financial assets will be subject to an additional "substantial understatement" penalty of 40%.

---

[211] Payments or the rights to receive the foreign equivalent of social security, social insurance benefits or another similar program of a foreign government are not specified foreign financial assets and do not have to be reported.

If a taxpayer accidentally omits Form 8938 when they file their income tax return, the taxpayer should file Form 1040-X, *Amended U.S. Individual Income Tax Return*, with their Form 8938 attached and attach a statement of reasonable cause to try to avoid any penalties.

> **Note:** Taxpayers that are **not required** to file an income tax return for the year, also do not need to file Form 8938, even if the value of their specified foreign assets is greater than one of the reporting thresholds.

> **Example:** Melinda is a U.S. citizen and full-time graduate student. Melinda does not work and has no taxable income for the year. She has a bank account in Canada that holds over $400,000, because she inherited a large sum of money and farmland from her brother, who died in January. Her brother was a Canadian citizen. Melinda must file an FBAR to report the value of the Canadian bank account. But she does not have to file a Form 8938, because she does not earn any income and does not otherwise have a filing requirement.

A Form 8938 filing requirement is triggered if the aggregate value of specified foreign financial assets is <u>more than</u> the following **reporting thresholds:**

- Taxpayers living **inside** the U.S.:

    o **Unmarried and MFS taxpayers:** The total value of specified foreign financial assets is more than $50,000 on the last day of the tax year or more than $75,000 at any time during the tax year.
    o **Married taxpayers filing MFJ:** The total value of specified foreign financial assets is more than $100,000 on the last day of the tax year or more than $150,000 at any time during the tax year.

- Taxpayers living **abroad**:

    o **Unmarried and MFS taxpayers:** living abroad must file Form 8938 if the total value of their specified foreign assets is more than $200,000 on the last day of the tax year or more than $300,000 at any time during the year.
    o **Married taxpayers filing MFJ:** for joint filers, the value of their specified foreign assets is more than $400,000 on the last day of the tax year or more than $600,000 at any time during the year.

The filing of Form 8938 does not relieve a taxpayer of the separate requirement to file the FBAR if they are required to do so, and vice-versa. Depending on the situation, the taxpayer may be required to file both forms, and certain foreign accounts may be required to be reported on both forms.

> **Example:** Asher is a U.S. citizen who resides in Costa Rica. He is not employed or earning any taxable income. Ten years ago, he received a substantial inheritance from his grandparents, which has been his only source of financial support. He currently holds $500,000 USD in a checking account at a bank in Costa Rica, but it does not accrue any interest. Since he does not have any taxable income, he does not have to file a U.S. income tax return (Form 1040 is not required). Asher only needs to file the FBAR, to report the funds in his Costa Rican bank account. He does not need to file a Form 1040 or a Form 8938.

Form 8938 filing requirement also applies to specified domestic entities, including a domestic trust if one or more of the trust's current beneficiaries is a U.S. citizen or U.S. resident alien and the asset value thresholds are surpassed.

A taxpayer does not need to report a financial account maintained by a U.S. financial institution or U.S. brokerage firm, even if the financial institution or fund invests in foreign stock. This also includes U.S. affiliates of foreign financial institutions. Examples of financial accounts maintained by U.S. financial institutions that do not need to be reported include:

- U.S. Mutual fund accounts
- IRAs (traditional or Roth)
- 401 (k) retirement plans
- Qualified U.S. retirement plans
- Brokerage and investing accounts maintained by U.S. financial institutions

The following assets are not "specified foreign assets" and do not have to be reported on Form 8938:

- Payments or the rights to receive the foreign equivalent of social security, social insurance benefits or another similar program of a foreign government,
- Directly-held tangible assets, such as art, gold, antiques, jewelry, cars and other collectibles,
- Foreign real estate, such as a personal residence or a rental property in a foreign country does not have to be reported as a "foreign financial asset," *unless* the property is held by a foreign entity.[212]
- Foreign currency, if it is directly held by the taxpayer and not held in a financial institution.

Example: Flavienne is a dual citizen of Germany and the U.S. She has funds deposited in three different German banks. As of December 31, 2023, bank account #1 had $5,000; bank account #2 had $3,000; and bank account #3 had $2,500. Flavienne is required to electronically file an FBAR by April 15, 2024 (October 15, 2024 with the automatic extension), because the aggregate value of her accounts is more than $10,000. However, she is not required to file Form 8938, because the value of her offshore assets is below the reporting threshold.

Example: Darius is a U.S. expat living overseas. He lives and works remotely in Mexico. At the end of the year, Darius has $385,000 in a Mexican bank account, because he is saving up money to purchase a condo in Cancun. Darius must file an FBAR as well as a Form 8938.

Example: Phineas is a U.S. citizen living and working in Sweden. He owns a house in Sweden, and also some very valuable artwork. The value of the house is $370,000 USD and the value of the artwork is $125,000. He owns the house and the artwork outright. He is not required to report the value of these assets on Form 8938. He also has a foreign bank account in Sweden, with the equivalent of $9,100 USD. His foreign bank account balance has never exceeded $10,000 USD during the year, so he does not have to file an FBAR, either.

---

[212] If real estate is held through a foreign entity, such as a foreign corporation, partnership, trust or estate, then the interest in the entity is a specified foreign financial asset that must be reported on Form 8938, if the total value of all the taxpayer's specified foreign financial assets is greater than the reporting threshold that applies.

Example: Khloe is a U.S. citizen who lives and works in Brazil for an online tutoring company that is based in the United States. Khloe lives with her grandmother, who is a Brazilian citizen. Khloe does not have a bank account in Brazil. Instead, she has a bank account in the U.S. and she uses her ATM card and credit cards to withdraw money and make purchases. She keeps a fairly large amount of Brazilian currency inside her home, in a safe, along with her personal jewelry. Since she does not have a foreign bank account or any other specified foreign assets, she does not have to file Form 8938 or the FBAR.

Schedule B, Reporting Foreign Accounts and Trusts

Schedule B of the Form 1040 is used to report interest and dividend income received during the tax year. However, the last part of Schedule B (Part III) is used by taxpayers who have financial accounts in foreign countries. This section of the form is where the taxpayer must disclose any foreign bank or investment accounts and whether or not the taxpayer received any distributions from a foreign trust. The reporting requirements for these taxpayers have increased significantly in recent years as part of FATCA, which refers to the Foreign Account Tax Compliance Act. The law addresses tax noncompliance by U.S. taxpayers with foreign accounts by focusing on reporting by these taxpayers and by foreign financial institutions.

In general, federal law requires U.S. citizens and resident aliens to report any worldwide income, including income from foreign trusts and foreign bank and securities accounts. In most cases, affected taxpayers need to complete and attach Schedule B to their tax returns. Part III of Schedule B asks about the existence of foreign accounts, such as bank and securities accounts, and generally requires U.S. citizens to report the country in which each account is located. On Part III, Schedule B, a taxpayer must check "yes" or "no" to the question of whether the taxpayer had at any time during the year a financial interest in or signature authority over a financial account.

A taxpayer who had a financial interest in a foreign account during the year must check the "yes" box even if they are not required to file FinCEN Form 114, *Report of Foreign Bank and Financial Accounts* (FBAR). There is no dollar threshold to report foreign accounts on Schedule B. Even if the taxpayer does not have an FBAR reporting requirement, the "yes" box must be checked if the taxpayer has any financial interest in, or signature authority over, a foreign account.

Part III Foreign Accounts and Trusts	You must complete this part if you **(a)** had over $1,500 of taxable interest or ordinary dividends; **(b)** had a foreign account; or **(c)** received a distribution from, or were a grantor of, or a transferor to, a foreign trust.	Yes	No
Caution: If required, failure to file FinCEN Form 114 may result in substantial penalties. Additionally, you may be required to file Form 8938, Statement of Specified Foreign Financial Assets. See instructions.	**7a** At any time during 2023, did you have a financial interest in or signature authority over a financial account (such as a bank account, securities account, or brokerage account) located in a foreign country? See instructions		
	If "Yes," are you required to file FinCEN Form 114, Report of Foreign Bank and Financial Accounts (FBAR), to report that financial interest or signature authority? See FinCEN Form 114 and its instructions for filing requirements and exceptions to those requirements		
	b If you are required to file FinCEN Form 114, list the name(s) of the foreign country(-ies) where the financial account(s) is (are) located: _____		
	8 During 2023, did you receive a distribution from, or were you the grantor of, or transferor to, a foreign trust? If "Yes," you may have to file Form 3520. See instructions		

For Paperwork Reduction Act Notice, see your tax return instructions.   Cat. No. 17146N   Schedule B (Form 1040) 2023

Note: If a taxpayer does not have a filing requirement, they are not required to file a tax return merely to report their foreign financial accounts on Schedule B. However, if a taxpayer is required to file a tax return, they must file Schedule B to report foreign financial accounts even if they would not be otherwise required to file Schedule B.

For reporting purposes on Schedule B, a "foreign financial account" includes securities, brokerage, savings, checking, deposit, time deposit, or other accounts that are maintained within a financial institution.

A financial account also includes a commodity futures or options account, an insurance policy with a cash value (such as a whole life insurance policy), an annuity policy with a cash value, and shares in a foreign mutual fund. A financial account is considered to be located in a foreign country if the account is *physically located outside* of the United States. This includes accounts maintained with a branch of a U.S. bank if it is physically located outside the United States. However, a branch of a foreign bank is not a foreign account if it is physically located in the United States.

Example: Olivia is a U.S. citizen who lives in Miami, Florida. She recently opened an account with Santander Bank, which has a branch in Miami. Oliva has no other bank accounts elsewhere. Later during the year, Olivia goes overseas to visit her grandmother in Spain, and she uses her ATM card to withdraw cash at a Santander branch in Spain. Santander is an international bank that has branches overseas in many countries, including Spain. Even though Santander is an international bank with branches in foreign countries, Olivia does not have to file an FBAR, because opened her account at a U.S. branch in Miami. Therefore, her account is treated as a U.S. bank account.

Form 5471: Information Return of U.S. Persons With Respect to Certain Foreign Corporations

When a U.S. taxpayer is an officer, director, or shareholder in a foreign corporation, they may have an IRS reporting requirement. Form 5471 is typically used to report ownership of a foreign corporation that exceeds a **10% threshold.** The categories of U.S. persons potentially liable for filing Form 5471 include:

- U.S. citizen and resident alien individuals
- U.S. domestic corporations
- U.S. domestic partnerships
- U.S. domestic trusts

The requirement to file Form 5471 is not based on whether the business generated any income. Form 5471 is an *informational* return, not a tax return. The penalties for nonfiling are severe. Each failure to file a required Form 5471 can result in a $10,000 penalty.

Furthermore, if Form 5471 is not filed within 90 days after the IRS has mailed a notice of the failure to file, an additional $10,000 penalty is charged for each 30-day period, or fraction thereof, during which the failure continues after the 90-day period has expired. This additional penalty is limited to a maximum of $50,000 for each failure to file.

Example: Breanna is a 15% shareholder in three separate foreign corporations. She inherited the stock when her German grandfather died two years ago. Breanna fails to seek proper legal advice and as a result, she does not file her returns on time, including the required Forms 5471 for her ownership in the foreign corporations. She later receives a notice from the IRS. Since she did not have any reasonable cause for her failure to file, she is assessed a penalty of $30,000 ($10,000 for each entity that she failed to report on Form 5471).

The Form 5471 is generally filed with a taxpayer's individual return. Even if a person is not required to file a tax return (for example, their income is below the filing threshold), the Form 5471 may still be required. Exceptions to the filing requirement exist in cases of constructive ownership, or an election to be treated as a domestic corporation.

	Differences Between the FBAR vs. Form 8938	
Data	**FBAR**	**Form 8938**
Legal Authority	**Authorized by the Bank Secrecy Act of 1970 (BSA).**	**Authorized by the Foreign Account Tax Compliance Act of 2010 (FATCA).**
Who must file?	U.S. persons, which includes U.S. citizens, U.S. resident aliens, trusts, estates, and other domestic entities.	Specified individuals, which includes U.S. citizens, resident aliens, and nonresident aliens who elect to be treated as resident aliens for purposes of filing a joint tax return; also applies to certain domestic entities.
Reporting thresholds (U.S. tax home)	$10,000 held in any foreign bank at any time during the calendar year. Based on the aggregate value of all reportable accounts.	$50,000 ($100,000 MFJ) on the last day of the tax year or $75,000 ($150,000 MFJ) at any time during the tax year.
Reporting thresholds (foreign tax home)	$10,000 held in any foreign bank at any time during the calendar year. Based on the aggregate value of all reportable accounts.	$200,000 ($400,000 MFJ) on the last day of the tax year or $300,000 ($600,000 MFJ) at any time during the tax year.[213]
When does the taxpayer have "an interest" in an account or asset?	Financial interest in an applicable foreign account, or signature authority on an applicable foreign account.	Any income, gains, losses, deductions, credits, gross proceeds, or distributions from holding or disposing of the account or asset that are (or would be required to be) reported, included, or otherwise reflected on the taxpayer's return.
What is reported?	The maximum value of financial accounts.	The maximum value of specified foreign financial assets.
How are values determined and reported?	Converted to U.S. dollars using the end of the calendar year exchange rate and reported in U.S. dollars.	The fair market value of the asset in U.S. dollars.
Due date	Due by April 15 (an extension is allowed to October 15).[214]	The same due date as the taxpayer's individual return, including extensions.
Filing procedures	File electronically through FinCEN's BSA E-Filing System. The FBAR is not filed with a federal tax return.	This form must be filed with the taxpayer's income tax return (Form 1040).
Penalties	Willful non-filing (most situations): up to the greater of $100,000 or 50% of account balances; "non-willful" violation civil penalties are up to $10,000 per violation (penalties are adjusted annually for inflation). Criminal penalties may also apply.	Up to $10,000 for failure to disclose, and an additional $10,000 for every 30 days of non-filing after IRS notice of a failure to disclose; up to a $60,000 total maximum penalty. Separate criminal penalties may also apply

---

[213] These thresholds apply even if only one spouse resides abroad. Married individuals who file a joint income tax return for the tax year will file a single Form 8938 that reports all of the specified foreign financial assets in which either spouse has an interest.
[214] These are the normal due dates. The due dates follow the same rules as for income tax purposes, so for 2023, the return due date is April 15, 2024, with the automatic extension until October 15, 2024.

Unit 17: Study Questions
(Test yourself first, then check the correct answers at the end of this quiz.)

1. Dylan, a U.S. citizen, often receives cash gifts from his wealthy German grandparents. At what monetary threshold would Dylan need to file a Form 3520 for receiving these gifts from abroad?

A. $10,000
B. $25,000
C. $50,000
D. $100,000

2. Part _____ of Schedule B (Form 1040) is completed by taxpayers who have financial accounts in foreign countries.

A. Part I.
B. Part II.
C. Part III.
D. Schedule B is not used for this purpose.

3. Which of the following forms is completed to report foreign bank accounts?

A. Schedule B (Form 1040) and FinCen 114 (FBAR).
B. Form 1116 and FinCen 114 (FBAR).
C. Schedule B (Form 1040) and Form 2555.
D. Only the FinCen 114 (FBAR).

4. Which of the following is NOT considered "U.S. person" for the purposes of filing an FBAR?

A. A U.S. citizen who lives in Israel.
B. A U.S. resident who lives in Russia.
C. A nonresident alien with $100,000 in U.S. investments that files Form 1040-NR.
D. A U.S. consular officer that lives and works overseas in a U.S. embassy.

5. Noriko is a U.S. citizen who is required to file Form 8938 with her personal income tax return because she has $800,000 in specified foreign assets. Noriko does not include a Form 8938 with her income tax return, but she later amends her personal tax return after the due date to include Form 8938. What potential penalty is Noriko subject to regarding the late-filed Form 8938?

A. $2,500
B. $5,000
C. $10,000
D. $60,000

6. As a general rule, how long should taxpayers keep records related to an FBAR filing (from the due date of the FBAR)?

A. 3 years.
B. 5 years.
C. 7 years.
D. 10 years.

7. When e-filing their federal return, a taxpayer who meets the requirements to file both Form 8938, *Statement of Specified Foreign Financial Assets,* and the FBAR (Form 114, *Report of Foreign Bank and Financial Accounts)* should do which of the following?

A. Attach both forms to their federal return.
B. File Form 8938 with their federal tax return and file Form 114 through FinCEN's e-filing system.
C. Attach only Form 114 to their federal return as it contains the relevant Form 8938 information.
D. Submit both forms separately to the Internal Revenue Service.

8. Regarding the FBAR reporting requirement, the IRS issued guidance on penalties for failing to file the FBAR that caps the maximum percentage of the penalty. In most cases, the total penalty amount for all years under examination will be limited to _____ of the highest aggregate balance of all unreported foreign financial accounts during the years under investigation.

A. 10%
B. 25%
C. 50%
D. 75%

9. Which of the following is a "specified foreign asset" for reporting purposes?

A. Real estate held in a foreign trust.
B. Artwork displayed in a foreign museum.
C. Jewelry held in a foreign country.
D. Payments or the rights to receive the foreign equivalent of social security.

10. Sophia is unmarried and lives in Texas. She is a U.S. citizen and has ownership of specified foreign assets, which she inherited when her Italian grandmother died. Which of the following foreign assets, all of which are located in Italy, may trigger the filing of the Form 8938?

A. A personal residence
B. A profitable rental property
C. Directly-held precious metals
D. A partnership interest in an Italian partnership

11. Amadeus, age 65, is a U.S. resident (green card holder) who lives in Florida, has a bank account located in Austria. He opened the account several years ago to send money to his elderly mother, Ursula, who is a citizen of Austria. He has signature authority on the account but does not withdraw money from it or collect any of the interest income on the account. On December 31, 2023, the account has a balance of $23,000 (which was the highest balance in the account for the year). He receives Social Security and otherwise does not have a U.S. filing requirement or any tax liability for the year. What is Amadeus's reporting requirement for this account?

A. Amadeus is not required to file any returns.
B. Amadeus must file Form 8938, *Statement of Specified Foreign Financial Assets*, with the IRS when he files his tax return.
C. Amadeus must file an FBAR, *Report of Foreign Bank and Financial Accounts*.
D. Amadeus and Ursula must both file an FBAR, *Report of Foreign Bank and Financial Accounts*, with the Treasury Department, and file Form 8938, *Statement of Specified Foreign Financial Assets*, with the IRS when he files his tax return.

Unit 17: Quiz Answers

1. The answer is D. Dylan must file Form 3520 if he receives gifts in one calendar year valued at more than $100,000 from a nonresident alien individual (in this case, his wealthy German grandparents). Form 3520, *Annual Return to Report Transactions with Foreign Trusts and Receipt of Certain Foreign Gifts*, is an information return, not a tax return because foreign gifts or bequests are not subject to income tax.

2. The answer is C. Part III of Schedule B (Form 1040) is completed by taxpayers who have financial accounts in foreign countries.

3. The answer is A. The FinCen 114 (FBAR) and Schedule B (part III) are both used to report foreign bank accounts and foreign financial accounts. Taxpayers with foreign financial accounts will typically need to complete Part III of Schedule B to indicate that they hold such an account, although they do not need to state the dollar amounts that the account contains. Unlike the FBAR, there is no dollar threshold on the duty to report foreign accounts on Schedule B.

4. The answer is C. Nonresident aliens are not subject to the FBAR filing requirement. All of the following are subject to the FBAR filing requirement if they hold foreign bank accounts or applicable foreign assets.

- A U.S. citizen or U.S. resident of the United States, (includes nonresident aliens electing to be treated as residents in order to file a joint tax return).
- A domestic entity, (corporation, estate or trust).

5. The answer is C. Noriko may be subject to a penalty of $10,000 for nonfiling of Form 8938. If a taxpayer is required to file Form 8938, but it is not complete and correctly filed by the due date (including extensions), a taxpayer may be subject to a penalty of $10,000. There would be *additional* penalties if the form is not filed within 90 days from the mailing of a notice from the IRS regarding a notice of a failure to file Form 8938.

6. The answer is B. Generally, records of accounts required to be reported on the FBAR should be kept for five years from the due date of the report, which is the year *following* the calendar year being reported.

7. The answer is B. The taxpayer must only attach Form 8938 to their federal return. The FBAR, Form 114, is not filed with a federal tax return or with the IRS. It is filed online through the Financial Crimes Enforcement Network (FinCEN) e-filing system.

8. The answer is C. In most cases, the maximum penalty amount for all years under examination will be limited to 50% of the highest aggregate balance of all unreported foreign financial accounts during the years under investigation.

9. The answer is A. Foreign real estate held in a foreign trust would be a specified foreign asset. If the real estate is held through a foreign entity, such as a corporation, partnership, trust or estate, then the interest in the entity is a specified foreign financial asset that must be reported on Form 8938. Answers "B" and "C" are incorrect, because directly held tangible assets, such as art, antiques, jewelry, cars and other collectibles, are not specified foreign financial assets. Answer "D" is incorrect, because payments or the rights to receive the foreign equivalent of social security are not specified foreign financial assets and are not reportable.

10. The answer is D. A partnership interest in a foreign partnership can trigger the filing of Form 8938 if the partnership interest is not held in a U.S.-based financial account. Answer "A" and answer "B" are not correct because a personal residence or a rental property does not have to be reported, if directly held (i.e., not held in a foreign entity). Answer "C" is not correct, because directly held precious metals, such as gold, are not specified foreign financial assets.

11. The answer is C. Amadeus is required to file an FBAR, even if he does not have any other filing requirement. There are two separate reporting requirements for taxpayers who hold certain types of foreign assets or who have certain amounts of funds in foreign bank accounts. An FBAR generally must be filed with the BSA E-Filing System if a taxpayer has more than $10,000 in offshore bank accounts. Taxpayers also must file a statement with the IRS if they hold foreign financial assets with an aggregate value that exceeds $50,000 ($100,000 MFJ) on the last day of the tax year, or that exceeds $75,000 ($150,000 MFJ) at any time during the tax year. In Amadeus's case, since the funds in his foreign account total $23,000, and he does not otherwise have a filing requirement, he is only required to file an FBAR.

Unit 18: Estate and Gift Taxes for Individuals

More Reading:
Publication 559, *Survivors, Executors, and Administrators*
Instructions for Form 1041, Form 706 and Form 709

Estates in General

An estate is a separate legal entity created when a taxpayer dies. The estate tax is a tax on the transfer of assets or property from an individual's estate to a decedent's beneficiaries after death. The Tax Cuts and Jobs Act (TCJA) made substantial changes to the estate tax exemption that will continue through tax year 2025. In 2023, the estate tax exemption is $12,920,000 per decedent.[215] This exemption is indexed for inflation at the current levels through 2025. The top estate and gift tax rate remains at 40%.

What this means is that most estates of up to $12.92 million in 2023 are free of *estate* tax, and from that point on, anything additional above that is taxable, at progressive rates that start at 18% and rise to 40% at taxable estates that are $1 million above the estate tax exemption.[216]

The same exemption level applies to the generation-skipping transfer tax (covered later). The deceased spousal portability election remains available in 2023 (covered later). Separately, the 2023 annual *gift* tax exclusion is $17,000.

Note: Sometimes, the estate tax is called a "death tax" or an "inheritance tax." The estate tax is *not* an income tax. It is a tax that is imposed on the transfer of property after a person's death. Estate and gift taxes are often considered together because they share the same lifetime exemption amount. However, the *estate tax* applies to transfers of the decedent's property after death, while the *gift tax* applies to transfers made while a person is alive.

Note: For Part 1 of the EA exam, you will be required to understand how estate and gift taxes affect individual taxpayers, especially the surviving spouses and other beneficiaries of those estates. For Part 2 of the exam, you will be tested on the income tax treatment of estates and trusts as legal entities. It is possible that questions will overlap, and therefore we cover the concept of estate taxation from various perspectives.

Personal Representative or Executor

When a person dies, a personal representative (an executor or administrator appointed by a court), will typically manage the estate and settle the decedent's final financial affairs. If there is no executor or administrator, another person with possession of the decedent's property may act as the personal representative. If a probate court proceeding is necessary, the judge will appoint an executor if one is not named in the decedent's will. A trustee can also administer the affairs of a deceased individual if the deceased individual had a valid trust at the time of their passing.

---

[215] This exemption may be less in situations where the exemption has been reduced due to prior taxable gifts.
[216] Be aware that some states have inheritance taxes of their own. Currently, about half of the U.S. states impose some type of inheritance or estate tax. Most states that impose estate taxes match the federal exemption threshold, but some states are much lower. Property left to a surviving spouse is exempt from the tax in all but six states.

Note: Under U.S. law, a "personal representative" is a living person appointed by the courts to administer an estate after a taxpayer has died. *Executors* are appointed when the decedent has a will, and *administrators* are appointed when the decedent dies without a will. The IRS also uses the term "personal representative" to refer to anyone filing a return on behalf of a decedent, regardless if that person has been appointed by the courts or named in a decedent's will.

Example: Dominik is 64 and unmarried. He has one 23-year-old daughter, named Jacqueline. Dominik dies on November 3, 2023. Thankfully, Dominik had a will when he died. In the will, Jacqueline is named as the sole beneficiary and the executor of her late father's estate. Jacqueline seeks the help of a licensed tax professional as well as an attorney to help her navigate the probate process. The attorney and the accountant will help Jacqueline file all the necessary paperwork with the court as well as the IRS. Jacqueline will sign her late father's final personal income tax return as the executor.

The personal representative is also responsible for determining any estate tax liability before the estate's assets are distributed to beneficiaries. The tax liability for an estate attaches to the assets of the estate itself. If the assets are distributed to the beneficiaries before the taxes are paid, the beneficiaries or the executor may be held liable for the tax debt, up to the value of the assets distributed. After a taxpayer dies, the following tax returns may need to be filed by the personal representative of the estate:

- **Form 1040:** Final income tax return for the decedent (for income received before death).
- **Form 1041**: *U.S. Income Tax Return for Estates and Trusts*: Fiduciary income tax returns for the estate for the period of its administration.
- **Form 706**: *United States Estate (and Generation-Skipping Transfer) Tax Return*: If the gross estate exceeds the applicable threshold. This return is used to report tax on the taxable estate (the gross estate minus certain deductions).

The personal representative (including a trustee) or executor must sign each required return. A personal representative should sign the decedent's final income tax return as "Personal Representative."

IRS **Form 56,** also known as the *Notice Concerning Fiduciary Relationship*, is an essential form to file to inform the IRS of the creation (or termination) of a fiduciary relationship for another party. An executor should submit the form to establish their authority to act on behalf of the estate. This form should be filed as soon as the estate's EIN is received, as it ensures that the executor will receive any important notices from the IRS.

Example: On April 3, 2023, Loretta Johnson, a widow with no children, passes away. She had not filed her tax return for the year 2023 before her death. In her final will, she named her nephew, Axel, as her executor. Axel takes on the responsibility of handling Loretta's final affairs, including his late aunt's taxes. To do so, he must first request an Employer Identification Number (EIN) for Loretta's estate. Once he receives the EIN, he completes Form 56, Notice Concerning Fiduciary Relationship, to establish his authority as the executor of Loretta's estate. On Form 56, Axel provides Loretta's information in Part I, including her name and Social Security number. He also includes his own information and the newly obtained EIN of the estate. After signing the form, Axel is now able to act as the authorized representative of Loretta's estate, including managing any tax matters that may arise. If any notices are generated by the IRS, they will automatically be sent to Axel, as he is the executor.

If the taxpayer's final income tax return is a joint return, then the surviving spouse would sign as a "surviving spouse" without the need to file Form 56 for the final 1040 (joint) return that includes the deceased spouse.

The executor or "personal representative" must include fees paid to them from an estate in their gross income. Fees paid to a trustee of a trust that is administering the affairs of a deceased individual will also be gross income to the trustee. If the executor is not "in the business" of being an executor (for instance, the executor is a friend or family member of the deceased), these fees are reported on the executor's individual Form 1040, as "other income" on Schedule 1.

If the executor is in the "trade or business" of being an executor, (such as a self-employed estate attorney), the executor would report the fees received from the estate as self-employment income on Schedule C.

Example: Patricia is a licensed CPA, but she only does audit work and does not prepare tax returns. Her uncle, Duran, dies in 2023. In his final will, Duran names his niece, Patricia, as the executor of his estate. Patricia has never served as an executor before, but she agrees to be the executor of her uncle's estate as a favor to his family. The fees she receives from the estate, if any, would be reported as "other income" on the Schedule 1 of her personal income tax return (Form 1040), because she is not a professional executor.

Note: A personal representative or executor of an estate cannot be held liable if an insolvent estate does not have enough assets to cover any of the income taxes due or debts. *However*, the executor must be sure that any income taxes are paid before any assets are distributed to the beneficiaries of the estate; otherwise, the executor might be held personally liable for the tax debt.

Example: Jacinta, who was 53 years old, passed away unexpectedly in 2023, leaving behind a valuable estate. At the time of her death, she was unmarried. Her oldest child, Silas, who is now 27 years old, was named as the executor of her estate. Silas has two younger siblings, Rebecca and Sasha, who are both under the age of 18 and still minors. All of the siblings are equal beneficiaries of the estate, but since Silas is the only legal adult, he is named the sole administrator of his mother's estate by the probate court. Silas distributes a large amount of stock and cash to himself and both his sisters before he has had his mother's assets properly appraised. After the appraisal is done, Silas realizes that his mother's estate has a filing requirement and an estate tax liability. Since Silas distributed assets to the beneficiaries before determining the correct amount of tax due, he may be held personally liable for paying the estate tax himself.

Final Income Tax Return (Form 1040)

A decedent's final *income* tax return is filed on the same form that would have been used if the taxpayer were still alive. The filing deadline is April 15 (April 15, 2024, for the tax year 2023) of the year following the taxpayer's death, the same deadline that applies for individual income tax returns.

The personal representative must file the final individual income tax return of the decedent for the year of death and any returns not filed for preceding years. If an individual died after the close of a tax year, but before the return for that year was filed, the return for that year will not be the final return. The return for that year will be a regular return, and the personal representative must file it.

Example: Huxley was unmarried when he died on April 20, 2023. His adult child, Janna, is the executor and sole heir of her father's estate. Huxley earned $74,000 in wages before his death, so a final tax return is required for 2023. Janna asks her accountant to help prepare her father's final Form 1040, which will include all the taxable income that Huxley received before his death. The accountant also helps Janna with the valuation of her father's estate. After determining the fair market value of all her father's assets, her accountant concludes that Huxley's gross estate is valued at approximately $16 million on the date of his death. As this exceeds the filing threshold for estate tax purposes for 2023, an estate tax return (Form 706) is also required to be filed, and Janna is responsible for filing both returns and signing them as the official representative of the estate.

Example: Esmeralda dies on February 28, 2024. At the time of her death, she was unmarried and had not yet filed her prior-year tax return. She earned $89,000 of wages during 2023. She also earned $18,200 of wages between January 1, 2024, and her death on February 28, 2024. Therefore, Esmeralda's 2023 and 2024 tax returns must both be filed by her executor. The 2024 return will be her final individual tax return, because that is the year that she died.

On a decedent's final tax return, the rules for deductions are the same as those that apply for any individual taxpayer. The decedent's year of death is *not* treated as a short tax year. In other words, the full amount of the applicable standard deduction or any applicable credits may be claimed on the final tax return, regardless of how long the taxpayer was alive during the year.

For example, a decedent who died in the middle of the year would still be eligible for EITC (the Earned Income Tax Credit), if they otherwise qualified, even though their final return covers less than twelve months.

Example: Ruthie, age 59, was unmarried when she passed away on July 30, 2023. Her only brother, Vernon, is named the executor of her estate. Ruthie earned a small amount of wages, $8,300, in the months before she died. Her income is below the filing requirement, so a return does not have to be filed. However, taxes were withheld from Ruthie's wages, so Vernon files an individual tax return in order to receive his late sister's refund. Ruthie is allowed the full standard deduction in 2023, as well as the EITC, even though she was only alive for part of the year.

Income in Respect of a Decedent (IRD)

Income in respect of a decedent (IRD) is any taxable income that was *earned* but not *received* by the decedent by the time of death. IRD is not taxed on the final return of the deceased taxpayer. IRD is reported on the tax return of the person (or entity) that receives the income.

This could be an heir, or the surviving spouse. If IRD is paid directly to a beneficiary, it is reported on the beneficiary's income tax return (Form 1040). If IRD is received by the estate itself, or if there is no designated beneficiary for the income, then the IRD is reported on the estate's Form 1041. IRD retains the same tax nature that would have been applied if the deceased taxpayer were still alive. For example, if the income would have been short-term capital gain, it is taxed the same way to the beneficiary. There is no step-up in basis for IRD items.

For *self-employment* tax purposes only, a decedent's self-employment income will include the decedent's distributive share of a partnership's income or loss through the end of the month in which death occurred.

Wages paid to a deceased employee's estate or executor/administrator <u>in the year of death</u> are not subject to income tax withholding, but employment taxes, such as FICA, must be withheld. Wages paid <u>*after* the year of death</u> generally are not subject to withholding for any federal taxes.

> **Example:** Zahid was owed $15,000 of wages when he died on December 27, 2023. The final check for these wages was not remitted by his employer until several weeks later (in January 2024, the following year) and was received and cashed by his daughter and sole beneficiary, Jolene. The wages are considered IRD to Jolene, and Jolene must recognize the $15,000 as ordinary income, the same tax treatment that would have applied for Zahid. However, since the wages were paid in the year *following* Zahid's death, the amounts are not subject to FICA or federal income tax withholding.

IRD can come from various sources, including:

- Unpaid salary, wages, or bonuses
- Amounts distributed from retirement plans distributed by the payor before the taxpayer's death, but not yet received by the decedent at the time of death.
- Deferred compensation benefits
- Accrued but unpaid interest, dividends, and rent
- Dividends declared *before* the decedent's death, but payable *after* death
- Outstanding income owed to a self-employed decedent (accounts receivable) is considered IRD but is not subject to self-employment tax.
- Gains on the sale of property sold before death but not collected until after death.

> **Example:** Wallace, age 65, sells a rental property that he had owned for many years to a private-party buyer on June 1, 2023, for $120,000. The buyer promised to deliver a cashier's check to Wallace the following week. Two days later, on June 3, 2023, Wallace dies, before receiving the check from the buyer. Wallace's adjusted basis in the rental property was $100,000 at the time of the sale, and he had owned the property for six years. The buyer of the property gives the $120,000 check to Wallace's daughter, Sheri, who is her father's only heir. The gain from the sale ($20,000) is IRD to Sheri, and she must report the gain on her own return. There is no step-up in basis, because the home was already sold by Wallace, so there is no "asset" for Sheri to step up, but Sheri is the one who received the gain from the sale. The sale generates a long-term capital gain, which Wallace would have recognized on his own return, had he lived long enough to collect the check. The income is reported and treated the same on Sheri's return, since she is the one who received the sale proceeds.

> **Example:** Jasper is a self-employed architect who reports his income on Schedule C. Jasper usually bills his clients monthly. Jasper is married to Zelda, who is a homemaker and does not work in his business. Jasper dies on December 27, 2023, with several unpaid client invoices outstanding at the time of his death. Jasper's surviving spouse, Zelda, receives all the payments from Jasper's outstanding invoices the following year, in January 2024. Since the outstanding accounts receivable was *earned* by Jasper while he was alive, but not *received* by Zelda until after his death, then it is considered IRD to Zelda, and it would be taxed as ordinary income to her in 2024, but not subject to self-employment tax, because Zelda is not self-employed.

Example: Reginald, age 67, decides to cash out his traditional IRA in order to take a nice vacation. He contacts his IRA trustee and requests a $12,000 distribution in the form of a check on February 1, 2023. The trustee tells Reginald that the check will take 7 days to deliver to his home. Two days later, Reginald dies. The $12,000 check for the IRA distribution is received by Reginald's daughter, Selma, who is the executor of his estate. The distribution is treated as IRD to Selma.

In rare instances, IRD must be included in the decedent's estate and may be subject to estate tax. This may happen with a very wealthy person. If the decedent's estate was large enough to be subject to estate tax, this can result in a form of double taxation: once at the estate level and again when the beneficiary receives the income.

If a beneficiary receives IRD and the income is also subject to estate tax, the beneficiary can deduct the tax on Schedule A of their individual income tax return as a miscellaneous itemized deduction. This is called the "IRD deduction" or "Estate Tax Deduction." A beneficiary must claim the IRD deduction[217] in the same tax year in which they actually receive the income.

If the value of the decedent's estate isn't subject to estate tax (because it falls within the estate tax exemption), the IRD deduction is not permitted.

The Estate Tax Return (Form 706)

An estate tax return is filed using Form 706, *United States Estate (and Generation-Skipping Transfer) Tax Return.* This return is due nine months after the death of the decedent. A six-month extension is allowed. After the taxable estate is computed, it is added to the value of lifetime taxable gifts. The applicable estate tax rate is applied to derive a tentative tax, from which any gift taxes paid or payable are subtracted to determine the gross estate tax. The maximum estate tax rate is 40% in 2023. Less than 1% of taxpayers are affected by the estate tax.

However, all or a portion of the gross estate tax may be eliminated after applying the Basic Exclusion Amount. The estate tax exclusion is $12.92 million in 2023.[218] The assessment period for estate tax is three years after the due date for a timely filed estate tax return. The assessment period is four years for transfers from an estate.

Example: Wilhelmina was age 60 and unmarried when she died in 2023 and left an estate valued at $9 million. She had no children, and her only heir is her 48-year-old brother, Donald. Wilhelmina had not previously used any of her basic exclusion amount to avoid paying gift taxes, so the entire exclusion amount of $12.92 million is available to her estate. As this amount exceeds the entire estate's value, no estate tax is owed, and an estate tax return (Form 706) does not need to be filed. All of Wilhelmina's assets shall pass tax-free to Donald (no estate tax will be owed).

There is a special rule that applies to widows and widowers. A surviving spouse can add any unused exclusion of a predeceased spouse who died most recently to their own estate tax return. This is also known as "portability," or the Deceased Spousal Unused Exclusion "DSUE"), which we will cover later.

---

[217] The "IRD deduction" is short for Income in Respect of a Decedent tax deduction. The IRD deduction is a miscellaneous itemized tax deduction, not subject to the 2% of AGI floor. The IRD deduction was not suspended by the TCJA.

[218] This threshold is much lower for nonresident aliens at $60,000 in 2023. However, nonresident aliens are only potentially subject to estate tax upon their death for assets located within the United States. Form 706-NA is used for nonresident aliens.

Form 1041, Annual Income Tax Return for Estates and Trusts

An estate is a legal entity that exists from the time of an individual's death until all assets have been distributed to beneficiaries. As investment assets will usually continue to earn income after a taxpayer has died, this income, such as rents, dividends, and interest, must be reported.

Most estates are administered and distributed within 12 to-18 months, but sometimes, if the decedent was a famous or wealthy person, the estate may not terminate for years, and sometimes, even decades. Probate litigation can drag on for a long time. If there is a dispute about the will, or between the heirs, the estate cannot terminate until the legal dispute is resolved.

Example: Geneva Jones is a popular writer with many bestselling novels. She is unmarried and has no children, but she has five adult siblings. Geneva dies without a will on January 19, 2023, at age 52. The estimated value of her estate exceeds $25 million, and her novels continue to sell briskly after her death. Geneva's siblings are her only living relatives and are therefore equal heirs of her estate. The siblings immediately start to squabble over their late sister's assets. All five siblings petition to be named the executor. The probate court is forced to appoint a professional executor, and the litigation will likely drag on for years. The estate is still generating revenue during this time, so the Form 1041 will need to be filed every year by the professional executor, in order to report the ongoing income of the estate until the legal dispute between the siblings is resolved.

Note: "Probate" is the court-supervised process of settling a decedent's estate. It takes longer to probate an estate that owes estate taxes because a taxable estate cannot be closed until either the estate obtains an IRS transcript showing the acceptance of the estate tax return, or it receives a final closing letter from the Internal Revenue Service.[219]

Form 1041 is an annual fiduciary return used to report the following items for a domestic decedent's estate, trust, or bankruptcy estate:

- Current income[220] and deductions, including gains and losses from the disposition of the entity's property, and excluding certain items such as tax-exempt interest (collectively, *distributable net income* or DNI),
- A deduction for income either held for future distribution or distributed currently to the beneficiaries (income distribution deduction), and
- Any income tax liability.

Expenses of administering the estate can be deducted either from the estate's income on Form 1041 in determining its income tax, or from the gross estate on Form 706 in determining the estate tax liability but cannot be claimed for both purposes.

Schedule K-1 is used to report any income that is distributed or distributable to each beneficiary and is filed with Form 1041, with a copy also given to the beneficiary. If the beneficiary of the estate is a person (and not an entity, like a charity) then the beneficiary would report the distributive income on Form 1040, Schedule E.

---

[219] The IRS no longer *automatically* issues Estate Tax Closing Letters. However, an estate or trust may request one by paying a fee to the IRS. The IRS recommends waiting at least nine months after the filing of an estate tax return to request an Estate Tax Closing Letter.

[220] "Current income" may include IRD (if it was received by the estate, rather than a beneficiary).

Example: Andrae owned three valuable rental properties before his death on July 1, 2023. The gross value of his assets on the date of Andrae's death was $2 million, so an estate tax return (Form 706) does not have to be filed. The income from the rental properties that was received while Andrae was alive would be reported on his final Form 1040, Schedule E. The rental income that was received by his estate *after* his death would be reportable on Form 1041, *Annual Tax Return for Estates and Trusts.*

Example: Annabelle is 67 years old and unmarried. She dies on January 31, 2023, and her only heir is her adult son, Nolan, who will inherit his mother's entire estate. This includes her primary home valued at $400,000 and a rental property worth $240,000 which brings in $3,000 of net income each month. Since the total value of Annabelle's assets falls below the estate exemption amount, no estate tax return (Form 706) is required. However, a Form 1041 must be filed to report the rental income earned by the estate after Annabelle's passing. Only the rental income that was earned in January will be reported on Annabelle's last income tax return (Form 1040), while the remaining rental income that was generated after her death will be reported on the Form 1041. Her executor will be responsible for filing her final income tax return (Form 1040) as well as the tax return for her estate (Form 1041).

Estates and trusts are allowed some of the same tax credits that are allowed to individuals. The credits are generally allocated between the estate and the beneficiaries. However, estates are not allowed the Child Tax Credit, or the Earned Income Tax Credit.

However, the Earned Income Tax Credit, Child Tax Credit, and any other applicable credits can be claimed on the decedent's final return.

Note: Just like individual taxpayers, estates and trusts are subject to the Net Investment Income Tax (an additional tax of 3.8% on net investment income). The basic provisions for this tax are similar to those for individuals, and it must be reported on Form 8960, *Net Investment Tax: Individuals, Estates, and Trusts.*

The due date for Form 1041 is the fifteenth day of the fourth month following the end of the entity's tax year but is subject to an automatic extension of five-and-one-half months if Form 7004 is filed by the original due date. The tax year may be either a calendar or a fiscal year for an estate, subject to the election made at the time the first return is filed. An election will also be made on the first return as to the accounting method (cash or accrual) of reporting the estate's income.

Form 1041 is required to be filed for any domestic estate that has (1) gross income for the tax year of $600 or more, or (2) a beneficiary who is a nonresident alien (with any amount of income). If the estate has no income-producing assets, and generates no income, no income tax return is necessary.

Example: Petra is 76 years old. She dies on July 1, 2023. At the time of her death, she owned a home valued at $675,000 and a vacation home valued at $900,000. She had $80,000 in a non-interest bearing checking account. Petra also owned 5 acres of undeveloped land in Texas valued at more than $1 million. She had purchased the land as an investment several years ago but was not currently using it for anything. While her estate is valuable, it has no income-producing assets. Therefore, there is no need to file Form 706 or Form 1041 for Petra's estate since the assets fall below the exemption amount and do not generate any revenue.

The Gross Estate

The gross estate is based upon the fair market value of the decedent's property, which is not necessarily equal to the assets' cost. The gross estate includes:

- The fair market value of all tangible and intangible property owned partially or outright by the decedent at the time of death,
- Life insurance proceeds payable to the estate or, for policies owned by the decedent, payable to the heirs,
- The value of certain annuities or survivor benefits payable to the heirs, and
- The value of certain property that was transferred within three years before the decedent's death.

The gross estate does not include property owned solely by the decedent's spouse or other individuals. Lifetime gifts that are complete (so that no control over the gifts was retained) are not included in the gross estate.

Example: Cristiano is wealthy and regularly gives money to many of his close relatives. The IRS allows every taxpayer to gift up to $17,000 in 2023 to an individual recipient, annually, without having to file a gift tax return. On January 10, 2023, Cristiano writes 10 individual checks for $17,000, giving a check to each of his siblings, as well as his parents and grandparents. None of the gifts are taxable to the recipients, and no gift tax reporting is required for Cristiano. Two months later, Cristiano dies. Since the cash gifts were "completed gifts" the $170,000 (10 checks × $17,000 each) he gifted to his family members is not includible in his gross estate.

Deductions from the Gross Estate on Form 706

After calculating the gross estate, certain deductions (and in specific situations, reductions) can be made to determine the taxable estate. These deductions may include:

- Funeral expenses paid from the estate,
- Administrative expenses for the estate, such as court fees and legal costs (if not already deducted on Form 1041),
- Debts owed at the time of the individual's death,
- Marital deduction (the value of property passing to a surviving spouse),
- Charitable deduction (the value of property passing to eligible charities),
- State death tax deduction (inheritance or estate taxes paid to any state).

The following items are *not* deductible from the gross estate:

- Federal estate taxes paid,
- Alimony paid after the taxpayer's death; these payments are treated as distributions to a beneficiary.

Property taxes are deductible on Form 706 only if they accrue under state law *prior* to the decedent's death.

Special Rule for Medical Expenses

If a person passes away with unpaid debts, including medical expenses that are unpaid at the time of death, those debts can be deducted from the total value of their estate on the estate tax return. Any outstanding medical expenses at the time of death are considered liabilities of the estate. However, if these medical expenses are paid by the estate within one year after the individual's death, the personal representative has the option to treat them as if they were paid by the deceased when *incurred,* instead of when they were actually paid, and deduct them on Form 1040 instead of potentially on Form 706, if it results in a better tax outcome to the estate. This election can also be made by filing an amended return.

Example: Jimena, age 76, died on April 1, 2024, after a long battle with cancer. She had filed her 2023 return just two days prior to her death (on March 30, 2024). She incurred $42,000 of medical expenses, half during 2023 (the prior tax year) and half during 2024. When she died in April, all her medical bills remained unpaid. The estate's executor is her adult son, Ralph. After consulting with an estate attorney, Ralph pays the entire $42,000 medical bill on July 10, 2024, with funds from his mother's estate. Ralph, the executor, elects to file an amended return (Form 1040-X) for Jimena for 2023, claiming $21,000 as a medical expense deduction on Schedule A (the year the medical expenses were *incurred*). The remaining $21,000 will be deducted on Jimena's final income tax return (her 2024 Form 1040, which will be due the following year).

The Marital Deduction

Transfers from one spouse to the other are typically tax-free. The marital deduction allows spouses to transfer an unlimited amount of property to one another during their lifetimes or at death without being subject to estate or gift taxes.

Note: The marital deduction is NOT the same thing as the Deceased Spousal Unused Exclusion, or DSUE, which is covered in the next section. The DSUE is an *election* that is generally only available to U.S. citizen spouses.

To receive an unlimited marital deduction, the spouse *receiving* the assets must be a U.S. citizen and must have outright ownership of the assets after the passing of the decedent. The unlimited marital deduction is generally not allowed if the transferee spouse is not a U.S. citizen (even if the spouse is a legal resident of the United States).

Example: Lorenzo and Margie are married, and both are U.S. citizens. Lorenzo dies and leaves his wife, Margie, all his assets, which total $15 million on the date of his death. The transfer is tax-free to Margie because of the unlimited marital deduction. Margie's estate may or may not owe tax when she dies, but the transfer of assets to a surviving spouse is generally a nontaxable event, provided that the surviving spouse is a U.S. citizen.

Note: If the receiving spouse is not a U.S. citizen, assets transferred tax-free are limited to an annual exclusion amount. Noncitizen spouses can only receive $175,000 in 2023. This is true even if the spouse is a legal U.S. resident (a green card holder). This is one of the rare instances where U.S. citizens are taxed differently than legal U.S. residents.

Deceased Spousal Unused Exclusion (DSUE)

The DSUE is an election to transfer the unused portion of the decedent's predeceased spouse's basic exclusion (the amount that was not used to offset gift or estate tax liabilities). A "portability" election must be made to claim the DSUE on behalf of the surviving spouse's estate. Once "ported" to the surviving spouse, the surviving spouse can use the DSUE amount to help shield future asset transfers from estate tax.

This election is made by filing an estate tax return. Portability is *not* automatic: Form 706 <u>must be filed</u> in order to make the DSUE election, even if no estate tax is owed. The Form 706 is due nine months after the death of the first spouse. A six-month extension is allowed.[221] The surviving spouse must be a U.S. citizen. The DSUE is not available to nonresident alien spouses.

> **Example:** Myron died on January 13, 2023, and left a gross estate valued at $19 million. All of his assets were transferred to his wife, Juliet, under the terms of his will. Juliet is a U.S. citizen. As a result, none of his estate was taxed because of the unlimited marital deduction. None of the $12.92 million basic exclusion amount available to Myron's estate was used (and none had been used to offset gift tax liabilities during his lifetime). Juliet then died later in the same year, on December 20, 2023. Assuming Form 706 was timely filed for Myron's estate, electing the DSUE, and Juliet had not used any of her basic exclusion amount, Myron's unused basic exclusion is added to Juliet's basic exclusion, for a total exclusion amount of $25.84 million between their two estates. If Juliet's estate is valued at less than $25.84 million at her death, the full amount can be excluded, and no estate tax will be owed when Juliet's assets eventually pass to her heirs.

Inheritances

For federal income tax purposes, inheritances are generally not taxable to the beneficiary, although the beneficiary may be responsible if there is a related estate tax liability that has not been satisfied.

> **Example:** Caruso's aunt, Georgina, died and left him $175,000 cash in her will. Georgina's estate was only worth $1.5 million, so the estate did not have an estate tax filing requirement, and no estate tax return (Form 706) was filed. Caruso is a U.S. citizen. He does not owe any federal tax on this inheritance, and nothing has to be reported on Caruso's return.

> **Example:** Raquel dies and leaves her entire estate to her son, Atticus. At the time of her death, she had a significant cash balance in her personal bank account as well as several valuable rental properties in New York. Raquel's estate is worth over $15 million, so the estate has a filing requirement, but Atticus ignores his accountant's advice and simply withdraws all the money from his late mother's bank account. He also sells all the rental properties and uses the money to take several lavish trips. Although inheritances are generally not taxable to the beneficiary, the fact that Atticus took possession of his mother's assets without filing her required estate tax return or satisfying the estate tax liability would make him directly responsible for the tax. The IRS can come after Atticus in order to satisfy the estate's tax liability.

---

[221] Revenue Procedure 2022-32 allows for a late estate tax return if it is filed solely for the purpose of making a "portability" election. This Revenue Procedure extends the time to make the DSUE election to five years after the first spouse's date of death.

Inherited retirement accounts are treated a bit differently. Distributions of retirement plan benefits or distributions from taxable IRA accounts to the decedent's beneficiaries are generally subject to income tax when received, although inherited IRAs are not subject to an early-withdrawal penalty, regardless of the beneficiary's age. Qualified distributions from a Roth IRA or of previously nondeductible contributions to a traditional IRA are generally not taxable.

The decedent's surviving spouse may elect to defer taxation by rolling over the assets of a taxable IRA to another IRA or to a qualified plan (i.e., the surviving spouse is allowed to treat an IRA inherited from a deceased spouse "as their own").

Example: Benjamin, age 55, dies on September 1, 2023. He was unmarried at the time of his death and did not have any children. Benjamin's only sister, Chanel, age 43, is named as the beneficiary of his estate, which consists entirely of a $170,000 traditional IRA account. There are no other assets. Since Chanel is a non-spousal beneficiary, she is not allowed to rollover the funds from her deceased brother's IRA into her own retirement account. Instead, she is required to either distribute the funds as a lump-sum, or make a new inherited IRA account in her name and transfer the funds to this account (this is also called a Beneficiary IRA). When Chanel starts withdrawing the money from the inherited IRA, she will not be charged a 10% early withdrawal penalty, even though she is under age 59½. She will only have to pay income tax on the withdrawals.

Basis of Estate Property

Although cash inheritances are not subject to federal income tax, money received from the sale of inherited property may be taxable. The basis of property inherited from a decedent is generally one of the following:

- The FMV of the property on the date of death,
- The FMV on an alternate valuation date, if elected by the personal representative,
- The value under a special-use valuation method for real property used in farming or another closely held business, if elected by the personal representative,
- The decedent's adjusted basis in land to the extent of the value excluded from the taxable estate as a qualified conservation easement.

Example: Paul, age 66, dies on February 1, 2023. Paul's adult son, Easton, is the executor of his late father's estate. Paul owned a large collection of collectible figurines and rare comic books. Paul's will directs that the estate be split equally between Easton and his four siblings. The fair market value of Paul's collectibles on the date of his death is $500,000. The collectibles are the only valuable asset that the estate owns. Since the estate's total value is less than the exclusion amount, Easton does not file an estate tax return (Form 706) or elect the alternate valuation date. On November 15, 2023, the siblings all agree to sell their late father's collection using an auction house. The entire collection sells at auction for $552,000. Collectively, Paul's children (his heirs) must report a capital gain of $52,000 ($552,000 sale price minus the $500,000 basis, based on the collection's FMV at the date of death).

Alternate Valuation Date: If elected, the alternate valuation date is six months after the date of death. The estate value and related estate tax must be <u>less</u> than they would have been on the date of the taxpayer's death. However, for any assets distributed to a beneficiary after death, but prior to six months after death, the basis for these assets is the fair market value as of the date of distribution.

Jointly Owned Property: Property that is jointly owned by a decedent and another person will be included in full in the decedent's gross estate unless it can be shown that the other person originally owned or otherwise contributed to the purchase price. The surviving owner's new basis of property that was jointly owned must be calculated.

To do so, the surviving owner's original basis in the property is added to the value of the part of the property included in the decedent's estate. Any deductions for depreciation allowed to the surviving owner for his portion of the property are subtracted from the sum.

If a property is jointly held between spouses as tenants-by-the-entirety,[222] or as joint tenants with the right of survivorship, one-half of the property's value is included in the gross estate, and there is a step-up in basis for that one-half.

The other half is stated at the surviving spouse's cost basis, net of any deductions for depreciation allowed to the surviving spouse on that half. If the decedent holds property in a community property state,[223] half of the value of the community property will be included in the gross estate of the decedent, but the entire value of the community property will receive a step-up in basis.

> **Example:** Bong-Cha and Hyun-Shik are married and live together in Texas, which is a community property state. They hold their personal residence as community property, and both of them live in the home together. They purchased the home for $450,000 eight years ago. Bong-Cha dies on December 15, 2023, and the house is valued at $630,000 on the date of her death. Hyun-Shik's basis in the house is now $630,000. The entire house gets a step-up in basis to the FMV on the date of one spouse's death because it was held as community property. If Hyun-Shik decides to sell the home at a later date, he would use $630,000 as his basis for determining whether or not he has any gain on the sale.

The Estate Tax

The estate tax may apply to a decedent's taxable estate, which is the gross estate minus any allowable deductions. The maximum estate tax rate in 2023 is 40%. In 2023, an estate valued at less than $12.92 million would generally not have an estate tax return filing requirement. Estates that are valued at more than this threshold are required to file Form 706, *United States Estate and Generation-Skipping Transfer Tax Return.*

> **Example:** Fabio is a U.S. citizen who dies on May 3, 2023. The fair market value of all his assets on the date of his death totals $8 million. Although his estate is valuable, the combined assets are worth less than the exemption amount ($12.92 million in 2023). His estate is not subject to estate tax, and Form 706 does not need to be filed. Fabio earned $210,000 in wages before his death, so his executor will still be required to file a final Form 1040 for the income that Fabio earned while he was alive (from January 1 to May 3, 2023). A Form 1041 also may need to be filed if Fabio's estate earns gross income of $600 or more in 2023.

---

222 "Tenancy by the entirety" is a form of property ownership for married couples. In general, "tenancy by the entirety" means that if one spouse dies, the other spouse will automatically own the real property without the need to probate it.
223 Community property law exists in nine U.S. states: Arizona, California, Idaho, Louisiana, Nevada, New Mexico, Texas, Washington, and Wisconsin.

However, this threshold is much lower for nonresident aliens at $60,000. An executor for a nonresident alien must file a nonresident estate tax return, Form 706-NA, *United States Estate (and Generation-Skipping) Tax Return, Estate of a nonresident,* if the fair market value at death of the decedent's U.S.-situated assets exceeds $60,000.

> **Example:** Yong-Sun is a citizen and resident of South Korea. Yong-Sun is a popular Korean recording artist, and his travels bring him to the U.S. quite frequently. Yong-Sun owns a vacation home in Hollywood, CA, which he uses at least once a year to entertain his celebrity guests. When he is not in the U.S., he uses a management company to rent out the home to short-term tenants. Yong-Sun dies on November 9, 2023. The Hollywood vacation home is the only U.S. asset that Yong-Sun owned. The house's FMV on the date of his death was approximately $450,000. Since Yong-Sun is a nonresident for U.S. tax purposes, his estate has a filing requirement. His executor must file Form 706-NA and report the value of the asset and pay any estate taxes owed.

Generation-Skipping Transfer Tax (GST)

In the past, wealthy families used various strategies to transfer wealth and assets to their grandchildren and other descendants. In response to this, Congress created the generation-skipping transfer tax, also known as the GST, to close this tax loophole.

The generation-skipping transfer tax (GST) may apply to gifts made during a taxpayer's lifetime, or bequests occurring after a taxpayer's death, made to "skip persons." A skip person is usually a grandchild, but it also applies to those who are more than 37½ years younger than the person making the gift or bequest. The most common scenario is when a taxpayer makes a gift to a grandchild.

The GST is assessed when the property transfer is made, including instances in which property is transferred from a trust. The GST is based on the amounts transferred to skip persons, after subtracting the allocated portions of the donor's available GST exemption. The GST exemption is the same as the estate tax basic exclusion amount, and the GST tax rate is set at the estate tax rates, with a maximum of 40%. The GST is imposed separately and in *addition* to the estate and gift tax.

> **Example:** Sylvester was diagnosed with terminal cancer, and is told that he only has a short time to live. He is unmarried and has only one adult daughter, named Glenda. Sylvester wants his daughter to be able to avoid the probate administration process when he dies. He meets with an attorney and sets up a grantor trust that names his adult daughter, Glenda, as the sole beneficiary of the trust, with his grandchildren (Glenda's two children) as contingent beneficiaries, who will only receive assets from the trust upon Sylvester's death if Glenda is no longer alive at the time of his passing. Sylvester then transfers all his assets into the trust. Unexpectedly, shortly after the trust is created, Glenda dies. On January 10, 2023, Sylvester dies, and the trust beneficiaries are his grandchildren. The revocable trust is now irrevocable. That means that any disposition of the assets that Sylvester placed inside the trust before his death cannot be revoked, nor can beneficiary designations be changed. The trust assets pass to his two grandchildren. Sylvester's grandchildren are "skip persons" for purposes of the GST, and the trust's property may now be subject to the GST.

Any payments for tuition or medical expenses on behalf of a skip person that are made directly to an educational or medical institution are exempt from gift tax and GST. There is no reporting requirement for this type of gift, regardless of the dollar amount.

The Gift Tax

The gift tax may apply to the transfer of property by one individual to another, whether the donor intends the transfer to be a gift or not. The gift tax can apply to both cash and noncash gifts. Gift tax is imposed on the *donor*, not the *receiver*, of the gift.

The recipient of a gift typically owes no taxes and doesn't have to report the gift unless it comes from a foreign donor. However, under special arrangements, the donee may *agree* to pay the tax instead of the donor.

As discussed previously, an individual taxpayer's liability for estate tax and gift tax is subject to a combined basic exclusion amount ($12.92 million in 2023), and the use of any portion of this exclusion amount to reduce payment of gift taxes during the taxpayer's lifetime will reduce the amount available upon death to reduce applicable estate taxes. The following gifts are not taxable and do not have to be reported:

- Gifts to an individual that do not exceed the annual exclusion amount. In 2023, the gift exclusion amount is $17,000 per donee.
- Tuition or medical expenses paid directly to an educational or medical institution for another person (the recipient does not have to be related to the taxpayer).
- Unlimited gifts to a spouse, as long as the spouse is a U.S. citizen.
- Gifts to a political organization for its own use.
- Gifts to a qualifying charity.
- A parent's support for a minor child. This may include support required as part of a legal obligation, such as by a divorce decree.

Example: Jurgen is 26, and Lynette is his mother. Both are U.S. citizens. Lynette gives her son, Jurgen, a gift of $17,000 of cash during the year. She also pays his college tuition, totaling $21,000. She writes the check directly to the college. Lynette also pays for Jurgen's medical bills by issuing an $18,000 check directly to his doctor's office. None of these gifts are taxable, and no gift tax reporting is required.

Example: Lincoln is single. In 2023, Lincoln gives his nephew, Jimmy, $39,000 to help start his first business. Lincoln tells his nephew that he does not have to pay it back. The money is intended as a gift, not a loan, so Lincoln is required to file a gift tax return (Form 709) since the amount exceeds the annual exclusion amount.

Example: Salman is a wealthy businessman, and he wants to support his two grandchildren, but he tries to make sure that his gifts are not subject to gift tax, GST, or estate tax. He also wants to legally avoid filing gift tax returns whenever possible. In 2023, he gifts each of his grandchildren $17,000 in cash, in the form of individual checks. He has one granddaughter in medical school, so he also pays his granddaughter's tuition in full, making the payment directly to the college for $54,195. His grandson also had a skiing accident during the year and broke his leg. The medical deductible after the insurance for the emergency care was $18,500, which Salman also paid directly to the medical provider on behalf of his grandson. There is no tax consequence for any of these gifts, and no reporting is required.

Gift taxes are reported on Form 709, *United States Gift (and Generation-Skipping Transfer) Tax Return.* Form 709 must be filed if:

- A taxpayer gives more than the annual exclusion amount to at least one individual (except to a U.S. citizen spouse),
- A taxpayer "splits gifts" with a spouse,
- A taxpayer gives a future interest to anyone other than a U.S. citizen spouse.

If a gift tax return is required to be filed, Form 709 is generally due by April 15 of the following year. However, if a donor dies during the year, the filing deadline may be the due date (with extensions) for the estate tax return, if earlier than April 15 of the following year. Taxpayers who extend the filing of Form 1040 for six months using Form 4868 are deemed to have extended their gift tax returns, if no gift tax is due with the extension.

If the taxpayer does not extend their individual return, the gift tax return can be extended separately by using Form 8892, *Application for Automatic Extension of Time to File Form 709 and/or Payment of Gift/Generation-Skipping Transfer Tax,* which also provides an additional six months to file Form 709, if filed by the original due date.

Note: A gift is considered a **present interest** if the donee has all immediate rights to the use, possession, and enjoyment of the property or income from the property, with no strings attached. A gift is considered a **future interest** if the donee's rights to the use, possession, and enjoyment of the property or income from the property will not begin until some future date. A gift of a future interest cannot be excluded under the annual exclusion. With a "future interest" the beneficiary typically does not become the legal owner of the property until the donor's death.

Example: Shepard creates an irrevocable trust for the beneficial enjoyment of Bethany, who is his long-time girlfriend. Shepard transfers an office building to the trust. The office building is currently rented to business tenants and is subject to a mortgage. The terms of the trust provides that the rental income from the property will first be used to pay off the mortgage. After the mortgage is paid in full, the net rental income is then to be paid to Bethany. Since Bethany's right to receive the rental income will not begin until *after* the mortgage is paid in full, the transfer in trust represents a gift of a future interest.

Applying the Applicable Credit to Gift Tax: After a taxpayer determines which of their gifts are taxable, the taxpayer must calculate the amount of gift tax on the total taxable gifts and apply the applicable credit for the year.

Gift Splitting by Married Couples

Both the basic exclusion amount and the annual exclusion amount apply separately to each spouse, and each spouse must separately file a gift tax return if they made reportable gifts during the year. However, if either spouse makes a gift to another person, the gift can be considered as being one-half from one spouse and one-half from the other spouse. This concept is known as *gift splitting.*

Gift splitting allows a married couple to give up to $34,000 (in 2023) to a single individual without making a taxable or reportable gift. Both spouses must consent to split the gift.

Example: Ignacio and his wife, Elinda, agree to split gifts of cash. Ignacio gives his friend a check for $21,000, and Elinda gives her niece a check for $18,000. Although each gift exceeds the annual exclusion amount of $17,000 in 2023, they can use gift splitting to avoid making a taxable gift to each donee. In each case, because one-half of each of the split gifts ($10,500 and $9,000) is not more than the annual exclusion amount, it is not taxable. However, a gift tax return is required to make these split gift elections.

Example: Gertrude gives her favorite cousin, Freddie, $25,000. Gertrude elects to split the gift with her husband, Maury, and Maury is treated as if he gave Freddie half the amount, or $12,500. Assuming they make no other gifts to Freddie during the year, the entire $25,000 gift is tax-free. However, a gift tax return is required in order to report the "split gift."

Note: A married couple can avoid filing a gift tax return if they each make a gift separately, such as by writing separate checks or giving separate property. In the example above, if each spouse had written separate checks for less than $17,000 each, then a gift tax return would not be required.

If a married couple splits a gift, each spouse must generally file their own individual gift tax return. However, certain exceptions may apply that allow for only one spouse to file a return if the other spouse signifies consent on the Form 709. Note that if gifts are made by a spouse from community property funds, the gift is deemed to have been made 50% by each spouse.

Basis of Property Received as a Gift

For purposes of determining gain or loss on a subsequent disposition of property received as a gift, a taxpayer must consider:

- The gift's adjusted basis to the donor just before it was given to the taxpayer,
- The gift's FMV at the time it was given to the taxpayer, and
- Any gift tax actually paid on the appreciation of the property's value while held by the donor (as opposed to gift tax offset by the donor's applicable credit amount).

If the fair market value of the gift is the same as or higher than the donor's adjusted basis for the gift before it was transferred, then the donee's basis will be the same as the donor's (transferred basis), adjusted for any gift tax paid on the donor's appreciation.

Example: Donovan gives his son, Maurice, 20 shares of stock on January 20, 2023. Donovan's basis in the stock is $500, and the stock has a fair market value of $8,600 on the date of the gift. Maurice's basis in the stock is also $500. This is called a "transferred basis."

However, in the event that the fair market value (FMV) of the gift is *lower* than the donor's adjusted basis at the time of transfer:

- When the recipient sells the gifted property, any gain will be calculated based on the donor's adjusted basis.
- If the recipient sells the property for a loss, their basis will be equal to the FMV at the time of the gift.

- If the recipient sells the property for a price higher than its FMV at the time of the gift, but lower than the donor's adjusted basis at that time, their basis will be equal to the selling price. This results in neither a gain nor loss on the sale.

> **Example:** Manuela receives an acre of land as a gift from her brother, Julian. Her brother's adjusted basis in the land is $50,000, and its FMV on the date of the gift is $40,000 (the land value has dropped since Julian bought it). A year later, Manuela sells the gifted land for $35,000 to an unrelated buyer. Since she sold the property at a loss, her basis in the land is $40,000, because it is *lower* than her brother's adjusted basis and the FMV on the date he gifted the property to her.

Generally, the value of a gift is its fair market value on the date of the gift. However, the value of the gift may be less than its fair market value to the extent that the donee gives the donor something in return.

> **Example:** Albus sells his son, Tanner, a house well below market value. Tanner only pays $10,000 for the house. In 2023, the fair market value of the house is $90,000. The home was transferred for much less than its full value. Therefore, Albus has made a gift to his son of $80,000 ($90,000 - $10,000 = $80,000). Albus is required to file a gift tax return because the gift exceeds the $17,000 threshold for 2023.

The Unified Credit (the Applicable Credit)

A taxpayer's gross estate tax is reduced by the *applicable credit*, also referred to as the *unified credit*. The unified credit is the combination of the lifetime gift tax exclusion and estate tax exclusion. For the 2023 tax year, the estate tax exclusion is $12.92 million. The applicable credit amount for 2023 is $5,113,800.

> **Note:** For taxable gifts, each taxpayer has an aggregate lifetime exemption before any out-of-pocket gift tax is due. For example, a taxpayer can give away up to $12.92 million during their lifetime *above* the annual $17,000 exclusion and still avoid paying any gift tax.

Just as with the basic exclusion amount, any portion of the applicable credit amount used to avoid payment of gift taxes reduces the amount of credit available in later years that can be used to offset gift or estate taxes. For example, if a taxpayer exceeds the annual gift tax exclusion amount in any year, the taxpayer can choose to either pay the gift tax on the excess or take advantage of the unified credit to avoid paying the tax in the current year.

> **Example:** Regina is a wealthy investor. She is unmarried and does not have any children. Two years ago, Regina gifted her brother $1 million in cash. She properly filed a gift tax return for the gift, and used $1 million of her basic exclusion to offset payments of gift tax. Regina dies in 2023 and leaves an estate valued at $20 million, all of which passes to her brother as her sole heir. Since she gifted $1 million during her lifetime, that reduced the amount her estate may exclude to $11.92 million (rather than $12.92 million), which is then subtracted from her $20 million taxable estate, to determine the amount of her estate that will be subject to the estate tax.

Unit 18: Study Questions

(Test yourself first, then check the correct answers at the end of this quiz.)

1. What is the main requirement for a surviving spouse to receive an unlimited marital deduction?

A. The surviving spouse must be a legal resident of the United States.
B. The surviving spouse must be a U.S. citizen.
C. The surviving spouse must have children.
D. The deceased spouse must have been a U.S. citizen.

2. Claude dies on May 4, 2023. His assets are valued at $60 million on the date of his death, so a Form 706 needs to be filed for his estate. When is the estate tax return due?

A. November 4, 2023
B. February 4, 2024
C. April 15, 2024
D. May 4, 2024

3. Eileen's aunt gives her a gift of a "future interest" on her estate. Eileen will have full use of the estate after her aunt dies. Which is the correct statement about this gift?

A. Eileen's aunt can use the annual gift tax exclusion for this gift.
B. The gift is considered a present interest.
C. Eileen's aunt cannot use the annual gift tax exclusion for this gift.
D. Eileen must pay estate tax on the gift.

4. Cash inheritances are generally:

A. Taxable to the beneficiary for any amount over $600.
B. Taxable to the beneficiary for amounts over $17,000.
C. Taxable to the beneficiary for amounts over $5 million.
D. Not taxable to the beneficiary for any amount.

5. Maximo is a legal U.S. resident (a green card holder). He dies on June 1, 2023, and leaves his entire estate to his wife, Jeanne, who is a U.S. citizen. Maximo's estate is valued at $50 million on the date of his death. What amount of tax must Jeanne pay on her late husband's estate in 2023?

A. $0
B. $15.52 million
C. $20.4 million
D. $37.98 million

6. Cristobal, a single taxpayer, has never been required to file a gift tax return. In 2023, Cristobal gave the following gifts:

- Tuition paid directly to a state university for his nephew: $18,000.
- Payment to General Hospital for his brother's medical bills: $19,500.
- Cash donation to a homeless shelter, a qualified 501(c)(3) organization: $50,000.
- Gift to the Libertarian Party (not a qualified charity): $25,000.

Is Cristobal required to file a gift tax return for 2023?

A. Yes, because the donation to the political party is not an excludable gift.
B. Yes, because each of the gifts exceeded the gift tax threshold.
C. Yes, because the political gift is a reportable transaction.
D. No, he does not have to file a gift tax return.

7. The executor of Celaya's estate is her sister, Elise. Elise decides to make a distribution of 100% of the estate's assets before paying the estate's income tax liability. Which of the following statements is correct?

A. The beneficiaries of the estate can be held liable for the payment of the liability, even if the liability exceeds the value of the estate assets.
B. No one can be held liable for the tax if the assets have been distributed.
C. Elise and the beneficiaries can be held liable for the tax debt, up to the value of the assets distributed.
D. None of the above.

8. Ahmed, age 73, died in 2023, after a long battle with Alzheimer's disease. At the time of his death, he had assets of $14 million and owed a mortgage totaling $2,500,000 on his main home. He also had outstanding medical debts of $300,000 that remained unpaid at the time of his death. He had not used any of his basic exclusion amount during his lifetime. Based upon the information provided, what is the *taxable* amount of Ahmed's estate that must be reported on Form 706?

A. $0
B. $4 million
C. $5.5 million
D. $6 million

9. Delia's estate has funeral expenses for the cost of her burial. How should the executor deduct these costs?

A. Funeral expenses are an itemized deduction on Form 1040.
B. Funeral expenses are deducted on Form 1041.
C. Funeral expenses are deducted on Form 706.
D. Funeral expenses are a non-deductible expense.

10. All of the following tax returns may include income in respect of a decedent (IRD) *except*:

A. The final Form 1040 for the decedent.
B. The decedent's estate, Form 1041, if the decedent's estate receives the right to the income.
C. The Form 1040 of any person to whom the estate properly distributes the income.
D. A beneficiary's Form 1040, if the right to income arising out of the decedent's death is passed directly to the beneficiary and is never acquired by the decedent's estate.

11. Cullen died in 2023. Following his death, the executor of his estate paid the following bills. Which of these is not an allowable deduction in determining Cullen's taxable estate?

A. Estate administration expenses, including lawyer's fees.
B. State inheritance taxes.
C. Charitable contributions.
D. Alimony paid after the taxpayer's death.

12. Which of the following items is not an allowable deduction from the gross estate?

A. Debts owed at the time of death.
B. Medical expenses of the decedent.
C. Funeral expenses of the decedent.
D. Federal estate tax.

13. Renata received 100 shares of stock as an inheritance from her brother, who died on January 6, 2023. Her brother's adjusted basis in the stock was $4,750. The stock's fair market value on the date of her brother's death was $26,200. Her brother's estate was valuable, and a Form 706 will be filed for the estate. The executor of the estate elects the alternate valuation date for valuing the gross estate. Six months later, on July 6, 2023, the stock's fair market value had dropped to $23,100. Renata finally received the stock on August 26, 2023, when its fair market value was $23,500. She sold the stock a week later for $23,450. What is Renata's basis in the inherited stock, in order to determine her taxable gain on the sale?

A. $4,750
B. $22,200
C. $23,100
D. $23,450

14. When is an estate tax return (Form 706) due?

A. Four months after the close of the taxable year.
B. Six months after the close of the calendar year.
C. Nine months after the date of death.
D. Twelve months after the date of death.

15. Sandy and Matthew are married and have combined assets valued at approximately $15 million. They are both U.S. citizens. On July 10, 2023, Sandy dies. The FMV of Sandy's estate is $7 million on the date of her death. Matthew is the executor of his wife's estate and her sole beneficiary. Since the value of Sandy's estate was below the $12.92 million threshold, Matthew decides not to file an estate tax return, and he declines to take the portability election. What future impact does this have on Matthew, the surviving spouse?

A. There is no taxable effect on Matthew in this scenario.
B. Since Matthew declined to file an estate tax return, he did not elect portability. There will be estate tax due upon Matthew's death, assuming that the value of his assets does not decline, and there will be no deductions for estate tax purposes.
C. Matthew will owe estate tax in 2023 on his inheritance.
D. Sandy's estate will owe estate tax in 2023. Her estate tax return must be filed by the executor.

16. Which of the following statements concerning the deceased spousal unused exclusion (DSUE) is correct?

A. A portability election can only be made by filing Form 706.
B. The DSUE allows an unlimited estate tax deduction for a surviving spouse.
C. The predeceased spouse must have died from natural causes.
D. The maximum DSUE available for a spouse who dies in 2023 is $17,000.

17. Luciana made a cash gift to her nephew totaling $48,000 on March 20, 2023. Luciana is required to file a gift tax return. Assuming no extensions are filed, when is her gift tax return due?

A. March 20, 2024
B. April 15, 2024
C. October 15, 2024
D. December 31, 2024

18. In which case must a gift tax return be filed?

A. A married couple gives a gift of $17,000 to an unrelated person.
B. A married couple gives a gift of $25,000 to a related person with a single check.
C. A single individual gives a gift of $17,000 to an unrelated person.
D. A wife gives a gift of $40,000 to her husband who is not a U.S. citizen.

19. Which of the following is *not* income in respect of a decedent (IRD)?

A. Wages earned before death but still unpaid at the time of death.
B. Vacation time paid after death.
C. IRA funds that were distributed before the taxpayer's death, but not received until after death.
D. A royalty check that was received before death but not cashed.

20. Emma's father dies during the year. Emma is the sole beneficiary of her father's traditional IRA. Emma is 46 years old when she takes possession of her father's IRA. Which of the following statements is correct about the distributions from the inherited IRA account?

A. Emma can avoid taxation by rolling over the IRA to her own IRA account.
B. Any distributions are taxable to Emma but not subject to an early withdrawal penalty.
C. Any tax on the distributions must be paid from her father's estate.
D. The distributions are taxable to Emma, and also subject to an early withdrawal penalty because Emma is younger than 59½.

21. Bruno, age 71, pays $19,000 of college tuition for his favorite granddaughter, Margaret, age 25, directly to her college. Bruno does not claim his granddaughter as a dependent. Which of the following statements is correct?

A. The gift is taxable, and Margaret must report the gift tax on her individual tax return.
B. The gift is not taxable, but Bruno must file a gift tax return.
C. The gift is not taxable, and no gift tax return is required.
D. The gift is taxable, and Bruno must file a gift tax return.

22. Esther is the executor for her father's estate. He died on November 5, 2023. Which of the following dates would be the alternate valuation date for his estate (if elected)?

A. April 15, 2024
B. May 5, 2024
C. August 5, 2024
D. October 15, 2024

23. In general, who is responsible for paying gift tax?

A. The estate.
B. The donor.
C. The gift recipient.
D. The executor.

24. Jeffrey gives $27,000 to his girlfriend, Rachel, in 2023. Which of the following statements is correct?

A. The first $17,000 of the gift is not subject to the gift tax, but the remainder is subject to gift tax, and Rachel is responsible for paying it.
B. Rachel is required to file a gift tax return and pay tax on the entire gift.
C. Jeffrey is required to file a gift tax return, Form 709.
D. Jeffrey may choose to report the gift on his individual Form 1040, Schedule A.

25. All of the following gifts are excluded from the determination of the gift tax, regardless of the amount, except:

A. A gift made to a political organization.
B. A medical bill paid directly to a hospital on behalf of a relative.
C. A gift made to a qualifying charity.
D. A cash gift given to a nonresident alien spouse of a U.S. citizen.

26. Mildred died on February 20, 2023. Her estate is valued at $24 million, so an estate tax return must be filed. Which of the following assets would *not* be included in the calculation of her gross estate?

A. Life insurance proceeds payable to Mildred's children.
B. The value of real estate transferred to Mildred's son five years before her death.
C. The value of property owned jointly by Mildred and her spouse.
D. The value of Mildred's traditional IRA.

Unit 18: Quiz Answers

1. The answer is B. The surviving spouse must be a U.S. citizen in order to receive an unlimited marital deduction. This means that the spouse *receiving* the assets must be a U.S. citizen and must have outright ownership of the assets after the passing of the decedent. The marital deduction allows spouses to transfer an unlimited amount of property to one another during their lifetimes or at death without being subject to estate or gift taxes. The unlimited marital deduction is generally not allowed if the transferee spouse is not a U.S. citizen, even if the spouse is a legal resident of the United States.

2. The answer is B. The estate tax return for Claude's estate is due on February 4, 2024, nine months after the date of Claude's death. If required to be filed, Form 706, *United States Estate (and Generation-Skipping Transfer) Tax Return,* must be filed nine months *after* the date of a decedent's death. Any estate tax would be owed at this time. An executor may request a six-month extension to file Form 706, but the tax would still be owed on the earlier date.

3. The answer is C. A gift of a future interest cannot be excluded under the annual exclusion. A gift is considered a present interest if the donee has all immediate rights to the use, possession, and enjoyment of the property or income from the property. A gift is considered a future interest if the donee's rights to the use, possession, and enjoyment of the property or income from the property will not begin until some future date. "Future interests" include: reversions, remainders, and other similar interests.

4. The answer is D. For federal income tax purposes, cash inheritances are generally not taxable to the beneficiary, although the beneficiary may be responsible for a related estate tax liability that has not been satisfied.

5. The answer is A. Jeanne will owe no estate taxes related to the value of Maximo's estate. The marital deduction allows for an unlimited transfer of property from one spouse to another during his lifetime or from his estate after death without being subject to gift or estate taxes. To qualify for this unlimited deduction, the spouse *receiving* the assets must be a U.S. citizen, a legal spouse, and must have outright ownership of the assets.

6. The answer is D. Cristobal is not required to file a gift tax return. None of the gifts are taxable gifts, and therefore, no reporting is required. Tuition or medical expenses paid for someone directly to an educational or medical institution are not counted as taxable gifts. Nor are gifts to a political organization or gifts to a qualified charity.

7. The answer is C. Elise and the beneficiaries can be held liable for the tax debt, up to the value of the assets distributed. The tax liability for an estate attaches to the assets of the estate itself. If the assets are distributed to the beneficiaries before the taxes are paid, the executor and the beneficiaries can be held liable for the tax debt, (up to the value of the assets distributed).

8. The answer is A. After calculating the allowable deductions from the gross estate, Ahmed's net estate is valued at $11.2 million. This amount is less than the basic exclusion amount of $12.92 million for 2023, so no estate tax is applicable in this case. However, because the *gross* value of his estate is more than 12.92 million, an estate tax return (Form 706) is required to be filed.

Gross value of the estate: FMV of Assets	$14,000,000
Mortgage debt	($2,500,000)
Medical debt	($300,000)
Net Estate	**$11,200,000**

9. The answer is C. No deduction for Delia's funeral expenses can be taken on Form 1041 or Form 1040. Funeral expenses may be claimed only as a deduction from the gross estate on Form 706. If an estate tax return is not filed, then the funeral expenses are not deductible.

10. The answer is A. The final Form 1040 for the decedent would not include IRD. Where IRD is reported depends on who received the income. If paid to the estate, it should be included on the estate income tax return (Form 1041).

11. The answer is D. Alimony paid after a taxpayer's death is never deductible from the gross estate. It is merely considered a distribution to a beneficiary. Deductions from the gross estate are allowed for:

- Funeral expenses paid out of the estate.
- Debts owed at the time of death.
- Estate administration expenses.
- The marital deduction, charitable deduction, and state death tax deduction.

12. The answer is D. Federal estate tax is not deductible from the gross estate. The other items listed are allowable deductions from the gross estate. The decedent's unpaid medical expenses represent liabilities that can be deducted from the gross estate. Alternatively, if the expenses are paid by the estate during the one-year period beginning with the day after death, the personal representative can elect to treat all or part of the expenses as paid by the decedent at the time they were incurred and deduct them on the decedent's final tax return (1040).

13. The answer is C. Since the alternate valuation date was elected by the executor, Renata's basis is the fair market value on the alternate valuation date, or $23,100. This is the basis that she must use to calculate her gain or loss on the sale of the stock. The basis of property received from a decedent is generally the fair market value of the property on the date of the decedent's death. However, an executor has the option of choosing an alternate valuation date, which is six months after the date of death for valuing the gross estate.

14. The answer is C. Estate tax returns are due nine months from the date of death, although the executor may request a 6-month extension of time to file.

15. The answer is B. Since Matthew declined to file an estate tax return, he did not elect portability. No estate tax is due after Sandy's death because the value of her estate is below the exclusion amount. However, all her assets passed to her surviving spouse. Matthew's estate is now in excess of the annual exclusion amount. Assuming there is no change in the value of Matthew's assets and no applicable deductions upon his passing, there will be estate tax due upon his death. He could have avoided this scenario if he had filed an estate tax return and elected portability.

16. The answer is A. The portability election allows a surviving spouse's estate the right to use a deceased spousal unused exclusion (DSUE), which is the remaining unused portion of the previously deceased spouse's basic exclusion amount. The portability election must be made by filing an estate tax return for the deceased spouse, even if no estate tax is owed.

17. The answer is B. Luciana would be required to file her gift tax return by April 15, 2024, the filing deadline for 2023 individual tax returns. Gift tax returns are typically due on April 15 of the following calendar year (the same as the individual income tax filing deadline), and payment of the tax is also due then, although the filing may be subject to a six-month extension. If the donor died during the year, the filing deadline is the earlier of (1) the due date for the donor's estate tax return (with extensions) or (2) April 15 (with a six-month extension available via a personal income tax return extension or by filing Form 8892).

18. The answer is B. In order to make a gift to one individual in excess of the annual exclusion of $17,000 and avoid using any of their basic exclusion amounts; a married couple can use gift splitting. Gift splitting allows married couples to give up to $34,000 to a single person in 2023 without making a taxable gift, but they each must consent to the gift, and each may be required to file a gift tax return. Gifts to a spouse generally do not require a return to be filed, unless the spouse is not a U.S. citizen. Even if the receiving spouse is not a U.S. citizen, the limits are higher than the normal gift limit ($175,000 for 2023). Therefore, a $40,000 gift to a spouse (even one who is not a U.S. citizen) would not have to be reported on a gift tax return.

19. The answer is D. Since the royalty check was received before the taxpayer died, it is not considered IRD income. Income in respect of a decedent is taxable income earned but *not received* by the decedent by the time of death. The fact that the royalty check was not cashed has no bearing on the nature of the income, and it should be reported as taxable income on the decedent's final income tax return (Form 1040).

20. The answer is B. Any IRA distributions from an inherited IRA are taxable to Emma, but not subject to an early withdrawal penalty. Distributions of retirement plan benefits or distributions from taxable IRA accounts to a decedent's beneficiaries are generally subject to income tax when received. The decedent's surviving spouse may be able to defer taxation by rolling over the assets of a taxable IRA to another IRA or to a qualified plan. However, a child or other beneficiary is not allowed this same treatment. Qualified distributions from a Roth IRA or of previously nondeductible contributions to a traditional IRA are generally not taxable.

21. The answer is C. Bruno does not have a gift tax return requirement. Tuition or medical expenses paid directly to a medical or educational institution for someone else are not included in the calculation of taxable gifts, and there is no reporting requirement.

22. The answer is B. If elected by Esther (the executor), the alternate valuation date is May 5, 2024. An estate is normally valued on the date of the decedent's death. However, an executor may elect, under certain requirements, an alternate valuation date for an estate, which would be six months after the date of death.

23. The answer is B. The donor is generally responsible for paying gift tax. Under special arrangements the donee may *agree* to pay the tax instead.

24. The answer is C. Jeffrey is required to file a gift tax return. Gift tax reporting must be done by the donor, not the recipient, of the gift. The first $17,000 of the gift is not subject to gift tax because of the annual exclusion. The remaining $10,000 will be shown as a net taxable gift on Form 709.

25. The answer is D. Although a full marital deduction is allowed for a spouse who is a U.S. citizen, a transfer of property to a noncitizen spouse is limited. This is true even if the receiving spouse is a legal U.S. resident (a green card holder).

26. The answer is B. The value of property transferred to Mildred's son five years before her death would not be included in her gross estate. A taxpayer's gross estate includes the following:

- The FMV of all tangible and intangible property owned partially or outright by the decedent at the time of death.
- Life insurance proceeds payable to the estate or, for policies owned by the decedent, payable to the heirs or beneficiaries.
- The value of certain annuities or survivor benefits payable to the heirs or beneficiaries.
- The value of certain property transferred within three years before the taxpayer's death (not five years, as stated in answer B).

Index

V

W

This page intentionally left blank.

About the Authors

Joel Busch, CPA, JD

Joel Busch is a tax professor at San Jose State University, where he teaches courses at both the graduate and undergraduate levels. Previously, he was in charge of tax audits, research, and planning for one of the largest civil construction and mining companies in the United States. He received both a BS in Accounting and a MS in Taxation from SJSU and he has a JD from the Monterey College of Law. He is licensed in California as both a CPA and an attorney.

Christy Pinheiro, EA, ABA®

Christy Pinheiro is an Enrolled Agent, Accredited Business Advisor, and bestselling financial writer. She is a graduate of San Jose State University. Christy worked as an accountant for the state of California as well as two private CPA firms before going into private practice. She is the author of multiple books on taxation, bookkeeping, and tax practice management. Her finance and tax articles have been nationally published.

Thomas A. Gorczynski, EA, USTCP

Thomas A. Gorczynski is an Enrolled Agent, a Certified Tax Planner, and admitted to the bar of the United States Tax Court. Tom is also a nationally known tax educator and currently serves as editor-in-chief of EA Journal. He received the 2019 Excellence in Education Award from the National Association of Enrolled Agents. He earned a Master of Science in Taxation from Golden Gate University and a Certificate in Finance and Accounting from the Wharton School at the University of Pennsylvania.

This page intentionally left blank.

Made in the USA
Monee, IL
11 June 2024

59752463R00260